PUBLICATIONS

of the

State Department of Archives and History

———

THE PAPERS OF
WILLIE PERSON MANGUM

———

Willie Person Mangum. From an oil portrait, painter unknown, in the possession of Mangum Turner of Winston-Salem, North Carolina.

THE PAPERS OF
WILLIE PERSON MANGUM

EDITED BY
HENRY THOMAS SHANKS

Volume Four
1844-1846

Raleigh
State Department of Archives and History
1955

CONTENTS

Contents

PREFACE

The letters in this volume are for the years 1844-1846, years of great optimism and great disappointment for the Whigs. During the first nine or ten months of 1844, the Whigs were confident that Clay would be elected President. His defeat in November was a severe disappointment to them, especially to Mangum, who, as chairman of one of the committees, helped to direct the campaign. The letters for 1844 throw light on the thinking and campaign methods of Mangum and his friends. Among the revealing letters are several from Mangum himself to his co-workers and of other important Whig leaders including Clay himself to Mangum. Not all of the letters for 1844 are concerned with the political campaign, but most of them are.

For the period after Clay's defeat and after Mangum gave up his position as president *pro tempore* of the Senate in March, 1845, there are fewer letters. Nevertheless these throw light on Whig reaction and activities on the issues of the day, national and local, especially on the Texas question and Polk's financial program.

In 1846 the number of letters increased. Many of these concern the Oregon and Mexican crises. They reveal something of the role which Whigs, such as Mangum, played in preventing a war with England and in attempting to prevent, and, after it started, to end the War with Mexico.

Some valuable letters from Mangum to J. Watson Webb for the years 1842-1847 were discovered too late to include in this and the previous volume. Along with some other papers discovered after the publication of the volumes in which they logically belonged, these letters will be included in the last one of this series.

H. T. S.

Birmingham, Alabama
February 1, 1955

LIST OF ILLUSTRATIONS

A CALENDAR OF MANUSCRIPTS IN THE MANGUM PAPERS FOR THE PERIOD 1844-1846 OMITTED FROM THIS VOLUME

1. January 6, 1844. Charles Hughes, of Marion, Alabama, to W. P. Mangum presenting additional certificates in support of his petition for a pension. MS in the Library of Congress.

2. January 15, 1844. William Huntington, of Marion, Alabama, to Thomas Clancy asking him to show an enclosed letter (this enclosed letter is not in the Mangum Papers) to his friends in Hillsboro to fill in additional data in support of Hughes' pension claims and send the same to W. P. Mangum. MS in the Library of Congress.

3. February 22, 1844. William F. Smith, of Pleasant Hill, Wake County, North Carolina, to W. P. Mangum asking his aid in obtaining a pension for Elizabeth Griffis whose husband, Joshua Griffis, fought in the Revolutionary War. MS in the Library of Congress.

4. February 27, 1844. H. W. Miller, president of the Wake Clay Club, to ———— inviting ———— to be present April 12, 1844, to help his club and others welcome H. Clay on his visit to Raleigh. This letter is similar to the one published in this volume. MS in the Library of Congress.

5. May 16, 1844. R. W. Thompson, of Terre Haute, to W. P. Mangum introducing Judge John Law, of Vincennes. MS in the Library of Congress.

6. May 23, 1844. J. F. E. Hardy and others, of Asheville, to W. P. Mangum inviting him to a Whig rally in Asheville July 4, 1844. MS in the Library of Congress.

7. May 26, 1844. J. W. Brown to W. P. Mangum explaining that since his brother had to leave for the West he would be unable to accept Mangum's invitation to dinner Monday. J. W. Brown gave his return address as Washington. MS in the Library of Congress.

8. June 9, 1844. Benjamin Drake, of New York, to W. P. Mangum inviting him to a Whig rally in New York City, the date to be selected at Mangum's convenience. MS in the Library of Congress.

9. June 12, 1844. James W. Pegram and others, of Richmond, Virginia, to W. P. Mangum inviting Mangum to a public dinner for John M. Botts, June 20, 1844. MS in the Library of Congress.

10. June 19, 1844. John P. Wetherill and others, of Philadelphia, to W. P. Mangum inviting him to a political dinner on July 4, 1844, at Philadelphia. MS in the Library of Congress.

11. July 1, 1844. Robert B. Gilliam and others, of Granville County, to W. P. Mangum inviting him to a Whig barbecue at Brassfields, July 6, 1844. MS in the Library of Congress.

12. July 8, 1844. A. Myers and others, of Anson County, North Carolina, to W. P. Mangum inviting him to a mass Whig meeting July 18. MS in the Library of Congress.

13. July 10, 1844. Samuel Pleasants and others, of Richmond, Virginia, to W. P. Mangum inviting him to a political barbecue July 25 at Howard's Grove near Richmond. MS in the Library of Congress.

14. July 13, 1844. George F. Davidson and others, of Iredell County, to W. P. Mangum inviting him to a Whig mass meeting at Statesville July 22. A postscript is added to explain the change of the date from the 25th to the 22nd for W. A. Graham's convenience. MS in the Library of Congress.

15. July 23, 1844. C. H. Wiley and others, of Granville County, to W. P. Mangum inviting him to a Whig barbecue at Oxford July 30. MS in the Library of Congress.

16. July 23, 1844. C. H. Wiley and others, of Granville County, to P. H. Mangum informing him that W. P. Mangum would attend the Whig barbecue at Oxford July 30 and inviting him to be present. MS in the Library of Congress.

17. July 29, 1844. S. L. Venable and others, of Mecklenburg County, Virginia, to W. P. Mangum inviting him to a mass meeting of both parties "some day hereafter to be agreed on." MS in the Library of Congress.

18. July 29, 1844. John C. Taylor and others, of Granville County, to W. P. Mangum informing him that the barbecue would be given July 30. MS in the Library of Congress.

19. August 2, 1844. M. A. Williams and others, of Franklin County, to W. P. Mangum inviting him to attend a public discussion at Franklinton August 13 and 14. William H. Haywood, Geo. C. Dromgoole, and R. M. Saunders were invited by the Democrats. MS in the Library of Congress.

20. August 3, 1844. J. J. Daly and others, of Mecklenburg County, Virginia, to W. P. Mangum inviting him to attend a "general Mass-meeting and Whig barbacue" at South Hill July 30. MS in the Library of Congress.

21. August 22, 1844. F. W. Venable and others, of Mecklenburg County, Virginia, to W. P. Mangum informing him that the mass meeting scheduled at Clarksville had been postponed to October 2. MS in the Library of Congress.

22. August 29, 1844. Committee of Whigs of the Lynchburg Congressional District to W. P. Mangum inviting him to a Whig Convention at Lynchburg October 8. MS in the Library of Congress.

23. August 29, 1844. William P. Bynum and others, of the "Clay Club of Rutherford County," North Carolina, to W. P. Mangum inviting him to a mass meeting at Rutherfordton October 11 and 12. MS in the Library of Congress.

24. September 1, 1844. J. M. Leach and others, of Davidson County, to W. P. Mangum inviting him to a *Whig Mass Meeting*" at Lexington October 2. MS in the Library of Congress.

25. September 4, 1844. Haywood W. Guion and others, of the Second Congressional District, to W. P. Mangum inviting him to a mass meeting at Cowan's Ford on the Catawba River October 24 and 25. MS in the Library of Congress.

26. September 10, 1844. James W. Osborne, H. W. Guion and others, of the Second Congressional District, to W. P. Mangum inviting him to speak at a mass meeting at Hickory Grove, Mecklenburg County, North Carolina, October 24 and 25. MS in the Library of Congress.

27. September 20, 1844. H. E. Royal and others, of Sampson County, to W. P. Mangum inviting him to a Whig "festival" at Holly Grove in Sampson County October 10. MS in the Library of Congress.

28. September 20, 1844. George Moore and others, of Chapel Hill section of Orange County, to W. P. Mangum inviting him to a barbecue at Captain King's muster ground on the first Saturday in October. MS in the Library of Congress.

29. September 27, 1844. T. G. Coffin and others, of Guilford County, to W. P. Mangum inviting him to a barbecue October 25 and 26 at Jamestown. MS in the Library of Congress.

30. September 30, 1844. R. P. Latham and others, of Craven County, to W. P. Mangum requesting him to use his influence to obtain a discharge from the United States Army for Henry Hinton in order that he may help support his destitute sister and brother. MS in the Library of Congress.

31. October 3, 1844. Grisham Choise and others, of Franklin County, to W. P. Mangum inviting him to a barbecue at A. S. Brooks' in Franklin County October 18. MS in the Library of Congress.

32. October 3, 1844. James G. Stanly and others, of New Bern, to W. P. Mangum inviting him to a "Whig Mass Meeting" at New Bern October 22. MS in the Library of Congress.

33. October 6, 1844. David A. Barnes and others, of Northampton County, to W. P. Mangum inviting him to a Whig "mass meeting" at Jackson November 1. MS in the Library of Congress.

34. October 14, 1844. P. Hamilton and others, of Granville County, to W. P. Mangum inviting him to a Whig meeting at Williamsboro October 30 and 31. MS in the Library of Congress.

35. October 22, 1844. M. Campbell, of Statesville, to W. P. Mangum requesting his assistance to obtain the pension papers of Isaac Marshall, a Revolutionary soldier. MS in the Library of Congress.

36. October 26, 1844. J. H. Haughton and others, of Chatham County, to W. P. Mangum inviting him to a Whig mass meeting at Pittsboro November 2. MS in the Library of Congress.

37. October 26, 1844. Jesse P. Smith, of Chapel Hill, to W. P. Mangum inviting him to address the two literary societies of the University at the commencement of 1845. Mangum had not replied to a similar letter written in August. MS in the Library of Congress.

38. November 7, 1844. E. H. Carrington, of Adair County, Kentucky, to W. P. Mangum requesting information about the wills and distribution of the property of John Lay, Sr., and Thomas Sellers, Sr., deceased. MS in the Library of Congres.

39. November 16, 1844. Charles Hughes, of Marion, Alabama, to W. P. Mangum giving information to support his claim for a pension for service in the Revolution. MS in the Library of Congress.

40. December 10, 1844. William B. Hawkins, of Memphis, to W. P. Mangum asking his assistance to obtain an appointment in the navy. MS in the Library of Congress.

41. December 26, 1844 or 1845. Memucan Hunt, of Texas, to W. P. Mangum introducing Colonel Thomas William Ward, commissioner general of the land office of Texas, who planned to visit New York. MS in the Library of Congress.

42. January 9, 1845. Thomas E. Clinton, of Washington, to W. P. Mangum inviting Mangum and his friends to see his "gun fired and Mr. Von Schmidt's Steamboat run by a new propeller." MS in the Library of Congress.

43. January 30, 1845. E. D. Bullock, of Mobile, to W. P. Mangum, requesting his assistance with the General Land Office to obtain a patent for his client, James T. Vivian. Major Harris committed suicide December 16 or 17, 1844. MS in the Library of Congress.

44. January, 1845. Samuel Smith, of Hillsboro, to W. P. Mangum requesting his assistance in obtaining a pension for his father's Revolutionary services. MS in the Library of Congress.

45. February 1, 1845. J. A. Spencer, of New York, to W. P. Mangum introducing General Leavenworth, who planned to visit Washington and the South. MS in the Library of Congress.

46. February 18, 1845. James L. Gillespie, of Oxford, North Carolina, to W. P. Mangum requesting a copy of a map of Texas printed by the Senate. MS in the Library of Congress.

47. February 28, 1845. Thomas Turner, of Windsor, to W. P. Mangum requesting his assistance in obtaining a pension for his uncle, Benaiah Turner, who was in the Revolutionary War. MS in the Library of Congress.

48. March 11, 1845. Statement of Sally Walker, no place, asking Henry Weatherspoon to settle her account of $12 with Hugh Woods. MS in the Library of Congress.

49. April 23, 1845. Charles Hughes, of Marion, Alabama, to W. P. Mangum about his pension request. MS in the Library of Congress.

50. August 25, 1845. Charles Hughes, of Marion, Alabama, to W. P. Mangum requesting him to return a letter he sent Mangum and W. A. Graham about his pension claims. MS in the Library of Congress.

51. October 27, 1845. R. Haywood, of Tuscaloosa, Alabama, to W. P. Mangum requesting his assistance in obtaining an appointment for A. D. Hughes to West Point. MS in the Library of Congress.

52. November 1, 1845. Hugh Waddell, of Hillsboro, to W. P. Mangum asking for letters of recommendation for Mrs. Benjamin Rounsaville, who planned to move to Arkansas. MS in the Library of Congress.

53. November 28, 1845. Petition of Mary A. Bland, of Orange County, North Carolina, to the House of Representatives of the United States certifying that she was the only heir of William Hendricks, and asking for a donation of land for his Revolutionary services. MS in the Library of Congress.

54. December 5, 1845. James A. Cain, of Ruffins Mills, North Carolina, to W. P. Mangum about the claims of Mary A. Bland for Revolutionary bounty land of her uncle, Captain William Hendricks. MS in the Library of Congress.

55. December 22, 1845. A copy in Mangum's handwriting of a letter of Alexander F. Vache to W. P. Mangum. The original is included in this publication. MS of the copy in Mangum's handwriting is in the Library of Congress.

56. January 5, 1846. Charles R. Eaton, of Granville County, to W. P. Mangum asking him to pay for his subscription for the *Weekly Union* and *National Intelligencer*. MS in the Library of Congress.

57. January 30, 1846. James A. Cain, of Ruffins Mills, North Carolina, to T. L. and A. Thomas Smith, Washington, D. C., about the pension claims of James Cain for his Revolutionary services. Included is a certificate of William F. Collins, comptroller, Raleigh, on the records in his office for James Cain's pension. MSS in the Library of Congress.

58. February 17, 1846. J. W. Norwood, of Hillsboro, to W. P. Mangum asking assistance for pension claims of Mary Bland. He also encloses a statement of the relation of Mary Bland to William Hendricks, who originally came from Pennsylvania. MS in the Library of Congress.

59. February 21, 1846. J. H. Kirkland, Raleigh, to W. P. Mangum asking assistance to obtain reimbursement for his mother-in-law, Mrs. Sarah Bass, for the Revolutionary services of her father. MS in the Library of Congress.

60. March 12, 1846. Samuel Smith, Hillsboro, to W. P. Mangum asking assistance for obtaining a pension for his father for his Revolutionary service. MS in the Library of Congress.

61. John C. B. Ehringhaus, Elizabeth City, North Carolina, to Asa
Biggs asking his assistance for Carl Hinricks, Ehringhaus' brother-
in-law and a New York City merchant, who seeks a patent for a
friend. MS in the Library of Congress.

62. March 25, 1846. Mary G. Young to W. P. Mangum asking assistance to obtain a pension for the Revolutionary service of her
father, William Christian. MS in the Library of Congress.

63. April 20, 1846. John F. Poindexter, Germanton, North Carolina,
to W. P. Mangum asking his assistance in obtaining a West Point
appointment for Reuben D. Golding, of Germanton. MS in the
Library of Congress.

64. April 23, 1846. T. L. Clingman, Morganton, to W. P. Mangum introducing a friend, D. John Dickson, of Buncombe County, who
"is on his way north." MS in the Library of Duke University.

65. April 25, 1846. Joseph P. Santmyer, Alleghany County, Maryland,
to W. P. Mangum inviting him to become a member of the Mt.
Savage Mechanical Lyceum. MS in the Library of Congress.

66. May 6, 1846. W. A. Duer, Morristown, N. J., to W. P. Mangum
asking his support for a position of regent of the Smithsonian Institute. MS in the Library of Congress.

67. May 29, 1846. Thomas Russell and others, Harpers Ferry, Virginia,
to W. P. Mangum asking him to deliver an oration on July 4 for
the Virginia Lodge No. 1 of the I.O.O.F. MS in the Library of Congress.

68. July 21, 1846. Charles Paist, Wittenberg College, Springfield,
Ohio, to W. P. Mangum informing him that the Excelsior Society
had elected Mangum an honorary member. MS in the Library of
Congress.

69. July 31, 1846. John Peabody to W. P. Mangum and other members
of Congress to accept Miss Woodside, Peabody's wife's aunt, as
housekeeper. She lived on Missouri Avenue in Washington. MS
in the Duke University Library.

70. July, 1846. Invitation of Thomas B. Bailey and others, of Hillsboro, to Martha Mangum to a "party," July 31, 1846. MS in the
Library of Congress.

71. August 2, 1846. Martin Stevenson and others, New Bern, North
Carolina, to W. P. Mangum asking him to speak October 28 at the
dedication of the "New Hall" of the Eureka Lodge No. 7, I.O.O.F.,
at New Bern. MS in the Library of Congress.

72. September 13, 1846. Alexander C. Blount, New Bern, to W. P.
Mangum renewing the request in the preceding letter (no. 69).
MS in the Library of Congress.

73. November 7, 1846. William D. Cooke and others, Raleigh, to W. P.
Mangum inviting him to deliver an address to the Manteo Lodge
No. 8, I.O.O.F., at a date convenient to Mangum. MS in the Library
of Congress.

CHRONOLOGICAL LIST

of the

MANGUM PAPERS (1844-1846) INCLUDED

IN THIS VOLUME

PAGE

SYMBOLS USED TO DESIGNATE DEPOSITORIES
OF MANGUM PAPERS

———

(The location of papers from other collections is indicated by footnotes.)

WPM-D   Willie P. Mangum Papers at Duke University, Durham, North Carolina.

WPM-LC   Willie P. Mangum Papers in the Library of Congress, Washington, District of Columbia.

WPM-NC   Willie P Mangum Papers in the State Department of Archives and History, Raleigh, North Carolina.

WPM-UNC Willie P. Mangum Papers, Southern Collection, University of North Carolina, Chapel Hill, North Carolina.

THE MANGUM PAPERS
1844-1846

1844

WPM-LC

J. Watson Webb to Willie P. Mangum.

[2 January, 1844]

My Dear Sir.

Permit me to introduce to your favourable acquaintance Mr. *Freeman Hunt*,[1] the editor of the Merchants Magazine, one of the very best publications of the kind ever got up in this City. Mr. *Hunt* is politically & personally, the friend of Mr. Clay; & yet takes the liberty of entertaining & advocating his own views in relation to the tariff etc. etc.

If you can be of any service to him you will greatly oblige

Your friend & obt. Srvt.

J. WATSON WEBB

Jany. 2. 1844.

Hon. W. P. Mangum.

[Addressed:]

      Hon: W. P. Mangum
        Washington City.

Mr. Hunt.

WPM-LC

C. H. Wiley[2] *to Willie P. Mangum.*

OXFORD, N. C. Jan. 5th. 1844—

Dear Sir:

If you can spare a few hours to the subject of this letter, your kindness will greatly oblige a friend.- I am becoming dissatisfied with my location; not that I have not met with sufficient en-

---

[1]Freeman Hunt, 1804-1858, a native of Massachusetts, had little formal schooling. Beginning as an office boy in a print shop, he soon rose to head the firm of Putnam and Hunt, which in the late 1820's and early 1830's published numerous small magazines. He moved to New York and established the *Merchants' Magazine and Commercial Review*. After 1850 this was called *Hunt's Merchants' Magazine*. This was his love; he worked on it until his death in 1858. In politics he was a Whig. *D. A. B.*, IX, 384.

[2]Compare the letter from Wiley to W. P. Mangum June 19, 1841. See above, III, 174-175.

1

couragement, according to the capabilities of the place; but because the Country cannot afford encouragement. I have, it is
said, done well for a young man, that is, succeeded well, & yet
what is it?—no man possesses stronger attachment for his native State than I. No one can more respect her laws, & law observing people; no one more admire her patriotism or venerate
her ancient renown.- Often, often have I wished that my lot
had been to be born with those means by which I could make
myself useful & valuable to the place of my nativity, instead
of being one of that class who must look for a location useful
to them. So tender & sincere is my regard for the good Old
North State, that in preparing to leave it, I feel myself called
on to make this apology. But as I said, I am one of those who
have their own way to carve: & I too am resolved to make my
way by my profession & the pursuits of literature. I am unfortunately, so constituted, that my chief happiness consists in the
study of books, the history of Governments &c &c.- Such tastes,
no man in the provincial situation, can gratify to any great extent, unless possessed of an easy fortune.- Nor is there any hope
of a young man's ever accumulating much in a country like this
at the law: & if he abide here, he must spend a life of drudgery
for a poor subsistence & in his old age - must reflect that he has
neither founded a fortune, nor explored to any extent the Treasure House of knowledge.- My desire is to settle in a City: I
could there gratify my tastes, & there have hopes, by industry
& steady habits of rising into a lucrative business. Besides the
insuperable argument of necessity which induces me to look
out for such a situation, & the inducements which it holds out
to a man of literary turn, there are other cogent reasons, operating on my mind.- A large city is a sort of focus of talent &
accomplishments of all sorts: man is brought into frequent collision with man, mind grapples with mind: & thus we are improved both by having our own intellectual powers developed
& polished, & by the constant aids of foreign lights, surrounding
us on every side.- Besides, I believe that great events are on the
wing & should I live the usual allotted period of man's existence,
I shall expect to see mighty changes in my day.- I wish to be
where I can get the earliest insight into the progress of these
changes & be prepared to act my part.- As a great, but in my
opinion bad man, asked "Where am I to go?" Now the labour
which I wish to impose on you, in addition to that of reading

this letter, is this: I wish you to give me some information for which your position will eminently enable you.- If I go hence, I must have the means of certain support where I settle.- This I propose to make in two ways: First by getting into the office of an old Attorney as a junior partner, or secondly, by getting an engagement as assistant Editor to some political Whig, Clay paper. As to my qualifications for the former, I can say, I have the habits & principles of a son of the Old North & can get recommendations from the first lawyers in our State. As to my fitness for the second, [I] can say, that I have had some success at all sorts of writing: political, literary, & dramatic—Few of my age are better *practiced*, at least, with the pen, & this is all I will say—Would you do me, the very great favour of looking out for a location for me? If you could spare the time (I know you have the will) to exert yourself a little for me, you will be conferring a favour—that will, at some day, return upon you with interest. You see men from all the cities: Will you make some enquiries, & give me a recommendation? I should think, in the ensuing campaign, a vigorous Whig pen in St. Louis, in Louisville, or Nashville, might "do the State some service." I merely suggest this as a hint.—

Expecting an answer, I have the honour to remain,

Most respectfully & truly, yours,
C. H. WILEY

[Addressed:]

Hon. Willie P. Mangum
Washington City
D. C.

WPM-LC

Perley S. Chase to Willie P. Mangum and Enclosure.

MANCHESTER, Jan.ʳʸ 5th, 1844.

To the Presdt. of the U. S. Senate—

Dear Sir Agreeably to a vote of of [sic] the New Hampshire, State Washingtonian Temperance Society[3] in Convention as-

³The temperance movement began in Concord, New Hampshire, in 1827. Reverend Nathaniel Bouton, as the leader, began the movement. In 1830 he organized the Temperance Society. By 1841 numerous societies had been formed. Franklin Pierce became a sponsor of the movement. By 1847 a referendum was authorized. Petitions poured into the legislature and by 1855 a temperance law was passed. Everett S. Stockpole, *History of New Hampshire*, IV, 251-256; R. F. Nichols, *Franklin Pierce: Young Hickory of the Granite Hills*, Philadelphia, 1931, 57, 123-124, 125-126.

sembled at Manchester, N. H. on the 3d & 4th days of Janry. 1844, I transmit to you the following Resolutions, which were adopted by the Convention, and signed by the President & Secretary of the above named Society.

I am very respectfully your
Obt Servant
PERLEY S. CHASE   ) Cor. Secretary

Hon. W P. Mangum
Presdt. Senate

1. Resolved—That this Convention regards with deep interest the welfare of the American Sailor, and has heard with great pleasure of the generally successful efforts in the Merchant Service to abolish the use of alcohol.

2. Resolved—That in the opinion of this Convention, the honor of our Country - the welfare of the sailor, and the good of society require that the Spirit Ration of the Navy should be at once & utterly abolished; that while the use of alcohol is chiefly abandoned in the Merchant-Service, its continuance on board our Ships of War, is alike injurious & disgraceful.

3d. Resolved—That copies of the foregoing votes, attested by the President & Secretary be forwarded to the Presiding Officers of each House of Congress, with a request that the same be communicated to their Respective Houses & printed for the information of the members.

ANTHONY COBLY) President
(
PERLEY S. CHASE Cor Secretary.

[Addressed:]

Hon. W. P. Mangum
Presdt. U. S. Senate
Washington, D. C.

L. W. Wilson[4] to Willie P. Mangum.

NEW YORK Jany 6, 1844

Honble. W. P. Mangum,
    Sir,

Pardon the liberty of one who was once honoured with a slight acquaintance with you, while Judge of the Superior Court of N. Carolina for addressing you. But well knowing your ardent love of Country as well as the only *policy* that possibly can render our beloved Country *prosperous & happy*, I shall without further preliminary make you acquainted with the low, *small* potatoe conduct of Loco foco Henshaw[5] - In the first place he commenced his *Great reform* by descending to remove Whig, Master Joiners, Master Labourers &c out of the Navy yard, at this place & appoint in their stead men entirely unquallified to fill their Stations, but Strong Loco focos; never was there a set of men, placed on public duty, that were more faithful public servants than those removed by Mr. Henshaw, and every Whig he is turning out with all possible dispatch, as fast as he can make the even semblance of a cause. Capt. Frelon, a loco foco of hot blood who is ordered to the U. S. S. Preble, had the privilege of choosing his forward officers; a few days past, a man by the name of Berry of the Same Stamp, applied to Capt. Frelon to be made Carpenter of his Ship the reply was, go and get a line from Mr. Murphy,[6] & you shall be appointed. Murphy is a member of Congress from Brooklyn District and is a man who is in the habit of doing the Kennel work for the Party—This information I had from Berry who was then waiting at the Bank door in Brooklyn to receive the promised check that was to be honoured by Secretary Henshaw; what contemptable small business say you, for the Secretary of the Navy of the greatest Republic that ever existed to stoop to, but what then could be expected from appointments made by the Accidental President & a traitor to his professed principals—

---

[4] Unable to identify.

[5] David Henshaw, a railroad pioneer and a Democrat, was appointed Secretary of the Navy by Tyler in the summer of 1843. His appointment was not confirmed by the Senate, the vote being 8 to 34.

In October, 1843, a number of workmen were discharged at the several navy yards. According to Whig partisans, these removals were due to the fact that the workmen were Whigs. Henshaw denied the accusation. *Niles' Register,* LXV, 135, 388.

[6] Henry Cruse Murphy, 1810-1882, held several offices in Brooklyn and New York State before he entered Congress in March, 1843. He served from 1843 to 1845 and 1847 to 1849. He was owner and editor of the *Brooklyn Eagle. Biog. Dir. of Cong.,* 1346.

Please bear in mind that when Secretary Badger made removals in the Navy Yard, there was *uncontrovertible proof* that the incumbent, had been guilty of the most barefaced Pilfering, and some of these Sir are yet retained in the Service of the Govt. to wit Comdr. Renshaw & Saml. Hart Naval Contractors had the Proofs Sir charged on these men, been proven in a Court of Civil or Criminal Justice, they would long since have been consigned to ignominy - but they were of the party & it required the hardihood of a traitor to retain & reward them for their villany.—

Some months Since, charges was made against the Master Sail Maker of this yard, which could have been established without the least doubt, & resulted in his discharge from the Service, but he belonged to the party & Secretary Henshaw, Sent the persons to Sea who made the charges & is now carrying on a Court of enquiry in the yard, which I am told will result in the acquittal of Van Voris, this *information rely on*, and I give it you, that our party may not be accused of participating & confirming the appointment of a man so incompetent to the Station & a mind that cannot possibly soar above little things.—

Driven from N. Carolina by misfortune & from a Lucrative Situation by Vanburen, I was by the recommendation of Judge Badger, placed in employment in the Navy Yard at this place & have had an opportunity of making myself well acquainted with much abuse of public confidence in many public officers, I am now discharged, because & only because I was consistent in my political principals & prefer Mr. Clay to any other man that I know of for the next President. I have always lived & enjoyed affluence until Vanburen drove me to day labour & as I am not one of them, they would condescend to employ me in the Yard if I would work as a day labourer at the m[ost] menial employment - to old Nick with them - Any information that I can give you from this quarter please ask for & you will confer a favour on me by replying to this.-

Very respectfully Sir Yr Obt. Servt
L. W. WILSON

[Addressed:] Honble Willie P. Mangum

Senate U. States
Washington City.

Willie P. Mangum to Charity A. Mangum.

Monday evening
WASHINGTON CITY, 8th. January 1844.

My dear Love.

I recd. a letter from you this evening, saying, that you had received but one letter from me.- I am astonished - as I have written *three*, & one upon business.

I have been unwell, until within a Week past. I am not now *entirely well*.- Three weeks ago, I was more alarmed, than I have ever been in my life. -

The cold with which I left home, fastened upon my lungs, and I suffered extremely.—Two Doctors attended me three weeks, or thereabouts.—

I have been much reduced, but for some days past—say— eight or ten, have been improving most rapidly.—I am so well, that I hope, to be entirely so.— I live with the utmost care, except that I fear, my cold bathing is carried too far— As I have the brush run over my body every morning, dipt in Cold Water— The doctors advise it.- I was very much hurt to hear, that you had received but one letter from me. - I know it gave you much concern - & I would not have given it without cause. - I fear, My Love, that you take these things too much to heart.- You ought to know - you must know - that whatever may happen - that whatever defects of temper or otherwise, I may exhibit - that you are dearer to me, than all the world, our dear children, not even excepted; dear as they, and every one of them are to me.—

I wrote about the *hiring*, which I hope has come to hand— I wrote about the blacksmith's tools. - If none are got, *they must be* - Mr. Wyche at Henderson will procure what may be wanted.—

You will write to "Mr James Wyche" at Henderson depot to get such tools, as Mr. Wilkins will direct, send by the first mail— He will get them & write to you by the first mail.-You will then send for them.—

I have not been able to go to Baltimore to get the things I want— If I do not go next week, I shall write to Petersburg for them, though I prefer to get them myself.—

I hope the Children go on well.— Give my *Love* to Sally,

Patty, & Mary & say to them to improve what they can.—To my son - say that I expect him to learn to spell, & read & write me a short letter *before long.*—

I write in great haste, as I have to go to a Caucus. - I live with Gov. Morehead of Kentucky - Nobody else—

Always My dear Love, feel that you are dearer to me than all others - because such are my feelings - & because you have always, deserved to be so.

Your affectionate husband
WILLIE P. MANGUM.

P.S.

I should have got well much sooner, if I had not made it a point to go to the Senate every day - & for nearly a week, a servant had to help me up stairs.—

I shall try to get well, & hope it will be so.—

ever dear, accept my love,
W.P.M.—

WPM-LC

Willie P. Mangum to Charity A. Mangum.

WASHINGTON. 8th. Jan: 1844.

My dear Love-

I have written by this mail, more at large, for you to receive on Saturday. —

I now write by Franklinton - But do not know, that you will receive it. —

I have been long sick, & much alarmed on account of my lungs.- I am getting well, & for more than a week, have been rapidly recovering.- My Love to the Children & a kiss to each.- and always My Love, feel sure, whatever may happen, that you are dearer to me than all the world, our dear Children not even excepted.

Your affectionate husband
W. P. MANGUM.

WPM-LC

Willie P. Mangum to Daniel Webster.

Monday morning, 8th Jan. 1844.

My dear Sir

A friend has sent me, some 150 miles, a saddle of mutton, beautiful to the eye, the most beautiful, I ever saw.

I propose with a few friends to look into it, *to morrow evening.*[7]

Will you do me & them the favor to aid us with your counsels?

I can promise you but little except the company of some dozen of our friends.

The donor of the saddle is in the City.—If I could keep the mutton, I cannot keep my friend - & therefore, you will join us prepared to excuse very hasty preparation on the part of new beginners.—

I had hoped to make this request in person, last night, but was not well enough.

Say at 5½ oclock. Will you join us?

With great respect,
Very truly yrs.
WILLIE P. MANGUM.

Mr. Webster.

WPM-D

Daniel Webster to Willie P. Mangum.

Monday, Jan. 8. [1844]
2 o'clock.

My Dear Sir;

It will give me pleasure to be one of those who shall sit in judgment on your mutton tomorrow.

I shall present myself at the hour proposed.

Very truly Yrs.
DANL WEBSTER.

Mr. Mangum.

---

[7]After Webster resigned as Secretary of State, he practiced law in Massachusetts until December, 1843, when he went to Washington on a visit. In Washington the Whigs were not too cordial. Choate, who held Webster's seat in the Senate, persuaded Mangum and others to work out some kind of reconciliation with Webster. This dinner was probably a part of that reconciliation. See Fuess, *Life of Webster,* II, 140.

WPM-LC

John McLean[8] *to Willie P. Mangum.*

BALTIMORE Jan 9, '44

My dear Sir

Our friends in this quarter are very solicitous to know the ultimate course of the Whigs in regard to the *implied* overtures of "Capt Tyler." Will they *ground their arms,* and take him and his friends into full-fellowship? Are his past political offences to be *sponged,* and the *Traitor* and his gang again to be taken in full-communion with the Whig Church?

May I ask the favor of you to advise me upon these matters; and as far as is consistent with your official duties to inform me of the probable issue of the important nominations now before the Senate- My relations with Mr Monroe of the "Patriot" and other Whig Editors will enable me to make profitable use of the information, and be of essential service to our friends in the Senate—

You may rely on my *discretion* and high regard for your honor in every thing that I may do either politically or personally—

faithfully your friend
& obedt servt
JOHN MCLEAN
(of N. Y)

Hon. W. P. Mangum.

[Addressed:]

Hon. Willie P. Mangum

President S. U. States

Washington

D. C.

---

[8]A New York business leader who took much interest in education and politics. He was a graduate of Columbia College, commissary-general of New York, and regent of New York University. He engaged in the lumber industry. *Manual for the Use of the Legislature of the State of New York for the Year 1854,* 370; M. H. Thomas, *Columbia University Officers and Alumni, 1854-1857,* New York, 1836, 118; Longworth, *New York Directory, 1835-1836,* 434.

WPM-LC

Charles F. Mayer[9] to J. McPherson Berrien.

BALTIMORE,
12 Jany. 1844.

Dear Sir;

When in Washington today I was desirous of saying a few words to you on a matter which I deem of interest to our Party - but your engagements and my own prevented me. Allow me now to mention it. To myself with others of the Whigs the question of Mr. Spencer's appointment as Judge,[10] seems to involve very important considerations for our prospects in New York as well as for our Party dignity. The eminent talent of Mr Spencer for the station being conceded, his rejection would be inflicted only as a penal retribution for imputed political instability - chiefly his supposed inconsistency with the professions of the Syracuse Convention.[11] That imputation I learn can be most satisfactorily explained away. But without treating of any exculpation, may we not, even assuming the deflection to exist, doubt the propriety - the expediency - of affixing the same stigma of a rejection - for a stigma it will be, where the qualification of mind and knowledge for the position is unquestionable? The publick may say that his sin was not more flagrant than Mr. Taney's, - and that as in Mr. Taney's case, so in the present there could be no question of the Judicial rectitude that was to have been expected, and in Mr. Taney's Judicial career has been exhibited.-Ought Mr. Spencer (especially under the exposition that can be given in his defence as to the Syracuse affair) to be marked with the reprobation of the Senate? The Whigs wield the power and, whatever cunning views our enemies may act on, would bear the responsibility and the odium - and the Democrats will, in Senate and out of it, watch results to turn them against us. They will see their triumph possibly in the reaction of the punishment, as it will be deemed, imposed by the Whigs on Mr. Spencer, by rejecting him. We have, in

---

[9]A lawyer and civic leader of Baltimore. Livingston, *Law Register*, 1851, p. 437; 1860, p. 367; Scharf, *Chronicles of Baltimore*, 471, 537, 543, 629.

[10]John C. Spencer had served in Tyler's Cabinet as Secretary of War and as Secretary of the Treasury. In January, 1844, Tyler appointed him justice of the United States Supreme Court. Because of Spencer's loyalty to Tyler, the Clay Whigs of New York, including Thurlow Weed, succeeded in defeating this confirmation. Lambert, *Presidential Politics in the U. S., 1841-1842*, 93-94; *D. A. B.*, XVII, 449-450.

[11]In their state convention which met at Syracuse, October 7, 1841, the Whigs of New York approved the resignation of members of Tyler's Cabinet after the split over the bank bill. *Hillsborough Recorder*, October 21, 1844; Chitwood, *Life of Tyler*, 251.

Mr. Van Buren's instance, already suffered the force of reaction from such a form of rebuke as now hangs over Mr. Spencer. I allude to this latter experience only to show how much reaction is to be regarded as an element among the political forces which give tendency and purpose to political movements In finding a point for the reaction here some think that in Western New York, where the Spencer family have had great influence, an interest Democratic, Conservative, and otherwise, might rally to blight us there very seriously; while the rejection might become a test generally of passionate rally elsewhere in the State of New York under the urgency of Mr Spencer's friends and favoured, as is natural, by himself. I have never seen good flow from the passion of Party whether that was actually the sole impulse or could be plausibly so interpreted by the adverse Party. And I very much fear that the rejection of Mr. Spencer would be regarded as the scorn of Whigs stimulated by impassioned discontent with him politically - and making political considerations a test for Judicial preferment. I make these allusions as only what our enemies and many even of our brethren *may* conceive. It may be a fair inquiry whether a Judicial station would not be the proper disposition of Mr Spencer even if he be politically restless, and might not be the appropriate sedative of the temperament, he may be supposed to have.

I hope, my dear Sir, you will pardon my intruding on you these thoughts. They are expressed to you in no officious spirit but merely as the reflections which my solicitude for our party's just ascendency has stirred up: and which in that feeling I believed I might be warranted in laying before you.

You are wiser and better informed than I can be in all these matters - but I know your kindness, and I am sure of your indulgence therefore for my speaking to you from the bosom of the People, whose various sentiments you always like together [*sic*].

> I am, my dear Sir,
> with great respect,
> Your's truly
> CHARLES F. MAYER.

The Honorable
    J. McPherson Berrien
      Washington City,

WPM-LC

J. Watson Webb to W. H. Morrell.[12]

[12 Jan., 1844]

Dear Morell

I returned from Philadelphia on Monday, & have since been so constantly occupied, that I could not find time to reply to your letter in relation to Talmadge. While as you well know, I have for nearly three years, known him to be a *knave*, I have never, since I brought forward the name of Mr. Clay in February '42 and called upon the Whigs to rally upon it, but on *one occasion* referred to T. and his utter worthlessness. Of course in this, I have acted from *policy* to the Whig Party; and this policy I shall not abandon until I perceive the *possibility* of his nomination. I shall then, should such a contingency arise, both during its pendency & after its occurrence, denounce him as a disgrace to any party and far less worthy of confidence than even *John Tyler* himself. Have no fear therefore, on this head; & tell Mr. Mangum, Morehead, and other friends that they have nothing to apprehend from the Cou. & Enq. on this subject, and that I am as well satisfied that it is the true course, as I am that it would be dishonorable in me to do or say or permit to be done or said any thing in my columns in *favour* of his nomination.

I am glad to hear that my article on abolition & the right of Petition, has done good. I felt that the views I expressed were just to all parties; & feeling so, I hope good would result from their being clearly & fearlessly expressed. I therefore, ordered a copy of the paper containing them to be sent to every member of Congress. I think however that to pursue the subject would do harm instead of good; but in relation to this, I am ready to be advised, and if it should be deemed advisable, will cheerfully publish whatever you or others may write, or will resume the discussion myself.

We all feel that it is *impossible* for the Senate to confirm Spencer; & the hope is that the place will be kept open for *John Tyler's* successor to fill. Who that will be, we all know. Next winter, the Locos may feel desirous of having the place filled; & to guard against *Treason* in our own ranks, why cannot our

[12]See above, III, 401n.

friends agree *definitively* with the Loco Foco Senators, that if *Tyler* will not give us a good Judge this Winter, it shall be deemed a vacancy not to be filled until his successor comes into office?

As to the Vice Presidency, you know precisely my feelings & views in regard to Mr. Webster. He could be delighted to see *Evans*[13] nominated; & as the vice President cannot be taken from a Slave State, why not agree that the Delegates from the New England States, shall make the nomination to the Convention, if they are found to be all right? New York should be put out of the question. *John Sargeant*[14] is just the honest whig suitable for the Station; though I should prefer Clayton or Mangum if the[y] dwelt in a non-slave State. But if it is said, *Evans* would unite the whole East, & give us Maine & New Hampshire, why little *Matty*[15] might in that contingency, be left without a solitary State! Would not this be a glorious result? But be this as it may, the *honest* whig who can most strengthen the ticket, & who in case of such a contingency as occurred to Harrison, would be qualified to succeed him, must be selected. You well know that when run up Mr. Clay's banner, I wrote to him that I would neither ask for nor take an office; my whole object therefore, is success by fair & honorable means & with *honorable* men, and my views & opinions are all openly expressed and may be quoted at all times. I have no other secrets in my politics than to preserve the secrets of my party & my friends when committed to me.

Ask Mr. Mangum if he recd. a second letter from me, though a long one, in relation to the Tariff & other matters. I have just given Pennsylvania *Repudiation* a *scoring*. "The preservation of the Public Faith" must be inscribed in indelible letters on the Whig Banner, & it alone would insure success. As ever your friend.

J. WATSON WEBB Ja y 12—1844

P.S. Please to take notice that this letter has a date although written after 2 A.M. I had thought it should be Jany 13.

---

[13]George Evans, Senator from Maine and close friend of Webster.
[14]See above, III, 92, 219n.
[15]Martin Van Buren.

WPM-LC

Henry L. Brooke [16] & others to Willie P. Mangum.

RICHMOND VA. 17th. Jany 1844

Honble W. P. Mangum
of the United States Senate

Dear Sir,

We are instructed by the Whig Central Committee of the State of Virginia to invite you to attend a general convention, of the party to be held in this City on the 7th, February next—

The objects of this convention are to nominate Electors to vote for a President & Vice President of the United States; to embody and promulgate in the form of an address to the people of Virginia, the political principles and measures of governmental policy, on their approval of which, the Whig party intend to place their hopes of success at the next Spring & Fall Elections; to provide a more effective organization, of the party throughout the State; and to diffuse a warmer spirit of patriotism and a more just appreciation of the importance of the establishment of the principles, and policy thus recommended, to the success of our free institutions and the welfare and prosperity of the nation—

The assembling of such a convention with such views, and for such purposes, has been deemed by the committee an occasion of sufficient importance to excite the interest, and invoke the aid of the purest virtue and most distinguished talents of the nation. - And in selecting from amongst our public men those whose political course has been most strongly illustrated by enlightened patriotism and distinguished services to the party, and the Country, we are happy to assure you that the Committee have found no one, in their opinion, more conspicuous than yourself, or whose presence on the occasion referred to would give sincerer pleasure to the Whigs of Virginia, and impart a higher degree of enthusiasm to the convention—

---

[16]A Richmond attorney. Livingston, *Law Register*, 1851, p. 588; 1860, p. 927.

With high consideration we have the honor to be your obt Serts

HENRY L BROOKE)   Committee
FLEMING JAMES)   of
JNO H PLEASANTS)   Invitation

[Addressed:]

Honble. W. P. Mangum
of the United States Senate
Washington City
D. C

WPM-LC

Hugh Waddell to Willie P. Mangum.

WILMINGTON
Jany. 18th /44

My dear Sir!

I beg leave to present to yr. particular attention my young friend Gaston Meares[17] Esqr. son of our late excellent friend Wm. B. Meares Esqr.—He visits Washington with the view of determining his final location as a member of the Bar.—

Knowing that Washington is the center of our system, he very naturally supposes that correct information from all points may there be had.

Will you be so good as to introduce him to gentlemen from the West & South who may be of service to him.—

I need not say he is every way worthy of such a father & such a name as he bears.

Yours truly
HUGH WADDELL

Hon. W. P. Mangum

[Addressed:]

Hon. W. P. Mangum
Washington

Mr. Meares

---

[17]Gaston Meares, 1821-1862, was a student at the state university in 1838-1839, a lieutenant colonel in the Mexican War, and a member of the state legislature before he moved to Arkansas, where he became a lawyer and planter. He was killed at Malvern Hill in 1862. Grant, *Alumni Hist. of U. N. C.,* 422; Battle, *Hist. of U. N. C.,* I, 798.

WPM-LC

William Cain, III, to Willie P. Mangum.

Marion [,Alabama,] 19th Jany 1844—

My dear Sir

On the 17th Int. I started your negroes to North Carolina all except Willie whom I have resolved to sell he had been run away two months before I arrived & I see that he is unwilling to do only as he pleases and all his brothers seem in a great measure to act from the same spirit so far as I can see them they have no thought of being controlled farther than they think proper; a common overseer will find much difficulty in manageing them. My reasons for sending them in are first Willies rascality. Judy has a Child & if she is hired the Child will not be taken care of & the hire will be small and Hulda would hire for nothing as she is troubled with the complaint I told you about altho she looks well at other times it continues for about 5 to 8 days in every month and I fear the others might be crippled or injured in some way or other.

I have no Idea how long I shall remain here as I propose remaining untill I can see my way clear in my business—

I should be glad to hear from you and should you write direct to Macon Marengo County—

I hope under all the circumstances, you will approve of my proceedings as I have done what I thought best—The negroes all wished to return to North Carolina The mails have not passed here in a week—

Yours most sincerely
Wm. Cain Senr

[Addressed:]

To The

Honble.

Willie P. Mangum

acting Vice-President U.S.

Washington City,

WPM-LC

Thos. Kirkpatrick[18] to Willie P. Mangum and Enclosure.

New York Jany 19 1844

Dear Sir

You may think me presumptious in addressing myself to you on such a subject as I am about to Communicate but your kindness to me while in Washington together with my ardent desires for the success of our cause must be my apology,

I have been in this City since I left Washington, and find a great feeling exists here in relation to the persons who either have been or will probably be shortly nominated to the Senate for the offices of Naval Officer and Appraisers in both of the offices named there has been good unexceptionable (and especially the appraisers) and devoted Whigs removed and their places supplied by brawling Locofocos- Jeremiah Towle will undoubdedly be nominated for Naval officer: a man who has secured his situation by low intrigue and I doubt not bargain likewise, and his character can be tolerably Judged of, When he employs such men as Jonathan D. Stevenson to procure the vote of the Locofoco- Sneether-[19] for him, the man who palmed himself off upon Major Swift of Philadelphia as a Mr Jarvis, to to get information in Connection with Glentworth to ruin the Whig party in the fall of 1840, by their story of a Great election fraud, there is likewise supposed to be an interest in the proceeds of his (Towles) office agreed to be given to George D. Strong who paid the Editor of the Democratic Review $250 to insert a Laudatory article (With an Engraved likeness) on the life and character of John Tyler. this was done the more effectively to Humbug Tyler as to their devotion to him- but they succeeded only in part, the arrangement was that Towle was to be appointed Collector of the Port in the place of Edward Curtis, who was to be removed and Strong (who is I understand in Washington interceeding for Towles, Confirmation and that of his Brother in law McKibben[20] for Appraiser) was to be Naval officer. Vice, Towle Promoted, to Collector, but they were frustrated by a friend of the Presidents from this

---

[18]Probably owner of Thomas Kirkpatrick & Co., jewelry store in New York City. Bonner, *New York*, 787.
[19]Worthington G. Sneether. See above, III, 467n.
[20]John S. McKibben was appointed appraiser of New York. Longworth *New York Directory, 1847-1848*, 266.

city who hastened to Washington and broke up their arrangements.- Towle has always been one of the the Dirtiest and small-
est of our opponents here, and has manifested, his friendship for
Whigs by removing from office every Whig in his department
but one who is only saved as being useful in carrying on the
Business of the office, but who will undoubtedly be removed if
he (Towle) should be Confirmed- our friends call loudly upon
the Senate to reject him and the Whole Batch of Van Buren
nominations of the same character, especially as it is understood that in most cases Whigs would be nominated in their
place Which would make a material differance to us here in the
forthcoming Campaign- I am told by Mr. Kelly a Confidential
friend of the President (whom I believe you know something off
from Major Morell that the President told him that the Senate
would oblige him by rejecting some of the Persons who he would
be obliged to nominate, and amongst the Rest was Towle for
Naval officer- N. Y. McKibben for Appraiser, N. Y. Rantoul for
Collector of Boston and James D. Watson for Postmaster at
Albany. this latter personage I know well, and a more obse-
quious fellow or tool of Van Buren does not exist. My name
has been mentioned here since my arrival in Connection with
the Albany Post office and I was informed by Mr. Curtis[21] that
my name had been mentioned to the President by a Mr. Parmalli
who had been authorized to give him the names of Three or
four prominent persons for the office, whether this be so or not,
I have no other means of knowing than his word, but I know
that I have never made application to the President for that, or
any other office, but I have no hesitation in saying that who
ever his successor may be, he ought not to be confirmed, as the
successor of Soloman Van Rensselaer, that he does not enjoy the
Confidence of one fourth of the Citizens of Albany, and in a
party view I would not trust Whig Documents in his hands- as
in my opinion if it would subserve the Interests of his Master,
they would be *Accidently lost*. therefore who ever gets the nomination it could not be Worse for us as a party.-You will perceive by the Enclosed slip that there is somewhat of a sketch of
some of the persons named in my letter. the author of the Article is the Mr. Kelly mentioned elsewhere- I pray you again
to pardon the liberty I have taken, and if one as Humble as my-

---

[21]Edward Curtis.

self could occupy your attention for a few moments I should be truly happy to hear from you in this place where I shall remain for some length of time—

I remain my dear Sir
Your obliged friend
THOS. KIRKPATRICK.

Hon. Willie P. Mangum   )
    Washington D. C.   )

P.S. Since writing the above I have learned that Towle got his appointment by an act of servitude to Tyler- he if you Recollect was one of his Witnesses in relation to the veto, and to give the Letter which he Wrote and to show his *perfect disinterestness* indited [sic] It to W. P. Hallet in this City wherein he stated that in the Summer of 1840 he (Towle) was traveling in the West and accidently met Tyler and during the Conversation he Tyler stated to Towle that he was opposed to a Bank of the U. States, for this degrading Service he expected and was not long in receiving office up to this time Towle had never known the President. Strong is advocating his claims as an importer, and has a Son in McKibben's office who I stated before is his Brother in Law and has another son in the office of Towle—so you can judge after enquiring into the Character of Strong how much safety there would be for the Revenue. I will on Monday send you more testimony in the shape of a report to the Legislature of this State, in Febuary showing their Transactions with the Commercial Bank in this city of which Strong was President.

T. K.

[Addressed:]

Hon. Willie P. Mangum
President of Senate
Washington
D. C.

Enclosure—Newspaper Clipping

Correspondence of the Subterranean[22]

WASHINGTON, Jan. 10th, 1844.

Friend Mike—I wrote you a letter some time ago, from this place, in which, among many other things, I took occasion to

---

[22]The New York *Subterranean* was published from 1843 to 1847. Mike Walsh and George H. Evans edited it in its first two years. In 1845 L. N. Carr took it over and in 1847 Corbett and McNally. Fox, *New York Newspapers 1820-1850*, 97.

speak of the position of the President, and the villainous manner in which he had been swindled by political sharks out of the favors which should have been dispensed only among his early and true friends. It was my intention at that time, and if I am not mistaken, I promised to analyze the characters of these most despicable rascals, and expose the means by which they wormed themselves into executive favor, and its consequent advantages. I propose to do so now, partially, and I do not know that I can commence better than by beginning with the clique that performs its scoundrelism, and enjoys its plunder in your city. I allude to the notorious firm of Strong, McKibbin, Towle, Graham, Redwood Fisher, and that last of all fag ends, Barnabas Bates.

Take these fellows individually, without regard to their present accidental position, and it certainly appears reprehensible in a writer, to treat them with more gravity than would be bestowed upon so many rats! But when we consider them collectively, with reference to the influence which their accidental station gives them, and the mischief it enables them to perpetrate, they are entitled to the dignity of a much more weighty opposition. If they remained in the position for which nature assigned them, I would puff them back to their original obscurity with contempt; but inasmuch as they are based upon a temporary pedestal, they must be overturned with a lever, if nothing else will serve. In studying human nature with reference to such characters as these, it is amusing to see how easily mankind will be deceived in their estimate of man, in measuring them by the position which chance or conspiracy has thrown them into.

Here are six fellows that pass for great men, who could not arrive at mediocrity as chimney sweepers, or maintain a tolerable honesty in tending the door of a Punch and Judy show; and yet, one has been the bearer of Despatches to the British Government, another jeopardizes a portion of the Revenue, the third had the consummate impudence to *ask* for, and received the responsible Naval office, the fourth perverts our liberal institutions as Post Master, the fifth, a tributary devil—a sort of jackal, helps him in the office, and the sixth and last, (God help us,) also perils the Exchequer in one of the departments in the New York Custom House, as he did the orphans the widows mites when formerly in another branch of the public service. It

is excessively mortifying to men of integrity and ability, to see
fellows like these, whom they could never meet, except as their
inferiors, occupying stations which should only be the award of
real merit. It appears singular that such creatures should be
able to achieve distinction and success, with the tremendous
drawbacks of stupidity, and more than questionable honesty
against them; but when we consider what the plain devil and
dissembling looks may do, joined to an immeasurable impudence, and a vehemence of hollow protestation, the mystery
partially dissolves; and when we go a little beyond the deduc-
tions of philosophy, and study facts, it vanishes altogether.

Let us see how those libels upon humanity attained that
prominence with the government which has apportioned spoils
to all of them, and now induces Towle, McKibbin & Co. to expect
a whig senate to confirm them in places which they occupy by
the most gross deception and fraud, and of which they have about
the same description of claim as Geo. Munday, the wandering
preacher. Not long since they were all of them, needy, shiftless,
desperate and unscrupulous *political black-legs*, eagerly engaged
in studying the tracks and chances, and ready to pounce upon
any scheme, however base and mean, that would afford them
an opportunity to finger and financier with unascertained
amounts. Geo. D. Strong had some special plans to carry out
for some mercantile houses here, which dealt in the manufactures of Sheffield, Birmingham and Devonshire, had the insolence to ask to be bearer of Dispatches to England, and preferred
as his claims to the appointment, the fact of having disgraced the
literature of the country, by writing two or three execrable con-
coctions of vapid trash, which he called novels, ("in one sense
they richly deserve that title, for they were novel enough, God
knows ["])—and the fact of his having been engaged in some
mysterious land speculations in Williamsburg, with McKibbin
and others, in which many unfortunates who were not acquainted
with the intricate science of windmill lots and water privileges,
suffered some.

John Lorimer Graham founds his claims upon his fraternity
with Tallmadge and other speculators, (of which I will speak
more at length in my next,) and to the fact of his having frequently drawn resolutions at ward meetings, for the laudable
object of giving himself notoriety, that would aid his meagre
practice of the law.

By the bye, just ask Jerry Towle whether Strong or Graham wrote the article, about a year ago, for the Democratic Review. I think he knows how much money it cost for the insertion, and who engraved the frontispiece[.] Jerry and his coadjutors consider it well got up, and well they may, for it paid the much better than some opperations which they lately attempted—but the unfortunate result of the Tennessee election proved fatal to their scheme. Should there be any doubt upon this matter, I will refer you to Silas M. Stilwell, who is a man of most unbounded integrity, and of great knowledge of *matters* and *things in general.* Should Silas, however, refuse to divulge, let me know, and perhaps I can get N. P. Tallmadge, who is considered (especially at the White House) an honorable man, to give the requisite information. In my next letter I will give the particulars of a most wicked fraud which was contemplated upon this administration, it was stupendous in its character, and I think it will be interesting to your readers—exhibiting the rarest specimens of political jugulary.

Redwood Fisher, the familiar devil, who fills the deputyship in the New York P. O., backs his modest pretensions with the proof that he has always been in place before, and like the prostitute who has braved the world for forty winters, offers us a reasoning that the public have tried and proved him to their hearts content.

Yours, &c.,

SOUNDINGS.

WPM-LC

David L. Swain to Willie P. Mangum.

CHAPEL HILL 19, Jan, 1844.

My dear Sir,

Mr. R. H. Graves[23] who is I believe personally known to you, having made one unsuccessful application for the payment of two Treasury notes,[24] the right hand halves of which have been lost under the circumstances disclosed by the accompanying Statement I take the liberty to request that the second attempt may be through your intervention.

---

[23]Ralph H. Graves, 1817-1876, graduated from the state university in 1836. In 1844 he helped organize the alumni association of his alma mater, became a tutor, the treasurer and librarian. Later he taught mathematics at Caldwell Institute. His son became a famous professor of mathematics at the university. Battle, *Hist. of U. N. C.,* I, 482, 486, 496, 795; Grant, *Alumni Hist. of U. N. C.,* 231.

[24]See below James W. McCulloh to Willie P. Mangum, February 23, 1844.

I have had some doubts under the instruction from the Treasury Department as to the proper place to make the newspaper advertisement required. The residence of R. S. Graves is unknown. The applicant R. H. Graves, and the individual Mrs. Thompson by whom the letter was placed in the Post-Office at Middleton Miss. both reside in this county, and the Hillsboro Recorder would therefore I presume be deemed the proper medium for advertising.

Of the honesty of the transaction no one who knows the applicant and reads his statement can doubt for a moment,—The Accompanying letter of your late colleague with respect to the character of Mr. R. H. Graves will probably be satisfactory to the Department. It contains no statement that I would hesitate to affirm by affidavit.

Mr. Graves is in need of money, has for some months been hedged about by technicalities which though doubtless necessary and proper, to the correct administration of the Treasury Department, are nevertheless vexatious, and I hope that further difficulties will not be interposed.

The University continues to prosper. The session opens with an aggregate number of 158- 47 of whom are Freshmen—Of the State of the Great World without our precincts I cannot claim to be either very minutely or accurately informed. Should your Session extend with [sic] the month of July, I may possibly be disposed to assume for a season the attitude of a Looker on in Venice.

Yours very sincerely,
D. L. SWAIN.

Honble. W. P. Mangum.

[Endorsed:]

> Letter from
> Gov Swain
>   President of University
>   to Hon W. Mangum
>   respecting Graves claim
>   19th Jany 1844.

WPM-LC

Willie P. Mangum to Charity A. Mangum

Sunday 21st Jan. 1844

My dear Love.

I send this book on fruit & ornamental trees, that I have not had time to look into—keep it. It may be useful.—

I have got well—at least, I have, I hope, entirely recovered from the cough & breast complaint that alarmed me.—

I shall write tomorrow. I write now, because, my letters so often fail.— My Love to our dear Children, & a kiss to William, if he learns his book, if he does not, he is not to have my kiss.—

W. R. Gales is here with his new *wife*,[25] & going home to-morrow.—How silly! I told him so.—

Always my Love, remember me with affection.

Yr. affectionate husband

W. P. MANGUM

Mrs. C. A. Mangum

WPM-LC

George Constantine Collins[26] to Willie P. Mangum.

BALTIMORE Jany. 22nd. 1844.

Hon. Sir.

I have arrived in this city, some days since and engaged John Murphy to print 50,000 copies of the "fifty reasons" in quantities of 5,000, at $150 per or $1500 the whole, in addition to this I am to pay $100 for stereotyping, &c.

Since my arrival here I have spoken twice, in the Clay Clubs as you may see by referring to the Whig papers of this City. I have been invited to speak on tomorrow evening, as you will also see, and on Wednesday to a Mass Meeting.

I have also the happiness to announce to you, that many of my countrymen have expressed themselves favorably of me and my principles, and also to report progress, in at *least six hopeful and useful converts.*

[25]Weston R. Gales married Mary Spies, daughter of John J. Spies, January 8, 1844. *Hillsborough Recorder,* January 25, 1844.
[26]George Constantine Collins, a New York merchant who also studied law under Josiah Randall, wrote several letters to Mangum in behalf of the Whig candidate. See below Collins to Mangum March 20, 1844 and March 24, 1846. See also *New York City Directory for 1845 and 1846.* Published by Groot and Elston, 1845, p. 84.

It would be well if you should communicate by mail your sentiments to some of your friends here, on the mode of conducting a political campaign, as I find that they are rather too personal towards individuals who do not at all stand in our way, but in whom we may perhaps find future friends, and voters: in order we may recommend to them *conciliation*. (Calhoun and others)—I have every reason to hope that the Whigs will succeed in electing four Congressmen at least, the utmost enthusiasm prevails, and 1840 is again revived! I have spoken to Senator Choate, who remained a short time in the Hotel, and requested his name &c. He declined but informed me that he would see you and Sen. Morehead on the subject, and then would act favorably, &c. On account of the first expense incurred, which will be the greatest, I sincerely request you to see a few of your friends, and use your influence in obtaining for me a few subscriptions towards the undertaking. Mr. Buffington[27] of Penn. treated me in an exceedingly kind manner, he gave me his name and subscription. Geo. R. Richardson[28] Esq. has examined the manuscript and it has pleased him so well that he will obtain for it the sanction of the State Committee, and introduce it into the Clubs of the City. If you could have a moment to spare, it would confer an honor on me, if you would examine a proof sheet; if you cannot, perhaps one of your friends could.

Excuse my Irish frankness, I have used plain language, but I do not the less respect you on that acct however this is not the time for Compliments or eulogies I am now in a different business. I hope it will be crowned with the best fruits of the richest CLAY. Hoping to hear from you shortly, I have the honor to be Hon. Sir—

> Your Obt. Servt. &
> Most devoted and humble friend
> GEO. CONSTANTINE COLLINS.

Hon. Willie P. Mangum, V.P. U.S.

P.S. Dont be offended at my presumption. I have seen you and I shall ever admire you. The books will be ready in seven or

---

[27]Joseph Buffington, 1803-1872, of western Pennsylvania, was trained as a lawyer before he entered Congress in 1843. He served until 1847. He was state judge in 1849, but declined an appointment by Fillmore in 1852 as chief justice of the Utah Territory. *Biog. Dir. of Cong.*, 757.
[28]George R. Richardson was the chairman of the Maryland Whig Committee. See above, III, 200n.

eight days and will have nice covers—drop me a line in a few day—Barnums Hotel.

[Addressed:]

>Hon. Willie P. Mangum
>Vice President of the United States,
>and President of the Senate.
>Washington City,
>D. C.

[Endorsed in pencil in autograph of W.P.M.:]
>To be answered.

———

WPM-LC

B. B. Blume[29] *to Willie P. Mangum.*

PETERSBURG Jany 23d 1844.

Honl. W. P. Mangum.

Dear Sir.

I regret that my situation makes it so *expedient* at least, to trespass on your time, which, no doubt, would otherwise be more profitably employed. But as my sickness of which I complained has already occupied three weeks of my time, I now feel it to be incumbent on me to make some arrangement for the support of my family—My design is to return to the practice of the Law. I have Memphis Ten. Cincinnatti O. & St. Louis Mo. under consideration - with a preference for the first— I hope you will add yet another favor to the many already extended to me - Please let me know *how* & *when* I can be admitted to practice in those states respectively - together with any suggestions you may be pleased to make— Also the residence of the Hone. (Judge) Thomas Maney[30] of Tenne. formerly of Murfreesboro, N°.Cᵃ. as I wish to address him - This much I can say for myself, in losing my property I have lost no character - & I am glad, yes happy, to add, my family are better contented than when they thought themselves at least independent— Some of your many friends can, & no doubt, will, give the desired information— The mode of practice - & the time of probation before license, are important with me now, without the

———

²⁹See above, I, 350n.
³⁰Thomas Maney was judge of the Sixth Circuit Court in Nashville. Livingston, *Law Register,* 1851, 560; *American Almanac,* 1844, 272.

means to sustain me during the time of anxiety. Trusting that you fully appreciate my feelings, & will pardon this liberty, I, am, dear Sir

Your friend & S.
B. B. BLUME.

[Addressed:]

Honl. W. P. Mangum
Prest. U. S. Senate
Washington City
D. C.

Willie P. Mangum to David L. Swain[31]

WASHINGTON CITY 27th. Jan: 1844

My dear Sir.

I received the enclosed[32] this morning which will be satisfactory. - I shall endeavor to get a draft for the amount on the Bank of the State of North Carolina, if I fail in that, I shall take one on New York, & enclose it to you, in a day or two. - A draft on N. York would be cashed at once, by any of the Banks.

We have nothing of much interest here, beyond what you see in the public prints.- Gen Saunders it is believed, will be placed at the head of one of the Departments, probly the Navy.[33] - Porter[34] will be rejected by the Senate, & it is said, that Anderson[35] from Tenn: [?] late a Senator, will have the other. -

We regret the necessity of so many rejections, & avoid it in as many cases, as we can. - But how can we endorse plain cases of moral turpitude? All the indications seem favorable to the success of Mr. Clay - Indeed, no one seems to doubt his success. - In that confidence I fear, the greatest danger lies. -

[31]The original is in the David L. Swain Papers, University of North Carolina.

[32]Not found in the Mangum Papers.

[33]After the rejection of David Henshaw as Secretary of the Navy by the Senate, Tyler appointed Thomas W. Gilmer to that post.

[34]John Madison Porter was appointed Secretary of War in March, 1843, in place of John C. Spencer who became Secretary of the Treasury. Porter had a good military record in the War of 1812. He had practiced law and served as a judge in Pennsylvania. His brother was governor of the state and his family was politically important. This appointment, therefore, was considered a bid by Tyler for the support of the Pennsylvania Democrats. Nevertheless, the Senate rejected him by a vote of 38 to 3. Lambert, *Presidential Politics in the U. S., 1841-1845*, 87-88, 92.

[35]Alexander Outlaw Anderson, 1794-1869, fought under Jackson at New Orleans. He practiced law at Dandridge and Knoxville before he was appointed by Jackson as land officer in Alabama. He served in the Senate from February, 1840, to March 3, 1841. In 1849 he moved to California, where he held several state offices until his return to Tennessee in 1853. In the Civil War he practiced law in Alabama. *Biog. Dir. of Cong.,* 640.

We shall be very glad to see you here this summer - Our session will probably run into July.

> With great respect & regard
> I am, dear Sir.
> Very truly y[rs].
> WILLIE P. MANGUM

[To] *Gov.* Swain.

WPM-LC

Spencer O'Brien[36] to Willie P. Mangum.

STEWARTSBORO' (TEN) 27th Jany. '44

My dear Sir;

I have just written for a friend & neighbour of mine Genl. Russwarm who forwards by this mail, a petition for pay, as the legal representative of his Father who was an Officer of the revolution. The Genl. was principally raised & educated in the Shocco region Warren Co. N. C.

If consistent with your other public duties & it should come in the way, any service you may be enabled to render him in the way of forwarding his claims, will be doing an essential service to one of the best of men, and most sterling of Whigs, besides obliging an old & 'consistent' friend who would *ride out more than 28 miles* to see Willie P Mangum Vice President of the U. S.

There is much speculation here as to who will be the Nominee of the Whig Convention for V. P.? The balance we all know.—Sir, I can assure you of one thing— There is no doubt of Tennessee giving to Mr Clay her support—and that too with a zeal she has never manifested for any other man— I mean that the Whig Party will make an effort for that great Patriot & Statesman, that will beggar all description - that in favor of Genl Harrison was feeble in Comparison. I heard a distinguished Democrat say today, that the nomination of Mr V. B. (now rendered certain) was the most suicidal policy that ever a party was guilty of.- A large majority of the Democrats in this State, left to themselves, would have been for Cass. It is pretty well known here that Polk visited the Hermitage to give the old Genl. that piece of information, but got the 'cold shoulder' for

---

[36]See above, I, 379n.

his pains. So as Judge Seawell used to say, they have to dance to music, not of their own selecting, without even seeing the fiddlers. 'Queen Deus^{De'}. [?] I wonder if Democracy after 1844, will not "stink in the nostrils of even *Warren* men"* This is the prediction here. All the accounts I hear from the old 'North State' are cheering.

By the way I do not know that it would be unbecoming in *you* to say to *me* what are your chances for the nomination? Your name I venture to say to you without fear of the imputation of flattery, is frequently mentioned most favorably in the connection— I say all this as a private individual having forsaken public life altogether with a determination not again to enter the Political arena. Yet, in my quiet pursuits I claim to think & feel as a man, who on all proper occasions should not shrink to vindicate the character of a much abased Country.

We had Baer[37] the Buckeye Black Smith in Nashville on the 8th. He is an original - perfectly so - and is calculated by his peculiar character to make himself felt wherever he goes. In an iminent degree he possesses the talent for swaying the multitude and they are sort of speakers now wanted. His effectiveness as such, more than atones for any violation of Academic taste. He told us he had enlisted for the War and intended to visit every State in the Union between this & the Presidential election.

So soon as you have leisure I should be gratified to hear from you. In the mean time present me respectfully to David Dickerson[38] Esqr.—whose neighbour I am & who can more particularly inform you of my whereabouts & whatabouts.

Very respectfully
Your Friend
SPENCER O'BRIEN.

* Extract from a Speech delivered by W. P. Mangum at Henderson in 1840.

W. P. Mangum Esqr.
    Washington, D. C.

[Addressed:] Honble. Willie P. Mangum
of the U. S. Senate
Washington City

Mail
D. C.

---

[37]Unable to identify.
[38]David W. Dickinson, 1808-1845, a native of Tennessee, graduated from the University of North Carolina before he began practicing law. He served in Congress as a Democrat from 1833 to 1835 and as a Whig from 1843 to 1845. *Biog. Dir. of Cong.*, 906.

WPM-LC

H. P. Hunt[39] to Willie P. Mangum.

TROY [N.Y.,] Jany 28th '/44.

D. Sir

I have presumed to trouble you with a suggestion in relation to the cause of Mr. J. C. Spencer, now before your body. Until today I have said nothing and so far as is in my power have induced our friends to say nothing, *assuming* as beyond question that the whigs of the U. States Senate would give an unanimous vote ag^t the Confirmation - A vote due alike to our principles, our party and the claims of a traitorous tool of a traitor. But rumors of bargaining and corruption have for several days been rife amongst us. *Unconfirmed* loco foco Office holders have been industrious in attempts to manufacture Opinions for a Whig Senate's Governance; And this induces me to speak to an unpurchased and unpurchaseable Whig on the subject. To you then my d. Sir I say unhesitatingly reject the foul offer. Take no counsel of expediency - expediency can never be taken into account at the sacrifice of principle—But, even as a matter of *expediency* there is in my humble judgment but one side to the question. Principle apart, every consideration demands his prompt rejection— What can John C. Spencer and all the rest of the Swiss Corps-who came amongst us for spoils and who by their stations & our Confidence sacrificed Mr. Clay in '/39, do either for good or for evil, when once stript of the adventitious importance given them by Whig generosity? Literally nothing. Nothing my d. Sir— As a proof of this look at the result of our Legislative Caucus the last work in nominating a Candidate for the Vice-Presidency and selecting delegates at large for the Baltimore Convention. But I forbear enlarging, knowing as I think I do, your uncompromising views and having answered my purpose in assuring you that you will be sustained in carrying out those views by every true Whig in this section of this State— You are at liberty to show this to our friends Crittenden and Morehead, having occasion to write Mr White[40] of Indiana

[39]Hiram Paine Hunt, 1796-1865, moved to Troy in 1831, where he practiced law until he entered Congress and after his retirement from Congress. He was in Congress in 1835-1837 and 1839-1843. *Biog. Dir. of Cong.,* 1350.

[40]Albert S. White, 1803-1864, a native of New York, moved to Indiana to practice law in 1829. Before entering Congress in 1837 he held several state offices and was an elector on the Harrison-Granger ticket in 1836. He served in the House of Representatives in 1837-1839, 1861-1863 and in the Senate in 1839-1845. He was president of several railroads. *Biog. Dir. of Cong.,* 1688.

on other matters today I have embraced the opportunity to express substantially the views given in this on the subject of the nomination in question—

It will afford me great pleasure to hear from you on the above or any other matter as leisure may offer—

I am now occupied in the Court of Chancery of my State, having gone back to my profession and quit politics, except so far as hard working in the ranks, for the maintenance of Whig principles and the elevation of Henry Clay is concerned—

With great Respect
Your friend
H. P. HUNT.

Honl. W. P. Mangum.

WPM-LC

John M. Clayton to Willie P. Mangum with Enclosure

(*Confidential*)

NEW CASTLE—DEL.
Jany. 28. 1844.

My dear Sir,

The enclosed letter is sent to me by Mr Michael the High Sheriff of the city & County of Philad[a]. who concurs with the writer Mr. Hamersley[41] that if Porter the Secretary of War is rejected by the Senate of the United States, it ought *not* to be by the vote of the Whigs. Hamersley is one of the strongest men in Pennsylvania, as I understand. From what I know of the State, I think it bad policy for the *Whigs* to reject Porter at this time.-[42] I go against Spencer, & I do not care if the Van Buren men reject Porter - but I hope the Whigs may not do it.- Mr Michael[43] who in my opinion knows the State of Penn[a]. bet-

[41]George W. Hamersley. See below Hamersly to Mangum, January 25, 1846.
[42]See above, 28n.
[43]Norton McMichael, 1807-1879, was a lawyer and journalist. He helped edit *Godey's Lady's Book* for many years. From 1843 to 1846 he was sheriff and in 1866-1869 mayor of Philadelphia. *D. A. B.*, XII, 142-143; *A. H. A. Reports*, 1901, II, 320-321.

ter than any other Whig I am acquainted with, says Porter *ought to be confirmed.*-

Faithfully your friend
JOHN M. CLAYTON

Hon: W. B. [*sic*] Mangum   )
   U. S. Senate.)

P.S. Please show Hamersley's letter to our friends.—

[Addressed:]

  To
   Hon: W. B. Mangum
    Prest. U. S. Senate,
    Washington.—

Enclosure

LANCASTER, [PA.] Jany. 25, 1844.

Dr Sir,

I am sorry to learn from Washington that there is a disposition amongst the Whig members of the Senate to reject the nomination of Mr. Porter as Secretary of War.[44] I think that it is decidedly the policy of the Whig party of this State to have him confirmed. We should thus secure the entire aid and patronage of that Department in the campaign of next fall; for Mr. Porter never will support Mr. Van Buren for the Presidency. In addition to this, I have no doubt in my own mind that if this question and one or two others now pending at Harrisburg are managed with a reasonable share of tact, we shall have the influence of the State Administration with us also in favor of Mr. Clay. I think that these influences are strong enough to turn the majority in this State to either side. They are therefore worth securing. On the other hand, I do not see where the Whigs are to profit by Mr. Porter's rejection. It will only be giving another victory to the Loco Foco radicals of the State, and be the means of providing a place for some bitter and malignant venter of our candidate and his friends. If you think with me in these things,

---

[44] In 1843-1844 Van Buren and Clay forces combined to defeat many of Tyler's appointees. Van Buren leaders felt that Tyler was trying to build up a party of his own through the cooperation of many Democrats. If he were successful in this program, Van Buren leaders felt that his success would impair Van Buren's chances in 1844. The Clay forces had been hostile to Tyler since the bank vetoes. Lambert, *Presidential Politics in U. S., 1841-1845*, 94.

I wish you would try to bring some influence to bear in favor of his confirmation. The nomination will be acted on very soon, and it is important that it should be exerted at an early day.— Can you not silence the frequent and bitter attacks of the "Forum" upon Mr. Porter? Did you receive the "Examiner" which I sent you, avowing its preference for Mr Clayton?

Very sincerely Yrs.
GEO. W. HAMERSLY.

M. McMichael, Esq.

[Addressed:]

> Morton McMichael,
> Sheriff's Office
> Philadelphia,
> Pa.

WPM-LC

Willie P. Mangum to Charity A. Mangum.

WASHINGTON CITY 29th. January 1844.

My dear Love.

I sit down by candle light to write you a line.- I have waited until *now,* hoping to hear from home, as I did hope last night, but have received no letter.- I am well, and have been very well, for the last two or three weeks.- Before that, I was more unwell, and even alarmingly so, than I have ever been.—

I hope My Love, you will write to me every week, or have Sally or Patty to do so. I am always anxious to hear from you, and when I fail, I feel most unhappy.- For, at last, My Love, whatever else may occupy me; I feel more interest in you & our dear Children, than all the world besides.- I am going out this evening to a party at Mrs. Seaton's, and write now a mere line, fearing that if I postpone until tomorrow, you may not receive it next Saturday.

Tomorrow, I will try to write to Patty, if I can get time.- Tell Sally, that I shall write to her not before I get a letter from her.— My mornings for the last week, have been occupied in sitting to have my portrait taken.- Gov. Morehead from Kentucky has engaged a painter to take me.-[45] I would have one

------

[45]He probably refers to the Lampdin portrait which was included as the frontispiece of Volume II of these papers. See below, 72, 131.

to carry home, if it were not, that I do not like to have mine taken, without yours.-

Gov. Morehead, whom you may remember to have heard me often say, is one of the best & most amiable men in the Senate, lives with me, & we are alone.-

Next week, I shall have to *Stand* to have a full length likeness taken for some gentlemen in the City of New York.- It tries one's patience.-

Give my Love to the Children- To Sally- Patty & Mary & William- & give William a kiss for Father, if he is a good boy.-

Mr. Clay will be elected-& every thing in politics, goes on well & promisingly.-

Always remember me, My dear Love, kindly & affectionately; & believe me, whatever may happen, My Love, as your most affectionate husband, & one who would feel it a misfortune yes the deepest misfortune,-to survive my love for my dear wife—

WILLIE P. MANGUM

To Mrs C. A. Mangum

WPM-LC

Thomas Kirkpatrick[46] to Willie P. Mangum.

NEW YORK Jany 29, 1844.

Dear Sir

In my last, I promised to send a report made to the Legislature of this State on the affairs of the Commercial Bank of this City of which Bank Geo. D. Strong was President. Owing to my being confined to the House ever since I have not been able to procure one but I enclose a Courier & Enquirer of this date, which contains an advertisement of the Receiver appointed by the Chancelor wherein the the Debts, and Judgements due the Bank are offered for sale, amongst the names of those who have swindled the widows & orphans, you will perceive the names of Geo. D. Strong and his Brotherinlaw John S. McKibbins. Towles name does not appear in the report but there is no doubt they are all interested alike in the offices here, and I state now what I did in a former letter, that our people [want] the Senate to reject them promptly, if any other information is

---

[46]See above, T. Kirkpatrick to W. P. Mangum, January 19, 1844.

necessary in relation to them I have no doubt it can be furnished for your early action

> I have Dear Sir the Honour to remain your
> obliged Friend

> THOS. KIRKPATRICK.

Hon. Willie P. Mangum
Washington D. C

> [Postmarked:] New York Jan 30

[Addressed:]

> Hon. Willie P. Mangum
> President of Senate
> Washington
> D. C

WPM-LC

Daniel Webster to Willie P. Mangum.

> Saturday Morng
> Feb. 3. '44

My Dear Sir

We very much wanted two Law Books, in Court, which were not to be had this side of N. York, & could not be obtained in season, except thr°. the mail. I therefore took the liberty of having them sent, under cover to you.

1 hope you will excuse this freedom; & send the Books into the Court room, or give them to Mr. Choate.

> Yrs very truly
> DANL WEBSTER

Mr Mangum

[Addressed:]

> Hon. Wm. P. Mangum
> President of the
> Senate of U.S.

WPM-LC

Josiah Randall[47] to Willie P. Mangum.

PHILA. 3 Feb 1844

Dear Sir

I think of visiting Raleigh when Mr Clay is there Can you drop me a line saying when the day of the celebration is, how long it will consume to go there from Washington and which is the best route. I hope every State in the Union will be represented.

Yours &-

J. RANDALL

Hble W. Mangum.

[Addressed:]

The Hble.

W. Mangum Esqr

Prest. of the Senate

Washington

City

Lewis Thompson[48] to Willie P. Mangum.

[4, Feb. 1844]

Sir

You will premit me the liberty that i take of writing to you for as your servant i take it, the kindness that you have allways bestowed on me have caused an abiding gratitude from me to you and as such i write to you now to enquire after your health and i hope that this may find you well as it leaves me at present. We arrived hear from the Spanish main a bout 10 days a go We have had several accidents since we left ower last port which was Curicoa [sic] we was grounded twice or thrice shot one man to peaces quite over board

Mr Mangum will do me the greatis kindness if he will send this letter for my wife, to miss Sarah Polk and she will send it

[47]See above, II, 236n.
[48]There are several letters in this collection from Thompson who was once Mangum's servant. See below Thompson to Mangum, April 9, 1846.

to her for me i hope you will excuse this liberty that your humbel and obedient servant have taken

> i still remain forever your
> Servant LEWIS THOMPSON
> Pensacola Feb 4th 1844.

PS

i will be in Washington in march

[Addressed:]

> To the Honbl.
>
> W. P. Mangum
>
> President of the Senate
>
> of the U. States
>
> Washington
>
> D. C

[Postmarked:] Pensacola
Feb 7

WPM-LC

Washington Hunt[49] to Willie P. Mangum with Enclosure.

> House of Representatives
> Feb 7. 1844

Dear Sir,

I consider it highly important that the information sought in the enclosed letter should be communicated, without reserve. If you will favor me with an answer you shall receive my profound acknowledgments.

The request comes from a friend of mine who is very competent to appreciate the "Magic of a name".

Hoping this fortunate child may be endowed with a goodly

---

[49]Washington Hunt, 1811-1867, a native of Greene County, New York, was admitted to the bar in 1834. Before entering Congress in 1843 he served as judge of the Niagara County Court of Common Pleas. He was in Congress as a Whig from 1843 to 1849. Then he served as comptroller and governor of New York. In 1860 he was offered the vice presidential post on the Democratic ticket but declined. He was a delegate to the Democratic National Convention in 1864. *Biog. Dir. of Cong.*, 1132.

share of those personal and political virtues which have won the admiration of his father and of the country,

I remain,
With great regard,
Yours,
W. HUNT

Honble. Willie P. Mangum.

[Addressed:] To the Honble.
Willie P. Mangum
President of the Senate.

Enclosure

NORWICH, CHENANGO Co. Jany 29, '44

Dear Sir.

A friend of Henry Clay, and of all who are his friends, residing in this village, has named his boy after the President of the Senate the Hon. Willie P. Mangum - but does not know what the middle letter *P* is designed to represent. I presume you can, without trouble, ascertain; and I will be much obliged if you will, at your leisure, write me, what mystery that important letter conceals. It is quite desirable that the child, when grown up should be able to tell *his name,* even if he does not know his father.

Your attention will much oblige
Your Obt. Servant
P. B. PRINDLE.

Hon. W. Hunt
House of Reps
Washington.

[Addressed:]

Hon. W. Hunt,
House of Reps—
Washington

WPM-LC

Asa Pedington[50] to Willie P. Mangum.

Maine Temperance Union,
AUGUSTA, February 9, 1844.

At the Annual meeting of the Maine Temperance Union, held at Augusta, on the 7th and 8th insts. the resolution, a copy of which we have the honor to annex was unanimously adopted by that body.

By an additional resolve, it became the duty of the undersigned to transmit the same to you, which we take pleasure in doing.

"Resolved, That the object of the Memorials on the spirit rations of the Navy, now in general circulation, which pray for the repeal of that law, and recommended that a substitute be furnished meets the hearty approbation of the Maine Temperance Union."

ASA PEDINGTON, Prest. M.T.U.

E. F. D[uren]
Recording Secretary.

A true copy from the records,
Attest:
E. F. DUREN.
Rec. Secty. M.T.U.

Hon. W. P. Mangum
Prest. Senate U.S.

[Post marked:] Augusta Me.
Feb 30

[Addressed:]
Hon. W. P. Mangum,
President of the Senate
Washington
D. C.

---

[50]See above, 3n.

Willie P. Mangum to Paul C. Cameron[51]

WASHINGTON CITY. 10th Feby: 1844.

My dear Sir:

Yesterday in the chair, I added a Postcript, to a letter by Mr. Haywood to you.-[52] His letter will give you all the information in regard to Col. Parrish's case.- It cannot for the present be changed, & the manifestation of any personal interest on my part would be decisive against him upon a renewed application.- Wickleffe[53] with good talents, & yet, more aptitude for business, is, in his nature & disposition, low, coarse, mercenary, in all things selfish, & extremely vindictive.-

He feels that he has the general contempt of the public here, & he has had many occasions to learn that I hold him in detestation.- J. C. Spencer always excepted, I regard him as the meanest of the mean- & in his official acts, I learn on all hands, that his arrogance & proscriptive spirit are rapidly on the increase; as he learns, that his prospects for other & more lucrative office *with the advice of the senate,* are daily diminishing.

Spencer by the inattention of two or three men, had nearly stolen a successful march on us- Eight days before the vote, his strength was 13 votes.- By the application of the whole power of the admn reinforced by individuals in various quarters, he increased it to twenty one.- The whole operation was conducted in silence & secrecy by Spencer & his Minions- & the vote fell upon us with absolute surprise.-

Spencer is a man of eminent intellectual ability—inferior to no man in New York.- In truth, he has the talent & cunning of the Devil himself.- Yet all fair minds must admit, that he is not as respectable a personage as his devilship—For the latter, after his first apostacy & fall, has at least, had the merit of con-

---

[51]The original is in the Cameron Papers, University of North Carolina.

[52]In the Cameron Papers, University of North Carolina, is a letter from W. H. Haywood, Jr., to Paul C. Cameron, February 7, 1844, saying that he enclosed a letter (the letter was not found) from the Postmaster General declining Haywood and Cameron's recommendation that Col. Parrish's post office be continued. Cameron had written to Mangum and Mangum had turned over Cameron's letter to Haywood. On Haywood's letter to Cameron, Mangum added this postscript: "P.S. I hold no intercourse with the P. M. & therefore Mr. H. acted for me—Judging from what I hear of *other cases,* the decision is not likely to be reversed. Very truly Dr Sir, Yrs W. P. M."

On February 19, 1844, the post office at Round Hill in Orange County was re-established, and Doctor C. Parrish was made postmaster. Note to Haywood from the Post Office Department, February 19, 1844. Cameron Papers, University of North Carolina.

[53]Charles Anderson Wickliffe, 1788-1869, a former governor and Congressman from Kentucky, was Tyler's Postmaster General from October, 1841, to March 6, 1845. He was a Kentucky Whig who for many years had been an enemy of Clay. He was sometimes called the "Old Duke." Van Deusen, *Life of Clay,* 337; *Biog. Dir. of Cong.,* 1697.

sistency; whereas Mr. S. undergoes a new apostacy with every
moon, if his interest may require it.-

Wise[54] has been permitted to pass— *All* willing that he might
have the money, which it is said, he much needs, & go out of the
country— Though a few of us, did not feel at liberty to endorse
him in person.-

Every thing here indicates the almost certain election of
Mr. Clay.- If we cannot beat Mr. Van Buren, we can beat no
one.- Every intelligent Whig here, desires the contest to be with
him.- The Whigs, therefore, have avoided in all cases, during
this session, & especially at the opening of it, to cooperate to
any extent with his unfriendly allies, to weaken him.- At the
meeting of Congress if the Whigs would have cooperated, *he*
nor *his* could have succeeded in the appointment of any of their
officers.- The Whigs- many of them- with that Bourbon
spirit- "That forgets nothing, & learns nothing," were ready to
do it, for the *wise* [sic] *reason*, that it would make temporary
mischief, & produce animosities, in the ranks of their natural
enemies.- That however, was prevented by the most decisive &
even violent action.- The consequence is, that Mr. V. B. is fixed
in the Loco-foco Saddle.-

We shall unhorse him at the first encounter, without presenting even a "sharp point".-

A compromize Candidate- Cass for instance, would have
greatly endangered us in Penn: & Ohio.- Whereas, as against
Mr V. B. these states are regarded as absolutely certain.-

What think you of Mr Calhoun's chivalry?[55] Has the world
ever seen so much bluster & gasconade issue in such puny &
pusillanimous results?

If you see your Father, present him my best respects & most
affectionate regards.- I will not revive painful recollections, by
saying how deeply & painfully, I was grieved & afflicted, at the
late deplorable & irreparable calamity that Heaven permitted
to fall upon his house & his old age.-[56] I learned from Doct.
Webb & others, that he bore himself up with remarkable for-

---

[54]Henry A. Wise, who had great influence with Tyler, was appointed minister to Brazil. He
had declined an appointment as Secretary of the Navy in 1841 and had been appointed minister to
France in 1843. This nomination to France was not confirmed. He served as minister to Brazil from
1844 to 1847. *Biog. Dir. of Cong.*, 1720; *Hillsborough Recorder*, February 22, 1844.

[55]After being defeated in the state Democratic conventions in New York and Massachusetts in
1843 and after being decisively defeated by the Van Buren forces in the organization of the House
of Representatives, Calhoun, on December 21, 1843, announced that he would not be a candidate
and would not have anything to do with the Democratic convention. As a result, South Carolina
refused to select delegates to the National Convention. Wiltse, *Calhoun: Sectionalist*, 144-147.

[56]Rebecca (Bennehan) Cameron, the wife of Duncan Cameron, died in early November, 1843.
John Struthers & Son to Duncan Cameron, Cameron Papers.

titude- *that* rather indicates to my mind, the intensity of hidden griefs— the more intense in proportion to the manly effort to repress their exhibtion. May God give strength, & sanctify the bereavement to the household. To Mr. Bennehan you will also, be pleased to present my respect & most kindly regards.- Will you all meet Mr Clay at Raleigh in April? I hear, that he designs to be in Raleigh on his birthday, the 12th. of April.- I hope old Orange "Will be there." Would it not be well for the patriotic ladies of Raleigh to be moved to offer a spendid banner to the county which shall send the *largest delegation* having regard to the *population of the respective* counties, & their *distance from the seat of Govt?*

The ratio to be settled by a comm.n of intelligent Gentlemen.- If you think there is anything in this thought, will you communicate with Mr Badger on the subject?

I trust, indeed, I am sure, that the hospitalities & affectionate regards of the "old North" towards her illustrious guest will be neither sparingly nor grudgingly tendered.-

With my best respects to Mrs. Cameron I beg you to accept the assurance of my respect & most

friendly regards
WILLIE P. MANGUM

To—
Paul C. Cameron esq.

WPM-LC

Robert Ransom[57] to Willie P. Mangum.

WARREN COUNTY Feby 10th. 1844

Dr. Sir
& friend

Suffer me again to call on you, to aid me, in procuring the situation at West Point, for my Son, *Robert* whose name has been enrolled in the proper department as an applicant for eighteen months or longer. He is a Boy of fine promise, and comes fully up in all particulars to the schedule sent me by the Secretary of War. (Spencer) I refer you to his preceptor Mr. Ezell of Warrenton, & my neighbours for his qualifications and

---

[57]See above, III, 84n.

moral character. I am as you are well apprised a very poor man, and a large family to support, or I would seek some other mode to Educate my Son. This District has with *one* or *two* exceptions been represented with the Sons of one family for a long number of years not of the same name but of same blood at West Point. Hoping you will see the Secretary of War, and use your influence *immediately,* as I can hope nothing from *our* Representative Mr. Daniel[58] to whom I wrote a month ago, & have not heard a word from. Hoping to hear from *you soon* I am as ever your friend respectfully and

truly
ROBT. RANSOM.

Honl. W. P. Mangum

[Addressed:]

The Honl. Willie P. Mangum
Washington
D. C

WPM-LC

Walter Lenox & others to Willie P. Mangum.[59]

WASHINGTON, February 14, 1844.

To the Hon. Willie P. Mangum M.C.

Sir:

The undersigned, Executive Committee of the Clay Club of Washington City, take the liberty to inform you, that the Whigs of Washington, emulating the spirit which animates their patriotic Whig brethren throughout the Union, have formed an Association under the name of "The Clay Club of Washington City," and are eager to lend all the aid that may be in their power to forward the good cause, and secure for it a glorious and enduring triumph by the election of HENRY CLAY to the Presidency. In their efforts for the advancement of the cause, they hope to have the co-operation of the Whig Members of Congress by their Executive Committee, and the object of this communication is respectfully to invite their co-operation.

The undersigned propose taking a suite of rooms on Pennsylvania Avenue, south side, between 9th and 10th streets, one or

---

[58]John R. J. Daniel.
[59]This is a printed circular.

two of which may be used by the Congressional Committee, if
they should deem it advisable.

We have the honor to be,

With great respect,

Your obedient servants,

WALTER LENOX,	GEO. W. HARKNESS,
JOHN A. BLAKE,	LEONARD HARBAUGH,
SYLVANUS HOLMES,	ISAAC BEERS,
RICH'D C. WASHINGTON,	R. H. STEWART,
SETH HYATT,	WM. THOMPSON,
SAMUEL BACON,	GEO. WATTERSTON,
R. S. PATTERSON,	J. I. HENSHAW,
JOS. BORROWS,	L. H. HEWITT.

[Addressed:]

Hon. Willie P. Mangum
Mrs. Scotts Ind. Avenue
Opp. City Hall.

WPM-LC

Horace T. Royster[60] to Willie P. Mangum.

PERRY COUNTY ALA Feb'ry 15th. /'44

Dear Sir

When I last saw you in Granville on your way to Washington you promised me if I had any business you would attend
to it cheerfully. I believe I then suggested to you, that in all
probability, I should send on a petition for the establishment of
a post office. I have settled myself North from Marion six miles,
And have a very extensive practice. My practice since June
last being worth Two Thousand Dollars. I have enclosed[61] you
a petition which you will understand by reference to it. I do
not know but what I ought to have enclosed to post Master
Genl. and requested your aid in the matter. Your attention to
this matter will confer a great favour on me. We have invited
Mr. Clay to visit us on his way to the Old North State I had the
Honour of being one of the Committee I understood on yester-

---

[60]A native of Granville County, North Carolina, Royster moved to Alabama where he practiced
law near Marion. He sent his son to the University of North Carolina. Grant, *Alumni Hist. of U.
N. C.*, 539.
[61]This enclosure is not in the Mangum Papers.

day he would be in Mobile by 25th. Int. We have not received
an answer from him yet. the friends of Mr. Clay are anxious
that he should not only come here, but further north he is invited to Tuscaloosa.[62] I feel more anxious to have the office
established prayed for, on account of the approaching Presidential election. The people in this region will be dissatisfied
with the nomination of Mr. V. I have an extensive intercourse
with the people not only in this but adjacent vicinities, and so
far as an investigation of their political feelings have been developed to me they (the Democrats) say almost unanimously
that if they cannot vote for Mr Calhoun, they undoubtably will
go for Mr Clay in preference to Mr Van Buren. It is my opinion that a supineness in the whigs have produced the result of
past defeat all that is necessary at present to produce among the
Whigs here, the spirit of the whigs of N.C., and I venture the
prediction that they will carry the state in the presidential election— Greater triumphs have been achieved in other states
where the odds have been more decidedly against us. A plan
that [has] system about it and carried on with determined energy
& unfaltering steps will accomplish wonders in any undertaking.
The region of Country expected to be benefitted by the office
wished know nothing about Politics, but what they are told by
Demagoges - they are mostly Loco's - but will vote for Mr
Clay in preference for Van—I know of but few who take papers, among them a Central Clay club has been determined on
in Marion and auxilliaries throughout the county, (One in this
region and will be at my office). I have nothing of news to write
you, only the people are perfectly sick of specie, it is flowing
into the Country by Thousands and Large planters are willing
to give specie checks on Mobile for Ala. money. Has the Large
influx of specie into this Country been the effect of the heretofore depreciated condition of our money or is it the effect of the
Tariff or what - Many speculations here about it. The ignorant
part of the community who are democrats, begin to say it is not
what they expected it to be, they prefer paper—The Gold Humbug has at last exploded, and the Whig Doctrine with respect
the currency, will be found to be the only safe and efficient one.
I am of opinion the name of Henry Clay will aid much our cause

[62]Clay's itinerary included New Orleans, Mobile, Montgomery, Columbus, Macon, Savannah,
Wilmington, Raleigh. On July 1, 1844, he wrote Stephen F. Miller, of Tuscaloosa, a letter explaining
his stand on Texas. *Niles' Register*, LXV, 331; LXVI, 105, 106, 372.

The Senate Chamber, 1844. Showing the seats of Senators. Mangum's appears twice as President and also in the front row, center. From the original stipple engraving in *The United States Album Embellished with . . . Appropriate Engravings . . . Twenty-Eighth Congress. . . .* Arranged and designed by J. Franklin Reigart, Lancaster City, Pennsylvania, 1844. Original in the possession of Miss Sallie Preston Weeks, Washington, D. C.

in this State Your attention to my request will be reciprocated by any favour in my power. I am Dr Sir

> With Sentiments of high regard
> Your friend & Obt Svt
> HORACE T. ROYSTER.

Any Documents which you may think worth sending direct them to Marion or Perry C. H.

[Addressed:] To,

> The Honbl. Wiley P. Mangum
> President of the Senate.
> Washington
> D. C.

Mail.

WPM-LC

Calvin Colton[63] to Willie P. Mangum.

CARLTON HOUSE, NEW YORK Feby 15—/44

My Dear Sir,

I stopped a day in Philadelphia, & our man, Mr. Reynolds,[64] talked very bravely in response to my suggestion of having some of my Tracts translated into German.—I am not sure whether it will be better to have it done here or there. If you will address me here on the subject, *as proposed,* it will doubtless facilitate the operation, if it can be started at all, as is quite probable.

I hope to send you a copy of my Tract, *Labor & Capital,* next week.

Allow me to say a word about putting Mr. True[65] to work— He will find enough to do *at once,* all or most of which would not otherwise be done. The importance of sowing seed *early* I need not speak of.—I am glad you are at the head of the Senate Committee.[66] A joint meeting with the Finance Committee of the

[63]See above, III, 235n.
[64]Possibly John Reynolds, a former editor of the Lancaster *Weekly Journal.* Philip Shriver Klein, *Pennsylvania Politics 1817-1832: A Game Without Rule,* Philadelphia, 1940, 221-222.
[65]Possibly Lambert True who was a clerk in the Washington post office.
[66]Mangum headed the Senate Whig Committee for the campaign of 1844.

House, (Mr. Winthrop, Chairman) might start the business, by the weight of your finger. —

Very Respectfully Yours
C. COLTON

Hon. W. P. Mangum

[Addressed:]

Hon. W. P. Mangum
Washington
D. C—

WPM-LC

Thurlow Weed to Willie P. Mangum.

ALBANY, Feb. 15, 1844

Hon Willie Mangum,

Dear Sir,

I am informed that the Whig Members of our Legislature have addressed a Letter to you, expressive of the high sense they entertain of the firmness and patriotism of the Whig Members of the Body over which you preside, as manifested in the Rejection of the nomination of Mr. John Spencer for a Judge of the U. S. Supreme Court.

The publication of that Letter in the National Intelligencer, and its re-publication throughout this State would do much good. Mr Spencer boa[s]ts that the Delegation in Congress from this State, were for him. The Whig Members of the Legislature and the Whig Press throughout the State, are with the Senate and *against* Mr Spencer.

If in your judgment there is no impropriety in publishing that Letter, you will render good service to the cause by sending a copy of it to Messrs. Gales & Seaton.

Very truly Yours,
THURLOW WEED

[Addressed:]

To the Honorable
W. Mangum
President of the Senate
Washington

WPM-LC

Will. A. Graham to Willie P. Mangum.

HILLSBORO'
Feby 17th 1844.

My Dear Sir

During the Canvass of 1840, I placed in your hands my Journals of the Genl. Assembly of 1834 & 1838, as also some other papers & documents - among the rest a Milton newspaper containing the speech of Mr. Brown on presenting the resolutions of the Legislature of 1838. I have never expected to have use for them again, but in the present canvass I find they may become necessary, and therefore I beg, if you can have them hunted up at home, that you will direct them to be sent to me— I have no plan of a campaign marked out as yet. I am invited to meet Mr Clay at Wilmington, and cant decline going tho' I presume but little can be effected in my line, on such an occasion. I had expected to be with him at Raleigh, & I suppose must be. When I was there at the Supreme Court, I attended a meeting of the Central Committee and suggested that they should invite Messrs Crittenden, Morehead, Foster & Jarnagan to meet with Mr Clay in Raleigh. For I very much fear that he will be so much taxed by calls on him to speak that he will be either exhausted, or compelled to give offence. I go tomorow to Guilford Co. Court, & after the Co. Court here the ensuing week will be at Granville. At each of which, if desired I will address the people. My impression is, that not much will be effected in Canvassing the Eastern Counties, and that the great contest must be in the middle & Western sections. As far as I can hear, our friends are sanguine and confident. The adversary doubting, but disposed to exertion. I think we have little to hope from division in their ranks. The friends of Mr Calhoun will hardly seperate, but will fall into the line of Van Buren upon his making some new promises or renewing old ones, that neither party will ever expect to be fulfilled. What say you?

We are hoping that Judge Nash[67] will be appointed to the vacancy on the Bench of the Supreme Court. I have not time to write more at the moment, and remain

With high regard
Your Friend & Servt
WILL. A. GRAHAM

Hon W. P. Mangum Prest. Sen. U. S.

[Addressed:]

Hon. Willie P. Mangum
President Senate U. S.
Washington City.

[Post marked:] Hillsboro N. C.
Feb 20

WPM-LC

Henry W. Miller to Willie P. Mangum.

RALEIGH Feby: 22nd 1844

My Dear Sir:

It affords me much pleasure to inform you that at a recent meeting of the 'Wake Clay Club' you were unanimously elected an honorary member thereof: - and I have been instructed to invite you to be present on the 12th April at which time we expect Mr Clay— It is our desire to give him a cordial and enthusiastic welcome.—Accept the best wishes of

Very Truly & Resply
H. W. MILLER.
Prdt: W. C. Club.

Honl. W. P. Mangum

[Addressed:]

Honl. W. P. Mangum
Washington City

---

[67]William Gaston, who was one of the three justices of the state supreme court, died in 1844. Frederick Nash was elected to succeed him. The other two justices were chief justice Thomas Ruffin and associate justice Joseph J. Daniel. *N. C. Manual*, 446.

WPM-LC

Washington Hunt[68] to Willie P. Mangum.

House of Representatives
Feb 22. 1844

My dear Sir,

I enclosed your letter to my friend Benjamin F. Rexford Esqr, who has made his son illustrious by conferring your name upon him. Perhaps I ought to add that Mr. R. is a member of the Bar of Chenango County in our State, of the highest worth and respectability.

I have just received a reply from him, in which he desires me "to convey to Mr. Mangum his grateful acknowledgements for his note, so full of beauty, kindness and generosity." He adds "It will not be the fault of the parents if the child so felicitously named shall fail to live and act in a manner becoming the name-sake, both of the chivalrous ante-Revolutionary Patriot of North Carolina, and the distinguished Statesman who presides over the councils of the national Senate" and "that he hopes to be able before Mr. Mangum leaves the Senate to have the pleasure of calling upon him personally, and assuring him of his high appreciation of this mark of favor, which is as gratifying as it was unexpected."

Praying you to accept the expression of my high regard and consideration,

I remain, Dear Sir,
Yours truly,
W. HUNT.

Honble.

Willie P. Mangum,
President of the Senate &c. &c.

WPM-LC

James Wm. McCulloh to Willie P. Mangum.[69]

Treasury Department
Comptroller's Office.
23.ᵈ Feby 1844.

Sir,

When the Report that was made on the 26.ᵗʰ Ultimo by the First Auditor in favor of Ralph H. Graves, for the principal and

---

⁶⁸See above, 38n.
⁶⁹See above, 23-24, and below, 227.

interest owing on two Treasury notes, of one hundred dollars each- the right hand half parts whereof have been lost; the said Ralph having delivered a bond of indemnity, in the form usually required, when payments are made on account of lost, or destroyed Treasury notes; I deemed it to be my duty, considering the circumstances of the case, as set forth in the papers delivered to prove the loss of the said half parts, and the relations of the parties who have been, are and might be immediately or remotely interested in the said notes and case- to suggest that evidence ought to be required, which would prove satisfactorily, that all who claim in the premises under Richard S. Graves, do so in good faith- because the said notes, with many others, were issued in his favor- and delivered to him, at this Department, as the Treasurer of the State of Mississippi.

Since that suggestion was communicated to the claimant- an affidavit, made on the the 10th. Instant by Eliza J. Thompson, sister of Richard S. Graves, had been furnished- and I am satisfied by its averments, and the statements that were previously made by her and R. H. Graves, of his and her good faith- but, I still deem it necessary, as the payment of said claim to him will be in effect a payment to Elijah Graves, that the said Elijah shall also state, under oath, all that he knew or believed concerning the appropriation and remittance of said two Treasury notes, or half parts thereof, at the date of said proceedings - that his good faith, in the premises, may also be thereby made manifest: and of this, I most respectfully apprize you, as through your kindness, the claimant has hitherto communicated with this Department.

With great respect
Your Obdt. Servt.
James Wm McCulloh
Comptroller.

[Addressed:]

To the   Honorable Willie P. Mangum
President of U. S. Senate.

Note)-[70]

It would seem that Elijah Graves must shew, that the *Treas: Notes passed into his hands* for valuable & bona fide consideration.

W. P. Mangum

---

[70]This note is in Mangum's handwriting.

WPM-LC

Septimus Tuston[71] to Willie P. Mangum.

WASHINGTON D. C.
February 24, 44.

To the Hon—
The President of the Senate,

Dear Sir

I deeply regret that the usual devotional exercises at the opening of the Senate should have been pretermitted in consequence of any apparent delinquency on my part. The "weekly interchange" required by the joint resolution will explain my absence from the Senate during the present week and the *"aequo pede"* of the clocks in both ends of the Capitol will account for the apparent tardiness of my colleague on the two past mornings. Be pleased Sir to overlook the past and unless Providence interposes there will be no similar omission in future. I thank you for the kind & generous spirit in which Mr Dickens[72] at your request communicated your wishes on the subject.

Most cordially & gratefully
Your friend & obt svt-
SEPTIMUS TUSTON

To the Hon Mr Mangum
President of the Senate
Present—

[Addressed:]
To the Hon Mr. Mangum
President of the Senate
Washington

WPM-LC

Willie P. Mangum to W. A. Graham.[73]

WASHINGTON CITY 26th Feby 1844

My dear Sir:

I shall write home immediately, & have a thorough search made for the documents you desire.[74] Last summer I made a

---

[71]Chaplain of the Senate.
[72]He refers to Asbury Dickins, secretary of the Senate at this time.
[73]The original is in the William A. Graham Papers, Department of Archives and History, Raleigh, N. C.
[74]See above, William A. Graham to W. P. Mangum, February 17, 1844.

partial search for them, for the use of Mr. Nash.— The whole of my papers, documents etc. were removed, during my absence from home, & placed, where they were almost inaccessible. I am sure, they are at home, & safe, & I fear too safely placed away to be found in my absence.

We think here, that your success is entirely certain, & yet none of the usual exertions should be remitted.—I concur in the opinion, that not a great deal can be accomplished by your presence in the East, but notwithstanding, I think, you ought to make an effort to pass through the Eastern Counties this spring. By judicious arrangements, it may be accomplished in a forthnight [sic].

I think, you will do well to go to Wilmington.—Though much may not be done, yet you will have paid them the Compliment of a visit. You will then be enabled to go to Newbern, taking the principal points on your route to Newbern, & then sweep through northwardly, say, Washington, Plymouth, perhaps, Williamston, Windsor, Edenton, Hartford in Perquimans Elizabeth City—Hence to Gates, Winton—Jackson & Halifax & thence homeward—

Afterwards, can't you set out at Fayetteville & pass through Deberry's district? The residue of the time should be given to the Midland Counties & the Mountains—The extreme West ought to be canvassed fully—If it shall be done, you will beat Hoke[75] there, farther than did Gov Morehead, his opponent— Hoke & his friends count largely upon breaking into the Whig ranks in the West.—I heard this while he was here on a visit— He did not come to see me. His time was busily applied to intercourse with the leading Loco-foco's, & I suppose, in garnering up, documentary matter for the Campaign. He however, said here that he must be beaten from 6 to 8,000 Votes.

My Hon: Colleague[76] is understood to be very busily engaged in writing letters & sending matter into the State, & especially, in the Counties west of the Yadkin. How much my dear Sir, I am disappointed in regard to his force, the intent of his calibre, & general ability.—That disappointment reaches his political friends.—The most elegant & consummate dandy in our grave & plain body, he undoubtedly is, & industrious, looking into the papers minutely, but constantly missing the Senatorial

---

[75]Michael Hoke. The vote for the two candidates was: Graham 42, 586 and Hoke 39, 433. Norton, *Democratic Party in N. C.*, 106, 149, 152.
[76]William H. Haywood, Jr.

pitch, & taking the merest microscopical & technical views of everything—fertile in suggesting difficulties & adroit & unsurpassable in *flushing* (as the sportsmen say.) mere shadows.— He made his *debut,* upon a question of remitting a forfeiture of $50, incurred by the Capt or Master of a Vessel from Maine, for some irregularity in his registry discovered at New Orleans.— The whole learning of the Case had been minutely & accurately examined, & was exhibited to the Senate with striking ability— the debate between him & Fairfield[77] of Maine (a very dull man.) ran through two or three days—that is, parts [of] 3 days. Huntington[78] assisting Fairfield in a short speech, designed to be exceedingly sarcastic & contemptuous—& the Vote was finally taken—though I could not vote with my colleague, yet I did feel for the North State, when *"her Senator,"* after brewing a storm in a teapot, got only 3, 4, or 5 votes to back the affluence & variety of his learning—The *rest* has been very much of a piece with the first exhibition *"ex uno disce"* etc. & yet he may be troublesome.—I stand upon terms of great civility with him, & unless he be disposed to strike in the dark, his dispositions seem well enough.—

As all this is contrary to my wont, it is designed only for your eye. For, I shall make it a point to observe great delicacy towards him unless he shall violate the Courtesies of our relations.

My Colleague was as well understood here in a fortnight, as he is in Raleigh.—He set out a very busy contriver—I think, he has remitted somewhat. The new Senator from Maryland, Pearce[79] after their first meeting in committee, asked me gravely, if my colleague was not educated at St. Omers College? Clingman, who obviously feels that he could not meet you without experiencing some unpleasant twinges, is very much disposed to make what reparation he may, by doing all he can for your election.—He has frequently urged me, to press upon you the expediency of going into every county in the Mountain Country.—He & Barringer will fill their districts with all the matter, that may be deemed useful.

We are getting ready much matter for distribution between

[77]John Fairfield, 1797-1847, was Senator from Maine from 1843 until his death in 1847. *Biog. Dir. of Cong.,* 955.
[78]Jabez Williams Huntington, 1788-1847, was Senator from Connecticut from 1840 to 1847. *Biog. Dir. of Cong.,* 1133.
[79]James Alfred Pearce, 1804-1862, was Senator from Maryland from 1843 until his death in 1862. A Whig in 1844, he later became a Democrat. *Biog. Dir. of Cong.,* 1394. Pearce here implies that Haywood was Jesuitical since St. Omer's was a Jesuit school.

$1600 & $1800 have been raised here to procure documents etc. rooms are engaged & the Clay Club have propose to furnish clerks to direct all the documents, that may be furnished & franked. In about a fortnight, the work will commence. Clay can't be arrested. Van Buren will be the candidate, & *is already* beaten in the public mind.—That is much. We feared early in the winter, that he might be driven off—But Benton, you know, is worth his Weight in gold[80]—He beat V. B. in 1840, & *his policy,* only makes assurance doubly sure, that the party will be beaten in '44.

The Whigs here, at the beginning of the session, declined all connexion that tended to weaken Mr. V. B. Everything turned out as they wished. The Calhoun men surrender with the most broken & pusillanimous spirit ever witnessed—They will generally fall in—not Calhoun himself but the paltrily ambitious men in his ranks, lest they may loose position.

Cass' friends are moving in Penn: New Jersey, & New York. Last week they carried the State convention of N.J. over which Geo. [Gen.] Wall (V.B.) presided with an overwhelming majority. That is working well. You will have seen that Capt Tyler's democratic Convention[81] will be held in Baltimore on *the same day,* that the general Loco or V.B. Convention is to be held. They will make terms, for an *old coat* with a twist of Tobacco thrown in; but if that cannot be done, (as I think, it cannot) his friends will set up for themselves, until the pieces of silver (not 30 an half dozen will suffice) are forth coming.

Some yet entertain fears that V.B. may be given up, but you & I, who know the master spirit of the party, know better.— To withdraw V.B. is to disband & to surrender the Contest.—

Gov. Morehead[82] went to Connecticut—all well there—Our friends don't doubt. He will return today or tomorrow.—

I hope Orange will send her full quota to Raleigh—I write, while Dayton[83] is speaking, & now must close.

Most Truly yr friend etc
WILLIE P. MANGUM

---

[80]Benton, as a leader of the Van Buren forces, was very unpopular with Calhoun's supporters.

[81]In April, 1844, " 'a large number of republicans' " assembled in Washington to organize a movement for Tyler's nomination. The meeting recommended a convention in Baltimore of the " 'Democratic republicans.' " The convention was held May 27. According to Tyler, about 1000 delegates from all parts of the Union were in the convention. In accepting the nomination, he referred to the convention as a "Democratic" convention. Tyler's friends suggested that he seek the nomination of the regular Democratic convention, but he refused to make the effort. Chitwood, *Life of Tyler,* 375-377.

[82]Gov. J. T. Morehead, Senator from Kentucky.

[83]William L. Dayton, 1807-1864, was Senator from New Jersey from 1842 to 1851, *Biog. Dir. of Cong.,* 891.

WPM-LC

Memucan Hunt[84] to Willie P. Mangum

(Private)

GALVESTON, TEXAS, 27th February 1844

To

Hon. W. P. Mangum, Pres't. U. S. S.

My Dear Sir,

I have the pleasure to introduce to your acquaintance, herewith, my esteemed friend W. D. Miller Esqr.,[85] Secretary of our secret embassy at Washington. Gen. J. Pinckney Henderson,[86] formerly of North Carolina, is charged with that important trust, which is for the purpose of accomplishing, if possible, the union of this country and the U. S.

Mr. Miller is formerly of Alabama, and brought with him to this country letters from Judge Martin[87] of N. C. to me. - He has been a member of our congress and for more than the last two years private Secretary of President Houston. There is no gentleman in Texas who more fully possesses my confidence in all the relations of life than Mr. Miller does. You will find him very inteligent and discreet;- No one possesses a better knowledge of the affairs of Texas than he does. I therefore refer you to him for the state of our local and foreign affairs.

Your respectful consideration to Mr. Miller during his residence in Washington will be a kindness to your friend,

MEMUCAN HUNT

[Addressed:]

Hon W. P. Mangum
Pres.ᵗ U. S. S.
Washington City

Introducing)
Mr Miller)

---

[84]See above, II, 226n.

[85]At this time William D. Miller was on his way to Washington to become Secretary of the Texan commissioners, Isaac Van Zandt and J. P. Henderson. In writing Jackson, February 16, 1844, Houston stated that he was directing his "Private Secretary and confidential friend, W. D. Miller, Esq., to convey my personal salutations and embraces to you, with authority to communicate everything upon every subject. Mr. Miller is a young gentleman who has been with me in my office since the commencement of my present administration. He knows all my actions and understands all my motives. I have concealed nothing from him—nor will he conceal anything from you." Bassett (ed.), *Cor. of Jackson*, VI, 263, 276-277.

[86]James Pinckney Henderson, 1808-1858, a native of Lincoln County, North Carolina, studied and practiced law in Lincolnton until he moved to Mississippi in 1835. After recruiting troops and fighting for Texan independence, he was appointed attorney general of Texas in 1836 and secretary of state in 1837. He represented the Republic of Texas in Europe in 1838 and in the United States in 1844. He was the first governor of Texas after her admission to the Union. From 1857 to 1858 he was United States Senator. *Biog. Dir. of Cong.*, 1086.

[87]He probably refers to James Martin, judge of the Superior Court of North Carolina from 1827 to 1835 or Francois Xavier Martin formerly of North Carolina and in 1844 chief justice of Louisiana.

WPM-LC

H. W. Miller to————[88]

RALEIGH Feby 27, 1844.

Dear Sir:

I have been instructed by the "Wake Clay Club" at one of its recent meetings to give you an invitation to be present on the 12th of April next at which time we expect to welcome our distinguished Countryman Henry Clay.—

I comply with the wishes of the Club most cordially & trust you will find it convenient to attend on that occasion.—Let me hear from you.—

I am Very Respectfully
H. W. MILLER
Presdt: Wake C. Club

————

WPM-LC

George Wallace McGiffin & others to Willie P. Mangum.

WASHINGTON HALL, Feb. 27th/44

To W. P. Mangum,
Dear Sir,

The undersigned, members of the Washington Litterary Society of Washington College,[89] are constituted a committee, to inform you of your election as an honorary member of their body. Permit us to accompany with this intimation, the assurance of our individual regard, and warmest wishes for your personal welfare and happiness.

With the highest regard for you and
yours we remain, your friends—
GEO. WALLACE McGRIFFIN
J. N. [torn]
J. H. OLIVER.

Hon W. P. Mangum

[Addressed:]

Hon. Willie P. Mangum
U. S. Senate,
Washington
D. C.

————
[88]This was probably addressed to W. P. Mangum.
[89]The future Washington and Lee University, Lexington, Virginia.

WPM-LC

Saml. S. Phelps[90] to Willie P. Mangum.

Washington 2ᵈ March 1844

Hon W. P. Mangum,

Sir — The bearer Mr. J. R. Lambdin[91] who has been introduced to me as a distinguished artist of Philadelphia, has applied to me as Chairman of the Comᵉᵉ. on Patents, & also to Mr Dayton[92] Ch.ᵐ of the Comᵉᵉ. on Pub Buildings, for the use of our Committee Room, as a Studio, when not wanted by us— I have consulted with the members of the Committees & find there is no objection as far as we are concerned to grant his application

Very Respectfully
Yr. Mo— obt. Sevt.
Saml. S. Phelps

Hon. W. P. Mangum
    Prest. of the Senate
[Addressed:]
        Hon Willie P. Mangum
            Senate U. S.
            Washington City

WPM-LC

O. H. Tiffany to Willie P. Mangum.

Dickinson College,
Carlisle Penna.
March 4th, 44.

Sir.

It becomes my pleasing duty to inform you of your election as an Honorary Member of the Union Philosophical Society of Dickinson College.

Yrs with much respect
O. H. Tiffany,
Corres. Sec. U.P.S.

Hon. Willie P. Mangum
    Pres. U. S. Senate
    Washington D. C.

---

[90]Samuel S. Phelps, 1793-1855, a native of Connecticut and graduate of Yale University, settled in Middlebury, Vermont, to practice law. After serving as paymaster in the War of 1812 and after holding several state offices, including judge of the Vermont Supreme Court, he entered the United States Senate in 1839 and served until 1851 and from 1853 to 1854. *Biog. Dir. of Cong.*, 1408.
[91]Lambdin, the famous portrait painter, painted one of the best portraits available of Mangum. This was included as frontispiece to volume II of these papers.
[92]See above, 56n.

WPM-LC

Isaac N. Jones[93] to Willie P. Mangum.

WASHINGTON [ARK.] 6th. Mar: '44

Hon. W. P. Mangum
    U. S. Senate
        Dear Sir
            Permit me to intrude a request upon you which from
its importance in a national point of view I hope you will excuse.

We live in a State which (from its representation in congress being entirely of Loco faith) is but poorly supplied with
ought but 'Loco' speeches, documents &c. Now will you do us
the favor to address us with whig documents of whatever kind
you think will be advantageous. We have here a Clay Club
which meets regularly the last Saturday of every month. In
this town we have 40 Whigs to some 18 Locos. There is a fair
prospect for the emancipation of this state at the next Election
from Locoism. I recd. from our Col. Sevier[94] (U. S. Senate)
Mr McDuffie's speech in answer to Messrs: Evans & Huntington upon the Tariff. But so far as I know no copy of those
gentlemen's speeches has reached here except in a newspaper.
Two or three dozn. of those speeches will be of great use to
the cause here.

I do not know whether you will recognize in my signature
one of yr. old acquaintances of Oxford No. C; But be assured
that (though I may have long since been forgotten by you) as
a citizen of my native State you have not been unnoticed by me,
to whom your elevation is a matter of no little gratification.

Very truly yr friend &c
ISAAC N. JONES M.D.

[Addressed:]

Hon: W. P. Mangum
    U. S. Senate
Mail. Washington City.

---

[93]Isaac N. Jones, a native of Granville County, was a student at the University of North Caro-
lina in 1816. He became a physician in Caswell County before he moved to Arkansas and Texas. In
Texas he was on the commission to survey the Texas boundary in 1839. Grant, *Alumni Hist. of
U. N. C.,* 328; George P. Garrison, (ed.), *Diplomatic Correspondence of the Republic of Texas* in
A. H. A. Report of 1908, II, 53.
    [94]Ambrose Hundley Sevier, Senator from Arkansas, 1836-1848; George McDuffie, Senator from
South Carolina, 1842-1847; George Evans, Senator from Maine, 1841-1847; and Jabez Williams
Huntington, Senator from Connecticut, 1840-1847.

WPM-LC

J. Watson Webb to Willie P. Mangum.

[9 March 1844]

My Dear Sir.

Dr. Peachy[95] of Williamsburgh, Virginia, was yesterday nominated Consul at Amoy, China. Mr. Brothers who is a Brother-in-law of the Dr. informs me that this is an act of personal friendship to an old neighbor - Dr. P. being a *Clay-Whig,* & at this time laboring for *Hill Carter* in that District.

I was writing to Mr. *Webster* on business last night, and took occasion to say that I had heard him spoken most kindly of by you & Gov. Morehead in the course of the Evening.[96] You may *win* him entirely to day, after you & the Governor have reached the *third* Bottle - a period when he & you, & all good fellows are in the melting mood. I feel quite sure that you can, if you will, Send him home an aroused & zealous *Clay man.* Believe me

Very sincerely & Truly
Your friend
J. WATSON WEBB
Saturday March 9/44

Hon W. P. Mangum.

P.S. I have arrived at the conclusion, much as I desire to see a modification of the tariff on every thing but *Iron & Woollen,* that it is safest to leave things untouched.

[Addressed:]

Hon. W. P. Mangum.

WPM-LC

W. J. Bingham[97] to Willie P. Mangum.

HILLSBORO' N. C. March 11th. 1844—

Dear Sir;

I addressed you a line a month or six weeks ago requesting of you the favour to send me a few grains of the 'Multicole rye',

---

[95]William S. Peachy was a lawyer of Williamsburg in 1851. Livingston, *Law Register,* 1851, 586.
[96]Webb was trying at this time to get the Whigs to select Webster as the Presidential candidate. See above, 9n, 14.
[97]See above, W. J. Bingham to W. P. Mangum, December 28, 1843.

which I observe from the Agricultural papers, is at the Patent office for distribution. I have now to request a greater favour.— A gentleman residing in Pinckney, Missouri, has been owing me about a hundred dollars for some years, & is, I have every reason to believe, *very good for the money.* But I can't *act on him* except through an agent in his neighborhood. Will you be so good as to learn from some one of the Missouri members what trusty agent I can employ, and give me his address?

I am happy to be able to inform you that Mr. Graham's health is steadily improving, and he is expected soon to be well enough to come home. I presume you are aware he has been confined at Greensboro' for more than a fortnight.— Things here as usual.—

Very respectfully,
Yr. obed't ser't
W. J. BINGHAM,

Hon. W. P. Mangum
    Washington

[Postmarked:] Hillsboro N. C. Mar 12

[Addressed:]

Hon. W. P. Mangum
Washington:
D. C.

WPM-LC

*J. Watson Webb to Messrs. Willie P. Mangum
and J. T. Morehead.*

[13 March, 1844]

Messrs. Mangum & Morehead

Gentlemen.

I greatly regret that my detention by my Loco Foco friend *Wilkins,*[98] who I beat at whist and who is about to send me a Barrell of *Monongahela* promised ten years ago, prevented my meeting you on Saturday evening when I am well satisfied you were in "good order & well conditioned." I am consoled however, with the reflection that you left W. "all right," & that I did not labour in vain in striving to have you understand each other

---

[98]He probably refers to William Wilkins, of Pennsylvania, who was Democratic Congressman at this time.

more fully. He will now doubtless leave Washington with
kindly feelings;[99] & his language on his way north & east, & the
impression he will everywhere leave that he is thoroughly with
us & for Mr. Clay, will give increased confidence in Mr. C's success; - not because Mr. Webster is with him, but because his
being with us will be attributed to *his* conviction of the certainty
of our success. Thus while he will influence and give actively
to the cause of his admirers, he will give additional confidence
to those who do not care for him, because his language will be
attributed to a conviction that Mr. Clay's election is inevitable.
Here & through that State, his direct influence upon the action
of those who admire him will be most salutary. In any event
his friends are with us after what we accomplished last autumn;
but they will now be *actively* instead of *passively* with us.

The new tariff Bill has created a panic here, & the Loco
Focos circulate every where that it meets Mr. Clay's views who
is now said to be angling for the South. I enclose a few lines
from the *Herald,* that most worthless of all prints, but which
the Locos always use when they think it can be useful. The enclosed is precisely the language used by one of Mr. Van Buren's
prominent friends yesterday and which you will find to be the
case of the party at the north. Much as a low tariff is my interest or the assumed interest of the Commercial part of our
community who are my chief support, I am now convinced that
we had better let things remain as they are and not risk any
change. This ground I shall assume broadly to-morrow, offend
whom it may among our shipping friends, and I sincerely hope
that if the House pass the bill reported, the Senate will reject
it without amendment. Let us go into the election with our own
issues *as they are* & then leave to Mr. Clay & his administration
the work of alteration. Mr. Henry Grinnell, brother of *Moses*
& one of the large Packet owners, said to me yesterday— "I
am opposed to the tariff, but I prefer it as it is, or even worse,
to their constant attempt at change.—We want stability & can
accomodate ourselves to any state of things if but assured that
it will be permanent."

I am so fearful of a radical alteration & of new issues for the
coming contest, that I would not even touch Rail Road Iron,
though it would save us $900,000 in the cost of on his [*sic*] Rail
Road.

---

[99]See above, 9n, 14.

My Brother whom you met at my room on Saturday night, is a thorough Clay man but was a neighbour of "his accidency" for fifteen years. He is now a resident of Troy, & is an applicant for the Post Office in that city. He told Tyler that there was not a Tyler man in that city - that *all* are for *Clay* or *Van Buren* - & that he is for Clay. The Captain did not like this, but for *auld lang syne,* half promised the office. *Tayloe* who is in all Tyler's secrets, said, that if *Davis* be rejected *before* the Baltimore Convention, a *Loco* will be appointed - if *after,* it will be given to my Brother. He like any body else takes it for granted that in no event can *Davis* be confirmed. I hope his nomination may *sleep* till after *Van Buren* is nominated.

Very Truly Your friend
J. WATSON WEBB.
March 13 / 44

_____

WPM-LC

M. H. Grinnell[100] to J. Watson Webb.

Thursday noon
14 March 1844.

Dear Col.

Your article of this morning, in regard to the Tariff, is in accordance with my views— I am truly glad that you have taken the ground of *no change in the present Tariff, and I* wish to God, our friends in Congress would stand upon the same platform. In my humble judgment its the only safe course for the Whig party to adopt at this time— *My interests,* you well know would be benefited if the *Free Trade principles* were fully carried out, but I cannot in my own conscience support *that* doctrine— I have not a dollars interest, directly or indirectly, in any manufacturing, but my whole property is in Ships - connected with Commerce—

My Motto is *"let well alone"* the Country is now prosperous, every branch of trade is improving, confidence being restored— and if Congress will only let the present Tariff alone, at least

_____

[100]See above, III, 248-249, 490.

long enough to give it a fair trial, I am sure that all will be well—

Yours Truly

M. H. GRINNELL

To

Jas Watson Webb Esq

[Addressed:]

To Col. Webb.

WPM-LC

Joseph L. Tillinghast[101] to Willie P. Mangum.

PROVIDENCE R. I. March 15 1844.

Dear Sir,

As chairman of the Corresponding Committee I have the honor of informing you that the Clay Club of the City of Providence, at their late meeting, unanimously elected you an Honorary Member; and this Committee is charged with the pleasing duty of informing you of your election.

I am, Sir, with the highest respect,

Your Obt. Servt.

JOSEPH L. TILLINGHAST

Hon. Willie P. Mangum

Willie P. Mangum to John M. Clayton[102]

WASHINGTON CITY 16th March 1844.

My dear Sir,

Yesterday, I wrote you a line and promised at length to day.-That, I cannot do, for want of time.

I repeat, that you in my opinion, ought to *Stand Still That* is Morehead's opinion, nor does Simmons[103] dissent from it- Simmons having been mentioned for the Vice Presidency, may have had some notions floating in his head on the Subject:- Yet I suppose, he does not think of it, seriously.- He did not know the contents of Mr. Sargent's[104] letter.-

---

[101]See above, III, 106n.
[102]The original is in the John M. Clayton Papers, Library of Congress.
[103]James T. Morehead, Senator from Kentucky, and James Fowler Simmons, Senator from Rhode Island.
[104]He probably refers to John Sergeant, who was recommended by some for the vice presidential candidate of the Whigs.

The contest, I think, is narrowed to *you* and *Massachusetts*.- Evans[105] cannot go it.- The Webster interest prevented him, & enlisted on his side his New York influence, & Bates, Choate,[106] & to my surprise, the member from Boston.- The whole thing was still-born. McLean undoubtedly desired it to the extent of giving some manifest "nibbles" at it, as has been his won't for the last ten years.- I don't think he was much encouraged in any influential quarter.- The thorough Whigs of his own State, were opposed to it.- Schenck[107] a fine spirited & highly gifted man, dryly said, "I think, I shd. prefer a Whig for the V. P."-Mr. Sergeant has never had a chance- and besides, it is an *unlucky* ticket, & Capt. Tyler believes in luck.-

Dennig, as well our friend from Washn. Co. Penn. are out of the question.— Tallmadge[108] has crippled himself, & his friends at home, are killing him outright. His course has been so objectionable, that it would have been fatal to his prospects, had his strength at home remained unimpaired.- Fillmore will be pressed with zeal & power.- Backed by the great State, it may render him formidable—

Yet, so general is the sense of public men here, that he is not suitable. I cannot think it will require much effort to dispose of him.

He has neither the talent, devotion or firmness & decision for so high a station- & besides, how many of my Constituents, & hundreds of thousands elsewhere, know, who Mr F is.- My old friend Gov Davis,[109] I fear, cannot make a good run.- He will fail in Virginia, Georgia, Tenessee, & I am very sure, his popularity has been much impaired at home:- In Penn: he cannot run as well, as several others.

I cannot lift my finger against him, as I was act & part, and I believe the first to move (certainly here) his nomination with Clay at the Faneuil Hall Convention in Sept.ʳ 1842. It was known that Webster was to leave here on the 1st. of Sepr. 1842, for Massachusetts.- The Convention was to be held the 11th or 13th of that month to nominate State officers.- Webster was in high feather, he had just concluded the treaty which had been ratified by a Whig Senate with an unanimous Vote of the Whigs, saving one,- He had made extraordinary efforts to restore cordial re-

---

[105]George Evans, Senator from Maine.
[106]Isaac C. Bates and Rufus Choate, Senators from Massachusetts.
[107]Ferdinand S. Schenck, Senator from New Jersey.
[108]N. P. Tallmadge, of New York.
[109]John Davis, of Massachusetts.

lations with the Whigs of the Senate which was steadily repulsed in those quarters, where he seemed least to desire it.-

Some of us thought, if, after having succeeded in the treaty, such relations should be restored, the knowledge of it should precede his return to Mass. that he would be armed with a formidable power, which I did not doubt wd. be used to crush or to disband the Clay Whigs.

Gov. Davis was saved up, as an antagonist power in that State, - and every New England member who was regarded as true, (& in those days, every one's position was well defined) was engaged to urge Clay's nomination at that convention, & to give us Davis, or any other, whom they might deem preferable for V.P. & he should have our hearty support— At least, I engaged my own, & spoke with entire confidence for my State.-You know what followed- & after I say, I wrote several letters to Mass. you can understand my position.- Yet, I do hope, Davis will decline without discontent, & yield gracefully to the force of circumstances.- I think, Abbott Lawrence[110] a preferable Candidate. He would run smoothly & by waving his Wand, the sinews of War, would spring from the bowels of the earth. Those sinews so indispensable in the north & east.- Whether, he is quite of the Calibre, I have my doubts.- Yet, in the event of the most disastrous contingency, I think the Country might expect from him a gentlemanly administration, surrounded by the talent and character of the Country- a thing so much needed, for the last 10 or 15 years.-

Now as to your humble self- you can do much more service to the Country in the State Department, where you will be called, if not otherwise, disposed of.-

I am for you, first, to avoid a bad nomination but if a good one can be had, I would prefer it. & leave you for other & higher service.- & yet I think, you can make a better run than any other- We however, are not so pressed, as to feel the necessity of determining the question upon our estimate of slight differences on the strength of the respective Candidates. We must avoid, placing unnecessary weight upon Clay.- Here is the whole of it, written in a gallop.- Webster leaves here in reasonably good temper, & will not make war on you, if you shall be nominated.

[110]Abbott Lawrence, 1792-1855, a Boston merchant who served in Congress in 1835-1837 and 1839-1840, was one of the commissioners that settled the northeastern boundary. He was a delegate to the Whig National Convention in 1844. He declined a post in Taylor's Cabinet but accepted the appointment of Minister to Great Britain. *Biog. Dir. of Cong.*, 1208; *D. A. B.*, XI, 44.

I put Col. Webb[111] in possession of all our views- he instantly surrendered Evans, & is ready to go for you with all his heart.

In truth, you are his first Choice, & he says, you can get along through the abolition Mires of the North, better than any northern man.

It ought to be Lawrence or you, if the thing can be managed without giving sectional offence.-

Davis would surely occupy a distinguished position in the eye of a new admn. & perhaps, might feel satisfied, if well assured of it-

After all, you must stand Still, or run the hazard of doing the party much damage, which I know you would not intentionally, for your right arm-

Very truly
yr friend
WILLIE P. MANGUM

To Hon. I. M. Clayton

I set out to write a page, & here you are on the fifth.

WPM-LC

William B. Reed[112] to Willie P. Mangum.

and Enclosure

[17 March, 1844]

My Dear Sir,

Not knowing Mr. Badger's precise address I take the liberty of asking you to direct and forward the enclosed. I leave it unsealed, for you as a North Carolinian to read in the hope that you too may be able to aid me in the object I have in view. Excuse the liberty I take and believe me

With sincere regard and respect
faithfully yrs.
WILLIAM B. REED.

Philad. March 17 1844
Hon. Mr. Mangum

---

[111]See above letters of J. Watson Webb to W. P. Mangum, March 9, 13, 1844.

[112]William B. Reed, 1806-1876, a native of Philadelphia and a graduate of the University of Pennsylvania, studied law under his uncle, John Sergeant, He went to Mexico and Panama as the private secretary of Sergeant in 1826. He held numerous state and local offices before he was appointed by Buchanan as Minister to China, where he helped negotiate the Treaty of Tientsin. In politics he was anti-mason before he entered the Whig party. In 1856 he went over to the Democrats. An able lawyer who had intellectual interests, he taught, on a part-time basis, American history at the University of Pennsylvania and wrote numerous articles on history. *D. A. B.,* XV, 461-462.

Enclosure

PHILADA. March 16, 1844.

My Dear Sir,

I am induced, at the instance of our common friend, Mr. Sergeant,[113] to revive a very slight personal acquaintance, and to ask a favour, which, I am very sure, if in your power, you will readily grant. I have consented, at the request of a very respectable literary Institution of this City, principally composed of Roman Catholic gentlemen, to prepare and deliver in the course of the next month or six weeks a Discourse or Eulogy on the Life and public services of Judge Gaston. Having undertaken the task, I wish to make the effort a creditable one, and to do full and minute justice to the subject. My principal difficulty is in obtaining a knowledge of the details of Mr. Gaston's public life after he left Congress, and of his services at home before he went on the bench, as well as afterwards so far as they had public interest.—Can you advise me on the subject, or put me in the way of obtaining the information I desire? I wish to do full justice to the subject. More than a little practical good may result from it. Judge Gaston's political opinions were eminently conservative, and a fair eulogy on his character will invoke a very decided defence of those opinions which now are a little out of fashion. My audience *must* listen and *may* profit. Do me the favour to give me an early reference to any materials that will aid me - any new information respecting his private life will be acceptable. Was not Mr. Gaston a decided Whig in his politics.

Apropos of politics, shall we not have the pleasure of meeting you in Baltimore in May? I am one of the senatorial Delegates from this State, and rely on meeting and conferring with many of our distant friends on the bright though somewhat perplexed prospect before us. I fear this detestable administration will give us trouble yet with its Texas and Anti-Anglican policy.

---

[113]John Sergeant was Reed's uncle.

I presume Mr Clay will soon be with you. Tell him his Pennsylvania friends are sanguine and active, well organized and perfectly united.

Very truly & Resp
Yrs.
WILLIAM B. REED.

Hon. George. E. Badger.

[Addressed:]

> Hon. George. E. Badger
> N. Carolina.

WPM-LC

S. H. Harris[114] to Willie P. Mangum.

CLARKSVILLE [VA.]
March 18th 1844

Dear Sir,

The late shocking accident on board the Steam Frigate Princeton[115] resulted as you know in the death of one of my wifes uncles Commo. B. Kennon of the United States Navy. At the time of his death and for several years previous he had under his care and protection a young man by the name of William Kennon a nephew of his and a son of my late Father in law Col. E. Kennon whom you no doubt will remember. He is now and has been for several years the clerk of the commander of the Washington Navy Yard; which appointment he obtained and held no doubt thro the influence of his uncle. Having lost his protection and being still under age, his numerous connections here and Mrs. Harris his sister among others, cannot but feel deeply interested about him. I am thus induced to approach you on the subject and solicite for him your notice and kind offices. I am aware Sir that your present political attitude may disincline you to ask any boon of the present administration; but I have thought it not unlikely that the exalted station which you now fill with so much distinction, might enable you

---

[114]See above, III, 43n.
[115]On February 22, 1844, Captain Stockton of the *U. S. S. Princeton,* a warship with the most modern improvements designed by John Ericsson of *Monitor* fame, took many guests, including the President and members of his Cabinet, on a trip from Alexandria to Mount Vernon. After the party had had a pleasant outing and were on their way back, the large gun, the "Peacemaker," was fired at the request of Secretary of the Navy Gilmer. An explosion occurred, instantly killing Secretaries Gilmer and Upshur, Commodore B. Kennon, and two other important guests. Chitwood, *Life of Tyler,* 397-398.

in many ways to forward the prospects of this young man. He is already favourably known to the President and I believe in the gay circles of Washington as a kinsman and protege of the late commodore. Should you therefore feel inclined to interest yourself in his favour it would not be difficult to obtain for him some permanent appointment under the government. I am not well informed as to his business qualifications, but infer from his letters and the very favourable opinions expressed by others, that he would fulfill the expectations of his friends in any station suited to his years. In stead of troubling you with this communication, I ought probably to have addressed myself to the Virginia Senators, but I am personally unknown to them. As to our representative Genl. Dromgoole[116] it is hardly to be expected that he would interest himself in favour of a man however meritorious who carries in his veins a mingled stream of Nelson and Kennon blood; two Whig families that have ever been, and always will be, I hope, opposed to him.

The excitement here is up and daily increasing in favour of Mr Clay, and it is not the least gratifying sign of the times to witness the gradual decline and removal of the old fashioned deep rooted prejudices against that distinguished statesman. We are up and a doing and I will just remark in passant [sic] that your name is frequently mentioned in connection with the vice Presidency. I may have been guilty myself of some indiscreetness, as the party leaders say, of thus expressing prematurely my preference. But who is to be the man? The old North State surely has claims, that must and will challenge the consideration of the national convention—

With high respect
I am Sir yours &c.
S. H. HARRIS.

Hon. Willie P. Mangum.

[Addressed:]

Hon. Willie P. Mangum
United States Senate
Washington
D. C.

---

[116]George Coke Dromgoole, 1797-1847, was Democratic Congressman from 1835 to 1841 and from 1843 to 1847. *Biog. Dir. of Cong.*, 921.

WPM-LC

Joseph Ridgway[117] to Willie P. Mangum

COLUMBUS, O. March 18.th 1844

Honl. Willie P. Mangum
    Pres.[t] of the U. S. Senate

Dr. Sir,

I have taken the liberty of enclosing to your address a volume for the Hon. Dan.[1] R. Tilden,[118] of the House. It contains matter that I think Mr. Tilden would prefer receiving through your hands than that of Genl. Jones-[119] the Speaker of the House. Will you have the kindness when the book comes to hand to drop a line to Mr. Tilden, or send it to him by one of your Pages.

We are preparing for the coming campaign, and entertain no doubts that we shall carry the State for Mr Clay triumphantly.

With high respect
I am, Your Obe[t] Sev.[t]
J. RIDGWAY

[Addressed:]

Honl. Willie P. Mangum
Prest. of the U. S. Senate
Washington City
D. C.

WPM-LC

J. R. Lambdin[120] to Willie P. Mangum.

[18 March, 1844]

Dear Sir

Will it be convenient for you to give me a sitting this morn-

[117]Joseph Ridgway, 1783-1861, was a plow manufacturer and a member of the Ohio legislature before he entered Congress in 1837. He served until 1843. *Biog. Dir. of Cong.*, 1462.
[118]Daniel Rose Tilden, 1804-1890, was a Whig Congressman from Portage County, Ohio, from 1843 to 1847. In 1848 and 1852 he was a delegate to the national Whig conventions. *Biog. Dir. of Cong.*, 1618.
[119]John Winton Jones, 1791-1848, of Virginia, was Speaker of the House of Representatives in the Twenty-eighth Congress, which was then in session. *Biog. Dir. of Cong.*, 1163.
[120]See above, 59.

ing? - by so doing you will greatly facilitate my operations, and add another to the many favours allready conferred on

Very truly your obed.^t

J R LAMBDIN

Hon W P Mangum.
Monday Mong Mar 18/44.

[Addressed:]

Honble W P Mangum

at

Mrs Cox's

WPM-D

George Constantine Collins[121] *to Willie P. Mangum.*

BALTIMORE March 20th 1844.

Hon. Sir:

I would again claim your attention, to the perusal of a few lines from my pen, hoping however that they will find you perfectly satisfied as regards my explanation respecting the draft. Since the publication of that anonymous letter in the Globe, my countrymen have treated me with *marked distinction,* and it has contributed very much to the advancement of the *"cause."* I have also the pleasure of announcing to you, that I have been enabled to pay the publisher $50 since I wrote you last, and I have the prospect of making further payments in a few days. Several letters have been recd from New York, requesting my immediate presence there, owing to the peculiar state of feeling now existing amongst the old countrymen, particularly the Irish, who very probably will act in concert with the *"Great Whig Party,"* at the approaching election. In order therefore, that I may leave here on Saturday I most respectfully request you to send me a little money, whereby I may be enabled to pay my expenses, and the amt. can be deducted on acc/ of the books in the Club— Be so kind as to send me a letter by the return mail as I shall await it impatiently.

I most humbly beg of you, not to lay any thing to my charge derogatory to my zeal in the promotion of the best interests of the Party, to which I have the honor to belong— When the first edition is payed for I will be able to get along without any as-

---

[121]See above, G. C. Collins to W. P. Mangum, January 22, 1844.

sistance - but owing to the great expense incurred by reason of eight weeks stay in Baltimore, the paying my family's expenses in Washington, and the stereotyping and composition— I have been and am embarrassed. Should you be able to obtain even $20, it would now be more serviceable than $100 at another time. Excuse my liberty I should not have addressed you on this, or any other subject, had I not known you to be possessed of every quality essential to the true gentleman and disinterested philanthropist. In the mean time, I have the Honor to be, Hon. Sir,

> Your most obt. Servt.
> and affectionate friend
> GEORGE CONSTANTINE COLLINS.

Hon Willie P. Mangum
  Pres. Sen. U. S. &
    V.P. U.S.

[Addressed:] Hon. Willie P. Mangum
        Pres of the U. S. Senate &
          V. P. U. S.
          Washington D. C.

WPM-LC

Reverdy Johnson to Willie P. Mangum.

BALT. 23 March /44

My Dear Sir,

The day I had the pleasure to dine with you at Mr. Coxe's, you mentioned Mr. Abbot Lawrence's name for the Vice Presidency, & I told you, I had thought of him before, & was greatly inclined to go for him - but you know what is the opinion of our friends upon the matter— If he is to be named, it is high time the public attention was called to such a situation. If it be deemed advisable, I will have it done here in our press— My personal preference is our friend Clayton, but I have all along supposed that the choice should be made from a non slave-holding State. Such is the opinion of Mr. Leigh, of Va. who has written me on the matter— Govr. Davis is perhaps very objectionable because of a correspondence which I am told he carried on with the Govr. of Va. relating to the Slave question. There is every reason for desiring a strong Southern vote—

Independent of its importance in the Election itself, it is all important, even when we succeed, as we are sure to do, to the quiet[ing] & settlement of the anti slavery excitement.

> Write to me, as
> soon as you have leisure—
> Truly yr. friend,
> REVERDY JOHNSON—

Mr. Mangum—

[Addressed:]

> Honble.
> Mr. Mangum
> In Senate
> Washington—

Willie P. Mangum and James T. Morehead to John M. Clayton[122]

> WASHINGTON CITY, 25th March 1844.
> 12 o'clock at night
> (all duly sober)

My dear Sir.

It is decreed that you must go to New York on the 12th of April, & make a speech.-

It is Clay's birthday.- The gentleman is not of much worth; yet Morehead & I say, you must go.- Have you new clothes? if you have not, we will raise a *"pony"* purse, & buy them-set me down for a round half dollar. Morehead will go a like sum.- If I had had a new suit[123] Mr. Tyler; perhaps, had not been President.- He had them not,- but he is lucky- they were given to him.

In a word- My dear sir- shake off the devil & his imps- shake them off, & go- You must go.- Public Servant as you are to be, you must obey instructions- *the instructions of friends*- They are imperative- Those from our enemies we may disobey & damn, without breach of any moral or religious obligation.

My dear Sir. You will go, if you are wise-

> You will go, if you are patriotic-
> You will go, if a friend to the Whig cause-

---

[122]The original is in the John M. Clayton Papers, Library of Congress. This letter was written by Mangum.

[123]Mangum was considered for Vice President at the Harrisburg Convention in 1839.

You will go, if you are a friend of "H. Clay".
You will go, above all, if you are a friend to J. M. Clayton
You will go. above all the alls, if you are a friend to your
very distinguished & most illustrious friends.

WILLIE P. MANGUM
J. T. MOREHEAD

My name is forged to the close and I claim the privilege of
signing it myself—

J. T. MOREHEAD

WPM-LC

Memucan Hunt to Willie P. Mangum.

GALVESTON TEXAS 27th March 1844

My Dear Sir; (Private)

I took the liberty of transmitting, under cover to you, by the
last mail which left for the U. S. a letter to our secret Minister
at Washington, and had intended to have addressed you a
note under the same envelop but for having been taken ill which
prevented me from being enabled to do so before the departure
of the mail.

The question of annexation has been and is now looked to
with the deepest interest in this country. Some of us are tolerably well advised as to it[s] prospects, but for one I feel somewhat distrustful of [a] favorable result. We have learned that
all the Whig and democratic senators from the slave States will
vote for its ratification. Mr Crittenden's vote as well as Mr
McDuffie's was regarded here as doubtful until recently, but assurances from Washington as late as the 7th instant affirm to
me that Mr Crittenden will vote for the treaty.[124] I learned
recently that Mr McDuffie would also. In addition to this vote
of the slave States we are assured that all the democratic senators in the North and West, with perhaps one exception will
likewise favor the treaty. If so it appears to me that there can

---

[124]Calhoun's treaty of annexation was signed April 12, 1844. Several weeks earlier, during
Upshur's negotiation, the sentiment for approval of a treaty seemed favorable. As sectional and partisan feeling mounted, ratification became more uncertain. The North Carolina Whigs had taken no
stand until Clay's Raleigh letter of April 27, 1844. After this, most North Carolina Whigs began
asserting that annexation would mean war. In the legislature 60 Whigs voted against a resolution
favoring annexation and only 7 voted for the resolution. Despite the advice of his Texan friends,
Mangum did not come out for annexation. The vote on Calhoun's treaty was a partisan vote. Only
one Whig, Henderson, of Missouri, voted for the treaty. All other Whigs, including Mangum, voted
against it. Pegg, "Whig Party in N. C.," 234.

be no doubt of its rattification, I ardently hope there will be none.

The slave interest in the U. S. and Texas is too small, it appears to me, to be seperated when we consider the prejudice and action which is constantly manifested and exerted against it by our northern neighbours and Great Britain. The government and certain politicians in the U. S. are doing much to increase the christian zeal and fanaticism in the non slave holding States of the U. S. and Great Britain against a continuance of the institution. I am satisfied that the slave interest is too small in Texas to be maintained, against the influence and money of England, for many years.

I was very much surprised when informed of Mr. Clay's indifference, not to say opposition, to a reannexation of Texas to the U. S.—The more so after an examination of the many records which are extant of his desire to re[ac]quire this territory for his country. I repeat that I am [a]stonished at Mr Clay's present attitude in reference to [the] question. What can he gain by it in respect to his popularity? His friends in the non slave holding States can answer best for him there. In the slave holding States I will use the presumption to assert, that if he continues to occupy the position he is now in that with the exception of Kentucky he will not get a majority in a single one of them for the Presidency. There is scarcely a county in the slave holding States, but from which, there are emigrants in this country. There kindred and friends in the U. S. simpathise in whatever concerns and effects them. If the annexation fail, it is a question of so much moment that the cause of the failure (after the alluring hopes which have been held out of its early consumation) will be inquired into by every one. My impression - the impression of every one with whom I have conversed is that if the measure is defeated that defeat will be in consequence of Mr. Clay's opposition. And I have not conversed with a man in Texas on this subject, however much he may have admired Mr. Clay before, but who hopes for his defeat in the next Presidential election if he proves to be the cause of the failure of annexation. What is to be lost by Mr Clay in the present attitude of parties in the non slave holding States— (save a few abolitionists)—by his comeing forward as the advocate of annexation? Mr Van Buren and all the other democratic candidates for the the Presidency are understood to be in favor of the measure and Mr. Clay's reavowal of his former opinions would leave the [pos]ition of the two great parties the same on the [que]stion.

Our Commissioners to Mexico who have [been] engaged several months in negotiating an armistice, or peace, arrived here on yesterday. They bring assurances, I learn, that Mexico is now willing to recognize our independence or enter into a truce for five or ten years (which is the same thing) provided this government will stipulate to remain seperate and unconnected as an integral part of the U. S. If the present negotiations at Washington fail to result in a treaty of annexation, I have no doubt these terms will be acceded to by this Government, and the oportunity thereby will be forever lost of reacquiring this valuable country by the U. S. - what a blunder it appears to me this would be in your Statesmen. If we are to become a part of the U. S. it must be very shortly. Twelve months delay, depend upon my assurance, will forever defeat the measure.

I took the liberty of presenting Mr. W. D. Miller, official secretary of Genl Henderson with a letter of acquaintance to you. Should you have a friend making a visit to this country at any time I should be gratified to render him any service in my power and if I can serve you in any way please command me.

I have the honor to be your friend
      and obedient servant
                    MEMUCAN HUNT

To
    Hon. W. P. Mangum
        Pres.ᵗ of the U. S. Senate

[Addressed:]

            Hon. W. P. Mangum
            Prest. U. S. Seante
            Washington City
                    D. C.

WPM-LC

B. W. Leigh to Willie P. Mangum.

RICHMOND, March 28. 1844.

My dear Sir—

I received your letter of the 25th, yesterday morning - and I thank you for it most heartily.

As to the selection of our candidate for the vice presidency, there are two points upon which common prudence and common sense must dictate to the Whigs an unanimous opinion - that the candidate to be run on the ticket with Mr Clay must be selected from a non-slave-holding State - and that the person must be such a one as in case of Mr Clay's death we may confide in for the administration of the government. This last consideration was wholly overlooked in the selection of Mr Tyler for the office at the Harrisburg convention in 1839 - and that was the capital error we committed - if the thought had occurred to any body, he never would have been nominated. But, in truth, well as I thought I understood his character, I had no conception of it - I had no idea of the inordinary, the unscrupulousness, the folly and knavery of his ambition, and I do not believe he had the least consciousness of it himself. I have always suspected, and I have no doubt of it, that it was Wise who put the idea of the succession to the presidency, into his head, and thus acquired absolute dominion over and direction of his conduct - and this without any view to the elevation of Tyler, but to accomplish his own purposes - to cross the Whig party in Congress, who had mortally offended his vanity by refusing openly and formally to instal him in the office of manager of the house of representatives - and to thwart Mr Clay, who had (some how or other, I could never understand exactly how) mortified his self love, or rather self-conceit; for he is the most vainglorious and presumptious being I have ever known; tho' if his cousin Bailey[125] shall be elected his successor in Congress, you will see his cousin german in vanity as well as in blood, without a tythe of his talent. The moment the presidency was held up to Tyler as possible to be attained, he went mad - stark mad. By the way, the ambition of the presidency seems to me a moral poison, of which it requires a very strong and firm

---

[125]Thomas Henry Bayly, 1810-1856, was elected as a State Rights Democrat to fill the vacancy caused by Wise's resignation. He served in Congress from 1846 to 1856. *Biog. Dir. of Cong.,* 681.

mind, and an unusual depth and energy of moral principle, to resist the effect. Swift says (in the Tale of a Tub) that there is a certain "serpent that wants teeth and consequently cannot bite; but if its vomit, to which it is much addicted, happens to fall upon anything, a certain rotteness or corruption ensues - these serpents are generally found among the mountains where jewels grow, and they frequently emit a poisonous juice, whereof whoever drinks, that person's brains fly out of his nostrils." That serpent is our selfish trading politician placed in conspicuous station - his vomit, his flattery of those whom he wishes to mould to his own purposes - and the poisonous juice, the ambition of the presidency, whereof whoever drinks that person's brains fly out of his nostrils. Tyler swallowed a drop, a single drop, which Wise distilled for him, and from that moment lost his senses. Mr Calhoun has taken phials full since 1824, and it is not wonderful that his brains are gone, and what is worse his heart too - you will soon see his capers in the office of secretary of state. That poor fellow Gilmer had taken a drop, and if he had had any brains (which he never had) you would have seen them spattered upon the walls of the capitol. Rives has taken a good large dose; and it gives me a higher opinion than I should otherwise have had of his understanding, to see how much discretion he retains.

To return to the vice presidency - I wrote a letter to Reverdy Johnson sometime in February, in which I took occasion to mention the subject; well knowing, however, that it would be agitated at Washington, and that as our candidate for the presidency was conclusively fixed upon, the candidate for the other office would be fixed upon there. The first person that occurred to me was John Davis of Massachusetts[126] - but his Latimer letter staggered me - not that that letter would have been sufficient to overcome *my* preference for him, but that, as I am particularly anxious to redeem Virginia from this Jeffersonian staterights democracy, which has been an incubus on the mind of the state, and is the vilest system of jesuitry that ever was conceived, and as that letter would probably be a stumbling block in our way at every step, I had *per force* given up my predilection for him. I then thought of our friend Clayton; and if I was

---

[126]Ex-governor John Davis, of Massachusetts, was seriously considered for Clay's running mate. He represented the high tariff views and, therefore, satisfied many in the North. At the same time his tariff views hurt him in the South. His anti-slavery views, however, were the chief reasons for his not being selected. *D. A. B.*, V, 133.

at liberty to follow my personal wishes, I should give him the
preference without hesitation - but Delaware is a slave-holding state - and besides, a very small state, so that he can bring
very little of local strength to the general cause; and tho' this
last consideration would not influence *me* in the least, yet we
know that it would have its influence in the election. Yielding
thus my own preferences, I looked to the large states, and the
large Atlantic states, to find a suitable person. You tell me,
that John Sergeant will decline—which I am sorry to hear, and
yet more sorry for the reason which enforces the propriety of
his declining, namely, that he is unpopular in Pennsylvania.
Is there any person in Pennsylvania whom it would be prudent
to take up? If there is, I should be very much inclined to go -
not for him - but for Pennsylvania; I have heard none suggested. Then as to New York - I was aware, that Talmadge
had loosened his hold upon the affections of the Whig party
generally - but I supposed that he was still the favorite, and
therefore the strongest man, of the Whigs in New York, and
was consequently very well content (the *expunge* to the contrary notwithstanding) that he should be put in nomination,
until the nomination of Filmore by the Whigs of New York,
suggested a doubt of Talmadge's weight in the "Empire." Yet
I do not hesitate to say, that I should prefer Talmadge to Filmore. I have no personal knowledge of Filmore's character -
from what I could gather from the National Intelligencer of his
conduct in the house of representatives, I had not formed any
very exalted opinion of his capacity - but he wrote a letter to
his constituents, containing a very severe and a very just reflection upon the conduct of Wise, without naming him indeed
but the application of the censure was not to be mistaken; and
then let Wise bully him into a false declaration that he had no
particular allusion to him. From that moment (as Lord Nelson
said of Gen. Mack) "my mind was made up as to the man" - and
I was grievously afflicted to fiind, that if we looked to the "Empire" for our candidate for the vice president, we must take
him - now, *I* will not, if it can be helped - which I am afraid it
cannot be. I never heard Evans seriously talked of; I thought
the demonstration which had been made in N. York to which
you allude, and its failure to make the least impression on the
public mind, had put an end to the movement. Among the
Whigs of Virginia certainly, and I believe of all the Southern

States, Webster has been "down among the dead men," ever
since his Fanuil Hall speech;[127] and it will be enough to damn
the hopes of any candidate that it should be known or suspected
that he preferred him. By the way, I really grieve for Webster - I grieve to see of how little worth the very highest abilities with which God can endow mere mortal man may be, when
perverted or blinded by his passions or his vices. I had, as you
suppose, the greatest admiration of his talents, as indeed I still
have - but I never thought him a wise man - to that character
virtue is an essential ingredient, and I never could put confidence in his virtue; and besides he always appeared to me to be
wanting in moral courage and energy, without which however
great a statesman may appear in debate, or even in council, he
is almost sure to fail in action, on all great occasions. If he had
resigned his office of Secretary of State the day after the Ash-
burton treaty was ratified, and come back into the Whig ranks
openly and heartily, he would have stood instantly upon such
high ground as he never before had attained to. How he should
have wanted judgment to see the vantage ground, which it
was open to him to occupy, and the vast and brilliant prospects
from which seemed so obvious to every body else, seems to me
quite unaccountable. I expected and predicted that he would
occupy it - but "he missed the figure." I suppose he was blinded
by his jealousy of Mr Clay, which is an old and ruling passion
with him, as well as with Mr Calhoun. I have lately heard
some stories impeaching his integrity and honor which have
shocked me - I hope they are not true - if they are, "twere better that he had been born a dog.—"

You see in this letter, how my mind has been speculating on
the subject of the vice presidency. I had never heard any
mention of Lawrence till I received your letter. I suppose you
know that I was more intimate with him and old Mr. Silsbee,[128]
while I was in Congress, than with any persons north of the
Potomac and the Ohio. And I have the utmost confidence in
him, and will go for him with all my heart. But there are one
or two considerations which must be weighed - considerations
affecting the question of policy, in putting him in nomination.
In the first place, may not the nomination produce disappoint-

---

[127]In September, 1842, Webster's friends gave Webster a dinner at Faneuil Hall. In his speech which followed he explained his support of Tyler and his refusal to follow Clay's friends from the Cabinet. In a rather defiant attitude he blamed Clay for the failure to work with Tyler. Fuess, *Life of Webster*, II, 119; Lambert, *Presidential Politics in U. S., 1841-1845*, 104.
[128]See above, II, 201n.

ment, disgust, discontent and disaffection, in the minds of Davis and Evans as well as Webster; and if *they* all oppose, or even *stand off*, how can Lawrence *stand up*, in New England? In the next place, the recent elections in Massachusetts and Maine, especially the former state, have made the impression upon my mind, that the abolitionists hold the balance,[129] and by throwing their weight into either scale can give it preponderance; and if this be so, tho' Mr L's known opinions on this subject will be a strong recommendation with us of the South, they may work against us with tremendous effect in New England. Is it possible to ascertain how old John Q. Adams would stand affected towards such a nomination? I suppose not, unless you can open some diplomatic communication with the devil. But if he is disaffected, he can do a world of mischief. That is another man of great talents without a particle of wisdom - talents effective for all sorts of mischief, but absolutely powerless for good. My serious apprenhension is, that he is for a dissolution of the Union.

Let me hear from you again immediately, and send me the first of the Baltimore papers in which the nomination of Lawrence is opened - and if you can get it, that letter of his about abolition.

Keep this letter to yourself - I cannot write a letter to you which is fit to be seen by any body else, except Archer*

With old and constant regard,

Yr: friend,
B: W: LEIGH

Hon. Willie P. Mangum

* I wish I could have a talk with him about Texas - I think I could shew him that *present action* is not adviseable

---

[129]The Liberty Party had considerable support in Maine. In special elections in Maine and Massachusetts in January and February, 1844, the votes for minor candidates determined the outcome. *Niles' Register*, LXVI, 23.

WPM-LC

Robert B. Gilliam to Willie P. Mangum.

Oxford N. C. March 29 1844.

Hon W. P. Mangum

Dear Sir,

I take the liberty of addressing you this letter, at the instance of Mr. Daniel R. Goodloe,[130] who is now in Washington City. Mr. Goodloe is anxious to procure some employment suited to his talents, and he very properly concludes, that a recommendation from a gentleman, with whose name the whole country is familiar would be of essential service to him. He has not yet, I presume, applied to you, owing as I have reason to believe, to very commendable motives of delicacy. He would be unwilling to make such an application to any one, who did not know him well, either personally or from reputation.

I have known Mr Good[l]oe intimately more than ten years, and during a large portion of that time he has resided in this village. He is a gentleman of highly respectable literary attainments, of pure morals, and in the whole range of my acquaintance, I know of no man whose conduct is regulated by a higher sense of honor. Of good talents and studious habits, the chief and indeed the only obstacle to his success hitherto, has been a want of energy, or perhaps it would be juster to him to say, a want of that self-confidence, without which a high degree of success in any pursuit is very difficult, if not unattainable. He is a ready and able writer in every department to which he has ever turned his attention.

I am thus particular in speaking of Mr Goodloe's character & attainments, that in the event of his applying to you, as he probably will, for a recommendation - you may be able to render him the service he desires.

I do not understand that Mr Goodloe is in search of an *office* under the government at Washington. I think it more likely

---

[130]Daniel Reaves Goodloe, 1814-1902, a native of Louisburg, North Carolina, was early apprenticed to a printer in Oxford and remained close to a newspaper thereafter. After serving as editor of the *Oxford Examiner* for a short time, he moved to Tennessee and joined the forces which fought the Creeks and Seminoles. He returned to Oxford, studied law under Gilliam, but was unsuccessful in his practice. Already holding anti-slavery views, he moved to Washington, where Mangum obtained a place for him with the *Whig Standard*. After its failure in the latter part of 1844, he became editor of the *Georgetown Advocate* and then the *Christian Statesman*. In 1853 he joined the staff of the anti-slavery *National Era* and edited it until the Civil War. In the war he held several posts in Washington and in 1865 returned to North Carolina, where he first supported Johnson's reconstruction plan. All through his life he wrote articles, pamphlets, and essays on the issues of the day. Despite his anti-slavery views, he returned to Louisburg and resided there until his death in 1902. *D. A. B.*, VII, 390-391; J. S. Bassett, "Anti-Slavery Leaders of North Carolina," *Johns Hopkins University Studies in History and Political Science*, ser. XVI, No. 6 (1898).

that he would desire employment as an assistant Editor of a newspaper, or as a teacher in a school. His services would be very valuable in either capacity.

I beg you will not take it amiss, that I inclose for Mr Goodloe a recommendatory letter, which I will thank you to hand to him, with such an *indorsement* from yourself, as may make it of use to him.

I am with high respect
ROB. B. GILLIAM
Oxford, N. C. 31st. March

[Addressed:]

Hon W. P. Mangum
Washington City

WPM-LC

John M. Clayton to Willie P. Mangum.

NEW CASTLE DEL. March 30, 1844.

My dear Mangum,

As soon as Mr. Atwell[131] of N. Y. delivered to me the letter of yourself & Mr. Morehead, I at once told him that whenever he should send me the letter of the Whigs of N. Y. inviting me to address them on the 12th, I would accept it.[132] This letter he said should be forthcoming as soon as he could return home.

On the next day after this, I was visited by a New York gentleman (a Fillmore man) who spent the day with me. He desired me not to go to New York till after the convention, alleging that it would infallibly be set down as an electioneering tour, make what professions or excuses I might to the contrary. I proposed to *decline* first and then go. He said that would play the d- - -l, as the New Yorkers meant to use me in case they could not get a man of their own.- on the 28th, a Pennsylvanian called, (a Sergeant Man) and told me the Pennsylvanians would rally on me as soon as they could prove by their votes in convention what they now (as he said) all knew,- that they could not get a Pennsylvanian. "But," said he "do not *now* go to New York, for it will be thought you are courting

---

[131]See below R. H. Atwell to W. P. Mangum, April 2, 1844.
[132]See above W. P. Mangum and James T. Morehead to John M. Clayton, March 25, 1844.

the New Yorkers, and mean to sacrifice "the Keystone" to the 'Empire State' and every body will say *you* are electioneering, while all the other *nominees* (as he called us) are staying at home, quietly awaiting the decision '*ex gratia modestia.*' 'My God!' (thought I) I shall be murdered in a gentlemanly way by Morehead and Mangum if I don't go, and I am sure to be burnt alive or boiled in oil, if I *do* go. In this dilemma I called a council of war, consisting of three old Whig friends, and I re- solved myself into a committee of five to wait upon and consult them. They drank three bottles of old Hock, three of champaign [*sic*] and four of Madiera, (to say nothing of six bottles more which they carried off in a riotous way) and then decided off hand that I was a d - d fool and ought to stay at home lest other people should find it out! But they were all drunk, and I scorn their decision - though I respect the conclusion they ar- rived at after they got sober, which was that I should keep in my house and mind my own business for thirty days, wearing crape on my *right* arm till the 1st of May[133] for the loss of the wines they had made way with - the toping varlets!—

So I wrote today to Mr. Atwell declining the New York in- vitation for professional reasons.

My dear Mangum, we are going to beat the Locos into bench holes, if we are prudent. My news from Connecticut is, that she will go whig in spite of the immense efforts on the other side, by 2000 at present and by 5000 in the Fall. New York will at the charter contest elect Harper "Native" - better for us just at this time than any other result. All is safe if we are discreet. I mean to devote myself to the work, but N. Sargent can tell you how important it is now, that I should be scrupulously delicate towards certain Gentlemen in the North. I *stand still* as you directed, and whenever you or Morehead shall write me a word "decline" I will go overboard instantly.

The Baltimore Young Whigs Convention[134] will be the most magnificent & interesting pageant the nation has ever exhibited. But tell Crittenden (God bless him!) I still think it ought not

---

[133]This was the day that the National Whig Convention opened in Baltimore.
[134]The Young Whigs' ratification convention met in Baltimore on the day following Clay's nomi- nation.

to have come *quite* so soon on the heels of the first of May.—

Ever faithfully yours
JOHN M. CLAYTON.

Hon. W. P. Mangum
    U. S. S.

[Addressed:] Hon: Willie P. Mangum
        President of the United States Senate,
        Washington.

Willie P. Mangum & others to Asbury Dickins[135]

[March-June, 1844][136]

To Asbury Dickens Esq.ʳ
    Secretary of the Senate.

Sir
    Should a vacancy occur in the clerkships in your office, it would be very agreeable to us that the appointment should be given to M.ʳ Stansbury,[137] whom we know to be qualified to discharge its duties and who, we do not doubt, would, if appointed, perform them to general satisfaction.

Washington, March 1844)

N. P. Tallmadge	A. S. Porter
Sam.¹ S. Phelps	H. Johnson
Albert S. White	W.ᵐ D. Merrick
T. Clayton	Geo. Mc Duffie
J. W. Miller	Daniel E. Huger
Richᵈ H. Bayard	Ephriam H. Foster
John Henderson	Alexander Barrow
Willie P. Mangum	W. C. Rives
Geo Evans	J. F. Simmons
I. C. Bates	Wᵐ Woodbridge
R. Choate	Wm. Upham
W. S. Archer	W. G. Fulton
J. W. Huntington	A. W. Lewis
Jn: Macpherson Berrien	J. A. Reeves
W.ᵐ L. Dayton	Spencer Jarnagin
J. J. Crittenden	John Brown Francis

------

[135]The original is in the Historical Society of Pennsylvania.

[136]Although this letter is not dated, it was written between March and June of 1844, because Henry Johnson, one of the signers, did not take his seat until March, 1844, and N. P. Tallmadge, another signer, resigned June 19, 1844.

[137]Probably Arthur J. Stansberry, the reporter for Gales and Seaton in the Senate. J. Q. Adams, *Memoirs*, X, 32; XII, 237.

[Endorsed in Dickins handwriting:] Willie P. Mangum
        1792-1861
        U. S. Senator from N. C., 1831-6,
        and 1840-53. President pro tem.
        U. S. Senate.
        See Appleton

WPM-LC

R. H. Atwell[138] to Willie P. Mangum.

NEW YORK April 2d. 1844.

My Dear Sir

Do me the favour to accept from me a couple of cards of "Wright's" Steel pens. You found them in writing for the young men of New York to our friend Clayton - very good.

Cannot you use one of these to induce Mr. C. to come amongst us on the 12th. he promised me when I saw him that on your & Gov Morehead's requisition he *would* come. I have just recd a letter from him saying that he will find it impossible to come, he has been "gazetted" and *must* come.

Very faithfully yours
R. H. ATWELL.

Hon. W. P. Mangum
    U. S. S.

[Addressed:]

Hon W. P. Mangum
    U. S. Senate.

WPM-LC

T. Hamer[139] to Willie P. Mangum.

WATSONTOWN [PA.] April 3, 1844.

Hon. & Respected Sir

In noticing the proceedings of Congress, on the subject of the *Oregon Territory*—I am at a loss to know how an American

------

[138]A merchant in New York City. *Longworth's New York Directory,* 1841-1842, 68.
[139]Possibly Thomas Lyon Hamer, 1800-1847, who represented Ohio in Congress in 1822-1839. *Biog. Dir. of Cong.,* 1256.

Citizen who has the rights and the honor of our glorious republic at heart can assume such a lukewarm timid and even cowardly position on this subject

They urge in long and loud speeches the impropriety of any action upon this question by the Americans lest they should give offence to England - and then they would resort to Arms and attempt to wrest from us that *territory* - which they have no claim upon under heavens, and well they know it too - yet give them an inch and they will take a yard and so in proportion untill finely they want all.

Had our forefathers asserted and maintained these rights in this way when oppressed by the Iron heel of tyranny at Boston where would American liberty have been - would it not have been cherished by her hired legon, the proud Eagle of Independence would have crouched beneath the infernal grasp of the of the [sic] the British Lyon— This Territory Sir is a part of the American continent and therefore it is a part of that soil for which our forefathers so nobly contended Now Sirs come out and take a decided stand & claim it at wonts [once] and you will be considered Americans otherwise you are cowardly traitors

T. HAMER.

Watsonstown Pa March 4, 1844

[Addressed:] Hon. Speaker of U. S. Senate
Washington City
D. C.

WPM-LC

G. C. Collins[140] to Willie P. Mangum.

NEW YORK April 3rd 1844.

Hon. Sir:

I arrived in this great Commercial Metropolis at 11 oC. last night, after a stay in Philadelphia of a few days, during which time, I had the honor of addressing the Whigs, and also of receiving $100 from the Nat. Clay Club for 1000 copies of my pamphlet I paid the publisher $50 thereof and sent Mr. Barrum[141] $20- leaving me on hand, when I left Pa— $30- Mr.

---

[140]See above, 25n.
[141]He probably refers to John M. Berrien.

Brady[142] an intelligent Irishman, Clk. of the Dist. Com. received me cordially- He is a glorious Clay Whig and at the same time a *Catholic* and Repealer- He is a very influential man, and was pleased with my position. I found there, the best feeling amongst the Whigs, and the most abject despondency amongst the other party. The Irish of Philadelphia in the event of the nomination of Mr. V. B. will go for Clay, almost unanimously. The Citizens requested me to return immediately after the election here to address the voters of each ward. The papers there noticed my pamphlet very favorably, I am confident it was not the composition or the Author which contributed to this, but the Subject, and the distinguished Statesman of whom it treats.

During my short stay here, I have had an interview with Horace Greely Esq. J. N. Reynolds & David Graham[143] Presidents of the most important committees of the city. During the conference, it was resolved that the Whigs should make a proposition, to the other party to divide the Aldermen, and toss up for the Mayor in order to defeat the Native American Party,[144] who have become quite formidable numerically, and who are I regret to say, actuated by the most bitter and malignant feelings, not only towards the civil but also the religious rights of the majority of the Adopted Citizens. The Pope is caricatured, and o Connell is made to kiss his toe &c. &c. Having had various confidential colloquies with several Whigs, they are becoming alive to the importance of shewing these men no confidence, I have no doubt, but, the Vans- started this matter, indeed, it is already a well authenticated fact, for political purposes in order that Many unwary Whigs might be caught in their traps. And as soon as they had them, leave them in the snares, and retire themselves. I have had an invitation to address a Mass meeting of the Adopted Citizens on next Saturday Night and accepted, it takes place at the National Hall, and

---

[142]Possibly Thomas Brady, a physician who died in 1850 at the age of 36. J. B. Nolan, *History of Southwestern Pennsylvania*, II, 1084.

[143]J. N. Reynolds declined being a candidate for the New York legislature in 1840 in order that he might give full time to Harrison's election. He was president of the Harrison committee of New York City. In 1844 he worked as ardently for Clay. *Hillsborough Recorder*, Nov. 12, 1840. See also below David Lambert to W. P. Mangum Sept. 29, 1844. David Graham, 1808-1852, a native of England, moved to New York City, when a small boy. In New York he was admitted to the bar in 1829 and almost immediately became successful, particularly as a criminal lawyer. He wrote numerous treatises on legal subjects and codified the state laws. In politics he actively worked for Clay. *D. A. B.*, VII, 471-472.

[144]By 1844 the Nativist movement had become strong in New York City. In their first election in 1842 the party received 9000 votes. In the mayor's race in the spring of 1844 the Whigs, in great numbers, deserted their party to vote for the Nativist candidate. The result was the election of a Nativist mayor and twelve aldermen. McMaster, *History of the People of the U. S.*, VII, 374.

THE MANGUM PAPERS 91

already seven distinguished Irishmen are cooperating with me. Having had an interview today with the Very Rev. Dr. Powers he has most cordially approved. I hope that we shall yet succeed, though the prospects are rather gloomy just now. The Con. Election has measurably assisted to this desirable end.

You will please excuse me, if I make a suggestion, relative to the Naval Officers of this Port, Jer.ʰ Towle- A certain Gentleman by the name of Kelly,¹⁴⁵ born here, has told me, that should he be convinced that the Senate would reject him, he would cause 1000 men to vote for us now and Clay hereafter. This Towle is a bitter *Loco*- of the V. Buren School. I really believe Kelly is a very influential Man, and would fulfil his promise, but at the same time, I would consider it highly presumptuous in me to interfere with the action of your Hon. body- I would however remark, that Messrs Graham and Reynolds believe Kelly to be actuated with the best motives, as for me, I have only suggested and this too by *request,* not being *otherwise interested.*

Senator, will you have the goodness to request your Treasurer to send my beloved Wife $10 or $20 on the Acct of those pamphlets, and should your opinions be already unfavorable towards Towle, if it would be within the Scope of your Senatorial character let me know- and I most conscientiouly believe, that good will result. No more from

Your Obt. Servt. &
humble friend
GEO. CONSTANTINE COLLINS

Hon. Willie P. Mangum

P. S. I most respectfully request a line,- City Hotel

Broadway

[Addressed:]

Hon. Willie P. Mangum
Pres. of the Senate &
Vice Pres of the U. S.
Washington D. C.

---

¹⁴⁵Unable to identify.

WPM-D

Reverdy Johnson to Willie P. Mangum.

BALT. 5 April /44.

My Dear Sir,

Have your recd. an answer from Mr. Lawrence about the V. Presidency to your letter to him? Let me know, & what he says. I have delayed noticing him in the Press here, as I desire, until I know if he would consent to his names being used—

The result in Connecticut shows,[146] if there was any doubt before, that our success in Novr. is certain. It is still all important that our selection of Vice President shall be a good one.

Virginia comes off next, - what do our friends there think will be result? Write me, if you can, by return mail.

Sincerely
Yr friend
REVERDY JOHNSON.

Mr. Mangum
   Washington.
   Some day next week I hope to be able to see you in Washington.

[Addressed:] Honbl.

Mr. Mangum
   In Senate
   Washington.

—————

WPM-LC

William Hayden[147] to Willie P. Mangum.

ATLAS OFFICE, BOSTON, April 6th 1844.

My dear sir—

I can hardly express to you the degree of gratification and delight with which I received and read your letter of the first instant. It is so entirely satisfactory, in regard to the feelings and

   [146]In the Connecticut election on April 1, the Whigs won a majority of 7 in the state senate and 24 in the state house. *Niles' Register,* LXVI, 146.
   [147]William Hayden was congressional correspondent of the *National Intelligencer* before he became editor of the Boston *Atlas* in 1841. At the time of this letter, he and Thomas M. Brewer were publishing the *Daily Atlas.* Ben Perley Poore, *Reminiscences of Sixty Years in the National Metropolis,* Philadelphia, 1886, I, 59; Fred A. Emory, "Washington Newspaper Correspondents," *Records of the Columbia Historical Society of Washington, D. C.,* XXXV-XXVI, 248-288.

HENRY CLAY,

Henry Clay, 1777-1852. From the line engraving by Peter Maverick, published 1822, after the painting by Charles King. From the original print in the possession of Mangum Weeks of Alexandria, Virginia.

intentions of our Southern & Western Whig friends in the Senate - and, withal, so full of kind, conciliatory and patriotic feeling, that I must confess it relieved me of a heavy pressure of anxiety, and made me feel that things would go on right again. Not that I have ever doubted the honor or fidelity of our Southern & Western friends in that body. I had carefully watched their course - and, from the past, was led to rely upon their future faithfulness. But I had no means at hand to satisfy those around me, upon that point. Great apprehensions were entertained here, that Tyler, and some of his coadjutors in the Cabinet, had so contrived the annexation matter as to bring it suddenly before the Senate, and to secure for it the support of the whole South. Startled as our community was with the suddenness of the development, the first impression was one of deep indignation. As soon, however, as time was allowed for reflection, our people began to consider how unlikely it was that gentlemen, who had been so faithful to the principles of their Party, and the interests of the Country, should be induced to disregard high considerations, on the occurrence of so important an emergency.

Just as the current of popular feeling was beginning to change, your excellent letter came to me. I have shown it, or otherwise caused its important purport to be made known, in the principal circles of our political friends in this vicinity. It has been pronounced, by all, to be perfectly satisfactory - and it has gone far to calm the public mind, upon the Texas and Tariff questions. I have been eagerly urged to publish it - but have refrained, as it would be manifestly improper to do so. I have, however, ventured so far as to depart from your injunction, as to publish an extract from it, in our leading article of this morning.

For the kind and friendly tone of your letter - its deference to the feelings and views of the North, on these great questions - for the true spirit of patriotism that pervades it - I most heartily thank you. Much of the acerbity that characterizes the discussion of most of the questions upon which local interests are supposed to be at variance, might be avoided, if leading men from the different sections would be governed by the same friendly, national feelings that are so well expressed in your letter.

All thoughts of [callin]g any Convention, so far as Massachusetts is concerned, have now been abandoned. The Whigs of our State are firmly attached to Mr Clay. We shall carry the State for him, as surely as the day of election arrives - and I most sincerely hope, and confidently believe, that his election, and administration, will dispel many of these sectional controversies, restore the Country to its wonted state of quiet and repose, and realize all the hopes which we so confidently repose in the full prevalence of Whig principles.

If, at any time hereafter, any views should occur to you, as likely to advance the cause of our Party, or promote the good of the Country and which it may be beneficial to make known here, I pray you freely to command my services - and, in the mean time, to believe me, dear sir,

> Very faithfully & respectfully,
> Your obt: servant,
> WILLIAM HAYDEN—

Hon. Willie P. Mangum.

[Addressed:]

> For—
> The Hon. Willie P. Mangum,
> United States Senate,
> Washington,
> D. C.

––––––––––

WPM-LC

James E. Harvey to Willie P. Mangum.

WASHINGTON
Saturday. [6 or 13 April, 1844]

My dear Sir

Accompanying this, you will receive the "Atlas" for which I scribble. The hasty notice which I gave your speech is *half* your own fault, for you did *not* furnish me with a reference to the Tariff Resolutions, from which I might have made capital. However you must take it, as it is, considering, that it comes from the *right spot*.

I am in position to touch very influential keys of this sort in New York, Philadelphia & Savannah & it will always afford me great & *sincere* pleasure to tune to your wishes, & in your service.

faithfully
Your friend
JAMES E. HARVEY

Judge Mangum.

My connection with the "Atlas" must not be spoken above a whisper or the d - d Locofocos may raise a hornets nest about my ears, as I have the means of letting out their Secrets, every day too often.

WPM-LC

J. Watson Webb to Willie P. Mangum.

N. YORK APRIL 11th. 1844

My Dear Sir.

Tyler is about removing Curtis.[148] Now for Curtis I care nothing; but I have it from my friend Col. *Clinton*,[149] that *Bob*[150] when he offered him the office, asked as a condition that he would agree to remove all obnoxious to his father. Clinton refused; upon which he said that if he would remove only the *Van Buren* men, he would be satisfied. To this too, Mr. Clinton objected as a degrading condition. He then told Master Bob that although a Calhoun man, the moment Mr. Calhoun was out of the question, he is thoroughly for Mr. Clay. This was quite astounding to Bob, & he had the folly to say that Mr. Calhoun "had disappointed his father & should be turned out in thirty days!" This last declaration you cannot use as *from me,* but it was made in presence of *Duff Green.*

Now, under the circumstances, can you not *reject* any person nominated in Curtis' place? This will not save Curtis nor do I desire to save him particularly. *Tyler* will certainly thrust him out the day after you adjourn. In the mean time by reject-

[148]Edward Curtis. See above, III, 163n, 223, 416.
[149]He probably refers to James Graham Clinton, half brother of DeWitt Clinton and Democratic Congressman from 1841 to 1845. *Biog. Dir. of Cong.*, 824.
[150]Robert Tyler, son of President Tyler.

ing any person nominated in his place, you put your finger on his profligacy and give power & strength, & *tone* to the Whig Party. Much is to be gained by thus *rebuking* corruption.

In to-morrow's paper I shall call upon you to refuse to administer the oath to Mr. *Niles*[151] without first instituting an enquiry into his capacity to take & understand it. *Quaere.* Has a magistrate a right to administer an oath to a child of five years of age? & if not, has the presiding officer of a deliberative body a right to administer an oath to a Lunatic? Being advised of the fact, it is I think your duty to investigate the state of his mind.

Please make my kindest repects to Messrs Morehead & Simmons, & say to them that the defeat of the Locos here, will do us much good & that they may hail it as another Cenn. affair.

Yours Very truly
J. W. WEBB

[Addressed:] To the Hon.
　　　　　W. P. Mangum,
　　　　　　　Washington City, D. C.

WPM-LC

John B. Thompson[152] to Willie P. Mangum.

FAYETTE HILL, SIMPSON COUNTY,
MISSISSIPPI 12th Aprl. 1844

Honor'd Sir,

My reason for thus adressing you on the present trivial occasion is, for the want of the knowledge of some known friend or acquaintance at the City of Washington, whome I could with propriety address, and I should not have taken this liberty with your honor had I not recollected to have seen you at my Fathers house (James Thompson's in the County of Onslow N. C.) some thirty years ago, I was then quite a Small lad, & as well as I recollect, you were quite young, probably not exceeding 20 years old— Your business with my father was to

---

¹⁵¹He probably refers to John Milton Niles, Democratic Senator from Connecticut, whose illness raised doubt as to his sanity.

¹⁵²The son of James Thompson, an active Whig in Onslow County, John B. Thompson represented Onslow in the North Carolina legislature in 1829 and 1831 before he moved to Alabama. *Hillsborough Recorder,* April 23, 1845, July 2, 1846; *Raleigh Register,* January 12, 1836; *N. C. Manual,* 734.

get pay for a little Grey horse by the name of Brilliant, which some gentleman living up the Country had sold in Onslow without informing the purchaser of the fact that half of said horse belong'd to your Father &c. &c.

In 1829 & 31, I had the honor to represent the County of Onslow in the General Assembly, each of those two years I had the pleasure of seeing the honorable J. C. Calhoun, at Raleigh, & the further gratification of an introduction, but have no doubt that I have escaped his recollection, probably in five minutes after being made known to him—

My next and last probable reference is to Joseph D. Ward, I received a letter from him I think in 1839, I was then living in Sumter County Ala., and have not heard from him since, he was then at the City of Washington, acting I think, as one of the Auditors, we were rais'd in old Onslow and near the same age. I should like to hear from him—

I have now done with flattery, and will tell you what I want; I now live in the State of Mississippi, Simpson County, and near the new post office, Call'd Fayette Hill, and a petition is getting up praying the department to move said office Eight miles So. Wt. from where it now is, to the inconvenience of your humble Servant and many other good Citizens.

I must therefore ask the favor of yourself, Mr. Calhoun and Mr. Ward, to request the department not to move the office, for if moved, it will only be to accommodate the contracter of the rout, and the whims of a few others— If either of you will say a word, it will be esteem'd and regarded as a special favor not only by me but many others—

Respectfully
Jno. B. Thompson.

N. B. If either of you have any extra publick documents, I should be thankful to receive a few of them— J B T

[Addressed:]

> The Honourable,
> Wiley P. Mangum
> Federal City
> Columbo

WPM-LC

John T. Towers[153] to Willie P. Mangum.

WASHINGTON, April 12, 1844.

Dr Sir:

Believing that you desired the continuation of the publication of at least one thorough Whig paper in this city, and that you deem it of importance to the party, I have thought proper to address you this note on the subject. In the first place it may be necessary to state the circumstances by which I find myself in my present position. Some short time after the stoppage of the "Independent," I was one of the persons spoken to in reference to its revival; I thought then, with many others, that as much good would be accomplished by delaying the establishment of another Whig paper in this city until the eve of the meeting of the 28th Congress, as by the revival of the Independent then, and that a certain loss would be avoided by the postponement; even upon the liberal terms proposed by the gentlemen who had the matter in hand. The conversation that occurred on the subject made me acquainted with the importance which was attached to it by the leading men of the party. During the past summer many good Whigs of the city thought it imperatively necessary that some thing should be done at once to combat and answer the daily libels of the Globe upon our champion and his friends, as well as to advance his claims. Concurring fully with them in their views. I did not hesitate to do what I could to meet the emergency by the investment in the cause of what little means I had accumulated; believing that I would not be permitted to suffer any serious pecuniary loss; and supposing such might be the case, I should still have the satisfaction of having contributed something to sustain the cause. The Whigs of the city have accomplished all I expected of them, and by the daily *evidences* of their good will, in subscriptions and advertising, are contributing materially to its permanent establishment—but many complain of the entire devotion of the whole paper to party - which prevents a larger increase of its circulation; besides the fact that a large portion of the reading population - clerks in offices—being on the same account, afraid to risk their places by subscribing. I presume you are aware of the heavy expense attendant on the *establishment* of a *daily* paper - and know also that *time* is as essential

---

[153]See above, III, 467n.

to it, as money. I have invested about $3000 in printing materials, and have expended about $800 more, above my receipts, besides somewhat involving myself. I knew what the undertaking would cost before I tried it, and am not disappointed at it. My expectation was to so far receive the patronage of our party in Congress by printing speeches and other matter during the canvass, as to make up my losses at least; but I had no idea that I should be apparently deserted by those whom I most design to defend; but such appears to be the fact. I have never appealed to the party for pecuniary aid, nor do I now; all I ask is an opportunity to *earn enough to meet my losses,* provided it is in the power of the party to do so, without detriment to themselves. If the "Standard" is thought to be of no advantage to the party, an intimation to that effect will be suficient to induce me to fall back upon our own local matters, and look to our own people to sustain it as a local paper; if otherwise, it is necessary that something should be done; I presume, in that case, no one would expect me to involve myself in further embarrassment by going on. Should it be desirable, and it can be done at very little sacrifice, the paper can be enlarged to the size of the other dailies of the city, in order to meet more fully the wishes of the friends of the paper. Excuse me for the liberty I have taken, but I feel it my duty to make known my grievances before I complain about them.

Very respectfully
JNO. T. TOWERS.

Hon. W. P. Mangum.

[Addressed:] Hon. Wm. P. Mangum.

J. Watson Webb to Willie P. Mangum.[154]

(Confidential.)

NEW YORK
April 13 1844

My Dear Sir:

I intend sailing from this City in the Packet of the 21st of April for Liverpool, to be absent until about the 1st of July -

---

[154] I have been unable to locate the original of this letter. Fortunately, Dr. Stephen B. Weeks left a typed copy which he compared with the original. On the typed copy in Dr. Weeks' handwriting is a note to the effect that the letter was unsigned and that it was in the autograph of James Watson Webb. See below, W. P. Mangum to J. W. Webb, April 20, 1844, in volume V. This letter was discovered too late to include in volume IV.

so that I will be here during the four last and most important months of the great contest. I have just written an article in favour of Mr. Clayton's nomination to the Vice Presidency, which will appear on Monday, to be followed up by my assistants during my absence. And having thus attended to my political duties, I must be held excusable if I run away for ten weeks to attend to my private affairs.

The object of my visit is to negotiate a loan for or make a sale of the stock of the Banellvill mining Company, chartered by the State of Maryland for the manufacture of Iron in the County of Alleghany. The sum I propose borrowing for them is $750,000; and there can be no doubt but who so ever succeeds in bringing into the County foreign capital to develop & bring into market the inexhaustable wealth of Forests & Mountains, does an acceptable & patriotic service to the Country. Since I saw you, I have visited the property in question, in company with Professors Silliman, Schoolcraft, Renwick[155] & others, who have made an official report upon its mineral resources which are really unexcelled. They report that Iron may be made at a price on this property in consequence of the contiguity of the Coal & Iron Ore which cannot fail to yield a large income to the manufacturers; & in consequence of the super-abundance of capital in England, it is only necessary to overcome the feeling against investments in the U. S. to win my success. To accomplish this, I intend to take letters which will insure a proper social position and satisfy capitalists that I am not an *adventurer,* & that whatever I state as facts, on my own knowledge, may be implicity relied upon. Mr. Webster, Govr. Cass, Judge Wilkins the Secy of War, Governor Seward & many private gentlemen, will & have written letters to our minister & consul, asking them to give me letters to any Banker I may designate, assuring him that he may rely implicitly upon any statement I may make. It would undoubtedly have added to my strength & chance of success if I could have taken similar letters from Mr. Clay & some others of our prominent men; but I did not feel justified in troubling them.

My object in thus occupying your time, is to ask you, in case you are of the same opinion with Mr. Crittenden, to address me a letter, stating that there is no danger of any alteration of the *tariff* at this session; and also, if such is your opinion, that noth-

---

[155]He possibly refers to Edward S. Renwick, Henry R. Schoolcraft, and Benjamin Silliman.

ing will be done in relation to Oregon or Texas. You will at once perceive that the prospects of a reduction of the duty on *Iron* will necessarily retard my negotiations; & consequently, if no such reduction is about to take place, I feel that there can be no impropriety in my request. At all events, if you should think otherwise, you will, I am sure, frankly say so, in the full conviction that I will appreciate your motives & take no exception to your decision. If on the contrary, you can with perfect propriety, write me such a letter as I desire, it will do me much good; & if our friend Morehead would join in it, I should not be unmindful of the kindness. If you should determine to write me a letter corroborating the declaration Mr. Crittenden on the floor of the Senate, you may further add to the kindness, by so wording the letter as to assume that my application will not & cannot be considered one from an adventurer or speculator, but when backed by my *word* will be entitled to consideration so far as facts & merit warrant it. My course too, in regard to the repudiating states & companies & companies [*sic*] might be referred to as evidence that I would not recommend any loan or investment which I did not feel would repay richly those who embark in it. Of one thing rest assured, I will not make any representation, for the truth of which I would not stake my life.

I have thus written your fully and frankly as if to an old friend who is familiar with my every thought; & in the same frankness I assure you most truly, that if you should decline giving me the letter I solicit, it would

[Rest of letter is missing]

WPM-LC

James Webb to Willie P. Mangum.

HILLSBORO N. C. April 13 1844

Dr Sir

I Rec'd from our friend Mr Cain a check for $650 for you. Please to say how I am to appropriate it.

Mr Cain does not know when he will return

Mr Graham is mending slowly We shall have a Blow up among the Whigs of Orange if the question of Division[156] of the County is not settled

Use your influence to bring about a compromise the Whigs about Hillsboro will not vote for Division Whigs over Haw River and they are determined on Division they have become rabid since the appropriation to build a New Court House

I have not time to say more when you come home we will talk freely on the subject. Yours obt

Sert
James Webb.

[Postmarked:]Hillsboro N. C. Apr 14

[Addressed:]

Honl. W. P. Mangum
    Washington
        City.

WPM-D

Henry Clay to Willie P. Mangum.

Raleigh April 14th 1844.

My Dear Sir,

I received here your favor of the 9th inst. and I am greatly obliged by the views opinions and information which it contains. It relieved me from some solicitude which I had felt. I think you need entertain no fears that your own opinions will not be fully sustained and supported by your constituents. Indeed throughout the whole of that portion of the South, which I have traversed, I have found a degree of indifference or opposition to the measure of annexation which quite surprised me. I have forborne to make any exposition of the sentiments which I entertain upon the subject; but it is my intention after my

---

[156]For some years before 1844 the citizens west of the Haw River in Orange County had been trying to divide the county and create a new county in the region that is today Alamance County. In May the county commissioners let a contract to rebuild the old courthouse. To the people west of Haw River this meant that there would be no division. The controversy increased. On May 23, 1844, the editor of the *Hillsborough Recorder* refused to publish any more letters from the Haw River section unless the writers' names were signed or the attacks on personalities were discontinued. On August 1 the voters were permitted to express their wishes on division in a referendum. The result was 1364 for and 1656 against division. *Hillsborough Recorder,* April 4, May 2, 23, August 8, 1844. Finally in 1849 a division was realized by the creation of Alamance County.

arrival at Washington to make such an exposition if I deem it necessary. I can easily avail myself for that purpose of any one of several letters of enquiry which have been addressed to me.[157] I do not entertain the slightest apprehension of any injury to our cause from the publication of my opinions. On the contrary I believe it would be benefitted and strengthened.

My reception at the Capital of your State has been cordial and enthusiastic, and attended by numbers, far surpassing my most sanquine anticipations.

> I am faithfully, your friend,
> and obednt. Servnt.
> H CLAY.

Honble. Mr Mangum

[Addressed:] The Honble Willie P. Mangum
&c &c &c
City of
Washington.

[Postmarked:] Raleigh N. C. Apr 15

WPM-LC

B. W. Leigh to Willie P. Mangum.

RICHMOND, April 17 1844

My dear Sir

I write merely to ask you, whether you received an answer I wrote you to your letter of the 25th March. The question is no otherwise important, than that I may be assured that *you* got it, instead of it's falling into the hands of other persons. There were somethings in it, on which I wished to hear further from you, tho' it was not very material that you should take the trouble of replying.

---

[157]Clay visited Raleigh on April 12-14 as a result of an earlier invitation from the Whigs of North Carolina. From April 11 through 13 a great celebration was held. From 3000 to 4000 people attended the meetings on the twelfth and thirteenth. Several out of state visitors were there, including Benjamin Watkins Leigh, who, with three others, made two and three hour speeches each in one day. On April 13 Clay spoke for two hours. Six other speeches and fire works were part of the program for the same day. On April 17 after consulting with Governor John M. Morehead, George Badger, and other North Carolina Whigs, Clay wrote his famous Raleigh letter on annexation. He sent the letter to Crittenden and asked to have it published in the *National Intelligencer*. In the letter Clay reviewed the history of the Texas question. He said we once owned Texas but gave up our claim to it and, therefore, had no right to reclaim it. He opposed annexing Texas if a considerable portion of a section of the Union opposed it, for it would break the balance between the free and slave states. He was also opposed to assuming the Texas debt. If, however, a foreign power should try to colonize or subjugate Texas, the United States should offer opposition. Clay reached Washington on April 26 and this letter was published in the *Intelligencer* the next day. On the evening of the same day Van Buren's letter on annexation appeared in the *Globe*. McMaster, *Hist. of the People of the U. S.*, VII, 327-328; Van Deusen, *Life of Clay*, 364-366.

The public mind here is very full of Texas.

Your friend,

B: W: LEIGH

Hon. W. P. Mangum.

[Addressed:]

Hon. Willie P. Mangum
Senator U. S.
Washington.

————

WPM-LC

Richard H. Atwell[158] to Willie P. Mangum.

NEW YORK April 17 1844

Confidential

My Dear Sir

When I was in Washington a few weeks since, you did me the honour to express your views somewhat freely, in relation to the candidate for the vice-presidency, and I take the liberty of saying a word or two to you, in order, in return, to state what my impressions are, in relation to the direction that will be given to the vote, of the State of New York, in the Balto Convention - after having taken a little time to look about, I believe that out of the thirty six votes, of this State, thirty, or thirty-two, will be cast in *good faith* for Millard Fillmore, and it is quite possible that all may be on the *first* ballot. Two Districts in the City of New York, would by their representatives vote for some other one, but they will probably be instructed to vote for him, which I think would not take place, if Mr. *Clayton had come amongst us.* The people of this State so far as I can learn, entertain not that strong and ardent feeling for Mr. F. that Mr. Clay commands, but an *esprit de corps,* which will enable their representative to "back up" their choice with great effect. I do believe that Millard Fillmore would run *well* in this State, but I do *not* believe that the affections of the Whigs are so *concentrated* upon him as to render it *dangerous,* to leave

———

[158]See above, 85, 88.

him off the ticket,[159] - except so far as the loss, (if any) of the additional votes he could bring in the Western part of the State, might be considered so.

Almost, if not entirely, the Whig vote can be controlled by Mr. Clay, and it must be *very* strong man that can keep *him*, when I say *almost* I mean, *abolitionists* whigs, and anti masons, besides whigs regular, these irregulars, are the ones Mr. F. is said by some to control.

You will meet with many "lobby members" of the Conventions from N. Y. and some actual ones, who will talk *large* about our state, as to the necessity that *their* particular Candidate should be nominated, in order to secure success here, that defeat will be more than probable without him, &c. &c. these statements must not be believed. I am but a very humble individual myself, but I have the vanity to think that after a little "comparing of notes" with my fellows, and the masses, I can gather as good or better evidence of public opinion in the party, as the *delegates* and "maybe a little better," for they frequently are exposed [*sic*] more to be biased, than one who does not have a vote upon the matter, neither would you be justified in my opinion - as a member of the Convention, - in believing that Mr. F. would bring contempt, upon the ticket, he *is respected* in this State.

But by no means my Dear Sir, must Mr. Talmadge be permitted to be nominated. I believe it would lose us the electoral vote of the State, such is the present feeling against him, *as such nominee,* I am constrained to say that Abbot Lawrence is apparently less appreciated here than Mr Fillmore is at the South and West, he is not enough known in New York State however much he may be in the South though certainly there is a most powerful argument in his favour in the fact (if it be such) that the Mercantile and Commercial interests of the Country will be conciliated, *and put in motion* by the nomination of him. I belong to that class, and have reason to know, that they move with great power, when the mass of them can be put in motion, though it must be confessed, that as we say of G. and the old Webster *Clique,* where *they are* - as a general thing,

---

[159]Fillmore wanted the vice presidential nomination, but Weed and others decided that he was needed more to head the state ticket for governor. On June 16, 1844, Weed wrote: " 'I am accused of all sorts of wicked designs in opposing Fillmore's nomination for Vice-President . . . as I knew I should be, but I determined to do my duty to the Party and take the curses. I knew that if F. was nominated for V. P. we should have some unfit man for Governor.' " Fillmore was defeated for governor by Silas Wright by 10,033. Van Deusen, *Thurlow Weed,* 132-133, 136, 362n.

through the series of years that make up a generation, "The Masses" *are not to be found.* These things must not be disregarded by those who have the laying out, a line of policy, on a large and prominent scale, for the whole Whig party, through the nation.

Upon this point our "great Captains" opinion would be in our estimation of great value. Webb your *protege* is making a fool of himself again, he might as well expect to push the Pallisade into the north river, as to destroy the influence and *power,* in this State of "the Boys"[160] see if we dont nominate our candidate for Governor, and *elect him too.*

I have the honour to be very faithfully yours,

RICHD. H. ATWELL.

Hon. W. P. Mangum.

WPM-LC

Memucan Hunt to Willie P. Mangum.

GALVESTON, TEXAS,
18th Apl. 1844

My Dear Sir,

As I have before done on two occasions, I again take the liberty to do, that of inclosing to your care a letter for my esteemed friend Gen'l. Henderson.[161]

The British and French Ministers have both conveyed to the government of Texas notes protesting against a treaty of annexation to the U. S. A.[162]

Captain Elliot[163] the Chargé d' Affaires of Great Britain left here a few days since for the U. S. He informed me that his family was at Natchez, where he expected to spend some weeks, or months. My impression is that the government of Great Britain, would be exceedingly gratified to witness a dissolution of the U. S., and may think, that in connexion with this great question of reannexation, auspicious movements for that end can be made. May an allwise Providence prevent such a

---

[160]Webb did not go along with Weed and Seward. He advocated the nomination of Webster for Vice President.
[161]He refers to James Pinckney Henderson, one of the commissioners from Texas to Washington.
[162]For a fresh discussion of the influence of the action of England and France on annexation, see Wiltse, *Calhoun: Sectionalist,* 151-155, 170-171, 200-201, 209, 215.
[163]Captain Charles Elliott.

calamity to my native land, and to mankind in general. The Government of the U. S. can not keep too scrutinising an eye on the movements of her great commercial rival Great Britain.

The Count de Saligny, Chargé d' Affaires of France is now in this City; he confident that Texas will never again be united to the U. S.

Your Minister Gen'l. Murphy[164] is likewise here.

Just before the departure of Captain Eliot the President, Genl. Houston, had a long private interview with him, and it is said wrote a despatch to our Minister at Washington instructing him, if our negotiations had not gone too far, to withdraw and return home. This despatch was placed in the hands of Captain E., as I learn, with the desire that he would cause it to be transmited himself.[165] I have no confidence in President Houston, and never make any lasting calculations on any thing that he may either write, or speak. I believe, however, that he is anxious to see Texas annexed to the U. S.

> I have the honor to remain with
> great respect your friend and obedient sv't
> MEMUCAN HUNT

To Hon. W. P. Mangum
  Prest. U. S. Senate

[Addressed:]

> Hon. W. P. Mangum
>   President of the
>   U. S. Senate

———

WPM-LC

James R. Wood[166] to Willie P. Mangum.

NEW YK. Apl. 19, 44

Dear Sir

By a vote of the Board of Management of the 7th Ward Democratic Clay club, you were unanimously invited to be present

---

[164]W. S. Murphy.

[165]Sam Houston's motives are hard to evaluate. He may have desired to maintain permanent independence of Texas or he may have been playing England and France against the United States to force ratification. Wiltse, *Calhoun: Sectionalist,* 158-159; Justin H. Smith, *The Annexation of Texas,* New York, 1941, 160-169; Marquis James, *The Raven: A Biography of Sam Houston,* Indianapolis, 1929, 349-351.

[166]James R. Wood was a New York surgeon. *Longworth's New York Directory,* 1844-1845, 386.

and address the club on the occasion of the presentation of a Banner to the club by the Whigs of the Ward.

By order of the Board
JAS. R. WOOD Pres

Wm. R. Loudon sec
To Honl. Willie P. Mangum.

———

"Justice to Harry of the West."[167]

Seventh Ward Democratic Clay Club.

NEW YORK, April 18, 1844.

Sir,

You are hereby notified that a Regular Meeting of the above Club will be held at CROTON HALL, corner of Bowery and Division St., on the Evening of Wednesday, the 24th instant, at 7 o'clock.

By order of
JAMES R WOOD, President.

John Cromwell,   ) Secretaries.
William R. Loudon,)

A magnificent Banner will be presented to the Club, on the above evening.

Seats reserved for the Ladies.

———

WPM-LC

Edward S. Tod to Major W. B. Morris & others.[168]

MEMPHIS April 20th 1844

Gentlemen

I had the pleasure of receiving a communication from you containing certain interrogatories in relation to the location

---

[167]This letter was printed on the same sheet with the preceding letter.
[168]In 1842 Matthew F. Maury, an advocate of direct trade between the South and Europe, wrote an article for the *National Intelligencer* advocating a navy yard at Memphis. The Tennessee legislature, thereupon, petitioned Congress, and F. P. Stanton, a Tennessee congressman, made it his project. After two naval surveys, Congress appropriated the money to begin the construction, which began in October, 1845. It proved a wasteful project, and, despite pressure from Memphis, the project received smaller and smaller appropriations until it was finally discontinued. Only one ship was built at the navy yard. Gerald M. Capers, Jr., *The Biography of a River Town Memphis: Its Heroic Age,* Chapel Hill, 1939, 82-85.

of the Naval depot & dock yard on the fourth Chickasaw Bluffs -
to which I hasten to reply

1st During the *second* visit of the Commissioners appointed
to examine the harbor of Memphis I was requested by D.
Morrison Esq to make an estimate of the number of cubic yards
of embankment necessary to raise the Batture in front of
Memphis to high water mark, which I did by accurate measure-
ment - and found that about five hundred and fifty thousand
cubic yards would be required I do not remember the precise
number but it would not vary much from my statement - this
estimate was handed by me to the commissioners & agreed to by
Mr. Morrison - the lowest price at which in my opinion the embankment could be made is twenty cents per cubic yard as the
hauling would be from three hundred to six hundred yards for a
great portion of the work - the cost at this price would be one
hundred & ten thousand dollars - the estimate handed to the commissioners at their first visit was made, by Mr. Morrison himself
and was published in their report

2nd In answer to the second interrogatory I reply that from
information which I have received from some of the oldest &
most respectable citizens in Memphis the depth of water where
the Batture now is was more than forty feet at low water before the year 1828 at which time the formation began—

3rd I should consider that for the location of a naval depot
& dock yard the preference is decidedly to be given to Fort
Pickering both on account of permanency & cost of forming the
yard, as regards permanency I would state that I have seen
rock formation at low water both a short distance above the
proposed site & and at the lower part of it, the Table Bench at
the Fort has remained unchanged since it has been known & before it was cleared a few years ago it was covered with timber
of a large size of at least 125 years standing which could be
determined by counting the rings formed each year during the
growth of the tree - the table bench is one hundred & ninety
feet wide in the narrowest part of the proposed site extends
about two thousand feet along its front & is up to high water
mark—

4th I have made an estimate of the number of cubic yards
necessary to be removed from the Bluff in order to reduce the
grade of that portion of it coloured pink on the plat herewith
sent to five & one quarter degrees and find it amounts to two

hundred & sixty five thousand - the part proposed to be graded is five hundred feet wide at the edge of the Bluff & four hundred where the grade strikes the surface of the ground which is six hundred feet from the edge of the Bluff the grade is proposed to be carried by embanking about two hundred feet across the table bench to the water's edge—

Proposals have been made to do the grading required for ten cents per cubic yard by W. B. Morris & W. W. Hart Esqrs who are men of Judgement in such matters & who offer to give any security that may be required for the completion of the work - at the price proposed the grading could be completed for twenty six thousand five hundred dollars

5th The title of the proposed site is beyond dispute there can be obtained for the purposes of government a tract containing a little more than one hundred acres on the following terms that portion marked 33 acres belonging to J. C. McLemore is proposed to be given unconditionally to the government, that part marked 28½ acres belonging to John Sugg he proposes to donate on condition of their purchasing from him a tract of forty acres lying immediately South of the 28½ acres tracts & adjoining thereto and comprised between the river bank and the eastern line of the proposed site extended south to the southern boundary line of his tract for one hundred & fifty dollars per acre or for the sum of six thousand dollars for the tract, which is deemed a fair price for land in that situation and is lower than lands have sold a mile from the river immediately back of it—

This would make the total cost of the one hundred acres of land and the grading as proposed amount to thirty two thousand five hundred dollars

6th I think that if the site proposed at Fort Pickering had been within the corporate limits of Memphis the commissioners would have undoubtedly chosen that place in preference to the one at the mouth of Wolf

7th The distance from the mouth of Wolf River to the site proposed at Fort Pickering is about 2½ miles the town extends about one & one half miles below the mouth of that River, leaving a distance between the lower part of the town and the site proposed about one mile - the ground between the two

places is a plain well adapted for building & without doubt will
in a few years be covered with houses.

Yours with Respect
EDWD S. TOD
Civil Engineer

Messrs Gen. Eastim Morris
W. W. Hart
W Howard
Major W. B. Morris.

[Endorsed:]

B. Mr. Tods Reply.

_____

WPM-LC

A. W. Gay[169] to Willie P. Mangum.

KNAP OF REEDS, GRANVILLE, April 20th—1844

Dear Sir.

The Whigs of Granville have this day nominated me as one
of their candidates for a seat in the next Legislature; and I
suppose I shall feel it my duty, tho' with great reluctance, to
accept the nomination.

That I may be prepared to sustain the whig cause in the approaching contest, I thought it not amiss to apply to you for
such documents as you may judge best suited to the purpose.
I shall specify a few of the points upon which I most desire information.

1. The history of the late Bank of the United States - especially its aid in conducting the fiscal operations of the government and its beneficial influence upon the currency and general
business of the country. If the speeches delivered by Mr. Calhoun in the Senate on Jackson's veto of the Bank and the removal of the Deposites can be readily procured, they would
probably furnish all the information necessary. Calhoun would
be an important witness in Granville.

_____

[169] A physician who entered the race for the legislature. He was defeated. See A. W. Gay to
W. P. Mangum, December 4, 1845.

In connexion with the above I should be glad to have a copy of the Sub-Treasury bill, approved July 4th. 1840: also Clay's Bank bill vetoed at the Extra Session.

I think of making the bank question the special issue. I am confident that question is stronger by twenty per cent in Granville than the whig cause. I have always been rather ultra bank - perhaps more so than Mr. Clay.

2. The Tariff. I suppose I shall have little trouble on this question; because Van Buren is more of a Tariff man than Clay. But I should like to have some proof as to Van Buren's latest. views on the Tariff.

3. The Bankrupt law. All the difficulty I anticipate on this question is the fact that Clay was instructed to vote for its repeal and disobeyed. Was he instructed unconditionally?

4. Annexation of Texas. On this question I am yet uncommitted. I presume it cannot be made a party question. I know nothing of the views of either Clay or Van Buren on this question. The ground which I think of taking in relation to the matter is this.

Personally I am in favor of Annexation if it can be effected without too great a sacrifice. But, if it is to involve us in a war with Mexico and England and the Indians, and occasion a dissolution of the Union, then I am apposed to it.

5. Expenditures of the government for the last 15 or 20 years, - especially the exact financial condition of the government on the 4th. of March 1841, and what it has been ever since. This you know is a matter of the first importance, and, on every point it is essential that I have the most indisputable documentary proof.

6. Gerrymandering of the state[170] by the last Legislature. Would it be best, before the people, to take the ground that the next Legislature, if whig, should remodel the Congressional districts of the state? The excuse given by the other party for that act is that the same thing was done by a whig Legislature

---

[170]As a result of the census of 1840, North Carolina lost four seats in the national House of Representatives. The legislature which apportioned the seats was under the control of the Democrats, who proceeded to gerrymander the state to their advantage. Orange County, which usually cast majority votes for the Whigs, was put with the Democratic counties of Franklin and Warren. Since the section around Greensboro usually voted for the Whigs, the counties near Greensboro were lumped together so that they would not help other divided districts to go Whig. In 1844 the Whigs gained control of the legislature and redistricted the state to their advantage. Under the 1844 plan, Orange, Guilford, Caswell, and Person composed the Seventh District, and Halifax, Warren, Franklin, Wake, and Granville were placed together. C. C. Norton, *Democratic Party in N. C.*, 73, 145; *Hillsborough Recorder*, May 30, 1844.

of Massachusetts in districting that state since 1840. Is this true? What are the real facts of the case?

I hope, Sir, you will not regard me as being too troublesome in making these inquiries and requests. The approaching contest is one of unequaled importance. Those who may be called upon to sustain the whig cause, ought to be thoroughly prepared. I have no means of obta[in]ing the requisite information except through you. Never having desired or expected to become a candidate, I have not preserved such Newspapers or documents as might have been useful at the present time.

I shall be glad to hear from you soon. On the 7th of May, being court week, the candidates for this county will have to address the people and declare themselves and avow their principles.

I was in Raleigh last week when Mr. Clay was there. Such an assemblage I never saw. But Mr. Clay will tell you all about it. I understand that many of the other party came to him, told him they had seen their error, and should hereafter support him.

Direct to Knap-of-Reeds, P. O.
Granville,

Truly Yours &c.
A. W. GAY.

P.S. What apology or excuse can be given for the whigs in electing John Tyler? We shall have that matter thrown at us continually

OXFORD May 7th 1844.

The within was written in anticipation of what I expected to occur on the 20th ult. but the day was so rainy, that nothing was done. The nomination was made today and, as I anticipated, I am one of the nominees. I hope you will send me such documents as you may think suited to the purpose. In relation to the Texas question, I suppose I shall need nothing but what I shall find in the papers. I see no Washington paper, except the Congressional Globe.

Yours &c.

A. W. GAY.

[Addressed:]

Hon. Willie P. Mangum
Washington City
D. C.

WPM-LC

B. W. Leigh to Willie P. Mangum.

RICHMOND, April 22, 1844

My dear Sir—

I have received your letter of the 18th. I was very much delighted with my visit to Raleigh - for, as you may suppose, I was quite at home among the North Carolinians, and the North Carolina Whigs were there in all their glory. The Whigs estimated that there were about 8000 or 9000 whigs present*—The democrats, I understood, struck off a nought, and said there could not be more than about 800: but having put forth their estimate on Saturday morning (the 13th), pains were taken to ascertain *the quantity of meat consumed* at the barbecue that day, which was found to be above 7000 lbs averdupois; whereupon some wag among the whigs said, that if 800 whigs consumed at one dinner 7000 lbs of *meat,* Van Buren would not be a *breakfast* even for them. Clay was in fine spirits, and in the best humour - he made an excellent speech, but as he was not excited by the collision of debate, he did not rise to any of *his* high flights of eloquence; and I told our friends so, but they could not believe me - you, who know him will. There was not a single personal remark in the speech, and but only one personal allusion, and that was to Tyler; so slight, however, that it did not strike even Duncan Cameron, acute as you know he is, until I called his attention to it. The very slightness of the allusion marked his contempt more strongly than the most laboured invective could have done. I don't know whether I shall be able to see you as I pass through Washington on my

way to Baltimore. I will if I can— Meantime, if there is any
thing I ought to be informed of on the subject of the Vice presidency, write to me, and send your letter to Baltimore by the
mail of monday the 29th - I shall be in Baltimore the evening
of that day.

                                        Yrs truly
                                        B: W: LEIGH

Hon. W. P. Mangum.

* There were 600 from your county of Orange.

[Addressed:]

                    Hon. Willie P. Mangum
                    Senator U. S.

                    ———————

                                        WPM-LC

        C. F. Welles, Jr.[171] to Willie P. Mangum.

                    ATHENS BRADFORD COUNTY PA.
                                        April 23, 1844
Honl W P Mangum
    U. S. Senate

        Dear Sir
            Though personaly an entire Stranger to you I feel
that you are not so to me from your long & brilliant career as
a Member of the Senate which has given me strong confidence
in your judgment & opinions in relation to Government matters.
The object of this letter you will see is to get your opinion in
relation to the probable result of the Orogan, Tarriff & Sub
Treasury question, more especially the Orogan; Will the Mad
Caps of the Country & Congress—belonging to Polks party overthrow the more Conservative portion of his friends & force the
Government to Settle the Orogan question by War in claiming
all & no compromise
        Will your honorable body pass the Sub Treasury bill as it
came from the house? Will the party in power repeal the present excellent Tariff or Materially alter the Same.

———————
[171]Unable to identify.

My object in making these enquiries are first I am now a partner in a mercantile house in this place doing a Somewhat extensive business in produce &c & if we are to have war, Sub Treasury & repeal of the present Tariff, I wish to Curtail very much or stop entirely. Again I am disposed to do a large lumbering business the ensuing year in which I should probable invest some 15 to $25,000 in Cash and this operation depends entirely upon the issue of the Orogan question if War is to come I should not invest one dollar in any article to be sold in 1847

The business of the country is now healthy & good & the prospects for the ensuing year are very fair indeed unless the insane infatuation of the Locofoco party shall plunge the Country into war & inflict upon the same the Sub Treasury & repeal the Tariff. When I say the Country is almost unanimous against war for anything North of 49 parralel I say what nineteen twentieths of the Sensible people will bear me out in. The war fever is raised by the paid agents of men who have or expect to get office, men who have no business & never will have but to steal from the government. This 54.40 War Cry rises in the large cities & towns by office expecants & Country Editors who in fact know nothing of public opinion except the little cliques who rule every loco foco paper catch up the cry & echo it back & from the Editor the pot house politician catches the cry & reiterates it to his base associates & so goes the cry. What interest have these men in the welfare of the country? Their interest is in war that they may rob & plunder from others. What care they about oragon, nothing. all they want is to live on the spoils of war or office These are the men who back the Allens Capes Hanegans and their Coworkers in crying out for 54. 40.[172] Shall we be ruled by such men - heaven forbid

Sir by giving me your opinion in answer to the questions put in this letter you will confer a lasting favour on one who claims

[172]By July, 1843, the American settlers in Oregon had established a temporary government to protect themselves. Petitions from various state legislatures began pouring into Congress asking for the establishment of a territorial government and for the acquisition of the territory up to 54° 40′ N. By April, Senator Edward A. Hannegan, of Indiana, William Allen, of Ohio, and others were belligerent in their demand for all of Oregon.

a close political relationship with you & the grand Whig Army
of the Union

Most Respectfully Your
obt Servant
C. F. WELLES JR
Athens
Bradford Co
Pa

[Postmarked:] Athens Pa. Apr 24

[Addressed:]

Honl. W. P. Mangum
U. S. Senate
Washington City
D. C.

WPM-LC

Wesley Hollister[173] to Willie P. Mangum.

RALEIGH N CAROLINA Apl 23d 1844

Dear Sir

Enclosed are keys belonging to the Hon H Clay - they were
drop[d] by his Servant on his recent visit to this place & I was
not able to learn to whom they belonged until it was too late
for me to forward them direct to Mr Clay & as they may be of
some importance to him—& not knowing of any more direct
way to send I take the liberty of troubling you with them - believing that you will [know] where to direct them that they
may reach him most speedily.

Very Respectfully
Your obdt Servant
WESLEY HOLLISTER

Hon W P Mangum

---

[173]Wesley Hollister was president of the Raleigh and Gaston Railroad. Moses N. Amis, *Historical Raleigh from its Foundation in 1792: Descriptive, Biographical, Educational Industrial, Religious*, Raleigh, 1902, 116.

WPM-LC

B. L. White[174] to Willie P. Mangum.

WILLIAMSTON MARTIN Co: April 23d 1844.

My Dear Sir.

I have taken this liberty to ask of you a piece of friendship if in your power. If my memory does not deceive me, my late deceased Brother (Willie N. White) often during his last days of affliction spoke of your tender friendship to him.

In this case I have through my representative (Mr. K. Rayner) put a claim into his hands to see if there is not justly due me by government, for Military Services rendered by my Father— Mr. Rayner has written to me on the subject, he proposes some questions which I am not at this time able to answer satisfactorily— Will you if you can recollect that at any time you ever heard my Brother speak any thing on the matter previous to his death, I believe you were with him during his last illness—

The claim rests upon the following grounds, my father was commissioned Lieut. Col. in the late war by President Madison, he was stationed at Charleston S. C., and Genl. Pinckney was the commander, whether he served during all the war, I am as yet unable to say, - if therefore you can assist my Representative in the establishing of this Claim, I will take it as one of the greatest favours.

I have settled in old Martin, and happy to inform you that I am doing as well as the times will admit.

We are preparing to try and do something for "Harry of the West." I would be glad to receive some speeches from you whenever it is convenient to send them.

Resp your friend
B. L. WHITE.

Honl. W. P. Mangum
U. S.

---

[174]Brother of Willie N. White, who married Mary (Cain) Sutherland, Mangum's sister-in-law.

WPM-LC

John Walker to Willie P. Mangum.

BROOKSVILLE April 24th 1844

Hon Mr Mangum

Dear Sir

Pleas Confer a favour upown me. by sending me documents or political papers, for election pourpose, for the Loco Focos ar Sending Kendals Lies into This town and we want truth to face them. The Whigs of this State are Waking up and Shall try hard to give the vote to Henry Clay That Noble Patriot, but we want truth to Circulate among the people, we have evrything To face all those miserable Abolitionist. They and the Loco Focos go Hand in Hand Circulating falsehoods and. Ministers Professing to preach the gospel Abusing Hon Henry Clay, but Clay must be Elected he will be and no mistake. in my humble opinion he will Carry Maine.

Verry Respectfully Yours
JOHN WALKER

Brooksville Me
April 25th

[Addressed:]

Hon Willie P Mangum
Senator in Congress
Washington
D. C.

_____

WPM-LC

Lewis Eaton[175] to Willie P. Mangum

NEW YORK Apl 27. 1844

Hon W. P. Mangum

Dear Sir

This will be handed by John G Brown Esq of Buffalo, he goes as delegate to the Baltimore Convention, he is a Zealous

---

[175]Probably Lewis Eaton, who was a member of Congress from New York from 1823 to 1825 and the state senate from 1829 to 1832. *Biog. Dir. of Cong.*, 932.

& an efficient politician and understands the state of parties well in our state any attention you may pay him will much Oblige

Yr friend & obt Set.

LEWIS EATON

[Addressed:]

Hon W. P. Mangum
Pres. U. S. S
Washington D. C.

_____

WPM-LC

Micajah Mangum to Willie P. Mangum.

RICHMOND 29th. April 1844

Dear Kinsman

Through the politeness of my old friend Capt. Wm. Claibourn I address A few lines to you to let you know that I feel gld to hear I have one relation[176] of the name of Mangum left to tell the history of my Ancesters as far as I am informed. My grand father's name was Micajah Mangum whos name I bear he came to this country before the revolutionary war was wounded at Yorktown and shortly arter the war died in Isle of Wight County Va leaving three daughters and one son my father Joseph Mangum who went up the country to Goochland County about 35 miles above Richmond on James River where he married Elizabeth Humber in the year 1796 where he lived till 1817 - when he left Virginia for Alabama (my mother died in 1807 - leaving 5 children 3 girls & 2 boys) he caried my brother with him & left me a prentice at the coach making business— I am now the only one of the name and family now in Virginia I have been married thirteen years and have had no children and I feel as tho I had found some lost treasure in hearing that you were of the old stock full of that warm feeling towards friends and relations that ever characterized my old father and familly - and if you should pass thro the city of Richmond I beg the favour of you to let me see you as

_____

[176]Willie P. Mangum's ancestors came into North Carolina from Sussex County, Virginia. See Stephen B. Weeks, "W. P. M.," *Biog. Hist. of N. C.*, V, 237-238.

my heart would rejoice to see once more some relation of my father's. I am A humble Coachmaker and make A very comfortable living clear of debt and many warm friend and I know of no enemy— I shall expect you to let me know when you pass thro Richmond that I may see you - and may the blesings of heaven be with you and familly is the fervant wish of your intruding relation—

MICAJAH MANGUM.

[Addressed:] To

The Hon. Willie P. Mangum
Washington City
D. C

By the politeness of Captn.
Wm. Claibourn.

WPM-LC

William Kinney[177] to Willie P. Mangum.

STAUNTON Monday Morng.
29th Apr 1844.

My dear Sir.

Presuming that my friends Archer and Morehead are, or will be in Balto: when this would arrive at Washington, I venture to address it to you, knowing it will give you pleasure.

As Genl. Ritchie[178] would say, the sky in Virginia, is bright and brightning.—

So far as we have heard from *our Gain is*   our loss.

2 in Buckingham, and the Senator		1 King & Queen.
2 Norfolk County		1 Southampton
1 Caroline		1 Tyler
1 Matthews of Middlesex	12	
1 Wythe	accomac	1
1 Montgomery	Mecklenburg	1
1 Floyd	Rappahanock	1
1 Pendleton	Randolph	1
1 Franklin	Brook	1
	Wood & Ritchie	1
1 Giles of Mercer, tho' returns not complete		

---

[177]An attorney who by 1860 had retired. Livingston *Law Register*, 1851, 580; 1860, 920.
[178]Thomas Ritchie, editor of the *Richmond Enquirer*.

which makes a difference of 22 on joint ballot, last year the Loco's had 24 on joint ballot, we want but 1 more (and I have every reason to believe we shall get from 4 to 8 more) to produce a tie, our gain in the popular vote has been great in every county heard from—The Whig in Bath came within *one* vote, and it is said he will contest the election - in Alleghany the Loco was only 10 votes ahead and one precint to hear from

Goggin[179] is certainly elected to Congress over Gordon by from 150 to 200 majority

The prospect for redeeming the old Dominion is good, very good - nothing can defeat us but the Texas question, that I fear will be a fire brand among the Whigs.

With all respect and esteem
In haste Truly yours
WM. KINNEY.

[Addressed:]

Honl.
Willie P. Mangum
U. S. Senate
Washington City.

WPM-LC

S. P. Walker[180] to Willie P. Mangum.

Tuesday Night. Apl. 30.[181] [1844]

Dear Sir

I drop you a line, the crowd, the spirit, the enthusiasm of 40 is nothing in comparison with the present. thousands are pouring in hourly: and at this moment while Graves of Ky[182] is addressing some 10000 persons in front of Barnum's a delegation from New York City 2000 strong with banner & music are entering the square. The whole 27 congress appear to be present.

---

[179]William L. Goggin, Whig Congressman in 1839-1843, 1844-1845, and 1847-1849, and William F. Gordon, a Democratic Congressman in 1830-1835. *Biog. Dir. of Cong.;* 1018, 1024.

[180] See above, I, 428n.

[181]This letter should be dated 1844 because the contents show that it was written on the eve of the National Whig Convention which met in Baltimore on May 1, 1844. April 30 fell on a Tuesday in 1844.

[182]William Jordon Graves, of Kentucky, 1805-1848, was in Congress in 1835-1841. *Biog. Dir. of Cong.,* 1029.

The *East, Ohio & Inda.* stand firm for Davis.[183] Fillmore
gains, and so does Frelinghuysen. McKennan[184] is brought out
today, but nothing is known, more than you can conjecture
about the matter of the V. P. at Washington.

Mr. Clay is expected to come. I hope you can all get here.
They say here, that Carter is elected.

With respect & Esteem
S. P. WALKER

[Addressed:]

Hon. Willie P. Mangum
or Hon. John T. Morehead
Washington
D. C.

WPM-LC

P. U. Murphey[185] to Willie P. Mangum.

U. S. Ship Ontario
NORFOLK May 2d 44

Dear Sir

I send you by the boat a box of fine terrapins, knowing that
you will enjoy them. I was in hope, that I should of been able to
of visited Washington before this! but my duties have prevented
it, as I have not had a leave from the Dept for nearly seven
years. I shall try and get off for a few days about the middle
of this month, if I can get through with, the surveys I am now
on.

---

[183] John Davis, of Massachusetts.

[184] Thomas M. T. McKennon, 1794-1852, of Pennsylvania, had been in Congress as a Whig in
1831-1839 and 1842-1843. He was a presidential elector in 1840. Under Fillmore he served as
Secretary of the Interior. *Biog. Dir. of Cong.,* 1267.

[185] Peter Umstead Murphey, 1810-1876, the son of Archibald D. Murphey, attended Bingham
School and the University of North Carolina before he became a midshipman in the United States
Navy in 1831. He served until 1861, when he resigned to join the Confederate Navy. In the Civil
War he served the Confederacy at Norfolk, in the North Carolina waters, and commanded the *Selma*
at Mobile Bay. After the war he lived in Mobile. Hoyt (ed.), *Papers of Murphey,* I, 389n.

I should of sent you more oysters had the boat continued running a little longer, as they had just commenced geting *good* at the time she stoped her regular trips.

Yours truly
P. U. MURPHEY
U. S. N

Honble Judge Mangum
    Washington
        D. C.

N.B. Kindest regards to all of my friends

[Addressed:] The Honble. Willie P. Mangum
    Washington
       City
       D. C.

WPM-LC

Isaac N. Jones to Willie P. Mangum.

WASHINGTON ARKS,
5th May, '44

Hon
    W. P. Mangum.
       U. S. Senate.

       Dear Sir.

          Permit me to acknowledge your kindness in having sent me the speeches of Messrs. Evans & Bates, of which I recd 3 or 4 copies each. They are eagerly sought after by the sober thinking democrats of our vicinity. I have less & less doubt of the vote of this State going for Mr. Clay.

          Mr. E's speech is *gigantic*, especially when contrasted with the *effort* of Mr. McDuffie.[186] That of Mr. Bates is not less convincive, except from the fact that the *grounds* taken to debate upon (or rather) the heads of his remarks are fewer. His speech so far as it goes is admirable.

---

[186]For the speeches of George Evans, Isaac Bates, and George McDuffie on January 19, 29, February 21, and May 30, 31, 1844, see *Cong. Globe,* 28 Cong., 1 sess., 159-160; Appendix, 104-109, 141-144, 294-298, 353-363, 745-753.

If I dare presume so far, I would ask you to present my un-
feighed thanks to Mr. Evans; & say to him that his doctrines;
so ably advocated as they have been by himself; need only to
be known as he knows them, to be the sentiments of the majority of the South, and also that he will much oblige me by
sending to me as many of the copies of it, as he may find it
convenient to put into the mail bags. And as one good turn deserves another will you be kind enough to remember my address & send me such matter as will help the cause of the
country & H.C.

As the Post offices have not my most entire confidence as
the means of conveyance of Whig documents; I will thank you
to say to me what you send that I may know whether all is recd.
R. River has been unusually high especially below the Mouth of
Little R. Crops much damaged. We are planting our cotton
again & may make 2/3 of a crop if the season is good. The
worms too have done much damage.

Excuse my tedious epistle and believe me to be

Yr obt. St. & Frnd
ISAAC N. JONES

[Addressed:]

Hon Willey P. Mangum
U. S. Senate
Mail.   Washington City.

WPM-LC

J. H. Haughton[187] to Willie P. Mangum.

PITTSBORO' 23 May 1844

My Dear Sir,

As I am soon to open the canvass for a seat in the Legislature, I find myself in need of some Dockuments, & knowing
your great zeal & efficiency in the cause of Clay & the Country,
I take the liberty of requesting you to send me such papers &
dockuments as you may deem important particularly on the

---

[187]John Hooker Haughton, a native of Chatham County, after graduating from the University of
North Carolina, became a lawyer at Pittsboro. He served in the legislature in 1844-1845, 1850-1851,
and 1854-1855. *N. C. Manual*, 551-552; Grant, *Alumni Hist. of U. N. C.*, 265.

following subjects to wit: An official statement of the appropriations by the last & the present Congress & every thing connected with the subject of expenditures during the last & present administration.

The speeches of Messrs Evans, & Simmons & Berrien on the Tariff if they can be had in pamphlet form or any others that you may think best on this important subject—

Gov. Morehead of Ky speech on the Bank question & also the report of the Jackson Committees in 1825 & 1832 I think, setting forth the great advantages that have resulted to the Country from the U. S. Bank.

Please present my respects to Messrs Clingman, Barringer & Rayner & say to them that I would thank them to cooperate with you in sending me such dockuments & speeches as they may think proper—

We consider here the coming campaign as of peculiar importance in this Country, because by increasing our majority handsomely Chatham may hold the balance of power in this Congressional District.

Whatever I can do towards the consummation of such an object shall be done.

Mr Graham addressed our people last week (on Tuesday of Court) in a very able & masterly manner & with fine effect.

From the signs of the times I should not be surprised if he were to beat Hoke 15,000 or 20,000 votes.

Please excuse my troubling you, in asmuch as I have no *representative* in Congress—

The nomination of Mr. Frelingheysen is received by the Whigs in this & all other parts of the State as far as I have heard from with general & entire approbation.

> With great respect,
> Your obt. servt. & friend
> J. H. HAUGHTON.

Hon: W P Mangum.

[Addressed:]

Hon. Wille P Mangum
U. S. Senate
Washington City
D. C.

WPM-LC

Willie P. Mangum to Charity A. Mangum.

WASHINGTON CITY 27th May 1844.

My dear Love.

I have time only to write you a line. - This is the day of the Van Buren & Tyler Conventions.

By the miraculous Telegraph, information of what they are doing at Baltimore, 40 miles off, is communicated in less than ten seconds.—

I am well.— We shall adjourn on the 17th of June. I hope to be at home by the 22nd or 23rd of June.— The time of adjournment is not fixed, but it will be, on friday next.

I think we shall have a called session, but by postponing ten days longer, we should not.— Yet that day will be fixed, as I think, many desire a called session.

My Love to the children, & a kiss to William, & believe me My Love, as I alway am

Your affectionate husband
WILLIE P. MANGUM

To Mrs. C. A. Mangum.

WPM-LC

Willie P. Mangum to Priestley H. Mangum.[188]

WASHINGTON CITY 29th May 1844

My dear Sir.

I have time only to inform you that James K. Polk of Tenn. has received the unanimous nomination for the Presidency by the Demo. Convention now sitting at Baltimore. The Magnetic Telegraph brings the information here every instant.— It is *a literal disbanding of the party* for this Campaign.— The sole object is to keep the party *in harness* for '48.— I think it probable Silas Wright of New York will be the nominee for Vice President.— He, Woodbury, & Gov. Morton of Mass. are now pushed. We know not the result.— No matter who may be

------
[188]A part of this letter has been previously published in Charles Warren, *The Supreme Court in the United States,* (1926), II, 135.

nominated, We will literally crush the ticket. They feel it. They know it.—

The Texas treaty will get 16, 17 or 18 Votes at the most.[189] The party *Count much* on Texas & its excitements.— They will be mistaken I think.— We shall adjourn the 17th June too early by ten days.— For unless we vote upon the joint resolutions, which we shall hardly do, we shall be called back again if Tyler shall have vitality enough to *hope*.— The *least* can inspire him & his Palinurus John Jones[190] to hope strongly.—

I have never Witnessed stronger excitement than here, for two days.—

The Telegraph is in rooms on the North end of the Capitol, under my room.— Every new turn at Baltimore, comes here in less than the twentieth part of a second - absolutely a Miraculous triumph of Science.—

Yesterday evening from 4 to 7 oclock, more than a thousand people were in attendance at the Window, at which placerds in large letters, were exhibited, upon the receipt of each item of news.— To day from 7 to 900 were attending, when the news came that Polk was unanimously nominated.— I was out of my seat, at a window above, observing, & ready to enquire.— Someone cried out "three Cheers for Clay." The air resounded with the outpourings of 500 pair of strong lungs—in three hearty cheers— A call was made for three cheers for Polk - & the feeblest wail of some twenty or thirty voices were heard, in modest, subdued & conquered strains - & they were in *literal truth* a majority of them - boys who had with equal zeal joined for Clay.—

Poor Tyler is dead - He feels so.— They have stolen *his theme*.— It reminds me of a drunken story of the noted John Holmes of Maine, who with inimitable burlesque once told in the Senate, of a fight between two beggar boys, at the head of the avenue, whose strife grew out of one having stolen the *pathetic tale* of the other, to get coppers.—

I was the first to tell Benton of the late Atto: Gen: Butler[191] having withdrawn V. Buren & enquired if he had expected such a result. He answered no he had not supposed they were

---

[189]On June 8 the Senate voted 16 to 35 against the treaty. *Niles' Register*, LXVI, 241.

[190]He probably refers to John W. Jones, Congressman from Virginia, who at this time was serving as Speaker of the House of Representatives.

[191]In the Democratic Convention at Baltimore after Van Buren failed to obtain the two-thirds majority and it became evident that he could not win, Benjamin F. Butler, Van Buren's manager from New York, withdrew his candidate's name. This brought harmony to the convention and the nomination of Polk. Wiltse, *Calhoun: Sectionalist*, 180; *Niles' Register*, LVI, 218.

so d - d fools as to have done so. With great excitement, he said, they had nothing to do, but to die for their principles & he repeated, with encreased & encreasing excitement. They are, as the printers say, all in pi.— I hope Graham goes on well— Haughton of Chatham writes me that he made a masterly speech at Pittsboro & with fine effect, & expressed the opinion that he wd. have a majority of at least 15,000 Votes.—

He must go to every County in the Mountain region.—

I regretted to hear that Willie had the meazles— I hope you are all well—

Affectionately Yrs.
WILLIE P. MANGUM

To P. H. Mangum esqr.

—————

WPM-LC

William S. Ransom[192] to Willie P. Mangum.

WARRENTON June 1st. 1844

Dear Sir

I understand that each State is entitled to two Cadets at West Point besides one from each District and that this is about the time their appointment is made and that the Senators are advised with in making the selection. If I have been correctly informed I must beg you to interfere in behalf of Robert Ransom Jr.[193] and endeavour to get Mr. Haywood to co-operate with you—he is well acquainted with my brother and his circumstances—has always been friendly, though never intimate, with my family and I have no reason to believe he would not aid in placing a promising young man in a situation to become useful and honorable to himself - his family and Country— Mr. Geo. Hawkins's time will expire this month and my brother and self more than a year ago sought through Mr. Daniel[194] and others to procure a Warrant from the War Department for Robert and were not much disappointed when D. recommended the son of a wealthy Loco, for both of us had openly opposed his election. Robert is now sixteen years old and as perfect in person as any one of his age I ever saw— He is prepared to join the Sophimore Class at Chapel Hill, but his father is unable

—————

[192]See above, II, 394, 501; III, 241-244.
[193]The future Confederate general.
[194]John R. J. Daniel.

to send him there. His brother is there through the liberality of his Society and receives the first distinction separate— Robert is equally as smart & I doubt not would be distinguished at any institution of the sort for good scholarship - application & gentlemanly demeanor.— If you should from this statement of facts find it convenient to your feelings to interest yourself in this matter you will greatly oblige Robert—brother and myself— If it will not be imposing too much labor and trouble you will confer a favor by giving us some early information on this subject.

You of course take great interest in our little political operations here and doubtless are desirous that that the Whig majority in N. C. should be larger than ever, therefore it is that I will inform you that in ten days Delegates from the Counties of this District meet in Louisburg to appoint an Elector— I shall go as one from this County and will be at a loss who to select— Manly - Moore & Joyner[195] are all candidates in their respective counties, and no other political aspiration - no professional engagement should be an obstacle to our Elector— His time should be devoted to the acquisition of such knowledge as will be necessary to use not only in advocating our principles but in refuting such falsehoods as Kendall will be sure to scatter through the land— His principles must not only be orthodox but he must have ability to expound and zeal to enforce them—The loss of time nor of money should be of no consideration— Hence I have thought our Country-man Geo: E. Spruill[196] not an unsuitable man. What think you of him? I trust we shall all be of one opinion when we meet. If the Whigs here will only hold together a little while longer we can carry the District. Even in this County we are gaining slowly— Nash or any such man can defeat Daniel next year, but I fear his party will never run him again.

With sentiments of unaltered friendship I remain

Most Respectfully yrs &c
Wm S Ransom

[Addressed:] To

The Hon: Willie P Mangum
Washington City

---

[195]He possibly refers to Charles Manly, Bartholomew F. Moore, and Andrew J. Joyner. No one of these was selected.
[196]See above, I, 217.

WPM-LC

J. R. Lambdin to Willie P. Mangum.

PHILA June 6th 1844

Dear Sir

I have this day drawn on you in favr. of A. B. Enystron - [not legible] at 5 days sight for Sixty five dollars, the amount of balance due on a/c of the Portrait: -[197] and hope that it may suit your convenience to meet the draft at maturity. I have written to Mr. Cranch (artist)[198] requesting that he will varnish the portrait before it is sent to North Carolina; and enclose the letter with the request that you may give it the proper direction on its arrival in Washington.—

Our Whig friends are in high spirits. - I have just heard from the western part of the State and they are there verry confident of carrying this State by 20,000 majority.—

With sincere regard

I am truly yours
J R LAMBDIN

To

Honble W P Mangum
Washington
D. C.

[Addressed:]

Honble W P Mangum
Washington
D. C.

---

[197]This portrait is reproduced on the frontispiece of Volume II of this publication.

[198]He probably refers to Christopher P. Cranch, 1813-1892, son of the jurist William Cranch. Young Cranch attended Columbian College in Washington, entered the ministry, and became a successful Unitarian minister in Boston. Then he turned to art and lived in Washington until his marriage in 1843 when he moved to New York. On three separate occasions he studied in Europe. Although not a great artist, he became a person who mingled with the intellectuals at Harvard and who was constantly preaching the "gospel of beauty." *D. A. B.*, IV, 501-502.

WPM-LC

Willis Hall[199] to Willie P. Mangum[200]

ALBANY June 7th 1844.

My Dear Mangum

As chairman of the executive committee of the Clay Club of this county I earnestly request your attendance at a meeting of that club to be held a week from next Thursday— You have numerous friends and admirers here to whom you are personally unknown, and who will be delighted with an opportunity of meeting you face to face—

I take for granted that Congress will adjourn on Monday the 17th inst. which will give you an opportunity of reaching here by a regular conveyance by Thursday afternoon This meeting is intended to be the first of a series of meetings, which it is hoped will be continued weekly until the election- This is a very central point- a thorough fare where our rail road and canal terminates, and steam boats leave for New York two or three times a day and loco motives for Boston as often.- Many strangers are here constantly- A good fire kindled and kept up here will at least warm our own State- You will pardon me that I am thus importunate, with you not to refuse- when you consider the importance to us of having a full attendance at our first meeting-

We shall certainly have a very hard fight in this State- But if our friends from abroad will lend us their helping hand we shall certainly beat them-

> I have the honor to be
> with the highest respect and regard
> Your friend & servant
> WILLIS HALL

Hon. W. P. Mangum)
)
President of the Senate)

P. S. Should you find Thursday inconveniently early the meeting may be called for any later day that will suit your convenience-

---

[199]See above, III, 282n.

[200]In the campaign of 1844, Mangum received many invitations to Whig rallies. These invitations are in the Mangum Papers, but to conserve space I am omitting most of them. I am making reference in the front of this volume to those omitted. I am, however, including enough to show the geographical distribution of the invitations.

WPM-LC

Circular letter of Augustus Reese
and others to Willie P. Mangum.

MADISON, [GA.,] 7th June, 1844.

Dear Sir:

The Whigs of Georgia contemplate holding a STATE MASS CONVENTION at this place on *Wednesday, the 31st day of July next,* and have delegated to the undersigned Committee the pleasing duty of inviting some of the distinguished Whigs of the Union to meet and hold counsel with us upon that occasion. In the performance of this pleasing duty, the undersigned most respectfully solicit you to accept the invitation hereby extended in behalf of the Whigs of Georgia, to be with them in their Convention.

The restoration of our Government to the healthy and beneficient action in which it left the hands of its founders, is an object devoutly to be desired by every Patriot; and, as Georgia was one of the first States of the Union that checked the mischievous spirit which was defeating the hopes inspired by our triumph of 1840, she appeals to you, Sir, to aid her, by your presence and your counsel, to sustain her position in the coming contest.

We have the honor to be,

> Very Respectfully,
> Your Obedient Servants,

> AUGUSTUS REESE,)
> ELIJAH E. JONES,)
> CHARLES WHITING,) Committee
> ERNEST L. WITTICH,) of
> C. R. HAULEITER,) Invitation

Hon. W. P. Mangum,
 Raleigh,
  N. C.

[Addressed:] Hon. Wiley P. Mangum
   Red Mountain, North--Carolina.

Henry Clay to Willie P. Mangum.[201]

ASHLAND, June 7, 1844

My Dear Sir,

I take the liberty of troubling you herewith, with a package containing my speech, delivered at Raleigh in April last. You will oblige me very much if you will have it put under another cover if necessary, give it your frank, and transmit it to its address without delay.

Are our Democratic friends serious in the nominations which they have made at Baltimore of candidates for President, and Vice President?[202] I have supposed that their object was to get rid of the Convention, and ultimately to get rid of Mr. Polk, and bring out Mr. Van Buren, or retaining Mr. Polk as the candidate for the South West, to bring Mr. Van Buren out in some form, as the candidate for the North. In that way they might calculate to be able to throw upon Mr. Polk all the Democratic votes for Texas, and upon Mr. Van Buren all the Democratic votes against Texas. But nous verrons. It is of very little consequence to us what their real designs may be; for no matter how many candidates or who they bring out, we must beat them with ease if we do one half of our duty.

Your friend truly and faithfully,
(Signed) H. CLAY

The Honble W. P. Mangum

WPM-LC

*Printed Circular from Vandalia Committee
to Willie P. Mangum.*

VANDALIA, ILLINOIS, June 8th. 1844.

Hon Sir

The Whigs of Illinois, having resolved to assemble *en masse* at this place, on the 17th proximo, we have the honor to solicit a visit from you, on that occasion. Your well known and pa-

---

[201]The original is in the possession of Miss Anne L. Turner and Mrs. John A. Livingston, Raleigh, N. C.

[202]At the time of Polk's nomination, many Whigs, including Clay and Mangum, underestimated Polk's popular appeal. Crittenden, however, appreciating the appeal of the Democratic platform, wrote Clay on June 17, " 'we have a *great* battle to fight.' " Van Deusen, *Life of Clay,* 367.

triotic devotion to those cardinal principles, on which the future prosperity of our country, and the permanency of our institutions depend, causes us to believe that your presence would cheer up the so "oft defeated but never conquered" Whigs of Illinois, and add even greater intensity to the enthusiasm which now fires the bosom of every true friend of [the] Union and of the *Great Statesman of the West* - Henry Clay.

We have the honor to be,
Yours &c.

Q. C. ALEXANDER,
F. REMANN,
LEMUEL LEE,
WM. M. BLACK,
C. H. HODGE,
Committee of Invitation.

Hon. W. P. Mangum

[Addressed:]

Hon. W. P Mangum M. C.
Washington
D. C.

WPM-LC

William Stevens to Willie P. Mangum.

BURNET, VT.
[June 10, 1844]

Dear Sir   In perusing different publications respecting the annexation of texas I have concluded to present for investigation my views in some respects according to the information collected. Mexico it appears are the rightful owners of the territory of Texas except that part which has heretofore been disposed of by them, and much of it no doubt [under] orthority to obtain settlers to form a colony. the latter becoming disaffected revolted and declared themselves independent and have thus far sustained it, but until reconciliation between the former and the latter should be concluded and ratified by the former under an agreement in writing and ceded to the latter they have no just claim to the remainder of the territory, as all title comes from a well organized and a regular instituted Government, and it appears that the Texas territory has heretofore been ceded by such a Government, or Governments. Therefore the present system by Tyler cannot be recommended for reasons, first, it sets the example of force which is not of a moral principle, Second, it leaves an open space for revolt and establishes the principles of Aristocracy, Furthermore the Acknowledgement of Texas independence by the United States Government or any other power gives them no title. Accept by Mexico whome & reasonable compensation should be granted if required and paid by the Texas Government or the United States as the agreement may be at or after annexation. Such a system in my view would do honor to this Republic and set an example to posterity on whose heads may the honor and glory ever rest who follows its precepts. My request is after the above has been investigated by the Senate, the same may be done by the house of Representatives, and then to be left with the Secretary of State to remain in that department.

                              Yours respectfully
                              WILLIAM STEVENS

[Addressed:] To the President of the Senate
                    In Congress
                    Washington City
                    District of Columbia.

                                                    WPM-LC

        James W. Pegram & others to Willie P. Mangum.

                                    RICHMOND June 12 1844
Dear Sir
        In behalf of the Central Clay Club of this City we are charged with the agreeable duty of asking the favor of you to visit this city and to address our club, after the adjournment of Congress.
        In view of the interesting character of the political contest now at hand, we trust you will not allow any small amount of

personal inconvenience to deprive the Whigs of this portion of Virginia of the benefit of your valuable co-operation, to the extent now solicited.

Hoping you will permit us to report to our associates your acceptance of our invitation, and the day on which we may expect your arrival, we assure you of the high respect with which we are

Your obt. Servants,

JAMES W. PEGRAM)
TH: NELSON) Committee &c. &c.
A. MOSELEY)

Hon. W. P. Mangum.

[Addressed:]

> Honble. W. P. Mangum
> Senate U. S.
> Washington City.

WPM-D

W. S. Archer to Willie P. Mangum.

[Possibly June 1844]

Dear Mangum

I am going to write to Gen. Pegram tonight, that I will arrive in Richmond to dine with him on tuesday before which day I cannot leave here.—

Shall I say, that I may bring you with me? He will have Leigh and others of the best to meet us.

Truly
W. S. ARCHER.

Hon. Mr. Mangum.

[Addressed:]

> Hon. Mr. Mangum
> Ind. Avenue.

WPM-LC

R. B. Gilliam to Willie P. Mangum.

LOUISBURG, N. C. June 13. 1844

Hon W. P. Mangum,

Dear Sir,

Our friends have most unexpectedly nominated me as presidential elector for this district. As reluctant as I am, on several accounts, to engage again in active politicks, yet having accepted the nomination I feel it to be my duty to prepare myself for the Campaign. If it will not impose too much trouble upon you, I will thank you to forward me a *copious assortment* of such Documents as throw most light upon all the subjects of difference between the two parties— The Speeches of Mr Phelps and of others on the Tariff—of Mr Benton, Mr Choate, and Mr Rives[203] on the Texas treaty - and such others as you may recommend on other subjects, would be desirable.

Congressional documents in relation to these subjects, for the sake of reference might be of service.

Any expense incurred will be promptly met by me upon your return, which I presume will be in a few days.

Should I be in Oxford on your return it would give me very sincere pleasure to see you at my house.

Mr Hoke has passed through this place, but has left no impression.

I am with high respect
R. B. GILLIAM

Louisburg N C
June 14 1844. Free

[Addressed:]

Hon. W. P. Mangum
Washington City.

---

[203]He refers to the speeches of Samuel S. Phelps, of Vermont, T. H. Benton, of Missouri, Rufus Choate, of Massachusetts, and W. C. Rives, of Virginia.

WPM-LC

B. B. Blume²⁰⁴ to Willie P. Mangum.

MEMPHIS TENN. June 15th. 1844.

Honl. W. P. Mangum

Dear Sir.

I arrived here safely & in due time— I found the Bar greatly crowded - but think the number but a slight obstacle to final success— Many inexperienced professional men "wend their way to the western wilds" expecting a profession alone to place them in prosperity— Hence there are but few men of business - fewer perhaps than in the Courts in the "Old States"— Much of the population, in this section of the State, are among the finest specimens of the "American Planter"—The state of agriculture is improving fast, & I have recently met with many gentlemen who say that they are "settled for life"—

Could you furnish me with any thing calculated to do good to the Whig cause, it might be well to send it to me— There is no waveing in the ranks - & the State is certain— But this is a great thorougfare & much good can be done here, which will tell in other States— Politics do not belong to my trade - but as I have leisure, I think it due to my country, to be doing a part of the work before the people— The great importance of this contest should awaken every friend to law & to the honor of his country, to the use of all his powers— I write this, because the servant neglected, as I think, to place my former letter in the office— Your obliged friend

B. B. BLUME.

[Addressed:]

Honl. W. P. Mangum
Prest. U. S. Senate
Red Mountain
N. Ca.

²⁰⁴See above, I, 350n.

WPM-LC

S. A. Wales[205] to Willie P. Mangum.

EATONTON GEORGIA
29th June 1844

Hon Willie P. Mangum

Dear Sir

Will you permit a Stranger to occupy your attention for a moment.

I am very anxious to hear from No. Carolina - as to the probable vote of the State for President—

Will you do me the kindness to give me your opinion in regard to it.

In this State we have just had a Convention to nominate Electors— Delegates were in attendance from all parts of the State. The prevailing opinion at the Convention was, that the vote of Georgia would be given to Mr Clay, by a majority of from 3 to 5000. The only difficulty we have, is the Texas question—

Your reply if you favor me with one shall not be published

Very Resply Yr Obt Servt
S. A. WALES

[Addressed:]

Honl. Willie P. Mangum
Red Mountain P. O.
Orange Co
No. Carolina.

WPM-LC

George S. Yerby[206] to Willie P. Mangum.

EASTVILLE NORTHAMPTON COUNTY
VIRGINIA June 29th 1844.

Dear Sir

Although I am a stranger to you I know you very well politically- I have long known you as a distinguished leader of

---

[205]Samuel A. Wales was the chairman of a general committee of Putnam County, in which Eatonton is located. He endorsed Calhoun's position on slavery. He was also chairman of his county's Whig Committee. *Niles' Register,* LXXII, 389; Boucher and Brooks (ed.), "Correspondence of Calhoun," *A. H. A. Report* of 1929, I, 382-383.
[206]Unable to identify.

the Whig party & a zealous & able advocate of Whig principles & warm personal & political friend of Mr. Clay's. Therefore it is that I presume to write to you upon political Matters & I feel very sure that you will pardon me for so doing. When I inform you as I now do that I too am a Whig of many years growth & that my object is simply to gain information respecting the prospects of the Whig party & our distinguished candidate Henry Clay, in different parts of the union, but specially in the Old North State. For give me leave to tell you that the Locos rely with seeming confidence on old Rip Van's Electorial Vote for Polk & Dallas - but I fear every confidence that at this time— He is wide awake & will go for old Harry Clay. As Chairman of the committee of correspondence of our Clay Club I am very desireous to gain all the information I can from Various parts of the Union & I am quite sure that you can form as correct an opinion as to the probable result of the pending contest as any other Gentleman of the Whig party

Was any answer ever more unexpected or wonderful than the nomination of Polk & Dallas & to none I am sure, more so than to the Nominees. One is constrained to enquire- What Services has Mr. Polk at any time rendered the country to entitle him to the highest honours in the gift of a free people? Of what peculiar Qualifications & fitness for so responsible and so important a Station can He boast? None that ever I have heard of. I have never estimated the man any thing over & beyond a good County Court Lawyer and a pretty fair Stump Speaker- Be this just or otherwise- He cannot lay Claim to any thing like Statesmanship-

I have also regard him as the tool & sycophant of Andrew Jackson & Martin Van Buren and ready at all times to do their bidding and I believe that he has justifyed every measure- every corrupt act & every outrage - that so peculiarly distinguished & characterised Jackson & Van Burens administrations & their party in & out of Congress. What possible chance can such a man stand of being elected President of the U S - Whose qualifications & Claims are so small if not contemptable?

Do you think it probable (I had like to have said possible) that Ja⁵ K Polk Esqr.- Who is Anti Tariff- Anti distribution- Anti one term for the Presidency &.c. &c. Who is for Annexation- right or wrong- just or faithless to Mexico- Union or Dissolution of the States- War or no War- Who in fact seems to be Anti every thing that will preserve the Honour of the Nation & promote the interest of the people, will defeat the election of such-a man- such a Statesman & Patriot as Henry Clay-A man who from his youth up has kept the Republican faith & whose career has been Brilliant & Noble beyond any example in Modern times— A man who has served his country- Long-served it well & served it faithfully- Who has twice saved the Union (which union I regret to see the Calhounites endeavouring now destr[ucti]on) & if elected President will endeavour I doubt, not to established permanently, sound Republican & American principles & Measures. I think it is not probable from the very bottom of my Heart I say *God forbid that he should.* Although I fear he is a more formidable opponent than Mr. Van Buren-Cass or Johnson would have been.

But to return to the object I had in writing this Letter which is to ascertain your opinion & connection as to the final result of this contest, & I will not trouble you farther with my own speculation & feelings.

Will Polk & Dallas carry in November Next NORTH CAROLINA? For the sake of the country-answer No. & answer correctly. Will they carry either- Georgia- Tennessee- Maryland- Indiana- Ohio- New York or Pennsylvania. To cut the matter short-What states will Polk & Dallas carry- What states will Clay & Frelinghauysen carry & which states are doubtful? I greatly fear we shall loose Virgina- in consequence of the Texas Question- which is seized upon to Humbug the people- But our Leading Whigs- Do not think so.

What effect will the Texas Question have upon the Presidential election- in the South- North & West? But I have punished you quite enough. In conclusion- Let me entreat you to exert all Your Great Powers & influence to secure Mr. Clay's Election. I am my Dear Sir

Yr. Obt. Servt.

George S. Yerby

[Addressed:]

Hon.[1] W. P. Mangum
United States Senator
Red Mountain
North Carolina

WPM-LC

QUESTIONS ASKED OF THE CANDIDATES
AT ANDERSON COURT HOUSE, ON SALE DAY IN JUNE.[207]

[July, 1844]

RESOLVED, THAT IN THE OPINION OF THIS MEETING THE QUESTION OF THE ANNEXATION OF TEXAS, IS ONE of paramount importance at this time; we hereby call on the several candidates for Congress and the Legislature in this district to make known through the public prints, whether they are for or against immediate annexation, and whether they will support for the presidency, HENRY CLAY, MARTIN VAN BUREN, or any other man, opposed to the immediate annexation of Texas.

(We have not the resolutions passed at Pickens at hand, but they are of the same purport.)

QUESTIONS ASKED OF THE CANDIDATES FOR THE LEGISLATURE, through the Anderson Gazzette, by "Many Voters."

Mr. Editor - To those candidates for the Legislature who have responded to certain inquiries heretofore addressed to them by a portion of their fellow citizens, and to others who may be disposed to answer, we beg leave to propound a few additional interrogatories, touching Federal and State policy.

1st. Do you or not, concur in the resolution adopted at a public meeting of the citizens of Beaufort District, in this State, & openly approved of in other quarters declaring that they will "dissolve this Union sooner than abandon Texas?"[208]

2nd. Do you or not, approve of the proposition made at public meetings in several of the middle Districts of this State, to hold a State Convention in Columbia for the purpose of effecting an organized resistance to the laws of the United States or the proposition to hold a Southern Convention at Nashville, Tennessee, to devise means for the immediate annexation of Texas to the Union; or to dissolve the Union and annex it to the Southern States?

---

[207]This is a printed circular of the questions asked at Anderson, South Carolina.
[208]In South Carolina talk of secession grew after the tariff was raised in 1842. Cotton prices went down to 6.2 cents. An effort to lower the tariff in 1843-1844 failed. In June the Texas treaty was defeated. All of these events caused grave concern. Rhett, Hammond and Holmes began playing on the prejudices of their people. They called for a Southern Convention. George McDuffie, in a speech in Richmond, denied that his state had any intention to secede but opposed the tariff in such strong terms that many considered it a call for nullification. Calhoun was alarmed for fear that the hotheads would defeat Polk and annexation. He, therefore, got Polk's promise to lower the tariff and began undermining Rhett and his Bluffton movement. These questions and answers are a part of this secession fight in the summer of 1844. Wiltse, *Calhoun: Sectionalist,* 187-190.

3rd. Do you or not, concur with Mr. McDuffie in believing the State of South Carolina possesses the power, and should exercise it, of laying a Tariff on all domestic manufactured goods, imported into this State from our sister states?

4th. Do you or not, approve of the course of the Democratic majority in Congress in admitting members to seats who were elected by general ticket, contrary to a law of the United States, remaining on the Statute Book, requiring them to be elected by Districts?

5th. Are you or not, in favor of so altering the law so as to give the election of Presidential electors to the people?

6th. Are you or not, in favor of increasing the jurisdiction of the Ordinary in matters of real estate. If yea, to what extent?

7th. Are you or not, in favor of dividing the election District of Pendleton, in whole if possible, and if not, as to *Representatives* only?

8th Do you or not, approve of the amendment to the constitution passed by the last legislature and to be confirmed by the ensuing one limiting the term of the Judges to sixty-five years of age?

9th. Are you or not, in favor of curtailing expenditures, by abolishing the offices of Superintendant of public works, and Adjutant-General?

Believing it to be the duty of every aspirant to political preferment to answer any question, touching public matters if asked byt single individual, a full and explicit answer to the above interrogatories is expected and requested from each candidate for the legislature by

MANY VOTERS.

TO THE VOTERS OF PENDLETON DISTRICT.

Fellow-Citizens: - The Undersigned candidates for your suffrages at the approaching election for the Legislature, having compared notes, and finding that they fully concur in opinion in order that their views may be more generally known, take this method of responding to certain inquiries addressed to them by meetings held at Anderson and Pickens, on sale day in June, and certain others asked by "Many Voters," through the columns of the "Anderson Gazette," of the 28th ult.; copies of each of which are appended above.

We answer, 1st. That we are in favor of the annexation of Texas to the American Union, as a matter of great national importance, as soon as it can possibly be done consistently with the honor and interest of the country.

2d. Regarding all the candidates for the Presidency as in favor of annexation, and only differing as to the proper time and mode, we do not hestitate to say, that we will vote for no man for the Presidency who is opposed to the annexation of Texas to the Union; but it is due that we should say in this connection, that we will under no circumstances, vote for James K. Polk, having no confidence in him, and regarding him as wholly unworthy of the trust in every point of view. His name has hitherto remained unknown to fame - he has made no sacrifice - performed no service for his country, to entitle him to so distinguished a position. Most of the little character he acquired during his short career in Congress, was by his advocacy of measures deadly hostile to South Carolina, and destructive to the dearest interests of the Southern States. He has originated no great measures for the benefit of his country, nor has he evinced his adherence to any other political principles than his party leaders, for the time being, have seen fit to dictate to him. He is destitute of the commanding talent - the stern political integrity - the high moral firmness, and the broad and enlightened patriotism that it is absolutely essential the Chief Magistrate of the Union should possess at this crisis; and having been twice rejected for the office of Governor in his own State - having no hold upon the confidence or affections of his countrymen at home, and no talent to command respect for us abroad he is not the man for the times or for the Union, and we at least, are unwilling [to entrust] him with the chief command of our Army and Navy.

If the Presidential election were to turn on the annexation of Texas, as an abstract proposition, losing sight of everything else, then should we be in favor of the election of John Tyler as the author of the present effort at annexation; but if it should turn (as it unquestionably will) upon other matters, in connection with the Texas question - if to select a man for President who has served his country long and faithfully - one whose genius has entered into the very spirit of our institutions - whose great talents and commanding eloquence has eclipsed his contemporaries of the same time, and reflected honor upon his country for near half a century - one who enjoys the confidence and affections of his countrymen in an extraordinary degree - who, in the language of the Charleston Mercury, in 1837, "is a bold, brave, high-minded, honorable man." If to get a man for the times, and for the Union - one who would restore peace and good will at home, and command respect for us abroad - a republican of the old school, and a patriot and philanthropist in the broadest sense of the terms - one who has the nerve and ability to allay sectional prejudice and political strife, and preserve our glorious Union, with all its blessings of civil and religious liberty; and who, by noble deeds, has *earned* the Presidential office, (without approving all his political principles,) be objects worthy of our approbation, then we are in favor of HENRY CLAY, as possessing all these in an eminent degree.

In answer to the inquiries propounded through the "Anderson Gazette," by "Many Voters," we reply:

1st. *We do not* concur in the resolution adopted at a meeting of the citizens, of Beaufort District, in this State, and approved elsewhere. However we may be in favor of the annexation of Texas, we are not willing to dissolve this Union to obtain it.

The preservation of the Union of these States is an object near our hearts, believing that upon its perpetuity depends the last hope of freedom throughout the world. We would rather, in the language of the immortal Jefferson, in the Declaration of American Independence, " suffer whilst evils are sufferable," than dissolve the Union cemented by the blood of our fathers.

2nd. *We do not* concur in the proposition to hold a State Convention in Columbia, for the purpose of resisting the laws of the United States; (or, as we understand it, to Nullify the Tariff;) nor in the proposition to hold a Southern Convention at Nashville, Tennesee, in reference to the annexation of Texas. We do not think our grievances sufficient to justify the one, or that the other would have the slightest influence in effecting the object desired - but would rather operate as a fire-brand whose ultimate effect would be to dissolve this Union.

3d. *We do not* concur with McDuffie in believing that a State of this Union possesses the power to lay a Tariff on the importation of domestic manufactures, or that it would be expedient to exercise it, if we did possess the constitutional power.

4th. We do not approve of the course of the Democratic majority in Congress in admitting members to seats who were elected by general ticket, in direct violation of the law of the land, nor do we approve of their course in *expunging* from the journals the patriotic protest of the Whigs made upon that occasion. We regard their conduct as in a high degree disorganizing and revolutionary - setting the laws of their country at defiance - trampling the Constitution under foot, and leading directly to anarchy and despotism.

5th. *We are in favor* of so altering the law as to give the election of Presidential electors to the people, as being decidedly more democratic, and in accordance with the spirit of our institutions. In a Government like ours all power is vested in the people and should, in all cases, emanate directly from them.

6th. *We are in favor* of increasing the jurisdiction of the Ordinary in matters of real estate, *to any extent* the representatives of the people may in their wisdom think proper, as being a great saving to every class of our citizens, and desirable in every point of view.

7th. *We are in favor* of dividing the [election distri]ct of Pendleton in whole, or as to *representatives* [only, for we] would rather have "half a loaf than no bread."

8th. *We do approve* of the amendment to the Constitution limiting the tenure of the Judges to sixty-five years of age, as being a means of securing to us at all times more active and efficient officers.

9th. *We are in favor* of abolishing the office of Superintendant of Public Works, and of retrenching public expenditures in every practical way. The office of Adjutant-General, we are disposed to think, might be dispensed with by requiring the more faithful discharge of their duties, and increasing those duties to some extent, of Division and Brigade field-officers.

We have thus, fellow citizens, in the discharge of what we considered our bounden duty to you as candidates for your suffrages, answered fully and frankly the various questions you have been pleased to propound to us, with others; and pledge ourselves, if honored by you with seats in the Legislature to carry out, as far as may be in our power, the various reforms in the laws of the State suggested by your interrogatories, and approved by us; having an eye singly directed, at all times, to the honor and interest of our common country.

We have the honor to remain,

Most respectfully, your fellow-citizens,

J. P. REED,
J. E. CALHOUN,
A. W. HOLCOMB,
CHESTER KINGSLEY,
J. OVERTON LEWIS,
SAMUEL MILWEE,
W. G. SPEED.

July, 1844.

————————

WPM-LC

Robert B. Gilliam to Willie P. Mangum.

OXFORD July 1st. 1844.

My dear Sir,

Your political frends are exceedingly anxious that you should attend a Barbecue to be given at Brassfield's in this County, on Saturday the 6th inst.— Permit me to say, that your presence on that occasion would exert a very decided influence upon publick opinion in that section.

The democratick party have been making heavy demonstrations upon this County, with a view as well to carry the County election, as to operate upon the presidential contest. At a recent meeting at Brassfields, they were represented by two orators, one domestic, the other imported. I was not present, but I understand, one of them relied greatly upon *your authority* to prejudice the people against Whig measures, and the Whig Candidate for the Presidency. I shall attend myself and take such part in the discussions, as the State of my health will enable me to bear without too much hazard; but my presence will be a matter of the least possible importance, if we shall be so fortunate to have your co-operation. Before making the request I have well considered the distinguished position occupied by you in the councils of the Country, and I cannot perceive in that circumstance, any thing to prevent you from giving your influence and talents to the advancement of the great cause of which you are one of the acknowledged leaders.

If it could be understood immediately that you will attend the barbecue, it would insure the attendance of an immense concourse of people.

I am with high respect
ROBT. B. GILLIAM

N. B. Brassfields is in the Southern part of the Country near Wilton (Carters). If you could be at Wilton the evening of the 5th, I will endeavour to meet you there.   R. B. G.

We have understood that you will be expected to attend a meeting of the Clay Club at Forsyth's on the same day.

If we had been aware of it, we could have made a different arrangement - but now it is too late. The Clay Club can very conveniently postpone its meeting to a subsequent day— The barbecue *cannot* be postponed. I would most earnestly request that you will not permit *any* consideration to interfere with your attendance at Brassfields. It is a matter of the last importance.

Yours truly
R B G

[Addressed:]

Hon: Willie P. Mangum
Red Mountain
Orange Co.
N. C.

WPM-LC

John Cameron to Willie P. Mangum.

July 1st. 1844

Hon. Wiley P. Mangum
Dear Sir
I have been requested by Messrs Gilliam, Littlejohn & others of our mutual friends in this place to earnestly request,

that you will consent to meet them at a Barbecue to be given at Brassfields on Saturday next. We are already aware that you have given your consent to attend on that day at Samuel Forsyth's, but trust that the urgency of the case will be deemed a sufficient excuse for your altering that arrangement. At the Barbecue given by our opponents at Brassfields on thursday last, the time was entirely occupied by Messrs. McRea & Venable[209] to the entire exclusion of the Whigs who were present as invited Guests. This course of the other party induced our friends here to make arrangements for a similar entertainment, to be free for all parties & numerous invitations have been sent out to their leading men requesting them to attend & take it turn & turn about. I am further requested to say that *this is the only real debateable ground in the County*. What Gilliam calls the Flanders of Granville, that the other party will doubtless be there in force & that if you ever wished to strike a good blow for the Whig cause this now is the time, & this the place. Gilliam says that if you will come to this place on Friday that he will take you over on Saturday morning in his carriage or that if you prefer he will meet you on Friday evening at Carters.

With sentiments of the highest esteem & regard I remain

Yrs. truly
JNO. CAMERON

[Addressed:]

Hon: Wilie P. Mangum
Red Mountain
Orange Co
No. Ca.

WPM-LC

Richard Hines to [*Willie P. Mangum*]

RALEIGH 4th. July 1844

My dear Sir,

You will see from the last Whig papers in this place that we have appointed Whig mass meetings to be held at Wadesborough on Thursday the 18th. inst and at Statesville on the 25th. both

---

[209]He probably refers to Duncan McRae, of Cumberland, and Abraham W. Venable, of Granville.

of which we are extremely anxious you should attend. Here we have but one opinion that no other man in the State can produce the same effect by his presence and speech as yourself we are therefore the more anxious for you to attend the above meetings and as many others as your convienience will admit-

Our friends here are all willing to do and doing all in their power except Mr. Badger who seams to take a very deep interest in the canvass but as far as I am informed has as yet contributed in no way to its success- Do you think it would be desirable for him to be active in the campaign except with his pen? We yesterday raised a subscription to have ten thousand copies of Mr. Clay's speech at this place published which we hope will have a beneficial effect.

The Loco's are exerting themselves to the uttermost to carry this state if possible and seam certain of reducing Mr. Graham's majority to a very small one if he is elected. Whilst the Whigs in all parts of the State except Bertie and Beaufort are not as active as they ought to be- Mr. Barringer informs us there is much luke warmness in his neighbourhood but he promised to do his best to arouse them as does Mr. Clingman Caldwell[210] &c. Rely upon it if we are not up and adoing we shall be hard pressed both to elect the Gov: & Legislatures-

Saunders was met by Stanly at Greenville as we are informed greatly to the advantage of the Whigs. He failed to meet his appointment at Beaufort and Williamston, Cherry and Stanly[211] attending and addressing the different meetings. He attended at Windsor where we are informed he was triumphantly met by Cherry who promised accompany him to the rest of his appointments.

Rumour which we credit says that Henry Haywood and Saunders[212] are to canvass the whole Western part of the State. They have all certainly promised to attend the mass meeting at Charlott as well as McDuffie and Calhoun- If you could happen there at the time it would impose great restraint upon them-

We find it impossable to arouse our papers here but Loring promises to run the whole set up Salt River and being very angry will no doubt do his best, Hale is also doing his best-

By appointment all the candidates for this county were to

[210]Thomas L. Clingman and Tod R. Caldwell.
[211]Edward Stanly and W. W. Cherry.
[212]Louis D. Henry, Will. H. Haywood, Jr., and R. M. Saunders.

meet here last Saturday and all attended except Thompson.[213] Manly made one of the most affective Electioneering speeches I ever heard both the matter and manner was first rate. Miller made a first rate speech in reply to Wilder[214] but a little too spicy he has fine abilities but is rather servere- We calculate with much confidence on electing part of our ticket, and hope to elect Manly Miller & Hinton[215] but probably shall not get more than one or two. our prospects are certainly improving at present.

The Whigs have given Hoke[216] too much credit as a gentleman of liberality entitled to all kindness &c. He is as great a demagogue as the state contains and has made the most of every kindness extended to him by the Whigs. As for instance when he has not been answered he and his friends say it was because he was an over match for the Whigs and they afraid &c.

He ought to be met at every cross roads and receive no quarters as he gives none—Rely upon it he is playing his cards greatly to our injury at present, and some of our friends begin to despair of Graham's election but I can but think they are alarmed without cause.

The declining health of eldest daughter compels me to leave in a few days for Old point Comfort to try the benefit of sea Bathing and I may be compelled to be absent much of the summer- In my absence Gov: Morehead will act as Chairman of the central committee. How would it do for the Gov: to attend the mass meeting in the Western part of the State. I shall certainly return to the election. If you have any acquaintances at Old Point you would much oblige me by inclosing me a letter to them, as I have no acquaintance there nor none of my friends here.

I have the Honor to be with
sentiments of great Respect
Very sincerely & truly yours

RICHD: HINES

---

[213]George W. Thompson was in the legislature in 1844-1849. *N. C. Manual*, 831.
[214]Gaston H. Wilder was in the legislature from 1842 to 1847 and 1852 to 1857. *N. C. Manual*, 831.
[215]He refers to Charles Manly, Henry W. Miller, and C. L. Hinton.
[216]Michael Hoke, the Democratic candidate for governor, was defeated by W. A. Graham.

WPM-LC

Jonathan Worth[217] to Willie P. Mangum.

ASHEBORO' July 8th 1844

Hon. W. P. Mangum

Dr Sir

We have learned within a day or two past that Judge Saunders is to address us on the 16th Inst. being Tuesday of an extra Term of the Supr. Court- No electoral Candidate has as yet been appointed in this district and in looking round for a proper person to reply to him, it turns out to be the universal wish of all us that you should be the man. As he is a member of Congress, well versed in the political questions of the day and has thought proper to publish appointments and travel out of his own County and district to make Texas speeches, we see no impropriety in your meeting him. Great apathy prevails among the Whigs of this County- and we are apprehensive that we shall not be able to get them to the polls in August- If you should see in it no impropriety and should find it convenient to reply to the general here, we think it would do much to re-animate our party There is no defection from the Whig ranks here- our danger is merely that Mr Graham will not get the full Whig vote, by a failure of the voters to go to the polls-

A Clay Club was held here to-day and it is at the request of all the Whigs present that I make this invitation- It is not in consequence of any public resolve in the meeting but at the individual request of the Whigs present—

Yours with great respect

JONATHAN WORTH.

[Addressed:]

Hon. Wile P. Mangum
Red Mountain N. C.

---

[217]For a sketch of Jonathan Worth see J. G. de R. Hamilton (ed.), *The Correspondence of Jonathan Worth*, Raleigh, 1909, I, v-xiii. and *D. A. B.*, XX, 536.

WPM-LC

S. Starkweather[218] to Willie P. Mangum.

N. YORK 9 July 1844

Dr Sir

I have just completed my pressing business which had accumulated, in my absence, and gave way last evening to the pressing invitation of my friends to appear before our citizens— It was hard work & I admit I came to scratch with reluctance But the worst is over and day after to morrow I leave for the interior. My work is laid out & I hope to perform it with success, no exertion shall be wanting on my part There is great excitement throughout the State. The Whig party were never so united. One heart seems to be with them all— The ability of the locos to lie is making Polk a harder candidate for us than Mr V B would have been They swear he is Tariff, *to the hub,* & every thing else which he is not but should be. I am anxious to hear from the south & see that you are moveing I think we shall lose Virginia but if it is by a small majority it will do no harm. But if contrary to expectation we carry it, and you carry the old north State likewise we may give her the next president But I have little or no hopes of your State, or that you will make a decent fight you know Senator some gentlemen are great on paper, some in the parlor but in the field, why they leave that to others. I do not intend to give up, however, but hope you may do better than my forebodings warrant. *We shall carry this state but* have to fight every inch of the ground & intend to do so. I will write you from the interior by & by & tell you to a *dot* where we are. Wishing you all prosperity,

I am truly yours

S. STARKWEATHER.

[Addressed:]

Hon Willie P Mangum
Red Mountain
Orange Co.
N Carolina.

---

[218]See above, III, 316-318, 479-481.

Mordecai Manuel Noah, 1785-1851. From the oil portrait by J. W. Jarvis in the
Shearith Isreal Synagogue Collection, New York City.

WPM-LC

John M. Morehead to Willie P. Mangum.

RALEIGH 10th July 1844.

Honl.
    Willie P. Mangum

        Dear Sir

A mass-meeting of the Whigs is appointed to take place on the 18th. Int. at Wadesboro—& another on the 25th at Statesville—

It is very desirable that some speaker from a distance should attend these meetings to rouse up our friends—which I assure you, is very much needed.

And no person of my acquaintance can do this more effectively than yourself. The week between the 18th & 25th you can visit Charlotte & be present at least, which I have no doubt will have some tendency to keep the Democracy who hold a mass-meeting on 23rd in check. It is probable there will be other meetings that you may attend.

Most extraordinary efforts are making to carry the elections of this State - Haywood receives whole bags of documents by the mails & the press here is engaged striking off tracts, & they are sending them off by the small waggon loads - to different parts of the State— While the Whigs seem to think the opposition not very serious & are not so zealous as they should be. I know of no person likely to go to these meetings from this quarter, unless you do so—

I think a meeting would do much good about Pattersons Store in the neighborhood of John Long's about the 29th or 30th July—If you think so get it up- Randolph, Chatham & Guilford, would attend— Let me hear from you—

                Yrs. Sincerely
                J. M. MOREHEAD

[Addressed:] Honl Willie P. Mangum
          Red Mountain
          Orange
          N. C.

WPM-LC

John Kerr[219] to Willie P. Mangum.

RALEIGH July 12th 1844

Dear Sir.

A few days since I had a public political discussion with Genl R M Saunders, at Williamsboro' in Granville.— In the course of that discussion, Genl Saunders used substantially the following language in regard to yourself when speaking of the action of the Senate upon the treaty recently negotiated by Mr. Wheaton.—

"I affirm" said he, - "that in regard to this treaty, Wilie P Mangum betrayed the interest of North Carolina, and William H Haywood supported that interest, and if Wilie P Mangum has friends here I desire that they will inform him of what I now say. I expected when I came here to have met him—"[220]

I feel it my duty to make to you this Communication, that you may take such course in regard to the subject of it, as you deem best.- Allow me to add, that I think you owe it to yourself no less than to the Whig Party, to give us the benefit of your able service in public discussions during the pending presidential canvass—

You may not be aware of what I know to be the fact - that you are the object of the bitter and unrelenting hostility, of the leaders of Loco focoism, in North Carolina and they let no opportunity of inflicting an injury upon you pass without improvement—

I trust you will not deem me officious in addressing *you* this letter,- The regard I entertain for you, both personally, and as

---

[219]John Kerr, 1811-1879, the son of a Congressman by the same name, practiced law at Yanceyville until he entered Congress in 1853. He was a Whig, a trustee of Wake Forest College and the state university. Later he was judge of the superior and supreme courts of North Carolina. *Biog. Dir. of Cong.*, 1406.

[220]In the winter of 1843-1844, Henry Wheaton, American minister to Berlin, made a trade agreement with the German Zollverein by which duties on tobacco and lard imported into Germany were reduced, raw cotton was put on the free list, and rice was admitted at a low rate. In return, the United States reduced its rates on goods imported from Germany. The treaty was presented to the Senate in April, 1844. It was contrary to the existing tariff law but Tyler proposed to have the Congress change the existing law if the Senate approved the treaty. Under these conditions the Senate Whigs laid the treaty on the table. Chitwood, *Life of Tyler*, 332-333.

one of the most distinguished & highly honored members of the party with which we both act- has prompted me to do so—

Very Sincerely your
friend & obt Svt
JOHN KERR

Hon W P Mangum

[Addresed:] Hon. Wilie P Mangum
Red Mountain
Orange County
N Carolina

WPM-LC

R. W. Lassiter[221] et als. to Willie P. Mangum.

OXFORD, July 14th, 1844.

Hon Willie P. Mangum,

Dear Sir,

At an informal meeting of some of your friends in this place, the undersigned were appointed a committee to invite you to a barbecue to be given at Oxford the last tuesday or wednesday of the present month, both as a token of respect for your eminent services, and to give you an opportunity of aiding the Whig cause in this county, by addressing on that occasion as large a portion of our fellow-citizens as can be got together. We hope you will do us the honor to accept the invitation, and designate on which of the above mentioned days, or on what other day, it will be most convenient for you to attend.

We would be urgent in this matter, as we cannot but believe it is one of considerable importance. Democracy is making a desperate struggle in Old Granville, and without the most strenuous exertions on the part of the whigs, we fear, will be successful. Permit us, then, to add to the wishes of those whom we represent, our most earnest, individual solicitations that

---

[221]R. W. Lassiter was a representative of Granville County in the state Whig convention in 1846. He was a state senator in 1864 and 1868-1869. *Greensboro Patriot*, January 24, 1846; *N. C. Manual*, 624, 625. Mangum attended this rally.

you will favour us with your presence on the occasion alluded
to-

With sentiments of the highest
consideration, we have the honor to be
your obedient servants,

R. W. LASSITER
JNO. R. HERNDON
R. H. KINGSBURY
R B GILLIAM

[Addressed:]

Hon W. P. Mangum
Red Mountain

WPM-LC

Chas. E. Russ et als. to Willie P. Mangum.

FLAT RIVER July 15th 1844

Dear Sir.-

At a meeting of the Clay Club of Flat River, held on the 6th.
instant, it was unanimously resolved, that your name should be
enrolled among the honorary members of our Association. A
committee of three being appointed to notify you of the fact.
We cherfully perform the task, feeling that we are honored in
paying a tribute of respect to one who stands so high in the
estimation of his countrymen one who, in the times that tried
men's soles, stood side by side with Henry Clay in dispelling
the cloud that overshadowed our beloved country, in preserving the union and battling on the side of the people against the
encroachments of executive power and usipations and we feel
sure that you could not give your aid or countinance to any man
or party that could conspire either against law or liberty- We
salute you with great respect and would add our fervent wishes
that many years be added to your honored age, and that you
may survive not only to witness the elevation of your great

compatriot Henry Clay to the presidency, but to see our beloved country once more free, prosperous, and happy.-

We remain with perfect respect your Friends
and fellow citizens

To Hon Wilie P. Mangum

CHA.ˢ E. RUSS)
CARTER WALLER) Committee
MOSES ROBERTS)

[Addressed:]

Hon. Wilie P. Mangum
Orange N. C.

WPM-LC

James E. Harvey[222] to Willie P. Mangum.

WASHINGTON
July 23d. 1844

Dear Sir

I take the liberty to enclose to you a Circular which I have found it necessary to issue, in Consequence of a very unceremonious removal from office "ordered" by the acting President immediately after the adjournment of Congress— I am ignorant of any cause for this Summary proceeding, save, my refusal to subscribe to the flagitious schemes of one corrupt & ambitious and the fact of having published the result of my reflections upon that vile iniquitous plot - the annexation of Texas. If any matters connected with the purposes of my "Circular" should fall under your view, I shall greatly esteem any consideration that may be bestowed in my behalf.

At the suggestion of several friends, and with a sincere desire to be useful in the Campaign, I am now devoting my services to the congressional Committee here, in disseminating Whig Doctrines & Documents in all parts of the Country. Your State has been, so far liberally served with this matter, but if any section has been neglected or should you regard it as essential to provide those regions already partially supplied, with additional light, I shall feel particular pleasure in fulfilling

---

[222]See above, 94. Harvey, a journalist, was a close friend of Mangum and of other Whig leaders including Seward who in 1861 recommended him for minister to Portugal. In this collection are several valuable letters from him to Mangum. For his connection with the Fort Sumter incident see J. G. Randall, *Lincoln the President*, I, 342-343; Bancroft, *William H. Seward*, II, 145.

your wishes in that respect and shall immediately devote myself to its completion at your notification— I have volunteered
for the purpose of being useful and it is a feeling of duty and
desire that will prompt me to take any part however arduous,
that will accomplish the most good to the cause. Mr. Willis
Green[223] has supervised us since the adjournment - He has been
aided by Mr. Causin of Md. and occasionally by Mr. Merrick
& Mr. Dillett.[224] Mr. Garret Davis will join us about the middle of next month, after the Elections, at which time Mr. Green
will probably return to Kentucky. Our force consists of Eight
or Ten and We act harmoniously & with proper energy and
spirit. We have intelligence from all sections, exhibiting a degree of resolution and enthusiasm akin to that of 1840 and a
power fully equal to a glorious triumph. Nothing has contributed to inspire courage and confidence, in a greater degree
than the result in Louisiana.-[225] Opening the canvass as she
did, it was all-important that we should maintain a respectable
party stand - at least, that we should not suffer a disastrous defeat. More than this, the sanguine had not anticipated and the
timid dreaded much worse— The result has proven the stability
of Whig principles and has conferred the highest honor upon
the integrity and firmness of the Senate- Of all states, Louisiana from her contiguity of Territory, familiarity of intercourse
and that almost invincible argument of interest, which had circulated its influence, through the personal exertions of speculators & scrip holders, was the most liable to be approached &
the most susceptible upon the issue of anexation and that *she*
therefore should have repudiated the plot itself and disgraced
its chief actors and friends, is a victory over which we may rejoice for its own intrinsic Consequence & more for the moral
effect which it will spread in the Southern Country.

Our accounts from western New York verify altogether the
newspaper statements as to the extent of the feeling abroad
and the numbers actually engaged in the canvass— there is
every good reason to hope for a more decisive majority than
was given to Genl. Harrison and with the exertions that are

---

[223]Willis Green, of Kentucky, was a member of Congress from 1839 to 1845. *Biog. Dir. of Cong.*, 1032.
[224]He refers to John M. S. Causin, a Whig member of Congress from Maryland in 1843-1845, William D. Merrick, Whig Senator from Maryland in 1838-1845, James Dellet, Whig congressman from Alabama in 1839-1841 and 1843-1845, and Garrett Davis, Whig congressman from Kentucky in 1839-1847 and Senator from 1867 to 1872. *Biog. Dir. of Cong.*, 797, 884, 896, 1307.
[225]In the election in Louisiana on July 1, the Whigs had candidates in only two congressional races, and they won in one of those. In the legislature the Whigs won 8 of the 17 senate seats and 34 of the 60 seats in the lower house. *Niles' Register*, LXVI, 336, 352.

employed in every corner of the state, it is impossible to fix upon a numerical result- The changes from Locofocoism are surprising and we gain hundreds of responsible & valuable men, without the loss of a single soldier.

In Missouri, the efforts are directed to secure the Legislature. It may be necessary, for the accomplishment of that object to yield the Governor & members of Congress, which are really unimportant when compared with the two Senators depending upon the Legislature- Those who are best informed, most active & therefore most competent to judge, give strong assurances, that we shall attain the great point - It is said Benton's strength will not exceed 35 which is about a third of the Legislature.

An unfortunate local issue has arisen in Indiana which may cost the Whigs so dear a price as the Legislature, which elects a U. S. Senator - [226] but little question exists as to her final vote and nothing will be wanting to place her in position now.

Alabama, will do much more than has been anticipated & it is not at all improbable that we shall be able to divide the Delegation in the House, which would be a great and an unexpected accession—

The Locofocos in Pennsylvania and the Tariff states are resorting to every species of falsehood to help their Candidates - Saltmarsh the Mail Contractor who has just passed through the Keystone region, says that at a Polk meeting he saw a banner streaming from a lofty pole, inscribed "Polk & Dallas - a High Tariff and Protection." It is a desperate chance & no means however disgraceful has any terror for men reckless in every state of society and utterly unprincipled in the game of politics—

I shall be much pleased, if I can be of Service to you in any way and trusting that you will pardon this lengthy infliction.

> I remain
> Yr Fr & St
> JAMES E. HARVEY

What will North Carolina do?

Hon. W. P. Mangum.

---

[226]In Indiana the state election in August resulted in the Whigs obtaining a majority of 10 in the lower house and the same number as the Democrats in the upper house of the legislature. *Niles' Register*, LXVI, 444.

WPM-LC

J. M. Edwards[227] to Willie P. Mangum.

N. YORK July 25, 1844—

Dear Sir.-

On my return from Washington I found that numerous applications had been sent from different quarters - asking for copies of the likeness we made of Hon Henry Clay - when he was in Washington.* After a little reflection, and consultation, we concluded the best manner of complying with these requests would be to copy the original likeness and set them in gold pins, of a small and not very expensive size, and accordingly have made known to the public our intentions. As soon as the pins are finished I will send one for your disposal and shall feel honored if it meets your approbation. You will find that the *copy* diminutive as it is, is superior to the *original* in many respects.— I shall also send one to Mr Clay- which I hope will please him tho he told me, "he did not think it a likeness at *all-*" Will you, sir, do me the favor to redirect a number of copies of the "Express"[228] containing the advertisements (which I send you under *double* envelopes) to the principal *Clay Clubs* in N. C.— I am unable to obtain their address.

Very Respectfully

J. M. EDWARDS.

Hon W. P Mangum

* of which several *letter writers* made mention in their correspondence.

WPM-LC

John B. Bobbitt to Sally Mangum

LOUISBURG, N. C. 27th. July, 1844.

Miss Sally:

We have heard frequently, during the last and present year, that you intended to visit this Village; but as yet your Friends and school mates here find themselves disappointed. They fre-

---

[227]Probably a New York engraver.
[228]He probably refers to the New York *Express*, a Whig newspaper that ran from 1836 to 1850. Its editors and publishers were James and Erastus Brooks. Louis H. Fox, *New York City Newspapers, 1820-1850: a Bibliography*, 42.

quently ask: when is Sally Mangum coming? To this we reply: Soon.

Now, to the end, that you may not make an indefinite postponement, I write you to come and stay with us one, two, or more months; and, moreover, if you will say when you can come, I will send for you at any moment. I will also, during your stay with us, send you to see your Friends in this section.

In regard to our schools, we have more Boarders than we have had for several years; Say twenty five, half of them young ladies.

Of Domestic news, I have not much to say. The Political Atmosphere in this neighborhood seems to be strongly impregnated with effluvia from the Ponds of Texas. Polk and Dallas also are much boasted of in this Demo. County: Clay too is much talked of by the minority *here*.

In conclusion: give our respects to your Friends, and accept the same for yourself.

Yrs. respectfully

JNO. B. BOBBITT

Miss Sally Mangum)
Louisburg N C July 9 1844   Paid J B B 10

[Addressed:]

Miss Sally Mangum
Red Mountain
Orange County, N. C.

WPM-LC

Daniel R. Goodloe[229] to Willie P. Mangum.

WASHINGTON July 27th 1844

Dear Sir-

Presuming that you are somewhat burdened with correspondence in these exciting times, I have hitherto abstained from writing you, in obedience to your kind request, until the present moment. You may remember, that before leaving here, you suggested that the Central Committee at Raleigh, and in the

----

[229]See above, 84n.

different counties of the State, might perhaps be induced to subscribe for a number of copies of the Weekly Standard,[230] and
that you would write to them suggesting the utility of such a
course. As I am aware, that in the multiplicity of your engagements, you would be likely to forget a matter of so little consequence I have taken the liberty, at the request of Mr. Towers
to address you a line upon the subject, and to solicit the favor
of you to write to Mr Badger or some other member of the
Committee calling attention to the paper. I believe that they
can no where purchase more reading matter (such as it is) at
so cheap a rate. It is now sent for seventy five cents until the
first of December with such of the back numbers as are on hand.
The editor can well afford the Weekly at the cheap rate at which
it is now furnished, since it only requires an extra outlay for
the paper. The same number of hands in all the departments
are indispensible whether the weekly is printed or not; so that
if the circulation of it could be extended it would become his
principle source of profit. Subscriptions have very much increased recently, and a letter *patronising* (not patronage) by
distinguished Whigs in different quarters would soon place it on
a permanent basis, and enable the editor to issue a permanent
country edition. The value of a whig paper here of a strong
party cast is so much better understood by you than by myself, that I will say nothing upon that head.

Mr. Green of Kentucky[231] remains here yet, and he with
his documentary corps are busily at work. At your suggestion
I have frequently called at the folding room to inquire about
the documents sent to N. Carolina. I have also conferred with
Mr Green as to the proper course to pursue in the editorial
change of the paper. I fear that I have a proclivity to fall into
the channel he points out, and that a good Christian would
rather curb the indulgence of a censorious spirit, than yield to
it. He advises me to make offensive war upon the locofocos, and
to spare them upon no occasion. You will perhaps think, if you
look into the standard, that I have acted upon his advice; but
I have not. I resolve from day to day to be more guarded, and
less harsh in my expressions, but reading the Globe and other
unscrupulous locofoco sheets, provokes me into the use of language of which I feel ashamed in cooler moments. I by no

---

[230]See above, III, 467n.
[231]Willis Green. See above, James E. Harvey to W. P. Mangum, July 23, 1844.

means think, however, that truth or justice or propriety demand, that I should have a mantle of charity as large as the Intelligencer's. I think it well enough to call things by their right names, though I am conscious of exceeding the line of propriety every day. I have not felt entirely at ease for repeating the charge of Toryism against Mr Polk's Grandfather;[232] though I have not a rational doubt of its truth, and think it an objection in some degree to him; but I have a repugnance to it. I wrote a long account of the whole affair which appeared in to-days Standard in which I think I have fixed it beyond controversy. I place the justice of the allegation upon the ground that the locofocos had boasted of Mr. Polk's revolutionary ancestry. Dwelling upon the subject so long yesterday afternoon, in writing the article, has disgusted me with the subject, and it affords me no little relief to make this confession to you. And this confession, by the way, is my apology for talking so much about myself.

I have not taken lodgings at Mrs. Scott's as upon reflection, I thought the expense too great, and Mr. Towers is slow in paying me my stipend. I regret to have named it to her, but in other respects am doing very well. I trust you will give me credit for appreciating your unparalleled kindness and generosity to me- which lays me under an unredeemable load of obligation. I shall be very proud to receive a line from you, sir, should your leisure permit. Present my respects to your family and believe me to be with great respect your obliged and obedt sevt

DANIEL R. GOODLOE

I presume you have heard that Bryant and others of New York have virtually broken off from the locofoco party. The New York papers are filled with the sparing between the Plebeian and Post.[233] I should think there was little chance of healing the breach. Great interest is felt here in regard to the

---

[232]In the campaign of 1844 many Whigs, especially in Polk's native state, North Carolina, asserted that Polk's grandfather, Ezekiel Polk, had been a traitor in the Revolution. Ezekiel Polk, according to this story, deserted the company of which he was captain and placed himself under the protection of Lord Cornwallis. Concerned with the charge, the North Carolina Democrats delegated W. W. Holden to write a refutation of the charge. Ezekiel Polk, therefore, became a significant issue in the campaign in North Carolina. Norton, *Democratic Party in N. C.*, 141-142.

[233]The New York *Plebeian*, a Democratic paper, was edited at this time by Levi D. Slamm, and William Cullen Bryant was editor of the New York *Evening Post*. Bryant opposed the Baltimore Democratic platform because of the annexation plank. He did support the ticket but with misgiving. The *Plebeian's* editor threatened to drive Bryant from the Democratic party because of his Federalism and opposition to Annexation. The *Post* replied that annexation might lose New York for Polk. Fox, *New York City Newspapers: a Bibliography*, 82; New York *Evening Post*, July 27, 1844.

N. C. elections. I think the signs are decidedly favorable at this time judging from the tone of the public press in every quarter. The Whigs seem to be losing nothing in any part of the South, while rapid accessions are made to the ranks in the North- particularly in New York and Pennsylvania.

[Addressed:]

Hon. Willie P. Mangum
Red Mountain
Orange County
N. Carolina

WPM-LC

Thos. K. Thomas[234] *to Willie P. Mangum.*

LOUISBURG Aug 4th 1844

Hon W P Mangum

My dear Sir

A number of the leading and most distinguished Whigs of this county have urged me as the Secretary of the Louisburg Clay Club to write you and to request you if you could with any degree of convenience to yourself, to meet our political adversaries at Franklinton on the 13th instant. It is an important point; they expect to operate on the people of four counties; its geographical situation is not more favorable to their views than its political aspect. Parties in that region are unsettled; it is now loco foco but with proper exertion a great revolution might be wrought. Mr Gilliam, our elector will not be able to attend; The democrats will have a number of speakers there may be some distinguished Whigs there;[235] several have been invited, but it is universally wished here that you may be able to attend and stand up before the people at that populous region as the champion and advocate of the Whig party.

Mr. Jeffreys[236] the Senator elect from this county attack with some vehemance your course on the Tariff and Bank dur-

---

[234]Thomas K. Thomas, a citizen of Franklin County, represented his county in the state Whig Convention in 1846. In 1833 he petitioned the legislature to support internal improvement and education for the purpose of decreasing the migration from North Carolina. *Greensboro Patriot,* January 24, 1846; Coon, (ed.), *Doc. Hist. of Educ. in N. C.,* II, 619-621.

[235]Abraham W. Venable was the chief spokesman for the Democrats and Henry W. Miller for the Whigs at the gathering. *Raleigh Register,* August 27, 1844.

[236]William A. Jeffries was state senator in 1844-1845. *N. C. Manual,* 610.

ing the late canvass in this county; the humblest member of the Whig party in Franklin would be able to vindicate you from the malignant shafts that this democratic pet might level at you; but the juvenal Senator will no doubt continue his detraction until he receives such a castigating as you alone could give him.

The returns from the election[237] are coming on well; Franklin done all she could under the circumstances; we have fearful odds against us, at best and greatly to our discomfiture my brother John E Thomas the Whig candidate in the Commons was taken sick few days before the election and was not able to be out on the day. Had he been able to have canvassed the county and to have attended on the day at the usual place where candidates in this county go, I think Graham would have gotten 25 votes more in this county than he did. As it is we are beaten, but not conquered; we will give Clay 40 votes more in this county than we gave Graham- if you will come to Franklinton and make a speech. Is this sufficient inducement? Besides this you will effect much in an important part of Granville County.

I am aware that others have written to you on this subject and I have no doubt but that you will attend if you can with convenience. In conclusion of this allow me to express the great obligation I feel myself under to you for the trouble you have taken in conveying to me my Bee hive cuts. I regret that you should have been so troubled with them, and I must beg that you will receive my sincere gratitude for your condescention and kindness Believe me dear Sir your obedient Servant

THOS. K THOMAS

Louisburg Aug 5th 1844   Paid 10

[Addressed:]

> Hon Willie P Mangum
> Red Mountain
> No Ca

---

[237]In the state as a whole, W. A. Graham, the Whig candidate, defeated Michael Hoke, the Democratic candidate for governor by a vote of 42,586 to 39,433 in the August election. In the state senate the Whigs won 26 out of 50 seats and 71 out of 120 in the lower house, which gave the Whigs a majority of 24 in the two houses together. *Hillsborough Recorder*, August 22, November 7, 1844.

WPM-LC

S. H. Harris to Willie P. Mangum.

CLARKSVILLE [Virginia] Augst. 5th. 1844

Dear Sir

Accompanying this is a letter from a scientific gentleman (probably not unknown to you) bearing testimony to the utility of my brothers invention, in the application of steam as a propelling power. He will if deemed necessary explain the nature of his engine and the principles upon which it acts. Viewed in reference to its practical results I cannot but hope that he has made a discovery which may ultimately tend to modify, if not entirely change, the mode of applying steam to machinery.

Robert will state to you the object of his visit and allow me to hope that you will give him your advice and influence in forwarding his schemes.

The Whigs of *this region* are waiting anxiously to hear from you and much good to the cause is anticipated from your expected visit. We are much cheered by the news from the old North State and with a little help from yourself and other distinguished leaders, we will endeavour to follow the example of N Carolina in Novem^r next. We shall be much gratified to have the priviledge of extending to you our hospitality should you visit this part of Virginia again- And I am desired to say that a visit from Mrs. Mangum or the young ladies would be particularly agreeable to Mrs Harris.

With high respect
I am yours &C

S. H HARRIS

[Addressed:]

Hon. Willie P. Mangum
Orange County
N. C

Robt. Harris

WPM-LC

P. C. Cameron to Willie P. Mangum.

ORANGE Co. Aug 7th. [1844]
Wed: afternoon 5 o'clock.

My dear Sir/

As in a 1840, the old North stands first, foremost, and freest! I have *just* returned from Raleigh - leaving it after all the intelligence for the day had been received. At the moment of my departure, according to the list kept by Mr. Loring[238] the Whigs had a majority of 24 in the House, and of (2) two in the Senate! The Governors majority for the Whig ticket, is so far *decreased* cannot say how much. Hoke is doing *better* than any one of his party before him! The impression at Raleigh seemed to be, that Grahams majority would not exceed 4,000. The old Wheel Horse Dobson[239] is defeated in Surry! Avery is defeated in Burke![240] he you know was a pet child of "Romeo's"! Mr. Augustus Moore is defeated as a candidate for the Edenton Senitorial District - a *loss* to us. I hope that Graham may make out his 5,000 & tho' I think our majority will be larger than reported above it is as large as we need. I send you the last Register. Gales makes a might to-do over "Nat Palmer!"[241] Another *such* an issue from his press & he will defeat Clay in Novr!

Yours

P. C. CAMERON.

[Addressed:]

Hon W. P. Mangum.
at Home.
Orange Co.

---

[238]Thomas Loring, editor of the *Raleigh Register.*
[239]William P. Dodson was in the state senate in 1827, 1830-1834, 1836-1837, and 1842-1843. *N. C. Manual,* 815-816.
[240]Isaac T. Avery.
[241]He probably refers to Nathaniel J. Palmer, the former editor of the *Milton Spectator.* He became a leader in education and in the Baptist denomination. Holden, *Address on the History of Journalism in N. C.,* 16; George W. Paschal, *History of Wake Forest College,* I, 308-311.

WPM-LC

Robert Ransom to Willie P. Mangum.

WARREN Co. August 8th. 1844

Dr. Sir

At the request of our friend Co¹. Robt. W. Alston,[242] I write to ascertain, when it will suit your entire convenience, to see us at your House he is particularly anxious to go and see you, the latter part of this Month if, you have no arrangement that calls you from home. You will therefore, please inform me by return mail, when it will best suit your convenience to see us.

You will see that our little Band has done well we have gained fifteen whigs in Warren against the most oppressive and tyrancial opposition ever practised in any Country. The Loco.ˢ rallied every voter from Pedlars to Boys. Yes German pedlars that were not Citizens, & beardless boys. Still we gained fifteen votes, we have done well, considering there never was but *two* Whig speeches made in the County.

With Great respect and high regard
I am Yrs.

ROB. RANSOM

Honl.

Willie P Mangum.

[Addressed:]

Honl. Willie P. Mangum
Red Mountain
Orange County
NO. CA.

By way of Franklinton.

---

[242]Formerly from Warren County, North Carolina, Robert W. Alston, 1781-1859, was a planter in Florida at the time of this letter. See below R. W. Alston to W. P. Mangum, December 26, 1844, and Groves, *The Alstons and Allstons of North and South Carolina,* 132.

WPM-LC

S. Starkweather[243] to Willie P. Mangum.

N. York 9 Augt 44.

Dr Sir

A matter of business brought me home from the country, for a day. I leave again in the morning to resume my labors. You may have seen that I have been through the State on the great thoroughfare I am now to take the Southern tier of counties Every moment confirms the opinion that we are gaining ground daily. I think the State good for *25,000* as it now appears. The vote must be a strong one past all doubt. I have seen veteren old democrats come entirely over while sitting under the truth. We have sufficient to show you are all right But how is this! You or rather the president of the Senate was boasting that the old North State would carry all before it and so I have very imprudently stated, now I see but a small gain in 18 counties of less than 400, from which I infer you will not carry the State by more than 1000 more than in 1840. When gentlemen talk of coats & suits despising Hats & small matters, we hold them to a strict accountability— Now I dont want to be too sure but I tell you to stand a little back and you will see the Empire State come in with about 30,000 if we have fair play you can have no idea of the ingagedness of our friends in the country One cannot stop at the corner of a street where they are wont to meet without being solicited to make a speech.

The women come out and ask you to stop & talk to their husbands & sons. This is what makes us strong. The Whigs are indolent as a party in ordinary times, when they arouse all is safe.

Truly yours
S. Starkweather.

We are looking for you north soon. If you come drop a note into the post office with your frank on it & it will find me somewhere Tell me in it how long you are to be with us and where you are going.

S. S.

[Addressed:] Hon W. P. Mangum
Red Mountain, North Carolina.

---

[243]See above, 154.

WPM-LC

Henry E. Rochester[244] *to Willie P. Mangum.*

ROCHESTER, NEW YORK, Augt. 15, 1844

Hon. Willie P. Mangum.

Dear Sir—

My Father *Col. Nathaniel Rochester,*[245] an officer of the Revolutionary Army in North Carolina died in this City in 1831 in the 80th. year of his age— In behalf of my aged mother, now 76 years old, I take the liberty to solicit the favor of your kind offices in procuring the necessary proofs of my father's services in the revolutionary war to entitle his widow to receive a pension— Nathaniel Macon, Judge Cameron & other known intimate friends of my father are no more, so that I am under the necessity of troubling one, who though well known by reputation, is personally a Stranger to me. I am induced to beg the favor of you, from the circumstance of your residence in Orange Co., and having an impression that you was an acquaintance of my brother *William B. Rochester,* formerly a member of Congress from this State, & who was lost at sea off the coast of North—Carolina, while on his journey home from the South in the ill-fated Steamer *Pulaski.*

It is possible the evidence of my father's services may be found in the public records of your State, but as such may not be the case, I furnish such particulars of my father's history, gathered from memoranda left by him, as will enable you to direct your inquiries to the proper sources for information. My Father was born in Westmoreland Co. Virga. Feb. 21. 1752— His father John Rochester was born at the same place- In the autumn of 1768 my father went to reside in Hillsborough, Orange Co. N. C. where he was engaged in the mercantile business with James Monroe & Col. John Hamilton until the commencement of the Revolutionary War- In 1775 he was appointed a member of *"the Committee of Safety"* for Orange

[244]Colonel Nathaniel Rochester, the founder of Rochester in New York, left three sons. One of these was Henry E. Rochester, who was a business leader in Rochester. Harriet A. Weed (ed.), *Autobiography of Thurlow Weed,* Boston, 1883, I, 346.

[245]Nathaniel Rochester was born in Virginia in 1752, moved to Granville County, North Carolina, and then to Hillsboro, where he engaged in mercantile business with several men, including Thomas Hart. A member of the Provincial Congress which met at Hillsboro in 1776, he was appointed by that body as major of the Orange militia. He became the paymaster to a battalion of minute men in the Hillsboro district. In 1782 with Thomas Hart he moved to Maryland, where he set up a flour and rope factory. In 1808 he was a presidential elector and member of the Maryland assembly. In 1810 he moved to New York and established a flour mill at Fallstown, the future city of Rochester. *Biog. Hist. of N. C.,* III, 341-343.

County, whose business was to promote the revolutionary spirit among the people—to procure arms and ammunition - make collections for the people of *Boston*- and to prevent the sale & use of East India Teas- In August of the same year he attended, as a member, the first provincial convention in N. Carolina— This Convention ordered the raising of four Regiments of Continential Troops - organized the minute men & militia System, & directed an election for another convention to meet in May 1776 to adopt a constitution &c— At this first Convention my father was appointed a major of militia & Paymaster to the minute-men & militia- In Feb. 1776 he was dispatched by Col. Thackston, his commanding officer, with two companies of Infantry & one of Cavalry in pursuit of Genl. McDonald who had collected a large body of Scotch (about 1000) in Cumberland Co. with the view of transporting them to join the British in New York, their destination was Wilmington- On reaching Devo's ferry, about 20 miles from headquarters, my father met about 500 of these Scotch, with McDonald, on their retreat, they having been met and defeated by Col. Caswell (afterwards Gov. of your State) at Moore's bridge— My father took McDonald & the 500 prisoners- Being a sparsely settled Country & unable to procure provisions for so many, he was obliged to discharge all but about 50 who were officers with whom he returned to head-quarters, where he found Col. Alexr. Martin— Marshall, in his life of Washington, mentions that Col. Martin took these prisoners— In May 1776 my Father attended, as a member, the Convention at Halifax, where a constitution was adopted- Six more Regiments of Continental Troops were ordered to be raised & their officers appointed, among whom my father, was appointed Commissary General, with the rank & pay of a Colonel for the N. Carolina line. after the adjournment of of the Convention he went to Wilmington to attend to his duties, taking with him Abishai Thomas as his Deputy, who was afterwards employed in one of the Departments of the Genl. Govt.- In the fall of this year (1776) my father was elected a member of the Legislature, which he attended in the winter of 1777— Nathaniel Macon was also a member. This Ligislature appointed my Father a Commissioner to establish & superintend a manufactory of Arms at Hillsborough- In 1780 he was appointed Colonel of Militia-

I am unable, from any minutes left by my father, to State the periods of his service, beyond what can be gathered from the incidents in his life above detailed. His father died in Virginia in 1754- His mother married a second husband *Thomas Critcher* about the year 1756 who removed with his family in the year 1763 to Granville Co. N. C.— By the second marriage his mother had three sons, *Thomas, James & John Critcher,* and two daughters who married Elijah & Charles Mitchell. His sister *Philis Rochester,* married a Mr. Saml. Morse & settled in Granville Co. N. C.— It is possible one or more of these brothers & Sisters may still be living, and if so will be able to give you information by which you can learn whether any of the revolutionary acquaintances of my father are living by whom his services may be proved- I will add another circumstance in my fathers history which may aid the object I have in view - In 1778 he engaged in business with Col. Thomas Hart, Father-in-Law to *Henry Clay,* and *James Brown.* Col. Hart then resided two miles west of Hillsborough where he had a considerable estate in Lands, Mills &c.

The inquiry may arise in your mind - "Why was not this Pension sought at an earlier day?" The only reply I can make is that it was owing to mere thoughtlessness. My Mother is comfortably provided for on the score of property but nothing beyond. If my fathers services in the Revolution really merit a pension, we think it alike due to his fame as a Soldier of the Revolution and as some recompense for the services rendered his country that his widow at least should enjoy the reward of those services- It is proper I should add also, that my Father was married in *1788* to Sophia Beatty of Fredericktown Maryland, his present widow who claims a Pension-

Should you be so fortunate as to find proof of my father's services, you will much oblige my mother by having it taken in due form & forwarding it under cover to my brother *Thomas H. Rochester* of this City,- I request you to give it such direction as my business calls me away from home a good deal- Any expense you may incur in the matter will be fully reimbursed, & I will avail myself of the opportunity to do so through the Hon. Thomas J. Patterson M. C. from this District— For your personal services in the business I will hold myself under great obligations to you, & will be most happy to fulfill in any way in which you may be pleased to command my humble Services—

> With Sentiments of high regard & respect
> I am your Obt. Servt.
> HENRY E. ROCHESTER

WPM-LC

Jesse P. Smith[246] to Willie P. Mangum.

CHAPEL HILL Augt. 15" 1844

Dear Sir.

It is my very agreeable duty, as President of the Dialectic Society, to inform you that you have been selected by that body to deliver an oration before the two literary Societies at the ensuing annual commencement. Next commencement day is the fiftieth anniversary of the Institution and we feel assured that your acceptance would add dignity and importance to the occasion. The Dialectic Society cherishes the hope that you will comply, believing that an oration from you would confer honor upon her and gratify the wishes of your friends throughout the State.

> Very respectfully
> JESSE P. SMITH

[Addressed:]

> Hon Willie P. Mangum,
> Red Mountain
> Orange Cy
> N. C.

WPM-LC

Henry E. Rochester to Willie P. Mangum.

ROCHESTER N. Y. Augt. 16. 1844

Dear Sir.

Allow me to presume so far upon the mutual interest which we feel in the approaching Presidential election, as to give you, on this envelope, a brief view of the aspect of political matters in this Section of the Union—

---

[246]After graduating from the University in 1845, Jesse Potts Smith settled near Fayetteville and became a lawyer and planter. Grant, *Alumni Hist. of U. N. C.,* 575.

We have just learned the final result of the State election in Indiana,[247] by which it seems the Whigs have a majority in both branches of the Legislature by which we secure a U. S. Senator- We have not learned sufficient from Illinois[248] to know the result - we have expected a defeat in that State, & if the result *should* be favorable to the Whigs, (which we can hardly hope) it will add strength to our now confident hope of electing Mr. Clay-

In this Section of New York the Whigs now & always have had a very large majority- In regard to the State at large I have no fears— With a *full vote* in this State the Whigs have *always* been in the majority - and from present indications we have reason to believe *every* Whig will vote this fall & secure a large majority-

Our opponents are distracted, disheartened & I might almost say dispairing- The result in your *noble State* has done much to produce this feeling among them.

There is great enthusiasm among the Whigs, quite as much as in 1840, & I see no reason why the result must not be as triumphant—

The abolitionists as a political party at best are no very formidable body & in the present contest will be lost sight of. They are, as you are aware I presume, hostile to Mr. Clay- but the nomination of Mr. Polk leaves them in a dilemma— There is no considerable number of them ever seriously thought of voting for Mr. Burney-[249] and it is now generally believed the most of them will take their places in the ranks of the two prominent parties—

in haste

yours &c.

H. E. Rochester

[Addressed:]

Hon. Willie P. Mangum

U. S. Senator

Red Mountain

Orange Co.

N. Carolina.

---

[247]In Indiana the Whigs and Democrats elected the same number of state senators, but the Whigs gained 55 out of the 100 in the lower house. *Hillsborough Recorder*, August 22, 29, 1844; *Niles' Register*, LXVI, 444.

[248]In Illinois the Democrats gained a large majority in the legislature and six out of the seven Congressional seats. *Niles' Register*, LXVI, 428; *Hillsborough Recorder*, August 22, 29, 1844.

[249]James G. Birney, the candidate of the Liberty Party.

WPM-D

David L. Swain to Willie P. Mangum.

CHAPEL HILL, 20. Aug. 1844.

My dear Sir,

I understand there are some vacancies in the Military Academy at West Point, that will be filled from the States at large on the recommendation of our Senators. - If this be so, my nephew Newton Coleman[250] at present a student of the University wishes to be advised of the fact, that he may in due season obtain and submit testimonials of his qualifications. - I would not myself be willing to speak as confidently in his behalf, as if he were unconnected with me, and yet I should feel bound to testify strongly.

Yours very sincerely,

D. L. SWAIN

[Addressed:] Honble. Willie P. Mangum,
Red Mountain
N. C.

[Postmarked:]
Chapel Hill, N C
Aug 21

WPM-LC

B. S. Gaither[251] & others to Willie P. Mangum.

MORGANTON 21st Aug: 1844

Hon. W. P. Mangum

Sir. We the undersigned, have been appointed as a committee to invite our Whig friends to attend a mass meeting to be held in Morganton on the 18th & 19th days of October next.

We take great pleasure in expressing to you the general wish of the Whigs in this region of the State that you would honour us with your presence on the occasion referred to & indulge the hope that you will not permit any slight circumstance to prevent your attendance.

You have no doubt observed the falling off in the Whig vote for Governor in this section of the State & will concur with

---

[250]A native of Buncombe County, Newton Coleman was a student at the University in 1844-1845. He became a lawyer and a member of the legislature as a representative of Buncombe in 1848-1849 before he moved to Missouri, where he continued his practice of law. *N. C. Manual,* 517; Grant, *Alumni Hist. of U. N. C.,* 123.

[251]This letter is written in Tod R. Caldwell's handwriting. The same is true of the following letter which he wrote on the same paper.

us in the belief that immediate & continued action should be had in every county in the State & particularly in the West where symptoms of disaffection have been shewn.

We have the honour to be
With great respect, Yr. obt. Svt.
B. S. GAITHER & others, com.

My Dear Sir.

On the preceding page you will receive an invitation from a committee to attend a mass meeting at this place on the 18th & 19th days of October next, to which I hope you will pardon me for adding my individual solicitation that you will favour us with your presence on that occasion. Our people will enter into this p[torn]t with a great deal of spirit & enthusiasm. I hazard little in sa[ying] that if we [torn] a favourable response from you & others [whom] we intend [to] invite, a larger concourse of persons [will] be congregated here at that time than has ever been witnessed in Western North Carolina. And I farther believe that if we can have such a meeting as we desire this Congressional will give Mr. Clay at least 5,000 majority. It will take very little I assure you to kindle such a fire of Excitement in Mr. Clay's behalf, in the bosom of our Mountain [torn] as never before burned in favour of any man either living or dead. The Polk men in this region are already disheartened and if we can only have such a gathering as we wish they will give up the contest without a "show of fight" and any man of them instead of electioneering for Polk, will be afraid on account of his own future personal popularity and ashamed to be seen with a Polk ticket in his hand - I feel assured, that when you recollect, in addition to what is above said the vote of No. Carolina for the last years has depended in a great measure upon us of the "Western Reserve" & that in any emergency we have been looked to [torn] so that it is upon that now for us to do our very best [torn] our earnest solicitation.

Minerva sends her love to you & all the family & joins me in the request, if you can make it convenient to [come] up, that you bring your family up with you [torn] will be a pleasant season to visit o[ur] mountains.

> With much respect
> I am Sir, Yr. obt. Svt.
> TOD. R. CALDWELL

Hon. W. P. Mangum.

P.S. An early answered is requested.

[Addressed:]

> Hon. W. P. Mangum
> U. S. Senator
> Red Mountain
> [Orange] County
> [N. C.]

WPM-LC

Nathan Sargent to Willie P. Mangum.

PHILA. Augt. 21. 1844

Hon Willie P. Mangum

My dear Sir

I received a few days ago, a letter from Mr Stanley[252] informing me that in consequence of a recent accident which happened to him, it would not be in his power to attend to the collecting of North Carolina's quota of the fund for the National Prize Banner- say $150- and he suggested the propriety of my writing to yourself upon the subject, believing that you could put to work the proper men in order to raise it. Mr. S. was, at the time he wrote, on the eve of departure for the sea shore. The accident he had met with, was being upset in a gig by which he had been much lamed. We have heard from nearly all the members of the Committee, from the different States, responding affirmatively to the call upon their respective States, for their contributions- *all* the Southern States save N. C. & La. I am getting up the banner, & intend it to be a very magnificent one- worthy of the State that shall win it.

---

[252]Edward Stanly.

The campaign is being carried on in this section of the country with great vigor & labor. In this & some other northern States, the Locos, with an audacity unparalleled, claim Mr Polk as the friend of protection, & denounce Mr Clay as opposed to it! And they ding this into the ears of their ignorant men in so confident a manner, that thousands really believe it, & cannot be persuaded to the contrary even by Polk's own declarations! But, nevertheless, we are making converts rapidly- Many of their prominent men have avowed their determination to vote for Mr Clay who still act with the party. Among these is Geo. M Hollenbach, of Luzerne Co. who was the Van Buren elector in 1840, & who was chairman of a democratic meeting the other day- after he had declared his intention to vote for Mr Clay.

If they unite, cordially on Shunk,[253] as their candidate for Governor, they will elect him; if not- & Gov Porter manifests a disposition to oppose his nomination- we shall elect Markle. Since my return from Washington, I have been keeping up a steady fire of hot shot, grape, cannister & ball, through the U. S. Gazette, the political department of which is under my charge- I am also occasionally on the stump.

We have been some what disappointed in Graham's vote, as well as at the result in Indiana. We looked for a larger majority.

With the best wishes for your health, accept the assurance of the cordial respect of

Your friend an

Obdt Servant

N. SARGENT

Nicholas Carroll[254] *to Willie P. Mangum.*

180 Prince St-

NEW YORK- Sunday 8th Sept. /44

My dear Sir

As a Lieutenant of the Great Captain I appeal to you. We are in danger - We see it undismayed. We thank God there *is* time to meet it- we believe, to ward it off.

---

[253]Thomas R. Shunk was the Democratic candidate. He won over James Markle, the Whig candidate, by a majority of 4,397. David R. Porter had been governor from 1838 to 1845. *Niles' Register*, LXVII, 112, 117.
[254]See above, III, 132n.

Silas Wright is nominated for Governor. He is the strongest
man the destructives *can* boast- he is the hardest man for us to
beat. He gives them that which before they lacked- strength &
union. With *any other* nomination our success was assured. The
field was to us an easy one. Now that field is studded with their
serried legions- and their consuls & proconsuls and *all* their subordinate officers are at their head, disciplining & marshalling
the banded forces- already flushed with anticipations of sure
victory. Their insolent challenge - ringing in our ears- our
blood boils to accept it & defy them. We approach the encounter
calmly & sternly- and like Spartacus in the Roman Arena we
cry out "Let them come- we are armed."

In the dread pause before the battle- we survey the field-
know every point of defence- and strengthen every breach or
weakness in our entrenchments.

The 'Natives' reversed affairs in the Spring.[255] I came home
then from Washington- traveling without rest to be here & in
season deposite my ballot among the '5000' who believed their independent course due to their principles & their own self vindication. The son of an Irishman- whose family at home even to
martyrdom, & here in '76 & subsequently, had proved their devotion to civil & religious liberty- could not- as a Catholic in belief & creed- he could not have done otherwise- I voted against
a party mercilessly proscriptive against foreigners- and maliciously vindictive towards my faith & religion. But reflection
& time- those "safe & sober moralists"- have thoroughly changed
the action & the views of the successful party. It is but their
due to declare that they have reformed our City Government
and fully discharged all their honest pledges. Then it was a
local matter- now it is changed- and *such* a change. Then it affected New York City only- now this Party are connected perhaps with the result of the Presidential election.

Last spring the Whigs (proper) cast 5.000, Tammany 20.000
& the Natives 24.000 votes- within 1000 of the *other* parties
united vote. Now the Natives are in the field to nominate members of Congress- State Senator & Assembly Ticket- The City

---

[255]The Nativist party originated in New York City. In 1843 the Whigs were defeated because
of the Irish and Germans. Many Democrats and Whigs, therefore, organized the Native American
Party to keep the government out of the hands of aliens. This party elected the mayor in 1844.
The same result was obtained in Philadelphia. In eastern cities the Nativist party almost absorbed
the Whigs. Strong feeling resulted in a petition to Congress to deprive aliens of the privilege of
voting until they had lived in this country twenty-five years. The fear in 1844 was that this party
might be a deciding factor in such states as New York and Pennsylvania. The Democrats accused
the Whigs of voting Native in local elections to gain the Nativists' support for President. Lambert,
Presidential Politics in U. S., 1841-1845, 180-197; McMaster, *Hist. of People of U. S.*, VII, 380-385.

sends *four* delegates to Congress- 13 to the Assembly & with *two* other counties makes the State Senatorial District. In the 3ᵈ District (Phoenix's) they have nominated John C. Hamilton (the worthiest son of the immortal Alexander) a thorough- staunch Whig- *devotedly* Clay- divested of herisies- uncontaminated by any 'isms' past or prospective- and in no manner *allied* to pipe-layerism, Scottism or Websterism. In the 4th (my residence) they propose to nominate Thos. M. Woodruff- an Independent Democrat- quasi Clay, in favor of the Tariff- against annexation & irreconcilable to Tammany. In the 5th the nomination will lay between a candidate of the *same* stamp or a Whig- In the 6ᵗʰ. they have nominated Hamilton Fish, our present excellent member. This will give us 1600 majority in the 3,ᵈ 300 in the 4ᵗʰ. 300 in the 5ᵗʰ & 500 in the 6ᵗʰ. They propose to give us ½ the Assembly ticket the other ½ Independent Democratic and *all* pledged to vote for *our* U. S. S. The State Senator will be a mutual nominee. With this Union we sweep everything- *without* it we may go out of New York in an overwhelming minority- say 10.000.* With this Union we will secure at least 12 to 1500 on our Electoral vote- without it we are whipped "horse- foot & dragoon." The course we propose (in favor of uniting) is to let them make the nominations, advising with us as they proceed- and then upon the eve of the election rally unanimously in their favor. The ONLY objection to *this* course is presented by the ambitious who are desirous of Independent Nominations, that they may be conspicuous, and by those whose absorbing fore[?] thirst for Spirits- hankered after longed for as "Daphne by the eager Day God," whose selfishness & venality now present the *only* barrier to this arrangement. God of Heaven is it to be borne- at this time- when the state is no less than the salvation of the nation - is this to be endured for an instant? Before my love for Henry Clay, which has known no laggard's soul since my boyhood- should couple itself with one solitary selfishness to defile the sanctuary where I have nursed it in all trials, & kept it pure & holy under every ordeal, I would go dig paving stones to give bread to my family.

If in Union with *this* Party there was even a temporary yielding of principle- the emergency & the occasion, would more than justify the momentary forgetfulness. What have they to suffer, in comparison with the sacrifice the *Catholic*

Whigs offer as an oblation on this altar of "union for the sake of the Union." It is we, if any, who for the time being look the result, rather than the principle, full in the face & to clutch that, will drive the dagger, if needed, into our own breasts. But there is no abandonment- no retreat from principle. It is *Duty* now to effect this Union- not grudgingly- reluctantly but cheerfully & earnestly- with a devotion & a love of our cause which will strew the thorny way- if it be so- with flowers- and render its performance dear to us hereafter, as the memory of acts whereby we *saved* our country in an hour of peril.

not exaggerated.

Elsewhere- everywhere the news is cheering- Vermont has proved true- of a verity she is "the star that never has set." Maine will do well- *All* the Eastern States- But here- & New Jersey and Pennsylvania- *there* is the danger. From this strait we must be suddenly relieved- Pause- there is no time for pause "the war has been declared" and the enemy, like dragon's teeth have sprung from the earth & like Pallas ready armed.- United- wary & untiring we can beat them 20.000 in this State- But we require *all these* qualities, acting in concert, to beat the foe. *You are not* needed now by the 'glorious old North.' You have taken care of her. Do- do come here- come among us & give us the benefit of your advice, counsel & direction- Look at the stake - The result here may be the election of Henry Clay- it might be his defeat- From a contemplation like the latter I shrink as from an accumulation of horrors that appals patriots & rejoices friends & traitors only. I would hear your trumpet tones peal out here to *awe* or to assure - whichever might in the exigency be most important. I remember, that you have told me that there have been times of trial since '41, [illegible] when your "coming— was more effectual *even* with Senators than reasoning." I have seen enough recently to convince me that with our 'dogs in the manger' *threats* are more formidable weapons than argument or entreaty. It is usless to invoke patriotism in a heart that has no answering chord to any divinity but self-

If you cannot come *at once*- please answer this by return mail- The time for action is narrowing down to days- The danger of defeat has been thrust upon us at the instant and

upon the echo we sound the alarm- Come- do come if you can-
but write, if you cannot, by the return mail & believe me

Faithfully- sincerely

Yr friend & sert.

N. CARROLL

Hon. Willie P. Mangum
  Private and *important*

WPM-LC

Hamilton C. Jones to Willie P. Mangum.

LINCOLNTON Sept 9 1844

My Dear Sir

I was once indebted to you for your good offices in electing
me solicitor, and for that I have endeavoured to show my gratitude in a substantial way. But my term is now out, and I shall
be before the next legislature for a renewal of the lease. Mr
Guion[256] is my competitor and as Mr Waddell is his brother in-
Law it is calculated that he will endeavor to take the whole
Orange delegation with him for Mr. G. If there is any man in
the west of North Carolina who has worked harder and sacrificed more than I have I do not know who he is. I laboured
seven long years at the Watchman at a dead loss (knowing it
too) for the consolidation of the Whig party in the west; and
all know that I had a prime agency in effecting this purpose:
besides that; I gave up one of the most lucrative practices as a
Lawyer of any one in my circuit which I have totally lost and
have only returned to the practice as a solicitor- I have many
suits of consequence scattered along this circuit but they will
not sustain me without my office. If I am ejected I shall therefore have to begin anew in a new circut You can see how disastrous must be all my prospects in this view of the matter-
Please lay these matters upon your members and let them
understand why I do not think Whigs ought to proscribe me:
If I have done any thing culpable or am incompetent- or negligent, and any respectable member of the profession will say so
of me I will not complain: but I understand that it is put on

---

[256]Haywood W. Guion, of Lincolnton, 1814-1876, after graduation from the University of
North Carolina, became a lawyer and the author of a scientific treatise called *The Comet.* An active
Whig, he was chairman of the committee which invited Mangum to the Whig rally in 1844 and
a delegate to the State Whig Convention in 1846. Battle, *Hist. of U. N. C.,* I, 422; Grant, *Alumni
Hist. of U. N. C.,* 241; *Greensborough Patriot,* January 24, 1846.

no such ground but simply because Mr. Guion is a good whig and a gentleman and wants the office. I admit such to the fact but I submit to those who know me if they have any thing to complain of me in my conduct of the office: of a proper bearing in other respects. As to wanting the office I am ashamed to say that notwithstanding a good deal of good fortune and some very good *strikes* I am still much in debt and do not know what I shall do without it. Please talk to such of your delegation as you can approach on the subject and write to me whether I may expect anything from that quarter"—

What do you think of my classmate Mr Polk for president- We never thought him any great things atho he got the first honor- the vote of the class would have put Hu Waddell ahead of him as a man of genius altho he did get the honor. He was certainly a very ignorant man of all the current knowledge of the world when he quit college and whether he has gathered as much as Old Hickory knew when he was made President I would not pretend to say. But some how or some other how in my ruminations on this matter I had supposed that it required something like distinguished qualities to entitle a man to that office- Some one asked Wm. Cost Johnson if it was a fact that he was for James K Polk for President. He answered no sir: I cant go that "for he is under the standard" on being asked to explain: he said there is an old statute still in force in Maryland that any man may take up and *cut* any stallion *under fourteen hands high* running at large. He considered Mr P. under 14.- I will vouch that Mr. Clay goes ahead of Mr. Graham in the west. Probably by a large difference.

Very truly
Yours
H. C. JONES

[Addressed:]

Honble. Willie P. Mangum
Red Mountain
Orange County
N. C.

WPM-LC

Colin McIver to Willie P. Mangum.[257]

FAYETTEVILLE, 10th Septr 1844.

My dear Sir,

Although, since the origin of our acquaintance, in this place, more than thirty years ago, I have, occasionally had the privilege of enjoying a few *personal & private interviews* with you, at Washington City and elsewhere; & those, all of a pleasant character; yet, I feel some regret, in not being able to say that I have ever been favoured, even to the amount of a single line, with any of the productions of your *pen.* An occasional note from you, I have, once & again, attempted to elicit; but, as yet, I have herein been unsuccessful. Will you *pardon* me, my dear Sir, for making *one effort more;-* (if unsuccessful, probably the last,)- not, I assure you, with the least desire to provoke you into that state of mind, in which a Judge, of a former age, yielded to the wishes of his petitioner, lest he should be wearied by continual importunity;- but, because it would be truly gratifying to me, to possess some evidence, *in a tangible form.* that, at least, so far as *you* are concerned, political preferment has not superinduced a foregetfulness of former days. It is true, indeed, that, in each of my former communications, I did solicit, from you, a particular favour; & I suppose, that, for reasons perfectly satisfactory to yourself, you judged it best not to grant that favour: but, yet, there was no need, that you should, therefore, remain silent. I should be unworthy to be called a *disciple* of CHRIST, & still more unworthy of appearing, publicly, before men, as his *Ambassador,* were I incapable of bearing in such a matter, a refusal, without suffering my equanimity to be, in the least degree, disturbed. But, I will not ascribe your silence to any apprehensions of this kind. I will rather take it for granted, that my letters reached you at inconvenient junctures, when the *public interest* pre-occupied all your time, & absorbed all your attention; & that, when intervals of leisure afterwards occurred, if my letters met your eye, you had concluded, that the proper season of responding to them, had passed away. This probably was especially the case, in relation to my last communication. It was written about a week before the opening of the last Session of Congress, & the original, or first-written draught of it,

---

[257]Compare C. McIver to W. P. Mangum, November 27, 1843.

was forwarded to your residence, in Orange; & a duplicate copy of it, was sent to the City of Washington.

Ever since I became capable of serious reflection, I have been in the habit of tracing the hand of Divine Providence, in reference to all the occurrences of my life; &, in taking a retrospect of the last forty years, I do not recollect, that I have ever met with a disappointment, of any kind, which was not, afterwards, over-ruled, to my advantage. With truth & confidence, I can apply this remark, to the failure of the object I had, in view, when I last wrote to you; &, should a similar disappointment again occur, I doubt not, but it will be speedily followed with a similar result.

While *I* was employed, at & about home, in the exercise of various duties, I was happy to know, that *you, & your fellow members of the Senate,* were *so faithfully & so ably served, in the office of Chaplain,* by my very worthy & excellent Brother, *The Rev.ᵈ Septimus Tuston.* I am sure, however, that *he* will not consider it incompatible with the highest fraternal regard for him, or be disposed to question the sincereity of that regard, should I venture to say that I think he has occupied the station here alluded to, sufficiently long; & that he might, now with propriety, at least for a season, yield the special field of labour, to some other *brother-* (or, shall I presume to say, to a *Father* in CHRIST?)- who might be desirous of promoting the spiritual welfare of his country, in the same sphere.

From what I have herein said, you will, doubtless, naturally infer, that, while I am well pleased that I was disappointed, last winter, it would, nevertheless, be quite gratifying to me, if through your kind influence, I could, for the next session of Congress, be chosen chaplain to the Senate. It is ever so. Are you disposed to enquire, *Why* I wish the appointment, during the ensuing Session, rather than at another time?—I will tell you.— I have, now, & have had ever since the close of last winter, a little book ready for the press, which I am desirous to dedicate to *a* President of the United States. For reasons, which, I presume, need not be stated to a man of your discernment, *I will not dedicate it to John Tyler.* I wish, therefore, to be in Washington, when the expected inauguration of Mr. Clay shall take place, that I may have the pleasure of waiting on him, in person, to ask his permission to prefix his name to my forthcoming volume; &, in such an event, I think, there would be a peculiar appropriateness in my waiting on him, for such a purpose, if, at the same time, I shall have received the appointment alluded to.

Having said this much, it is proper, that I should here add a few words, as to the subject-matter of my book. It contains upwards of 500 sententious, aphoretical maxims, designed to guide the habitual course of action, of those, who, in conducting the affairs of State, would desire to regulate their practice by the principles revealed in the Bible. Such a work, you will readily say, - if well executed, - would be a very suitable pocket-companion for every member of Congress. That you may form some idea of the character of the work I here speak of, I will fill the next page of this sheet, with some of the maxims it contains by way of specimen.

I hope this will reach you, at an interval of leisure; & find you free from other engagements, at least so far as to admit of your devoting a few moments to the gratification of an old friend.

Anxiously expecting the pleasure of an early communication from you, I remain, with unfeigned esteem,— My dear Sir,—

Yours truly,
Colin McIver

A few political maxims

1. Religion & piety are the best securities of a nation.
2. Righteousness supports the government; & will never shake it.
3. National repentance & reformation, bring national plenty, peace, & prosperity.
4. Nothing contributes more to the making of a Nation considerable abroad, valuable to its friends, & formidable to its enemies, than religion reigning in it. For, who can be against those that have God for them? And He is certainly for those that are sincerely for [Him].
5. Government is a burthen:- It is a burthen of care & trouble to those who make cons[tant] duty of it; &, to those who do not, it will prove a heavier burthen, in the day of account, when they fall under the doom of the unprofitable servant, that buried his talent.

6. They that humble themselves shall be exalted; & those are most fit for government, who are least ambitious of it.

7. Those make out the best title to public honours, that lay out themselves the most for the public good, & obtain mercy of the Lord to be faithful & useful.

8. Better to die in honour, than live in bondage.

9. Those that are employed in public trusts, must not think to benefit themselves only by their toils & hazards, but must aim at the advantage of the community.

10. An interest in the affections of the people, is a great advantage; & a great encouragement to those that were called to public trusts, of what kind soever.

11. *Seest thou a man diligent in his business,* & dutiful to his superiors, willing to stoop, & willing to take pains? He stands fair for preferment.

12. Those are unfit & unworthy to rule over men, who are not willing that God should rule over them.

13. Men's preferment, instead of discharging them from their obedience to God, obliges them so much the more to it.

14. A good ruler cannot think himself happy, unless his country be so.

15. Two things recommend a man to popular esteem, greatness & goodness.

16. We do not hinder our success by preparing for disappointment.

17. Acts of sincerity are seldom acts of policy.

[Addressed:]

> Honble. Wyllie P. Mangum Esqr. M. C.
> Red Mountain P. O.
> Orange County
> North Carolina.

WPM-LC

Thomas Williams, Jr., and others to Willie P. Mangum.

CIRCULAR.[258]

[Sept 11 44]

Sir:

The Whigs of Alabama having determined to hold a General Mass Convention of the State in this place, on *Thursday the*

---

[258]This is a printed circular.

24th of October next, to make one more struggle for the redemption of our fair and beautiful state from the thraldom of Locofocoism, - we, a committee appointed by the Clay club of this city, have the honor to invite your presence and aid on that occasion; believing as we do that the co-operation of our distinguished fellow Whigs will greatly assist us in effecting a consummation so devoutly to be wished. We shall wait with much anxiety for your reply.

Very truly yours, &c.

COMMITTEE:

THOS. WILLIAMS JR.,	JESSE P. TAYLOR,
J. J. HUTCHINSON,	B. S. BIBB,
J. C. BATES,	S. C. OLIVER,
S. D. HOLT,	M. ASHURST,
R. C. CUMMINGS,	WM. RIVES,
T. J. VICKERS,	R. J. WARE,
GEORGE RIVES,	R. C. BUNTING.

Montgomery, Ala., Sept. 11th, 1844.

[Addressed:]

Hon. W. P. Mangum
Raleigh, N. C

If misdirected the P. M. will please forward.

———

WPM-LC

Henry Clay to Willie P. Mangum and Enclosure.

ASHLAND [Ky.] 11ᵗʰ. Sept. 1844.

My Dear Sir,

I was very happy to receive your favor of the 23ᵈ of July. Your election did not turn out quite [as] well as you anticipated, and its result was the reverse of what was anticipated when I was at Raleigh, at which time no fears were entertained for the election of the Governor, but great apprehensions were entertained about the Legislature. What is the present state of your prospects? Our opponents are manifestly making great exertions every where, and affect if they do not feel great confidence in the issue of the contest. Their whole system now seems to be directed to the propogation of the most detestable libels and lies. Is it producing any effect in North Carolina? If I am to credit the enclosed letter it is doing us mischief there. Do you know the writers of it? The old story to which they allude I thought had been buried so low that it could never rise[to] the surface again. Our friends at Washington have been getting up an abridged history of all the facts, documents, and proofs respecting that old story, and if you think it worth while I wish you would write to Green and have some of them distributed in your State. The Blair letters to which the enclosed refers, or rather copies of them are in the possession of Benj. Watkins Leigh of Richmond with authority to show them to any gentleman that may be desirous of perusing them. The truth is that so far as relates to the charge against me, they contain strong corroborative proof of its falsity: but they are sportive, playful, and written in all the familiarity of private correspondence, to the violation of which in any case I do not wish to give my sanction.

I am greatly obliged to you for the friendly solicitude you entertain about my health, and I am happy to inform you that it is now very good. I hope this letter will find yours equally so. Owing to the great extent of my correspondence, I am obliged to obtain the assistance of one of my sons who writes this letter as my amanuensis upon my dictation.

I am always, your friend
And obedient servant-

H. CLAY.

The Honble - Willie P. Mangum.

[Addressed:]

The Honble - Willie P. Mangum
President of the Senate
Red Mountain
Orange County
North Carolina.

Enclosure

HALIFAX N. C. 27th. Augt. 1844

Hon: H. Clay

My dear Sir,

As much has been said in relation to your letter addressed to Mr. Blair many years ago, in regard to the election of the Hon: J. Q. Adams to the Presidency, when & where you were accused of bargain & corruption in that election;[259] We have thought proper to ask of you, if you ever in a solitary instance refused directly or indirectly to permit the letter to be published, if not, we respectfully ask will you now give your consent to publish it?

Since the Hon: L. Boyds'[260] expose of the matter in Congress, the Whigs have been losing ground in this State, and we have no doubt unless the letter is published Polk & Dallas will carry it in Nov[r]. next.

An answer at your earliest convenience is requested—

Respectully

Yr. obt. Svts

MAJOR A. WILLCOX[261]

W. H. HARDEE

[Addressed:]

Hon: H. Clay

Lexington

Ky.

———

WPM-LC

Robert Ransom to Willie P. Mangum.

Sept[r]. 12th. 1844

D[r]. Sir

& friend

Your letter in answer to my two,[262] was recd. and all arrangements made to start to see you this day. But our worthy

---

[259]At the time of the election of 1824 Clay and F. P. Blair were close friends. Clay wrote Blair several letters during the time that the election was in the hands of the members of the House of Representatives. Because of the constant reference by the Democrats in the campaign of 1844 to Clay's part in a "corrupt bargain" in 1823, the Whigs insisted that the correspondence with Blair be published. Finally on October 7, 1844, Benjamin Watkins Leigh sent to the Richmond *Whig* for publication his letter and copies of two letters which Clay had written Blair in 1825. In 1827 Clay had received certified copies of the Blair letters. He sent copies of these to Leigh in the summer of 1844. *Niles' Register,* LXVII, 84-85; Van Deusen, *Life of Clay,* 180-184.

[260]Linn Boyd, of Tennessee, was a member of Congress as a Democrat in 1835-1837 and 1839-1855. *Biog. Dir. of Cong.,* 729.

[261]Major A. Willcox was a member of the North Carolina legislature in 1825 and 1838. *N. C. Manual,* 641, 717.

[262]See above, Robert Ransom to W. P. Mangum, August 8, 1844.

and venerable friend Col. Alston, begs me to say to you, that he is compelled to defer the Visit, until the first week in Octr. He finds that he must go to Petersburg on business that cant be delayed, and hopes he will not incommode your arrangements, if he does, he wishes you to inform him. He says he will certainly be at your House by the 7th. or 8th. of Oct^r.

I have no news from this county of Dogmatical arristocracy, we gained 22 votes for Graham, and will add as many more for Clay. Our Watering places are full to overflowing, a large majority for Clay.

Hoping this may find you rapidly recovering, & able to do battle in our Heavenly Cause, I am, as ever your devoted friend. With Great respect.

ROBT. RANSOM.

Honl.
Willie P. Mangum

[Addressed:]

Honl. Willie P. Mangum
Red Mountain
Orrange County N. C.

WPM-LC

Circular of Maine Whig State Central Committee

CIRCULAR.[263]

MAINE, September 16, 1844.

The State Committee of the Whigs of Maine, deem it their duty to address this brief note to their friends in other States, in relation to the result of our recent State Election. We do this not for the purpose of extenuating our defeat,[264] or of promising to remedy the effect, by the next Election in November. We presume that no one seriously believed that we should succeed over both the other parties, although some indulged the hope that we might defeat the choice of Governor by a majority

---

[263]This is a printed circular.
[264]The results in Maine were:
Whig candidate for Governor 24,777
Democratic candidate for Governor 28,863
Anti-Slavery candidate for Governor 3,689
Naturally the Democrats rejoiced that they carried the state over the combined votes of the two opponents. The Whigs, on the other hand, tried to explain away the defeat. *National Intelligencer,* September 14, 1844.

of the people, but probably some may be disappointed by the amount of the majority against us. We confess we have been somewhat disappointed in the result, so far as the relative votes of the parties are concerned, - But we beg leave to observe,

1. That we are much more disappointed by the decrease in the Whig vote, than by the increase of the other party. The whole vote of the State will about equal the vote of 1840. The natural increase of population would give our opponents all the increase which they show by their recent vote. It is quite clear that many thousand Whigs have not voted, for the sum total of the whole vote of all parties against the "Democratic," is less than the Whig vote of 1840.

2. We feel bound to say that this failure to bring out the full vote was unexpected, and it is the principal object of this letter to give you this information, in order to enable you to take such measures as may be necessary to prevent a like result in your State. The preparation on the part of the Whigs generally, was, as we believed before the Election, ample and thorough. We had many public meetings in every County, which were well attended *by the Whigs,* and the great doctrines of the party fully explained and defended by able, eloquent and untiring advocates. We have had more and better speaking than ever before. Our meetings have been full and enthusiastic. We have no doubt that among thinking men, we had many changes in our favor. The arguments presented to the people, were clear, calm, cogent, unanswerable and *unanswered.*

3. Since the Election we are satisfied that we had not a thorough, perfect and effective *detailed organization.* We had Committees enough appointed, but our efforts and our zeal were expended too much in public gatherings and Club room discussions. We needed more of the school-district organization, and that accurate and effective arrangement, by which every individual in every neighborhood is brought out to the polls. We are satisfied that nothing short of this kind of organization, under the charge of active, discreet and perservering men, will secure a full vote of the Whig party anywhere. We have relied too much upon public gatherings and able arguments. The *Whigs* have been there in great numbers, but our opponents have taken great pains, and generally with success, to keep their party away from Whig meetings

4. Our opponents commenced and carried out a system based upon misrepresentation and calumny - denouncing Mr. Clay especially. They appealed constantly to the lowest and vilest passions and prejudices, and particularly relied upon exciting the hatred of the poor against the rich - the *employed* against the *employer*, the laborer against the man who furnished capital. They represented in every place, and to every person whom they could reach, publicly or privately, that the protective system of the Whigs was a scheme devised to increase the profits of Capital, and to depress and injure the working man - a tax on the farmer for the benefit solely of the rich manufacturer. They repudiated the principle of protection as an element in the formation of a tariff, and advocated the revenue principle as the only allowable mode, viz: - such a duty on every article as will produce the most revenue, irrespective of the effect on the industry of the Country. They particularly denounced the duty on iron and sugar, and represented Maine as suffering grievously for the benefit of Pennsylvania and Louisianna. We think our friends in those States ought to understand these facts. It is only since the day of the Election, that we have learned the extent of the influence brought to bear, to poison the minds of the laborers against the tariff doctrines of the Whigs. The same influence will be noiselessly, but unless met and counteracted, effectively used in other States.

5. Our opponents were furnished from some source, with a plentiful supply of money - whether it came from English Manufacturers or Texas bond holders, or office holders or seekers, or from all, we know not. The fact is certain. And doubtless the same fund will supply in the same manner, all the money which can be used advantageously in every other State.

We have felt it to be our duty to make this communication to you in a spirit of frankness, to put you into possession of the facts recited, and in the hope and belief that you may from these facts and suggestions, derive some hints which may be of advantage in preparing for the coming contest in your State. If in any degree the result of our Election has disappointed any of our friends abroad, we can only hope that our experience and observation of the mode and manner of conducting the campaign by our opponents, may enable them to avoid our errors, and to redouble their diligence, to secure the great - the

vital point, a perfect, systematic and *detail* organization, by
which it shall be beforehand rendered certain that every voter
will be at the polls. We would especially hope that the *business
men,* who are most directly and deeply interested in the success
and permancy of Whig principles, will in each State enter into
the contest with the spirit, activity and personal effort, for
which they were distinguished in 1840.

JOSIAH S. LITTLE,	)	
GIDEON TUCKER,	)	
J. WINGATE CARR,	)	Maine
WILLIAM C. HAMMATT,	)	Whig State
MOSES L. APPLETON,	)	Central
RICHARD F. PERKINS,	)	Committee.
AARON HAYDEN,	)	
E. WILDER FARLEY.	)	

WPM-LC

Nathaniel J. Palmer[265] to Willie P. Mangum.

ROSEBOROUGH, Sept. 17th 1844

Dear Sir.

We are about to establish a Female Institute of high character in Milton[266] to be under the Patronage of the Baptists or
friends of the Baptist cause in four different Associations.
Twelve of the Trustees to reside in the bounds of the Beulah
Association and Six in each of the other Associations. This is to
request that you will permit us to use your name as one of the
Trustees in the Flat River Association. We do not ask you to
assume any responsibility, but simply to give us the influence
of your name and countenance in the promotion of the interests
of the Institution. The Baptists, are the most numerous and
in the aggregate the most wealthy denomination in the State
and I rejoice to see that they are about to take that stand in

----

[265]See above, I, 414n.
[266]Four Baptist associations obtained from the legislature, December 24, 1844, a charter for
the Milton Female Institute. In the charter W. A. Graham, Calvin Graves, and Willie P. Mangum
were among those designated as members of the board of trustees. The school was opened January
1, 1845. In 1849 the charter was amended to permit the same trustees to operate the Beulah Male
Academy. G. W. Paschal, "Baptist Academies in North Carolina," *N. C. Hist. Review,* XXVIII, 51;
N. C. Laws, 1844-1845, 148-150.

the promotion of education which will elevate their character and extend their influence. Judge Settle, Mr. Kerr and other gentlemen of high standing will be numbered with the Trustees.

I should be pleased if you could visit Milton or Yanceyville before the Presidential Election. Our County Court meets the 30th of this month. Can you not be there then. The Baptist State Convention which will probably be the largest Religious Assembly ever convened in the State will meet in Raleigh on the Friday preceding the 3rd Sabbath in October. Please write to me on the receipt of this

Yours truly,
NATHANIEL J. PALMER.

Hon. W. P. Mangum.

[Addressed:]

> Hon. Willie P. Mangum,
> Red Mountain,
> Orange County,
> N. C.

Politeness of
G. W. Jomes Esqr.

WPM-LC

John Sergeant and others to Willie P. Mangum.

PHILADA Septr 17, 1844

Dear Sir,

It has been determined to hold a Grand Convention of the Whigs of the Eastern Counties of Penna in the City of Philada on Tuesday the 1st. day of October.— The importance of the State Election which takes place in the following week authorizes this appeal to the patriotism of our Whig brethren throughout the State and the Union.— We invite you earnestly & specially to come amongst us on this occasion.- It is an invitation not tendered as a matter of form.— We sincerely desire the opportunity at our own home to testify anew our high sense of your public services and to have the opportunity of exhibiting to you the enthusiasm of the Whigs of Pennsylvania.

We are, very respectfully
Your friends,

JOHN SERGEANT	CHARLES GIBBONS
JOSIAH RANDALL	SAM W. WEER
WILLIAM B. REED	JAS. TXAGUAIN[?] [BRYNAIS]
HENRY WHITE	JACOB STRATTAN
JOS R CHANDLER	ALEXANDER H FREEMAN
MELOR MOWBOYD [illegible]	JOHN H WITHERS

Hon: W. P Mangum

   North Carolina—

Free

J. R. INGERSOLL

[Addressed:]

       Hon. Willie P. Mangum
         Red Mountain
         Orange Co.
         North Carolina

WPM-LC

R. J. Mitchell[267] *to Willie P. Mangum.*

[Sept. 27, 1844]

1842.   Hon. W. P. Mangum,
July 22.   To R. J. Mitchell Dr.

To Subscription to the Oxford Mercury
    from 29th Dec. '41. to Sept. 8th. 1843.—$5.00

OXFORD, N. C. Sept. 27, '44.

Dear Sir: - Enclosed I send you your account up to the end of
the time I was publisher of the Mercury. You will confer a

---

[267]The *Oxford Mercury and District Telegram* was published by John Cameron 1841-1843.
C. H. Wiley was the editor. *Check List of U. S. Newspapers in Duke General Library,* IV, 590.

favor by forwarding it as early as convenient. If you wish to pay for the present year, I am authorized to receipt for the same.

Yours very respectfully,

R. J. MITCHELL

Hon. W. P. Mangum.

[Addressed:]

Hon. W. P. Mangum
Red Mountain
Orange Co.
N. C.

WPM-LC

David Lambert to Willie P. Mangum.

NEW YORK, Sept. 29th. 1844

Hon. Willie P. Mangum,

Dear Sir,

You will probably be somewhat surprised at receiving a letter from me dated at this City, and perhaps still more when I inform you that I have taken up my residence here- I effected the exchange into the Custom House here through Gov. Van Ess[268] which I had expected to effect thro' Mr. Ferris had the latter been confirmed as Collector- My family have not yet joined me but I expect Fredrica and our oldest boy early next month- I presume you have heard that we have had the misfortune of losing the infant-

New York is in a state of great excitement now in reference to politics- Meetings of both parties are held almost every night- The Whig meeting of Thursday night was really a great affair- The papers have doubtless given you some account of it and also of the outrageous assault made on a portion of the Whig procession by the infamous wretches of the *Empire Club* - Cassius M[arcellus] Clay of Ky. is here, and with Mr. Webster

---

[268]Cornelius Peter Van Ness 1782-1852, a former governor of New York and minister to Spain in 1829-1837. Tyler appointed him Collector of Customs at New York in 1844. Polk at first retained him in this office, but Van Buren soon had him removed. M. M. Quaife (ed.), *The Diary of James K. Polk During His Presidency, 1845-1849.* 1910, I, 95; F. J. Jameson (ed.), *Correspondence of John C. Calhoun,* A. H. A. *Annual Report* for 1899, II, 532, 1004, 1038, 1039.

will address a meeting at Syracuse this week- Leslie Combs[269] has been here and is doing his best. J. N. Reynolds[270] is making a great noise, and our good friend Jos. Hoxie continues to sing Whig songs and make speeches.

Meanwhile the Democrats are not idle- They are exerting themselves to the uttermost, and have certainly made a great hit in the nomination of Silas Wright, while our friends picked out one of their feeblest men in Fillmore,[271] who has no personal popularity and labors under the disadvantage of not being generally known-

I confess I am by no means sanguine that the Whigs will carry the State- The leaders certainly are indefatigable, but there is nothing like the enthusiasm that was displayed here in 1840. The event however must soon be known-

Capt. Tyler made an excellent appointment in the case of Gov. Van Ess-He is an excellent officer, and gives his time exclusively to the legitimate business of his office- I know not when so large a proportion of the public revenues could be deposited in safer or more competent hands

Should any thing occur here of a political character likely to be interesting I will take the pleasure of addressing you again soon

Meanwhile believe me
Respectfully & truly yours
DAVID LAMBERT-

We are in the midst of a violent equinoctial gale which will probably do serious damage to the shipping- I am residing close to the Battery and it is a beautiful sight to look out at the bay, covered with shipping, dashed in every direction by the waves. I never saw so rough a Sea in the Bay as at this moment-

[269]Leslie Combs was a Kentucky Whig who served as a member of the Kentucky legislature and who wrote pamphlets and made speeches against Jackson. He was an ardent supporter of Clay. Bassett (ed.), *Cor. of Jackson*, III, 379, 380, 439, 440; *D. A. B.*, IV, 328.

[270]J. N. Reynolds had been very active in the campaign of 1840. He declined being a candidate for the New York legislature in that year in order that he might give more time to the election of Harrison. He was president of the Central Democartic Republican Committee of Tippecanoe and other Harrison associations in New York City. In 1844 he supported Clay with the same enthusiasm. *Hillsborough Recorder*, November 12, 1840.

[271]Seward had selected Millard Fillmore to be the Whig candidate for governor. Wright won by a majority of 10,030, and Polk carried the state by a 5010 majority. *Niles' Register*, LXVII, 208.

WPM-LC

S. Starkweather[272] to Willie P. Mangum.

Sunday 30 Sept 1844

My Dear Friend,

As I told you some time since we have been much distressed by Mr. Clay's letter relative to Cassius M Clay,[273] but are partially recovering from it- I have just met and old most intelligent friend from michigan who says the state was safe before but that now he thinks we have little or no chance - Yet I hope our friends will rally again. The great meeting here last thursday has been powerful in its effects and an entirely new feeling is among us It was most unfortunate that Van Buren was withdrawn Polk is a much harder candidate for us—

The contest with us will be hard & close. If N. Jersey & Pennsylvania go against us by small votes & we carry Ohio N York is safe- But if we lose all these States & by a discouraging vote next month all is lost.

Yours truly
S. STARKWEATHER

[Addressed:]

Hon W. P. Mangum
Red Mountain
Orange Co
N Carolina

WPM-LC

John H. Pleasants and others to Willie P. Mangum.

CIRCULAR.[274]

To
Hon. Willie P. Mangum

RICHMOND, October 1, 1844.
Sir,

The undersigned have been designated as a Committee of Invitation by the Central State Whig Committee, to act in con-

[272]See above, 154.
[273]In the course of the campaign of 1844 many attributed Henry Clay's opposition to annexation to abolitionism. Clay's cousin, Cassius M. Clay, gave grounds for this accusation. In traveling in the anti-slavery regions and speaking for his kinsman, Cassius Clay encouraged the anti-slavery people to believe that Henry Clay was opposed to slave expansion. The South, as a result, became less enthusiastic about Clay's candidacy. Henry Clay, therefore, repudiated his cousin. Van Deusen, *Life of Clay*, 371-372; Poage, *Henry Clay and the Whig Party*, 140.
[274]This is a printed circular.

junction with the Williamsburg Committee, in inviting guests to the York Town Convention, on the 18th and 19th of October, in pursuance of the request of the latter; and in discharge of that duty, have the honor of requesting your presence on the occasion.

We beg leave to say that we regard the York Town Convention as of very great, and perhaps decisive importance. We feel persuaded, from the most authentic intelligence, that it is quite within the power of strenuous exertion to retrieve that Congressional District to the Whigs, and to replace it where it stood in 1840. To succeed in this effort, is almost certainly to succeed in securing the vote of Virginia to her native son, Henry Clay - an object, next to that of his election, not only of high political importance, but of the greatest personal solicitude to every Whig. We therefore emphatically ask your cooperation.

We have the honor to be &c.

> JOHN H. PLEASANTS,
> SAML. F. ADIE,
> JAS. W. PEGRAM,
> JOHN A. MEREDITH,
> R. T. DANIEL,
> THOS. NELSON, M. D.
> A. L. WARNER, M. D.

CIRCULAR—#2.

RICHMOND (alias Great coon Den) Oct. 1st[275]
1844
Little Coon Den 1. P M

My Dear Judge

In haste I drop you a few lines & to forward you an invitation by the request of the Committee— Come my good Friend, come! Come do, and you shall be protected from all Edmond's & such trash—

I shall write today to friends Crittenden, (slim Jim) Morehead, Garret Davis, Genl. Combs, Foster and Jarnagan, also Schanks of Ohio, (I don't know that I have spelt his name right)

------

[275]This letter is written on the same sheet as the preceding printed invitation.

consequently have but little time to say much to you— I have a
long message from Jno. H. Pleasants to you which you shall have
at another time— Suffice for the present, he desires his best respects to you— I have sent to you occasionally the Enquirer,
Time & Compiler & Whig Standard, and to day send you the Enquirer, Compiler & Standard— We are all well— My old Gourd,
& Alexander desire their best wishes & respects to you— May
this find you & family well

Yr Friend
W. CLAIBORNE

To Hon. Willie P. Mangum

[Addressed:]

To
Hon. Willie P. Mangum
Red Mountain
N. C.

WPM-LC

A. M. Burton[276] to Willie P. Mangum.

BEATYSFORD 2nd. October 1844

My dear Sir

Having just emerged from an attack of fever it might be
supposed that the politics of the country occupied but a small
portion of my time or thoughts; The approaching Presidential
election is a subject of too much importance to every American
to be disregarded.

You will I am certain acting upon the principle pardon the
liberty I take in making a suggestion to you; the great Western
reserve as it is properly called will have a meeting at Morganton on the 17. 18 & 19th of this month they are very desirous
that you attend it, Allow me then my dear Sir to ask and entreat you in my own name and that of the whigs of No. Ca that
you make this small sacrafice to the great cause in which we
all feel so deep an interest.

---

[276]Alfred M. Burton, the son of Continental Congressman, Robert Burton of Granville County,
graduated from the University. He married Elizabeth Fullenwider and moved to Beatty's Ford, where
he practiced law most of his life. *Tyler's Quarterly Historical and Genealogical Magazine*, II, 274-
277; Grant, *Alumni Hist. of U. N. C.*, 87.

The impression I am fearful is gaining ground in the Western part of the State, that the Whigs in the Middle and Eastern part of the State do not care for the West except on the day of Election; this may produce a paralysis which would be dangerous to our cause.

I do not know any gentleman in the state who has it in his power to render as great service in counteracting this dangerous state of feeling as yourself. Let me therefore beg of you to come.

Spend if you can some time amongst us, and if convenient make my house your head quarters; you are hereby invited and solicited to spend as much time with me as convenient- there is yet much to be done in this month; if we can prevent any sectional jealousy, or allay the excitement which I am fearfull may arise *all will be well and safe.*

You will please to understand me as writing without authority or consultation with any one; it, my letter is the offspring of my own judgement, and observation; if ever it is in the cause of freedom as I verily believe, I may have too much feeling but it is in a noble cause-

Since I have become a farmer by profession I never hear from you; yet I examine and approve your course; God grant you success

Accept assurances of my high regard
I have the honour to be very truly your friend
and Obt Sevt
A. M. Burton

[Addressed:]

The Honble. Willie P. Mangum Esqr.
Red Mountain
No. Ca

Mail)   The post master at Hills^{bo}. will please
forward as soon as possible and oblige a friend.

WPM-LC

Nicholos Carroll to Willie P. Mangum.

180 Prince St
NEW YORK Oct. 7th 1844

My dear Sir

I am grieved to learn of your illness.[277] I hope it will not tye
you to your bed & room when your spirit is thirsty with the
great excitement.

I am very sure I can beat your doctor this morning in the
remedy I shall minister to your ailment.

We are sure of the vote of New York - of the State of New
York. The very best feeling prevails throughout and we were
never so united as at this moment. Reconcilement has been the
order of the day, and those who have been alienated within all
the past four years now centre like brothers to a common standard. In the City we will do the *best we can* and as the avowed
& open design, of those who have hitherto been straight laced
& puritanical in their creed, to yield up all prejudices and go
in the brodest & strongest sense for *Union,* is now manifest, why
may we not hope for success *even* in the City? When we can be
strengthened by so doing we *coalesce* with others - and stand on
our own ground *only* where we cannot gain by alliances. The City
has been canvassed even to the obscurest alley & lowest den
and the inmates, floating & resident, polled to a man. Of this
we are *assured,* if the vote is *honestly* cast we have the City by
2,000— The great importance which *attaches* to the election in
this City is that 13 members of Assembly will probably determine at all events 1 and perhaps 2 U. S. Senators. That is the
state here. But the State - the 36 Electoral votes are sure for
Henry Clay - It has been good for us that Mr Wright was nominated— Every nerve of the Whig Party has been called forth
and they are in the field *night* & *day* with all their energy and in
the majesty of *that* might which can insure the best half of
520.000 votes—

New Jersey *is not* in Capt Stockton's breeches pocket. We
only fear colonizing— Preparations to effect this have been

---

[277]During the summer of 1844 Mangum attended a great many mass meetings and became the
leader of the Whig program in North Carolina. As a result, he was exhausted and became seriously
ill in August. His recuperation was slow, for his lungs were affected. His illness prevented his par-
ticipation in the rallies until near the end of the campaign. *Hillsborough Recorder,* September 5,
24, 1844; *Raleigh Register,* October 1, 1844.

made to a very great extent but it will be met by an over-whelming effort by the Jersey Blue, now thoroughly roused & incensed and they will defend their ballot boxes *with their lives*.

It is a deep matter of regret that already a determined spirit of violence has been apparent. The Whigs have determined to carry out the adage "forewarned - forearmed."

Pennsylvania we hope the best - Appearances are in our favor— If we are beat there it will be because it has been made *apparent* to the people that James K. Polk is a protective Tariff man & Henry Clay a Free Trade disorganizer. Delaware has filled her cup of glory full for treason was rife there - oh Judge beware Bayard, nor has Maryland been wanting—

The East and North are *all right*. We will have Vert. Mass. R. I. Connt. N. Y. & N. J. - then Del. Md. will Virginia join the Line? then N. Ca. Geo. La. Tenne. Ina. Ky. & Ohio- This is our count.

I wish your complaint had been more civil & given us the pleasure of your society for a while— My dear Judge there is no heart beats for Henry Clay in this quarter, that warms to him *un*selfishly that does not include you in the same warm home

The news of your convalescence will be as agreeable to them as the tidings of a State in doubt voting Whig.

I wonder if your physician wont order you North to recruit so as to be here on the 23d of this month. We are to have a sort of National Convention & Festival then and from appearances it *will* be enormous & will give an impetus that will carry us gloriously into & past the Ides of November. Why can't you come?

At all events dear sir regard your health first & foremost- A good many of us feel as if we would *like* to nurse you if we could help you along - but any way we want to hear that you are better - that you are *well*

With earnest & respectful esteem & regard

Faithfully
Yr friend & sert.
NICHS. CARROLL

Hon Willie P Mangum

The Young News State Convention at Rochester on the 2ᵈ numbered 60,000 & upwards— It was very - very enthusiastic. There were thousands there, speaking almost literally who had

voted for Van Buren in 1840- This is a pregnant fact. Mr
Clay's last letter (I am glad *it is his last*) will put us on the
highest ground in these quarters & its effect is already telling
for us *everywhere*.

I enclose a table of Maryland's vote - 1500 *non* residents
voted in Balt. City. The *fact* is *pregnant*. By fraud and violence, the party leaders have maped out their operations. The
result in Maryland is most happy considering the unhallowed
means used by the Locos. A Maryland friend assures me that
$200,000 & upwards were used by the Locos in that State. They
will make *us* no fight there in November- If New Jersey &
Pennsylvania do their duty *tomorrow* the game *is* played. Mr
Clay will sweep everything like Prarie fire. *22* States then
would be a small count- I shall watch & pray & enclose you the
earliest returns

WPM-LC

Walter A. Mangum to Priestley H. Mangum.

[OAKLAND MISSISSIPPI]
October 9th 1844—

Dear Sir,

This is to inform you that we are yet in the land of the
living, but I dont know how soon it may be some of us next.
The people are dropping off every day around us like the leaves
from the trees- This morning Mrs. William M. Sneed departed
this life at 7 oclock, & her husband has been very low. Albert
Sneed, his wife & 2 of his children are very sick & I have but
little hopes of him, - We have had more sickness this season
than we have had in 5 years past all together & more fatal,
nearly all the sickness is disposed to *Congestion,* it is not un-
comon for a man to be in good health & die in 3 hours, There
has dyed about 100 persons within 10 miles of me since the 1st
of last June- We are looking forward to frost for releaf, it would
be useless in me to attempt to describe the distress on the Mississippi river anywhere within 50 miles- There is no doubt our
sickness is produced by the great overflow- You know Alexander Murphy who married Womacks daughter he was living
in my County & he, & 3 of his children is dead - his wife & their

2 other children came near to dying— She is now with her mother some 70 miles north of me— I have had some little sickness but of the common order both in my White & Black family- Our crops are good particular cotton my crop will make 400 lbs picked Cotton to the acre— I have delayed mailing this letter till today the 17th - inconsequence of the illness of my wife- She is at the point of death of Congestive fever, I think there is a great probabilty the next time you hear from her, it will be of her death- Capt Sneed & his wife is thought to be some better this morning - but very ill - Thos. Gooch is quite sick - I am determined to leave the Mississippi vally - *do write* me the health of your country this season & *particularly* the health of yours & Willie's family-

We have no frost yet & our sickness still rages with violence—

Yours with respect &c.
W. A. MANGUM

To P. H Mangum

[Postmarked:] Oakland Mi Oct 21ˢᵗ

[Addressed:]

> Priestley H. Mangum Esqr.
> Hillsboro
> Orange County
> [North] Carolina

WPM-LC

William Churchill[278] *to Willie P. Mangum.*

NEW YORK Octr 11 1844

My Dear Sir.

I have been pained to see in the Newspapers notices that you had been seriously ill, but without mentioning in what manner you were afflicted, or its extent. This causes me great anxiety, which is shared by all the members of my family, and I hear frequent expressions of interest from those who have not, like us, had the pleasure of social intercourse with you.— *With them,* this may be mainly induced by their estimate of the

---

[278]He was a manufacturer of bird cages in New York City. *New York City Directory for 1845 and 1846*, p. 75.

important services you would continue to render the great interests of our country at this interesting period.—

Will it, - my Dear Judge - be trespasing to ask you to let me know how your health is: if you are able to write without inconvenience?

The Whigs here are in high spirits and I think are better organized and quite as earnest as in 1840.—

Being just recovering from severe illness, - I have not been able to work for the good cause so much as I wished to do, in a humble way, nor to attain full data upon which to form a positive judgement of the vote of this state. But from all I can learn of intelligent individuals from the interior and in the City, I have strong hopes that New York will go for Mr. Clay - notwithstanding the strength of the Loco foco candidates for Gov. and Lieut Govr.—

My family are in usual health and unite in earnest wishes for your speedy restoration to health with,

> My Dear Sir
> Yours Faithfully
> & Respy
> WM. CHURCHILL

To Hon W. P. Mangum
 Red Mountain,
  N. C.

[Addressed:]

Hon. Willie P. Mangum
Red Mountain
North Carolina

S. Starkweather to Willie P. Mangum.

N. YORK. 13. Oct 44.

Hon W P Mangum

Dear Sir

If you accost the Whig watchman here, "with what of the night?" he responds be of good cheer, all is well, the day is beginning to dawn. The late election in Cont. has put that State beyond doubt. we have carried N Jersey, Del. Maryland, are carrying Ohio, & proved our powers to carry Penn.—

These results have rendered N. York unqualifiedly safe. Ohio will give us a good vote probably 7000. At least so it looks this morning- I write you to say *N. York is safe.* Your friend N P Tallmadge & his brother L. B. the judge, have gone fully over to John Tyler & so I knew they intended last winter but you would not believe it - we have had some fears of Georgia, but this mornings mail has relieved us though the vote will be close. Can you not give your neighbor a little aid. Gen. Clinch went from these a little discouraged about three weeks since But like a noble Roman as he is went home to share in the conflict. The Whigs are in high spirits and full of exultation but be assured they will not relax in their exertions until the closing of the balot Box

You may say to all friends N. York is safe. Mr. Clays last letter was called for & has saved us.

> In haste truly Yours
> S. Starkweather.

[Addressed:]

> Hon. Willie P. Mangum
> Red Mountain.
> Orange Co
> N Carolina

_____

WPM-LC

James C. Mangham[279] to Willie P. Mangum.

Bethel
GLYNN COUNTY GEORGIA 13th October, 1844
Honerable W. P. Mangum

Dr Sir I am well & a bold plebian & truly hope this may find you & your sweat family in the same good health - please excuse my Boldness in atempting to trouble you with reading my imperfect Letter the time has been when I felt proud to heare of your High Station in Life, but now feel mortifyed to find you side with Mr. Clay - you as a southern Man 2d in command. In administering the general government, & could turn the tables in my oald beloved state are you to yield to the will of the self styled whigs of the grate Union - may God for Bid it, you have been chided By Mr Clay on the Senate floor, you in the Last

_____

[279]See above, I, 84.

Whig Convention have been over Lookt by that party an ordinary man taken in your stead, for your Honours sake your
countrys sake come and go with us we will Doo the Good -, can
you Indorse the public conduct of Mr Clay & vote for him for
president Oh that your God may Guide you Right, it is a Lasting Lorel on the Braw of him that will leave the wrong & cleve
to the right way It was a Democratic government Delivered to
us by the Blood washt Band, and for the sake of your free
Blood that follows after you, I would not try to have you change
policy as knowing you have Sterling worth, but the wisest man
may be Deceived - the south would a have been pleased to a
have made you president some years ago - and would yet if you
would take the right side- My heart feels what I write if you
help Clay to the presidency. Dont, pray dont fasten on us a

Institution for a [illegible] may endanger the Union, not alter
our glorious Constitution, that has been the first step taken
always, to overthrow all republics. Doo examine both sides of
policy - and chuse impartially for your God & your country
there will be more rejoicing over the return of one Neglected
sinner than over 99 just pursons- I Battled with you in your
virgin policy for our Crawford in vain - for Jackson Twice -
for Vanburen Twice, the 2d time in vain, and Now for my
Country - and think with success-, T. B. King - put me Down,
and there I am Content to stay - I have Laboured 40 years for
the public in Glynn County, Ga— have never changed my policy for the sake of office Neither do I wish you to Doo it but I
can tell you that the flatterey of J. M. Berrien, will never benefit you, Neither will the Clay party - his ambition is known -
the former - Deceipt is known Clays changes & British Guilt is
known - Mr. Berriens federalism is known - his changes is
known - he was opposed to the last war - would Brook the British insults - and oppression - the Decendence of Britons &
France, here - is whigs - the first from hatred to Jackson the
2d from Hatred to Jackson & Vanburen, from giving payment
by the french of the 25 millions of Francks - the 3d party is
under T. B. Ks Controll, same stripe yankeys. - Soft sawder
& Ham oriaturecrates (these 3 partys rules the County - and
trys to rule the whole seaboard of Georgia - but cant Cum it - I
wish you to answer this Letter - or the Next will be but short -
as I will [illegible] then write and to the purpose— I Love you

and all that has my Blood in there vains- Both the Carringtons
& Mangums— our worthy old Gramp is for us

I am your obt Sevt

JAS. C. MANGHAM

Jackson do-Benton do- [several lines are badly torn]
Colquet Cooper Black
Gilmer - Seborn Jones
Black, Cheves Chappel
Oald - Virginia
Honest John Tyler and
his friends - all the South,
that has rightly Judged - is for us
the northern Whigs [illegible] against us
then Let us be unitted at the South for
the sake of our Dearest rights
and not promote the whigs for the sake of office
Nor suffer Adams & Clay to Dictate save the republic
for Gods sake & your Country sake

Adams calls on 3/5 Negroes - Clay says one
thing yonder yesterday - says another thing here to Day,
Oh our Best Blood is in Texas holding out thare
Hands to us as Drownding men for help—

Doo grant it.-

[Addressed:]

To

the Honble W. P. Mangum
Red Mountain
Orange Co.   North Caro.

[Postscript]

I Nurst you on my knees many be the times I have workt
for your father under the whip as a poor orphan. I have been
abused by your uncle Nathaniel Carrington many years - I
pray for you all in Common with the rest of my Countrymen. I
must quit - though have not said half anough if I am Drunk
you must Excuse it, for it is with Ignorance and not with spirits
for I have not taken a Drink for the sake of Drink in 73 years.
During which time I have watcht every public man in the union
Even the old Roman Jackson - watcht Clays Disobedience to
his State and you to yours - both was wrong.

WPM-LC

Jas. Auchincloss[280] to Willie P. Mangum.

NEW YORK, Octr. 15. 1844.

Dear Sir,

Not knowing a solitary individual on whom I can bestow it
more worthily than your good self, I have placed in the hands of
Mr. Phenix[281] a walking stick cut from off the broad acres of
the noble old "Farmer of Ashland." Your acceptance of which
I have to request. It will go to Washington when Phenix starts
for his Congressional labors, and, doubtless, if he is chary of his
eloquence ordinarily, he will be unusally impressive when he
presents it to you in propria persona.

In offering you this souvenir I wish, my respected Sir, that
I had something more worthy of your acceptance, as I am
sincerely desirous of testifying my respect for you as a man and
as a Statesman of unfaltering integrity: When others have
wavered you have stood by your "gun." Would, alas, my dear
Sir, that I could say as much of some who were in times of yore
the very "embodiment" of Conservatism if not "of Whiggery."

> With true regard
> and unqualified rspect,
> I am Dear Sir,
> Yours always,
> JAS: AUCHINCLOSS.

P. S. I trust that you have entirely recovered from your indisposition, and that you will be found at your post by and by
completely restored in health.- We are extremely anxious relative to this State for Mr. Clay, but have strong hopes of carrying
it. *Joshua A. Spencer* told me a few days ago that it would go
by *20.000* for Clay. If the Locos do not cheat too much we shall
carry it- but still we are exceedingly anxious, as you may suppose.

J. A.

Hon. Willie P. Mangum,
    Red Mountain,
        Orange Co.
            No. Ca.

---

[280]See above, III, 216n.
[281]See above, III, 135n.

WPM-LC

Nicholas Carroll to Willie P. Mangum.

180 Prince St—[NEW YORK CITY,]
Tuesday Oct 15th/44

My dear Sir.

The elections of the past week have assured us that the old Whig States are true but we gain *nothing*—

While there is nothing to dishearten there is proof positive that we want the whip & spur unceasing- There is no time for laying on our oars. At the utmost we foot up 133 votes as *sure.* Mr Clay's election I consider certain That is not enough. When the Sun went down on Wednesday night he was President elect- But this is not enough- We owe to him - to the country that he should not be *bolstered* but magnificently supported- We have lost 15 members of the 29th Congress, outrageously lost them. We have Vert. Mass. R. I. Connt. N. J. Del. Md. N. Ca. Geo. La. Tenn. Ind. Ky. & Ohio- We have for the next congress In Maine 2 members in Vert. 3. in R. I. 2 in Geo. 5 in Pa 10 in Ala 2 in La. 1. Ill. 1 in Ohio 9 - 35 members. We expect 10 in Mass. 4 in Connt. 18 in N. Y. 3 in N. J. 5 in Md. 7 in Va. *5 in N. Ca. 1 in S. Ca. 4 in Miss.* 7 in Ind. 7 in Tenn. 7 in Ky 2 in Michigan - 80 members - making 115 members- 112 in a majority- There will be 5 'Natives'- The impression is that in effect they will be Whigs - but we must not count *on this* - we must have 115 *straight out reliable Whigs-*

Upon N. Y. Pa. or Va. will probably depend the bestowal of 'the purple.' We *believe* New York under *all* contingencies will vote for Mr Clay by at least 10,000. Indeed that is the *worst* aspect the case presents. This estimate is predicated on a Loco majority of 2,000 in this City. The events of the past week has *determined* that, Mr Clay will go out of this City & County by 2 to 4,000— How so? Why I can't tell except that the Native Ticket will elect their Assembly ticket—a State Senator & 2 members of Congress We will elect 2. There will be no *Union* yet somehow this result is now *generally* understood. Tammany is great on cheating & fraud- But *they* took *their* lessons from the the men who are now the wire pullers *for* the Natives.

We can say earnestly & truthfully that we are full of hope- We cannot be sure because the trial must be made first. Since

Wright was nominated - the first blush of his giant like strength
has been succeeded by a determination to beat *him*. His actual
& life-long consistency in opposing Internal Improvement State
or Federal will cost him thousands of votes. The Total Abstin-
ence men will 5 out of 6 of those associated as sons of Temperance vote against him on that ground alone. This is a queer
fact - but nevertheless *true*. You may judge of their importance
from the fact that only a *portion* of them were out in procession
yesterday and they numbered some 4,000. I think if you were
here & could understand all the moves of the chess board you
would *bet* on our winning.

But we can't afford to lose an *electoral* vote- We must not
do it- It is not *too* late to save the 29th Congress. If a *true* canvass of the chances for carrying a majority of the whole has
been made out- our friends should be informed *when* there is
a chance of making a fight & by united effort to carry disputed
ground.

Many *stories* are told of Pennsylvania: that we lost one
Whig County, Bucks, by the lie that Markle could not read or
write;[282] another by representing him as the avowed advocate
of destroying, root & branch, the Catholic Church; they say
too "Shunk will vote for Clay" - this was one mode of attack -
while he lent himself to the story by stumping *for the Tariff as
it is* without amendment, modification, or repeal. It is feared
that *3000* Natives voted for Shunk. It is feared that in 7 counties
the abolition vote is 3,300. It is proved that some 6 to 7000
whigs voted for Shunk- Now we *dont* say that Mr Clay will
carry Pa - but we do say that Henry Clay's vote will be more
than 10,000 over Shunk's vote. My advices from Va. carefully
collected assures us of that State. The evidences of this result
are quite strong. I don't know what your information as regards Va. is - but I know that *we* feel *surer* of the vote of New
York than of Virginia.

I mean to betray no fear - but I want no stone left un-
turned - for we cannot spare the vote of *a man*. Victory at *all*
cost & *every* hazard, would be *meet* - but to triumph even to
the extinction of Loco-ism is the *aim* of *New York*.

We want to see you very much- We want to hear of your
health & well being- We want to know that you are better -
convalescent - well- It is a real disappointment that we are de-

[282]See above, 161, 179-180.

nied the pleasure of welcoming you here but we will be cheered to know that your health is surely & rapidly mending- With sentiments of respectful affection & esteem

> Faithfully
> Yr friend & Sert.
>
> N. Carroll

Judge Mangum

WPM-LC

J. Watson Webb to Willie P. Mangum.

New York
October 18 1844

My Dear Sir.

On my return from Europe six weeks since, I found here your kind letter of the 20th April last, which arrived after I sailed, & which should have been forwarded to me. I ought to have acknowledged the rect. of it sooner; but my return was the signal for a general furlough to my assistants, & I have consequently been alone with the work of three persons on my shoulders. I now however, am compelled to write you on a matter of business.

In March last, *Alexander Powell*[283] of no inconsiderable notoriety, commenced an action against me for *Libel* laying his damage at $10.000! — now the scamp is bringing the matter to trial. Of his worthlessness there can be no doubt; & it is equally true that we published no more than what his conduct justified. But I am without proof. You kindly gave most of the facts in his case to my worthless compatriot who so timely went to *Wisconsin;*[284] and to you therefore, I apply in my difficulties, satisfied that you will do all in your power to get me out of them. Will you at your earliest convenience let me hear from you on this subject?

Politically things look as well to me as I could desire; but then I am more sanguine than my friends & not easily driven from a position which my judgment tells me is right. Acting

---

[283] See above, III, 467n.
[284] He probably refers to David Lambert, who formerly was a correspondent of Webb's paper and in 1844 became the editor of a Wisconsin newspaper.

James Watson Webb, 1802-1884. From the oil portrait by Henry Inman in the possession of Vanderbilt Webb of New York City.

on my own judgment & in opposition to the opinions of my friends, I assure you that this State will give more than 15.000 for Clay. How much more I will not say lest you should think me demented. I am almost as confident of Penn. & Virginia; though the latter is somewhat doubtful by all accounts. The truth is, Clay will have many if not quite Harrison's majority in the Electoral College. Our Native Americans in this City & Phil^a. will generally act with us.

Truly your friend
J. WATSON WEBB

Hon. W. P. Mangum.

Willie P. Mangum to Albert B. Dodd.[285]

/NORTH CAROLINA/
RED MOUNTAIN, 18th. Octo: 1844.

My dear Sir.

Will you pardon the liberty of one - an entire stranger to you, personally - who begs to introduce to you, the son of one of his best friends?

M^r. Sterling R. Cain,[286] who will hand you this, was arrested some two years ago, at one of our Colleges, in his Course, by bad health. - He is the son of my brother-in-law, & in whose well doing, I feel a deep interest. - Since he left school, he has been engaged in agricultural labors, & seems to be well, & robust. - He desires to finish his Collegiate Course at Princeton, The "Alma Mater" of some of the most distinguished names that ever graced the public history of N^o. Ca: - Indeed, one of his uncles - the brother of his mother - who is now the Chief Justice of the Supreme Court of N^o. Ca: is a graduate of Princeton College. -

He may have to devote some months, in a private Course, to enable him to join one of the classes in College. -

Will you be so obliging, as to aid his inexperience by your valuable *advice & Counsels?* -

[285]The original is in the Historical Society of Pennsylvania. Albert B. Dod was a Presbyterian preacher and professor of mathematics at Princeton University. In 1844 the University of North Carolina conferred the D.D. degree upon him. Battle, *Hist. of U. N. C.,* I, 485; *D. A. B.,* V, 338-339.
[286]Sterling Ruffin Cain was the son of William Cain, Jr. and Mary (Ruffin) Cain. He died in 1853. *Hillsborough Recorder,* October 12, 1853; Groves, *The Alstons and Allstons of North and South Carolina,* 423-424.

He has talent & decision of Character, & is Capable under favorable circumstances, of reflecting honor on himself & his family. -

I am sensible of the great liberty, I have taken in writing thus freely to one known to me only by reputation, & so freely making requests - But to that distinguished reputation, I trust, you will ascribe quite as much of this burthen, as to my boldness. -

May I further ask, that your Counsels & friendly guidance may be given to him *freely*, as far as may be compatible with your public duties, & personal convenience?

With profound respect
I am My dear Sir
Your Mo. ob^t. Ser^t.
WILLIE P. MANGUM

To Professor
Albert B. Dodd

*

[*Endorsed:] Hon: W. P. Mangum
Willie P. Mangum
Pres. pro tem. U. S. Senate, and
Acting Vice-President during
part of the Presidency of John
Tyler.

———————

WPM-LC

Dennis Heartt to Willie P. Mangum.

HILLSBOROUGH, Nov. 11 1844-

Dear Sir:- According to promise I send you all the returns I am in possession of; but the complexion of them is not so favorable as we could wish.

Our own state has done very well. In 52 counties Clay has gained upon the Whig vote for Governor some eight or nine hundred. Twenty-two counties remain to be heard from. Clay's majority will doubtless be over 4000.-

The returns from the state of New York are somewhat discouraging. Forty counties heard from give to Clay (of majorities) 7,029 - to Polk 15,850; carrying Polk 8821 ahead; neerly all of which, the Nat: Intel: says, is a gain upon the vote of 1840. The 18 counties that remain to be heard from gave to Gen. Harrison a nett majority of 11,490; but as so large a Whig majority is not now expected in those counties, the result is uncertain; it is to be feared the state has gone for Polk. The Whigs thus far, it is said, have gained four members of Congress.

Maryland - all the counties heard from - gives Clay a majority of 3283.

Virginia - Eighty-five counties heard from give majorities for Clay 12421 - for Polk, 15232. Same counties in 1840, gave Harrison 29,274 - Van Buren 29912. From this it appears that Virginia has gone for Polk.-

Georgia - 16 counties give Clay a majority of 1904 - being a gain of 527 on the October election - not enough I fear to redeem the state.

Connecticut. The Intelligencer says that returns from all except five towns have been received, and Clay's majority so far is 3,066.

New Jersey- all the counties having been heard from - has given her vote for Clay by more then 1000 majority; and has also, it is believed, elected four Whig members to Congress.

Rhode Island has gone for Clay of course- Clay 7279 - Polk 4777.

The above hasty sketch comprises all the intelligence of the elections I now have - I regret that it contains so little to encourage our hope of success.

Yours, respectfully,
DENNIS, HEARTT.

[Addressed:]

Hon. Willie P. Mangum.
Red Mountain.
Orange.

All gone hell-ward

WPM-LC

Thomas L. Ragsdale[287] to Willie P. Mangum.

WASHINGTON CITY.
12th. Novr. 1844.

My Dear friend,

Had Mr. Clay been elected I know that you would have procured me justice. I had an abiding confidence in his generous noble spirit; and I am aware that I was under your protection. I am not under the less obligation to you, and my confidence in his magnanimity is not diminished by the result. No man in America suffered more than I did under the wrong use of Whig power: but notwithstanding this, I can do Mr. Clay justice even now when thousands of Whigs are damning him as the destroyer of their Party.

If Mr. Polk turns out any whig on account of his honest expression of his opinions- democrat as I am - I say he ought to be damned for it. If he can be persuaded whipped kicked into it by some of the demented Loco focos, then I shall despair of the Republic. Res *nolunt* male administrari; and if he administers them *male,* the vis medicatrix rerum will must react - for it is the law of nature. It is not whig principles that destroyed the Whig Party-: it was the bad administration of them.— At a glance you will see the whole of my private position. I can now tell what I have suffered. I have been forced to sell even my clothing piece by piece. I have been compelled to suffer for want of even a meal of victuals- yet under all this I have still sustained the bearing of a gentleman. I knew well that your purse the purse any noble Whig or democrat was open to me - but to receive their money would have choked me. I can now speak out trumpet tongued without degradation. I now return any money I may borrow.

I must now stand up as a No. Carolina southern gentleman Even Southern Whigs would resent my conduct if I appeared otherwise. I want decent clothes, I want to pay my way in a decent boarding house. Send me two or three hundred dollars.- Some of my loco foco *friends,* who a week or two ago passed me without a nod are now bowing and scraping to me, damn them. I want your friendship. As for Mr. Tyler he would reinstate me

---
[287]See above, III, 305n.

now; but I would not touch him or his Secy. of War with a 40 foot pole.

Wm A. Bradley told me to go to Piney Point the past summer and pay him when I could and when convenient and that too when I told him I did not see that I could ever pay- I went, he treated me like a Prince. Politics cant separate *me* from such a man-. I cant utter all I feel. I am interrupted- Yours ever

THOS. L. RAGSDALE.

Hon. W. P. Mangum.

[Addressed:]

> Hon. W. P. Mangum.
> Red Mountain.
> Franklinton
> N. Ca.

WPM-LC

Walter R. Johnson[288] *to Willie P. Mangum.*

PHILA. Nov. 12 1844.

Hon. & dear Sir

The report on American coals of which 11000 extra copies were ordered to be printed by the Senate at the last session is nearly through the press. Many applications for it have been made to me by parties furnishing the coal, by scientific & practical men, & by those interested in mining operations, - to none of whom have I been able to give more than a conditional promise to comply with their wishes in case the kindness of gentlemen of the Senate should dispose them to afford me the use of any *surplus copies* for that purpose. Should this be your case, I should esteem it a great favour, as I have at present none to offer to the hundred or two of applicants, who have asked to be supplied. Will you do me the kindness to state what number

---

[288]On June 11, 1844, the Senate Committee on Naval Affairs first ordered the printing of 1000 copies of Johnson's report and six days later increased the order to 10,000. The title of the report is: "A Report to the Navy Department of the United States on American Coals Applicable to Steam Navigation, and to other purposes," by Walter R. Johnson. *Senate Doc.,* 28 Cong. 1 sess., Doc. No. 386. 607 pp.

of copies, if any, you can probably spare, without in any degree interfering with your own distributions?

I am with high respect
Your obedient Servant
WALTER R. JOHNSON.

Hon. Willie P. Mangum

[Addressed:] Hon. Willie P. Mangum
U. S. Senator.
Red Mountain
Orange Co
N. C.

WPM-LC

J. C. Barrett[289] to Willie P. Mangum.

NORTH MT. PLEASANT MISS. Nov. 29th 1844

Hon. W. P. Mangum;

My Dear Sir;

Although I have not the pleasure of a personal acquaintance with you; yet I hope you will not think it presumption in me in requesting you to forward to me such papers documents to me during the approaching session of congress that you may deem interesting.

The representatives from this state as you know are all Locos and consequently the whigs hardly ever receive any thing. I am a whig of the hard cast and am very desirous of such documents and such others as you may think profitable. In complying with the above you will confer a favor on me that will be greatfully received.

Most respectfully
Your obedient servant
J. C. BARRETT

---

[289]Unable to identify.

P S. My address is North. Mt. Pleasant. Miss. Set me down as
one of you constituents. J. C . B.

[Addressed:]

Hon. W. P. Mangum. M. C.
Washington City
D. C.

Charles Gibbons[290] to Willie P. Mangum.

PHILADELPHIA Dec. 2 1844

Dear Sir

A number of applications have been made to the National
Clay Club from various sources, urging them to adopt some
means of carrying into effect the proposition of a suitable testimonial of Whig gratitude to Henry Clay. We have declined to
act in the matter, on the ground that it will probably be considered by the Whig members of Congress.

I have been directed by the Club to confer with you on the
subject and to ascertain if the members of Congress who represent the Whigs of the Union, will not, at an early day take the
subject in hand. We all feel that something is due to Mr. Clay,
whose private character has been so fiercely, and it *may* be said
hereafter, so successfully assailed. He received a majority of
the legal votes of Penna. *and we can prove it.* But the law gives
us no remedy. I am sir Very Respectfully

Yr ob st
CH: GIBBONS
Presdt. Natl. Clay Club.

Hon. W. P. Mangum.

WPM-LC

Will. H. Haywood, Jr., to Willie P. Mangum.

[2 Dec. 1844]

Hon Willie P Mangum

My Dear Sir

My family are going to Newbern to spend the winter and
I shall be obliged to accompany them thither before I start for

---

[290]Charles Gibbons was a Clay supporter who practiced law in Philadelphia. Livingston's *Law
Register*, 1851, 548.

Washington. It is therefore probable that you will appoint the Committees of the Senate before I reach my post and as you kindly intimated to me during the last Session that my position might be changed this Session if it were personally desirable to me I seize upon a moment of leisure to say that I would prefer to be removed from *Navy Committee* and put upon the *Judiciary* Committee in place of it.[291] If thought to be well suited to *Claims* I have no objection to remaining there and performing the *labors* of that station: The Jud^y Com: occurs to my mind, as I think you will probably allow the Democrats *two* Members on it and we had but one last Session So there appeared to be more room for a change therein than upon others. If you should not feel at liberty in the discharge of your duties as Prest of Senate to do this, may I solicit *Mr Wrights* place on *Com: of Commerce* for though not so well qualified for it as I am for the other (Jud'y) I can perhaps make myself reasonably so by study & c. You will understand me however as not wishing to have this indulgent recollection of my personal preference for a station on or off of any Committee to interfere in the slightest manner with your duty to others or your deliberate & impartial judgment in executing your own office.

The hope of seeing you here on your way to Washington delayed this note until today- I hope to reach W. City by Monday next or the day after it - There is nothing of particular interest going forward here that I know of. I have the honour to be your

Obt Servt.

WILL. H. HAYWOOD JR
Raleigh 2 Dec 1844.

WPM-LC

Edward Stanly to Willie P. Mangum.

Term will expire 10 January, 1845
[Inserted by Stanly]
RALEIGH Dec: 2nd 1844

My Dear Sir,

I hope you would pass through Raleigh on your way to Washington City - but I know you would have been pained to

---

[291]Haywood was appointed on the commerce and claims committees of the Senate. He was not made a member of either the naval or judicial committees. *Cong. Globe,* 28 Cong., 1 sess., 12.

meet your friends in these gloomy times without the ability of giving any consolation.

I have no time to write on politics & though I hold up my head amidst Locos, I have no heart to write at present.-

But while the power is probably in our hands I wish you to aid in giving a rebuke to a malignant, vile Loco-foco.[292] The Collector at Ocracoke will be nominated to the Senate this Session I think. Sylvester Brown is his name. He had a Tyler meeting in April & sent his son a delegate to the Tyler Balt: convention. The whigs,- I among them,- suffered him to remain in office & he was very active & influential for Mr Arrington in my contest. Let the Senate remember him— not only for this, but for official misconduct which can be proved on investigation.—

I write to request you to learn as soon as you can, & before you are engaged in the business of the Session, when Brown's time expires- an inquiry from some officer at the Treasury Department will bring the information.—

Nothing new.- the Whigs are still unconquered & feel unconquerable: though heart stricken for our country & our glorious "old chief" - dearer to us now than if he had been successful-

We shall have a meeting & pass some resolutions in testimony of our high regard & for Mr Clay.

Remember me kindly to Messrs Crittenden, Morehead & & &—

Let me hear from you of the matter referred to above.— & believe me

Yours as ever
EDW. STANLY

Hon: W. P. Mangum
  U. S. Senate
    Washington City

[Addressed:]

    Hon: W. P. Mangum
      U. S. Senate
       Washington City

---

[292]See below Stanly to Mangum, December 10, 1844.

WPM-LC

C. L. Hinton to Willie P. Mangum.

RALEIGH Dec 2nd 1844

Dr Sir

Some weeks since I wrote you respecting the appointment of Thomas Loring as post master at Busbee's store, I feel some interest in it as we are loosing ground in that precinct and I think that Loring settlement there would have a good effect- I learned that Busbee had resigned his commission as P. M. and the Office is not kept up—

Nothing of importance before our Legislature, the Whigs are firm, and I believe determined to try & keep the party together— A vote for circuit & supreme court Judge will take place to day,

Very respectfully

C. L. HINTON

Nash & Caldwell are elected Judge of the Superior & circuit courts

[Addressed:]

Hon. Willie P Mangum
Washington City
D. C.

WPM-LC

Daniel R. Goodloe to Willie P. Mangum.[293]

December 3 [,1844]

Dear Sir: I negelected to ascertain from you when I might expect to know the result of your friendly efforts to obtain me a place as clerk to one of the Committees, or assistant to Mr. Dickens the Secretary to the Senate. Fearing that you would be at a loss to find me out in the event of success, I address you this note to say that a line or verbal massage sent to the "Standard Office" which stands within a few rods of Colemans upon sixth street, will be duly received.- I feel reluctant to trouble

---

[293]Compare this letter with the one of Goodloe to Mangum, June 11, 1845.

you with a call as I presume you are much occupied with business or company at this time.

I have the honor to be

With great respect

Your obliged and obdt. servt.

DANIEL R. GOODLOE.

The Standard office is south of the Avenue upon the east side of sixth street.

[Addressed:]

Hon. Willie P. Mangum
National Hotel.

WPM-LC

D. L. Swain to Willie P. Mangum and Enclosure.

RALEIGH, 3, Dec. 1844.

My dear Sir,

I would have transmitted the enclosed papers at an earlier day, if I had not indulged the hope of meeting you on your way to Washington.

If the affidavit of the Rev^d. E. Graves, supplies the only deficient link in the chain of testimony required by the accompanying letter of the 23rd Feb. last, from Comptroller of the Treasury Department, I presume no further delay will occur in the payment of a claim so obviously fair.[294]

R. H. Graves the applicant is at present Prof. of Mathematics in the Caldwell Institute at Greensboro; and the remittance may be made either directly to him, or under cover to me.- I suppose it is scarcely necessary to remark, that my agency in this business has been prompted by no motive, but regard for Mr. G. than whom I do not know, in my opinion a purer man.

Your very sincerely

D. L. SWAIN.

Honble W. P. Mangum.

[Addressed:]

Honble, Willie P. Mangum,
Pre's. of the Senate,
Washington City

---

[294]See above, 23-24, 51-52.

7 Oct., 1844.

Enclosure

The State of Mississippi Carroll County SS

This day personally appeared before the undersigned, Judge of the Second Judicial District of the State of Mississippi, Elijah Graves who being first duly sworn deposeth and saith that some time in the month of February of the year 1843, according to the best of affiants recollection, affiant sold to Richard S. Graves a negro woman named Phebe, and her three children for about the sum of twelve hundred dollars: that affiant at that time was indebted to Ralph H. Graves in and about the sum of six hundred dollars, two hundred dollars of which debt due to R. H. Graves, the said Richd S. Graves agreed to pay for affiant as part of the price of said negroes. In compliance with said agreement, said R. S. Graves informed affiant that he had forward two halfs of two $100 United States Treasurer notes, left hand halves, N°s 26 & 27 letters B. & C. which were received by R. H. Graves and the right hand halves of same were forwarded by Mrs. Elizah J Thompson about the same time at the request of Rich^d. S. Graves, which your affiant is informed have not been received but are lost. Said halves sent by R. S. Graves were mailed at Jackson Miss, & those by Mrs Thompson at Middleton Miss. That said agreement between affiants & R. S. Graves was entered into in good faith by the parties, said that the payment made by said Richd S. Graves to said Ralph H. Graves was upon good and *bona fide* consideration and on behalf of said affiant as before stated -

Sworn to & subscribed before
me this 7th of October 1844

E. GRAVES

Witness my hand & seal
Benj. F. Caruthers   (Seal)
Judge of the 2d Judicial
District of the State of Miss.

WPM-LC

Edward Stanly to Willie P. Mangum

RALEIGH Dec: 10th. 1844

My Dear Sir,

I received your favor in reply to mine, & thank you for your prompt attention. *Pray bear in mind, what I suggested to you.*

Our friends here & in the country so far from being disposed to despair, are more resolved than ever to fight on - Clay's defeat will but add fuel to the flame of their hate of Loco-focoism.-

I only write at present, to thank you for attending to my request[295] & to suggest to you to send some docs: or speech to the Whigs of the Legislature, if you have a chance before they adjourn. - I think we shall adjourn early in Jany: there is a disinclination on the part of our friends to pass political resolutions, because we have not a majority in both branches - my own opinion is otherwise: we ought to give "line upon line & precept upon precept:" to let the people understand that Whig principles still exist. We shall at all events make a move relative to the 4th instalment[296] - at this time a most important matter for us - I hope before you adjourn, you will try Billy Haywood on that point, by resolutions in the Senate-

And now I wish to trouble you to deliver a message for me. I have seen to day, a paper informing me that Col: Benton was re-elected to the Senate. & I really felt happy at hearing the intelligence. I wish you, to say to Col: B. that his manly conduct in the Texas matter,[297] has raised him high in the estimation of every patriot Whig in the land, & I think the country ought gratefully to remember his services.— I differ widely with him, in political matters, I think upon some subjects we can never agree & I never expect to ask any political or other favor at his hands; I have often in public speeches spoken well of his conduct, & he will not I hope, with entire indifference understand, that hundreds of Whigs, in this State, admire & thank him for his eminent services, in exposing the Texas conspiracy.—

[295]See above Stanly to Mangum, December 2, 1844.

[296]In the House of Representatives Garrett Davis, of Kentucky, introduced a resolution directing the Secretary of Treasury to pay to the several states $9,367,614.99—the fourth installment of money in the treasury, for deposit with the several states. The Democrats moved to lay this motion on the table. *Raleigh Register,* December 10, 1844.

[297]Benton held that the consent of Mexico should be secured before annexation. In the campaign of 1844 he said the Texas question was brought up to defeat Van Buren. He accused the speculators and stock jobbers of purchasing Texas script at the rate of two to seven cents on the dollar and of urging annexation to make their investments pay off. His speech was widely circulated in the campaign. Lambert, *Presidential Politics in the U. S., 1841-1844,* 173, 179.

Besides, his treatment of Tyler, has shown he not only spoke like a prophet, but evinced a noble contempt, for treachery.- I know you entertain as high an estimate of Col: B, as I do.

I will write to you again soon—Mrs S. desires to be kindly remembered to you.- best regards to Messrs Crittenden, Green, & &.—

As ever very truly your's
EDW. STANLY

Hon: W. P. Mangum.
    U. S. Senate
    W. City

WPM-LC

William Prescott to Willie P. Mangum.

LYNN (MASS.) Dec. 14th. 1844.

Dear Sir,

Believing that a discrepancy and a misunderstanding exists among the people relative to the import of the terms *Tariff, Revenue, Fee Trade, Protection* &c. as used by our statesmen; also as to what constitutes the true policy of the country relative to the duties on imports, the various interests connected therewith, and the numerous questions growing out of the same; And, believing also, that a definite understanding in relation to these intricate subjects would conduce to the harmony and welfare of the people of this country, as well as be gratifying to all concerned; I have drawn up a series of questions for the purpose of submitting them to several distinguished statesmen and politicians of the different and opposing political parties in the United States for their examination and decision.

I therefore take the liberty to transmit a copy of them to you, and hope to receive your views upon the same at an early day.

Question 1st What do you understand by the term *Free Trade,* as used by the statesmen of this country & Europe?

Question 2nd What do you understand by the term *Protective Tariff,* as used by the statesmen of this country & Europe?

Quest. 3rd Are you in favour of abolishing all duties on imports, or do you know of any statesman that is? and if so, who?

Quest 4th If you answer the third question in the affirmative, what method would you recommend to raise money to defray the current expenses of the government?

Question 5th Are you in favour of a *horizontal* tariff, (so called) or are you in favour of discriminating duties with incidental protection?

Quest. 6th Are you in favour of a *protective* tariff, and if so, what great interests require *most* protection, if any? or do you prefer a tariff which will raise the necessary revenue only?

Quest. 7th Do you believe the *present* tariff, (that of 1842) to be just and equal, bearing alike on all the great interests of the country? if not, wherein is its operation unequal, and in what particular should it be altered or amended? Are you in favour of a large surplus revenue, and what would you do with it?

By communicating to me your views upon & answers to these several questions at your earliest convenience, and also any additional suggestions in relation to revenue, finance, protection &c. &c. you may think the importance of these subjects demands, you will very much oblige an inquiring public and especially, Dear Sir,

Your Friend and
Fellow Citizen,
WILLIAM PRESCOTT.

Hon. W. P. Mangum
    U. S. Senate.

[Addressed:]

Hon. W. P. Mangum U.S.S.
Washington City
D. C.

Charity A. Mangum to Willie P. Mangum.[298]

December 14, 1844.

My dear Husband

I received your letter on last Saturday and was so much relieved by the getting of it. I had hoped that the weather being

----

[298]The original is in the possession of Mangum Turner, Winston-Salem, N. C.

so much better than was expected that you would arrive safe
at Washington but could not help being uneasy.

I had as well acknowledge my weakness if it has to be called
so. After you left home no person but my Family saw me. I had
born so much better than I thought I would that when you left
home I could hold out no longer and had such a violent headache
and had to keep my room until next morning. P. Nash sent his
young man hoping to see you and tune Sallys Piano before you
left home. I could not see him but had the Piano tuned. He has
improved it greatly. I was very glad to learn that I had not
humbled the young gentleman that tuned. Cousin Abner had
not touched mine-

Cousin Abner Parkers Family has been in great distress for
a week looking every day for Mary's death. Dr. Smith attending her constantly. She would not let any person see her except two or three of her own family. The sight of more company than usual would throw her into violent storms- Her
mother stayed a day and a night from her when she was so bad
looking for her death any moment. For a day or two she has
appeared to mend and they have hopes of her recovery. I heard
several persons say that saw Cousin Abner that they had never
seen a man so disturbed before that he walked constantly day
and night. I have not been to see them as I understood I could
not see Cn'y, but sent every day for three or four days until
I found she was better if she continues to mend I hope to see
her in a few days.

William came very soon to Mother to get your kiss when he
saw your letter he ran to me to get Father's kiss.

You must be certain to let me know by your next letter if I
am to let Mr. Crabtree have five hundred weight of pork and
what Mr. Riley is to have and if I am to keep it. I know you
ought to keep part of it if you wish him to work well. We have
killed the hogs over the river. They were not as heavy as expected. I do not think you can spare Mr. Crabtree as much as
five hundred. He says you promised it. I desire to know. I let
Augustine Mangum have something more than two hundred.
He wants one more hundred.

You must certainly know what you desire so I can do what
you desire. William has gone to live with Jesse Parker. The
very place he ought to be- I do not know what to do about sleep-
ing. I cannot sleep upstairs. I have slept but very little since

you left home. I do not think I can get along through the winter upon so little sleep. I have a strong notion of moving in the new house. You must write before Christmas if you wish another chimney built quickly. I know it would be best to build one chimney near the barn to the lower house. Jesse Parker was to see him the other day to get him to build him two chimneys. If you wish yours done you can merely write soon-

Our children are all well as usual and send their love to Father. Farewell my dear husband and know I cannot be content while I am so much far from you-

Your devoted wife,

C. A. MANGUM,

W. P. MANGUM

————————

WPM-LC

E. D. Bullock[299] to Willie P. Mangum.

MOBILE Dec*. 17*th*. 1844.

My dear Judge.

I should have written you on my return to my friends but I left a few days after on my country Circuit and only returned a few days since. Shortly after my arrival here I received a letter from Walter advising me that you were perfectly restored to health. This I assure you gave me great pleasure as I feared that your lungs were seriously effected. I am happy to tell you that I found my family quite well all indeed having escaped the diseases of our fated climate. Mr. Gaines[300] is still absent in Missi: attending to the Court of Commissioners, which will expire by Law on the 19- of this month. The commissioners will be here in a few days on their way to Washington City to pass upon such claims as they have examined.

Our community has quieted down since the defeat of our noble chieftain. I have never in all my life witnessed such sore disappointment as has been manifested among the true friends of Mr Clay. I do not believe that any community has in its bosome more devoted friends of Mr Clay than ours & hence the

————————

[299]See above, III, 27n.
[300]See above, III, 27n.

sore disappointment that many feel. But fraud and practise'd villany have turned the tide against us and we must await some other time to buckle on our armour in the defence of those principles which alone can perpetuate our system of Government. I am at a loss to conjecture what will be the final result of the Locofoco rule in our land. The prospects in our community were cheering at the certainty of the election of Mr. Clay, all men seem to place implicit reliance upon the upright and glorious policy that would have propounded to the country in the event of his election but now all capitalists hug their money closer than at any other previous time and trade the life and soul of our Country has been fearfully shocked at the result of the Presidential contest. I hope that you and your noble peers that stood by the law and constitution in 1832 3- & 4 will again be and remain at your post to check the mad & merciless career of locofoco misrule. I should be most happy to hear your views about the coming administration and do not forget to place me upon your list. No one feels more delighted than I do to hear at all times of your good health & happiness. Be pleased to send me such documents as you may have of interest.

My Partner & myself have written a long letter to Thos. H. Blake Conn: of the General land office at Washington City in behalf of a client of ours, Mr. James T. Vivian of Washington County Alabama, who has employed us to procure for him a Patent to a certain piece of land lying upon the waters of the Tombigbee River in Washington Co. It is a matter of great importance to us and I must beg your influence in our behalf. You will see by reference to the letter now sent on to Mr Blake *that we have furnished all the evidence that was demanded in a letter written by Mr Blake to the Hon. B. G. Shields* a copy of which is annexed to our letter, before alluded to. We are unknown at the land office and you will confer a great favor if you will at some leisure moment as early as may suit your convenience, call at the land office and interpose your influence in our behalf. If you should not on the reception of this letter find it convenient to call on Mr Blake, will you address him a note upon the subject.

I had the pleasure to hear from Missi: on yesterday and am happy to say that all are well.

I hope my dear Judge that the ladies of your household are

all well and be pleased when you write to bear to them our sincere and devoted wishes for their health and happiness.

I am Yours most truly,

E. D. BULLOCK.

Hon. W. P. Mangum
    Vice Pres^t—

[Addressed:]

Hon Willie P. Mangum
    Vice Pres^t.
    U States Senate
    Washington City
    D. C.

WPM-LC

B. Hl. Kosciuszko[301] *to Willie P. Mangum.*

[19 December 1844]

To the Hon.
    P. M. [*sic*] Magnum
President of the Senate.

Sir

I beg You thousand & thousands pardon that having not the honor to be known to You, I permitted myself to trespass on Your valuable time with my correspondence; but being informed by *Public voice* (and it is saying *"Vox Populi* vox Dei") of your high character, I hope that when You will peruse my Epistle, You will excuse not only my boldness, but You will sympathize with my unhappy state—

I am unhappy nephew to Gen¹ *Kosciuszko.* and it is now Seven Years I am in this my adopted Country in the City of Washington and I am a Citizen- I am known in the Senate to the Hon Senator Crittenden as well to the Hon. Henry Clay, to whom on my first arrival at America I remitted a letter of Introduction from a distinguished Gentleman, and I was received by Mr Clay very kindly, from him I learned in what consist the welfare of this Country, & that only Whigs party could produce it- I hoped to see Mr Clay to be Our President,

---

[301]He was a nephew of the American Revolutionary hero, General Thaddeus Kosciuszko. In 1838 his request for a grant of public land was referred to the House Committee of Public Lands. Adams, *Memoirs,* IX, 469.

& certainly if he was I would be very happy in all my circumstances- but I am deprived together with many & many good citizens of that happiness—

1840 I enjoyed when our beloved Gen¹ Harrison was elected President- but how long that happiness- One month & all gone- *President died* Cabinet scattered, & my mind was so troubled that I got mental sickness and almost four Years I was deprived of all my senses- It is some more than four months I am recovered entirely from that unhappy sickness which sickness not only exhausted my resources I only have, but delayed my case in the Court of the D. C. for the amount of $5,000 left by my Uncle *Kosciuszko* which amount belongs to me as I am sole Survivor. Altho' I was out of means but I rejoiced to be well, because I hoped that wile my case will be decided I will be able to get by my industry & work the Sustenance for my little family as well I will pursue my case, and then I will be independent- but unhappy I am I got the unhappy sickness *Consumption* & it is three months I cannot leave my bed- & so at once deprived of my health I have lost the dearest gift *independence*.

In such my unhappy state I address myself to Your noble feelings to help me with some Dollars, & be assured not only my everlasting gratitude but that such Your noble deed shall have the reward of Almighty- Noble Senator Crittenden helped me with little amount on the 7th of the instant—

With high respect
Sir
Your most obedience Servant

B. H. [?] KOSCIUSZKO
Lieut Col. of the late Revolutionary
Polish Army.

Washington
19 December 1844.
The Crown *is my Star.*

[Addressed:]

To the Hon.
P. M. Magnum
President of the Senate
present.

WPM-LC

J. Watson Webb to Willie P. Mangum.

PHILADELPHIA
Dec. 20th 1844

My Dear Sir.

My friend Theodore E. Tomlinson,[302] well known & appreciated by all our Whig friends in New York, has just taken to himself a partner for life, & visits Washington on a Wedding excursion. Of course he desires to know *you*, & it affords me great pleasure to present him to your favorable acquaintance.

Very truly your friend
J. WATSON WEBB

P. S. I shall be with you next week. For God's sake *reject* Atwood.[303]

Hon W. P. Mangum

[Addressed:]   National Hotel

To the Hon:
W. P. Mangum
Washington
Mr. Tomlinson.

WPM-LC

Robert W. Alston[304] to Willie P. Mangum.

TALLAHASSEE MIDDLE FLA. 26th. Decr 1844

Honble Wiley P. Mangum

Dr Sir

You will recollect when I had the pleasure of meeting, you last summer, & before I left N. Carolina I promised to write you on my return home - which I should have done at an earlier period, but for having business in the Southern part of the Territory from which I only returned a few days since—

---

[302]A New York attorney. *Longworth's New York Directory*, 1844-1845, 345.
[303]Henry C. Atwood was nominated by Tyler for surveyor of revenue for the port of New York in December, 1844. He was not confirmed. *Executive Journal of Senate*, VI, 381.
[304]Robert W. Alston became collector of customs at St. Marks, Florida, in 1849. *American Almanac*, 1850, 106.

My intention of Visiting Washington is defeated by the defeat of our favourite, for the Presidency, which you are aware is the result from the most conclusive evidence, that much corruption was practiced at the Ballot Box, by the admission of *Thousands,* and *Tens* of *thousands* of Illegal Votes, smuggled in by the improper, interfearance of the friends of aur opponents, as well as a misrepresentation of principal, to suite the climate in which the Votes were located, which were wanted by the opposition to Elect their President. But I cannot believe any party, or set of men can remain united under an organization of such contradictory opinions as those advanced by the Loco Foco party are, and Judging from the expression of the news paper press up to this this [*sic*] time, we may well immagine that their troubles have already commenced and I am of opinion, that the sooner their plans are disconcerted the better for the country. It appears to be matter of doubt with many, who is to be the Ruling Spirit with the ensuing administration, whether it is to be Genl Jackson, Mr. Polk, or Mr Calhoun. I would like very much to have a hint from you, of your opinion of the matter. At any rate I immagine the friends of Mr Clay will not be very highly favoured. Save and except, what may be slightly cared for, by Mr. Tyler, who it is thought will still retain some influence with the new Kitchen cabinet— But in this crush, of the anticipated success of the Whig party, it becomes our duty to do the best we can, under the circumstances for our Whig friends, & our country, and as I have but little chance of doing much good for either especially out of Florida. I am perfectly willing to leave all important public matters, to you and our Whig friends who fill the more exalted stations of public confidence, and to request you to do as much as you can to obtain for us immediate admission into the Union of the States, and especially to obtain for us the appointment of officers of the Territory, who are citizens of the country, for the reasons, as given when in conversation with you last Summer. It is at all times unpleasant to complain of public men, and especially of officers of the Judiciary. But it is nevertheless some times our duty to do so, and I am sorry to say that those among us, are charged with incapacity and a palpable abuse of the priviledges confered, I therefore hope they will be Removed, and some of our own citizens appointed, and for the office of marshal I understand Capt. Daniel Byrd of Jefferson County will be urged by the Democrats who I have no doubt is competent consequently if his name should be sent up to the Senate I hope it will be your pleasure to urge upon your Whig friends the importance of his confirmation, as he meets my own views better than any one of that party I have any knowledge of. I donot know who will be urged for Judge. I understand however, Thos. Baltzell is spoken of by the Branch Clicke, we donot want him. Col. T. H. Butler is also spoken of, who was formaly a member of congress from S Carolina. he I think would give satisfaction. Branch as Governor is not a favourite with either party, and if we can git a sutable Gentleman who is a citizen of Florida we would gratly prefer him.

I regret exceedingly being placed in a position which I presume will preclude me from getting the office of collector of the port of St. Marks- but presume it would be perfect Vanity to ask a favour of the approaching administration - however if you find an opportunity of obtaining for me the appointment, I would be Very willing to accept of it—

I Remain Very Respectfully Your Friend

RBT. W. ALSTON.

N. B. You will please regard this as confidential

R. W. A.

[Addressed:]

> Honble Wiley P. Mangum
> President of Senate
> Washington City
> D. C.

Willie P. Mangum to Sally, Patty and Mary Mangum.[305]

Monday 30th-Dec. 1844

My dear Daughters

I send you a copy of Graham's Magazine-[306] I have not had time to read it. The engravings are fine-

[305]The original is in the possession of Mangum Turner, Winston-Salem, N. C.

[306]Graham's magazine was established by George R. Graham, who bought out Samuel C. Atkinson's *Casket* in 1839. About the same time, he bought Wm. E. Burton's *Gentleman's Magazine.* The combined magazines bore the title *Graham's Lady's and Gentleman's Magazine.* The titles varied slightly thereafter. A typical number in the forties "contained three or four short stories, a light essay on manners, a biographical sketch, a literary article, a considerable amount of poetry . . . an out-door sketch of Frank Forester, a travel article, fine arts and book-review departments, and a chat with the editor; besides the color fashion plates, and one or two art plates by well-known engravers." Its writers were among the most popular of the day, Poe, Hawthorne, William Gilmore Simms, and Bayard Taylor. Its circulation was one of the largest in the country. Mott, *History of American Magazines,* I, 544-555.

I am well- My love to Mother and all

Yrs affectionately

W. P. Mangum

To Misses
  Sally, Patty and Mary Mangum
  My love to Billy-

Willie P. Mangum to David Lowrie Swain[307] and Enclosure.

Washington 31st. Decr. 1844.

My dear Sir.

I transmit herewith, a letter from the Hon: Joel Crawford.[308] of Geo. to Gen: Clinch,[309] & Gen: C's note to me, & beg that you will give such information touching *expense* &c. as the nature of the enquiries may seem to require.

I have in general terms, strongly advised the sending of Mr. Crawford's sons to North Carolina, but have said that I will give in a few days, more specific information. As to the preparatory school- Is not that, at Hillsboro good & efficient? What might be the probable expense? Is Mr. Bingham's school full? If not, is not the latter prefereable? I think, his charge pr. annum is $150, if more please advise me.

I recd. last fall, while confined by illness to my bed, a note from you requesting the appointment to West point a young friend of yours which has not been acknowledged. I transmitted to the Department the name of the young gentleman with the usual request &c. &c. What has been the fate of it I know not as yet.

Be pleased to send a Catalogue of Students & the Course of of Studies in the University, if you have a spare copy.

With great respect & regard
I am, My Dear Sir.
Yr. friend & Obt. St.
Willie P. Mangum.

---

[307]The original is in the David L. Swain Papers, University of North Carolina, Chapel Hill, N. C.
[308]Joel Crawford, 1783-1858, a lawyer and soldier, served in Congress as a Democrat from Georgia in 1817-1821. *Biog. Dir. of Cong.,* 859.
[309]General Duncan L. Clinch, who served in the War of 1812 and the war against the Seminoles, was a Whig Congressman from Georgia in 1844-1845. *Biog. Dir. of Cong.,* 991.

Enclosure

EARLY COUNTY Nov 17th 1844

Dear General,

I have often wished to have with you, a conversation at length, on the merits of Chapel Hill the University of N. Carolina. You have had at least one son at the Institution, since its administration has been placed under the presidency of Gov. Swain.—Permit me in the form of a letter (since we may not soon meet) to have what you may choose to say of Chappel Hill.

I have three Sons aged 12, 14 & 16—all pretty sprightly boys, of sound constitutions, but none of them likely to attain gigantic size of body—acircumstance, all things considered, which I have no cause to regret. If properly trained they will, I think, make effective men in any honorable and useful walk of life.

I am in persuasion at least, "a utilitarian"—I have a thorough contempt for all unnecessary embellishments of either mind or body—Sooner than see a son of mine raised up to manhood, fribble in manners & a pedant in mind, I would consign him to the toils, the humblest toils of a workshop.

This remark will give you a hint of my purpose in educating sons & I hope you will do me the favor to write how far Chappel Hill is likely to advance the end I have in view.

My oldest son now at Montpelier, reads the Common Latin & Greek Classics with fluency, & has made some attainments in elementary Mathematics—My second & third, have commenced the study of latin.

Please let me know whether there is a good grammar or preparatory school at Chappel Hill—and what are the usual expenses of Boad, Clothing & tuition pr ann. not omitting to state whether there are instances at that place of wild Boy's spending their fathers money foolishly, & making boobus of themselves.

So it seems we have Mr Polk for our next president!! What think you of our American Democracy now? What incentive have the best or the worst educated men in the U. States (from the example of Clay's life) to take an eminently useful & distinguished part in the public service? No man among us can hope, by the most exalted & brilliant careers, for any other reward than a conscious satisfaction at having done his duty— and that, unless he has been particularly cautious or lucky, contervailed by condemnation of our insane public opinion.—

As early as 1820 I understand and expressed the belief that I should never see a really great man in the presidency of the U. States. But my hopes revived, on the subject, when Mr. Clay was brought forward last May under auspices apparently so favorable. But Sir, such is the condition on which Our Republic must exist.—if indeed it shall continue to exist.—I am mortified at the pitiful gullibility of the people; but we who are beaten must submit with as good grace as may be.

Be assured dear Sir, of the continued esteem & friendship of

Yr. mo obt.
JOEL CRAWFORD

Genl D. L. Clinch

N. B. Please address me at Blakely, Early County: Ga.

[Addressed:] Genl D. L. Clinch
                Jefferson County
                Georgia

———

Sketch of Willie P. Mangum.[310]

In the Senate, the Honorable WILLIE P. MANGUM presides. John Tyler, the Vice President, on the death of General Harrison became President of the United States. The Senate thereafter elected Samuel Southard, their presiding officer, he dying, they elected Judge Mangum their president. He lives, when at home, in Orange county, North Carolina. From his name, I should suppose that his ancestors were from Wales. However that may be, Judged Mangum's family is an ancient one in North Carolina, the name being found among the earliest settlers of that colony. He presides in the Senate and occupies the Vice President's room in the capitol. He is a man above the common size, of fair complexion and commanding air, rather grave in in his manners, but very agreeable and appears to be kind hearted. His voice is clear, sufficiently loud and distinct to be heard all over the Senate chamber and its gallery. On the whole, he is, taking him all and all, the best presiding officer, that I ever saw in any legislative assembly. He is always at

———

[310]This sketch is taken from *Mysteries of Washington City, during Several Months of the Session of the 28th Congress*, by a Citizen of Ohio [Caleb Atwater]. Washington, D. C. printed by G. A. Sage, 1844, 130-133.

his ease, always dignified and always agreeable. His appearance is that of a man about forty years old. He is a whig, unwavering and unflinching, yet like the Kentucky Senators, not a persecuting whig, often voting to confirm men in offices, who are not whigs, nor any thing else—long. He appears to look more to the interests of his country than his party. When I say this, I mean to draw no invidious distinction between Judge Mangum and others in the Senate. The feelings of senators must have been often severly tried by having to them the names of very incompetent men. Where the man is not decidedly a bad one though wanting decision of character, without which no man can be relied on, in any pressing emergency, the Senate let him pass as Hobson's choice, because they expect nothing better. In this way they have confirmed many nominations which I should have rejected at once, as destitute of a qualification, without possessing which, no man is fit for any office or any calling. So far as Ohio is concerned, not even one appointment of a citizen of that State, has been a good one, nor such an one as I would have made, during the last two years. I feel no hostility to any one of these weak men, but wish they had belonged to some other State, not to ours. Where the imbecility of a country is placed in the offices, it shows the strength of our institutions and the virtue of our people, which can get along tolerably well, though such weak men are appointed to offices. To have found so much imbecility, so carefully selected from the very surface of society, must have cost those a vast deal of labor, care and diligence, who have succeeded so well, so perfectly in hunting it up, and bringing it forward to the President and his secretaries for their acceptance and gratification! It is a strong argument in favor of the permanency of our institutions, which can bear such appointments. The Senate appear to be as hungry for the nomination of men well qualified for the offices to which they are nominated, as any trout ever was for a well baited hook—they jump at them in a moment and unanimously confirm them. The confirmation of CALHOUN'S appointment as Secretary of State is a case in point. The news spread like wildfire, and fell upon the ear like the roar of a water fall in the ear of a thirsty traveller, in the desert of Sahara.

Pp. 130-133. MYSTERIES OF WASHINGTON CITY, During Several Months of the Session of the 28th Congress. By a Citizen of Ohio. [Caleb Atiwater] Washington, D. C. Printed by G. A. Sage, E Street, Near Ninth.

1845

Willie P. Mangum to D. Francis Bacon.[1]

WASHINGTON CITY 2nd. January 1845.

My dear Sir

I have rec^d. your favors, the first of 25th. & the second of the 31st. Ult. for both of which pleased to accept my thanks. I have been waiting a letter from M^r. Pettis, giving in a more detailed form than did your first, the particulars, to enable us to see clearly our course.[2]

He has not yet written.

I conferred with M^r. Crittenden fully, upon the receipt of your first, showing your letter to him, feeling that it would not be in conflict with the cautionary reserve fit to be maintained. - I have opened the subject to no other person, feeling pretty sure that anything we may determine upon, will probably have the countenance of our friends. -

We both feel the weight, magnitude & real importance of the subject.

We are both decidedly in favor of movement provided we can see that it will not *deeply* implicate any of our friends, and that the result we seek, is to any important extent certainly attainable. —

The enquiry as *incidental* to other *legitimate* enquiries with a view to further legislation is clearly within the Constitutional Competency & proper functions of the Senate. -

The Committee or Commission to take testimony would not "eo Nomine" be *secret* - but as the Committee, or the Commission may determine whatever is Convenient, or calculated to accelerate their enquiries, the object *in that form* is attainable. -

---

[1] The original is in the Yale University Library, New Haven, Conn. In 1848-1849 D. Francis Bacon edited the *New York Daybook*, a Whig newspaper. Louis H. Fox, *New York City Newspapers, 1820-1850: a Bibliography*, 34. See also below Mangum to Bacon, January 11, 1845 and Bacon to Mangum, January 16, 1845.

[2] Charges of fraud in the presidential election of 1844 were made by both the Clay and Polk forces. Webster attributed the loss of Pennsylvania and New York to the fraudulent voting of foreigners. Calvin Colton maintained that there was fraud in New York, Pennsylvania, Georgia, and Louisiana. Justin H. Smith, *The Annexation of Texas*, 316-317.

As you spoke of coming to Washington, Crittenden & I both thought it expedient, as in oral communications we could more clearly see all the ground, and adapt our measures to the actual or probable state of the facts.

Will you come on immediately?

If we can make a strong & clear case, it will be of incalculable importance.

We doubt not that the Senate will cordially come up to any work, that may be deemed necessary to eviscerate these portentous frauds. -

We feel, that we & the Country owe you much for your indefatigable effort in this thankless, but patriotic & honest cause.

Your enclosures rec^d. this morning exhibit pretty clearly the field of operations - Yet it would be satisfactory to have somewhat more detailed information. - Again, Will you come to Wash^n.?

With great respect
I am dear Sir
Very truly y.^{rs}
WILLIE P. MANGUM

To
D. Francis Bacon
  New York.

WPM-LC

J. Watson Webb to Willie P. Mangum.

PHILADELPHIA
Janry 5th. 1845

My Dear Sir,

I am here in connexion with the Powell Libel suit,[3] which I hope to have postponed until Spring. If I succeed, I shall leave here on Wednesday for Washington.

I am writing in Randall's office[4] & at his request, merely to say that the Whigs here with one accord, beg that you will act upon the nomination of & J [torn] at once, as every day's de-

---

[3]See above, J. W. Webb to W. P. Mangum, October 18, 1844.
[4]Josiah Randall. See above, II, 236n.

lay is making for the benefit of Buchanan and the Loco Foco Party. Our friends think it all important to have King's weapon.

Your friend
J. WATSON WEBB.

Hon. W. P. Mangum.

[Addressed:]

To the Hon.
W. P. Mangum
Washington City,
D. (C.)

WPM-LC

William S. Mullens[5] to Willie P. Mangum.

FAYETTEVILLE, No: Ca.
9th of Jan, 1845

Hon Willie P. Mangum,

Dear Sir,

As Chairman of the Managing Committee of the "Fayette-ville Library Institute",[6] & under the instructions of the Committee, I take the liberty, which I trust you will excuse, of addressing you without the honor of a personal acquaintance with you. The Institute has been founded by the young men of this place with the design of gradually building up a Public Library & thus securing to all in the community the means of intellectual improvement. As a great assistance in the effort, I take the liberty of requesting you to forward to the Institute copies of such public documents as may be printed by the order of the

---

[5]William Sidney Mullens, of Fayetteville, graduated from the University in 1842. Later he moved to South Carolina and became a "brilliant speaker at the bar," the president of a South Carolina railroad, and a member of the South Carolina legislature. Grant, *Alumni Hist. of U. N. C.,* 447; Battle, *Hist. of U. N. C.,* I, 478.

[6]The Fayetteville Library Institute was incorporated in 1844. Johnson, *Ante Bellum N. C.,* 166.

Senate, if it shall be convenient to you to do so. Such a favour would very greatly oblige & aid us.

I have the honour to be with the highest respect

Your most obt. servant

WILL: S. MULLENS.

Hon Willie P. Mangum.

[Addressed:]

Hon. Willie P. Mangum
Washington Cty.

WPM-LC

Edmund Pendleton Gaines[7] to Willie P. Mangum.

Hd qr^s. Western Division
NEW ORLEANS, January 10th. 1845

My dear Sir:

I do myself the honor to introduce to your acquaintance and recommend to your attention Mrs Putnam, an amiable Tennessean, the widow of D^r. James R. Putnam[8] late of this city; with whom Mrs Gaines and myself have been acquainted for several years.

Mrs Putnam has been advised by several of her much respected friends of Tennessee and of this place in whose judgment she has confidence, to visit the city of Washington during the present session of Congress, with the view of making some such disposition of the Patent right granted to Dr Putnam on the 6th of May 1841 for new and useful improvements in Machinery for removing Bars, and other obstructions from the U. S. inlets, harbours and river, as will at once test the utility and establish the value of the discovery, and render the same serviceable to our Naval, Military and commercial interests, and available to the widow and young family of the projector in a pecuniary point of view as the principal fortune left to them for their support.

---

[7]At this time Gaines was a major general commanding the western division of the United States Army. *D. A. B.*, VII, 92. This letter was not signed by General Gaines himself.

[8]He was living at 118 Canal Street in 1842. He was listed as a dentist. *Gibson's Guide and Directory of the State of La. and the Cities of New Orleans and Lafayette,* New Orleans, 1835, p. 171.

Knowing as I do the deep interest which you take in whatever discoveries, and improvements tend to lessen the expense of our commercial intercourse whether foreign or domestic, and being convinced that the proposed improved means of deepening our ship channels and inlets by Steam power will contribute much to the attainment of the all important objects of *Defence* and commericial prosperity- objects not less dear to our agricultural and manufacturing friends of the central and Western States and interior districts of the Union than to the shipping and other merchants and traders of our large Sea Port towns, I think it my duty to desire your attention to Dr Putnam's plan.

Not a ship nor a steam boat can be lost or damaged by a Snag or a shoal- or other obstruction, without affecting more or less the interests of the farmers and planters or mechanics of the interior. And in war such obstructions might even in the presence of the invading foe cost us more vessels and more men, than the foe could, in the absence of such obstructions, take or destroy in Battle.

I respectfully suggest the propriety of granting to the widow and family of Dr Putnam, a specific sum of money for her Patent right. And then authorise the construction of a Steam Boat upon a larger scale than that proposed by Dr Putnam, to be built of the best Oak and Iron- principally Iron- upon the principles of the British Mail Boats convertible into Steam Ships of War with a view on the approach of War instantly to exchange her ploughs and scrapers with her machinery to break up and remove obstructions from our Inlets, Harbours and rivers, for a complete armament, for driving into the vitals of an invading Fleet, an ample supply of *Red hot shot* and Paixhan shells.

Every Fort upon the sea board ought to be supplied with a Floating Battery of the above description, to be manned with U. S. troops and volunteers and employed in Peace on every description of service necessary and proper to deepen our inlets and ship channels and extend other facilities to commerce- in a word- *in peace to prepare for war*- and in war to cooperate with our Forts in repelling invasion.

Although I have not advised Mrs. Putnam to visit Washington, I am convinced that the efforts of her husband to establish an improved system of deepening our shoal waters of the South and East have so far succeeded as to entitle his widow and orphan children to a respectable compensation.

And as the whole subject of *navigation* and *commerce,* as
well as of *National defense* embracing the improvements to set
forth in the claim belong exclusively to the Federal Government, I hope you will concur with me in the opinion that an
act or Resolution should be proposed for giving to Mrs Putnam
and her children a specific compensation for her claim.

But should there be any doubts as to the utility of Dr.
Putnam's plan for deepening our inlets and rivers by steam
power, let measures be taken at once to test its utility and ascertain its value so that his widow & orphans may not suffer
the affliction of that *"hope deferred which maketh the heart
sick."*

For myself I have not a doubt that the proposed plan of
deepening our ship channels, inlets and rivers is worth ten
thousand times as much as any Dredging vessel or Dredging
machine ever invented or ever known in the United States; as
with it we can speedily deepen the inlets at the mouth of the
Mississippi river and all other inlets now navigable for small
coasting vessels in this State and in most of our other Southern
States and Territories to any extent the Government may desire; and that we shall accomplish this all-important work
without any expense to the United States beyond the original
cost and repairs of the Steam boats or floating Batteries of Oak
and Iron- *principally of Iron-* here recommended, as the work
will be done by the United States Troops, and volunteers in
actual service in their daily exercises and drills with the few
Guns that should be placed on each vessel- *Drills* which will be
enjoyed by officers and men, and which will contribute more
to their health and comfort, and vastly more to their efficiancy
and fitness for Battle than any recreations which our fashionable
Watering places afford to the votaries of amusement and pleasure;
as every vessel will have as many State rooms and as many
sources of comfort as the largest and best of Passenger Steamers.
But the transcendent utility of the system here proposed will
be seen in the fact that our steam Boats or floating Batteries employed in giving action to our machinery for deepening our
inlets and cleaning out our rivers *in Peace-* will upon the first
suspicion of an approaching foe, lay aside all such machinery,
and in place of *Ploughs, Log chains and Scrapers* and other implements propelled by Steam power in Peace, instantly take on
board their Paixhan Guns and all other implements of *War*

held in deposite at the Forts to which the Boats or Batteries belong, and by co-operating with such Forts or Martello towers, will triumphantly *defend* the ship channels which they shall have been deepening.

This is a plain matter of fact view of the subject suggested by no French or English Book of the last century, but by the mighty change which steam power applied to Ships of War, rail roads and Snag Boats has produced *in the art of War.* I thank my God that the subject of steam power to Harbour improvements and Harbour defence is no longer enveloped in mystery, nor liable to be thrust aside by any miserable or magnificent *humbug* such as that of the the submarine explosions, by which the weak *are made to believe,* and the wicked *affect to believe* that our inlets & Harbours are to be defended by magnetic *wire workers.*

Give us the proposed plan for deepening our inlets *in Peace,* by means necessary to their defense *in War-* preparatory to War- and moreover give us rail roads with Dr Morse's Magnetic Telegraph, and my life for it we shall soon prove to an admiring World that we know how to defend as well as how to Govern ourselves and our country, and by means applicable alike to the successful work of making our beloved Republic prosperous and happy in Peace and impregnable in War.

> With very great respect, I am, Dear Sir,
> Your friend
> EDMUND PENDLETON GAINES
> Major General U. S. Army
> commanding the Western Division

The Honble. W. P. Mangum
President of the Senate
Washington City D. C.

Willie P. Mangum to D. Francis Bacon.[9]

WASHINGTON 11th. January 1845.

My dear Sir

I received this morning a letter from I. H. Pettis, stating that on the 22nd. Decr. he mailed a letter at N. Y. to my address -

⁹The original is in the Manuscript Collection, Yale University. See above Willie P. Mangum to D. Francis Bacon, January 2, 1845, and Bacon to Mangum, January 16, 1845.

None such has been received by me. - He further, states that
upon my advising you of the fact he will transmit through you
a copy. I shall be glad to receive it.

M^r. P. likewise says that I may expect to see you in Washington in a few days, at which I shall be gratified

If the revelations can be made, that you so confidently believe within reach, & so as not to exculpate our friends *as* a
party, they cannot but be of very great importance. - They will
brace the Whigs to renewed & more desperately energetic efforts.

With great respect
Yrs Very truly
WILLIE P. MANGUM

I have rec^d. three letters from you, & written but once hitherto, which I trust, you received. The miscarriage of M^r. P's letter,
leads to this statement

W. P. M.

To
D. Francis Bacon
    N. Y.

_____

WPM-LC

Willie P. Mangum to Charity A. Mangum.

WASHINGTON CITY 14th. January 1845.

My dear Love:

It has been too long, since I have written to you, but writing
to the children, I have sent home every week, except one.—
My health has been perfectly good since I left home, except for
two or three days past. I have had some cold, which however,
has not annoyed me much.—

I recd. your letters in regard to Eliza Moore. I should have
had great pleasure in aiding her in the manner desired, if my
own affairs would have admitted of it.— The[y] did not, however.

The times are such, & prices of every kind of produce, is so
low, that everybody almost, needs every thing due them. I
hope, My Love, that you are well & in good spirits.— I desire

extremely to see you & the children.— If I were at perfect ease, I should enjoy more of real life & happiness to be at home with you & our dear children, than I could possibly enjoy here in ten times the length of time. I hope everything is going on well under the management of Cousin Meekins.— I have great confidence in his judgment, industry & good management.

The Winter here has been usually agreeable, & the Weather the finest I ever saw in Washington in the Winter.— Our Whig friends are sombre & melancholy, but in no wise, dispirited in regard to the future.— Mr. Clay writes me that he and his family are well, & that he bears with quiet & resignation the unexpected result.

Yesterday, we had a duel in the neighbourhood between Mr. Clingman of No. Carolina & a Mr. Yancey, a member from Alabama.—[10] Clingman challenged him for offensive language used in debate in the Ho. of Reps.— They exchanged shots without injury. Yancy then made suitable explanations & the matter was settled.

Clingman bore himself with great calmness & resolution, & went through whole affair in a manner most honorable to him.—

I hope, my boy William attends to his book a good deal.— He can do that & catch birds also.— Tell Patty I hope, she will not let him be neglected.—

Give my Love to Sally, & tell her that I cannot *yet* fix the day that I will meet her in Petersburg to attend the inauguration.

Give my Love to Patty & Mary - & also to my boy, if he has been good.—

For yourself, My Love, always feel & know that you are dearer to my heart than all the world, our dear children not excepted, and I regard it the greatest misfortune of my life, that my vexed circumstances through life, always affecting or souring the temper, have not suffered me always to manifest the full extent of my confidence in you & My Love & affection for

---

[10]In the course of the debate in early January, 1845, on annexation, Thomas L. Clingman accused the Democrats of unfair tactics in the presidential campaign of 1844. W. L. Yancey replied with a personal attack on Clingman accusing him of being deficient in honor. Clingman challenged Yancey. The duel was fought near Bladensburg, Maryland. After the first shots the difficulties were settled by consultation of the seconds. *Memorandum of the Late Affair of Honor between Hon. T. L. Clingman, of North Carolina, and Hon William L. Yancey, of Alabama. Printed by Yancey Feb. 13, 1848, for private circulation.* 8 pp. See also Stephen B. Weeks, "The Duello in North Carolina and among North Carolinians," *Charlotte Democrat,* December 23, 1887, in Stephen B. Weeks, *Miscellaneous Studies in Southern History, 1886-1897.*

you.— May God bless you My dear Love & our dear children - & Spare us many years for love, quiet & affection—

Your affectionate husband
WILLIE P. MANGUM

To Mrs. Charity A. Mangum

I have sent home a good many seeds.— The *names* & *places* ought to be entered in a book when they are planted.

Give my thanks to Patty for her pretty & agreeable letter to me, & say to Sally, I should like to have an opportunity of sending my thanks to her.

W. P. MANGUM

WPM-D

Reverdy Johnson to Willie P. Mangum.

ANNAPOLIS 15 Jany [1845]
/45 - 12 P.M.

My Dear Judge

I know you will be delighted to hear, that in the Whig caucus tonight, I was selected as Senator of Md., on the *first* ballot, having recd. a majority of all the votes— Make it known to our mutual friends—

Yrs most sincerely
REVERDY JOHNSON.

[Addressed:]

Honble
Judge Mangum
In Senate
Washington   [Postmarked:] Annapolis Md.
Jan 15

WPM-LC

D. Francis Bacon to Willie P. Mangum.[11]

NEW YORK, Thursday night,
January 16, 1845.

Sir,

I regret to be compelled to withdraw for a day or two my promise to meet you in Washington. I have been pushing the investigation and have made much progress since I wrote to you. I am backed and supported by some of the best, ablest and richest men in New York. I have obtained some important specifications against certain individuals as having planned, directed and *suborned*. But I wish especially to obtain a list of the names of the actual performers, with the details of their operations, specifying the places where the plurality of ballots were deposited. This I hope soon to obtain. No pains - no means will be spared to secure this. We deal with the highest order of our foes. The inducements which we offer are proportional. Tens of thousands are within our scope.

I have many important facts which you ought to know; but I can not do any justice to them by any other than an oral statement which I trust soon to give you, - on Sunday or Mon-night.

Excuse this hasty scrawl, and believe me

With great respect,
yours faithfully,

D. FRANCIS BACON.

Hon. President of the Senate.

WPM-LC

William H. Battle[12] to Willie P. Mangum

CHAPEL HILL Jan'y 18th 1845

Sir/

The Executive Committee of the Alumni Association of the University of North Carolina have, in pursuance of the duty

---

[11]See above, Mangum to Bacon, January 2, 11, 1845.
[12]After graduating from the University in 1820, William Horn Battle, 1802-1879, became an attorney, state supreme court reporter, judge of the superior and supreme courts of North Carolina and professor of law at his alma mater. Twice he revised the statutes of the state. *D. A. B.*, IV, 58; Ashe, *Biog. Hist. of N. C.*, VI, 20-25.

assigned them for that purpose, appointed you to deliver an address before the Association on the day preceding the next annual commencement of the University, and have instructed me to inform you of the appointment and to request your acceptance of it-[13]

The Association has been but recently organised and you are the first person appointed to deliver an address before it. In making the appointment the committee have adopted a rule to select a member of the class which was graduated thirty years before the address is to be delivered, and to invite specially all the other members who are living to attend.- We trust that you will assist in promoting the objects of the Association and gratify your numerous friends by accepting the appointment. Be pleased to let us hear from you at an early day.

With great regard
I am your's &C.
WILL: H. BATTLE

Hon. Willie P. Mangum
    Washington City

[Addressed:]

Hon. Willie P. Mangum
President of the Senate
Washington, City

WPM-LC

C. L. Hinton to Willie P. Mangum

RALEIGH Jany 19th 1845

Dr Sir

I dislike very much to trouble you with a third letter[14] about reestablishing the Post office at Busbees Store, but the solicitude of Mr Loring must be my apology for asking your attention to the subject at this time.- The particulars I presume you have not forgotten, Busbee has removed from his former residence

---

[13]Although Mangum did not attend this commencement, the LL.D. degrees were conferred upon him, James K. Polk, and James Y. Mason. William H. Battle reported that he was unable to obtain a speaker. In place of an address he and others read brief sketches of the lives of ten of the alumni who died during the year.. Battle, *Hist. of U. N. C.,* I, 496.
[14]See above, 226.

and the Post Office discontinued. Loring has purchased it and wishes to print his paper there, the situation is ten miles from this place- no other office nearer than this, it had been keep up I suppose for twenty year, Loring wishes to be Post master and I have no doubt is desired by the neighbours— I should have written to Judge Sanders about it, but I fear his strong prejudices to Loring would induce him to oppose it— Be pleased to write me on the subject-

Very Sincerely
Yr friend
C L HINTON

[Addressed:]

> Hon. Willie P Mangum, M. C.
> Washington City
> D. C.

WPM-LC

Geo. E. Badger to Willie P. Mangum

RALEIGH Jany. 21st. 1845

My dear Sir.

The letter for Judge Wayne[15] enclosed in the same envelope with this, relating to a question in our Circuit Court here, and therefore partaking of a public character, may properly be embraced by the *equity* of the Statute conferring the franking privilege on Senators and other dignitaries- I send it therefore under the protection of your name and beg you will cause it to be delivered to the Judge.

I suppose you *sometimes* see Crittenden- If so make my respects to him- and say for me that I should like to learn upon what terms he now is with his old master Capt. Tyler- I fear he cannot communicate the information as fully as I should desire to have it, except in a personal interview- and for this purpose, to say nothing of others of inferior importance, I beg he will come and see me- If he knew how much pleasure such a visit

---

[15]Judge James M. Wayne, of Georgia, 1790-1867, was appointed as justice of the United States Supreme Court by Jackson in 1835. He served until his death in 1867. *Biog. Dir. of Cong.*, 1675-1676; *D. A. B.*, XIX, 565. The enclosure is not in the Mangum Papers.

William Segar Archer, 1789-1855. From the oil portrait by G. P. A. Healy in the possession of the Virginia State Library, Richmond.

Benjamin Watkins Leigh, 1781-1849. From the oil portrait, attributed to William J. Hubard, in the possession of the Virginia Historical Society, Richmond.

would give Mrs. B. and myself, I think he would give us a call
at the end of the session- Tell him to be a clever fellow and do
it-

I beg you to excuse me for the trouble I give you and believe
me

most truly & respectfully
your friend & Servt.
GEO. E. BADGER

Hon. Mr. Mangum.

[Addressed:]

The Honorable
W. P. Mangum
Prest. of the Senate

Willie P. Mangum to Patty Mangum[16]

WASHINGTON 21st. Jan. 1845

My dear Patty,

I have but a moment before going into the chair today. I send
herewith two books for beginners in the French language- the
smaller one in six lessons. I wish you to begin and study it
closely, accurately and with care- You can learn enough to
translate French papers that may occur in your reading- I shall
send you a grammar and dictionary- You will not need them at
present.

I am well- I recd your mother's letter and was glad to hear
that all are well-

My love to Mother, your sisters, Sally and Mary and your
brother William.

Yrs affectionately,
W. P. MANGUM

---

[16]The original is in the possession of Mangum Turner, Winston-Salem, N. C.

WPM-LC

Redwood Fisher[17] to Willie P. Mangum

NEW YORK Jany. 30. 1845.

The Hble
    Willie P Mangum

        My Dear Sir

            I beg leave to call myself to your friendly recollection,
and to believe my solemn assurances that I have no earthly objects in writing you at this time, but to save our friends who
are trembling for their fate in case Mr Atwood[18] should be rejected by the Senate.

I am almost daily called upon by them and urged to write
to some friend in the Senate. Accordingly I have written to
Mr Huntingdon[19] assuring him, that Mr Atwood is a faithful
public officer, that our friends will be safe if he is confirmed,
and that should he be rejected no one can answer for the consequences, as in that case the whole torrent of Tammany Hall,
will in all probability find a passage into our Custom House,
and not only every Whig, but every moderate man be sacrificed.
I now my dear Sir repeat this to you, and you may rely upon
my knowledge in this matter.

Although I am sure you will believe me without my stating
to you my own Situation and views yet it may not be amiss for
me to say, that I shall be a private citizen in a few weeks. My
open vote, and known attachment for Mr Clay it is alike my
pride, and duty every where to avow, and of course I cannot
hold office under the new dynasty, having no spark of locofocoism in my composition. To our good friends Mess[s] Phillips
Phoenix & H Fish[20] my feelings and conduct are well known
and I can with great confidence refer you to them, for the confirmation of what I write, as well as regards Mr Atwood as myself.

Repeating therefore that I have no earthly motive but the
one stated in urging the confirmation of Mr Atwood I conclude

---

[17]Redwood Fisher was a former editor of the *Mercantile Advertiser and New York Advocate* in
1838. In 1845 he edited the *National Magazine and Industrial Record. William and Mary Quarterly,*
Ser. 2, Vol. IV, pp. 155-156; Fox, *New York City Newspapers, 1820-1850,* 65.
[18]See above, J. Watson Webb to W. P. Mangum, December 20, 1844.
[19]Jabez Williams Huntington, 1788-1847, was Senator from Connecticut from 1840 to 1847.
Biog. Dir. of Cong., 1133.
[20]Jonas Phillips Phoenix, Congressman from New York in 1843-1845, and Hamilton Fish,
Congressman from New York and future Secretary of State. *Biog. Dir. of Cong.,* 967-968, 1410.

fully confiding that you will place this letter to the true motive which has dictated it and subscribe myself with the greatest respect

Your obt St-
REDWOOD FISHER

WPM-LC

Samuel B. Williams[21] to Willie P. Mangum.

United States Hotel
NEW YORK Feby 5th. 1845

To the
    Honl. Willie P Mangum
       President of the Senate. &c. &c.

      Sir

          I most respectfully enclose to your address the petition of Sundry Gentlemen in favor of a reduction of postage throughout the United States, and request that the same may be laid before your honourable body—

deeming a few remarks not illy appropriate on a subject of this nature, I would observe that I am personally in favor of a credit system, as I conceive it is the only protection the educated part of the community, under our form of Government have over the uneducated, and in order to sustain that System, I am in favor of a tariff to prevent foreign merchandise coming into the country to an extent as to deprive our Banks of their special basis and so far to protect our manufacturers.

I am opposed to a distribution of the general revenue for State purposes- but would favor an appropriation of four or more Millions of dollars of surplus revenue for the expenses of the Post Office department, in order that Newspapers and pamphlets may be conveyed free of postage, and letter postage a mere charge of record—and charge the franking privilege now enjoyed to the general expenses.—

---

[21]Possibly a commission merchant in New York City. *Longworth's New York Directory*, 1847-1848, 443.

I trust you will deem the enclosed petition and remarks worthy your immediate action—and remain

Most Respectfully
Your obt Servt
SAM. B. WILLIAMS

[Endorsed in hand of W.P.M.:]

This accompanied a petition I presented this morning

WPM-LC

William G. Cochran[22] *to Willie P. Mangum*

PHILADELPHIA Feby 8th 1845

Hon: W. P. Mangum
   U. S. Senate.
      Washington City.

My Dear Sir,

I See from the morning papers that the President has nominated Mr. John M Read[23] of this City as Judge of the Supreme court of the United States in place of Judge Baldwin Deceased.

This is certainly one of the Very best appointments Mr Tyler ever made, and I hope the whig Senators will go for him unanimously, of course you cannot expect Mr. Polk to nominate any other than a *Loco.*

I have been a very active whig here, and I have not seen any of our friends, that are not in favour of Mr Reads Confirmation, I know him personally, and a more correct gentlemanly man I never knew-

This is the first of Mr. Tyler appointment I ever wished *particularly,* to see confirmed, and as a rebuke to him (Tyler) I should like to see it unanimous, to shew him that the Whigs were always *ready to go for* Gentlemen & competent men when nominated

[22]William G. Cochran was a wine merchant in Philadelphia. *McElroy's Philadelphia Directory,* 1852, 78.
   [23]John Meredith Read, 1792-1874, a graduate of the University of Pennsylvania, was city solicitor of Philadelphia, a member of the legislature, and United States District Attorney before Tyler in 1845 nominated him for associate justice of the United States Supreme Court. Because of his anti-slavery views, the Senate rejected the nomination. After that he was attorney general of Pennsylvania and justice of the Pennsylvania supreme court. *D. A. B., IX,* 427-428.

I shall take it as a personal favour if you will use your influence for him, and believe me Very Truly

Your old friend and obt servant

WM G COCHRAN.

P. S. let me know what you think of it.

WPM-LC

Edward Stanly to Willie P. Mangum

WASHINGTON Feby 10th 1845

My Dear Sir,

My young friend & connection Benjamin T. [*sic*] Guion,[24] is an applicant for admission as a Cadet at West Point. I fear it is not in your power to assist him, but he earnestly requests me to write to you in his behalf—

He is a fine, manly fellow, of good education, the Grandson of a Revolutionary soldier, and the son of a widowed mother, who has a large family in narrow circumstances. From the first district,- Clingman's there is no applicant. Probably you might have Guion appointed to fill that vacancy, if Clingman has no constituent who desires the place.

Genl Scott, as he has I think according to usage, the right of nominating a few, would take pleasure in pleasing you.- If you can see Scott, & it is not too late, say a word, on my part, & from yourself for young Guion. Arrington of course, will do nothing for any Whig family.—

Nothing new with us— We ardently hope the Senate will save us from the Annexation-with Texas.—

In haste

Your's truly

EDW. STANLY

Hon: W. P. Mangum

W. City

Don't forget Brown's case:-[25] one of the Vice Presidents of Tyler's convention went to the Capt: & he *in his presence sent*

----

[24]Benjamin Simmon Guion, of New Bern, 1826-1893, graduated at the University of North Carolina in 1848. He became the superintendent of the Western North Carolina Railroad and a major in the Confederatee army. Grant, *Alumni Hist. of U. N. C.*, 241.

[25]See above Edward Stanly to W. P. Mangum, December 2, 1844, and February 15, 1845.

his nomination to the Senate! I KNOW THIS.- It is already dividing them & the Locos:- let a Loco have it, he cannot help this.
but not a Tyler man & a corrupt man (of course) at that.-

[Addressed:]

> Hon: Willie P. Mangum
> U. S. Senate
> Washington City

WPM-LC

Louisa S. Childs²⁶ to Willie P. Mangum.

ROCHESTER Feb. 10th 1845

Dear Sir

When I recall to your memory the name of Mrs. Childs a
member of the little Mess at Miss Tolson's two winters ago, I
trust that I need not apologize for the liberty I take in requesting your frank for two Carolina friends.

Our little company has been scattered far and wide, and
you, I believe, are the only one remaining in Washington.— Of
Mr. Shepherd²⁷ I have heard nothing, of Mr. & Mrs Williams
very little, since we parted. Of poor Miss Gamble I heard that
she had sought refuge in the West-Indies against consumption,
but nothing more.—

The late Election closed the door against many anticipated
reunions of Whig friends.- Except myself, all were gay and
sanguine here untill the very last day of the campaign.- For
more than a year I felt a painful presentiment of our defeat,
and frequently urged upon Mr. Childs the possibility of a disappointment, but he laughed at my presages, and when I did
come it struck to his very heart.— It was a terrible blow to all,
but of all the causes that conspired to inflict it the Liberty party
was the most treacherous and detestable. Compared with them
the herd of foreign convicts and Paupers who were bribed to
roll the car of Loco-Focoism over the laws and liberties of the

---

²⁶Probably the wife of Timothy Childs, who was a Whig Congressman from Rochester, New
York in 1841-1843. *Biog. Dir. of Cong.,* 807.
²⁷She probably refers to A. H. Shepperd, Whig Congressman from North Carolina in 1841-
1843; Christopher Harris Williams, Whig Congressman from Tennessee, 1837-1843; and the daughter of Roger Lawson Gamble, Whig Congressman from Georgia in 1841-1843. *Biog. Dir. of Cong.,*
998, 1517, 1703.

nation are pure. But I did not intend to trespass on your time by useless political regrets or party phillipics, for without recuring to causes it is quite enough for us that the victory we so justly deserve was wrested from us.— Mr C sends his best respects.—

You will oblige me much by sending Mr Clingman's speech.-[28] I do not know him, but I am deeply interested in any one whose talents reflects honor upon my native state.—

Who will be our next candidate for President. I wish you would make us a visit and talk it over before you return to Carolina. We should be truly happy to see you. Yours, very respectfully

LOUISA S. CHILDS.

[Addressed:]

Hon. W. P. Mangum
Washington, D. C.

WPM-LC

W. A. Graham to Willie P. Mangum and Enclosure.

[13 February, 1845]

RESOLUTION Relative to the Re-Building of the Branch Mint at Charlotte.[29]

Resloved, That out Senators and Representatives in Congress be respectfully requested to urge upon their respective bodies the expediency and necessity of making a sufficient appropriation for re-building the Branch Mint at Charlotte, in this State.

Provided, That nothing herein contained shall be construed as sanctioning the former extravagant expenditures of the Branch Mint, or of recommending the Edifice to be furnished for the personal comfort of the officers, but that it shall be designed and constructed solely for the purpose of coining money for the public advantage.

---

[28]In early January Thomas L. Clingman made a strong attack on annexation and on Calhoun. Yancey replied and the duel followed. See above, 252n.

[29]On July 27, 1844, a fire almost totally destroyed the building and machinery of the mint. In 1846 it was rebuilt but because of competition with California gold and the decline in output in North Carolina gold mines, the Charlotte mint soon became of little importance. Robert L. Cherry, "The Charlotte Mint," *The Tarheel Banker,* XVI, No. 9 (March, 1939), pp. 21-23.

Resolved, That his Excellency, the Governor, be respectfully requested to transmit to our Senators and Representatives in Congress, a copy of the foregoing Resolution.

Read three times in General Assembly, and ratified the 8th January, 1845.

EDW. STANLY,
Speaker of the House of Commons.

BURGESS S. GAITHER.
Speaker of the Senate.

STATE OF NORTH CAROLINA, ⎫
  Office Of Secretary Of State. ⎭

I, William Hill, Secretary of State, in and for the State of North Carolina, do hereby certify, that the above is a true copy of resolutions passed at the last General Assembly of this State. Given under my hand, this 13th. day of February, 1845.

WM. HILL

Executive Department
RALEIGH, Feby 13/45.

Sir,

By the request of our last Legislature, I have the honor to transmit the foreging Resolutions-

Very respectfully
WILL. A. GRAHAM

WPM-LC

Edward Stanly to Willie P. Mangum.

WASHINGTON [North Carolina,] Feby: 15th 1845

My Dear Sir,

The worst part of the correspondence with friends is, that it imposes on us the duty of answering their letters. I know the nature of your engagements & do not expect or request an answer.—

I wish you to have, if you can speedy action on Brown's case.—[30] There will be probably in a few days, several applications from this district for his place & some from decent, honest men.— Arrington's favorite, is a Mr. Cananay, a trifling, bloated drunkard & gambler - some other decent nomination will be made should Brown be rejected: no matter whom - let him be rejected.

Jesse Speight was his patron & friend, in 1833 or 34, when a nullifier was turned out & he put in - this may do to whisper in the ears of Huger, McDuffie & Lewis[31] & will have its influence.- & I am afraid Jesse will exert himself with Polk & have him retained. He married in Greene Co., where Jesse formerly lived.- *Early action is very necessary,* for after rejection Polk will be excusable for preferring some Democrat, to a Tyler man, accused also of malpractice in office, as Brown is.—

Col: Tayloe formerly a member of the State Convention, one of the Com: who received Mr Clay in Raleigh & recently a Senator from Beaufort & Hyde, was the States rights man, turned out by Jackson for Brown.—

Do quickly, whatever is to be done with this case, & let me have a single line informing me of the result.— Call the attention of Messrs. Huntington, Baerrien & others to this case.—

Mrs. S. sends her kind regards.—
Very truly your's
EDW. STANLY

Hon: W. P. Mangum
   W. City

[Addressed:]

Hon: Willie P. Mangum
   U. S. Senate
   Washington City

[Postmarked:] Washington N. C. Feb 16

---

[30]See above, Edward Stanly to W. P. Mangum, December 2, 1844 and February 10, 1845.
[31]Daniel E. Huger, a states' rights Democrat in the Senate from 1843 to 1845; George McDuffie, a Calhoun supporter in the Senate, 1843-1846; and Dixon Hall Lewis, a states' rights Democrat from Alabama in the Senate, 1844-1848. *Biog. Dir. of Cong.,* 1126, 1222-1223. 1261.

WPM-LC

Quinby Williams[32] to Willie P. Mangum.

BALTIMORE Feby 19th. 1845

Honored Sir

It becomes my duty in my official capacity to inform you of your Election as an Honorary Member of the

Ogden Institute
Very Respectfully
QUINBY WILLIAMS,
Cor Sec.

Hon W. P Mangum

[Addressed:]

Hon. W. P. Mangum
Washington
D. C.

_____

WPM-LC

Tod R. Caldwell to Willie P. Mangum

MORGANTON 19th. Febry 1845

Honl. W. P. Mangum

Dear Sir. I rec^d. a day or two ago a letter from an uncle of mine in the State of Alabama, Cornelius Robinson Esqr.[33] informing me that he is an applicant for the office of Marshall for the Southern District of Alabama, and requesting me if I had any friends in Congress, to write to them and ask their influence in his favour. I do not suppose the President will be apt to consult the Whigs in regard to his appointments, but perhaps something might be done by a Whig thro' some democrat who is a personal friend-. If you can use any influence in behalf of Mr. Robinson you will confer a favour on me by doing so, he will not be objectionable to the President on account of his

---

[32]Unable to identify.
[33]From North Carolina, Robinson moved to Georgia where he married Kezziah Hardwick in 1816 and then moved to Alabama. *William and Mary Quarterly*, Ser. 2, Vol. III, p. 157.

politics, for he is a *good* democrat, and I think a gentleman well qualified for the discharge of all the duties of the office for which he is an applicant-.

We have no news of interest in our Mountain country, every thing seems to be moving on smoothly in the political world and the people are beginning to get over their disappointment in the result of the Presidential election and I am happy to say are Whigs as firm and as true as they were the day they voted for Clay & Frelinghuysen, they have no variableness or shadow of turning.- We are anxiously awaiting every day the news of the defeat of the Texas resolution by your honourable body.- Minerva desires me to send her love to you.-

                              I am, dear Sir, Your
                              Obt. Svt.
                              TOD R. CALDWELL

[Addressed:]

            Honl. W. P. Mangum
            Senate U. States
            Washington
                D. C.

                                        WPM-NC

Willie P. Mangum to Tod R. Caldwell

                              WASHINGTON CITY 20th. Feby 1845.
My dear Sir.

As events at Washington are rapidly Verging to a point of high & fearful interest I avail myself of a leisure moment to write to you a few lines.

I think now, & to day for the first time, that the joint resolutions for the Annexation of Texas will pass the Senate.- It will not pass without amendment, but so amended as to Meet with

favor from the democracy of the House.-[34] Benton's proposition
with probably some amendment, will most likely be added to
the joint reso: offering to Texas the alternative of accepting
the terms of the Resolution: or in the case of her refusal to open
negotiation with Commissioners & the stipulations to be submitted to both Governments for acceptance or rejection.-

The annexation in this form will excite deep feeling in the
North, North east & East. It will stir to its foundation the abolition & antislavery feeling, & lead not remotely I fear, to a state
of things to be deplored by every friend of the Country.- The
arrival of the President elect has given a powerful impulse to
party action on this subject.- He is for Texas, Texas, Texas; &
talks of but little else, as I learn.- He says that the Democrat
who shall falter, will have thrown upon him a fearful responsibility.- You cannot easily estimate the Weight of influence that
a New President backed by his party, can exercise, upon the
Weak the doubting, the Mercenary & the paltrily & measly ambition.- Benton, the manliest among them, will be compelled to
Compromise, or succumb, or be crushed.- The tone of the English
press- recking the most offensive & worst possible spirit, in
connection with her undoubted diplomatic movements & intrigues, to Combine Europe against our further aggrandizement,
& her efforts to poison the public mind of Mexico ag[t] us, as well
as the heads of as many in Texas, as her policy or money can
reach, give a vast momentum to the other popular & party considerations, in favor of annexation.- Though our Gov[t]. has done
much to disgrace itself in this matter, & ought to be held by our
countrymen to the strictest responsibility yet I will never recognize the rightful interposition of any European Power in a
matter of this sort.- I would repel it, as far as I might, with
the whole resources of our Gov[t]. & people. It is obvious that
the whole diplomatic Corps here, are adverse to the Course of
the party in power- *that* gives strength to it.- The foreign War

---

[34]On January 25, 1845, the House, by a vote of 120 to 98, approved the joint resolution. The
Senate Committee on Foreign Relations reported unfavorably on the resolution February 4. Thereupon, Benton proposed a substitute bill which would have left to the negotiation of the United States
and Texas the boundaries and the terms of cession. All of this delayed matters until only two weeks
were left before the adjournment of Congress. By Benton's action the Democrats were split and the
Whigs hoped to use this division for their political advantage. Annexation seemed certain. The only
question was its form. February 13 Polk arrived in Washington and things began changing. He apparently used patronage to influence Senators. Houston had already announced that if annexation was
not passed by March 4 he would take the stump against any other effort to join the United States.
Reports from France and Great Britain also influenced some to vote for the measure. Robert J.
Walker solved the problem by proposing that Benton's bill be added as an alternative choice either
of which the President was left free to adopt under the joint resolution. The amended resolution
passed the Senate 27 to 25 and the House 132 to 76. Wiltse, *Calhoun: Sectionalist*, 212-214; Chitwood, *John Tyler*, 359; Eugene I. McCormac, *James K. Polk: A Political Biography*, Berkeley, 1922,
312-316.

can grow out of this rapacious act- Mexico cannot, & England will not fight for Texas, but *she will* for Oregon.

The War Spirit is high with the democracy, especially the Western Section of it.- As War with G. Britain would bring to them more prosperity & money, than would Six inches of the richest Compost bring to the barren fields of Carolina, were it to descend from the Clouds!- Our Whole Atlantic board would be swept for the first year, as with a Sirocco of fire- & the float-interest w^d. sink into the earth with the oppressive Weight.-

I hope nothing, Committing us to War, Will be done on the Oregon question.- If we w^d. but be quiet, that Country would fall into our possession without an effort, as soon, at least, as *We shall* need it.-

Polk Keeps *Close* on his Cabinet, & holds up the matter, with a high demo: policy, until the Texas question shall be settled- He desires to avoid the responsibility of his Adm^n for that policy & the *form* of urging it for war, & yet indirectly, does all he can to push it through at this Session.- His great men obviously are- Walker, Buchanan, Cave Johnson & I think Saunders- Calhoun must walk the plank-[35] Every thing is yet uncertain, & famished Wolves would not work with more eager & greedy effort than do the different Sections of the democracy.

The Whigs are at ease, they are quiet, cherishing no excessive feeling, but as a mass devoted to the principles of their Cause- Three Will Vote for Texas- Foster[36] as sound a Whig as any, in other respects.- Henderson & Merrick always a little fishy, & possibly Johnson of Louisiana, who has not yet given sufficient evidence of his power to resist very strong action upon him.-

The old North has stood firmly.- How does Clingman get on among your religionists & churchmen?[37] He is a fine, bold, decided & talented fellow- of great use to us here.-

It was to be regretted that he had to fight, but it was unavoidable, & to have declined would have disgraced him here & destroyed his just Weight & influence.- Whereas now, even the upturned White eyes of the puritan of New England, look up-

---

[35]Calhoun's friends brought much pressure on Polk to have Calhoun appointed. On February 26 Polk finally told Calhoun that there was to be an entirely new Cabinet. According to some, Senator John A. Dix, a Barnburner from New York, agreed to vote for the annexation of Texas if Polk would agree not to bring Calhoun into his Cabinet. McCormac, *James K. Polk*, 289-290; Wiltse, *Calhoun: Sectionalist*, 213-214.

[36]He refers to Ephraim H. Foster, Senator from Tennessee, John Henderson, Senator from Mississippi, William D. Merrick, Senator from Maryland, and Henry Johnson, Senator from Louisiana. Foster voted against the resolution of annexation. The others voted for it. *Niles' Register*, LXVII, 401.

[37]He refers to T. L. Clingman's duel with W. L. Yancey.

on him with Confidence & respect.- I trust, no Court in No. Ca. (however muc[h] in the abstract, I abhor duelling, & abhor & scorn & detest the Wanton seeker of duels) will require a son of No. Ca to sacrifice his honor & public usefulness rather than resent an indignity & gross outrag[e]

Present my Love & most affectionate regards to your dear Wife, & accept for yourself the assurance

my high respect & friendship

WILLIE P MANGUM

To

    Tod Caldwell esq^r.

WPM-LC

J. Watson Webb to Willie P. Mangum

NEW YORK

February 21. 1845

My Dear Sir.

    William Paxton Hallett, who has been nominated as Consul to Liverpool, is a gentleman of character & intelligence; and although a Loco Foco, by far the most unexceptional appointment Mr. *Tyler* has made from the ranks of our opponents. I sincerely hope he may be confirmed, as Polk will certainly give us a Van man.- I hope to be with you next week.

Yours very truly

J. WATSON WEBB

Hon. W. P. Mangum

[Addressed:]

To the Hon

W. P. Mangum

Washington City

D. C.

Willie P. Mangum to William A. Graham[38]

WASHINGTON CITY 21st. Feby: 1845.

My dear Sir.

I have not written to you, because we have had nothing of interest, that did not mostly appear in the public prints. - Events are rapidly verging here to a point of great & startling interest. - I now believe, & yesterday for the first time, that the Resolution from the House annexing Texas, will pass the Senate, probably with amendment that will be agreed to in the House. -

It will produce deep & dangerous excitement in portions of the North & East. Besides the outrage upon the Constitution & past precedents, it will stir deeply the anti Slavery feeling, & shake profoundly the confidence of higher & better men in the perpetuity of our system. - This feeling will be confined for the most part to the North, North east & the East.

I think it likely the resolution will pass, to be submitted to Texas - if declined by her - then an alternative proposition to be submitted to her through commissioners - This alternative proposition will most probably be Benton's[39] - recently submitted - with an amendment requiring the Missouri Compromise to be recognized as the basis of any Convention or other arrangement - In this form three Whigs will vote for it - Foster. Merrick & Henderson. -

There is some difficulty in the Demo: ranks. but all will go it, in my opinion, except Tappan[40] - With him they have much difficulty - They will overcome it. - With two Presidents Polk & Tyler upon him, & the whole party, he will either Vote with them or decline to Vote - In either case, the measure will pass. Polk has given a strong impulse to party action on this subject since his arrival.

It is understood that he constantly says, that the Democrat who shall stand out, will have thrown upon him a fearful responsibility.-

Nothing is known certainly as to the new Cabinet.[41] There has been & still is raging the fiercest party strife between the different sections. - Calhoun I think, will go out - Prodigious

---

[38]The original is in the William A. Graham Papers, University of North Carolina.
[39]See above, 229n, 268n.
[40]Benjamin Tappan, Senator from Ohio from 1839 to 1845, had anti-slavery leaning. Nevertheless, he voted for the annexation of Texas even though Thomas Corwin, a Whig, had just been elected to succeed him. Garrison, *Westward Extension*, 152; *Niles' Register*, LXVII, 401.
[41]For a good discussion of the problems involved in the selection of Polk's Cabinet see McCormac, *James K. Polk*, 287-299.

efforts have been made in his favor & against Buchanan. - It is understood that the Vice President elect, without exactly co operating with Calhoun, is operating as far as he decently can agᵗ. Buch: - Mason may remain. - The great men here, & certainly the most busy in Consultation. & the most imposing by a Certain knowing & mysterious look full of portents - are Senator Walker - Cave Johnson - Buchanan & Saunders. Three of the four, if not all, may be in the Cabinet. Col. Butler was brought on for the War department - It is less likely, than it seemed to be a week ago, that he will get it.

Polk is in great difficulty, & tho, coming here with as he thought fixed resolves, he by this time, I apprehend, finds it impossible. to resolve upon anything. -

It is very sure the Cabinet will have but little force of talent. - It ought to be so. - Who would not regret to see the choice of this great & free people thrown into Shadow by over topping talent. -

If Polk shall not be firmer & more conservative than I fear, & will prove to be, we may not unreasonably indulge apprehension in regard to a war with England. -

She will fight for Oregon - not for Texas, or put herself to any trouble beyond diplomatic intrigues to counteract the rank & rapacious movement of this Country.

I write during the sitting of the Senate & with great haste, supposing these hints & scraps of intelligence may not be uninteresting to you -

With great respect Yr

friend & obᵗ. Servᵗ.

To Gov. Graham - Willie P. Mangum

[Endorsed on back:] 1845

Hon. Willie P. Mangum

WPM-LC

C. N. B. Evans[42] to Willie P. Mangum.

MILTON, N. C. Feb. 24, 1845

Hon. W. P. Mangum—

Dear Sir: As my subscription to the National Intelligencer expired on the 7th. inst., you will do me a kind favor to call on the Editors and have it renewed by paying the difference between our respective papers, which, I believe is $3, and for which I will account to you satisfactorily. I don't think the Editors ought to charge *me* any difference— I am sure if they knew how much I had the Whig cause at heart, what sacrifices I have made for it, and am still making, they would not charge me, provided they be Whigs of "the true grit," of which I do not doubt.

The democrats are making great efforts to put me down here in Caswell. They find I am not to be driven or run off, and now they seek to *starve me to death.* For this purpose, a "joint stock office" is to be established here, and Gen. Baz. Graves[43] is to edit and publish and [sic] democratic paper - "Milton Banner."[44] I will battle as long as I can stand, and if fall I must my expiring breath will be spent struling to strike another blow.

I think Mr. Rives, of Va., has delivered the ablest speech on the Texas question,[45] ever delivered in the Senate - perhaps I should accept [sic] Col. Th. H. Benton. Will you be so good as to send me a pamphlet copy of Mr. Rives' speech?

Your humble servt,

C. N. B. EVANS.

[Addressed:]

Hon. W. P. Mangum
Washington City
D. C.

---

[42]Charles N. B. Evans was a native of Virginia who did journalistic work in Columbia, Raleigh, Richmond, Hillsboro, Greensboro, and Milton. From 1836 to 1839 he was part owner of the *Greensborough Patriot.* In 1841 he bought the Milton *Spectator* and changed its name to the Milton *Chronicle,* which he published until 1861. From 1870 to 1872 he published the *Hillsborough Recorder.* In 1873 he returned to Milton and again published the Milton *Chronicle. A Checklist of U. S. Newspapers in Duke Univ. Library,* IV, 543, 556, 574-575; Johnson, *AnteBellum N. C.,* 769.

[43]For a brief sketch of Barzilla Graves see above I, 62n.

[44]*The Union List of Newspapers* and the *Checklist of U. S. Newspapers in Duke University Library* do not indicate that this newspaper was ever published.

[45]On February 15, 1845, W. C. Rives spoke in the Senate on the joint resolution of annexation. He said that he did not oppose annexation if it could be accomplished without violating the constitution and without disturbing the peace with other nations. Most of his speech was an attack on the unconstitutionality of acquiring territory by joint resolution instead of treaty. *Cong. Globe,* 28 Cong., 2 sess., appendix, 378-382.

WPM-LC

Calvin Colton to Willie P. Mangum.

Philadelphia, Feby 25. 1845

My Dear Sir,

Your *first impressions* of Mr. Clay[46] are very much coveted by me, & are wanted *now,* if you can find time to sit down a few minutes, & give me a sketch of them, & address them to me at *Philadelphia.* You will great oblige me by so doing, & I fancy there will be a charm in it—

Very respectfully Yours,

C. Colton.

Hon. W. P. Mangum.

[Addressed:]

Hon. W. P. Mangum
Prest. U. S. Senate
Washington
D. C.

WPM-LC

Thomas Ruffin[47] to Willie P. Mangum.

Raleigh, February 28th 1845.

My dear Sir./

Although reluctant to trouble you on such a subject at this juncture of political turmoil at Washington, I find myself under some sort of necessity to do so, for the better discharge of a public duty; and therefore I am sure you will excuse the liberty I take.—

You will remember that the Bankrupt Act of August 1841 provides, that as to debts "created in consequence of a defalcation as a public officer, or as executor, administrator, guardian, or trustee, *or while acting in any other fiduciary capacity,*" no person shall become a voluntary bankrupt.[48] A question is depending in the Supreme Court here, as to the proper construction of the clause in respect to debts created in any *other* fidu-

----

[46]At this time Calvin Colton was writing his life of Clay which appeared in 1846.
[47]Thomas Ruffin was at this time chief justice of the North Carolina Supreme Court.
[48]See above, III, 266n.

ciary capacity than one of those expressly mentioned, namely, as a public offer, executor &c.- Of course, it will be the duty of the Judges to put on the act the construction that to them may seem proper; but in doing so, it would be satisfactory to them to have the aid of previous adjudications by other respectable Courts & especially of those of the Supreme Court of the United States, if any such have been made. Mr. Badger tells me, that he thinks that tribunal a year or two [ago] held, in an opinion delivered by Ch: J. Taney, that "fiduciary capacity" did not include the relation of principal & agent between private persons *sui juris;* for example, where the debt arises by a collection of money by one *as the agent* of another. Now the Reports by Mr Howard for the last year are not to be had here; and it is to ask the favour of you to make the requisite enquiry upon the point, that I now trouble you.

You will oblige me very much by asking the Chief-Justice or some gentleman of the bar or Mr. Howard, what adjudications, if any, have been made on the point; and, if so, by being good enough to send me the substance of the opinion. Badger says he has an impression, that what he saw on the subject was in a newspaper; and it has occurred to me that possibly, if that be true, the adjudication might not have been in the Supreme Co but was made by the Ch. Justice in one of his Circuit Courts. Presuming that he will take pleasure in stating how the fact is, I trust I do not impose on you an unpleasant task in requesting you to ask the information from him, if you should find any difficulty in finding the case in the Reports, that are accessible to you.

You will be pleased to hear, that our friends Mr. Cain & Mr P. C. Cameron reached us night before last on their return from their long tour to the South: both in good health.

> With much respect & esteem,
> Dear Sir,
> Your friend & Obdt. Svt.
> THOMAS RUFFIN.

[Addressed:]

> Honble. Wilie P. Mangum
> Of the Senate
> Washington City.

WPM-LC

James Cass Williams[49] to Willie P. Mangum.

NEW YORK March 1 1845

Wm P Mangum Esq

Sir

I feel it my duty to state to you, the position R. C. Wetmore and M. O. Robert,[50] took immediately after the treachery of John Tyler to the Whig party disclosed itself.

The Tyler party was anxious to obtain an organ her[e] and the choice lay between two papers, the Aurora, and the New York Arena published by T. L Nicholls.

R. C. Wetmore, the man whom the Whig party had favored with an office, but four months before, was the agent to do the corrupt deed and he paid Mr Nicholls Two hundred dollars in cash for the good his paper had done, as the choice for the Government fell on the Aurora.

And now the same set, through the same influence ask the Whig Senate to confirm the appointment of P M Wetmore,[51] brother to R C Wetmore for the same office, all to aid Mr Roberts and Mr Benson men who by their connexion with Tylerism did more to injure the Whig Party than all others combined-

I hope Justice will be done these men by the immediate *rejection of Wetmore*

Yours Truly

JAMES CASS WILLIAMS

[Addressed:]

Hon¹. W. P. Mangum
In Senate
Washington
D. C

---

[49]Possibly a carriage trimmer in New York City. *Longworth's New York Directory*, 1844-1845, 380.

[50]See above, III, 161.

[51]Prosper M. Wetmore was appointed by Polk to be navy agent at New York. *Niles' Register*, LXVII, 34; *Exec. Journal of Senate*, VI, 394.

WPM-LC

Willie P. Mangum to Charity A. Mangum

WASHINGTON 3rd. March 1845.

My dear Love,

This is the last day of the session, & tonight I suppose we shall sit up all night. I have left the chair for a moment, simply to say to you, that I am not quite well- I have been too much confined to the Chair of late-

Tomorrow is the inauguaration of Mr Polk. & then my duties in the chair cease, or rather they will cease, when I swear in the Vice President tomorrow.—

We shall be kept here 7. or 8. or 10 days perhaps in Executive session, & perhaps longer.- I donot expect to get home before the 17th. or 18th. of the month & perhaps even later. I may write again next week if we are likely to be detained longer.

I wish very much to get home & see you & our children. I hope you are well. I have not time to say more.-

My Love to all the Children,
& believe me as ever,
your most affectionate husband
W. P. MANGUM

WPM-LC

J. Whitehorne[52] to Willie P. Mangum.

[7 March, 1845]

Sir,

Will you oblige me by Sitting for your portrait once or twice at your earliest convenience. From 10 o'clock until 11½ or from 2 until 5 o'clock or any time between those hours would suit me perfectly well

Very respectfully
J. WHITEHORNE.

Hon. W. P. Mangum.
March 7th 1845.

[Addressed:]

Hon. W. P. Mangum.
Present—

---

[52]James Whitehorne was a portrait painter in New York City. I have been unable to ascertain if the portrait was painted. *Wilson's Business Directory of New York City,* 1848, 185.

WPM-LC

Stephen Moore [53] *to Willie P. Mangum.*

HILLSBORO': Mar. 11, 1845.

My dear Sir.

I am just requested by my friend Jno. Stafford Esq.[54] to call your attention [to] a Letter he wrote you some time in Decem. requesting you to call at the Patent office and procure for him the specifications of a Patetents for a Th[r]eshing machine obtained by a man by the name of Parsons. The machine on which Louis H. Morse made the improvement, and also the time the Patent was granted. I will pay you at sight whatever expense attends it— Direct to John Stafford, Snow Camp Post office, Orange-

I must [ask you] if you will permit, that you call at the office of the National Intelligencer and Settle my subscription to that Paper up to this time and stop the paper. I regret the necessity that impels me to do so, but I am not able to take it any longer.

Your daughter Sally came to town yesterday, left your family pretty well, She has come up to attend a Wedding that comes off tomorrow night at Gov. Grahams - between Miss Mary Washington[55] and a Mr. Graham, son I understand of Mr. Jno. Graham.

Very respectfully
STEP. MOORE.

[Addressed:]

Honbl. W. P. Mangum

Washington City

D. C.

---

[53]A relative of Mangum.
[54]See above, III, 16n.
[55]Joseph Montrose Graham, the son of John Graham and nephew of Governor William A. Graham. Joseph Montrose Graham married Mary Washington, daughter of John Washington, of New Bern, March 12, 1845, at Governor Graham's residence in Hillsboro. *Hillsborough Recorder,* March 20, 1845.

WPM-LC

Thos. L. Ragsdale[56] to Willie P. Mangum

WASHINGTON.
13th. March 1845.

My Dear Sir,

Mrs. Weed, widow of Maj. Weed late of the M. Corps, has prevailed on me- much against my sense of propriety- to state to you that she has no doubt the death of her father R. M. Whitney[57] will be hastened if his nomniation be rejected. She heard of your kind feeling for the distressed; and she relies upon that to conciliate you and consequently your friends in his favor. I took the liberty to promise for you; that if you had no insuperable objections, you would be gratified to obey her wishes.

Having myself received so many unmerited acts of kindness from you, it is presumptuous for me to mention it to you. But Mrs. W. declares, that these numerous obligations already conferred, ought to prevent you from denying me on on [sic] the present occasion. I feel that I may be wrong in this; but it is impossible for me to say *no* to the request of a lady.

I am yr. obliged friend
THOS. L. RAGSDALE.

Hon.
W. P. Mangum
    U. S. Senator.

[Addressed:]

Hon. W. P. Mangum.

U. S. Senator
Washington

---

[56]See above, III, 305n.
[57]See above, II, 430n.

WPM-LC

Willie P. Mangum to Charity A. Mangum.

WASHINGTON CITY, 16th. March 1845.
Sunday evening, at 7 o'clock, P.M.

My dear Love.

I had supposed that the Senate would adjourn tomorrow, and in that event, I should have left here on Thursday morning, & stopt one day in Petersburg & got home on Saturday or Sunday evening next. I shall be compelled to stay at least two days; & most probably, three days after the adjournment—

Ten minutes ago, I heard, that Mr. Bates a Senator from Massachusetts, who has been sick for a fortnight, died this evening at 20 minutes after six oclock, this evening, - that is - forty minutes ago.- This sad event will keep us here until (probably) thursday or friday next, and in that case, I may not be expected at home before the Week of this coming in.— I shall be at home, as soon as I can get there.— I have never more desired to see you My Love, and our dear children.— My health is now good.— I have had a very bad cold, but am getting well. I went to Baltimore on friday evening to buy some articles of furniture, & returned last night.

I hoped by going, to get home, a day sooner. I trust my dear Love, you are all well.— I anticipate with much happiness, the long *recess,* that we shall be together, if our lives be spared.- At no period of our lives, My Love, have I felt that you were more necessary to my happiness.— *That* you know My Love, & *that* you must never doubt.

We are too old, & we have lived together too long, to think of any thing but ourselves our dear children, & our duties to ourselves our Connexions & the world - & the world to come—

Give my Love to our dear Children, & believe, me as ever.

Most truly & affectionately
Your husband
WILLIE P. MANGUM

To
Mrs. Charity A. Mangum.

WPM-LC

Nicholas Carroll to Willie P. Mangum

Confidential

Monday March 19th 1845

My dear Sir

I leave Washington this evening and there were many matters I wished to talk to you about before I left. I feared that I had already monopolized more than my fair proportion and I believe an poor man if he is proud grows more fastidious every day as his case becomes the harder.

You will recollect that in a conversation we had together on Tuesday last you mentioned that you should call on Mr Polk before you left and it would depend upon the look of things whether, if he gave you the opportunity you would ask him a favor— You were kind enough to say also that if he did give you the chance you would submit my name to him.

Judge I am brief for I wish to be earnest. I leave that to your own judgement & kindness. If you think it right to address Mr Polk, upon the subject, I shall abide the result. I do not wish to press the matter in any way— because if no other reason operated upon my mind than the Whig faith, which God Almighty has stamped upon my soul— I would in deep & earnest gratitude & love towards you & for you— leave in your hands without reserve— my own fate.

My dear sir you will appreciate the agony of my mind, so to speak, when I tell you that the sun never shone on one of my years, when fortunes were so fair as mine last October. Viewing the election of Mr Clay as almost assured, I wanted no office that he or any power could bestow. One short month brought with his defeat reverses that overwhelmed me— My own disaster was nothing— but my family's was intensively [?] severe.

I bent under it but did not break. You may judge how much I embarked in the hope of that charge' ship when I tell you it was my last plank. Pending my labors to obtain it my wife gave birth to another daughter, making four in all that call me father. I would have been where my duty called me. I was mistaken about the periods when its coming should be expected & my dear lady forbore to inform me of its birth, until she was hapily out of danger— the while she hoped & believed I would succeed. It was not my own fault that I did not. Now my dear sir I have given you a painful recital. It is so for me to make & I am very sure, from the knowledge I have of you— not un so far for you to hear. I would not lift the veil further. I cannot stand still I must move on. How?

If there is an opening in any leading paper in our State I would much rather throw myself in the way of so earning a livlihood than by adopting any other plan. Here in me is not a matter that exists today & expires tomorrow. The devotion of my heart, toward Henry Clay & those whom I recognize as coordinate Gods of my idolatry, has become in me a fixed & changeless principle. I would most fervently pray for full, free opportunity to prove to them, that I value their friendship & regard by a standard that circumstances cannot control. Now if I *see* such an opportunity and endeavour to reach it, p'vd that my friends must say that it is desirable, will they take the trouble to say so? If there is no such opportunity, then I must turn, amid the hord, to [illegible] and right cheerfully will I embrace any recourse for better men than myself are prostrate. If it occurs that I can establish myself with some leading press I shall then be in a condition to prove what Byron denies— that there is no being besides 'a woman and a dog' that is grateful— ay that a true man is grateful also.

If our friends in New York move at all with the set that are arranging for the next canvass, I deem it of the utmost importance to let the McLean & Scott folks move as much as they please, so we hold the check rein. Indeed I think the purpose I have nearest my heart will be best answered by suggesting now your name as *second* on the ticket that *may* be formed, until we force 'the obsolete idea' & the other candidates- to abide by the expressed will of a National Convention, and then we have them. They dare not assail you as second now- and then if, as I religiously believe, from long experience of Scott & Mc-Lean men, they should quarrel among themselves- we can then step in as mediators and heal the breach by naming *our* *second* as the *general first*. Indeed this seems so perfectly adapted to succeed that I shall, if not overruled, move in it very shortly. I can see already that the elements of intrigue are at work, and the best way to defeat them effectually is to appear to fall in with them readily. Our friends are not always safe. It would have been better this Spring where success was problematical to have permitted the nomination of a Federalist or Bluelight and let him try his chance to be soundly thrashed. Now we have put up, I fear, one of our kindred, to be sadly beaten- This gives an unnecessary advantage to the 'obsoletes' and permits them to claim places in the Lexicon from which they would be otherwise excluded.

I shall be able, soon after my return to New York, to give you a list of reliable & faithful *Mangum men*. Perhaps, so little do I believe you have ever thought of such a contingency, you will be somewhat astonished to learn their number and efficiency. We are bound if we strike at all to war for success. I think the probabilities are in favor of such a glorious result. For two years your own name as *first* shall be or should be locked up in the breasts of your friends—the while they moved on steadily in view of the ultimate result[.] To me it is very plain and I believe you will think it practicable within a year. I believe you to be perfectly unambitious as regards this high position. You will therefore be the least likely of any one, to be able to judge of your own prospects of success. A far off great men have, like the distant mountain, grown magnificent from the distance. Few have stood the test of close and daily observation. Mr. Clay, Mr Calhoun & yourself I put among those few. I only hope now that you will place no bar in the *way* of your friends- If they move they would not thank you if you flung a wet blanket over them. Possibly they may ask to extend your confidence to them- so far as to place implicit reliance upon their ability, integrity & zeal. That you will do so I shall, except otherwise directed, so state to them. Whatever is done will be faithfully related to you, in the order of its happening

My dear Sir I am & always have been ardent in any cause in which I once engage. The suggestions I made to you in relation to your own probable position in the next contest, were the result of cool reflections and conclusions that have been arrived at, in full view of the past- the present- and the *look* the future now means to my mind. I pledge myself without reserve, that if the blood hounds do not force Henry Clay's nomination again- by their incessant persecutions & slanders (not *yet* an 'obsolete idea')- I throw myself without reserve into the next contest for you, as *His Executor*

Should however you & other of our friends force upon us the selection of a Coxcomb or a Hunker for a candidate, we will hold you & them responsible and then you must excuse us if we should see fit to vote for *Bill* Allen of Ohio, or *Tom* Benton in preference to the *Federal* Whig nominee. Indeed I would think the Iron Despotism of their Jacobinism vastly preferable to the old grannyism of the other set. For one I must own a man for my leader, and not the shadow of a man- one whom I could bear with reviling him if he was angered, sooner than I would tolerate the mock dignity and pompous inanity of a vain glorious Executive.

I will hope however that we can have things arranged to suit the truly Democratic impulses of our Party. Not that Democracy which professes so much to liberality, and yet practices the most odious species of aristocracy- but which, like the pure well of truth, rises in every place when the Whig doctrines are received in moderation, & yet cherished with that affection, that would make martyrs of their disciples- if but a shadow of despotism crossed their paths.

I believe we have the power, and most fervently do I pray for its righteous exercise- Once unleashed, we can know no stopping place short of revolution, & the entire overthrow of the 'spoils Conspirators.' I believe their doom *is* written. They have taught us their plan of playing brag & *poker* We will, having been learning while we lost, profit by our bitter experience.

May I hope that you will give this matter your attention & I would solicit before you leave Washington a rejoinder, addressed to me at New York?

It is a pleasing duty in a heart sensitively alive to acts or expressions of kindness, to utter thanks for benefits received. But sometimes words are inadequate- to express the deepest feelings Towards you, dear sir, there will ever be in my heart the sincerest affection for you & the profoundest gratitude for your many kindnesses. The latter might well overwhelm me- for in nothing have I merited them- save in your good opinion of my fidelity & faithfulness to a common cause- which I am proud to say, my heart declares, has only awarded me ample justice. I only wish my roof tree was neighbor to your own, and that I could find work for a willing head & energetic hands in the old North State

Faithfully
Your friend & serv^t
NICHOLAS CARROLL

Hon. Willie P. Mangum

[Addressed:]

Hon: Willie P. Mangum
U. S. Senator
Washington

WPM-LC

William S. G. Brown[58] *to Willie P. Mangum.*

ERIE PENNSYLVANIA
March 19, 1845

Hon Sir

I trust you will pardon the liberty I have taken in addressing you, not having the pleasure of a personal acquaintance-

"The annexation of Texas at this time to the Union is of interest to all true and Enlightened friends of this goverment, and should it be (As It will be beyond doubt) finally annexed by an further action of the President and congress and the Consent of Texas to admission, I cannot but regard it as disastrous to this Union, but time must and will show the result of annexation, at this time—I am at a loss to know whether Texas will be in one State with the same name or of more than one, and at what time she will receive her first representation in Congress-

---

[58]Unable to identify.

"Please drop me a line in respect to the above for which I will feel gratefull-

Very truly your friend & servt
WILLIAM S. G. BROWN—

to
>   Hon Willie P. Mangum   )
>   Speaker U. S. Senate)

[Addressed:]

>   Hon Willie P. Mangum
>   U. S. Senator
>   Red Mountain
>   N Ca.

WPM-LC

Nicholas Carroll to Willie P. Mangum.

CROTON INSURANCE COMPANY
No 35 Wall St Apl. 29th /45

My dear Sir

On Tuesday 22d Inst. I was elected Secretary of of this Company. I first heard of the vacancy on the 16th. Sunday intervening I had but five working days. I had 22 competitors. Some of them had the start of me 4 to 6 weeks. On the first ballot I received 13 out of 16 votes and was instanter elected unanimously & by the same rule I had my salary fixed at $2,000. My dear Judge I wanted to tell you this for I did believe no one would be readier to congratulate me upon my fortunate success. I had intended to cross the Alleghanies & plant my family on the Praries. This is better- every way better It anchors me here where I belong- and if there is any good in me for myself & for my friends it can be best brought out here-

We want some Agencies in the 'old North State'. We have now Agents at three points: John Huske at Fayetteville, Wm. G. Bryan at Newbern, and Wm. C. Lord at Wilmington. We want Agents at Elizabeth City, Halifax, Plymouth and Raleigh. Do you know the gentlemen now acting as our Agents and can you recommend to us suitable persons to act as Agents at the places designated? The situation is a desirable one to the party receiving the appointment, fairly lucrative of itself and calculated to increase the Agent's business. The Company is in first rate condition, has been very fortunate, has a good Board of Directors, honorable officers and pays its losses promptly. You need not be afraid to say this to any one who should ask you respecting it and whenever it changes in any respect from the character I have given it above, I will leave it instanter & advise you of the change. I throw my heart & soul into it pledged to its success- My friends, God bless them, have rallied to my support and thrown their business influence in favor of the Company. They pledged themselves that my appointment would give the Company $55,000 this year in Premimums- this was $5,000 more than our friend Joseph Hoxie pledged to 'the Mercantile' to procure the Vice Presidency of that Company & he had three months to work in- while your servant was restricted to five days.-

We insure Marine & Fire- coasting, inland & foreign marine & fire risks by land & sea. If I do not impose too much trouble on you I would like to have the priviledge of saying to our Agents that they can refer to you as to the standing of the Croton Insurance Company of New York. I forward you copies of our charter &c.- You can say besides that we are a clever set of Whigs-

In politics we are all still. I see enough to know that Webster, McLean, Scott & their respective friends are at work - but covertly- Open action would prostrate them at once. The elements now at work no man can control. My mind as expressed to you, remains *unchanged*. If Mr Polk unadvisedly plunges us into War, the Great Harry will go into the House & rule the nation from there, mangle the White House. If we remain *at Peace,* the gentlemen now at work canvassing for the Presidency will use each other up and then you are the Candidate *they* uniting on you. I have not touched a wire here, that was *honest Clay-* that has not virbrated on the instant in answer to this electricity.

I live in the hope of welcoming you to New York this summer. I trust they will drive you out of your mountain home & force you North that you may judge for yourself that your friends are not local or sectional.

Mrs. C. desired me to present Judge Mangum with her regards & thanks for his efforts in her husband's behalf last win-
ter- and to say also that this event leaves her no regret that
those labors were ineffectual-

I shall be happy to serve you in any way and trust you will
command me in any matter that concerns you at the North

Hoping soon to engage a leisure moment from you for a reply, I am

Faithfully & truly
Yr. friend & servt
N. Carroll

Hon. Willie P. Mangum
    Red Mountain
        Orange Co
           N. Ca.

[Addressed:]

Hon. Willie P. Mangum
U. S. Senator
Red Mountain
Orange Co
N. Ca.

WPM-LC

E. D. Bullock[59] to Willie P. Mangum

Mobile May 3ᵈ. 1845.

My Dear Sir.

During my stay at your house last summer you kindly prof-
fered letters to Mr Abbot[60] of Boston and the Messrs Lawrences.
If you can now give me letters to them it will be of incalculable
service to me. After my return from the North last year I had
propositions made to me, without any solicitations on my part,
to embark in commercial life. These propositions I thought
but little of, until about the first of March when I had an offer
from a highly respectable and responsible House, engaged in

---

⁵⁹E. D. Bullock was an attorney in Mobile at this time. William Garrett, *Reminiscences of
Public Men in Alabama for Thirty Years,* Atlanta, 1872, 786.
⁶⁰George W. Abbot was a commission merchant in Boston. *Stimson's Boston Directory,* 1845, 50.

the General commission and agency business. All of my near
friends at once advised me to accede to their proposition which
I did.

The partners in the House are Col John McRae & F. P.
Ravisies & myself. Col McRae the Brother in Law of Mr
Ravisies is very wealthy & is the monied man of the House.
Mr Ravisies married the daughter of Samuel Strudwick Esq
of Marengo County, who is the Brother of Dr Strudwick of
Hillsborough. I mention these facts to apprize you of the
Honorable connection that I have made and to afford you an
opportunity, if you require it to learn the *character* and *responsibility* of the House. If we can through you and other
kind friends procure the confidence of those Houses it will open
the whole business world in Massachusetts to us. The goods
that are shipped to us will be sold and the proceeds invested
in cotton for the manufacturer & se[n]t on to Boston. In this
business there is not one dollar of risk neither do we buy but
sell all manner of goods & retain 5 per cent commission upon
the sales. We also advance 50 per cent upon all articles that
meet with ready sales in our market & 33-1/3 upon those that
are not so easily put upon the market.

Will you do me the favor to send on the letters to the place
as early as possible as I shall leave here by the West about the
5 or 6 of June. If this letter should not reach you in time to enable you to send the letters by that time, I will write the day
I leave to what point you can address them. It is of great importance to have them here before I leave.

My wife and little daughter are now at Mr Lyons in the
country, & will remain some two weeks for the benefit of their
health. I am grieved to inform you that her health has been of
late very delicate & a trip to the mountains is determined upon
for her.

I hope my dear Judge that you and Mrs Mangum & the
family are all well and if it is possible we will come to see you
as I shall probably visit Petersburg & Richmond.

With many assurances from my heart, of my continued love
for you and the Ladies I remain

Your Sincere friend
E D BULLOCK

The name of our House is
McRae Ravisies & Bullock

[Addressed:]

Hon. Willie P. Mangum
Red Mountain P. O.
Orange Co
N Carolina

WPM-LC

Nathan Sargent to Willie P. Mangum.

PHILA. May, 16, 1845

Hon W. P. Mangum

My Dear Sir,

You will probably recollect that a resolution was adopted
by the Senate to print 10,000 copies of Fremont's Journal.[61]
This was got up Mr Towers, or rather at his suggestion, & was
intended for him, to enable him to pay off some of the debts
incurred in publishing the Whig Standard. All that was necessary after the resolution was adopted was to inform Gales &
Seaton of the circumstances upon which they would have permitted Towers to execute the job. This Mr. Morehead said he
would do; but it seems he probably inadvertently neglected,
as Mr. Towers informs me, in consequence of which he is likely to lose the benefit of the job. This would be a *Serious* disappointment to him as well as to myself, & I suppose your young
friend who assisted him during last summer.[62]

I do not know whether you feel authorized to say any thing
to Messrs. Gales & Seaton on the subject, but if you do, I earnestly wish you would drop them a note just to inform them
what the design was in reference to that report. The least
intimation of the fact from yourself or Mr Morehead would, I
have no doubt, be sufficient. It is a matter of some importance
to me & I know it is to Towers, otherwise I would not have
troubled you with it.

[61]This was published by Gales and Seaton as document no. 174. *Senate Documents,* 28 Cong.,
2 sess.
[62]Daniel R. Goodloe. See the next letter.

Mr. Green[63] succeeded in obtaining $1,500 in N. Y. We staid there about two weeks before we could accomplish our purpose. Nothing could be obtained in Boston. I should have been able, I think, to have raised a few hundred dollars here, (by the aid of a letter from you to J. P. Wetherill)[64] but for the Pittsburg fire, which absorbed all the benevolent & liberal disposition, for the time being, of our citizens.

Is it possible, after the cavalier treatment Mr Calhoun received from Mr Polk, he will come to his aid & help him out of the dilemma his blunder has run him into? If Mr C. had the spirit he once possessed, I should think not, but I do not know how to count on him now. It is clear that an attack on the Tariff is designed- I hope it will be made, & be successful.- We must sometimes wish for evil as the cause of good.

Believe me my dear sir, Very sincerely
& Respectfully
Your friend & obdt St.
N. SARGENT

_____

WPM-LC

Jno. T. Towers to Willie P. Mangum

WASHINGTON, May 17, 1845.

Dear Sir:

I wrote you upon your leaving the city last March, in reference to the report of Mr. Fremont, which Gov: Morehead had the kindness to get ordered to be printed with a view to my executing it- thus enabling me to liquidate some embarrassing debts that were against me on account of the publication of the Standard. I presume you were told (by Gov. M.) of the manner in which the job was brought about at the time of its conception, and of course it is not necessary to speak more of it on that score. In my conversation with Col. Seaton the day after you and Gov. M. left the city, on the subject, (and having been told by Gov. M. to call on Col. S. and I would find it all right) he told me he had a conversation with you and Gov. M. the

[63]Willis Green. See above, III, 484n.
[64]J. P. Wetherill actively campaigned for Clay in 1842-1844. See above Johnson to Mangum, September 24, 1842, and J. P. Wetherill to Mangum, June 19, 1844.

evening previous, and that you would write him on the subject. Since which time I have heard nothing from Col. S. Col. S.
told me (as I stated in my former letter,) that he was willing
to do whatever his or my friends required, but preferred giving
a portion of the profits in money, and executing the job him-
self- but awaited the wishes of yourself and Gov. M. and, as I
understood, by which he should be bound. As the time is now
at hand when the job must be put in execution, I would ask the
favor of such a letter from you that I could show Col. S. as
would bring the matter to a definite conclusion. I would prefer, of course, to execute the job myself because I could perhaps make double out of it that will be made at his office; if he
gives a portion of the profits it may not liquidate the claims
against me- besides, had it not been for the kindness of Gov. M
towards me in interesting himself in attending to the passage
of the resolution it never would have been ordered to be printed
at all by the Senate at its last session— Gales & Seaton never
dreamed of this document, their greatest hope being to get the
money for the State papers appropriated, which would give
them a fortune without any thing else- and every thing else was
done that they asked, *besides* the appropriation. they so much
desired- thus putting them in possession of more work and
money than ever before at the adjournment of the session hardly
excepting the payment of the 20 per cent. Not satisfied with
all this, they hesitate to permit the disposition of a job that
was not designed for them, by the friends who had done so
much. With all due deference, I would make this suggestion
in order to bring the matter to a close- state in a letter to me
(that I may show Col. S.) whatever you may deem most pro-
per- either for my executing the job or otherwise- and leave
me to do whatever I can with him. Perhaps by my executing
the work I may be enabled to do with its proceeds some service to the friends who have got it through. Our Whig friends
here and in the adjoining counties urge the establishment here
of a large semi-weekly paper, and will assist in its support- I
am debarred the pleasure of acceding to their wishes by these
very pecuniary liabilities from which I wish to be relieved. I
am gratified also to see that so faithful a member of our great
party as yourself is destined to take so prominent a position in
the next issue before the People- may I have the privilege and

opportunity of being one of your advocates. The "Union" as
you see, no doubt, daily puts forth its Locofocoism unanswered;
and by the time of the next campaign, what it now *asserts* as
principles for its party may become its *maxims,* too deeply
rooted to be removed. Thus the necessity of a paper to meet its
issues, and expose the daily increasing corruptions of Locofocoism.

May I expect an early answer to the above, and such an
one as your sense of propriety may justify.

Yours very respectfully
JNO. T. TOWERS

Hon. W. P. Mangum.
  of N. C.

P. S.—The "Globe" has nearly completed the printing of the
document for the House, which renders it certain that its commencement by the Senate printers cannot be delayed much
longer.

J. T. T.

[Addressed:]

> Hon. W. P. Mangum,
>   Red Mountain,
>   Orange County,
>   N. C.

WPM-LC

George H. Colton[65] *to Willie P. Mangum*

NEW YORK - June 4th '45

Hon. Willey P. Mangum

Dear Sir. -

I intended to have written you a long time since- but
frequent necessary absences from Town, & an infinite pressure
of business while in town, have conspired to prevent me. I

---

[65]George Hooker Colton, 1818-1847, a native of New York and graduate of Yale, was one of
the literary figures in New York in the 1840's. In 1840 he wrote a poem "Tecumseh" and some
essays on Indians which helped Harrison's candidacy. In January, 1845, he published the first issue
of the *American Review.* He succeeded in obtaining writers such as Edgar Allen Poe, Rufus Choate,
Daniel Webster, and J. P. Kennedy to contribute. Mangum promised to write an article for him
but never did. Colton died in 1847. Frank Luther Mott, *A History of American Magazines 1741-
1850.* Cambridge, Mass., 1939, I, 751-752; *Appleton's Cyclopedia of American Biography,* I, 696.

felt it to be the less necessary, as Mr. Webber[66] was to see you, at your residence. He informs me, that he paid you a visit—in all respects a pleasant one- adding much to the interest of his account, by letting me know how kindly he was received & how interested you were still disposed to be in the Review.[67] Certainly, both for Mr. Webber, & myself, and in behalf of the enterprise, I have to render you my warmest thanks.

In respect to the subject on which you spoke of writing something for the Review this Summer- I hope you will not suffer it to slip out of your mind. It is earnestly desired to make this a truly national work-free from all Sectional prejudices- But as yet, I have not had a single article from any one Southern writer. May I earnestly solicit your assistance to obtain some articles in addition to your own. Will you write to Gov. Swain for this purpose- asking him to write on some national topic- to also Prof-Tucker, who, I think belongs to your State, would furnish something of interest. Any article of real value from any gentleman of your State would be welcome. It would [be] of great service, if some one of these gentlemen, of whom you spoke in your State could be prevailed to send on some piece soon.

May I hope to hear from [you] at your earliest convenience. The first instalment of your article—to appear in Sept. no.— should be in New York by about the 25th or 28th of July as I begin very early to put matter in hand for the succeeding month—being obliged to publish by the 1st of each month.

I am, Dear Sir-
Most Sincerely Yours
& with great respect
GEO. H. COLTON

Hon. W. P. Mangum
Red Mountain
N. C.

---

[66]Charles W. Webber, 1819-1856, a native of Kentucky and educated at home, went to Texas in 1838 where, as a member of the Texas rangers, he had numerous adventures. For a short time he studied medicine and then went to Princeton to prepare to be a Presbyterian minister. In 1844 he went to New York to take up journalism. There he met Audubon and fell under the influence of his writings on nature and the frontier. He wrote numerous articles and essays. He assisted Colton in the editing of the *American Review.* He went on several adventurous expeditions, his last being with William Walker in Nicaragua where he was killed. In 1847 he wrote a long pamphlet accusing Colton of "falsehood, imbecility, and shameful cowardice." D. A. B., XIX, 580-581; Mott, *A History of American Magazines,* I, 752-753.

[67]*The American Review: A Whig Journal of Politics, Literature, Art and Science,* became *The American Whig Review* in 1850. Established with the endorsement of numerous Whig leaders to strengthen the party after its defeat in 1844, it appeared first under the editorship of Colton and then James D. Whelpley, 1848-1849, and George W. Peck, 1850-1852. With the defeat of the Whigs in 1852, it went out of existence. The circulation ranged from 3000 to 8000, which in that day was a good circulation. Mott, *A History of American Journalism,* I, 750-754.

William Cain, Junior, 1784-1857. The brother of Mangum's wife, Charity Alston (Cain) Mangum. From an oil portrait, painter unknown, in the possession of Mrs. Annie C. Bridgers of Raleigh, North Carolina.

WPM-LC

D. M. Barringer to Willie P. Mangum

LINCOLNTON N. C.
June 7, 1845.

My Dear Sir.

Strange as it may seem to you, an attempt has been made to injure me in this District by a charge that I did not do my duty in the last session of Congress, in failing to use the proper exertions to carry through that body the appropriation for rebuilding the Branch mint at Charlotte, N. C.-[68] I know you are aware of the interest I took in this matter—& I desire you to write me whether I did not frequently see you on the subject desiring and urging your aid & influence to secure the measure through the Senate. [Illegible] was freely given and to state generally the interest & zeal I manifested for its success.

Please to address me at Concord N. C.

Your friend Sincerely
D. M. BARRINGER

Hon. W. P. Mangum

There is no danger in this District if the Whigs turn out— Fisher is the Democratic candidate.

[Addressed:]

Hon. W. P. Mangum
Red Mountain,
Orange Co
N. C.

WPM-LC

Daniel R. Goodloe to Willie P. Mangum

PRINCE GEORGE COUNTY MD. June 11 1845.

Dear Sir.

I have recently obtained the situation of teacher of a primary school in Maryland, and as it will enable me in the course

---
[68]See above, 263n.

of a few months to pay you, I have thought that it would be proper to inform you of the fact.[69] The school is situated about ten miles from Washington east of Bladensburg- The salary is $350.00 per annum, payable half yearly. I commenced teaching on the 4th inst. and shall receive the first payment in December about the time you arrive at Washington, I trust I shall at that time, without an accident be able to pay you.

I understand from my friends in North Carolina that a vacancy is likely to occur in the office of Clerk and Master for the county of Franklin, and if such is the case I will be an applicant.—If it should devolve upon the Judges of the Supreme Court to fill the vacancy I would thank you to speak to Judge Nash or Judge Ruffin for me, as you will probably meet them at Hillsborough. Or if you happen to see Judge Battle who resides in your county be pleased to name the subject to him.

I feel high gratification at the prospect of refunding the money you so generously lent me when the chance of repayment was so distant.

I shall ever remain your obliged and obedient servant

DANIEL R. GOODLOE

Hon Willie P. Mangum

[Addressed:]

Hon. Willie P. Mangum
Red Mountain
N. Carolina.

WPM-LC

James Webb[70] to Willie P. Mangum

HILLSBORO June 30. 1845

D Sir

I Recd your kind message by Mr J. Hancock on Saturday that you could spare me 5 Barrels Corn It will be a considerable

[69]The Washington *Whig Standard,* which Goodloe helped to edit, had been discontinued in 1844. See above, 84n.
[70]A banker who lived in Hillsboro.

accommodation to me I use a Bushel a day Let me know when I can send for itt or if you can send it to me

Yours Respectfully
JAMES WEBB

[Addressed:]

Honl. W. P. Mangum
Red Mountain
Orange

WPM-LC

Samuel Martin[71] to Willie P. Mangum.

CAMPBELLS STATION TENSEE 8. Jy/45

Honble W. P. Mangum
Vice President-

D Sir

I sent another Petition to your House care of our Senator Jarnagen[72] in which I again insist on the Nation making that canal from Beaufort to the Neuse River. I will never cease asking for that matter as long as I can write Justice & Good Faith say it must be & it shall be but I must wait untill my Postage resolution is passed.

My Plan was Sir for the defense of the South a Canal from the Dismal Swamp Canal passing by Newbern Fayetteville Columbia Augusta Milledgeville & so on round to nearly opposite red River this canal to be 80 feet at the Water line & 4 feet deep from this. I want ship canals from the Sea here will be a place men can live & on which Troops can be collected & munition of War & on which the[y] can be moved at the rate of 100 miles in 24 Hours on the line of canal could be stored the cotton Tobacco & Sugar of the South & in safety from a Coast enemy & from this line a forced march could be made of Cavalry & light artillery Steam will soon become general on Canals from this time I want a Branch from the Chatahache to

---

[71]Possibly Samuel Martin, who originally came from North Carolina after graduation from the University in 1819. Grant, *Alumni Hist. of U. N. C.*, 416.
[72]Spencer Jarnagin, 1792-1853, was the Whig Senator from Tennessee from 1843 to 1847. *Biog. Dir. of Cong.*, 1147.

the Tennessee river down Dark river to the Mississippi direct[?] through the State & one from Duck river by Nashville down Green River to the Ohio to meet the one from the Lakes no one doubts but England will get Cuba & if we get Texas soon will she lay her hands on it & I have no doubt she will be very willing we set the example of open & wilfull robbery on the weak & defenceless with the British in possession of the Havana she commands the Gulf in the same manner with Possession of Gibralter. She commands the exit & entrance in & from the Mediterrannean there will these canals be wanted & The[y] had better be begun in time she will be made ask our friend G. McDuffy what I wrote when he was making such efforts to recharter the U. S. Bank George will I think recollect it

SAMUEL MARTIN.

[Addressed:]

   Honbl.
    W. P. Mangum
     Vice Pres'ent U. States
     W. City

———

WPM-D

Charles Manly to Willie P. Mangum

RALEIGH, N. C 8th July 1845

Hon: Willie P. Mangum
  Senator U. States

Sir

 It becomes my duty as the Organ of the Board of Trustees of the University of North Carolina to make known to you that at the late Annual Commencement of that Institution the Senatus Academicus by unanimous assent conferred upon you the Honorary Degree of Doctor of Laws.—

It is proper for me to add that no Diploma issues for this Degree except where it is specially desired by the Recipient.

I have the honor, to be
Very respectfully
Your Obt. Sevt
CHAS. MANLEY

[Addressed:] Hon. W. P. Mangum
Red Mountain
Orange Co
N. C.

WPM-LC

P. H. Mangum to Ellison G. Mangum.[73]

HILLSBORO' July 24th. 1845.

Dear Sir,

I wished to see my friends on Flat River, but I am not very well & therefore can not be with you to-day.—

Things have taken such a turn in regard to the Cty Court Clerk's election,[74] that I am desirous my part of the County may be in possession of all the necessary information upon both sides;- And when they shall be thus informed, I am sure their good sense & independence of character will ensure such a line of conduct on their part that they will never have cause to be ashamed of what they shall have done.

It is known that we were all at first for Major Taylor's re-election, with all his faults; and that we thought that Jos. Norwood & Jno. W. Carr were doing wrong to become candidates for the office in opposition to Taylor, when it was known that Genl. Allison was a candidate & would make it a *party contest* necessarily, to almost an entire extent of the democratic strength. But all the candidates being out, we hoped that before the election, the competitors would narrow down to Taylor & Allison, & then we could keep the office from being made a political machine for partizan purposes.—

---

[73]See above, I, 332n.
[74]John W. Carr, Joseph Norwood, John W. Hancock, John Taylor, John Kirkwood, and Joseph Allison were the candidates. Carr, Hancock, and Taylor withdrew, but Taylor's friends insisted that he be kept in the race. The result was as follows: Allison 1455, Norwood 910, Taylor 403, Kirkwood 163. Allison was elected. *Hillsborough Recorder*, May 22, 29, July 10, August 14, 1845.

Contrary to all reasonable expectation, Major Taylor permits himself to be influenced into an arrangement with the other two Whig candidates, whereby he is ruled out of the Field, & he thereby is silenced, with his hands tied. Some of his friends were dissatisfied, & avowed their determination to run Taylor any how - & a good deal has been said & done to excite the passions, & but little that a dispassionate Judgment & a wise policy would dictate & sanction.—

I have been a good deal indignant & perplexed about this matter. After collecting all the information in regard to the arrangement that was to be had, I became satisfied that Taylor, altho' bitterly opposed to entering into the arrangement when first presented to him, did ultimately accede to the arrangement under the belief that he would certainly receive the nomination. In this, he failed; and it is not alledged by any person that the fifteen men chosen to determine the matter, did not act throughout fairly & honorably. Well, there being no unfairness, indeed no pretence of unfairness in the conduct of the *fifteen men;* what ought to be done? That is the question.—The most that could be said, I suppose, is, that in entering into the famous arrangement; Taylor thought he would *"chouse"* his competitors, & his competitors thought that he might be *"choused"*. This is all, I suppose, that an illiberal spirit could say. - Are the Whigs of Orange to sit still with their arms folded, to look quietly on this contemptible scuffle for show, between a few personal friends, however pure their motives may be? I learn that the great body of Taylor's friends above Hillsboro', & the most of them hereabouts, will not vote for Taylor - because such a course could have no other effect than to divide the Whig vote & elect Genl. Allison, but on the contrary they think that Jos. Norwood can be elected if the Whigs East of Hillsboro' will vote with them for Norwood.—

On Monday, I conversed with several of our personal friends West of Hillsboro' as far as the Over-river Country & Stony Creek; and this is the opinion in common, in the Whig ranks west of Hillsboro' - the immediate neighbourhood of the Messrs Clarks & Banes excepted.—

I submit to my neighbours & friends on the rivers, if this is not the course for us to pursue.—

Show this to Abner, Harrison,[75] & Willie P. Mangum.

Yrs. respectfully

P. H. MANGUM.

[Addressed:]

To Ellison G. Mangum Esqr.
Flat River
Orange.

WPM-LC

William K. Ruffin to Willie P. Mangum.

HAW RIVER August 2nd 1845

My Dear Sir-

I take the liberty of writing you a line upon the subject of our Clerks Election- I *know* that you wish *Allison beaten*—and I know that between the Whig Norwood & the Democrat Kirkland your choice will be determined by the chances of the Election - My own opinion is that Allison will be elected - and still further that his election will inure to the interests & the *permanent* interests of the Whig Party of Orange County. But we must (in duty bound, as every honest man is in duty bound) keep him out if we can— I have been upon a tour of electioneering for two days and I tell you the impressions that I have received - *Allison will be elected.* But your interest is to make friends with the respectable portion of the Republican Party (see how I catch the old Gentleman's phrases) —and I believe that Uncle John[76] will divide (& in our neighbourhood more than take his share of the Whig votes). His prospects are daily improving - and I assure you that as far as I know & believe that the contest lies between him & Allison— *Norwood is out of the question— He stands no chance—* Taylor, you know, *cannot* be elected - & understanding that his friends have been privately canvassing in the upper part of the county & supposing that they feel satisfied that there is no earthly chance for him, I hope that he will be induced to withdraw his name— If he will do so, I think Uncle John's election is certain—

Of course I have written to you the impressions that have been made upon me by the conversations I have held with my neighbours- They may be deceptive but I give them to you for what they may, in your estimation, be worth. I shall write to the same effect to Fulindry[?] brothers, John Ray, & Paul Cameron - and you & they & your friends must do what *you* think is right in the premises-

I flatter myself that I shall be able to spend a day or two with you before August Court- Above all things I should be pleased to have that time spent in your company. Allow me Dear Sir, to subscribe myself

With sincere affection your friend
W. K. RUFFIN.

[Addressed:]

Hon. Willie P. Mangum.

WPM-LC

John Cameron[77] *to Willie P. Mangum.*

Friday Morning. [Summer, August, 1845]

Hon: Willie P. Many there are, high on the roll of fame,
Among Columbia's chosen civic band!
None more than he, possess a heartfelt claim,
Great tho they be, in action, & in name;
Upon the warm affections of the land!
Meeting both friend, & foe, with heart upon his hand.

Theres a flourish for you my dear Sir! What a pattern of an office seeker I would make, though I am sadly afraid, that the sincerity which constitues the only merit in the above, would be so sadly wanting (necessarily) in many instances; that all my tact, & diplomacy, could not prevent the cloven foot of ridicule from showing.

---

[77]John Cameron's newspaper, the *Oxford Mercury and District Telegram,* was suspended in late 1844 or early 1845. In 1848 he became one of the publishers of the Wadesboro *North Carolina Argus.* He edited or published, with different partners, this paper until 1847. *Check List of Newspapers in the Duke University Library.*

Your high behest has been obeyed! Both hat & coat have been won; & I am almost afraid that it will be impossible to prevent you from throwing in the breeches too. If the "Cocoethes Admirandi" of all the botanists, & florists, be not excited to the utmost, & Dial's Creek become a favoured resort, for all the seekers after the rare, & beautiful, then will I eschew hat, coat, & breeches forever; & in Georgia Summer costume walk the world, with nothing save my shirt collar & spurs. Yea verily! the name and fame of Dial's Creek; depends upon the typography of next week; & should that in any wise come up to the merits of the production, from henceforth the denizens of St. Mary's District,

Will each & all, thank the Almighty giver,
That Dial's Creek doth run into Flat River.

They will become lions, Sir, men of note, whose "locum tenens" being known, will always be a passport to the very topmost crust, of the upper Ten Thousand - Hurra for Dial's Creek! & ten thousand welcomes from a world getting ready to admire, to that brightener of its solitudes, the matchless, & unparalelled Dialia - so much for fun. As for news, our gleanings so far are but scanty, & what we have gathered are by no means cheering.[78] Barringer is elected certain; Clingman I am afraid is beaten; the last accounts were certainly unfavourable, & should he get in, it will be by the skin of his teeth; Dockery will beat Worth, Meares, Haughton & Bond,[79] are all badly licked & Donnell will have to vail his bonnet, to the chivalric Mr. Clark. Asa Biggs too, will grow bigger, and bigger, before the admiring eyes of the frequenters of the Federal City, the Whigs of Rayner's district, not having had pluck & energy enough, to Outlaw him. The tempest of intestine commotion hath completely subsided; the Ocean of Orange is still; having scarce a ripple, or ground swell; to tell that the storm had ever raged. Every one see[m]s to be of opinion *now* that the result has been, pre-

---

[78]In the Congressional election on August 7, 1845, the results were as follows:

Dist.	Democrats	Whigs
1st	None	T. L. Clingman, James Graham (won)
2nd	Charles Fisher	D. M. Barringer (won)
3rd	David S. Reid (won)	A. B. McMillan
4th		Alfred Dockery (won)
5th	James C. Dobbin (won)	Jonathan Worth
6th	James I. McKay (won)	T. O. Meares
7th	J. R. J. Daniel (won)	
8th	Henry S. Clark (won)	R. S. Donnell
9th	Asa Biggs (won)	David Outlaw

Niles' Register, LXVII, 294, 400; *N. C. Manual,* 931-932.

[79]He probably refers to John H. Haughton and Richard C. Bond, candidates from the fifth and sixth districts.

cisely what he anticipated; though I very much doubt if the matter is altogether settled yet. *"Entre nous"*, Gorrell, Gilmer, Haughton & others, have written to Taylor, advising him to refuse to surrender the office & to leave the settlement of the matter, to the decision of the Supreme Court.[80] Taking the ground, that in as much as he has never at any time, vacated the office, he stands precisely where he did, at the passage of the New Election law, & is consequently entitled to hold under the old Regime. The general impression has been heretofore, that by consenting to submit the matter at all, to the abitrament of a Canvass; he waived his right to hold under the old law, & that having once waived it, he could not again avail himself of its provisions. This is a matter however for lawyers to decide, & to them I expect, it will be referred, if the old man meets with any farther encouragement. This is a thing known but to few, & as nothing is determined upon, it would be better, probably not to mention it. I should like to know your opinion about it ("sub rosa" of course) for I hardly know how to talk to him about it. I met a young gentleman the other day, who says he knew your young Kentuckian Webber,[81] at Princeton. He figured there as a Student of Divinity; & was considered a sprightly, & talented man, but having unfortunately taken it into his head, that the Spirit of Grace could only be thoroughly acquired, by the aid, & assistance, of the Spirit of Wine, that too got into his head; in other words, Webber got drunk one day; or by'r lady it may be it was night, whereupon he was advised, to relinquish his studies for awhile, & has I suppose, been Texas Von Webber, ever since. What a queer case he must have been? studying divinity by a Spirit lamp, & taking a bottle to bed with him, to help him say his prayers:

After a careful perusal of the dicta of Johnston, Webster, & Walker, upon the subject; I have come to the decision, that the word to be used as most thoroughly descriptive of your sentiments, upon realizing for the first time, the delights of Roast Turkey stuffed with mushrooms, should be *voluptuous*. The *elegant* voluptuary of the present times, holds a corresponding position with the Epicureans of old, those elegant savages, who

---

[80]See above, P. H. Mangum to Ellison G. Mangum, July 24, 1845.
[81]See above, 294n.

from the alembick of their own fertile imaginations, first distilled those imaginery wants, & equally imaginery gratification,
which have tended so much to refine the tastes, and enervate
the energies of mankind. The true voluptuary is a thing "sui
Generis." & ranks with the mere sensualist as Hyperion to a
Satyr. While the one, yielding to his brutal propensities, would
"leave an angel's bed, to prey on garbage; the other yields not
even to the fierce call of passion; unless the object be surrounded
with the imaginery halo, of elegance, & refinement. The one is
all animal, the other in a measure deifies the brute, making the
mind an active contributor to the pleasure of sense. In short,
tis Aspasia, to a common drab. So my dear Sir, you see, that
the next time you chance to regale yourself, upon triffles,
plucked from a Turkey's bosom, you are to consider yourself
as being *most voluptuously employed*.

We have just had a very fine & most seasonable rain, which
if it be general, will eventually knock another quarter off of
corn, & *to which* in part, you may charge this very boring epistle.

With kindest regards to Mrs. Mangum, & many bows to the
young ladies, I remain my dear Sir with the utmost esteem &
regard.

Ever Yrs. truly
JNO. CAMERON.

P.S.

By no manner of means let Davis know of the fame that
awaits him; or the fellow will annihilate me perchance in an
exstacy; & particularly I beseech, that this entire production
may be "Entre vous, si'l vous plait, monsieur." When will you
be up? If you make your visit soon, I think I can procure something to while away the short hours with; superior to the productions of either Maj. Palmer,[82] or Mr. Ellis. Do not deem me
either impertinent, or a humbug, from the manner in which
this rambling rigmarole is commenced; the truth is I had been
thinking of you, while smoking my morning pipe, & that jingle
of lines, in the way of an acrostic popped into my head. When
I afterwards concluded to take advantage of the rainy morn-

---

[82]Nathaniel J. Palmer.

ing to write; I determined to commence my letter, as never was letter commenced before. So that you see Hal, if there be aught of offence, in all ariseth from that d—d Yankee spirit of adventure—

WPM-LC

Thomas F. Davis[83] *to Willie P. Mangum.*

CHAPEL HILL, August 3rd. [1845]

Hon. Willie P. Mangum.

Dear Sir,

I have the honor to address you in behalf of the Dialectic Society, and to ask such contribution, as you may think proper, for the furtherance of a scheme in which her members are now engaged.

You are well aware, I presume, Sir, from your connection with this University, that its two Societies have for some time resolved to construct new Rooms suited to all their purposes.[84] The Halls heretofore in use have become too small and incommodious for their meetings and incapable of accomodating their libraries. This design has the cordial approbation of the Faculty and of the Trustees generally: I trust, Sir, of yourself among the number. Engagements have already been made with a view to the speedy commencement of the work.

The acting members of the Dialectic Society have found *themselves* incompetent to carry out their resolutions. We therefore appeal for assistance to the old members of Society, and particularly to you, Sir, as to one who has experienced her benefits, and not only is concerned, for the welfare of the In-

---

[83]Thomas Frederick Davis, son of Bishop T. F. Davis, who also graduated from the University, was a senior at the time this letter was written. Battle, *Hist. of the U. N. C.,* II, 494; Grant, *Alumni Hist. of U. N. C.,* 157.

[84]In 1837 members of the Philanthropic Society petitioned the trustees for a new hall. The next year the Dialectic Society made a similar request. In 1839 a special committee of the trustees recommended that as soon as the funds would permit, two buildings should be created. In 1844 a famous New York architect, A. J. Davis, who helped design the capitol at Raleigh, presented plans for altering Old East and Old West halls to meet the new needs. These plans were accepted. The Societies paid $1400 each and the state $6,560. The improvements were completed in 1848. Battle, *Hist. of the U. N. C.,* I, 511-514.

stitution, but who takes a kindly interest in the affairs of young fellow members, and we would entreat your aid.

I am, Sir, with high respect,
Your ob'd't serv't
THOS. F. DAVIS.

[Postmarked:] Chapel Hill N. C.
Aug 7

[Addressed:]

Hon. Willie P. Mangum

Red Mountain P. O.

Orange C'ty

N. C.

WPM-LC

E. W. Hall and others to Willie P. Mangum

UNIVERSITY OF N. CAROLINA. Aug. 1845

Sir

During our last Commencement, several of the Trustees, seeing the inconvenience arising from the limited size of our party room, and its incapacity to accommodate with any degree of comfort the large number of persons present, expressed a willingness to aid us in building a hall. At this suggestion the matter has been taken in hand, and we a committee on behalf of the students, are authorized to ask pecuniary assistance from such persons as we may think willing to subscribe. Please notice this as soon as possible, as we wish to make our calculations and complete the hall by our next commencement. Hoping that our scheme may meet with your concurrence, we sign ourselves.

Yours respectfully

E. W. HALL)	(? A. DANIEL
W K. BLAKE) Committee	(? C. DUKE
D. T. TAYLOE)	(? Y. MANLY

?

[Addressed:]

Hon. W. P. Mangum
Red Mountain
Orange
N. C.

WPM-LC

William Piper[85] to Willie P. Mangum

Augt 21st. 1845.

Judge Mangum.

Dear Sir.

Your proposition in regard to a school was unexpected to me. I have thought upon the subject I do not feel myself competent to teach a school as it ought to be done. I am willing if a school can be made to do my best, provided I can get a comfortable situation convenient for my family.

Your very generous offer in regard to a school, has led me to believe, that you regard my interest, and happiness. It is true my situation in life is an uncomfortable one, through the mishaps of fortune. I am advancing in life, with delicate health, my children all daughters, and nothing but my efforts, upon which I can hope, to sustain myself and family; which will be freely and fully exerted, whe[n] an opportunity offers, for them to be displayed. I hope you will pardon me, if I propose too much, when I say, provided a school cannot be made, that

---

[85]See below letters of W. P. Mangum to Charity A. Mangum, March 16, 1846, and William Piper to W. P. Mangum, March 24, 1846. William Piper was one of the agents for the sale of Rev. John A. McMannin's book entitled *A Pictorial Illustration of the Way of Life & Death*, which was published in 1844. *Hillsborough Recorder*, February 22, 1844.

if you will divide your hands, and plantations with Mr. Carrington and myself to manage, that with fortune in my favour I can so manage the part entrusted to my care, that nothing will [be] lost to you by the arrangement- Necessity has no law, I am anxious to obtain business, and submit this proposition without knowing what your arrangements for the next year are, trusting that you will believe it to be my anxiety to get business, that has induced me to be thus plain. I hope you will answer me, and if you think it would not be to your interest to employ me, provided a school can not be made, and of that I have my doubts, I shall remain as ever,

Your friend
Yours &c,
W. PIPER

[Addressed:]

Hon. W. P. Mangum

Jim

WPM-D

Henry Clay to P. Henry Langdon[86]

ASHLAND 13th Sept. 1845

My Dear Sir

I received and thank you for your kind and friendly letter. The trifling object which you requested is enclosed, with regrets it is not some thing more worthy of your acceptance.

I submit, with resignation and philosophy, to the political event to which you allude. It has long ceased to give me any personal concern. Perhaps I ought to felicitate myself on my escape from great responsibilities, in meeting which I may be have failed to accomplish all that my ardent friends anticipated. Whatever lingering regrets remain are excited for them and for our Country.

Recollecting with lively and grateful feelings my agreeable visit last year to North Carolina, I should be most happy to re-

---

[86]Langdon was one of those in Wilmington who helped entertain Clay while he was there.

peat it; but I am not now aware that it ever will be in my power.

Reciprocating your friendly wishes for my health and hapiness,

I am Your friend
And obed. Servant
H. CLAY

P. Henry Langdon Esq
    Wilmington N C

[Endorsed:] From the Honbl. Henry Clay   [Postmarked:]
                Ashland   Lexington, Ky.

[Addressed:] P. Henry Langdon Esq   Sept 14
                Wilmington
                North Carolina

WPM-LC

J. Pope, Jr.,[87] *et als. to Willie P. Mangum.*

MEMPHIS, TENN. Sept 15th. 1845.

Dear Sir:

You are doubtless aware that a Convention was held at this place, on the 4th of July last,[88] the leading object of which was, earnestly to awaken and stimulate public attention to the long neglected wants and resources of the South and West. In consequence of a somewhat indefinite notice, in the call of that Convention, no decided impression was made upon the public mind; and the result was, that, in some instances, there was no representation, and others a very partial one, of the States interested

---

[87]This is a printed letter. In the July meeting, J. Pope, Jr., of Tennessee, was chairman of the committee on local arrangements for the November Convention. Herbert Wender, *Southern Commercial Conventions, 1837-1859,* Baltimore, 1930, 61.

[88]In March, 1845, at a small gathering at Memphis of West Tennesseans and a commission from Arkansas, it was decided to hold an internal improvements convention at Memphis in July. On July 4, 1845, delegates from several states gathered, but, because of inadequate publicity and the hurried nature of the call, it was decided to postpone the meeting until November. Calhoun and other well-known political leaders were approached and induced to attend. The result was that at the November session 600 delegates representing 17 states were present. Calhoun became chairman. A series of eighteen recommendations were adopted: the strengthening of western defenses, federal aid to the navigation of the Mississippi and its tributaries, the building of strong forts on the Gulf, a navy yard on the Mississippi, and the apportioning of government land to build a main western railroad. The House of Representatives ignored the recommendation, but the Senate, under Calhoun's influence, appointed a committee which approved several of the recommendations. The convention was called the Calhoun Convention. *Hillsborough Recorder,* December 4, 1845; Wender, *Southern Commercial Conventions,* 49-69.

in the great objects proposed for its deliberation. Small, however, as was the Convention, compared with the magnitude of the subjects brought before it, much interesting discussion was elicited, and an intense and inextinguishable zeal was roused in behalf of the vast and diversified interests, for the development and guardianship of which the aid of the Convention had been invoked.

In justice to the States interested, for the reasons above stated, it was determined that the Convention should assume a preliminary form, and that the final consummation of its ob-objects should be postponed to a Convention to be held at this place on the 12th day of November next.

Among the projects which will primarily engage the attention of this Convention may be mentioned: The Atlantic and Mississippi Rail-Road, the Great Ship Canal, connecting the Illinois River with Lake Michigan, the National Turnpike Road through the State of Arkansas, the Military and Naval defences of the South and West, embracing Armories, Depots and Forts, the Improvement of Southern & Western Rivers, and the reclaiming of the banks of the same by Levees, the Facilities of Mail Transportation, the Condition and Improvement of Agriculture, and the Manufacturing Capabilities of the South & West.

It is expected that the Convention will studiously avoid every thing which will tend to excite or inflame party antipathies, and that the action of our National Authorities will be sought and urged only in cases where there is an entire unanimity of sentiment as to the powers conferred upon the General Government.

The undersigned were appointed a Committee by the Convention of July last, to invite the attendance of such persons as were presumed to be friendly to the objects proposed for its action. Among those who have advocated, with distinguished zeal and ability, the great interests of the South and West, the Committee are happy to find your name; and they earnestly and respectfully solicit your presence and co-operation in aid of the important enterprizes contemplated by the Convention of the 12th of November next. They would, further respectfully invoke your influence in procuring a full delegation from the district in which you reside.

With sentiments of distinguished regard,
Your obedient Servants,

J. Pope, Jr.
J. H. McMahon,
J. J. Finley,
E. M. Yerger,
J. P. Trezevant,
D. Morrison,
L. C. Trezevant.

[Addressed:]

Hon. W. P. Mangum
Red Mountain,
Orange Co.,
N. C.

WPM-LC

John H. Young[89] to Willie P. Mangum.

Orange Co. Sept. 16th 1845.

Dear Judge-

I wish to remove two houses at Buffalo Hill tomorrow and I ask the favour of you to assist me; - by sending as many hands as you can conveniently spare (if but one) you will much oblige.

Your obt. servant,
John H. Young.

[Addressed:]

Hon. W. P. Mangum
Present.

----

[89]John H. Young, a physician, 1819-1851, lived near Mangum. He married Mangum's cousin, Lucy P. Parker, daughter of Colonel Abner Parker. *Hillsborough Recorder,* January 28, 1841; February 18, 1851.

WPM-LC

Samuel Winfree and John M. Sheppard to Willie P. Mangum

CIRCULAR LETTER.

RICHMOND, 1st October 1845.

Sir,

The subscribers, after many years experience in the Tobacco Trade, have associated themselves in business this day under the firm and style of

WINFREE & SHEPPARD,

For the sale of Tobacco, Wheat and Flour.
They respectfully solicit consignments.

Very respectfully,

SAMUEL WINFREE,
JOHN M. SHEPPARD, JR.

HENDERSON, N. C. 1st November 1845.[90]

Sir,

The subscriber intends removing to Richmond about the 1st January next, and would recommend his friends in North Carolina to the House of WINFREE & SHEPPARD. He will give his personal and particular attention to all Consignments of Tobacco and other Produce entrusted to their management, with the assurance that their interest will be attended to with fidelity and dispatch.

Very respectfully

V. WINFREE.

[Addressed:]

Hon. W. P. Mangum,
Red Mountain
N. Ca.

---

[90]This letter in manuscript is written on the printed circular.

WPM-LC

William Hickey[91] to Willie P. Mangum.

(CONFIDENTIAL)

Office of the Secretary of the Senate U. S.

October 3d. 1845.

Dear Sir,

I hope that you have spent a pleasant summer and that yourself and family are in the enjoyment of perfect health, and, that in due time, we will have you again among us, ready to do battle in the good cause and in support of the best interests of our country.— As the session approaches we are admonished to prepare for your reception, and, on this occasion, to say a word to our friends, to prepare them for the rather extraordinary aspect which the interested and vindictive zeal of some of the ultra Locofocos, seem to threaten to some of our household.— Poor Dyer's place[92] was a mark for them, and they intended to have opposed his re-election, particularly a man of the name of Riell an Editor from New York, but our friend Dyer is gone and I hope is better off, leaving the place vacant. With regard to this place (as it is not expected that a Whig could be elected) two views will be presented to our Whig friends, - either to support Mr. Beall the Assistant Doorkeeper for the place of Sergeant-at-Arms, upon the principle of regular promotion (although he may not be personally so well qualified as he might be), or, on the other hand, to permit this Loco-Editor to be brought in upon Strong party grounds.— It is thought that if the Whigs would support Beall he has personal friends enough among the Democratic Senators to secure his election.—

It is also rumored that a push is to be made at our Secretary[93] because he is rather luke warm - Keeps whigs in his office - is too impartial in making purchases and giving out

---

[91]William Hickey, 1798-1866, held several government posts: draftsman for the coastal survey; chief clerk of the Department of War; executive clerk, reading clerk, assistant clerk, and acting clerk of the Senate. He wrote a treatise on the Constitution which went through several editions. Bessie W. Gahn, "William Hickey of Greenvale," *Records of the Columbia Historical Society of Washington, D. C.,* XXXV-XXXVI, 109-123.

[92]Edward Dyer was elected sergeant at arms and doorkeeper of the Senate. *American Almanac,* 1846, 193.

[93]Asbury Dickins was Secretary of the Senate at this time.

jobs of work &c, *whereas he ought to give them all to the Democrats par excellence.* Should they succeed in turning him out,
we would, of course, be all marked for proscription, and the
most hungry and pushing harpies be put in.- I considered it my
duty to mention the subject in time to one or two of *my known*
and *true friends,* in order that they might be aware of the consequences to us of an opposition to our friend Mr. Dickens.—
He has avoided proscription in the office, and of course, should
the other party now seek to proscribe him for his moderation
and justice, the gallant whigs, our friends, will I hope to a man
stand by him; whom, with his personal friends on the other
side, will secure his election.— I understand that Colo. Benton,
who is now here, has given a very emphatic negative, at the
threshold, to a party man who is seeking Mr. Dickens' place.
He is reported to have said - "Sir I would have you to know
that so far as I am concerned the Officers of the Senate are in
during good behavior, and I will tolerate no proscription in this
place for opinions' sake."— We will support and aid Mr. Dickens
in the Senate and out of the Senate with our best energies and
ability.

With apologies for troubling you on this subject I remain

> Dr. Sir, with the highest respect & esteem,
> Your friend and most obedient servant
> W. HICKEY

The Hon'ble Willie P. Mangum,
Senator of the United States.—

WPM-LC

T. L. Clingman to Willie P. Mangum.

(CONFIDENTIAL)

ASHEVILLE Oct 5th 1845.

My dear Judge

I write you this letter at the suggestion of Col. Gaither[94] &
several of our other whig friends and any reply which you may
make to it will be made public not further than may accord

---

[94]He refers to Burgess S. Gaither, who at this time was solicitor for the seventh judicial district
of North Carolina. Ashe, *Biog. Hist. of N. C.,* II, 93-99.

with your wishes. There is a great diversity of opinion here with respect to a proper selection of our next candidate for the office of governor. I say to you in confidence that a number of the best whigs in this district have said in my hearing & to others that they will not support Wm. A. Graham. These expressions I have endeavoured as much as possible to check & have been & shall continue to urge upon the whigs the necessity of supporting him if he should be nominated. We had great difficulty last year in this district in giving him the vote he got (& that was twelve hundred less than Morehead's majority). I then made for him all the exertion in my power & my friends here say that I lost by so doing more votes than I was beaten this year.[95] I know it myself & last year foresaw that I should make many enimies with the fishy whigs, (Hoke's friends of course). I do not regret this now & shall if Mr Graham be the nominee support him again, but the difficulty will be much greater to get him along than it was. Many intelligent men say that they will not support a man whose own brother would not support him but kept out of the district to avoid committing himself last year, as he has invariably done when not a candidate himself. In fact James Graham is viewed by the greater part of the whigs say three fourths probably in no better light than John Tyler himself.

As to who ought to be the nominee there is much diversity of opinion Some are for Rayner, others for Stanly, Manly &c.

The gentlemen to whom I have alluded at the beginning of this note are of opinion that you would make a better run if you would consent to undergo the labour than any one else. Something which you said to me last winter, which I have not thought fit however to allude to publicly made me suppose that you might possibly be willing to be brought out. Whether you would feel authorised to leave your present position filling it as you do with so much credit to yourself & honour to the State is a matter about which I cannot undertake to advise, I can only assure you that should you consent to run the western reserve will come out for you in all its whig strength & give you a larger majority than it would any one else of our party. I think a strong man & a vigorous canvass necessary to enable us to sustain ourselves next year. Afterwards a new presidential

---

[95]Clingman was defeated for Congress by James Graham, William A. Graham's brother. Although a Whig, James Graham had many Democratic supporters.

candidate will make the thing easy for us I believe because the floating vote will leave the democracy & come over to us in two years/I know of course that portion of the voters who go in for spoils &c & who will rally on some new man is preferred to staying in the ranks of Polks party because some of them will feel disappointed & others become dissatisfied with a very tame mercenary administration.

Please let me hear from you at once & direct your letter to me at Morganton where I expect to be two weeks from this time, Our course will be in accordance with your wishes should you intimate them. We shall begin at this place a series of meetings for the purpose of selecting delegates to our State convention. In these we shall expect no preference for any one till we hear from you.

Hoping that this will be soon

I remain truly yours
T. L. CLINGMAN.

Hon. Willie P. Mangum.

[Addressed:] Hon. Willie P. Mangum
Red Mountain
Orange Co
N. C.

WPM-LC

J. S. Skinner[96] to W. P. Mangum

Office of The Farmers Library
7th Octr. 1845.

My Dear Sir.

You will have to appoint a Serjeant at Arms for the Senate and my friend Mr. James B. Mower[97] long known to me as an efficient officer in the New York Post Office and perfectly well qualified, will be an applicant for the trust, I hope it may be in your way and inclination to give him your support, being

---

[96] In 1845 John Stuart Skinner edited the New York *Farmer's Library and Monthly Journal of Agriculture* for the *New York Tribune*. Three years later he moved to Philadelphia and continued the paper under a different name and under his own control. *D. A. B.*, XVII, 200.
[97] James B. Mower was in the New York post office. In 1848 he tried to have the Whigs nominate John McLean and Mangum for their candidates. See his letters to Mangum in 1847-1848.

well assured that his performance of the duties would be altogether satisfactory

For myself, I am much more agreeably fixed here, than when wearing a collar, that 'though it always chafed and sometimes almost choked me I yet had not the courage to slip— God send that I may never again by the power of an *"accident"* or otherwise be *poked* into such another predicament! one altogether repugnant to the feelings of a freeman and to which his poverty *may*, but his will- never will consent.

Very truly & constantly
Your friend
& ob't serv't
J. S. Skinner

Hon. W. P. Mangum
U. S. Senator.

———

WPM-LC

J. B. Mower[98] to Willie P. Mangum

Hon. Willie P. Mangum)   New York. 8th. Oct. 1845
U. S. Senator ）
Redmountain ）
N. C. ）

Sir,

I hope you will pardon me Sir, for again troubling you, with my application, for the office of sergeant at arms; but my good old friend Skinner, is such a right good fellow, that I thought, I could not refuse his kind offer, of a letter of introduc-

---

[98]See the previous letter.

tion to you, Mr. Senator, and I here take leave, again Sir, to enclose it to you.

I am Sir,
most respectfully
Your mo^t. ob^t.
Servant
J. B. MOWER

[Addressed:]

Hon. Willie P. Mangum
U. S. Senator
Redmountain
N. C.

WPM-LC

Thomas J. Green To The Electors of the
Western Congressional District Of The State of Texas.[99]

[25 October, 1845]

Fellow Citizens:

Some months since at the request of many friends, I consented that my name might be used as a candidate for the
United States House of Representatives, for the western district
of Texas. Since which time I have been absent from home upon a visit to the best of Mothers, now eighty years of age, whom
I had not seen during our protracted revolution and an only
son[100] from whom I had been absent the same period, as well
as to attend to some indispensable personal obligations which
a ten years service for the land of my adoption, had caused me
to neglect. It may not be out of place here to name one other
reason for this absence. When a prisoner of war in Mexico,
with my brave comrades, of Mier and San Antonio,[101] we found
ourselves denounced by our own President Gen. Houston, as

---

[99] This is a circular, printed at the office of the *Daily* and *Weekly Globe*, by Levi D. Slamm and
C. C. Childs.

[100] Wharton J. Green, later a Confederate officer and member of Congress. Born in Florida in
1831, he was educated at the University of Virginia and Cumberland University. He practiced law
with Robert J. Walker until the war broke out in 1861. Davis recommended him for brigadier
general, but the appointment was not confirmed. After the war, he returned to Warren County, North
Carolina, and later entered Congress. Ashe, *Biog. Hist. of N. C.*, II, 120-125.

[101] See above, III, 431n.

robbers and marauders upon that country which caused many
of those men to be lotteried for and murdered in a manner so
horrible as to shock the humanity of the civilized world.[102]
Many of the ballance were starved to death, piece-meal in the
cold dungeons of that country. Those who survived this catalogue of sufferings and blood, as well as those who perished,
had reputations more dear to them than life,— reputations
which they had gloriously won in fighting the battles of their
country,— reputations, the proudest heir-loom to their posterity,— reputations their country's pride and property. It
was my good fortune fellow citizens, to preserve through all
the trials and dangers of our captivity the written evidences of
this most unholy, murderous slander. The living appealed to
me to vindicate them.— the tears of fathers, mothers, widows
and orphans, called aloud upon me to preserve to them the
brightest, the only legacy of sons, brothers and fathers, whose
bones are now bleaching in an enemies country. Justice to the
true history of my own country, as well as duty to the living
and the dead left me no option. This bloody tale I have published,[103] and it is a circumstance not less flattering to myself
than the vindicated, that it has met universal favor with the
reading public of this country. My absence from Texas during
these few interesting months in her political existence, I trust
has neither been idly spent in her cause, but with zeal and
whatever of ability I possess has been devoted to advocating
her interest and reconciling and enlightening many unjust prejudices which heretofore had such a strong hold upon the popular thought of these states. To believe as I do, that I have been
of service to Texas, in this respect, is to me, ample compensation. A few weeks longer absence makes it proper that I should
address you upon some few points of great political concern-
ment, though I can hardly hope to do so satisfactorily in the
limited space of a letter, If however the presenting at this
time these questions to your consideration, invites your discussion and thereby evidences your public will, I shall feel
pround [sic] in having done so.

The surrender of your unappropriated Lands in Texas for the
payment of your public debt,— the liquidation of all just claims

---

[102]See above, III, 431, 434-435.
[103]Thomas Jefferson Green, *Journal of the Texian Expedition Against Mier;* New York, 1845.
482 pp.

against Texas,— the early settlement of private land claims,—
the subdivision of Texas into states under the resolutions of annexation,— the endowment of public schools— the improvement of your harbors bays and rivers and the western boundary
of Texas, are among many others, momentous questions for the
immediate consideration of the people of Texas, and a too early
discussion of them cannot be had.

Four weeks previous to the death of the illustrious Ex-President Andrew Jackson, in discussing with me the benefits of the
union to our respective countries, he said, *"It is impossible for
the United States to control the Indians and Texas to hold the
public lands. We must have them."* So far as I have been able
to learn, this will be among the strong reasons urged by President Polk, to procure our public domain by either the assumption of our debt, or a valuable consideration in some other
shape. Whether the people of Texas prefer to surrender their
one hundred and eighty millions of unappropriated acres for
the payment of seven or eight millions of dollars, most of which
was paid out of our treasury, at one-fourth of its face, and now
mostly due foreign shavers; or whether they will prefer an
average price per acre and settle their own debts and leave a
large surplus in their treasury; or whether they will prefer to
hold their lands and thereby control the meets and bounds of
their own and future states, are important considerations for
the people of Texas and cannot be too early entertained. While
the limits of this letter precludes me from more than a hint at
these important questions, I hope soon to discuss them at length
in person; and to abide your will thereon will be the duty of
your representatives.

In my frequent interviews this summer with President
Polk and his cabinet, I have invariably found them entertaining views the most liberal in all things towards our country
and that they will so continue to feel and act, no one doubts;
for they know and admit that it was your sweat and blood
which won our fair Texas back to the bosom of this great nation, when untold millions of money backed by the influence
and diplomacy of Adams, Jackson, Van Buren and Clay, failed
to accomplish it.

Should it be the will of the people of Texas to surrender
their unappropriated lands to the general government, they

cannot be too cautious in submitting their own private land claims to the endless adjudication of an United States *Land board*, who may do as has been done in other new States *adjudicate* the *first* owners into their graves and *delay* the *second* generation into penury. With the experience of Missouri, Florida and other states before us, let us substitute some plan by which the few survivors of our revolution, may be early guaranteed in some of the fruits of their hard fought battles.

Fellow Citizens, upon the subject of your Western boundary, I am proud to assure you, that President Polk has planted his foot upon the banks of the Rio Grande, from whence no power of Mexico, nor any diplomatic trick at *National reference,* will drive him east; and in this position he is backed by an overwhelming majority of his countrymen. There is one great controlling feeling, with the millions of this country, which was so boldly avowed by the republicans of the land, under President Monroe,— to submit to no European control in the affairs of this continent—

"No pent up Utica, confines our powers,
This whole boundless continent is ours."

This question of boundary, has been ably urged since the adjournment of the United States Congress.— The law of the Texas Congress, in 1836 *"defining the boundary of Texas,"* has been mainly relied upon, and those presses in this country who advocated a surrender of Texas to the Nuesses [sic] frequently answered that "this law of 1836 was an arbitrary declaration and not justified by the facts in the case"— In this they are mistaken— I was the member of the Congress of 1836 who drafted that law and which unanimously passed that Congress.— When some members of the committee proposed the Nueces as our western boundary, I objected upon the ground that we had driven the enemy beyond the Rio Grande— that beyond this line the commanding General Felisola, had passed under the conduct of our own commissioners Colonels Carnes and Teal, and that subsequently those of the enemy who ventures to the eastern bank of that river was defeated and driven back by Captain Erastus, (Deaf) Smith, near Lerado [Larado] and that we held to this boundary not only by virtue of Felisola's acknowledgment, but by conquest and actual possession. Those reasons were sufficient with the Congress of '36, and I am

proud to say that they are sustained by the overwhelming public voice of this country— Had I then yielded my opinion and
adopted the Nueces, the case might now be far different, and
Texas instead of her three hundred and fifty thousand square
miles would not have one fourth that amount.

With respect fellow citizens to my political creed, I am what
is known in the United States as a Democrat— My Father and
Grand Fathers before me were *Whigs* in '76 and *Republicans* in
'98 and proved their principles then as you have since done
in your struggle for liberty.

As to Texas politics, it is unnecessary for me to speak—
they are known to you all— my principles have been on all
occasions to fight the enemies of my country. When I have
seen that country year after year abused by a dastard enemy,
plundered and desolated and our own Chief Executive President Houston, foremost in falsely asserting to the enemy our
inability to redress these outrages,— When I have seen that same
Executive acting under a settled purpose to destroy that fair
portion of Western Texas, which has paid the heaviest tribute
both in taxes and blood, I have boldly and at all times, and on
all occasions, opposed this measure,— So likewise have I opposed his measures when I have seen him pandering to the
intrigues of a French diplomatist, who modestly asked to make
Texas a *"Franco Texian"* dependency,— So have I opposed his
nefarious attempt to put her under British vassalage,— His
correspondence with the blood-thirsty Santa Anna,— His denunciation of the brave men of Mier— His usurpation of the
law which gave them bread. His proclamation of piracy against
the gallant Commodore Moore and the Navy[104]— His extravagant friendship to our Indian enemies— His compound
frauds to defeat annexation, all, all, have I boldly opposed both
in and out of Congress. While I have many personal friends
in Texas, who have heretofore been the avowed friends of
General Houston, I beg that they will not deceive themselves,
as to my opinion of him. I have long since conscientiously believed that he was the most corrupt man personally and political·

[104]The Texas navy consisted of three vessels which at the time of the negotiations for annexation
were at New Orleans under the command of Commodore Moore. Money was sent to release the
vessels from creditors, but Moore failed to carry out the orders. Instead, he cooperated in a free-
booting expedition to make great profits for Texas and himself. Houston ordered Moore to surrender
the vessels and when he failed to comply, Houston pronounced him a pirate. Moore then challenged
Houston to a duel, but Houston ignored the challenge and demoted Moore. Marquis James, *The
Raven: A Biography of Sam Houston* (Indianapolis, 1929), 334-335; Alexander Dienst, "The
Navy of the Republic of Texas," *Quarterly of the Texas Historical Association*, XIII, 113-127.

ly I ever knew— This belief has never been disguised; on all occasions for the last nine years, have I spoken and published it.[105] His favors and his cowardly malice I have ever held in equal contempt, and between him and *his* principles and myself there can be no compromise.— When I have seen him proclaiming in his annual Message the most stupid untruths— When I have seen him swallowing at the bar of Congress falsehoods before they were cold from his lips,— When I have seen his blubbering lamentations over his Cherokee connections,— When I have seen him wallowing in the filthiest gutters of your capitol a disgusting bloated drunkard, and a majority of our countrymen folding their arms and countenancing these, and a thousand other of his enormities, my heart has bled for my country, but never have I despaired of a brighter day— That brighter day, fellow citizens, thanks to your republican principles, is at hand, when we can produly look to the President of this great Confederacy as our President, to the American Congress, as our Congress, and to this great Nation, as our Nation.

THOMAS J. GREEN,
City of New-York, Oct. 25, 1845.

WPM-LC

James P. Scales[106] & Others to Willie P. Mangum.

HILLSBORO' Nov. 15th 1845.

Judge Mangum

Sir

We the undersigned have the honor to inform you in behalf of the Adelphian Society that you have been elected an honorary member of that body.

The object for which our Society was instituted, is similar to that of other literary associations of the kind, and too well

---

[105]This hostility continued until the Civil War. In 1860-1861, when Texans were considering secession, Green vigorously campaigned for secession. At one place in the discussion when Houston was asked his opinion of Green, he replied: "He has all the characteristics of a dog except fidelity." James, *The Raven*, 409.
[106]A graduate of the University of North Carolina in 1829, James Scales moved to Mississippi where he became a speaker of the lower house of the legislature. He was a major in the Civil War. Grant, *Alumni Hist. of U. N. C.*, 548.

known to you to require any explanation on our part. An early answer is respectfully requested

Yours

JAMES P. SCALES
D. T. TOWLES
WM. MCKERALL
Correspon'd Committee.

To Hon. W. P. Mangum
> Orange
>> N. C.

[Addressed:]

> Hon. Willie P. Mangum
>> Red Mountain
>> Orange Cty
>> No. Ca.

Willie P. Mangum to William A. Graham[107]

ORANGE CO. 22nd. Nov. 1845.

My dear Sir.

I have been requested to ask the favor of you, to write a word touching the Sufficiency of two Notes, that will be presented next week, to the Cape Fear bank in Raleigh, for discount. -

The first - W^m. Forsythe, principal;- with S. P. Forsythe & James Bullock, & E. G. Mangum sureties. - The next E. G. Mangum principal - with Abner Parker & H. Parker sureties. - The first for $800 - The next for like sum.

I presume, you know enough of the parties. to render any statement of mine unnecessary. - At all events, the notes, as above, will be beyond all question, & as good as any in N. Carolina. -

107The original is in the William A. Graham Papers, University of North Carolina.

I speak from knowledge.

Yrs as ever, most truly
WILLIE P. MANGUM

To Gov. Graham
Raleigh

[Endorsed on reverse:] Willie P. Mangum 1845
Two Notes in Bank Cape Fear?

WPM-LC

Joseph B. Hinton[108] to Willie P. Mangum

RALEIGH N. C. Dec 1. 1845

Honl. & dear Sir,

Permit an old friend & admirer to say, in the pride & pleasure of a Carolinian, your honours wear well, for they have been fairly won. Another, indeed, may fill your vacant seat, but does the *Nation* think it is as nobly filled as when occupied by the Mangum of the good old North State? No indeed, no. We shall see the beginning of the end of the present state of things, by & by.

In the mean time, allow me to commend to your kindest regards and assistance, if possible, a gentleman who is every way worthy of both- I mean Edward Warner Esq. a promising young Lawyer of Washington City- the protege of the late Mr. Legare, in whose office he studied Law, & under whose patronage he went to the bar: besides a ripe schollar, Mr Warren is a gentleman in every sense of the word- He desires to be Door Keeper of the Senate- and if his political & personal friend, Mr. Choat, had not left the Senate, he would have a right to expect all that his Whig principles & the influence of his friend, Mr Choat, could do for him. His wife is a niece of ex Gov. Grayson of Md. & of the late Mrs. Stone of this City & my wife also. If you can feel free to aid Mr. Warner - it will greatly gratify us all- and if in Mr. Warner, the Senate gets an officer, I feel confident, that body never had an officer who gave more universal satisfaction, than he would.

------

[108]See above, I, 520n.

My best wishes for your health & happiness—ever attends you.

Yours most truly.
Jos. B. HINTON

Honl. W. P. Mangum.

[Addressed:]

> Honl. Willie P. Mangum.
> Senator in Congress,
> Washington.
> D. C.

WPM-LC

John Minge[109] to Willie P. Mangum.

PETERSBG. Decr 1 45

Dear Sir

I had intended to have visited Washington to see you in person but as circumstances prevent me, I must be permitted to call your attention to some of my grievances, as you perhaps know I have been without cause or even charge of error been dismissed from office and my place supplied by a man, to say the least of him, who stands charged with crimes and misdemeanors and who was the *only* applicant, shewing the settled policy of the administration, and no doubt can be left on the mind of any man that it is a case similar to the *one supposed* in the debate by Mr. Madison and others on the abridgement of the Executive power, and which Mr. Madison in his enthusiasm on the virtue of republicks declared "was not likely to happen, and if it did, would afford fair grounds for impeachment." I Sir have been displaced directly in the face of publick opinion as you might have known on yr visit here last spring both parties loudly and numerously demanded my continuance yet a few party hacks representing themselves as a delegation from the democratic party, in fulfilment of *promises of payment* to some hirelings of their party demanded the removal of every officer

---

[109]John Minge, 1796-1871, a graduate of William and Mary, married Mary Griffin Adams, of Richmond, and later became postmaster under Tyler. *William and Mary Quarterly,* Ser. 1, Vol. XXI, 32; XXV, 238; John Minge to _____, April 12, 1849.

in the district, and with the aid of Mr Dromgoole and Mr I W Jones to *certify* to fitness and capacity have placed in situations of high trust and responsibility, at least one if not two who are unworthy of the places they occupy, if the charge made against them be true and which are *uncontradicted* and these charges have been made by one of their own party and who is a Lawyer of eminence in this City and who receives and enjoys the respect and confidence of the most respectable part of our community, and the only means left his opponents of countervailing his influence was to charge him with monomania on the subject of gambling and cheating at cards, now, a very common substerfuge in criminal accusations.—

You will be surprised when I declare to you that my course in this affair, to wit, requesting yr particular attention to the confirmation of the present incumbent in the P. Office in Petersbg has not been directed by any malignity of feeling towards this individual, but in obedience to a duty I owe to my Country as well as to myself, believing as I do that the chains of the slaves may become musick to their ears unless manfully resisted when the first rivet is made, and fearfully should we look on these small encroachments on the citadel of our liberties when in our own history we know that perhaps this domain now our beautiful and beloved country has been lost to its mother for a paltry tax unjustly levied on a few pounds of tea, and Grecian history informs us that a counsel of its wisest men, maintained that government to be best, which soonest redress'd the grievances of its subjects, and in making this request of you Sir whose head & heart have ever dictated and whose hand is ever ready to do justice to the humblest individual, I have contributed *my mite smaller* perhaps than even "the widows" to prevent such great effects from inconsiderable causes, so when our beautiful government shall crumble into atoms and be lost in Chaotic confusion it shall not be said of me as was said of the Romans "their failure to resist the first approach to Tyrany rivited their chains."

I have no intimate personal acquaintance with Mr. Archer or I would appeal to him, I know him only as a man of high, noble and Chivalrous bearing as incapable of the least shadow of injustice or oppression as is water to run upwards and whose attention will be call'd to it on the least hint which you may give—

I owe you an apology for not calling on you when *hard pressed* as you told me but the truth is I had been lulled into security by a conversation which had been held with the President of his own seeking with Mr. Ritchie in which he distinctly told Mr. R he would not molest me, only a few days before this self styled delegation from the dem. party in Petersbg demanded my removal, I *was beheaded* before I knew the Guilotine had been built, and of course had no time to do so, tho' I shall ever believe from our conversation that you could have saved me—

Yrs. with great Esteem
Sincerely & truly
JNO MINGE.

WPM-LC

A. W. Gay[110] to Willie P. Mangum.

KNAP-OF REEDS, GRANVILLE COUNTY N. C.
Decr 4th 1845

Dear Sir,

I desired to call and see you before you left home; but was prevented by a continued press of professional engagements. I perceive that, by the new post office law of March 3rd 1845, "members of Congress may transmit, free of postage, any documents printed by order of either House of Congress."] Although I shall no more be a candidate, still I wish to keep myself informed on all the leading political topics of the day. On this account, I shall be greatly obliged to you, if you will be good enough to send me from time to time such documents as will give information on what will be the points of most probable discussion in the contests of next year, relating particularly to Texas, Oregon, and more especially the financial concerns of the General Government. You are doubtless aware that an important element in the political discussions of next summer in this state, will be your own political course, as the next General Assembly will have either to re-elect you or select some one in

---

[110]See above A. W. Gay to W. P. Mangum, April 20, 1844.

your place. As far as I can learn, I believe the whigs are disposed to sustain you and retain you in your present position. You will, however, be the object of violent attack by the opposite party. It will therefore be indispensable that your friends be, in some way, put in possession of such information as may best enable them to meet those assaults. I would suggest whether this could not best be done by speeches delivered by yourself in the Senate during the present session of Congress and circulated, before the canvass of next summer. Such speeches, if delivered will be industriously circulated by your friends in N. C.

As the Appendix to the Congressional Union is devoted entirely to such purposes, and will no doubt be widely circulated, would it not be well to prepare the speeches carefully for that paper?

Please excuse these suggestions if they appear to be out of place. They are prompted only by a desire for your re-election by the next Legislature.

Respectfuly yours &c.

A. W. Gay

P.S. Since the foregoing was written, I was called to your house late in the night on Friday last, the 5th to see your boy Alfred. I found him in a state of callapse; almost entirely unable either to speak or to swallow. Dr. Blacknal, who had been sent for on Friday, did not get there until Saturday morning. The boy had sunk so low that I soon found him to be moribund. From the history of his disease given by the family, it was evidently a case of low typhoid fever, which has been prevailing for some months past, complicated with an insidious kind of Pneumonia which often does not declare itself by any very unequivocal signs to an ordinary observer until irreparable disorganization of the pulmonary structure has taken place. I succeeded for a very short period before the arrival of Dr. Blacknal, in partially arousing the boy from his stupor; but he soon relapsed. As I had to attend to a patient dangerously ill at home, I left him with Dr. B. satisfied that he could not live long. He died on Saturday night. The boy was unwell before you left home, and continued somewhat so all the time; but nothing occurred to alarm the family until Friday. An unsuccessful effort was immediately made to get Dr. B. and I did not see him until two or three hours before day on Saturday morning. Dr. Young had gone off to be married.

It is not uncommon for Pneumonia to proceed so insidiously and to create so little suffering that neither the patient nor his friends are ala[rm]ed until all remedies are unavailing, especia[lly w]hen the pulmonary disease is associated with very low typhoid degree of fever.

Yours &c.

A. W. GAY.

[Addressed:]

Hon. W. P. Mangum.
Washington City.
D. C.

WPM-LC

Thomas J. Green to Willie P. Mangum

WASHINGTON CITY
Decr. 4th. 1845.

My Dear Judge:

Herewith I enclose[111] you a map of Texas, with the Land of Dr. Archer,[112] marked upon it, by which you can judge of its locality.- You will see that it is within 35 miles of the sea coast, crosses *Caney* & fronts upon the San Bernard river, which is navigable at many seasons of the year immediately from it, and at all seasons to within a few miles of it.- This tract of 1600 acres is a portion of Ira Ingrams, head right League of Land one of the first and most choice leagues in Austin colony.- It was purchased of s^d. Ingram, by the Hon Wm H. Wharton in 1834 at $2. per acre & one half subsequently sold to Dr. Branch T. Archer.— The Land is *cain brake and cedar and esteemed to be as good as any on the earth & entirely above overflow.*- It is

111This is not in the Mangum Papers.
112Branch T. Archer, 1790-1856, was a physician and local political leader of his native state, Virginia, before he moved to Texas in 1831. In Texas he supported statehood within the Republic of Mexico and later Texan independence. In 1826 with S. F. Austin and William H. Wharton, he went to the United States as commissioner to obtain money, men, and supplies for the war against Mexico. Under Lamar he was secretary of war for Texas. *D. A. B.*, I, 338-339.

in Latitude 29⁰ .30 minutes & quite one degree South of the best Sugar estates in Louisana.— The Sugar planters in the neighbourhood with crude wooden fixtures have made a better yield of Sugar than the Lousianians while the cotton produce of this region is uneaquelled. Another advantage of this kind of Land should be named- towit- that it is as easy to clear a plantation in *one* year on it, as it would be in heavy timber Land in *twenty*.- This Land is in the immediate vicinity of Capt. John Duncan, & Majr. Rugely, two wealthy gentlemen and large planters.- Capt. Duncan, sold the remaining part of this league of Land to Mr. P. Weaver, of Selma Alabama in 1838 at $4. *per acre in gold*.- Circumstances makes it necessary for Dr. Archer, to sell immediately and he will take for his 800 acres $2.000 or $2.50 per acre I do esteem this as one of the best bargains ever offered in choise sugar Lands whether it be purchased for immediate cultivation or as an investment; for I have not yet heard a good reason why our Texas Sugar Lands may not come up to something like the Louisana prices.—

There is a popular mistake about the cost of a sugar establishment which I desire to correct.— A a small planter can make sugar as well as he can make cotton, and with no more expence of fixture.—

Dr. Archer, and myself will go tomorrow to New York where we will be absent about a week and return *via* this place to Texas, when if you wish to make this purchase he can be seen.- Mrs. Wharton's portion of the Land was offered at the same price and can doubtless yet be had for that price.- The whole tract is capable of makeing a planting interest sufficient for 100 hands-

In haste your friend truly,

THOS. J. GREEN.

[Addressed:]

Hon. W. P. Mangum
Washington City.

Willie P. Mangum to Asbury Dickins[113]

Sunday 7th. Dec[r]. '45

My dear Sir,

I have just returned from Berrien & Barrow - All right. M[r]. Berrien has been approached both at home & here, in the manner you had supposed. - He promptly & resolutely rejected the overture. -

He said there, as he has just said to me, that upon no consideration, nor for any person, would he withhold his Vote from you - On the contrary, he goes for you as decidedly & as cordially, as any Gentleman in the Senate.

Yrs as ever

W. P. MANGUM

To As: Dickens esq.

WPM-LC

D. Clapp[114] *to Willie P. Mangum*

[15 December, 1845]

Hon. Wiley P. Mangum:

Dear Sir

I take the liberty to address you these few lines, and request a favor from you, which, if granted, will be a great accommodation to myself as p[ub]lisher of a public Newspaper.

What I have to ask is, that you [wou]ld send me any. and all public d[ocu]ments and speeches which would be of advantage to me in my business. And especially, I wish to get such documents and reports as will give any information on the Tariff, the amount of imports and exports &C. Also all documents giving information in reference to Oregon &c. &c., with all reports officially made to Congress during the present session.

You will excuse my presumption in making this request. The only apology I have to offer is, that our member from this Dist,

---

[113]The original is in the Historical Society, Pennsylvania. Compare this letter with the one from William Hickey to W. P. Mangum, October 3, 1845.
[114]See above, III, 97n.

(John Wentworth,) cannot be prevailed upon to send any thing of importance to a *Whig,* while I myself, have counted, on the arrival of one single mail at our place, not less than three hundred documents all franked by the said "Long John," to locofocos. And why I presume to address you is that I have had the pleasure of an introduction to your Honor; being a native of old Orange, N. C. and having emigrated to this state only a few years.

With this explanation I sign myself your servant and friend

D. CLAPP

Danville Ill. Dec. 15, '45.

P.S.   What favors you may [confer] upon me please direct to
     Danville Patriot
          Danville
               Ill.

[Addressed:]

Hon W. P. Mangum

U. S. Senate

Washington City

D. C.

WPM-LC

Chas. G. Percival[115] *to Willie P. Mangum*

CITY OF UTICA N. Y.
Dec. 16, 1845—

Dr Sir

I have the favor to ask that you will put my name on the list of those to whom you send Pub Doc[s]. as unless I can persuade some Whig to do so I shall stand a poor chance in this

---

[115]Unable to identify.

hot bed of loco focoism without a Whig M. C. within a hundred miles—

Very Respcty Yours
CHAS. G. PERCIVAL

Hon. W. P. Mangum

[Addressed:]

Hon. W. P. Mangum
U. S. Senate
Washington
D. C.

WPM-LC

Report of the Work of the Whig Republican Association 1845

CIRCULAR.

BOSTON, Dec. 16, 1845.

The Committee appointed by the Government of the WHIG REPUBLICAN ASSOCIATION, to make a brief Report on the doings of the Association, for the year 1845,

REPORT:

That at the commencement of the present season, under the discouragements of a recent national defeat, and the estrangement of some of our friends, it was thought hardly possible that our Head Quarters could be kept open, and the Whig flag kept flying over them during the year. Through the urgent solicitation of many of our strongest Whigs and their liberal contributions, and confiding in the liberality of the Whigs of Boston, and feeling, also, that it was most important that Massachusetts should present a bold front during the attacks on the Protective System of 1842, and on our general State Policy, the Government determined to carry on their operations for another year.

Their anticipations have not been disappointed. The Finances of the present year will cover every expense, and it is believed that the usefulness of the Association, to the City and the State has been greatly increased, without any additional outlay, especially as regards its influence with the Young Whigs, and the circulation of information by documents, &c.

During the past year, besides the regular subscribers, more than *a thousand young men* have enjoyed this means of acquiring political information; we have sent out over *five hundred thousand pages* of valuable documents into the City and adjacent towns, and many of our friends from the country towns send to our Head Quarters for statistics and political documents. - Thousands of Whigs from the interior, and from other States, have visited our Rooms, to which they are always welcome.

The Committee leave it to the Whigs of Boston to decide whether the Association shall continue its operations or whether their Head Quarters shall be closed and their influence be discontinued.

NATHANIEL HAMMOND,)
NATHAN W. BRIDGE,　　)
EBENEZER DALE,　　　)　　Committee.
JAMES FOWLE,　　　　)
HENRY W. CUSHING,　)

N. B. - *This Circular will be called for.* Those who wish to aid the operation of the Association by being considered subscribers for the ensuing year, and those who do not, will write *Yes,* or *No,* at the bottom. Subscription $3. Those under twenty-one, $1.

WPM-LC

W. G. E. Agnew[116] et als. to Willie P. Mangum.

PHILAD[a]. Decr 17, 1845

Dear Sir

At a meeting of the Board of Managers of the Home Missionary & Tract Society of the M. E. Church of the City & County of Philadelphia it was Resolved That W. G. E. Agnew President, Wm. H. Richardson T. Norris W. McMackin W. H. Reed W. P.

---

[116]In McElney's *Philadelphia Directory for 1852,* p. 2, he listed his occupation as teacher.

Hacker & Alex. Cummings be a Committee to provide Talented Popular Speakers for a course of Public Lectures [to be] delivered in this City The proceeds of which shall be appropriated to the relief of the poor & destitute without regard to denomination within the bounds of our Mission. In pursuance of the above object we now address you desiring to know if it would suit your convenience to deliver one Lecture for us in the course of the Winter on any subject that might meet your views.

We would urge this the more upon you in view of the great destitution among our populace during the Winter and the increased means of relief with which your valuable services thus rendered are calculated to supply us.

Knowing your Urbanity & benevolence we fearlessly leave the matter with you requesting an answer as soon as convenient that if favourable we may take the necessary measures to give it publicity

With great respect
We are Dear Sir
Yrs truly & Sincerely

W. G. E. AGNEW Prest
WM. H. RICHARDSON
THAD⁵ NORRIS
W H REED
W P HACKER
WM. McMACKIN
A CUMMINGS

Hon. Willie P. Mangum   )
)
   Washington   )
)
      D. C.   )

WPM-LC

Thurlow Weed to Willie P. Mangum

ALBANY, Dec 18, 1845.

Hon. W. Mangum,

Allow me, Dear Sir, to thank you, most ardently, for the enlightened and patriotic course you took upon Gov. Cass' Resolution.[117] The voices and the Votes of Whig Senators, on these Resolutions, while they diminish greatly the chances of War, serve to keep the Whig Party out of false position.

If our Whig friends would consent to leave the *responsibility* of a War with England, and upon the Tariff where the People have lodged the *power*, "there would be little of evil to apprehend from either of these crusades.

Very Respectfully & Truly
Your Obt Sert
THURLOW WEED

[Addressed:]

Hon. W Mangum,
U. S. Senate
Washington

WPM-LC

P. U. Murphey to Willie P. Mangum.

U. S. S. PENNSYLVANIA
Dec 20th 1845

My dear Sir

I am now at the head of the list of Passed Midm. & a vacancy has occured in the death of Commodore Elliott: which causes me to write you at this time—

The Commodore has been dead better than a week & the vacancy has not been filled— I feel most anxious to get my promotion, as you must know, & I hope you will assist me. I have seen a great deal of hard service, since I had the pleasure of seeing you, & am much altered, from my campaign in Florida. At this time, the war fever seems to run high, in the country.

---

[117]In the Senate in early December, Cass offered resolutions instructing certain committees to inquire into the conditions of the army, navy, and public defenses and to report what improvements were necessary. On December 15, when he supported his resolutions with a speech, he said that negotiations with Britain had failed and that Great Britain was assuming a menacing attitude. Military preparation, he said, was the best means to prevent war. Mangum replied that this action would only stir up war feelings. He would leave the matter to the President, who was in a position to ascertain the needs of the military forces. He felt that the country was ready to meet an emergency. His speech and similarly expressed views of Webster and Crittenden tended to allay some of the war feeling. *Hillsborough Recorder*, January 15, 1846; *Cong. Globe*, 29 Cong., 1 sess., 47-49; McCormac, *James K. Polk*, 585-586.

Should we have one, I hope the officers from the Old North State, (though few) will gain laurels for her.

I hope I shall have a chance of sending you a barrel of fine oysters ere long

Please remember me to my friends from the Old State.

Excuse this scribble

Yours truly

P. U. MURPHEY, U.S.N.

Judge Mangum.

[Addressed:]

Judge Mangum
U. S. Senate
Washington
D. C.

WPM-D

Alexander F. Vache[118] to Willie P. Mangum

NEW YORK December 22nd 1845

The Honble
Willie P. Mangum
U. States Senator

Sir,

I have the honor to invite you and your lady, to the first annual Ball of the "Texas and Oregon Association" on the 8th of January 1846, and in conveying to you this wish, I avail myself of the opportunity, at their request, to say, that although they differ with you in general politics, they nevertheless, appreciate, and honor the intergrity of a man who casts aside party distinction, and fearlessly and magnanimously comes to the aid of his Country when threatend with invasion by foreign foes - With such Americans, the character and safety of the United States, can neither be sullied or endangered, and with such

---

[118]Alexander F. Vache, a graduate of Columbia College in 1825, dabbled in politics at the same time that he practiced medicine. *Longworth's New York Directory, 1844-1845,* 354; Bonner, *The World's Metropolis,* 270; See below W. P. Mangum to Sally, Patty, Mary Mangum, January 1, 1846. See below, 344-345.

patriots, the Flag of the nation must ever victoriously and triumphantly flow to the unrestrained winds of Heaven.

Allow me to add that your recent speech, on Senator Cass' resolutions, has identified you with the distinguished men, who prefer defeat, to inglorious submission, and death, to apprehensive venality.

With profound respect
Your Obedt. Sert.

Alexr. F. Vache
The Corresponding Committee
29 Chambers Street

WPM-LC

Daniel Mallory[119] to Willie P. Mangum.

New York Decr. 22^d. 1845

Dear Sir,

I was rejoiced to see your name among the Committee appointed by the Senate to report on the claims of French Spoilations[120] prior to 1800. Indeed, I think a majority of the Committee are gentlemen who will be willing to do justice to this long protracted claim. I have no immediate interest in the matter, but I have friends who are large sufferers in the injustice and shameful neglect of our own government. The history of this business you are too familiar with for me to speak of it here. It is now almost, if not quite fifty years, since these aggressions took place. The consideration for these losses has been in the possession of this government for forty years if my memory serves me. Be that as it may our government received from that of France a full recompense for these claims, and no Subterfuge can be interposed with any show of fairness to withold any longer the amounts due to the claimants. Many, if not most of the original sufferers, have ceased to want, but there are yet a few who are in poverty. For the life of me I cannot understand the policy, let alone the justice, of a government like ours, refusing to refund the amount which it has long since

---

[119]He is listed as a "General Agent" in Wilson, *The Business Directory of New York City for 1848,* p. 27.

[120]See above, I, 418n.

obtained belonging to these claimants. In private life an individual would be ashamed to show his head in public who had received a large sum belonging to another and refused to refund it. If he had inadvertently used it, common honesty would require some acknowledgement with a promise to repay it at some future time, and this should be the course of this government. Let these claims be fairly stated and settled, and if the government is not able to pay at the moment let it issue their promise—fifty years ahead if advisable with 5 or 6 pr ct interest. Something should be done in common business to mark the just aspirations of their claimants. I have taken it for granted that one of your generous and noble nature would spurn an ignoble act let it emanate from what source it may; and what can compare in meanness thro' retention of anothers property, when the ability to make restitution is manifested.

I was very much gratified with the course you adopted on Genl Cass's resolutions. It has crossed my mind whether the early movement of these resolutions by him were not intended to place the Whigs in the wrong by the supposition that coming from the quarter they did they would be opposed Cass is a man of some genius, but sadly deficient in long sightedness as a Statesman. You recollect a question put to him by some designing friends of Mr Van Buren on his reaching this city from his French mission & as to his opinion of the utility & constitutionality of a U S Bank? and he had just returned too from the most crafty & subtle court in Europe; a friend who knows him intimately says he is deficient in moral courage, and is easily cowed, of this I know nothing. I do not even know his person. It is evident enough that he is commencing a game for the presidency.

I trust, and so does a large portion of the people that there is conservatism enough in the Senate to frustrate the folly and wickedness of some of its members who would for their own vile and selfish ends emboil this country in war with England. Should it take place there is not a town or city that would be reached with their Steam Marine that would not suffer and a majority would be destroyed. Can it be possible that a majority of Congress can be mad enough to bring about so deplorable a calamity? and all for what? It is worse than idle to suppose England is desirous of a conflict with us. There is every inducement for a contrary conclusion. Here in this city the agitation of it is producing disastrous effects. What then would be the reality? Should it come it will drive thousands and tens of thousands into hopeless poverty.

I trust that no apology is deemed necessary for the liberty I have taken in saying what I have on these subjects

I am very truly & faithfully
Your friend & obt. st.

DANIEL MALLORY.

To the Honb Willie P. Mangum
    U. S. Senate.

[Addressed:]

> To the honorable,
>   Willie P. Mangum
>   Senate
>   Washington.

WPM-LC

"A True American" to Willie P. Mangum

NEW YORK Dec 24th 1845

Dear Sir,

In the present state of affairs, I have one or two things to present to your notice. From all accounts brought over to this country from Europe we are informed that England is making extensive preparations as for war. All eyes turn towards Oregon as the moving spirit.[121] May I not ask if it may not be making preparations to send her ships to the coast of Oregon and of erecting forts on the Columbia river, and then saying to us *now* take Oregon if you want it. She might be urged to this by the course the American press have been pursuing- I would suggest one thing and then I have done- it is this Would it not be

---

[121]For a good discussion of the Oregon controversy and the danger of war with Great Britain see McCormac, *James K. Polk,* 555-611.

better instead of comming to any agreement in regard to Oregon, at the present time, with England, or of laying claim to the country and sending troop there, instead of this I say to go on colonising, and affording every facility for emigration there, to our citizens there, at the same time establishing a sett of Laws by which our citizens could be governed and protected as the English have already done. Also by sending occasionally a body of mounted riflemen into the country and building stockades in the country, especially along the banks of the Columbia river. The advantage of this you will immediately perceive. For every soldier you sent, in the former case, you would be obliged to send his provisions to him, and every bushel of wheat would cost perhaps from four to five Dollars by the time it reached him, and meat in proportion- while in the latter case the man who emegrates there raises his own corn and is at no expense to the government and he would be as good a soldier as the former as he would be defending his own property. As to the riflemen, if the British say what are you sending bodies of armed men into the country, we can say merely to defend our citizens as you do yours. Look at the British fur Company. By these means we can take quiet possession of the country and in a few years say to the English, now come to to terms. Leaving these few thoughts for your consideration

I remain

Yours respectfully

A TRUE AMERICAN

P. S. I direct to you as I have forgotten at the moment the name of *our* senator but I trust any Whig

[Addressed:]

TO The

Honorable Mr Mangum

Washington

D. C.

Willie P. Mangum to James K. Polk[122]

WASHINGTON 26th Dec. 1845.

To

The President of the U States

Sir

Two days ago Col. Ward requested me (as he was well warranted in doing, by reason of his knowledge of my former intimacy with some of his most distinguished & near relatives) to hand you a note to day, as he understood from me, that I intended to make a call.- Circumstances prevent my carrying out that purpose; & I take the liberty of enclosing his note, lest Col. W. may think me negligent or careless in this matter.

I am very sure, that if Col. W. shall succeed in his purpose, it will be gratifying to a large & extended Circle of relatives & friends in No. Ca.- all or nearly all, I am sorry to know, are democrats as well as agreeable to all- & as far as I know- of the delegation in Congress from that State.

With high Consideration
I am Sir
Your Mo. obt. Sevt.
WILLIE P. MANGUM

1846

WPM-LC

Willie P. Mangum to Sally, Patty & Mary Mangum

WASHINGTON, 1st January 1846.

My dear daughters.

I enclose an invitation[1] to a ball at New York on the 8th. inst. for you dear Mother & myself.— Will she come in time? I

---

[122]The original is in the James K. Polk Papers, Library of Congress. I did not find the enclosed note of Colonel Ward. This letter has been previously published by Miss Elizabeth McPherson in the *N. C. Hist. Rev.* XVII, 266.

Polk held a more kindly feeling toward Mangum than he did toward most Whigs. On one occasion he wrote in his diary that Mangum "though a Whig, is a gentleman, and fair & manly in his opposition to my administration." McCormac, *James K. Polk*, 336; Quaife, ed., *Diary of James K. Polk*, III, 381.

[1]See above, Alexander F. Vache to W. P. Mangum, December 22, 1845.

cannot ask you, as you are not invited.- This day is spent here in Visits - I have been out the most of the day- It is now 8½ oclock, at night.- I am nearer well than I have been, since my arrival.- We shall not have War.

Look at the invitation enclosed. & Misses Sally & Patty will lay it *before them & copy* it an hundred times, & see if they cannot begin to write as well.- The invitation & the note, show that I struck the right note- Many other evidences to the same effect.- I spoke without warning, & without expecting it.

Give My Love to your Mother & William, & believe me, as ever, with the strongest affection for all of you.

Kiss Mother for me.
W. P. MANGUM

Misses Sally, Patty & Mary Mangum

[Addressed:]

To
Misses Sally, Patty & Mary Mangum
Red Mountain
No. Carolina

—————

WPM-LC

James Cooper[2] to Willie P. Mangum.

HARRISBURG Jany 4 1846.

My dear Sir:

It is of very great importance to the Whigs of Penna. that the nomination of Judge Woodward[3] to the Bench of the Sup. Court should not be confirmed. I have not time to give you the reasons at present. But be assured that I do not over-estimate the importance of his defeat when I say that it is more than

—————

[2]James Cooper, 1810-1863, was a member of Congress in 1839-1843 and of the Pennsylvania legislature in 1843, 1844, 1846, and 1848. He was his state's attorney general in 1849 just prior to his election to the United States Senate. He served in the Senate until 1855. In politics he was a Whig. *Biog. Dir. of Cong.*, 846.

[3]George Washington Woodward, 1809-1875, was judge of the fourth judicial district in Pennsylvania from 1841 to 1851. In 1845 Polk nominated him justice of the Supreme Court, but the Senate rejected his nomination. He served as judge of his state's supreme court from 1852 to 1867 and as a member of Congress from 1867 to 1871. *Biog. Dir. of Cong.*, 1728.

probable it will change the relative positions of parties in this State.

Very truly & respectfully yours

JAMES COOPER.

Hon. W. P. Mangum.

[Addressed:]

Hon: W. P. Mangum
U. S. Senate
Washington.

WPM-LC

Francis B. Whiting⁴ to Willie P. Mangum.

ST. MARKS FLORIDA
January 5th, 1846.

Sir:

I trust you will pardon the liberty I take in troubling you with this communication, when the motives are made known: - I wish to call your attention to the appointment of Nathaniel W. Walker⁵ as Collector of the customs for this Port, made by the President during the recess of your honorable body.

I have known this man for nearly seventeen years and am well assured no Senator would sustain his nomination if his perfect unfitness for office was made apparent—

In the first place he left South Carolina for killing his half brother & though acquitted by Law, I know that he is still held in detestation by Genltmen cognizant of the fact: in proof of which you will please to refer to Col: Robert W. Alston of Quincy Florida, (with whom I presume you are personally acquainted,) formerly of Halifax N. Carolina.

I also on yesterday (Sunday 4th instant) saw the said Walker *gambling* in a Grog shop in presence of eight or ten persons.

---

⁴Whiting moved to Florida from Virginia after 1834. *William and Mary Quarterly*, Ser. 2, Vol. III, pp. 271, 275.
⁵In 1842 he was the speaker of the Florida lower house of the legislature. His appointment as Collector of Customs at St. Marks was confirmed January 3, 1846. Dorothy Dodd, *Florida Becomes a State*, Tallahassee, 1945, 383; *Executive Journal of the Senate*, VII, 14, 24.

I also assert without fear of contradiction, that this man is a notorious drunkard and entirely unqualified for so important an office and pledge myself to prove those & other serious charges against him whenever required by the proper authority.

I have written also to Col. Benton, Hon. D. H. Lewis and Hon. W. T. Colquitt on the same subject to whom you will please to refer.—

And beg to refer you to Gov. Call[6] & Geo K. Walker of Tallahassee & Col. Alston (above named) as to myself.

With great Respect
Yours sincerely
FRANCIS B. WHITING

Hon. W. P. Mangum.

[Addressed:] Hon. Willie P. Mangum.
United States Senate.
Washington City. D. C.

Willie P. Mangum to Sally A. Mangum[7]

Monday.
WASHINGTON 5th. Jany. 1846

My dear daughter Sally.

I was distressed to learn from your Mother's letter, that your health is not good.— I trust my dear, you will clothe yourself sufficiently.— In the Winter, you & your sisters ought to wear flannel next to the skin, coming high up to the neck, & down to the hips—& you ought to wear thick cotton pantalettes, pinning or buttoning to the flannel.— Let me entreat you my dear daughter, to array yourself in the manner described.—

I am now quite well—though I was quite otherwise, during the most of December.

I sat down to write you but a line, as I am in a committee room, & must be in the Senate in 5 or 10 minutes. I send you *a guide* to Oregon.— What say you, after reading it? Shall we

----

⁶Richard Call served as governor of Florida from 1835 to 1844. He was defeated for reelection in 1845. *Biog. Dir. of Cong.*, 937.
⁷The original is in the possession of Miss Preston Weeks, Washington, D. C.

go?[8] Will Mother be willing? Do press it upon her & request her to write me a definitive answer.— The sal-Aratus would make Letty perfectly happy.—

Does my boy go to school regularly? I hope he does, & is a good boy, & learns his books. Give your dear Mother, my love, & a kiss for me. & my love to Patty, Mary & my boy.

May God bless & protect you all, is the constant aspiration of

Yr affectionate Father
WILLIE P. MANGUM

To Miss Sally A. Mangum—

P. S. Let me know if you are all for Oregon—if so—We must be off early in March.

W. P. M.

_____

WPM-LC

Samuel Martin[9] to Willie P. Mangum.

CAMPBELLS STATION TENSEE 6th Jay,/46

Honorable Mangum

D Sir

Your State of N. Carolina is suffering a large drain on her Population not less than 20,000 must have left it during the last 5 months had the Canal been made as I have suggested to you much of this would have been saved. Those passing here say that in places corn is worth 1.25 p. Bushel had there been a Canal running from Newbern, Fayetteville & on to the Mississippi with one from the Mississippi through Tennessee & Georgia to Intersect this you could have had plenty of corn along the whole line for from 45 to 60 cents corn could be delivered in Liverpool for 75 p. Bushel & your People hav to leave their homes or starve. This is a most miserable state of things. Your other States gains by it but it is Unnatural to think of such matters, Corn is here selling from 12½ to 20 cents p.

_____

[8]Like many North Carolinians in this period, Mangum considered leaving his native state for a more prosperous region. He was importuned by his brother, Walter, to go to Mississippi and Texas. Thomas Jefferson Green tried to get him to buy the land of Dr. Branch T. Archer in Texas. So far as his papers show, he never went beyond the point of inquiry.
[9]See above, 297n.

Bushel. I hope you will think of this matter & of the few miles of Canal from Beaufort to Newbern if War comes as I fear it will it will make those think of Canals that scarcely dream of them at the Present Time.

SAMUEL MARTIN.

[Addressed:]

Honble. Mangum
U. S. Senator
W. City.

WPM-D

W. Claiborne[10] to Willie P. Mangum.

[8 January, 1846]

Dear Judge

I have ben quite indisposed since I parted with you on tuesday evening last— From the heavy freight of Pendleton Venison & other good things I took on board on Saturday last at the Columbian House, combined with additional freight with you on *tuesday last* viz, oysters Pendleton vension, Pullets, plum puddings &c., I found *that night,* that the ship would founder unless I through over board a part of the Cargo, consequently I took a *horse dose* of Epsum salts and the way the young Bucks and Fawns (about the size of grasshoppers) were skipping about the House all day yesterday was a caution— I feel much better today but for fear of a relaps, I wish you would come over (if convenient) & write my will— I send the Paper loaned me - do send, or bring me another.

Yr. Truly
W. CLAIBORNE.

Jany 8th 1846.
Thursday 5 P.M.

[Addressed:]

To
Hon. W. P. Mangum
Present.

---

[10]See above, 202-203.

WPM-LC

George W. Jones[11] to Willie P. Mangum

ORANGE CO, N. C.

Jany: 10th. 1846

Dear Sir

I desire you to cause to be forwarded to me the National Intelligencer as I do not think I can get along without it. I believe that the terms of subscription is Two dollars in advance per annum

If you will be so kind as to advance that amount for me I will pay it to Mrs. Mangum, which I suppose will suit as well.

I have nothing of interest to communicate- I learnt this evening by Moses Chambers[12] that Green Caldwell was nominated as the Democratic candidate for Governor.[13] He is just from Raleigh He said that they desired him on his arrival in Raleigh, to have his name enrolled as a delegate from Person which he declined saying that Graham was democrat enough for him. Bank transactions took him down there & not the nomination of a democratic candidate. The nomination however you will learn thro' the papers ere you receive this

I would be glad if you would send me a copy of your *speeches* as it is not in any paper I take - I have merely seen an extract in the Ral. Reg-

Yours Truly

GEO W. JONES

[Addressed:]

To

Honb^{le}

W. P. Mangum

Senator of U. S.

Washington City

D. C.—

[Postmarked:]

Red Mountain N.C.

Jany. 13th

[11]George W. Jones, of Orange County, was secretary of the Whig county meeting in 1844 and delegate to the state Whig convention in 1846. *Hillsborough Recorder*, June 6, 1844; January 8, 1846.

[12]Moses Chambers represented Person County in the state Constitutional Convention in 1835 and the legislature in 1831-1841. *N. C. Manual*, 758, 894.

[13]Green W. Caldwell, of Mecklenburg County, 1806-1864, graduated from the University of Pennsylvania in 1831 in medicine. He served as assistant surgeon in the United States Army for a few months in 1832. He then studied law and practiced in Charlotte. In 1836-1841 he was in the legislature and in 1841-1843 he was in Congress. He was Superintendent of the Charlotte Mint when he was nominated, January 8, 1846, by the Democratic state convention for governor. This nomination was due to the demand that a western Democrat be selected to carry that part of the state which normally voted for the Whigs. The nomination was a surprise to many delegates and to Caldwell himself. On January 20 he declined the nomination. Whereupon, James B. Shepard was selected to replace him. W. A. Graham, the Whig candidate, won the election by a larger majority than in 1844. Caldwell also served in the Mexican War. *Biog. Dir. of Cong.*, 776; Norton, *Democratic Party in N. C.*, 150-152; *Hillsborough Recorder*, January 22, 1846.

WPM-LC

J. R. Creecy to Willie P. Mangum.[14]

[10 January, 1846]

My Dear Sir

I will make no apology for thus troubling you feeling confident that if you can aid me you will-

MY Son Dr. Will Clinton Creecy now in his 21st year holds a commission as Midshipman in the Texas Navy, he was eighteen months in active service with Commodore Moore, was in all the Battles with the Mexican Steam Ships of War served with much credit, I am fully authorized to say, has a *strange* fondness for the Navy, and wishes to be *restored,* he was treated as was his commodore by President Houston- I ask of you Sir, if he can be *restored;* if he can *now* by the terms of annexation take his place in our Navy as a midshipman, or whether he can in any way without much delay be entitled or appointed as one,

I am unskilled, unitiated in the way of obtaining offices or appointments never having applied in any way to any one, and feeling as if I could not have any friends at Court, or rather among Courtiers- Some provisions may have been made for the officers of the Texan Navy in the articles of agreement (annexation) I am ignorant on the subject entirely- Can you spare time to ascertain for me, whether there is any chance or prospect for my Son; If he can get an appointment *at once* we are willing he should take it on any terms; he only wishes to be in the Navy in active Service if possible without delay- I am now living in this City, and will ever be *happy* to hear of your *happiness.*

Very truly

yr um ob

J. R. CREECY.

New Orleans 10th January 1846.

[Addressed:]

Honl. W. P. Mangum
United States Senate
Washington City.

---

[14]See below J. R. Creecy to W. P. Mangum, June 5, 1846, and W. P. Mangum to the Secretary of the Navy, May 27, 1846.

WPM-LC

Thomas J. Green to the People of Texas.[15]

WASHINGTON CITY, Jan. 10th 1846.

A friend has just placed in my hand a "Galveston Civilian" of the 13th ult., containing a letter from Gen. Sam Houston, purporting to be a vindication of his conduct in reference to the decimation of our countrymen in Mexico. Gen Houston in his letter, failing to adduce any evidence of his innocence of this enormous crime, has endeavoured to divert public attention from his guilt, by the grossest, false and vindictive—I had almost said unparalleled slander of myself. In this I would have erred, for it has many parallels from Gen. Houston himself. His publication of the gallant Commodore Moore to the world as an outlaw and pirate, at the identical time that his cannon were thundering against more than ten times his force, that of our common enemy— his reiterated slanders against the brave Generals Burleson, Sherman and Wharton, and almost every other distinguished man in Texas— his oft repeated ridiculous charges against ex-President Burnet, one of the purest men in any country— his vile denunciation of Gen. Stephen F. Austin, the father of his country—his perfidious slander of the spotless wife of his own bosom— yea, in his general character as an universal calumniator, countless parallels might be adduced. Though his charges against myself must meet that contempt from every honest man which has followed the habitual falsehoods of his whole life, yet the circumstances in which Gen. Houston and myself are now placed before the people of Texas, make it proper that I should appear before the public through the same medium. And I will ask what other redress is left me? It is well known that Gen. Houston holds himself perfectly irresponsible. If personal chastisement be inflicted upon him, as was done by the Hon. Branch T. Archer and Col. Jordon, he either pleads sickness or old age. If falsehood is proved upon him, as was done by Mr. Wingfield, and many others, he pleads drunkenness. It is due to myself then, that I should in this case prove his falsehood, and "out of his own mouth will I convict him."

---

[15]This is a printed circular. Compare it to the circular letter of Green to the "Electors of the Western Congressional District of the State of Texas," October 25, 1845.

Fellow citizens, it has been three long years and over, since the hard fought and sanguinary battle of Mier: a few days more will make three years, since that gallant little band of your countrymen was made to draw in a black-bean lottery, and each tenth man shot. Such a cold blooded murder astonished the whole civilized world, and put to the test the wisest politicians of the most civilized nations, to know what sufficient cause could be assigned therefor. Could it be that they had fought under the requirements of their own government, considering the disparity of forces and the circumstances of the case, the hardest fought battle in the annals of war? Could it be, that when captives, they had, while emaciated and worn down by the fatigues of a long and wearisome march, risen upon double their number of armed guards, overpowered and dispersed them uninjured, and then peaceably pursued their way homewards? No! these actions met the praises, not only of all civilized nations, but even the highest encomiums of semibarbarian Mexico. For what then could such a shocking murder have been perpetrated? Alone, upon the most authoritive evidence, that they were without the pale of those laws which govern civilized nations in war. Did that evidence exist? If so, who furnished it, and how came it to the knowledge of that government?

In this letter, fellow citizens, I must necessarily confine myself to a brief statement of this matter and refer every man, who wishes to know the whole history of it, to appendix No. 2, page 450 and appendix No. 6, page 477 of my work upon Texas and Mexico, in which, will be seen stated, all the evidence in the case and such evidence, as no man, so far as I have heard, of the thousands and tens of thousands in this country, who have read it, pretended to doubt. That evidence is—that Sam. Houston, the President of Texas, early in the year 1843 and soon after the battle of Mier, wrote a letter to Capt. Elliot, Her Britanic Majesty's Charge D'Affairs, residing in Galveston, which he, Houston, requested him, Elliot, to forward to Mexico and which he, Elliot, did as he was requested; in which Houston said, *"that though the Mier prisoners had entered Mexico, contrary to law and authority, yet he, Houston, begged mercy for them &c."* It is in evidence, that upon the receipt of this letter of Presd't Houston, that Santa Anna, the President of

Mexico ordered the decimation, showing, that the President of Texas was the highest, and sufficient authority for this horrible deed: because, that evidence had proclaimed them brigands and robbers.

Fellow citizens, these facts came to the knowledge of myself and companions, through the American and English ministers, while we were in the dungeons of Mexico, very soon after this sad tragedy in March 1843. After my escape from the castle of Perote and in October of the same year, I published them in the "Galveston News" and notwithstanding President Houston's then control of the Mails and Post Offices of Texas and the limited circulation of that journal, he, Houston knowing the truth of these charges and feeling a murderer's guilt, commenced his vindication by denying with uplifted eyes, that he every wrote or caused to be written, the letter charged to him. (See Lieut. S. H. Walker's statement, page 453.) This was President Houston's *first* defence of himself; but upon my receipt and publication of Gen. Waddy Thompson's and the British Minister's letters from Mexico, proving the falsity of his denial, he fled to the Presbyterian Church in the town of Houston, in November of the same year and made a speech, which was published in all his newspapers of that day, and which he said, *"it was not my friend's, Capt. Elliott's letter, that produced the mischief,"* thereby implying, that Elliott had written the letter. In said speech however, he goes on to charge all the consequences of that murder, to a letter, which Gen. M. Hunt had written to, and which was published in the "Houston Telegraph" of the 18th of Jan. previously. This is Gen Houston's *second* defence, and thus, up to this hour, so far as I am informed, Gen. Hunt and the Telegraph, stands charged by Gen. Houston, with the horrid butchery. On the 12th of December, which was about one month after his speech was published, in his annual message to Congress, he again changes his ground and said, that *"it was a retaliation on account of those under Gen. Somerville who robbed Laredo,"* charging this murder, to those who returned from that place with Col. Bennett. Thus you see, for the *third* time, in the short space of a few months, when pursued by the ghosts of these murdered heroes, he changes his ground of defence. Now, fellow citizens, after a lapse of nearly three years, when his control over the public intelligence

of Texas, is about to give way to an honest administration of
the mails, - when my work upon Texas and Mexico, has gone
the length and breadth of this great nation, and carried conviction to the mind of every man, who has read it, that Sam.
Houston is the wilful and malicious murderer of his countrymen of Mier, and just on the eve of the Congressional elections
and in my absence from Texas, he comes out in the "Civilian"
of the 13th of last month and charges this crime upon myself,
as having been the "first to incite the men" to the plunder of
Laredo. Thus, for the *fourth* time, Gen Houston, has changed
his defence. But fellow citizens, falsehood and crime will always convict itself, because it rarely ever tells one steady tale.
Gen. Houston, after changing his defence, as you have seen
four different times, comes out in his latest publication and for
the *first* time admits that *"he wrote the letter to Capt. Elliott."*
It cannot be forgotten, in Texas, how often, for the last three
years, both Gen. Houston and his partizans have denied this
fact, and it would have been better for him always to have
denied it; for then many of his blinded friends, would either
have believed or professed to believe, that he never had written
it. The cool effrontery of Gen. Houston's letter to the "Civilian"
can only be equalled by himself— See how he commences:

Mr. H. Stuart,
Dear Sir:— Believing that I should be delinquent in duty to
others as well as myself, if I were longer to remain silent,
touching the facts connected with the Mier prisoners, subsequent to their capitulation, I will now express myself."— Now
express himself! Thus after three years dodging about between
subterfuge and falsehood, he will now express himself. The
true reason for his expressing himself *now*, is the near approach to the Senatorial election and if, by the perpetration of
any possible falsehood upon myself, he can thereby prevent my
election, to the House of Representatives, he and his crimes,
may be saved from that fearless exposure in the U. S. Congress, which I have never failed to visit upon him in the Texas
Congress. My friendship for Western Texas has been as long,
constant and as ardent, as has been Gen. Houston's hostility to
that bleeding country and while he has done everything, to de-
populate and destroy it, I have stood by it, both in Congress
and the field.— While Gen. Houston's policy has been to sur-

render to the Colorado, mine has been to defend to the Rio Grande, and I am proud to say, that my position is sustained by the President of the U. S. But let Gen. Houston, slander me out of an election to the House of Representatives, and bargain himself into the U. S. Senate. What may Western Texas not expect, short of an attempt at a surrender to the Nueces?

Fellow citizens, the vindictiveness of Gen Houston's last defence can only be equalled by its stupidity. If the plunder of Laredo had been a sufficient cause for the decimation of your countrymen, and I had been the *"first* to incite the men to that plunder,"* why did not Santa Anna have me shot? His personal hostility to myself for the last ten years was well known, and the slightest pretext would have been sufficient for him to have practised his bloody vengeance upon my person. If Gen. Houston's charge be correct, I ask, in the name of common sense, why it was that innocent, unoffending men, were made to pay the penalty of my crime? Why it was that Majors Cocke and Dunham, Captains Cameron and Eastland, Este, Harris, Jones and Mahan, Ogden, Roberts, Rowan and Shepard, Thompson, Torry, Trumbull, Wing, and the "iron nerved" Whaling, were made to pay the penalty of my wrong-dong? This charge, like a badly counterfeited dollar, carries its own condemnation upon its face, and I should not have deemed it worthy of notice, but to show the recklessness of one who scruples at no falsehood to serve his ambition and hatred.

Fellow citizens, what Gen. Houston asserts in his letter, about promptly furnishing the Mier prisoners in Mexico, with the supplies which Congress had voted them, is as untrue as the balance of his letter, and I will take the journals of Congress and his *own* letter to prove it. The facts are these:— Early in December, 1845, and soon after the meeting of Congress, the destitution of our countrymen in Mexico, was pressed upon the attention of Congress by myself, the Hon. Wm. E. Jones, S. H. Maverick, and others, who had tasted some of the sweets of a Mexican prison. To the honor of that Congress, be it known, no time was lost in voting $15,000 for their relief, under the requirement that it should be forthwith furnished them. It was then deemed best by the Congress, for the good of our countrymen in prison, that this law should not be made public at the time. About two months after, and at nearly the

close of the session, the Secretary of the Treasury was called
upon by myself and others, to know what had been done in
carrying out this law. To our surprise and mortification, we
were informed, that not a dollar had been sent them, and no
measures taken to send them one. We saw then, full well,
that President Houston, would cloak his vindictive direliction
of duty under a law *then* not designed to be made public; and
just before the close of the Congress another law was passed
in open session, appropriating an additional $15,000. This law
was passed without the repeal of the former, and thus the Congress, under full consideration for the eminent services of these
men, voted $30,000 to their relief. We come now to the ques-
tion, how much of this money was sent to these men, and when
it was sent to them. Gen. Houston tells you in his letter, that
on the 19th of October, 1844, one draft was drawn for $3,740.—
Mark the time— *this is ten months and a half* from the passage
of the law. But he says that he sent Mr. Potter as a special
agent, (Mr. Hargous refusing to act as such) with $2,500. Now
I ask the question of every Mier man, did they ever receive
one dollar of this appropriation while in prison, No! On the
16th of September, the survivors were turned loose at the gates
of Perote, like so many cattle, with the exception, that the
"magnanimous Mexican nation" gave each man *one silver dollar* to bear his expenses to Texas. With that silver dollar they
started home, and at Jalapa, for the first time, they were furnished, through Mr. Hargous, $2,000. These are the historical
facts of the case, proved by the acts of Congress, now upon
your statute book, the assertion of every Texian then in Perote,
and the confessions of Gen. Houston's own letter. Was there
any possible excuse for this cruel delay, even had Mr. Hargous
refused to act as our agent? Was Mr. Hargous the only man in
Mexico through whom money could be transmitted?, Or was
it [at] all necessary that we should have an agent? I say not!
and Gen. Houston knew full well, that in one week from the
passage of that act, he could have placed the money in some
responsible house or bank in New Orleans, and with a certificate
of deposite and authority sent to Gen. Fisher, or Quarter Master
Fenton, Mr. Gibson, or any other officer in the Castle of Perote,
to draw for the same, could have been cashed in one hour at
that place, at a premium of six per cent. Thus, with this small

paper, which could have been sent to them in twenty days from the passage of the act, every $100 on deposit in New Orleans would have been worth to them in their cheerless and destitute prison, $106.

But fellow citizens, in these long ten months of witholding the bread of your dying countrymen did President Houston hear no complaints from them? Yes! not a sail that crossed the Gulf which did not bring from the miserable cells of Perote the lamentations of the sick and dying; and the bones of eighty odd noble souls now scattered from the bottom of the great ditch of Perote, to nearly every prison-yard in Mexico, is evidence of *"President Houston's friendship for the Mier men."*— Did President Houston hear no other complaints from the Mier men? Yes, indeed, be it told to their eternal honor! though it has been well said that starvation for the want of food is the greatest subduer of the physical man, yet, when these noble countrymen of ours heard that President Houston had his commissioners across the Rio Grande, signing their country away as the *"Department of Texas,"* though they were at that time living skeletons and daily depositing some of their comrades in that horrible ditch, they nobly wrote home, which should be written in letters of gold and engraven upon every patriot's heart, *"Let no consideration of us forfeit your country's honor: let us rot in these dungeons ere you concede one inch to these colored barbarians."*

All this is only equalled by one thing in the conclusion of Gen. Houston's letter, which I must think caps the climax of every assertion and assumption of his whole life— to wit: that *"The day will come when it will be shown, that he obtained the release of the Mier prisoners."* This beats "Coqueting" about Annexation, so far, that I cannot well conceive, how his most devoted followers can read it with becoming gravity. "The day will come." Was there ever so propitious a day for Gen. Houston to prove that thing as now, when the separate nationality of Texas is merged in this great confederacy and when he is staking everything, for a seat in that dignified branch of the Congress of this Union, which, should he succeed, it cannot fail to experience the disgrace of that success.

Fellow citizens, so much for Gen. Houston and the Mier men, and in conclusion, I must crave your further attention to

that part of his letter personal to myself.— Gen. Houston says
that in the sacking of Laredo, I was "the first man, who broke
open a house and incited the men to outrage." I know not what
milder epithet to give to this charge, than to say it is maliciously,
infamously false. It is known by the whole army, that on the
day of the sacking of Laredo, I did not leave the camp, which
was three miles below the town and that when those that had
participated in the sacking, returned to the camp, I was among
the most active, in getting them to return the articles to Gen.
Somerville's quarters, to be re-delivered to the alcalde, and
the well known fact that *every* Mier man, with many others,
did so return them, relieves them from *Gen. Houston's charge
of crime*, if crime it was. That some who returned from Laredo
with Col. Bennett, did not return the articles taken from the town
is also well known. These men are known to be Gen. Houston's
warmest friends, and they must settle with him, this high
charge of robbery which he brings against them. I will however defend these friends of Gen Houston, against his whole-
sale denunciations.

On the 8th of December 1842, Gen. Somerville's forces arrived at the Town of Laredo after seventeen days march from
their camp upon the Medina, having exhausted the whole of
more than three hundred beeves which they started with from
the San Antonio, Gen. Somerville, made a requisition for 8 or
10 beeves, which was barely rations for one day and then took
the backward track home. The men had been promised supplies,
upon the Rio Grande and now found that promise neglected.
They had by every law of war and nature, a right to be fed, and
if the Gen. did not do it, through his commissariat, they were
reduced to the alternative of doing so of their own accord,
though with becoming patience, they awaited a whole day, for
the General to comply with his promise, and did not attempt
to supply themselves until he had made a retrograde march of
three miles homewards. That these men took articles useless
and unbecoming soldiers was more the fault of their General, in
not telling them what was lawful to take, than in their not
knowing what was so lawful by the usages of war. Now I will
ask, did President Houston inform these men, what was proper by the laws of war to take, when in his address to the people
of Texas in July 1842, he called upon them to *"pursue the*

enemy in to his own country and chastise him for his insolence and wrongs." No! These are his identical instructions, published in all the newspapers of the day. *The Government* (says President Houston) *will promise nothing but authority to march, and such supplies of ammunition as may be needful for the campaign. They must look to the valley of the Rio Grande for remuneration.— The Government will claim no portion of the spoils; they will be divided among the victors. The flag of Texas will accompany the expedition.*" Thus much for President Houston's calumny of the sacking of the Laredo; and while the Texian army has been in the invariable habit, during our revolution of quartering upon our own citizens, while in the field, he would have them starve while in an enemies country, though called there by his own proclamation.

Fellow citizens, the manner in which Gen. Houston has lugged Mr. Hargous into his letter, shows a vindictive hatred of that gentleman, which he, Houston, has manifested in several of his *veto* messages on those laws of your Congress, which provided to pay him the money he furnished our countrymen of the Santa Fe Expedition while in Mexico. Wherefore, I ask, has Gen. Houston thus formally brought Mr. Hargous before his government? - There can be but one answer.— It is the same manifestation of his murderous intent which caused him to write to Santa Anna, that the *"Mier men had gone into Mexico without authority of law,"* and while I trust that the fatal consequences of his Mier letter may not befall this excellent gentleman, it is due, both to him and myself, to state the particulars of a transaction for which President Houston, in January, 1844, received the *unanimous* rebuke of the House of Representatives of Texas.

The facts are these, fellow citizens:— In June, 1843, while in the castle of Perote, I received, as was known to all my companions, several letters from my brother, Col. C. P. Green, of N. C., saying, that in July he would come to Mexico, to see how he could best serve me. On the 2d of that month, not content to wait the arrival of my brother, I escaped from prison, with fifteen of my countrymen. After weeks of suffering in the mountains, myself, Capt. C. K. Reese, and Interpreter, Dan Drake,

Henrie, of Brazoria County, Rd. Barclay, and R. Cornegay, of
Fayette County, and John Forrester, of the town of Houston,
met in disguise in the City of Vera Cruz; Capt. Reese had been
provided with some means through his father's factor, in New
Orleans, and Mr. Hargous furnished me with $130, and I be-
came responsible for the balance of the passages of my comrades on board the steamer Petrita, to New Orleans, which, in
all, amounted to $280. I distinctly told Mr. Hargous that it was
more than probable I would meet my brother in New Orleans,
and in expectation of which, I would draw for the $280 upon
him; but at the same time, I would draw a duplicate draft
upon the Government of Texas, that for a like purpose Gen.
McLeod and Col. Cooke had drawn the year previously in his
favor, for the Santa Fe prisoners, for several thousand dollars;
that I was satisfied that Gen. Houston, would neither pay the
one or the other, for he never was known to pay his own debts
voluntarily, and rarely under any circumstances, but that the
Texas congress would. When we sailed on the Petrita, John
Forester preferred to work his passage as fireman, thereby reducing my indebtedness to Mr. Hargous to $255. On my arrival
at New Orleans I had sufficient money to pay for the use of a
bed, and drink of grog each. The next day through the kindness of my friends, Col. W. M. Beal and Chas. Duroche, I was
enable to furnish some of them still farther. In a few days
after we sailed for Texas, I becoming individually responsible
for passages of four to Capt. Furguson. Upon my arrival in
New Orleans, instead of meeting my brother as I expected, I
received the melancholy intelligence that he was upon his death
bed, and from which he never arose. This fact was known to
the Supercargo of Mr. Hargous, in Orleans, and at my request
he sent the duplicate draft to the Government of Texas, which
he accompanied with some stupid complaints of my brother
not meeting him in Orleans. At this time I was a member of
Congress, and had exposed Houston's murder of our *decimated
Mier men.* and all other of his mal-practices coming under my
knowledge, with that unreserve well known to you all. Upon
the receipt of this draft for $280, expended upon our suffering
countrymen, President Houston laid it before the House of

Representatives, in a special message, with reflections against myself. Upon the presentation of which, the House *unanimously* refused to receive his message, and ordered the Clerk *forthwith* to return it to him: thus rebuking him in a manner never known before or since in the history of the Texian Congress. Did the Congress stop here? No! the draft for the $280 was incorporated in Mr. Hargou's Santa Fe outlay, without one dissenting vote, and if that gentleman has not yet received his whole dues, it has been on account of the constant hostility of President Houston and Jones, which their veto messages will prove.— For these facts I refer to the journals of Congress and the Hon. Wm. E. Jones, who was chairman of the Committee, as well as to every member of the House of Representatives, and challenge their denial.

Thus, fellow citizens, just upon the eve of your congressional election, while I have been here, at my own expense, in the absence of any authorized agent of Texas, working for her interest, and I trust not without effect, have I been arraigned before the public, in a hirling press, by the prince of calumniators, and it is now for every dispassionate man to say, whether I have proved him such by his own documents; and while a proper self respect would cause me to pass in silence the contemptible pensioned scribblers who may reiterate Gen. Houston's falsehoods, yet his position before the people of Texas, and my respect for them require of me a different treatment. My present duty then is to administer the antidote from the same cup, (the public press) out of which he has emptied his venom. Nor can I allow myself to believe that there are but the fewest number of editors, so dead to every principle of honor and justice, as to be the means of propagating the vilest falsehoods against me, without affording me the same means of proving them such.

THOMAS J. GREEN.

[Addressed:]

Hon. W. P. Mangum.

Washington,

City.

WPM-LC

John M. Botts to Willie P. Mangum.

Jany 13th 1846

Dear Mangum—

Being no longer President of the Senate, (a situation in which I wish you could have retained as long as it was agreeable to you,) you might find time if you ever think of me now, to drop me an occasional line to let an old and sincere friend to let him know what was going on in the *big world*.

Are we to have War? Did you receive a paper from me & did you read it? and what impression did it make on your mind? Will the resolution of the committee of Foreign affairs reported by Allen[16] pass the Senate or Not? I should be glad to hear from you and an answer to these several enquiries- and particularly tell me what has become of Morehead, & why he is not in Washington- I hope he is not sick-

Why don't the Whig party thunder against the War! are they afraid of a nick name- are they afraid of taking the responsibilty of preserving the peace of the world, & being called "British Whigs" Let them throw the responsibility of the war, (*which is cuning ruse*) on the authors of it, & we shall see after awhile, when the taxes are to be paid, & the battles to be fought, without seeing, what it is we are fighting for, where the shoe pinches-

I am afraid timidity, exercises more control over the policy of the Whigs in Washington than true wisdom- as you dont belong to the timid family- suppose you shake it off from their shoulders- & put them on the true track, & denounce it on every occasion—as an ungodly unnecessary & unprovoked war. that is provided you agree with me, as to the *"fixed facts."*

---

[16]William Allen, Chairman of the Senate Committee on Foreign Relations, on December 18, 1845, presented a joint resolution which advised the President " 'to give, forthwith,' the necessary notice for terminating the convention of 1827 with Great Britain." In April after two months' debate by the Senate, Allen moved that his resolution be laid on the table and that the Senate adopt the resolution of the House which directed the President to notify England that the convention would be abrogated. The Senate added that this notice would be given at the discretion of the President. Mc-Cormac, *James K. Polk,* 586, 599.

Do let me hear from you.

I am your friend very truly,
JNO M BOTTS.

[Addressed:]

Hon Willie P Mangum

U S Senate

Washington

WPM-LC

Henry M. Bickel to Willie P. Mangum.

PHILA. HALL. Jan, 14th, 1846—

Hon. Willie P. Mangum

Sir,

By order of the Philomathaen Society of Pennsylvania College, I hereby inform you, that you have been elected an honorary member of that Association.

The object of this society is, to cultivate and diffuse among its members liberal principles, and to promote the great objects of social, moral, and intellectual improvement.

An answer is respectfully requested. I take pleasure in subscribing myself

Your obedient servant
HENRY M. BICKEL,
Cor. Sec.

Gettysburg- Pa.

[Addressed:]

Hon. Willie P. Mangum LL.D.

Washington

D. C.

WPM-LC

William H. Haywood Jr., to Willie P. Mangum.

Friday Night 16 Jan 1846.

My Dear Sir

I am ready to start for home in the Boat to night but some of my friends are seized with a *panic* about Slidells nomination[17] and I have pacified them by a promise to pair off with you upon the question of confirming it viz: that if I am not here you will not vote against his confirmation and that I would make that arrangement with you before I left I am sure you do not feel any deep solicitude upon the question and it will be a sad disappointment to me not to go home in the situation of my family and affairs there. Wherefore I take the liberty of asking if you are willing to accomodate me by entering into this arrangement? If it will put you under the slightest embarrassment I shall not deem it at all unkind to refuse me. If otherwise as I hope may be the case I feel sure you will oblige me. An answer if you please

respy & truly yours
WILL H HAYWOOD JR

[Addressed:]

Hon. W. P. Mangum
Ebenbeck's
From Will H. Haywood Jr E & 8th

WPM-LC

John Hill[18] to Willie P. Mangum

WILMINGTON N C
19" Jany 1846

Honble. Willie P. Mangum

My dear Sir.

My son W^m is desirous of spending a portion of his vacation at the Cambridge Law School, in visiting the city of Wash-

---

[17]On December 22, 1845, Polk nominated John Slidell as envoy extraordinary and minister plenipotentiary to Mexico. The nomination was confirmed January 20, 1846. Mangum voted against confirmation. *Executive Journal of the Senate*, VII, 9, 33, 34, 35, 36.

[18]See above, II, 131a.

ington, seeing the great men of the Nation & listening to the interesting debates which are in progress in Congress, and I presume upon "auld lang syne" in introducing him to you, & in asking for him such civilities as it may be convenient for you to bestow upon him.

I hope the Friends of peace & of humanity, will be able to avert the calamities of war, which seem to be impending.

With a vivid recollection of by gone days, & with much consideration & respect

I am very truly
Yours
JOHN HILL

[Addressed:]

Honble W. P. Mangum
Washington City

Wm Hill

WPM-LC

J. C. Clark[19] to Willie P. Mangum

CHENANGO N. Y. Jany 19. 1846

My Dear Sir.

I see in a Philadelphia paper a notice of a rumour that Mr. Secretary Bancroft is about to commence a new order of things in regard to promotion of officers in the Navy. He is about to adopt the "jumping" system. When will locofocoism cease to lay its unhallowed hands upon the old well tried & glorious institutions of the Country? Is it not enough that we have seen the prosperity of the Country blighted - its industry crippled - its currency destroyed - and its law - its order, and its constitution disturbed & broken down by its ruthless— levelling & destructive spirits— But we are now doomed to witness the degradation of the gallant officers of our deathless Navy - and a fatal blow given to its prosperity. No, I will not believe it - un-

---

[19] John Chamberlain Clark, 1793-1852, was a Democratic member of Congress in 1827-1839. In 1837 he changed to the Whig party because of Van Buren's proposal of the Independent Treasury. He was reelected as a Whig and served from 1839 to 1843. In the latter part of his life he engaged in the lumber business. *Biog. Dir. of Cong.*, 816.

till the deed is actually consummated— Should the Secretary be so forgetful of his duty to the Navy and its brave officers, as to open the door to trickery & favoritism in their promotions, I trust the Senate will slam it back in his face.

Is it not enough to satisfy the aggressive restless & innovating spirit of the Secretary, that an officer standing fair on the Naval Register having at all times done his duty faithfully & devotedly, without a blot on either his Naval or professional reputation, should await the tardy movements of time & death to make a place for him in the usual & regular lists of promotions— But he would go counter to the instinct of Locofocoism and level up some favorites - some nephews - cousins - or cousins-cousins - to a grade [to] which they hold no just title - and at the expense of the lacerated feelings & wounded honor of men higher, as well on the list of merit & gallant service, as on that of the Navy— But even in this operation the instinct referred to, would be followed - for in levelling up *one* favorite - *all* above him on the register would be levelled down.

I cannot conceive a blow could be aimed at the Navy, more fatal to its interest or more unjust to the fearless men - who have shed so much lustre upon the Country— When it shall happen, that some demagogue commander, who instead of devoting his time & talents to the discharge of his proper professional duties shall prostitute them, by electioneering & catering for votes, to continue in power a corrupt executive, shall be elevated to office over the heads of his Seniors & probably betters - we may then bid "farewell & long farewell" to the order - the learning the efficiency - and the glory of the Navy

The country has furnished some examples of officers on shore "waiting orders" traversing it as partizon electioneers, & heralding from the stump the virtue & glories of their favorite candidate for the Presidency— Should the Secretary be permitted to carry out his plan as shadowed forth in the paper alluded to, these examples would be multiplied to a most disquieting extent. Among the officers of the Navy, instead of a generous rivalry, of who should best serve the country and advance the best interests of the Navy, the strife would be, who could do the most to advance his favorite political aspirant to power.- The aliment of this strife would be the hope and expectation of reward, in the shape of a post captaincy, at the expense of quiet, modest men of ten times their worth.

But I need not in talking with my old friend enlarge upon the disastrious consequences which would inevitably flow from the adoption of the suggested policy.

For many years I have known your friendship to the Navy & I have no fears that you will sit silently by, & see it desecrated.

It has given me much satisfaction to witness your course & that of most of our Whig friends in Congress in regard to the Oregon matter.— Every Whig in this region of the Country opposes it- The Whigs—honest confiding souls, have put their feet into not a few Locofoco traps, first & last, - But they have had sagacity enough to keep out of this Oregon pit-fall. The Locos have inflated their lungs to shout to the top of their bent, "Hartford Convention" - "British Whigs" - "Peace Party" & "all that sort of thing" - They may now puff it out & breath free again - as we stand "recti in curia" ready to fight like D - s if Polk will take the responsibilty of giving us guns & ammunition.

Will you have the kindess to present to Mr. Crittenden & Morehead my sincere regards and accept for yourself the assurance of my friendship.

J. C. CLARK.

———————

WPM-LC

Thurlow Weed to Willie P. Mangum

ALBANY, Jan, 19, 1846.

Dear Sir,

Excuse, I pray you, my importunities. Were our mutual friend Morehead at Washington, you would escape these inflictions, as I have his permission to tax his time.

I send you, in the Eve. Jour. Resoultions submitted to-day. They express the sense of our friends in this State upon the Oregon question.[20] We could not stand here upon weaker ground.

———————

[20]In 1845-1846 Thurlow Weed and the New York Whigs were uncertain about the course to take about Oregon. At times they blamed the Democrats for provoking a crisis and at other times they defended the American claim to Oregon. Weed wanted the Whigs to avoid a pacifist attitude or they might fall into another Hartford Convention trap. Van Deusen, *Life of Weed*, 146-147. See also the resolutions in the New York legislature in Jabez D. Hammond, *Political History of the State of New York*, Syracuse, 1848, III, 588, 590.

If we should attempt it the People would run away ahead of us. And we take this ground because we believe that a Northern Peace Party would tempt both our own and the English Government to plunge us into War. We think, too, that we stand best upon the record, and that therefore the ground taken is both right and expedient.

Without its Proviso, we should have hailed Mr Crittenden's Resolution[21] with the enthusiasm which Mr. Hillards speech excited. We know Mr. Crittenden would delight to follow him.

We are all grateful for the patriotic direction you gave to the first War demonstration made in the Senate, and we look with confidence to your wisdom and firmness in taking the Country and the Whig Party safely through this ordeal. Should Congress adjourn without advising the President to give the notice, in his own time and way, the Administration will go to the People with an issue that will overwhelm us.

With great respect,
I am truly yours,
T. WEED.

WPM-LC

C. P. Kingsbury[22] to Willie P. Mangum.

Camp near CORPUS CHRISTI, TEXAS,
January 22nd 1846.

Dear Sir:

The splendor of a Washington "assembly room," where we last parted, is removed almost as far from the frail and simple structure in which I am now writing, as is the Capitol of the Republic from the Army of Occupation. You will perhaps be surprised to receive a letter from me in this part of North America, where I have been exiled since last August. The campaign however, as you are aware, has thus far been pregnant with events of but little importance, and we can boast of nothing more glorious in the line of duty than the daily drill and

---

[21]Crittenden's resolution amounted to an instruction to the President to resume negotiations over the Oregon questions to see if an amicable settlement could be arranged. Wiltse, *Calhoun: Sectionalist,* 257.

[22]See above, II, 2n.

parade, which are poor equivalents for the "revels" that were anticipated in the "halls of the Montezumas." Yet one practical result even now, has been obtained- a knowledge of the soil, climate and resources of what has hitherto been a *terra incognita* - which may some day serve to dispel the illusions which have gone abroad, in relation to its qualities as an agricultural and commercial country. I will not now however, trouble you with the perusal of views and speculations which would occupy time known to be valuable, but come at once to the purpose of this letter.

In this obscure corner of the world, though almost forming a fraction of the United States, we hear but little, and that at a late day, of what transpires in Congress. But among the items of intelligence, that have traversed even Texas, is the rumor of the probable passage of a law creating two or three additional regiments of Dragoons. What basis may exist for this report, or whether among those who have circulated it, the wish is only father to the thought, I am of course unable to determine, but if there be truth in it, you will be able to advise me upon the points to which I desire to call your attention.

It is now nearly six years that I have been serving in the Army, and I am still a second Lieutenant. The regiments that are to be formed, will doubtless be officered from civil life, and by selections from the army. If in your opinion these regiments will be permanent, I have thought of applying for a Captaincy in one of them. The success of this application, which I would wish to keep private, would depend upon your willingness to give me your aid and influence. There will doubtless be swarms of politicians for the offices, and others who may have stronger claims than any which I could urge; and if you think there would be but little probability of success, I will at once abandon the idea. It might be deemed presumption in one of my present grade to apply for the commission, but I believe there have been cases on which such transfers have been effected.

There is nothing of interest that I can communicate in reference to the movements of the army. A few days since it was believed that a march to the Rio Grande was in contemplation, but the rumor has subsided, and if any such measure be anticipated or on foot, the knowlege of it seems to be confined to the

Commanding General. By the traders from Matamoros, through whom intelligence is frequently received, we have no later information touching the last projected revolution in Mexico,[23] than has been conveyed through the public prints. Gen. Arista[24] appears to be inactive in the Department of Tamaulipas, watching the current of events, and probably indifferent as to the result.

Every item of information that we receive here concerning the action of Congress upon our Foreign relations, is of absorbing interest. The debate on the resolutions of Mr. Cass,[25] created no little excitement in our belligerent community, and you will pardon me for adding that your speech was hailed with peculiar pleasure, gave most satisfaction, and received most approbation. Its views and sentiments, all agree in pronouncing as worthy of the occasion and of an American Senator. As an adopted son of North Carolina I could not but feel a lofty pride in the applause bestowed upon her Representative—and that Representative an early and valued friend.

If your leisure will permit, may I request you to give me your views upon the personal matter contained in this letter, the probabilities of a war with England, and the seeming duration of our banishment to Texas? The recent demonstrations of Gen. Paredes, to effect the overthrow of the administration, have put to flight our previous calculations as to the dispersion of the troops on this frontier, as the negotations may be retarded to an indefinite period.

Very respectfully and truly yours,

C. P. Kingsbury.

Hon. W. P. Mangum,

   U. S. Senate,

      Washington,

         D. C.

---

[23]Slidell's negotiations with Mexico were handicapped by the threatened revolt in Mexico. President J. J. de Herrera was inclined to receive Slidell as an envoy from the United States but delayed out of fear that General Mariano Paredes, his rival, would seize the government if Slidell were received. On December 31 Herrera was overthrown by a combination of the army, church, and monarchists and on January 2, Paredes was selected president *ad interim*. McCormac, *James K. Polk,* 395; Justin H. Smith, *The War With Mexico,* I, 95, 98-99.
[24]General Mariano Arista was in command of the Mexican forces in the state of Tamaulipas. In early April he took command at Matamoras and soon provoked the attack that led to the Mexican War with the United States. Smith, *War with Mexico,* I, 149.
[25]See above, 338n.

Jan. 23rd. A letter from Matamoras just received, states that Tampico is the only place that has declared for Gen. Paredes, and that his efforts are likely to prove abortive.

Abraham W. Venable[26] to Willie P. Mangum

BROWNSVILLE 22 January 1846

Dear Sir

I write amongst other things to request you to send me Fremonts report with the maps of his expedition as I observe many copies were printed for the use of the Senate. As my immediate representative sends me few or no documents if it will not be too troublesome please send me such as are most valuable & interesting. Our man J. R J Daniel has been exceedingly remiss on this subject- I approve most cordially of Mr. Calhouns views of the *Oregen Question*[27] as I take this occasion to express my gratification at the speech delivered by yourself on the motion of Mr Cass. I dislike a bullying attitude both in public and private life and am peculiarly opposed to a transfer of the treaty-making power from the President to the hustings & popular assemblies- I trust the honor of the country will not demand a war, but if it should I feel confident that the Whig & Democratic party will be merged in the American party presenting an unbroken front to the enemy. Accept sir assurances of my most sincere regard

Yrs truly
ABR W. VENABLE

Direct to Abrams Plains Granville N. C

[Addressed:]

Honble. Willie P. Mangum
Washington City.

---

[26]See above, II, 86n.
[27]In December Calhoun returned to the Senate determined to fight for a peaceful settlement of the Oregon question. As Secretary of State under Tyler, he had been conciliatory towards England. Now in December and January he began gaining Southern support for negotiating a peace. With the help of Benton, Webster, and other conservatives, he created sentiment for compromise. Wiltse, *Calhoun: Sectionalist,* 251-254, 257-262.

Thomas Lanier Clingman, 1812-1897. From an oil portrait by William Garl Browne, painted in 1877, in the Dialectic Society at the University of North Carolina, Chapel Hill.

Edward Stanly, 1810-1872. From a photograph in the North Carolina Collection, Library, University of North Carolina, Chapel Hill.

WPM-LC

J. S. Skinner[28] *to Willie P. Mangum*

[24 Januray, 1846]

My dear Sir

I shall leave here for the South on tuesday afternoon, proposing to touch at Hicksford Gaston Raleigh & Fayetteville in your State. Having it in view to make such personal observation as may assist me in promoting the more efficiently the agricultural interest of the Country, through the medium of the Farmers Library, which you have been pleased to favour with your patronage will you do me the kindness to give me a few *brief* notes of introduction to gentlemen known to you as zealous friends of that branch of industry—

It is only the public nature and value of the interest refer'd to that would justify me in troubling you so far— In any case be assured of the cordial respect & esteem of yours truly

J. S. SKINNER
24 Jany 46
Washington.

To the Hon
W. P. Mangum
Senate of the U. S.

WPM-LC

Edward Stanly to Willie P. Mangum

WASHINGTON [N. C.,] Jany: 27th. 1846

My Dear Sir,

I beg your permission to trouble you to call the attention of the Secy: of the Navy or the 4th. Auditor A. O. Dayton, to the settlement of the accounts of Robt: S. Moore, late a purser in the Navy, who died, little more than twelve months since. He was the son of Robt: G. Moore, the former efficient & able editor of the New Bern Spectator, since dead, & his wife & daughter have requested me to aid them, in having the accounts settled.-

---

[28]See above, 317n.

I know the nature of your engagements too well, to request that you should hasten your attention to the settlement of the account, but if you will write a note to the 4th Auditor, & say you feel some desire that the account of R. S. Moore, the late Purser should be settled, it will have the effect of hastening the action of the Department, on the subject. When you receive an answer, let me hear from you, that I may inform Miss V. S. Moore, the sister. Miss M. writes me that Lt. H. H. Lewis, a resident of Washington City, & Mr De Bree, a purser, who resides in Norfolk are acquainted with all the facts—it might be of service to ask the auditor to call on them for information.

After you shall have written to the Auditor, give me a line- possibly it may be necessary to present a claim to Congress should the Auditor refuse to allow all the claim— early action is therefore desirable. An expression of a desire on your part that the matter should not be neglected, is all that I wish to trouble you with.—

The Register has furnished you the account of our convention doings at Raleigh. The Locos will make a desperate effort for the Legislature, and I hope you will soon begin to stir up your friends in the counties of Surry, Stokes, Orange & Granville. If we work we can carry the State, if we do not, we shall lose it.—

I hope you received a copy of the correspondence, with H. T. Clark which I sent you:—

The Locos in North Carolina, are not so hot for Oregon, since the abolitionists have shown such anxiety on the subject.—[29]

> Very truly yours
> EDW. STANLY

Hon. W. P. Mangum
Washington City
    D. C.

---

[29]On January 5, 1846, a House committee recommended a resolution directing the President to give notice at once to end the joint control of Oregon. Giddings and other anti-slavery leaders proceeded to champion the whole of Oregon as a check on the expansion of slavery. Giddings said he had opposed expansion until slavery was expanded by the annexation of Texas and that he now supported the acquisition of all of Oregon to counteract the Southern expansion. This and other abolitionist speeches alarmed the Southerners. McCormac, *James K. Polk,* 587-588; Wiltse, *Calhoun: Sectionalist,* 257.

WPM-LC

J. R. Lambdin[30] to Willie P. Mangum

PHILAD" Jany 27th 1846.

Hon W. P. Mangum

Dear Sir

I presume upon your former kindness, in addressing a few lines to you on a subject in which I feel some solicitude, and which is likely to be brought before your honorable body shortly in what manner I am not able at present to say. The law of 1844-5 authorizing the painting of four pictures for the Rotunda[31] of the Capitol has been fulfilled so far as regards the commission given to Messrs Chapman & Weir- the third picture to be executed by Vanderlyn is, I understand, ready to be shipped from Paris, where it has been painted in contravention to the spirit of the law which required the pictures to be executed by native American artists- and as I have reason to believe was the intention of the framers of the bill- to be executed on the soil- the only way in which art can be benefitted to country.- The fourth commission was given to Mr Inman of New York- and has never progress even to the completion of a design.- his death which occurred on the 20th inst leaves the commission to be executed by some other hand.— I have given much attention to the subject of our western History- the character- manners, habits & scenery- and for some time past have meditated the painting of a large picture commemorating an important event in the settlement of the great west, but have been deterred from the fear of being unable for want of pecuniary ability, to carry it through. The death of Mr Inman has led me to look to Washington- and to my friends there to aid me in procuring a commission to fill the vacant pannel of the Rotunda.—[32] Should you think proper to present my claims in any way- you may be interrogated with the questions what

[30]See above, 59n.

[31]Henry Inman, Robert Weir, John Vanderlyn, and John G. Chapman were commissioned to make these paintings. Henry Inman, 1801-January 17, 1846, before his death, had begun a design of the cottage of Daniel Boone. Robert Walker Weir, 1803-1889, painted the "Embarkation of the Pilgrims." John Vanderlyn, 1775-1852, went to Paris and employed a French artist to help him with his "Landing of Columbus." John G. Chapman, 1808-1889, completed his "Baptism of Pocahontas" in 1847.

[32]After Inman's death, William H. Powell, of Ohio, was authorized to paint the western scene. He began in 1848 and completed his "Discovery of the Mississippi by DeSoto" in 1853. All of these paintings of Colonial America are in the Rotunda along with the four on the Revolution by John Trumbull. Federal Writers' Project, *Washington City and Capital*, Washington, 1937, 225; *D. A. B.*, IV, 18; IX, 481-482; XV, 153-154; XIX, 180-181, 612-613.

historical works has he executed? this may be answered by the asking of another- What works had Chapman Weir Vanderlyn or Inman executed before they were entrusted with the government orders?— I feel that within me which says, *I can do it,* and in a way that shall bring no discredit on American art.

Pardon me my dear Sir for this egotism- when I know the efforts that will be made by these who have no claims- and whose perserverance may yet accomplish what they desire— it makes me indeed anxious for an opportunity of bringing out that, which has been implanted by nature and cultivated with much application.—

If it be possible to get away from my professional engagements at home in two or three weeks I may have an opportunity in giving you my views in propria persona.

truly your friend and admirer

J R LAMBDIN

[Addressed:]

Hon W P Mangum
of N. C.
U S Senate
Washington
D. C.

WPM-LC

Priestley H. Mangum to Willie P. Mangum

HILLSBORO' Jan: 30th 1846.-

Dear Sir,

[torn] Lipscombe is desirous of having [torn] with Roberts tried the ensuing spring- and it will be necessary [to] take your deposition on the subject of the state of mind of the Grantor & bargainor, John Tilly sen^r. dec^d.—

I drop you this note, to ascertain from you, *some suitable place* for taking your deposition in Washington City, so that we may be able to give the opposite party the necessary notice. Will you write forthwith?-

I was at your House some days ago, when all were well, except Sally- who was but little indisposed.- The effect on her mind, I thought, consequent on the sudden death of Alfred.[33] I learn that she is much better since I came up.—

I have not yet removed to Wake- I expect to be off early in the Spring, if practicable.—

You take it for granted that I am always [torn] - and therefore, it seems, tha[t] what I say is always disregarded by you. But you may rely upon it, that if you at all desire to perpetuate your reputation; to attain that object you must use the ordinary & necessary means. - I perceive that the speeches of every man in Congress, & particularly those most distinguished in the Nation, suffer nothing to go from them abroad, thro' the papers, that is not prepared by their pen. It is obvious to every reader of observation.- Hence their reputation abroad is often more imposing, as it is more desireable, than at Washington with the audience who hear the speeches delivered. This latter reputation, tho' to be desired, is frail & unsubstantial- unless sustained by able speeches reported.- You don't do yourself justice in your late speech as reported.[34] It is not at all calculated to sustain your reputation- it [torn] random shot than a well [regu]lated fire- & there are about as m[any] different versions of it as there were reporters- & all because you will not write out your speeches as others do.— Every public speaker knows, that a good speech *as delivered* by the speaker is often a very ordinary one if reported *verbatim et literatum*- & the same can be made a good one by writing it out, without violating any of the rules of propriety.—

(I saw the Whig version only) -

I hope you are sending into the state more documents than formerly- You are aware that that has been a prolific source of complaints- Men, who are public servants are expected to notice their constituents; & if they do not, they may expect dissatisfaction- This is a progressive Whiggism, as well as a progressive democracy— a young Whiggism as well as a young

---

[33]One of Mangum's slaves. See above A. W. Gay to W. P. Mangum, December 4, 1845.
[34]Mangum's speech was published in the *Congressional Globe*, 29 Cong., 1 sess., 47-49.

democracy: & one is worth about as much, in these regions, as
the other.

Yrs truly.

P. H. MANGUM

[Addressed:]

To

The Hon:
Willie P. Mangum
(*Senate of U. S. C.*)
Washington City
D. C.

Willie P. Mangum to William A. Graham[35]

WASHINGTON CITY 31st. Jan: 1846

My dear Sir.

Permit me to introduce to you Mr. Skinner,[36] the editor of
The Farmer's Library published in New York. - I believe you
will remember him, having as I suppose, known him in this
City. - His reputation is so well known to you, that I need say
nothing, beyond a request that you will afford him the means
of seeing Mr. Cameron, Mr. Boylan, Majr. Hinton & such other
Gentlemen as are most likely to feel interest in the success of
his enterprize.-

Mr. Skinner goes South to make observations &C &C. on the
modes of Southern agriculture. - With great respect & regard

I am, as ever,
Yrs. Mo. truly
WILLIE P. MANGUM

To

Gov. Graham
Raleigh.

---

[35]The original letter is in the W. A. Graham Papers, University of North Carolina.
[36]See above, J. S. Skinner to W. P. Mangum, January 26, 1846.

WPM-LC

James E. Harvey to Willie P. Mangum.

[January 1846]

My dear Sir.

King of Geo.[37] told me to-day he had undoubted information that Pakenham submitted proposition to *arbitrate* the Oregon matter and that it was peremptorily refused-[38] As the best information nowadays is doubtful from the nature of things, would you tell me, if it has come to you in a reliable form? It is too important, to authenticate, without being nearly sure.

Do you get anything of Slidell further than what is before the world? or have you any item to increase my little stock of intelligence for the "dear people."

Yours faithfully
JAMES E HARVEY

Judge Mangum.

WPM-LC

R. W. Brown[39] to W. P. Mangum

WILMINGTON, N°. Ca
2ᵈ. Feby. 1846—

Honbᴸᵉ. W. P. Mangum,
Senate U. S. from N. C.

Dear Sir,

My purpose is not to intrude- but, to solicit your kind aid in behalf of our requirement here of a Marine Hospital.-

Since 1835 we have been *scuffleing*- suffering in various ways for the want of the fixture to accomodate & relieve our poor

------

[37]Thomas Butler King.
[38]On December 27, 1845, the British minister, Richard Pakenham, proposed to Secretary of State James Buchanan that the whole Oregon question be referred to the arbitration of some friendly nation. Anticipating such an offer, Polk had already decided to reject it. When Buchanan gave an unfriendly reply, Pakenham expressed the desire to settle the matter on almost any terms. McCormac, *James K. Polk,* 582-583.
[39]A close friend of Thomas Ruffin, he sent his son by Ruffin's home for counseling before he entered the University in 1830. When Clay came to Wilmington in 1844, Robert W. Brown was on the reception committee and one of the managers of the ball given in Clay's honor. He was very much interested in the development of internal improvements for Wilmington. In 1843 he wrote a long statement describing the trade of the city. Hamilton (ed.), *Papers of Ruffin,* II, 3; Sprunt, *Chronicles of the Cape Fear River,* 214, 218, 506-511.

fellows who come here in their arduous duties as seamen and having paid Hospital money all their lives- happen to be sick & find no place to lay their head- & to bear every expense! The cases of small pox when they occur are particularly hard- certain death in almost every case is the consequence- Sixty years ago my native place & 40 yrs. in active business I have witnessed large importations made here & in all cases the crews of Vessels have been req^d. to pay on the Hospital tax.- Our port, the chief in No. Caro'. has long deserved this arrangement, from the Governm^t.- it has now much increased & is daily expanding- our commerce is large & particularly the coasting- we had contributed & bo^t. a place 2½ miles below town- which for several years we have endeavored to make answer a temporary purpose- but, we can't stand it any longer- having laid out over $2500. We are willing to surrender all if the U. S. will fix it & keep it up. Our contributors could not object of course to get their outlay in money back again- but prefer to yield all if we can but see the needfull establishment- Later occurrences of last Summer & this winter since Xmas in cases of small pox- delay of vessels & death have produced another effort.

Why should it be, my Dear Sir, that when a poor fellow has paid his Hospital tax for 40. 50 years & happens here his first time & *sick* to find no place to lay his head! They all complain- say it is not so any where else & tis indeed hard to see them banished & to die! Our Petition is preparing to go on- annexed to it is copy of the act of Incorporation of "Wilmington Marine Hospital association" which will show how the property stands & that the right exists in us to transfer- We are not asking for public money or a share of the spoils, you know, but, purely a necessary- important item & return occasionally of monies paid in long ago- a little money will produce the means of relief & comfort to the hardy few who are largely deserving & entitled! Honble. Mr. Haywood understands our situation & he will be fully advised- as also Honble. Mr. Dobbin with other Gent^n. - for myself I take leave to add this hasty letter to you as a means of preparing you for the battle & I fear not the result-

Here we are within 3 Days of New York- Balt^o. Philad^a. New Orls. West Indies & without any preparation & quite a different condition from those other distant Western Waters- The Shipping of New York, lately suff^d. here- Massachusetts & *Maine* all interested largely- perhaps their representatives would aid you in our cause when y [torn] all others- our frds. get together- explain [torn] & understand the importance of our case—

Our Collector has taken interest with us & since his time of being here is fully aware of our wants. I gave him a plan of our place in question which he sent to Washington- Mr. Dobbin will have a full detail & can explain- Mr. Haywood has an idea of our deplorable fix from frequent conversations here at Govr. Dudleys-

Mo: respectfully,

Yr. Ob. Sert.

R. W. BROWN,

Our Board of Navigation are getting up a petition separately we sign it too- as a *Hospital* is desired *by all!* & willing to have it *somewhere*- Some few don't like the distance of our place from town- not over 3 & think not more than 2½ miles. Suitable in all other points I don't see why the mere convenience of a Doc- tor shou'd be largely consulted. Sever'l Gent^n. here who would take the place at reasonable annual pay- & then be idle greater part of his time—

[Addressed:]

Honble. W. P. Mangum,
Senator U. S. from No Ca-
Mail.   Washington City.

WPM-LC

James Manney[40] to Willie P. Mangum

BEAUFORD N^o. C^a
Feby. 2nd, 1846

Dear Sir,

I have just read your amendments to the Resolutions of the Honbl. Senator from Kentucky on the Oregon Territory.[41] They

---

[40]Member of the House of Commons from Cartaret County in 1834, *N. C. Manual*, 539.
[41]Crittenden's resolution authorized the President to notify Great Britain that the Oregon con- vention of 1827 was abrogated. Mangum proposed an amendment to the effect that the notice of termination of the agreement be accompanied with a proposal to submit the claims of the two coun- tries to arbitration. He added a second part which authorized the Senate Committee on Territories to report a bill organizing a territorial government for Oregon upon the expiration of joint occupation. *Cong. Globe*, 29 Cong., 1 sess., 239.

meet my entire approval- I would not alter a word were it in my power. If ever there was a time when it was right & proper for a Senator's constituents to communicate their opinions freely to him- this is, in my opinion, the most important. I have conversed freely and unreservedly with intelligent men of both political parties. We all, with *very few* exceptions, prefer an honorable peace, to an unnecessary & disgraceful war. Nothing could be more disgraceful, now and in all future time, than for two great civilized and protestant Christian nations to rush blindly and inconsiderately into a War, ruinous to both Nations, and distressing to the whole civilized world, for a Territory not worth five cents pr. acre. Arbitration is the proper and only mode in which the dispute can be settled— and I am surprised that the President should have entirely omitted to mention the proposal of Great Brittain to settle the dispute in this just and friendly manner.

I have read the correspondence of our diplomatists, with Mr. Packenham, with great attention- but I cannot arrive at the conclusion that our title to the whole of Oregon "is clear and unquestionable." It appears to me that England has a title to the Northern part of the Oregon Territory. I should think from the nature of the climate & productions that the northern half of Oregon would not be settled by a white population in two hundred years from this.

Our country now is nearly out of debt, and prosperous in every department of business. Ever since the Tariff of 1842 went into operation, Agriculture, Manufactures, commerce, & the Mechanic Arts have flourished. The revenue has increased under this Tariff, because the people have prospered in every department of business, and been enabled to purchase & pay for a vast amount of Foreign Luxuries- and Manufactures of Foreign Nations, paying duties or taxes into the National Treasury. The Polititions who put their shoulders to the pillars of this fair fabric, to overthrow it- are more *bold* than *wise*. They will be buried in the ruins- and the Elections of 1848 will satisfy them, that I am a true prophet.

When I was a young man I was opposed to a Tariff for Revenue with incidental protection to Manufactures. After studying attentively the arguments of our greatest Statesmen on both sides, I became a convert to the doctrine of the great Statesman of the West.-[42] whose fame will be brighter and more enduring than that of any of the great conquererors and desolators of the World in ancient, or modern times.

I have read with great satisfaction your remarks in the Senate, on the reference of the resolutions to give Notice, &C- Your sentiments are entirely worthy of a Senator of this great Republic.

My grandson's now playing about me, will probably live to see & form a part of a population of one hundred millions- what a brilliant prospect!

Patres conscripti take care of the Republic, let not reckless, and unhallowed ambition shroud it with "clouds and darkness."

I am
very respectfully
Yr friend & obt. Servt,

J. MANNEY

Honbl W. P. Mangum
Senate of the
United States.

[Addressed:]

Hon[bl]. W. P. Mangum
Senate of the
UNITED STATES.

WPM-LC

J. B. Mower to Willie P. Mangum

NEW YORK 5th. Feby. 1846.

My dear Sir
        private

On my arrival here, I was surprised to learn, that there was just getting up, a very serious and powerful opposition, to the confirmation of Mr. Laurence,[43] the present collector of this

---

[42]By 1844 many Southern Whigs accepted the tariff as a good thing. Cole, *Whig Party in the South*, 101-102.

[43]Abram R. Laurence was chairman of the Whig General Committee of New York City. See below Abram R. Laurence to W. P. Mangum, August 4, 1846.

port, and all, or almost all, from the friends of Mr. Calhoun & others, of the democratic party. And to the end, that they may gain time, to arrange & carry into successful effect, their determinations, they respectfully solicit, the Senators of your side of the chamber, to postpone action, on this nomination, till you further hear from us again. I have written to Mr. Clayton, on this subject & to Mr. Lewis.

> I am my dear Sir
> with the highest respect
> & good will, very long enter-
> tained for you.
> J. B. MOWER

Hon. Willie P. Mangum)

)

  U. S. Senate   )

)

  Washington   )

[Addressed:]

    Hon. Willie P. Mangum
    U. S. Senate
    Washington

              WPM-LC

Gouverneur Kemble[44] to Charles Fisher.

       COLD SPRING [N. Y.] 6th feby 1846.

My dear Sir/

  after having sent my trunk from Gallaturns to the rail road, in looking over some old cards to burn them, I found one with the name C. Fisher - had my trunk not already gone, I should certainly have remained another day to see you, and I now very much regret that the neglect of the servants, should have prevented our meeting, as I had much to say to you on the subject

---

[44]Gouverneur Kemble, 1786-1875, a graduate of Columbia College in New York, began business as a merchant. While visiting Spain he studied the process of casting cannons. Upon his return to the United States, he established a cannon foundry at Cold Spring, where, for the first time, cannons were cast in this country. He was a Democratic member of Congress from 1837 to 1841. *Biog. Dir. of Cong.*, 1173.

of copper, to which I have of late turned my intention [*sic*], without however abandoning my Iron interests— Could we have met, you would most probably have been able to satisfy me on the mines of North Carolina,[45] as it is, I want you to give me some information in relation to them, the facilities and cost of raising the ore - its average produce, and the possiblity of so selecting as to render it capable of transportation, with the cost of transportation to the nearest water carriage - what are the facilities of water power for crushing it, and in what district are the best mines - is there any body in the vicinity of Fayette Ville who could direct me in case of my coming to North Carolina, and whether you will probably be at home in the month of April.- I have long intended this visit, but when I returned home after my service in congress, I found it necessary to apply myself closely to my business here, after having abandoned it entirely for four years, and at the only time when I could have left home, you were absent in Kentucky; so, after proceeding as far as Washington I returned back again, until the last year I have thought no more of copper, but having thrown a venture at Lake Superior, it has induced me to collect information, and to investigate the subject more closely, and it appears to me that our Country presents a wide and interesting field, that from it, will hereafter the great supplies of copper be drawn, as yet both the smelting and manufacture have been little thought of - we have neither chemists who understand the theory, nor practical workmen for the manipulation - both must in the first instance be supplied from abroad - but when I first commenced the manufacture of Iron it was little better with that great branch of national industry - there was something more to be sure to be learned from books, but practical workmen were wanting, in every branch, and for many years, until we could create them here, we were entirely dependent on Europe- [But] the case is now reversed, and there are some branches in which we actually vie with them on equal terms, and if ten years hence we do it not in copper, it is our

---

[45]Prior to 1845 several small iron foundries were operated in Gaston, Lincoln, and Chatham counties. Elisha Mitchell and Denison Olmstead, the state geologists, reported the presence of a low grade iron ore in several counties. In Gaston County the High Shoals Manufacturing Company, supported by New York capital, continued to operate until 1854, when it failed. There was not much iron mining in North Carolina after 1840. Lester J. Cappon, "Iron making—a Forgotten Industry of North Carolina," *North Carolina Historical Review*, IX, 331-348.

own fault, and you must join me in this, when I think of the open field, that now offers, it makes me young again.

Yours truly

GOUV KEMBLE.

Chs. Fisher Esqr.

The only speciments that I have of copper ore from North Carolina are selected ones for the cabinet, but these give little information in relation to the average richness of the ore & the minerals with which it is associated.

G' K.

[Addressed:]

Hon'
Charles Fisher Esqr
Salisbury
North Carolina.

WPM-LC

John D. Hawkins[46] to Willie P. Mangum

Near HENDERSON
Feby. 13th. 1846

Dear Sir.

After I obtained your name as well as many other members of Congress to the recommendation to the Post-Mas-Genl. to put 4 Horse Stages on the Road from Raleigh to Columbia, I went to see Col. Johnson[47] accompanied by Mr Haywood Genl. McKay and Mr Dobbin, The Post Mas-Genl. was very willing to make the substitution if he could get the power which the present Law did not give (the present stages are 2 Horse) him. But he said if he did make the change of the 4 instead of the 2 Horse coaches, he would stipulate that the Great mail now going by Wilmington should be sent by Raleigh when he pleased.

---

[46]John D. Hawkins, 1781-1858, a graduate of the University of North Carolina and son of Colonel Philemon Hawkins, practiced law for a short time in Raleigh before he moved to Franklin County near the Granville County line. He owned and cultivated large plantations in that section. For many years he was presiding judge of the court of Common Pleas and Quarter Sessions. In 1834 and 1840 he represented Franklin County in the legislature. He helped promote the Raleigh and Gaston Railroad. Ashe, *Biog. Hist. of N. C.*, V, 160-162.
[47]He refers to Cave Johnson, Postmaster General under Polk, and Will H. Haywood, James J. McKay, and James C. Dobbins.

He said moreover He must send the Big Mail that way, as there were so many failures on the Wilmington rout. that the service would not put up with it. I understood Mr Haywood to say he would have nothing to do with taking the Big mail from the Wilmington Road. But at the close of the conference, it was settled down by the *Congress men,* and Col. Johnson, to which I assented, that I would cause two propositions to be made to the Department. First what price would be asked for substituting 4 horse coaches in place of the 2 now in use, And 2^{ndy}. if the Big mail was put upon that rout which should be at the pleasure of the Post Mas. Genl. at what price? I put Govr. Grahams letter of Terms as to the Rail Road in the hands of Mr. Dobbin and asked him to act for me. On my way Home I met Captn. Guion,[48] and I am notified since that he in behalf of himself and the other Stage Contractors to Columbia, agreed with the Post Mas- Genl. upon terms for 4 Horse coaches instead of 2, provided an act of Congress is passed giving power to the Post Mas. Genl. to contract for a time suited to the wishes of the stage contractors. Col. Johnson under the present Law could only contract for the unexpired term, which is so short the stage contractors could not incur the expense of new stages and additional Horses for that term especially as corn is very scarce in So. C. The Post Mas. Genl who doubted his power under the present Law to even substitute the 4 Horse coaches for the 2 now in use. But he agreed if the power was given him he would make the contract as desired by the Stage Contractors. Mr Haywood & Genl. McKay said that a law to that effect could be passed immediately. As the terms have been agreed upon by the Department, and the Stage Contractors, and nothing is lacking to consummate them, but the Law, to give the Power; I have written Mr Haywood & Genl. McKay and asked them to endeavour to have that Law passed as they proposed, and the object of this letter is to inform you of the result of my negotiations in the matter and to solicit your cooperation. If I can as an *humble instrument* in this matter aid

---

[48]Probably Haywood W. Guion, of Charlotte.

to sustain the Rail Road, it will give not only me, but many others great pleasure -

> I am most respectfully
> Your Humble Servt.
> JNO. D. HAWKINS

The Honble.
  W. P. Mangum.

[Addressed:]

> The Honble.
>   Willie P. Mangum
>   Washington City.

WPM-LC

Wm. Gibbs McNeill⁴⁹ to Willie P. Mangum.

NEW YORK 14th Feby 1846.—

Hon: Willie P. Mangum.-
  U. S. Senate.

Dr. Sir: Surrounded by a number of officers of our Navy I venture to address myself to you, in their behalf & fully sympathizing with them - in relation to the commission (appointment of) Comr. Moore to a Captaincy in our Navy.—

All that they ask is a little more time for Hon: Senators to reflect on the injustice which may result from the precedent - to say nothing of that which, in excited feeling - perhaps - they think will have been done them by the confirmation of Captn. Moore before his nomination shall be acted on.—

Omitting any argument: will you allow me to suggest that if he & others (or he alone) are to be introduced as part & parcel of the effects - *the public property* - of Texas; an increase of the numerical rank of Captains & others of subordinate grade would, measurably mollify the excited (& as some think) outraged feeling of the Navy: - That is - if it be determined to introduce ("annex") Comr. Moore to the list of Navy Captains -

---

⁴⁹William Gibbs McNeill, 1801-1853, a native of Wilmington, North Carolina, attended West Point. A successful engineer, he surveyed most of the railroad routes of the East. In 1837 he resigned from the army to promote other railroads. *D. A. B.*, XII, 152-153.

do it (not by filling a vacancy) but by special Legislation *in-dividualizing* (if there be such a word) & creating a place for him by *increasing* the number of Captns.

You will excuse this when I tell you that hearing that gallant arm of the National defence - so well represented by those present - express confidence in the justice of Senator Mangum: I am called on to write for them because I almost claimed relationship! "The Old North State" - drank with "three times three". - (Loco-foco as I am I had to lug in "Hon. Mr. Crittenden" & I am not the only *democrat!!* (shade of my Federalist Father do not hear it!) who am prepared to go for him "right, or wrong, dead, or alive"—politically speaking—

Most res'y. I am truly &c
WM. GIBBS MCNEILL

[Addressed:]

> Hon: Mr. Mangum.—
> U. S. Senate.—
> Washington City.

WPM-NC

Note of Willie P. Mangum on the "History of Ivory Crucifix"

14 Feby 1846.

The following is a most remarkable work- I have for hours, sat looking at it, in a sort of dreamy solemn idealism.- It speaks to the Senses of the heart, with an eloquence beyond the pulpit; & when is superadded, the back ground view (a painting) of the City of Jerusalem, with the heavens overcast with angry clouds, & the fierce, avenging, & forked lightning is seen bursting & descending in a red & wrathful stream of fire to "rend the Vail of the temple" it is absolutely magnificent, appalling & dissolving to a mind & heart of the slightest devotional cast.

I am tolerably well.
W. P. MANGUM

HISTORY
OF THE
IVORY CRUCIFIX,
or
STATUE OF CHRIST,
Carved from a solid Block of Ivory
By a monk in the Convent of
St. Nicholas,
at
Genoa, Italy.

WPM-LC

J. Watson Webb to Willie P. Mangum

[16 February, 1846]

My Dear Sir.

More enquiries- to whom did Mr. Buchanan say that the People possessed all the facts in regard to the Oregon affair? I answer that he told Mr. Calhoun & Mr. W. S. Miller[50] the member from this City. To Mr. Miller he made his declaration after the 1st of January- I do not know when he spoke to Mr. Calhoun. To both his declaration was precise & full, that *all* the correspondence was in the possession of Congress; & both of these Gentlemen repeated it to me. Mr. Miller's Brother who is here, says further that *Buchanan* deliberately *lied*. He and the Brother, was in Washington at the time. Send for Miller, & Mr Calhoun, & you will have facts enough. Miller will give you other names to whom he made the same declaration. I believe to Campbell member from the Cty.

Yours ever.

J. Watson Webb
Feby. 16 1846

Hon W. P. Mangum.

[Addressed:]

To the Hon:
W. P. Mangum.
U. S. Senate
Washington.

---

[50] William Starr Miller, Congressman from New York City in 1845-1847. *Biog. Dir. of Cong.* 1316.

WPM-LC

William Hooper[51] to Willie P. Mangum

COLUMBIA S. C. Feb. 17 [1846]

My dear Sir

Will you be good enough to send me a list of the two Houses of the present Congress, as I suppose you have it in pamphlet form. We are, you may be sure watching your proceedings with deep interest & some anxiety; and our comfort is to think that it is, as you & others every now & then give us a hint, namely: that a game is playing- that the President & his backers have no notion of going to war- & are only making a *fair show* for some party purposes. I read, with much pleasure, last night, Mr. Clayton's speech, at least the concluding part of it. I was glad to hear from Mr. Preston this morning that his *private advices* from Washington increase the hope held out by the papers that we shall get thro this business without a war. What a war it would be to us! You will be interested to hear about your old friend- Col. Preston.[52] Academical habits seem to set easy upon him- He goes to prayers most punctually every morning & evening- and lectures his classes 4 times a week very diligently- too much so, for his strength- for I am sorry to tell you that his health appears much worsted by a severe attack last summer, and as he himself says he "is very easily put out of tune." He appears easily fatigued. He has to live very carefully & abstemiously. I hope as the cold weather withdraws, he will be better. He is very popular as a president & I think will continue so. Pray give me what circumstances you know of the late fatal duel between our countrymen Jones & Dr Johnson.[53] The unhappy *cause* we have heard, to our infinite astonishment, & our great sorrow, for our friend Devereux's sake, as well as the immediate parties concerned. We learn from N. Ca that Mr D. had gone to Washington to see Jones Is it true that Jones & his second & Dr. J.s second are in custody, or have they been

---

[51]See above, III, 23n.
[52]W. C. Preston was president of South Carolina College from 1846 to 1851.
[53]Dr. Daniel Johnson and Thomas F. Jones, both of Perquimans County, fought a duel at Bladensburg, Maryland, February 2, 1846. The duel developed from the infidelity of Jones's wife. Johnson, a physician, refused to fire. Jones, a lawyer and near sighted, shot and killed Johnson. Jones and his second were arrested, but no action resulted from the arrest. The duel produced great excitement. Both men were prominent and respected in their communities. About 300 people witnessed the shooting. *Hillsborough Recorder*, February 12, 1846; Stephen B. Weeks, "The Code in North Carolina," *Magazine of America's History*, December, 1891, 451; *Raleigh Register*, February 6, 13, 1846.

discharged? We learn that Dr J.s body was brought home to his friends. Is it true that he reserved his fire, & protested, to the last, that Jones's jealousy was *groundless?* This is stated in a Baltimore print. But *can this be possible?* The accounts we have rec[d], *direct from Raleigh,* (said to be on the best authority) make the proof *ocular, personal!* Would that there could be a "loop to hang a hope upon," for poor Devereux's sake & his family's.

Excuse me for intruding upon your public cares with this letter, which your uniform courtesy & kindness assure me you will do-

Yours very truly &
Respectfully
W. Hooper
S. Ca. College

[Addressed:]

The
Hon. W. P. Mangum
Washington
D. C.

WPM-LC

J. Whitehorne[54] to Willie P. Mangum

New York Feb 17th 1846

Dear Sir,

I write to beg your influence in procuring the picture for the Rotunda which was to have been painted by N. Inman[55] but which has never, even had a beginning. My only recommendation is the Design of the senate, a proof engraving of which you will see in Washington in the course of four weeks- at which time I hope to see you myself.

I suppose that it will be left open to competition for some months. May I hope for any influence that you, Sir, or any of

---

[54]See above, J. Whitehorne to W. P. Mangum, March 7, 1845.
[55]See above, 375n.

your friends may bring to bear upon the Com^tee to whom this subject is referred?

I shall remain in W. long enough to paint several portraits. If you, sir should wish to employ my pencil I should be pleased to know it previous to my leaving home, that I might make my arrangements accordingly—

Yours in F. L. & T.

J. WHITEHORNE

Hon. W. P. Mangum -

[Addressed:]

Hon. W. P. Mangum.
Washington
D. C.

Politeness Hon. Ely Moore)

WPM-LC

J. B. Mower to Willie P. Mangum

19th. Feby. 1846.

[NEW YORK, N. Y.]

Dear Sir

private.

I have been much occupied, since my return home, about my own affairs. But I am not unmindful, of the topic, we familiarly discussed, at your lodging. I have in my walks, found a few old friends, of both parties, who unhesitatingly declare, their decided preference, for the Judge, over the *General*[56]- And their reasons, are unanswerable. From the very nature of things, who is best able, who is, the most proper person, to be at the head of a Government, like ours, founded on universal suffrage; him, who has been tried, as a representative, executive, and Judicial office, displayed, the very best administrative talent, in each. Or him, who has, from his youth, been ac-

---

[56]He refers to Judge John McLean and General Winfield Scott.

customed, to hold the sword, in his hand. Who has always commanded, knows nothing, of being commanded. Unaccustomed, to mingle, with the great body, of the people; knows nothing about them, nor of *Human nature-* He is very irritable, vain, and pompous, very credulous, and visionary, beyond all comparison. Irritable, as I will show you. During the Embargo, in 1809. or- 10. the Government desired, a cession, of a piece of Land, at the battery, in this city, and because, it was not done in time, and manner, to suit Col. Scott, (now General) Dewitt Clinton, (afterwards Governor) then being mayor, of the city, was challenged, to mortal combat. That story, would not read well now, when it is known, that the General, refused to meet General Jackson, with his hands untied. Besides Sir, there is, a prejudice among the people, of taking the President, from a slave state. General S must hail from Virginia. The people, are quite willing, to take the vice-President, from a slave holding state. I desire, you should most distinctly know, from me, that I disclaim, any ill will, towards the General. We are on the very best of friendly terms. But I place these facts, before you, my friend, as they are freely talked, among the people. It is also due to truth, to inform you, that Mr. Calhoun, just now, stands well, in our community. The people generally, are quite pleased with his acts, on the Oregon question. And Sir, I assure you also, that you may ride, from Washington, to this City, stop one day in Philadelphia, mingle with the business people, and with a few calls, on personal friends, and you will not hear, the name of Mr. Polk, mentioned, in any other way, than with contempt, if mentioned at all.

I salute you Mr. Senator, with
a great deal of Respect & good
will,
Your friend.
J. B. MOWER

Hon. Willie P. Mangum

   U. S. Senate

     Washington

       D. C.

WPM-LC

T. L. Clingman to Willie P. Mangum.

ASHEVILLE Feb. 21st 1846

My dear Sir

I should have written to you some time since in reply to your favour but that I know that situated as you are a letter even from a friend is often a burden. In the first place permit me to thank you for the many favours which I have received from you in the shape of interesting documents. Your course on the Oregon question allow me to say is just what it ought to be, I am much pleased to see that you were the first of the Senators to take what seems to me the true position on that question, and I am strongly inclined to believe that manner in which you expressed yourself at the beginning of the discussion has had a favorable effect in preventing some of our Northern friends from taking an extreme anti-war position which as our political enemies hoped, would have weakened us as a party, For however silly [and] weak may be the views of our executive (and I believe that the history of governments does not present a greater climax of absurdity and wickedness than would be the system of Mr Polk reduced into practice) yet it ought always to be kept prominently before the public mind that in the event of actual collision with a foreign nation all parties here would support our government, Your resolutions on this subject it seems to me are just what they ought to have been and point to that course which I think alone it is practicable to take.

With respect to party politics here we are all in a state of much quiet. What the Locos will do now that Caldwell has declined I have no means at present of knowing.[57]

Should they decline giving us opposition I shall think it fortunate for us for with all the effort which the active Whigs in this part of the state would make for Gov. Graham he would I fear if opposed by a respectable man fall smartly behind the party strength, We found in 1844 that many of these persons who voted against us in August who were called Whigs could not be gotten back in November for Clay with all our efforts, though as you may remember we gained nearly a thousand

---

[57]See above, 350n.

votes, on the gov., election. Should we be crippled in the same manner again I fear we might be placed in a minority in some of our counties. This however, you understand is not for the public to know, but on the contrary we tell the Locos that their men are afraid of our candidate.

As to Gov. Graham himself the promient Whigs have no objection, and as for myself it is hardly necessary for me to say to you that I entertain the same feelings towards him that I did in 1840 when I took occasion to defend against the assaults of *your very particular* friend Mr. Shepard.[58] Should we have opposition you may rely upon our doing here all we can for him and the Whig party of the old North State

How the Legislature is to be no one can tell, If we can get out the right men we can easily carry the state. Should we get the majority of the Legislature I may without any impropriety say to you as I do to my friends that I am for you if you are willing to serve, against any man in the State even if he were from old Buncombe itself, I consider this much due to the fidelity and ability you have shown to principles of the Whig party, Should you find time to write to me occasionly it would always as you know give me the greatest pleasure to hear from you

                                        I am very truly yours
                                        T. L. Clingman

Hon Willie P. Mangum.

                                                        WPM-LC

Daniel S. Hill[59] *to Willie P. Mangum.*

                                        Louisburg No. Ca.
                                        February 21st 1846

Hon Willie P Mangum

    Dear Sir

        If you have any spare copies of Fremonts Expedition through the countries west of the Rocky Mnts &c. I would be glad if you would send me one, or procure me a copy & let me

---

[58]See above, III, 81n.
[59]See above, III, 387n.

know the price & I will remit the amt. to you on its reception.
The Oregon question is discussed very fully & sapiently by our
Loco-foco fire eaters hereabouts, but there is an evident wincing
under the developments made by the corespondence between
our valiant Secretary of State & the British Minister published
by the House They claim the Resolutions passed by the House
as carrying out the views of the President, which of course *they*
do not believe I think so far as I can understand; Public sentiment in our community is decidedly opposed to war & in favor
of fair honest compromise Either by negotiation or arbitration
and unanimously condemn the course of Mr Polk on the subject. as you remarked the other day if the people had confidence
in those who had charge of the negotiation they would rest
satisfied let the issue be what it may, but those who aided to
elevate him & especially those who know him best have no
confidence either in his honesty his firmness or his patriotism
& I see some of the Northern Papers, (the Journal of Commerce
for instance) have confessed it. Of course the leaders here who
get their cue from the standard Union &c are obliged to believe & think & talk as they are ordered to do by their mas-
ters

The Party have not yet brot out their candidate for Govr.
since Green W Caldwell did not prove to be as *green* & *verdant*
as Wheeler supposed him. I understand he tried to be nominated
for Govr himself[60] indeed a Democrat informed me that he
wrote to some of the leading Democrats in the state soliciting
their influence in his favor before the convention & when he
found it was no go, he made a virtue of necessity & came out in
the Standard with great self sacrifice & refused to have his
name brot before the Convention

If we get up a *big* barbecue in our county will you come
to it this summer? it will be given with especial view to your
benefit & approbatory of your course in Congress If there is
any way to fix it I will send you a vote from Franklin we have
done such things notwithstanding there are just 2 to 1 against
us. Any thing that I can do, you know I will do for your success, & I have the consolation to know that in none of our reverses could I reproach myself after it was over for not having

[60]The *Raleigh Register*, March 6, 1846, stated that after Caldwell declined the nomination, the Democrats had trouble finding a candidate. "McKay did not want it. Saunders had been appointed as minister to Spain. Col. Wheeler's alarm lest he might be made Governor 'before he could get there,' was soon removed, as nobody seconded the motion." He refers to John H. Wheeler.

done all I could to advance the good cause If you have anything that can be used to our advantage in any way send them & I will send you the amt.

Success to our cause
your Respectfully
DANL. S. HILL

[Addressed:]

Hon. Willie P. Mangum
U. S. Senate
Washington City.

WPM-LC

Washington Hunt to Willie P. Mangum.

Feb 23 1846

My dear Sir.

This picture has been sent to me by the Editor of the Whig Review, and he desires some of your friends to give an opinion of its merit. In the main I think it a capital likeness.[61] If I were disposed to find fault, I would object to the stern solemnity of expression. But this gravity is dignified and Senatorial, and I have seen you wear that serious look on many occasions. I think this must have been taken after the election of 1844, when your mind was sorrowful in contemplation of the degeneracy of the times, and the doubtful future on which we were about to enter. Yet it is evident that you did not "despair of the Republic."

I have conversed with Gov. Morehead who will prepare a sketch of your Life & Character in time for the April number of the Review. He takes up the subject *con amore* and no man can do it better justice.

In haste, dear sir,
Yours truly
W. HUNT

Hon. Willie P. Mangum

---

[61]The portrait of Mangum was a daguerreotype by Anthony, Clark & Co., engraved in mezzotint by T. Doney and published in the *American Review*, 1846, and later reproduced in the *Portraits of United States Senators, with a Biographical Sketch of Each.*, Claremont, N. H., 1856.

WPM-LC

J. Watson Webb to Willie P. Mangum.

[25 Feb. 1846]

My Dear Mangum

You know all about our Yacht bill. It is out of position in the House, & I have written to Butler King, to see you & get it started in the Senate. For my sake, & to save the friendship of two hundred gentlemen who will *talk* & *act* as we desire, I entreat of you to bring it forward in the Senate & push it through. *You* can do it, & to *you* shall be the glory.

Ever yours
J. WATSON WEBB
Tuesday night.

Hon. W. P. Mangum

P.S.

Have I not given C.[62] & his friends a dose *this time?*

[Addressed:]

W. P. Mangum
Senate U. S.
Washington City.

[Postmarked:]
New York, Feb. 25.

WPM-LC

William B. Lewis[63] to Willie P. Mangum.

WASHINGTON D. C.
Feb. 27th 1846.

Sir

The members of "The Cambrian Benevolent Society" of this city having been given to understand that you are of Welsh descent,[64] have instructed me to request the honor of your com-

----

[62]He probably refers to Calhoun.
[63]He ran a clothing store in Washington at this time. *The Waashington Directory and National Register* for 1846, published by Gaither & Addison, Washington, 1846, p. 57.
[64]See above, I, 84n.

pany at their Festival in honor of St. David to be held on Monday 2d day of March next—

The Society will assemble at the store of Messrs Owen, Evans & Co at 6 o'clock P.M. and will from thence repair to the Swan dining rooms, near the residence of John C. Rives Esqr.

Very respectfully
Your obt. St
WILLIAM B. LEWIS
Corresponding Secy.

Hon. W. P. Mangum
   U. S. Senate—

[Addressed:]

Hon. W. P. Mangum
U. S. Senate.

WPM-LC

Henry W. Moncure et als. to Willie P. Mangum[65]

RICHMOND, 4th March, 1846.

Dear Sir,

You have already been made acquainted, through the medium of the public press, with the death, so sudden, sad and tragical, of JOHN HAMPDEN PLEASANTS.

We desire not to enter into any particulars connected with this melancholoy event. It is sufficient to say, that Mr. Pleasants fell a victim to the merciless requirements of a code of honor, which, false as it is, has yet the powerful sanction of public opinion, and of the society in which our fallen friend was born and reared. Yet it is but justice to his memory to say, that he went upon the field with no desire to take his adversary's life; that, in his last moments, he declared that previously to the combat he had extracted the ball from his pistol

---

[65]This is a printed circular letter set in heavy mourning borders. Thomas Ritchie, Jr., editor of the Richmond *Enquirer*, accused Pleasants of abolitionist leanings. A duel followed, and Pleasants was killed. *D. A. B.*, XV, 8.

to lessen the chances of a fatal result, and that his only object in the encounter, was to repel the imputation which had been cast upon his courage. Such a course, extraordinary as it appears, was only in keeping with the lofty magnanimity and forgetfulness of self, which had ever been a distinguishing characteristic of one of the most chivalrous and magnanimous spirits of the age.

You, Sir, are familiar with the public course of John H. Pleasants for the last twenty-five years. The founder of the Richmond Whig, the gallant champion of our political principles, the man whose splendid genius commanded alike the admiration of friends and foes, it is unnecessary that we speak with minuteness of his political history to any one acquainted with the affairs of Virginia. But it may not be so generally known, that an interesting family were entirely dependent upon the labors of his mind, and that this sudden and appalling bereavement has left an aged mother and two young and promising children unprotected and destitute.

To that mother, to those children, his last thoughts were given. Expressions of love and gratitude to her who gave him birth, exhortations to his children to pursue the path of virtue, honesty and truth, fell from his dying lips. Shall we not receive the mother and the children as a precious legacy? Shall we not seize with eagerness an opportunity to manifest our gratitude, for the illustrious services of the deceased, and our sympathy with the surviving members of his household?

The people of Richmond having commenced the good work of contributing to the relief of this destitute family, appeal to you, Sir, (as an old and tried friend of the cause to which the whole life and brilliant powers of Mr. Pleasants were devoted,) to give your generous aid; and, as a friend of humanity, to visit with your bounty the widowed mother and orphan children of a man whose own heart was ever open as the day to the call of charity, and to whom the children of affliction and want never appealed in vain.

Contributions may be forwarded to either of the subscribers, trustees appointed to receive the same.

Respectfully,

HENRY W. MONCURE,
HENRY LUDLAM,
JOSHUA J. FRY.

[Addressed:]

Hon Willie P. Mangum
U. S. S.
Washington City
D. C.

WPM-LC

Samuel F. Man[66] to Willie P. Mangum.

PROVIDENCE 14th. March '46

Hon. W. P Mangum.

Dear Sir

The "law and order" leaders[67] in this State have spared no pains to impress the public mind with the belief that Senator Simmons, *as a whig,* has lost cast with whig Senators. They assert, that it is a subject of general remark, as well as deep regret, amongst *Whigs* in Washington, that Mr. Simmons should have so conducted, as to have forfeited the good opinion of his Senatorial brethren.[68]

They allude to his vote upon Allens resolution as the act, which has strengthend, what before was rather impression, as to his defection.

Please, per return post, if it comports with your feelings, state Mr. Simmons' standing - and particularly as a firm & unflinching whig, and whether any vote or act has in the least impaired confidence in him in this respect

Very truly & respectfully
Your obt. Servant.

SAML. F MAN

---

[66]A student at Brown University in 1812-1813, he became a Whig and in 1844 he was vice-president of the national Whig convention, which met in Baltimore. *Niles' Register,* LXVI, 147; *Historical Catalogue of Brown University, 1764-1904,* Providence, 1905, 599.
[67]See below S. F. Man to W. P. Mangum, March 17 and 21, 1846.
[68]See below S. F. Man to W. P. Mangum, March 17 and 21, 1846.

P.S. Please say how far I may use yr reply - Shall I publish it? Please direct to Providence.

[Addressed:]

Honr. Willie P Mangum
U. S. Senate
Washington
D C.

WPM-LC

Willie P. Mangum to Charity A. Mangum

Monday evening.
WASHINGTON CITY, 16th. March 1846

My dear Love.

Two or three days ago, I received a very pretty letter from our dear daughter Sally, and a day or two after I recd. one from you, saying, Sally would write the next week. - I don't know how it came about; but I was greatly gratified to hear that Sally was improving, that the rest of the family were well. - I have not written because I intended to be at Hillsbor°. Supr. Court, if the state of the business before Congress had admitted of it.—

It did not, however—& yet I intend God willing, to go home in the month of April & stay a week. - From present appearances, the session may run, until late in the Summer.—

As to Polly's roses, I intended to carry them home. - That failing, I thought it best not to send them, unless by some safe hand, & none such offered, - because they might be a month on the road, & perhaps never get home.—

Tell the girls they must lay out their own borders & beds, & let us see how much taste they have. - I have a great many seeds that [I will] try to get off tomorrow by the mail.—

I hear that some movement has been made [the o]bject of which is to deprive Mr. Piper of his school.-[69] I am sorry to hear of it.- It is unpleasant to have to interfere in such matters, as the selfishness of people, will neither view, such interference with justice, nor listen to reason, & will think every thing of the

---

[69]See above, 308.

sort an evidence of unfriendliness.- I certainly have no such motive nor object, yet I wish William to go to school to one *Competent* to *teach* and *manage* him.- Davis Hester cannot be fit for either the *one* or the *other*.- I fear Meekins and Col. Mangum[70] have failed to use the influence & energy which was due to the subject & the neighborhood.- I do not understand what is either *done* or *intended*.- Talk to Mr. Piper on the subject & ask him to write to me.-

I desire him to make a school & will subscribe $50. rather than be without a good School.—

At the same time that I will do this- I wish to do it, in a way, to give as little offence as possible. -

Tell my boy that I hope he learns his book well, & say to Mr Piper & to him, that I think he ought to begin to use the pen- to make letters & to write a little- It would amuse him, & he would not only be not kept too closely to his book, but would learn to use the pen & to write, just as well as if he were further advanced.- At his age, he ought to be taught *how to hold a pen*, & to use it.- Shew this to Mr Piper.-

I hope our daughters Patty & Mary not only attend to their books, &C. but that they also work & go in the open air enough to promote health.

I have generally been well, until within the last two weeks- I have had cold but am now nearly well.-

I hope to see you in a Month. In the meantime give my love to the Children, & say, that I very much desire to see you all.—

I trust my Love, that you are well and cheerful.- You must think of me often & Kindly, & with the assurance of my ever constant love

& all the regards of an

Affectionate husband

WILLIE P. MANGUM

To Mrs. C. A. Mangum-

---

[70]Meekins Mangum and Ellison G. Mangum, cousins of Willie P. Mangum.

WPM-LC

Samuel F. Man to Willie P. Mangum.

PROVIDENCE. 17th March. 1846

My Dear Sir

Your very acceptable letter of the 14th inst[71] is before me. The flattering exordium, is highly appreciated and be assured, Sir, that the remembrance of the social enjoyment, that I experienced during my visit in Washington in your society, has made an indelible impression on my mind, which I shall cherish whilst memory lasts; the reccollection of it is amongst the most pleasing incidents of my life.

There is a fierce political contest before us in this State. I am engaged in it to the extent of my power. For I deem the continuance of the Law and Order party's ascendancy, a fatal blow, to our prospects as *whigs.* That organization is thoroughly hostile to the formation of a whig party here, which by its insidious wounds has been prostrate ever since its organization. Indeed in their selections for office, even in our National Counsels, whig. democrat or trimmer, all stand upon a level- the only test is, fidelity to Law & order dictation, and the most subservient is the most eligible. With such a party I cannot harmonize, my whig principles forbid. If you have received a pamphlet, which reflects upon Mr. Simmons honor, the act has not been committed by him in our State, which will justify the charge. I have been intimate with Mr Simmons for *thirty years,* and the first dishonorable act as a politician or a man is unknown to me.

The opposition to Mr. Simmons does not proceed from his recent course in advocating the release of Dorr.- *this* is made the occasion to gratify an old grudge, and break him down; for this purpose is the Law & order party continued- *this* it is which gives it vitality. The men engaged in the work, are trimmers of the true Tyler stamp and Mr. Simmon's straight forward and independent course does not square with their diplomacy.

---

[71]See above, S. F. Man to W. P. Mangum, March 14, 1846.

I did myself the pleasure to address you a few days since, making enquiries of you as to Mr. Simmon's standing, which you have anticipated.

But if any thing further occurs to you. & particularly as to his vote upon ALLen's resolutions which affects him as a whig, it would afford me great additional pleasure to receive it.

I troubled Gov. Woodbridge- Senator Jarnigan and Gov Morehead, by the same mail. You ask "And yet where shall the man be found who shall charge him with delinquency?" It is upon this very point, that the Law and order men are making head way against him. They assert, and several of them have recently returned from Washington, indeed the story is common throughout our state, that Mr. Simmons has lost his standing in Washington as a *whig*. with *whig* Senators; And that consequently he has greatly impaired his usefullness in his present position.

I have ventured to brand the story, as false, but as they have just returned they claim to know, better than myself, and it was on this account, that I took the liberty to write you. A leading article in the National Intelligencer would place this thing beyond a question, for no whig in this State gainsays what appears in that Journal.

I know not how the thing can be accomplished but it would be of inestimable service to the friends of Mr. Simmons. I have ventured to suggest it, in the hope, perhaps presumptuous, that a thing can be brought about.

The money power of the State is against Mr. Simmons. His political opponents, are nondescripts, who are on any side for power.

What talent- and money- and will can do, will be done against him. Social, political- pecuniary and business relations are all brought to bear, backed up with a very influential and somewhat talented press, Pardon me for repeating, that if any thing occurs to you which will aid us in our labors, which are truly Herculean in this contest for Mr. Simmons, I flatter myself that you will communicate it.

With my thanks for your kind and timely letter, and the assurances of my high regard.

> I am dear Sir Your much
> Obliged and Obt. Sevt.
> SAMUEL F MAN

To Hon.
Willie P Mangum.
Washington

P S. Would you permit the publication of your letter.

> S. F M.

WPM-LC

J. B. Mower to Willie P. Mangum.

NEW YORK 20th March 1846.

My dear Sir

I congratulate you most grave, respected, and respectable Senator, on the prospect, of a speedy and honorable adjustment of that worn out name, Oregon. That small person, who fills & so fills, so large a place, rode in, on the Texas horse, and will gallop out, on the Oregon, on the very hobby, that promised so much good Capital, to this administration.

Is it not Sir, a very important affair, that this country, has got such a body, as is known to the Government, by the name of the *Senate,* 52 or 54 Senators, all, all, [sic] Honorable men, it is most devoutly, to be hoped-[72]

Where would we be, just now, without such an anchor? Since my return home, I have called, on several prominent men of the Whig party, & some *old fashioned Republicans* like myself. I found, every one, very kindly disposed, towards the judge,[73] the most influential person of all, without my saying one word,

---

[72]At this time many Senate leaders were trying to check the warlike moves of the administration forces on the Oregon question.
[73]Judge John McLean, the perennial candidate.

for any candidate, declared off handed, for the judge, as the
safest, strongest the very best candidate, for the Whigs to rally
on in 48. He deplored the idea of bringing the General[74] out,
as ruinous in the highest degree, to the Whig cause. He was
decidedly & firmly opposed to that move. And Sir when you
come to look at the question, as it must shortly present itself
to you; And if the Whigs avail themselves, of the event that
will most assuredly, cast their shades before them. The Candidate, of the Executive, must come from a *non* slave holding
state, and the Vice President, from a slave one. You are aware,
I presume Sir, that we are to have, a state Convention,[75] to alter
our Constitution. And it is considered, that the old party ties,
will be severed, that Western New York, will be Whig and
abolition, this union, will control, the balance of power, and
make New York, a whig state.

These fanatic abolitionists will support the judge, but they
will not go for the General. You must look at men, and things,
as you find them. I am stronger in my opinions, since my return, from seeing, reading and hearing, what passes every day,
before me. And if the Whigs will only act, with common prudence, sagacity, and honesty, the road is clear, for a most splendid triumph.

The tongue of slander, hath not, nor never can, assail him.
His character, is without a blot upon it. Look at him, I repeat
again to you Sir, at the Head, of that most vexatious, and per-
plexing, departments of the Government, the General P. O. and
behold him, coming out of it, with a solid, and healthful popularity; such as no one, ever enjoyed before, or perhaps, ever
will again.

Then Sir, I ask you, if he was so successful, in this most difficult of offices, coming out of it, as he actually did, with such,
an abiding popularity, how can he, but excel, in this, his new
position, surrounded, as he would, most certainly be, by such a
Galaxy, of kindred- spirits, as yourself, J. M. Clayton, W. C.

---

[74]General Winfield Scott.
[75]The state constitutional convention of New York convened on June 1, 1846, and remained in
session until October 9, 1846. The changes were in keeping with the trends of the day. The number of elective officers was increased, the system of representation was altered so that members of the
upper and lower house were elected by single districts. Jabez D. Hammond, *Political History of the
State of New York*, III, 609-670.

Rives & others, of the like stamp- away with doubt,—away with fear—you must triumph, you will prevail.

I am my dear Sir,
most truly
Your friend
J. B. MOWER.

Hon. Willie P. Mangum
U. S. Senate,
Washington.

[Addressed:]

Hon. Willie P. Mangum
U. S. Senate
Washington

WPM-LC

Saml. F. Man to Willie P. Mangum.[76]

EARLS HOTEL. PROVIDENCE 21. Mar. '46

My Dear Sir

Yours of the 14th is just at hand. I feel most thankful, for the free use which you permit of what you have written as spoken on the subject of Mr. Simmon's standing. But so far as you have expressed yourself to the Editor of the Journal, we may rest assured, nothing of it will appear in *his* columns, *His* is the organ of Law & order, and *the* great object of that party particularly the leaders, is to break down Simmons

Our friends are ignorant of what "pamphlet" you have received by mail breathing a spirit of bitterness against him. We know of but *one* pamphlet which is in print, and that is from the pen of Dexter Randall Esqr. an old and bitter locofoco; but it dropped "still-born" If you have received any other pamphlets, it would be very acceptable, If you would forward it strongly envelloped, you would confer a great favor, *or* if it is Randall's. please say so - but we do *not* wish a copy.

We think that we have passed the Rubicon, for we have formed and published a strong whig ticket of thirteen representatives from this city. The success of this ticket determines the reelection of Mr. Simmons.

[76]See above, S. F. Man to W. P. Mangum, March 14, 17, 1846.

It's is almost, if not quite certain, if the candidates are bullet proof- but we cannot overlook the fact, as was significant and with an air of triumph thrown into our teeth by a Law & order man this morning on the appearance of the ticket, that "we should remember that the whole money power of the city will be brought against us"! This is true, they have & every effort will be made to *crush* the candidates.

Time alone, will determine with what success.

Other than this, there is no danger, our course is clear and our haven near

Very truly yours. with great respect.

SAML. F MAN

To . Hon¹
Willie P Mangum
Washington

WPM-LC

William Albright[77] to Willie P. Mangum.

SANDY GROVE N. C. 21st March 1846

Hon. Wilie P. Mangum

My Dear Sir

I take pen in hand to inform you that we are in reasonable Health & hope these will find you in the enjoyment of the same

My further object is to ask you to forward to me if you have it in your power Secretary Walkers Report,[78] and other documents that might be of use to us in the Next Campaign. I have not Recd the first Document or other paper during this Session from any member of Congress, nor has there been the first one sent to this office for any person. you will please also, if convenient, to send such documents to Daniel Hackney.[79] St. Lawrence P.O. Chatham County N. C he will probably be one of our candidates for the County. I think it stands our Whig friends in hand to distribute information as much as they possibly can, between now and the Next Election. The Locos are

---

[77]See above, II, 278n.
[78]Robert J. Walker's report as Secretary of Treasury in December, 1845.
[79]Daniel Hackney, of Chatham County, was a delegate to the state Whig convention which met in Raleigh in January, 1846. *Hillsborough Recorder*, January 22, 1846.

determined to take the State & Elect a Loco Senator next session, Should the Tariff be altered I want a Copy of the new act. I write in haste, the mail is coming.

Very Respectfully yours
WM. ALBRIGHT.

My Respects to
Genl. Dockery.

[Addressed:]

Hon. Wilie P. Mangum
Washington City
D. C.

WPM-LC

John G. Roulhac[80] to Willie P. Mangum.

MARIANNA FLO. 21 March 1846

Mr. W. P. Mangum

Dear Sir

Since the House of Representatives gave the Seat of Mr. Cabell[81] to Mr Brockenbrough this part of the State has been left to the tender Care of the Loco Focos to supply us with documents which they have used well in Loading the mail with speechs essays &c &c none have supplyed the wants of the Whigs.

An exciting canvass for the seat in the next House of Representatives is about to commence in the State and we are very much in want of the aid of Documents speechs &c &c to use during the summer that we may be enabled again to return a Whig to the House. An occasional supply from you & such other members of either House of such as you may have to spare would give pleasure & be of great service in this County & probably in most of the others in the State.

---

[80]John Gray Roulhac, 1797-1858, graduated from the University of North Carolina with high distinction at the early age of fourteen. In 1846 he moved to Florida, where he became a planter. Grant, *Alumni Hist. of U. N. C.*, 536; Helen M. Prescott, *Genealogist Memoirs of the Roulhac Family in America*, Atlanta, 1894, 64.
[81]Edward Carrington Cabell was a representative from Florida from October 6, 1845 to January 24, 1846, when he was replaced in a contested election by his Democratic opponent, William Henry Brockenbrough, who served until March 3, 1847. Cabell, a Whig, served again from 1847 to 1853. *Biog. Dir. of Cong.*, 739, 773.

I know you have a large constituency to supply, yet hope you may have some to spare for us. Almost the entire population of this County are North Carolinians & would much prefer to receive favours of this kind from the Representatives of their Mother State than from others—

I have enclosed you a list[82] of a number in & about town should you have time & opportunity to supply them with such things as may be useful in the approaching Canvass.

Should you wish it I can supply you with names & Post offices in some of the adjoining Counties.

I am very respectfully
Yr M O Sert

JNO G. ROULHAC

[Addressed:]

> Hon. Willie P. Mangum
> U. S. Senate
> Washington
> D. C.

WPM-LC

George C. Collins[83] to Willie P. Mangum.

PHILADELPHIA March 24th. 1846.

Hon: Sir.

I ought to have long since congratulated you on the noble effort made by you in the Senate Chamber relative to the Oregon Territory. I take this opportunity of doing so from the bottom of my heart. Nothing would afford me greater pleasure than to contribute my mite towards placing you before this Republic as the next Whig Candidate for the *Presidency,* and I am happy to say that I am not alone in this matter. I have lately been to Harrisburg and other surrounding towns delivering Lectures in order to defray my expenses whilst pursuing the study of the Law in the office of Josiah Randall Esq. of this City. And I discovered that your name stood prominent for that high office. A great majority of the people are in favor of

---

[82]This list is not in the Mangum Papers.
[83]See above, 25n.

our claim to the whole of Oregon. I would not suggest a thing
to a Senator, unless I felt a deep and profound regard for his
welfare. Let me then say with great humility and with a due
sense of my uttter worthlessness, when placed near you in the
scale of comparisons. *"Vote for the Notice."* The masses are
alive to that question. I shall never forget your kindness towards me, perhaps the day might come, when I shall have it in
my power to render you some service. I only expect the arrival of that happy moment.

I observe a likeness of you in this month's "American Review," which is pronounced by the publisher a *"fine likeness."*
I hope you will excuse me for my freedom, when I say I think
it is a *poor likeness.* Painters generally flatter the original,
but in this case, the artist has fallen far short of doing you justice - *"Sat dictum est"*

Since the defeat of Mr. Clay, I have had many, yea un-
exampled difficulties, wherewith to contend. I had only $200
saved, after the sale of my furniture in Washington. Mr. Randall threw open his office to me gratis, and I embarked in the
study of Law with a wife and 4 small children and $200 in
Cash. I have now spent 16 mos. and there remain but 8. When
I trust I shall be admitted. Alfred du Pont of Delaware sent me
$400 to assist me, and I earned about $600 which have enabled
me with great self-denial to pass so far on my journey. I propose delivering another Lecture in the Museum of this city on
Thursday Evening next on Christopher Columbus. I have already recd. from there many favors, but I know I may with
confidence expect a little assistance from you, say $5 or $10 by
the return mail. I shall give my countrymen and others tickets
for the Amount, and in the mean time shall never fail to regard
the generous Senator from N. C. in whom I more than once
found a friend, with sentiments of devoted attachment.

> Believe me Hon. Sir
> I am your Obt. Servt.
> And ever devoted friend
> GEO: C. COLLINS.

Hon. Willie P. Mangum
Senator from N. C.

WPM-LC

"A True Whig" to Willie P. Mangum.

PROVIDENCE March 26. 1846

Hon Willie P. Mangum

Dear Sir.

I deem it necessary to address you at this time on a subject which to the people of R. I is one of momentous importance, and as you are *somewhat* implicated I trust you will feel some little degree of interest in what I may say. Mr Simmons has within a few weeks been in our state *electioneering,* and purports (as I no doubt he has) to have brought letters from you, stating that you have the fullest confidence in him as a *"Whig,"* and also that the present Law and Order party of this state, ought to be broken up, and the parties fall back as they were before our troubles with T. W. Dorr.[84]

You cannot, nor can any one unless they have lived or been among us some little time. know the state of things in our state. We are on the eve of an election which our best and ablest men think to be, one, if not the *most* important of any that ever occurred in our state. the Dorrites are the same that they ever were and if they get the power. would carry out all their plans. and in my opinion sap the foundation of our country. but let me say and perhaps I ought to have said it in the commencement. what part Mr. Simmons our present senator has taken in this election. Where was James F. Simmons during the Dorrite troubles in this state, was he shoulder to shoulder as he ought to have been with his fellow citizens. willing if need be die in defence of our institutions. our hearth sides and all that was dear to us; No; he was where nothing would trouble him, and where he at least was secure from any harm that might happen to any of us who were defending ourselves from a band of ruffians willing to do anything if they could but carry out their designs.

Did not the Law and Order party. or in other words the Conservative party of this state beat them at the ballot box and with the bayonet; and think you that they will now sit down and suffer themselves to be governed by such a set of

---

[84]See above, III, 335; IV, 405.

rascals. without first exerting all their powers to defeat them as in 1842; if you would come to R I I am satisfied you would not say the Law and Order party, ought to be abandoned. the party is composed of Whigs and Democrats, but I will guarrantee to say seven eighths of them are Whigs. *true Whigs*. and I trust and I *know* Mr Mangum is one of this same kind of Law and Order Whigs. but what I wished in particular to call your attention to in this letter is. the part James F. Simmons has taken in order to secure his re-election to the U. S. Senate. far be it from me to say anything which will injure Mr Simmons in any way. but when I see him doing as he is *now* doing. I cannot and I will not suffer his conduct to go unrebuked. I have the greatest respect for his talents. and heaven knows I would not injure him in the least. last Spring just before our election Mr Simmons came out without consulting any of his friends who had always supported him. and who always would have done so. formed an alliance with Chas. Jackson our present govenr and went over with the Dorrites. he publicly addressed them in this city. and urged them to use all means in their power. to elect Jackson as Gov over Fenner[85] the then incumbent. he did this without consulting any of his former Whig friends. he had as he has since said thought *"his* party was not strong enough to re-elect him" and so he went over to the Dorrites. who as you very well know. are the very worst of Democrats. real Jacobins. Mr Jackson was elected Gov. the only man on their prox. This spring Mr Simmons has left his seat in the U. S. Senate. where his services are greatly needed. has come to R. I. stationed himself at one of the public houses of this city. and has been making a Prox for Representatives to our State legislature for the city of Providence. when he is a native of Johnston. has gone over entirely to the Loco Foco's. and there is not a Dorrite. or a Loco Foco in the State but what will vote for him. he has succeeded in getting 12 so called *Whig* representatives from this city to stand as candidates to the legislature to be supported by the Dorrites. and if he goes to the U. S. Senate another Six years. he goes there as a Loco Foco. Dorrite Senator.

I cannot think Mr Mangum would uphold Mr Simmons in this act of his. he has been guilty of so base conduct. as to

---

[85]James Fenner was governor of Rhode Island from 1843 to 1845. *Biog. Dir. of Cong.*, 1151.

merit the scorn of the whole whig party. I trust he will be defeated. there is not a Whig in the State. who is *really one*. that will [vote] for him. he has said *since* he went over to the Dorrites that if the Whigs would pledge themselves to support him, as Senator he would sink the Dorrites. where they never would be heard from again. think you the Whigs of R. I. will support such a man; if he can wear two faces at home. it is certainly not much to say he can wear them abroad.

let me assure you my dear sir. I love the Whig party and what is more I love my Country. I would spill my blood for her honor, and in her defence, but I cannot nay I will not uphold those men, who are willing to be anything provided they can have an office. if such men as Jas. F. Simmons were at the head of our government I fear we should soon go to ruin. I have written to you because you ought to know the whole facts in the case. I do not profess to understand letter writing. but I have deemed it important you should know all about this affair. I assure you I have the best wishes for the Whig party. and always mean. so long as it is, what it is now, to support it. but I cannot uphold Mr Simmons in this act of his merely to secure his seat in the Senate. If you wish to know more of the details of this matter Mr. Greene[86] our other Senator. I have no doubt would gladly inform you. With the best wishes for the Whig party and with a fervent desire to see Whig principles carried out. I remain with great respect, Your most Obt. Servant

"A TRUE WHIG"

Let me repeat what I have said. If Jas. F. Simmons goes to the Senate. another time he goes there supported by the Loco Focos.

[Addressed:] Hon. Willie P. Mangum

Washington. D. C.

---

[86]Albert Collins Greene, 1791-1863, served in the Senate from 1845 to 1851. *Biog. Dir. of Cong.*, 1032.

WPM-LC

D. Francis Bacon[87] to Willie P. Mangum

NEW YORK, March 28, 1846.

Dear Sir,

Arrangements have been made by a large and respectable Committee of the unchanged friends of Henry Clay, for a celebration of the birth-day of that patriotic statesman on the evening of Monday, April 13, by a grand festival at Niblo's Saloon. At a large meeting of that Committee on Thursday the 26th inst. a resolution was unanimously adopted inviting your attendance on that occasion, as the guest of the Committee; and the undersigned, Chairman of the Committee of Management, was instructed to urge this invitation most earnestly upon your notice, and to express the ardent wishes of a large body of the friends of Mr. Clay, for the gratification which would be afforded by your presence among them at the proposed entertainment.

In communicating to you this urgent request of my highly respectable and patriotic associates, I am but repeating the wishes which I have had occasion to express to you formerly at personal interviews. It is a long time since you have visited this great metropolis; and a renewal of your acquaintance with it, under auspices so favorable, must be productive of great enjoyment and benefit to yourself, as well as to the numerous friends whom you would find here.

I have observed, with great regrets, notices of a recent illness which you have suffered; but I have inferred that your indisposition was not so serious as to have materially impaired your strength, and trust that your convalescence has already proceeded so far as to make the brief ride to this city both easy and beneficial to you. I presume that it would contribute greatly to the perfect restoration of your health and to the refreshment of a mind tasked as yours has been with the peculiarly harrassing and momentous labors of the present Session.

I assure you that during the proposed visit, no demand shall be made upon you for any exertion incompatible with your health or feelings. Preparations will be made for your comfortable accommodation at a quiet and elegant Hotel up town;

---

[87]See below W. P. Mangum to D. Francis Bacon, April 10, 1846.

and the evening's entertainment will be altogether devoid of the crowd, noise and bad air of an ordinary meeting. The number of persons admitted is limited (by the size of the Saloon) to six hundred: the hours will be early,- the company good and orderly, and the whole entertainment neat and elegant in the extreme.

If you can arrange public engagements so as to leave Washington on Saturday, April 11, you will enjoy Sunday here as a day of rest, and will have Monday for visits and rides about the city as may suit your convenience; and if the emergencies of National Affairs should forbid a longer stay among us, you can be in Washington again on Tuesday evening, with the loss of only two days' attendance in the Senate.

The proposed celebration has no other objects than those which appear on the face of the plan. It is simply a grateful and cordial commemoration of the public services and manly worth of our much-wronged patriot-chief, designed to encourage half-despairing honesty here and every where, and to assure the world that though such a man may be cheated of the station which his capacity deserved, he retains a degree of popular affection and veneration, worth more to him than a whole lifetime in the Presidential office.

The invitations given by the Committee are very few,- limited to yourself and seven of your associates in the Senate, to the Representative of the Ashland District in the House, to the two Senatorial Electors on our Clay ticket in this State in 1844, and lastly Mr. Fillmore and Mr. Frelinghuysen.

Trusting that this communication may receive your most favorable consideration and that you may signify speedily your acceptance of the invitation, I am

Yours with great respect

D. FRANCIS BACON.

(at the "Carlton House"

New York city.)

Hon. Willie P. Mangum,
    in the
Senate of the United States.

WPM-LC

Wm. G. Webster to Willie P. Mangum.

NEW HAVEN CONN. Apr. 6. 1846

Sir,

In the *U. S. Album*,[88] the *arms* of N. Carolina are delineated without a *motto*. Will you do me the honor to inform [me] whether that State has no motto, or what it is?—

Pardon the liberty I have taken, & believe me Sir, with true respect, Yr Obedt. & humble Sert.

WM G. WEBSTER

Hon. Willie P. Mangum.
Senator.

[Addressed:]

Hon. Willie P. Mangum
Senator.
Washington City.
D. C.

WPM-LC

John Hogan[89] to Willie P. Mangum

Confidential

UTICA. N. YORK April 7th. 1846

My dear Sir

I hope you will excuse me in meddling or speaking in relation to the course & policy of the Whig party in this (N Y). State. Let me here say to you that from all that I can gather from Gent in your party in this state our friend Gen Scott will not be the perference of his party. *mark that.* of course I cannot speak further on that subject *I have only to say let Gent take care of themselves* as nothing appears more improper than a Gent belonging to an opposite party to interfere with a party

---

[88]*The United States Album, Embellished with the Arms of Each State and Other Appropriate Engravings, Containing the Autographs of the President and Cabinet, Twenty-Eight Congress, Supreme Court and Other Officers of Government.* Arranged and designed by J. Franklin Reigart, Lancaster City, Penna. 1844.

[89]A lawyer and land agent, he became quite prosperous after the Erie Canal was opened. Alexander C. Flick, *History of the State of New York*, New York, 1935, VII, 32.

to which he does not belong. but I suppose that it is not an unpardonable sin for one to express an opinion to a friend as I do in this case. The weather here is fine & vegetation on the movement & should we have no more snow or cold our crops will be good.

Since I left Washington my health has improved much. I hope in a few days to enjoy tolerable health. Now can you tell me what is to become of the Oregon question will you take a vote on it this week or will the discussion be put off. Did you make the call for my papers yet I hope so. I hope your health continues improving and that our mutual friend Gen Speights's[90] health will also improve.

I will write you again in a few days I send you some of our State papers. be good enough to say to Gen Speight that I will write him I hope you will both keep me advised as to the progress of Gen Cass & friend Allens[91] as to 54.40

>accept Sir my best wishes
>I remain your Obt-
>humble Servant
>JOHN HOGAN

Hon. W. P. Mangum

[Addressed:]

>Hon Willie P. Mangum
>Washington
>D. C.

---

[90]He refers to Jesse Speight, former Congressman from North Carolina and in 1846 Senator from Mississippi. *Biog. Dir. of Cong.*, 1553.
[91]William Allen, Democratic Senator from Ohio, was chairman of the Senate Committee on Foreign Relations.

WPM-LC

William H. Thomas[92] to Willie P. Mangum.

WASHINGTON CITY
April 8, 1846

Hon. W. P. Mangum
of the Senate.

Dear Sir.

The adverse report of the Committee on Indian Affairs, on my claims for furnishing Cherokee Indians in the years of 1836, & 38, having been adopted yesterday, allow me to ask of you the favor to obtain permission for me to withdraw the papers from the files of the Senate.[93]

I had supposed that upon the evidence I last forwarded to you not only of the supplies furnished but the services rendered my country no objections would have existed to the passage of a resolution authorizing the Secretary of War, to settle with me on the principles of equity and justice, for, provisions furnished the Indians or for my services, I did not suppose that it would have been considered necessary that I should sustain the loss of my time and then not be compensated for provisions furnished the Indians which became necessary in consequence of the means adopted to restore peace, but it seems the Senate have thought otherwise. I therefore desire my papers, to be returned.

With the highest respects
your obt servt
WM H. THOMAS

---

[92]A descendant of the Maryland Calverts and a relative of Zachary Taylor, Colonel William Holland Thomas became, at an early age, a merchant in the Cherokee country of North Carolina. From childhood a friend of the Cherokees, he was made a member of the tribe. As the Cherokees' business adviser, he spent much of his time in 1836-1841 and all in 1841-1848 in Washington working for the Cherokee claims. Upon his return to North Carolina, he was elected to the legislature and served until 1862. He supported the South in the Civil War. He was also largely responsible for building the Western North Carolina Railroad to Murphy. "Colonel William Holland Thomas" *The University of N. C. Magazine,* No. 5 (May, 1899), 291-295.

[93]June 12, 1846, Mangum introduced a joint resolution in the Senate for the relief of Thomas. *Cong. Globe,* 20 Cong., 1 sess., 965.

After the Cherokees decided to migrate to the West under the treaty of 1835, the eastern branch of the tribe obtained, through Thomas' aid, the right to remain in western North Carolina. Under the settlement Thomas was given, as the agent, their part of the money due for improvements. At various times until 1861 he bought up tracts on the Oconachee River in Swain and Jackson counties. Since the state refused to recognize Indians' right to own land, Thomas kept the titles in his own name. James Mooney, "Myths of the Cherokees," in *Nineteenth Annual Report of the Bureau of American Ethnology to the Secretary of the Smithsonian Institution, 1897-1898,* Washington, 1900, I, 157-159.

WPM-LC

Nicholas Carroll to Willie P. Mangum

Office of the Creton (Mutual) Insurance Co.
No. 35 WALL-ST., NEW YORK, April 8th 1846

To Hon Willie P. Mangum -

My dear Sir

Some days since I was informed that you had been invited by the Young Men to be here on the 13th.[94] of this month- to be their guest at a supper given in honor of Henry Clay. Some wiseacres have attempted to connect this honest expression of *personal* attachment with *ulterior political* views. I can assure you 'the movement' as they call it has nothing to do with the next Presidency. Whatever course the friends of Mr Clay may take with reference to that, you know them *well enough* to know that their action cannot be transmitted. If they *choose* to nominate him all the powers of earth & hell could not prevent them and if they have no such active idea at this time nothing half so sure to bring it forth as opposition- come the latter from whatever quarter it may. Denunciation, intimidation, meanance or threats will as sure, as there is a God in Heaven place Henry Clay in the field again with or without Regular Nomination & utterly regardless of his assent or dissent— Men cannot be dragooned like horses to wheel into or out of line at the word of command or tap of the drum—I have never met any class of men so hard to curb as the Young Men of New York, none so easy to direct, guide & lead by argument backed by kindness. Coax them and they can be moulded, so the request be reasonable & right- all the inmates of Pandemonium can not drive them. I believe the question of the next Presidency is yet to be determined. It is a thing of chance & conjecture and the result will be mainly reached through circumstance & that present design would be as brittle as pipe clay. "Enough for the day is the evil thereof."

You will I hope in no wise be guided in coming here or not coming by any remarks or assertions made by these 'would-be-conscience-keepers-of-the-Party.' They and their ordinary course is beneath contempt- We feel that their day has been & is past

---

[94]See above D. Francis Bacon to W. P. Mangum, March 28, 1846.

Paul Carrington Cameron, 1808-1891. Mangum was tutor of Paul Cameron while reading law under his father, Judge Duncan Cameron. From the oil portrait by William Garl Browne, painted in 1887, in the possession of the Dialectic Society at the University of North Carolina, Chapel Hill.

forever- Their power is gone and the 'Young Men' of New York are their own men- the instruments & tools of no faction- ready to do battle whenever 'the trumpet' calls them forth

For yourself personally & politically they have warm affection & regard, and being on the Com⁰. I know the feelings which induced them to ask you here- and they will regret that any circumstances should prevent your presence *here*- but they would be grieved indeed if any feeling on your part, that yourself & others were by your presence at a *personal* festival to be used for a *political* movement, should deter you from coming to New York & being in person & spirit present with them at the social Board

Faithfully
Yr friend & sert,
N. Carroll

WPM-LC

Louis Thompson⁹⁵ to Willie P. Mangum.

U. S. Frigate Potomac, Very Cruz, Mexico, April 9th 1846

Most Respected & esteemed Sir

Mr. Mangum

Once more I take the liberty of writing to you and hope that This may find you enjoying good health it may surprize you to find me writing so far out of the country in so short a time since I wrote you from New York although at the time I left New York, I was doing very well indeed and getting $25 per month. and was there in charge about eight months and part of the remaining four months I was in England and the old countrys Mr. Mangum. You will please excuse me for troubling you with this statement but I feel it a duty I owe you as you have always shown so much kindness towards me as well as to promote my welfare that I have resolved within myself. to communicate the same to you whereever I go or whatsomever my employment may be. I shall always write to you I hope you will grant me that permission.

⁹⁵See above, 37.

Capt. Aulick received orders for the Frigate potomac. and wrote to new york for me and I came Immediately on as far as Baltimore, and finding there was no conveyance from washington to norfolk. I taken the baltimore route to norfolk and arrived in norfolk on the day he appointed. My pay here is 24 dollars per month and out of that I have left enough sufficiently to school my children. the balance I believe I can save up to a dollar. Our cruze is said to be short about six or eight months. and by next winter I am in hopes to be in washington. please make my humble respects to Mr. Crittenden. Govr. Morehead. and Mr Barrow. as a token of my gratitude I should be much pleased if the Judge would be so kind as to forward my Mothers letters on to me that she may write to me and one line from the Judge. would afford me more pleasure than any thing else in the world. I have taken the liberty of enclosing a letter for my mother. therefore I feel myself under many obligations

With great respect Believe me dear Sir your devoted Servant

[Addressed:]   Louis Thompson.

Hon. Wilie P. Mangum   [Post marked:]
    U. S. Seante   Pensacola Apr 27
    Washington, Dist Columbia,
        U. States.

WPM-LC

Willie P. Mangum to D. Francis Bacon.[96]

Washington City 10th. April 1846.

My dear Sir.

I received in due course of mail, your letter inviting me to be present at a dinner to be given in your City by the friends of Mr. Clay in honor of the anniversary of his birthday, and as a testimonial of their abiding respect, & affection for that great & good man.— I had hoped that the condition of the public business before the Senate would admit of my availing myself of this occasion to visit your great City: & to meet a body of Whigs who

---

[96]This is a rough draft in Mangum's handwriting. It is a reply to D. Francis Bacon's letter to W. P. Mangum, March 28, 1846.

have not only deserved but commanded the respect of the whole Country.

Such however, is the important character of pending questions, that I dare not leave my post. I am constrained therefore to deny myself the pleasure of participating with the imperial guard of the Whig party, in testifying their respect for the man who above all others, has clustering around him the confidence & the affections of the intelligent & patriotic portions of his Countrymen & whose name & whose deeds will descend to posterity with a lustre neither enhanced nor diminished by the giving or the withholding of the first official station.— His history constitutes a large portion of our National renown enduring, ineffaceable, perpetual which as the tooth of time will spare, may defy the fangs & the poison of detraction & Calumny.—

Be pleased my dear Sir, to make known to those whom you represent my acknowledgements & my profound sense of the honor they have done me, & accept for yourself

the assurance of my high
respect & Mo. friendly regards
WILLIE P. MANGUM

To Dr. D. Francis Bacon.

———

WPM-LC

John Cameron[?][97] to Willie P. Mangum.

HILLSBORO: 23d April, 1846—

My dear Friend

After having jolted about from Pillar to post the major part of the winter, until I was thoroughly sick, sore, & sorry, at the bare idea of locomotives or locomotion, I have at length set seriously to work, to endeavour to effect what you so earnestly impressed & urged upon me last Fall; namely: the getting into my hands the means of circumventing the *Locofocos* & thereby securing to myself much personal emolument, & to the *Whigs great glory.*

———

[97]See above, III, 4n.

In other words I have made formal propositions to the controllers of the Whig press in Raleigh, agreeing for a reasonable number of half pence, by way of compensation, to do all the political drudgery, as well as take all the kicks, and cuffs, which make up the ordinary allowance of a political editor. So far the idea seems to take very well! Our friends so many as I have seen of them, seem pleased with the project, & flatter me, that although not of much value now, I will improve & in time both draw well & carry a gay head in the harness- I have written to Clingman & to Guion[98] in the western part of the State, requesting an expression of opinion from them as to the amount of encouragement likely to be obtained up there. It is necessary I find that we should have some data of the kind to be guided by, as the times are so hard, that otherwise the editorial gentlemen would not find it to their interest probably, to make such an offer, as could with prudence be accepted.

Graham *has given* to some extent, & promises his further aid, the active young whigs about Raleigh are clear for it! You must write to some of them & stir them up. get Barringer too to write to some of *his* leading friends & Dockery & James Graham, urging them on in the cause; & request them, if possible to obtain for me some estimate of the amount of additional aid to be procured in their respective districts, to a press in Raleigh, whose tone & temper may entitle it to be considered as the Organ of the Whig party. I have taken the liberty of using your name, as my friend & adviser; & in as much as at your instance I have aimed my head at the stone wall. I shall certainly expect your assistance either in getting through safely, or butting my brains out gallantly. The negotiation for the present is pending with Lemay,[99] though I believe *now,* it could be more favourably, & readily effected with Gales,[100] *"entre nous"*) & if it can be done, I think it would be better, in as much as it is easier certainly to increase the circulation of a paper already established, with a large patronage, than to give a *sufficient* circulation to one which has to be built up almost from the beginning.

My only difficulty now, in effecting an arrangement immediately, is the absence of any proof that the Whig party, as a

---

[98]He refers to Thomas L. Clingman and Haywood W. Guion.
[99]Thomas J. Lemay was editor of the Raleigh *Star* at this time.
[100]Weston R. Gales published the *Raleigh Register.*

party, will certainly take the matter in hand, & just as soon as I can obtain a sufficient expression of opinion from leading men in the State to establish that fact, I will have the matter going in less than a month.

I *know* there is great & general dissatisfaction throughout the State at the present State of affairs, nor do I flatter myself that the satisfaction would be any greater, Should I come into the administration, unless my own crude efforts be assisted from time to time, by the various talent with which the Whig party abounds. The main advantages which will accrue to *us* are these. In the first place there is nothing in the whole course of my career, upon which the enemy can lay hands, as an excuse for affecting to doubt the purity of my sentiments, or for attempting to invalidate the truth of my Statements. I have never been anything but a Whig! & I have only been before the public long enough, to make it perfectly apparent, that I was one without shadow of turning. Even Democrats have given me credit for being honest, & stating nothing but my real sentiments! So that if fairly upheld & put forward by the leaders of our party, the editorial columns of the journal, no matter by whom written out, would be subjects of *faith* to one side, & could only be effectually attacked by the other, in a fair & legitimate manner, as against an adversary of acknowledged candour, all shuffling, & rascality would only in the end recoil upon themselves, making their own men doubtful, & the winning[?] of ours firm.

In speaking to our friends in Washington, do not I pray, let your personal partiality induce you to draw such a picture of *my merits,* as will only lead to disappointment upon a personal interview. I am nothing you know but a good Whig, possessing but few qualifications, & rusty in the exercise of them devoted however to the cause, & ready if it is desired to bear its flag through good or evil report, from this time forth! The mail is about closing, & I must spur up my pen, which has been travelling already at such a rate, that I am afraid you will be unable to read. I wish you would write to Clingman & such others as you may think it expedient to address, also drop me a line expressive of your sentiments & so worded, that you would not be averse to its being shown to a few friends.

I suppose you have had news from Dial's Creek since I
have? Our friends here are all well, the Small Pox or whatever it was, is dying out; & all hands are revelling in the luxury
of nothing to do, & nothing to eat! I saw Graham a few days
ago he was in fine health & fine spirits. I am afraid however
if our friends are not more active, that he will be disappointed
as to the result in Orange. Old Allison & the Locos are working
the wires all the time in Secret, while *we* are *not certain* that
one of our men will run. I would be glad, Waddell would consent, though *I* cannot urge him knowing his situation. If *he* will
take the lead, the rest will all follow! Remember me to my
friend Jeames the President, & tell him if perfectly convenient
I will go as Minister to *Chaney* [*sic*] be Consul at Gibralter or
enact the part of *Great Plenipotentiary* at the Court of the *Grand
Turk.*

Present my regards to Barringer &c. & believe me ever

> Yrs. truly & sincerely
>
> J. CAM.
>
> [John Cameron?]

WPM-LC

A. H. Shepperd[101] to Willie P. Mangum.

GOOD SPRING Apl. 26, 1846

The Hon W P Mangum

Dear Sir

As my Representative is rather busy in attending to his
peculiar friends, may I ask the favour of you to procure and
send me the last compilation of the pension laws &c embracing
the decisions of the Commrs. & attorney Genl upon the various
questions that have arisen: such a compilation I perceive has
been published by order of Congress & many extra copies directed to be published. If you cannot procure a copy in the
Senate perhaps some friend in the House would oblige you.

How is the Chairman of the Committee on Foreign Relations?[102] Does he recognize & relish the *striking likeness* of him-

---

[101]See above, I, 16n.
[102]William Allen, of Ohio, a Democrat, was chairman of the Senate Committee on Foreign Affairs.

self which has been painted in such vivid & lasting colours by the Senator from Kentucky?— No news here & nothing do I ever hear except from the news papers from Washington. 1 suppose Graham can beat two Democrats, although one would I think be an overmatch for him— Is he not a singular standard bearer for the party that sustains the Tariff principles of the Act of 1842[103] - Why, I pray you has he never even offered an apology for his course in the Senate on the subject of the Tariff, I mean not his opposition to the law as it passed, that he has justified mainly on the ground that it *surrendered distribution,* yet who does not know that the bill vetoed by Tyler & which *preserved distribution* was the great Whig measure of the session- *This the Govr. also voted against.* Why I repeat has he never noticed in any way the reasons of his action on this bill?— He will have to do so in the coming campaign- Untill quite lately I thought of continuing in private life but recently I have thought seriously of becoming a candidate for the Genl. Assembly.—

> I am Dr. Sir
> Very respy
> Yrs A. H. SHEPPERD

Should you have a spare copy of your Speech would be glad to have it. A.H.S.

[Addressed:]

> To/
>
> The Hon. Willie P. Mangum
>
> Senate of the U. S.
>
> Washington
>
> D. C.

---

[103]W. A. Graham was opposed to protection, but for party reasons he gave lip service to the tariff. Statement of Dr. J. G. de R. Hamilton, University of North Carolina, who is editing the William A. Graham Papers. See also A. H. Shepperd to W. P. Mangum, May 20, 1846.

WPM-LC

L. D. Dewey[104] to Willie P. Mangum

NEW YORK April 27- 1846

Hon Senator Mangum,

Sir,

Permit me to renew a request made in a letter of
March 2ᵈ, that you would favor me with an "opinion" of the
importance of the bible and the Sabbath, to be published in
connection with the "Advice" of chief Justice Hale to his children and like opinions from other distinguished Americans, for
the benefit of our youth. The great influence which the eminence of their names will impart to such a work, makes it very
desirable to obtain such opinions, and I am happy to say that
already a hearty response with much commendation of the
plan has been received from very respectable sources. I express the more freely my wish and hope to receive a tribute to
so good an object from your pen. If your many duties will admit of bestowing but a few lines they will be greatly appreciated,
as they will have much influence. A few strong words, or
page or two of your warm testimony in favor of the virtue and
true honor which it is the design of the bible and the sabbath
to promote, will, thus sent forth, bear on the best interests of
our youth in our country for years and years to come.

If received in the course of May it will be in season.

Respectfully yours

L. D. DEWEY

WPM-LC

J. B. Mower to Willie P. Mangum.

NEW YORK 28th. April 1846.

My dear Sir

I congratulate you, your friends, and all the good people,
of the nation, that you have at last, settled this Oregon "foot-

---

[104]L. D. Dewey was a New York publisher who in 1831-1834 published the New York *Whig.*
Fox, *New York City Newspapers, 1820-1850,* 115.

ball," so far as the Senate, & House, are at present concerned.[105]
And now we shall see, what Mr. 54.40, one day, & 49.50, the
next, will say, or do.

Permit me Sir, to call your attention, one moment, to the
Sub Treasury,[106] which is about, to be fixed upon us. I beseech
you, to strive, to put off, the specie clause,[107] to the 1st. of July
1847, the one half of it. The other half, to the 1st of July 1848,
which will be only 4. months, before the Presidential election,
and then, if you don't lick, "the rascals, naked through the" nation, then, I can't see, one atom ahead. Provided always, you
take, that good & popular citizen, of Ohio, John McLean, for
your candidate. The Whigs, if they desire to gain the ascendancy, and keep it too, in the U. S. must either, change their
views, or their leaders,. For, where so many, emphatically
truisms, can be said, of such a distinguished man, as Henry
Clay; the rabble, the great mass, the floating, dirty, drunken
population, of this free country, will always have a thousand,
tens of thousand, falsehoods, and lies, to tell of this, and against
this, American orator, & statesman. The whigs generally, as a
party, rely too much, on the respectability of their candidates,
the intelligence of the people, and the justness of their cause,.
You had at the last election, all the elements of success, in your
own hands, but your people, were so cock sure, of triumphing,
that the voters, were *presumed to vote*, who never came to the
polls, but would come, had they been draged there, as the democrats, haul their creatures, to the hustings, on election days.
Bonaparte, never won a battle, by presumption. There is another
reason, why Mr. Clay, should not be the Whig Candidate, in 48.
having a view to success. It is predicted, by those who pretend
to know, that the abolition vote, in 48. will be nearly, or quite,
1/6th. of the whole electoral vote, of the U. States, say 45.
votes, that might defeat any Candidate, but more especially one,
from a slave state. Mr Calhouns friends here, are thinking, of
bringing him forward, as a candidate, but the same facts, stare

[105]On February 9, the House of Representatives passed the resolution authorizing the President
to " 'cause notice to be given' to Great Britain that the convention of 1827 would be abrogated at
the end of twelve months." The Senate changed it to authorize the President to give notice " 'at his
discretion.' " McCormac, *James K. Polk*, 592-600.

[106]In his message to Congress, December 2, 1845, Polk advocated the reestablishment of the
Independent Treasury which had been abolished in 1841 by the Whigs. Polk's supporter, Dromgoole,
of Virginia, introduced a bill on March 30, 1846, calling for building fireproof vaults for safe keeping of public money. Under the bill only specie would be accepted in payment of government obligations. With minor changes the bill passed the House April 2 and the Senate August 1. McCormac,
James K. Polk, 669-672.

[107]The Senate added a clause postponing for six months the proviso requiring payment of government obligations in specie. McCormac, *James K. Polk*, 672.

him in the face, as well as Mr. Clay. But Sir, just so sure, as your people bring out, fairly before the American people, Mr. McLean of Ohio, just so sure, your party, are in the ascendant and I know, he will have one of the most profound & respectable Cabinets, this nation ever had, I will not except, James Monroe's.

May you, and I, live to see this, & much more good, meeted out, to our great & growing country, and your health & happiness, in particular, shall be my constant & devout prayer.

Most truly your friend
J. B. MOWER

Hon. Willie P. Mangum
   U. S. Senate
     Washington

[Addressed:]

Hon. Willie P. Mangum
U. S. Senate
Washington,
D. C.

WPM-LC

John Cameron to Willie P. Mangum.

HILLSBORO: 7th. May 1846—

My dear Friend

Permit me to put my right foot foremost & return you my sincere thanks, with all the genuflexions of a truly oriental salaam, for that copy of Fremont, both on account of the work itself, & as evidence of your kind recollection. I wish it was in my power to send you something in the way of news or fun that would afford you half as much satisfaction, in return.

But the truth is that as far as incident is concerned a man had as well be shut up in an iron cage, or wander thro the alleys of some city of the dead, as frequent the promenades of our sombre little burg: The Small Pox has been declared "hors du combat," by the descendants of Dr. Hornbook, but though relieved from our apprehensions, we are not yet freed from the inconveniences, incident to a knowledge of its presence. The country folk are still too much alarmed to bring us in anything to eat, & in a general way.

Our only dependence to keep us all frisky,

Is Salt hog & turnip tops, washed down with whiskey.

So far as our county politics are concerned, we are still somewhat at a loss. All the Old Whig candidates will run again I think with the exception of Waddell, unless Pratt's[108] health should render it impossible for him to go through the fatigues of the campaign, in which case James Patterson is spoken of to fill his place. In the Senate it will be either Holt, Mebane or Faucett. I am sorry that Waddell can't make it convenient to run; as I should then look upon the Senate as certain, as even old Santa Ann acknowledged that they have no body to watch him, & his Superiority is so generally admitted, that I do not believe, that they could organise anything like an efficient opposition. With the others the thing is at least doubtful, though either of them, I think ought to beat Berry. The Locos will run Berry Sid, Smith Bill Patterson. Patterson McDade & somebody else I dont know who: McDade is spoken of as the most dangerous, as he is very popular at Chapel Hill & will very likely cripple our vote there a good deal as far as he himself is concerned, which with the party vote will probably put him ahead of the rest of his Squad. I can hardly think there is any danger to be apprehended from the rest, if our men will only exert themselves; but the Clerk's Office is doing its prittiest, & the wires of the Loco foco Telegraph have been vibrating for a week or two. Such a laying of heads together, such planning & arranging has not been seem for some time. They intend to carry the County if they possibly can, so as to have the call in the Selection of a member of Congress, which *distinguished position,* the present *Solicitor,* would have no objection to holding, as I am informed.

If he should cut Sid out, there will be heart burnings in the Wigwam certain. In the Sheriff's election Nichols[109] says that he

---

[108]In Orange the Whig candidate for the state senate was Hugh Waddell. Dr. M. W. Holt, Giles Mebane, C. F. Faucett, and John Leathers were the Whig candidates for the lower house. The Democrats nominated John Berry for the senate and William Patterson, H. McDade, Sidney Smith and William N. Pratt for the lower house. Waddell, Mebane, Faucett, Leathers and Sidney Smith were elected. *Raleigh Register,* June 2, 1846; *Hillsborough Recorder,* June 4, August 13, 1846.

[109]For sheriff of Orange County, the Democrats nominated James C. Turrentine and the Whigs Richeson Nichols. Turrentine was elected. *Hillsborough Recorder,* August 13, 1846.

certainly will be elected though I believe he is the only one who is satisfied of the fact.

It will be a fair race between them, Nichols pledging himself to withdraw the minute a Loco foco takes the field. Our friends are all well! Your Nephew Wm.[110] is about to take a wife tis said, from our Judge Bailey's family; though when the affair is to come off is not known.

He has bought the carriage & horses, & the sugar plums so I suppose it cant be many months off. Perhaps you may go home in time for the frolic.

Poor fellow his lassie ought to be kind to him, for he was very much shocked at poor Mitchells death, to whom he was as much attached I believe as he could be to any one; & a little affection now, kindly displayed would go a great way with him. I have heard nothing from West or East yet, & Lemay I understand wont move until he has some inkling of what the harvest is to be:

Mrs. C- sends her respects & says that as we are a little nearer down town than we were, she hopes to have the pleasure of seeing you sometimes, when next you come among us. I suppose you received my letter by Robin Jones: Write me if you have leisure, & believe me ever

Yrs very truly
JNO. CAMERON

To
    Hon: W. P. Mangum.

Bring all the money home from Washington that you can, for scarcely[?] the cent is there here to be had.

WPM-LC

Willie P. Mangum to Charity A. Mangum

WASHINGTON CITY, 11th. May 1846.

My dear Love.

I have not written to you for a long time, as every week, I supposed, I would get off the next, for home—. And now I in-

----

[110]He refers to Mangum's nephew-in-law, William Cain, who married Sarah Jane Bailey, daughter of John L. Bailey, July 21, 1848. *Hillsborough Recorder*, July 23, 1848.

tend it, as soon as possible- for, from appearances, no correct notion can be formed, when we shall probably get away from this place.- We are getting into, or *have* got into, a War with Mexico - & I fear, that may bring War with G. Britain.

I know not what ought to be done with the administration- They deserve any & all sorts of punishment.

I have not enjoyed scarcely any health this Spring.- I was confined ten or twelve days with severe bilious fever, brought on by cold.- I have not been well since- I was confined in April.- To leave here for a fortnight would I think, be useful to me- I have received a letter from Sally- I will write to her.-

I have nothing to write, except to say, I am in ill health & spirits.-

I do not intend to come to Congress any longer than my term, even, if so long. Were it in my power to come by unanimous vote.

I hope to see you all soon.-

In the meantime, give my Love to the Children & believe me as ever

Your affectionate husband
W. P. Mangum.

I had hoped to leave here this Week. The news on Saturday night from the Mexican frontier make that impossible. & when - I cannot say—

W P. M.

Mrs. C. A. Mangum

WPM-LC

Elipht. Nott[111] to Willie P. Mangum.

Union College May 15th 1846.

Dear Sir

Having been somewhat conversant, from my position and occupation as a teacher and experimenter, with many of the improvements which have been introduced during the last half

------

[111]Eliphalet Nott, 1773-1866, a Presbyterian minister, was president of Union College in New York for sixty-two years. In addition to his work as a minister and college president, he made a number of inventions involving heat. *D. A. B.,* XIII, 580-581. This letter was L.S., not A.L.S.

century, and which have so greatly contributed to the multi-
plication of the Comforts, and the amelioration of the Condition
of the human race; and feeling a deep interest in whatever concerns the growth and glory of our own Country - I have thought
that perhaps I might be justified in addressing a few lines to
some of the leading members of Congress, in relation to a
Marine instrument recently introduced called the *"Sectional
Dock"* and which in my judgement is destined ultimately to
change the method of raising vessels not only, but also of laying
them up and repairing and launching them: And which, if
this be so deserves the attention of Congress especially during
a season when there is time and means for making such changes
and improvements in our Marine instruments as the advanced
state of science and practical skill may be found to call for.

It would not be easy without drawing nor is my purpose to
attempt to convey by letter an account of the instrument in
question - but by an expression of opinion to bespeak your attention to its merits, when the question of appropriations for
Dry Docks shall come before you - an instrument in the introduction of which every maratime nation has an interest- For
were the exposure of the hull of a vessell for inspection cleaning and repair, alone in question, the Sectional dock would, I
apprehend, on account of the diminished expense it occasions
as well as the increased Convenience and Safety it affords -
Supersede the use of each and all the other Docks hitherto
known to the public But there are other and very important
naval purposes to which this instrument may be successfully
applied - and this being the case it is very important at a time
like the present, that the attention of those charged with the
care of the public interests should be directed to an examination
of the question - and the object of this letter is to bespeak in
its behalf that attention - and this is done under a full belief of
its claim to superiority over every instrument of the kind
hitherto in use- And should it be so, your influence in favour
of its adoption will I doubt not be secured - and should it not
be so, it is not desired

It is because I have thought the public interest might be
materially promoted by inviting leading minds to an examination of the marine instrument in question - that I have taken

the liberty to do what might otherwise appear not only uncalled for but obtrusive

I have only to add that I am with Sentiments of respect & esteem

Yours &c.

ELIPHT. NOTT.

[Addressed:]

To the Honourable
Willie P. Mangum
U. S. Senator
Washington City
D. C.

WPM-LC

Fabius Stanly[112] to Willie P. Mangum.

NEW YORK

May 16 /46

Dear Sir

War has been declared. Our country will soon look to the actions of her officers. I have an innate feeling - long kept quiet - that desires duty fraught with difficulty, teeming with danger.

Experience assures me that I am calm and decisive in danger, competent in professional emergencies.

The time has arrived, when I hope, I can solicit your influence, as a Senator from N Carolina - to obtain for me a command will need no apology.

There will doubtless be many small vessels fitted out for the West Indies and the Pacific Ocean. I believe it my duty, as it is my highest ambition to command one of them.

I remain-

Your Obt'. Sert'.

FABIUS STANLY

Hon.

Judge Mangum.

---

[112]Unable to identify.

WPM-LC

A. H. Shepperd to Willie P. Mangum.

GOOD SPRING May 20 - 46

Hon. Willie P. Mangum.

My dear Sir

I have too long delayed tendering you my thanks for your prompt attention to my request for a Document, which I have received accompanied with Capt. Fremonts Book— This journal carries with it the strongest evidence of the truth of the narrative from the remarkable absence of all grouping of extraordinary & startling occurrences, & that too in the midst of a wilderness abounding with Mountains Indians & Buffaloes- Oh what a book a *real* Yankee would have made out of such a tromp- You speak of Candidates for the Presidency, for myself I am strongly inclined to go for Benton as the *best* man among *them*. No one of the Whig party can come it - & we must look amongst the enemy— If Scott would not straddle & swagger so much like a Virginian he might get along *tolerably* well, McLean's Methodistical cant might help him somewhat but really, My Dr. Sir what task or inclination can the Whigs have for success even if it were practicable with this that or the other make shift of a Candidate when by a fair experiment they have established the fact of the nations unwillingness to be governed by one, who was prepared to reflect the highest honor on that once most exalted station— I say again why should we think of a contest with such a candidate as we must now look about for among the whigs-

Let the thought be at once utterly abandoned & let us all unite for Benton. Calhoun is certainly doing his prettiest this session, now & then however, I find him splitting hairs about internal improvement, & on that subject he has dodged & bungled more than any other, *trying to get away from himself.*—

Your anticipation seems to be quickly realized for it seems that we are already at war with Mexico - what will Polk do? surely in the midst of all his apparent purposes of bravery in a fight with somebody he never could seriously have thought of doing so far I cannot be mistaken in believing that so great is the timidity of his character he would feel alarm for his personal safety if the seat of war was not [*sic*] nearer than Mexico.—

I regret having mentioned to you my apprehension as to the result of a single contest in our State for Governor: it would be truly mortifying to the whigs to fail in a single contest with either of the individuals spoken of as the Democratic Candidate & such a fate I sincerely pray may not await us— I spoke of Mr. Grahams vote on the Tariff[113]- do not understand me as objecting so much to the vote as to his course before the public on the subject- In all his addresses he has merely said that he voted against the Tariff as it passed & became the law assigning for reason first that some of the duties were too high, & its surrender of distribution & alleging that if his amendment to restore distribution had been seconded he would have gone for it, yet but a few days before he had voted against the great whig measure for raising revenue & at the same time preserving distribution &c &c - the reasons, all the reasons that the Governor has ever given for voting against Tylers tariff would have seemed to require his support of the first Bill: that too he voted against, but has taken care to allude only to his course on that which became the law by obtaining the signature of the President. - But enough - He can & must beat such candidates as the Democracy are able to bring out.

I shall be glad to hear from you if it be but a line. Do mention me to Crittenden Morehead & Barrow. I am yr. friend &c

A. H. SHEPPERD

[Addressed to:]

Hon Willie P. Mangum

U S Senate

Washington

---

[113]See above A. H. Shepperd to W. P. Mangum, April 26, 1846.

WPM-LC

James S. Russell[114] to Willie P. Mangum.

BEREA May 22 1846

Dear Sir

I am again candidate in Granville and we shall no doubt have a desperate contest, and as I have become somewhat rusty in political matters, I am driven therefore to request of you the favour to send me such documents and other information as in your opinion will best enable me to conduct a campaign. Sub Treasury Tariff and Oregon questions will be discussed, in Granville, together with such subjects as may arise between now and the adjournment of Congress whatever expence may attend your compliance with this request, you will please inform me

Yours Respectfully

JAS. S. RUSSELL
Berea
Granville Cty
N. Carolina

[Addressed:]

Hon. W. P. Mangum
Washington City.

WPM-LC

James Lynch[115] et als. to Willie P. Mangum

NEW YORK, May 22nd. 1846

Sir

On the 20th. instant, a meeting was held in this city in the Park, in pursuance of a call from the Mayor addressed to the citizens of the City and County of New York to respond to the action of the National Government in relation to our difficulties

---

[114] James S. Russell was a member of the legislature in 1840-1841, and 1846-1847. *N. C. Manual,* 623, 624.
[115] James Lynch, who graduated from Columbia College in New York in 1799 and who died in 1853, was a lawyer and justice of the Marine Court of New York City. M. H. Thomas, *Columbia University Officers and Alumni 1754-1857,* New York, 1936, 118.

with Mexico: At a preliminary meeting a Committee had been appointed, composed of distinguished members of each of the political parties to make arrangements and prepare Resolutions, the Officers of the meeting were selected from the several parties and some of the whig officers attended under the impression that the Resolutions were to be limited to the expression of an opinion that as War existed, it was the duty of every good citizen to sustain the administration in measures necessary to bring the same to a successful termination, and particularly to reinforce the army on the Rio Grande. When the Resolutions were read to the meeting it was discovered with surprise that they justified the existing war[116] on the ground that submission to the wrongs to which our country had been subjected by the authorities of Mexico would be deemed pusillanimous by the civilized world, and that it was declared in the Resolutions that the War is *just and necessary*. It can hardly be necessary to say to you that the Whigs of the City of New York unanimously do not concur in those sentiments, and the question is now presented as to the expediency of a formal public declaration to that effect at this moment. The Whig General Committee have had the subject under consideration and have appointed the undersigned a Committee to consult some of our leading friends in Congress.

There are some amongst our Whig friends who are unwilling to remain for a moment under the imputation that the Whig party have concurred in the Resolutions referred to, and are anxious without delay to call a public meeting, for the purpose of expressing their dissent, whilst others on the score of expediency would prefer to await the further action of our friends in Congress, and the further progress of the events on the Rio Grande, on the ground that there are strong symptoms of a lurking dissatisfaction among the friends of the administration which will probably be soon developed; as well against the measures which have produced collision, as against the inefficient manner in which the military movements have been conducted, in addition to which the class of our friends last

116Many Whigs had insisted that annexation would lead to war, and their opposition had been put on that ground. They held that war was unnecessary and was brought on by the rashness of Polk. On the day of Polk's war message, the House of Representatives passed a resolution with a preamble which asserted that by "act of the Republic of Mexico a state of war exists." In the Senate the Whigs and Calhoun objected to this preamble. They held that war did not exist until Congress acted. Mangum declared, in the course of the debate, that if the Democrats would separate the political question from the bill for supplies, money, and troops, the Whigs would support it. Wiltse, *Calhoun: Sectionalist*, 282-284; McCormac, *James K. Polk*, 415-416; Pegg, *"Whig Party in N. C.,"* 237-238.

mentioned, apprehend that in the excitement at a public meeting there is danger that some ardent friends might express opinions which would be unpopular and might tend to re-unite the friends of the administration.

Having viewed with great satisfaction the course taken by our friends in Congress on this War question and being under the impression that you have well considered what should hereafter be done, we should be much gratified to have the benefit of your advice on this occasion at your earliest convenience, as it is not improbable that the action of the Whig party in this City may have a considerable effect upon our friends in other parts of this State.

> We have the honor
> to be Most Respectfully
> Your Obt. Servts.
>
> JAMES LYNCH Chm
> M. L. DAVIS
> JOHN CROMWELL
> JAMES S. THAYER
> JAMES BROOKS

To the Hon.
Willie P Mangum

WPM-LC

Thomas G. Polk[117] to Willie P. Mangum.

HOLLY SPRINGS, MISS - PI

Honble. W. P. Mangum.

My Dear Sir.

I renew an old No. Ca. acquaintance by asking a favour from your hands, which I hope will be granted if *consistent with your feelings.*

The last Washington papers, brought us the Presidents Message & the Bill for the increase of the Army, as well as the appropriation for its support— True to the principles of my fore-

---

[117]See above, II, 340n.

fathers, I stop not to enquire by what means this War has been brought upon us - by whom - or for what purpose- It is sufficient for me to know that the country is at War, and I am anxious to enter into the service in defence of her honor & the maintenance of her rights. May I then ask, if consistent with your feelings, & a knowledge of who I am, that you would with other friends to whom I have written place my name before the President for the appointment of Brigadier General— I have written to Haywood - Speight & Chalmers & some others— Some of my friends have voluntarily written to the Secty of the Treasury & I learn also the President—

I should be pleased if you would speak to Mr. Calhoun, with whom I have an acquaintance & also to Mr. Benton who may possibly recollect me - at least he will know who I am. Take what course you may deem advisable & you will confer a favour on your very

Sincere friend &
obt. Sevt.
Thos. G. Polk

[Addressed:]

> Honbl. W. P. Mangum
> Senate
> Washington City.

WPM-LC

O. F. Long[118] to Willie P. Mangum.

Hillsboro May 25th, 1846

Dear Sir

Long. Webb & Co have purchased and fitted up the Union Hotel and as we intend the House. shall be first rate. we wish to have some of the leading Journals of the country. You will therefore confer a favour on us. by calling at the office of the "Nat: Intelligencer" & "The Union" and request them to send

---

[118]Osmond Fitz Long, 1808-1864, a graduate of the University of North Carolina and a native of Randolph County, studied medicine at the University of Pennsylvania. After marrying Frances Helen Webb, daughter of Dr. James Webb, in 1832, he moved to Hillsboro, where he associated with his father-in-law in his many businesses. *Carolina Watchman*, October 13, 1832; Grant, *Alumni Hist. of U. N. C.*, 375.

their tri-weekly papers to the "Union Hotel, Hillsboro, No Ca"
- and you will confer a further favour by paying the subscription to each for one year which we will settle on your return—
    We expect to bring out our candidates this week. As usual
the Whigs are Blundering about. Nobody knows what we will
do for candidates- The Democrats are well prepared for the contest[119]- Capt. Berry will be their candidate for the senate - Sid
Smith & some kindred spirits in the commons- Rick Nichols has
a foolish notion of trying to be Sheriff and I fear will injure the
whig cause

Yours Respectfully

O. F. LONG

[Addressed:]

Hon. W. P. Mangum
Washington City.

Willie P. Mangum to the Secretary of the Navy[120]

SENATE CHAMBER 27th. May 1846

To The Hon: Secretary of the Navy.

    Sir.

    I enclose to you a letter addressed to me by Mr. Creecy,[121]
in behalf of his son.

    I have learned, that the administration has taken a proper
interest in the officers of the late Texan Navy, & therefore do
all that is proper on my part, by refreshing your recollection by
simply inviting your attention to the subject.

    During the past Winter, I received several communications
in regard to young Mr. Creecy, in all of which he is represented
as a young man of Spirit & much promise.

I am Sir with much respect

Your Obt. Sert.

WILLIE P. MANGUM

---

[119]See above John Cameron to W. P. Mangum, May 7, 1846.
[120]The original is in the Historical Society of Pennsylvania, Philadelphia, Pa.
[121]See above J. R. Creecy to W. P. Mangum, January 10, 1846. The enclosure here referred
to was not found.

WPM-LC

Willie P. Mangum to Charity A. Mangum.

WASHINGTON CITY
Thursday morning, 4th June 1846.

My dear Love,

Mr. Gordon of Guilford County will probably hand you this.- He leaves this morning & in a few minutes, & promised me last night, that he would endeavour to go home by our house-

I am just out of bed & undressed to write a line—— I am tolerably well.- My health is much better, than it was during the latter part of the Winter & Spring. I had hoped My Love to see you all before this time—But the follies, Wickedness & War of this administration rendered it impossible.- I have not given it up, - because we may be kept here a long time yet.

We ought not to leave before we settle all with England, for two wars would almost ruin the Country.

Mr. Gordon is a plain, ingenious & worthy man. Of course, you will treat him kindly— I send by him a few books for Sally & Patty - & Mary & William.- He wants a copy of the Patent report, & perhaps several- Give them to him.-

Give my Love to the Children.
Your affectionate husband
W. P. MANGUM

Mrs. C. A. Mangum

WPM-LC

J. R. Creecy[122] to Willie P. Mangum.

NEW ORLEANS 5th June 1846

My Dear Sir

Your very kind and friendly letter of the 27th was recd. this morning; from my heart I thank you; but of how little avail are all my exertions, to obtain even so small a boon as I have asked from the "powers that be! God save the Nation! To show you

[122]See above J. R. Creecy to W. P. Mangum, January 10, 1846, and W. P. Mangum to the Secretary of the Navy, May 27, 1846.

how I have been *understood* or *misunderstood;* I enclose a letter recd. yesterday from the Honl. Secty of the Navy.[123] My son never was a Citizen of *Louisiana,* never expects to be; and in my first letter to the Secty. I mentioned *particularly* that he was a native of No. Carolina and had been for the last eleven years a resident of Mississippi; and that he had been a midshipman with Comm. Moore, 18 ms. in the Texan Navy; and had returned from Texas (after being dismissed with Comr. M. by Gov. Houston) to Mississippi, where he had remained, until he came to this City and volunteered in a company from Natchez about three weeks since, he is now at Matamoras- I do think the "wants of the service" will require *'ere long* a "few more" appointments; and that this little favor might be granted, to me, Mississippi or Texas, or No. Carolina, but I did not ask it for Louisiana.—

The war has caused me to give up the idea, of publishing a paper for the present; and under authority from Genl Gaines, I was actively engaged in raising a Regiment for the Army of *"Invasion,"* when a damper arrived upon the old Genl*. acts[124]- and we are now in a state of most unenviable suspense and expense! I am requested to "hold on" a few days by Genl. G. in the hope that his *"doings"* will not be finally repudiated - but the administration appear determined to kill off the old veteran in some way; and I have but little faith in the establishment- The people will force the Government into the entire conquest or occupation of Mexico; and to settle all disputes about the next President; Genl. Scott, Mr. Polk &c &c may furl their banners, for Genl. Z. Taylor is the man already selected for our next chief— Excuse me for enclosing an article[125] written by yr. humble Sert. and published in the Jeffersonian a few days since;

---

[123]The enclosure was not found.

[124]On August 2, 1845, word reached New Orleans, where General Edmund P. Gaines was in command of the Western Division of the Army, that Taylor had been surrounded in Texas by the Mexicans. Without considering the extent of his authority, Gaines immediately called on the governor of Louisiana for two regiments of the militia. His action was declared illegal by the Adjutant General, but the troops were accepted. In May, 1846, when Taylor was fired upon by the Mexicans, Gaines requested several Southern governors to hold their forces in readiness. He also accepted volunteers. Polk dismissed him June 2 and ordered a court martial. James W. Silver, *Edmund Pendleton Gaines: Frontier General,* Baton Rouge, 1949, 258-265.

[125]The enclosure was not found.

it may aid in preventing Northern troops from being sent to untimely graves in this war—

> I will not take more of your time.
>> With best and warmest wishes
>>> Yr friend
>>> & much obliged
>>> J. R. Creecy.

[Addressed:]

> For the
>> Honl. W. P. Mangum
>> U. S. Senate
>> Washington
>> City.

Willie P. Mangum to Messrs. Gales & Seaton[126]

Senate Chamber. 6th June '46

To Messrs. Gales & Seaton

The turn which the debate of yesterday took upon great principles will fix men's positions to some extent.—I participated with the view of postponing immediate action, & had to pursue a course of remark extemely liable to be misunderstood[127]—The subsequent part of the debate attracted so much attention, that I desire to see my remarks before printed.— The "Union" makes me express opinions, which I expressly disclaimed.

I avoided *expressly* expressing any opinion in *advance* upon those important points afterwards so much debated.

---

[126]The original is in the Ford Collection, New York Public Library.
[127]On June 5, 1846, the Senate debated Cass's resolution requesting the President to inform Congress if any army officers had called volunteers or militia organizations into the service of the United States without legal authority. This was directed against General Gaines. Mangum took the position that the resolution was unnecessary for the law was explicit on calling men into service and that if Gaines had done anything wrong, it was the President's responsibility to court martial him. *Cong. Globe*, 29 Cong., 1 sess., 930.

Will you do me the favor to enclose the remarks written out, & I will return them whenever desired.

Yours truly
W. P. MANGUM

[Addressed To:]

Messrs. Gales & Seaton
Intell. Office

[Endorsed:] W. P. Mangum
June 6, 1846

WPM-LC

J. B. Mower to Willie P. Mangum

NEW YORK 8. th. June 1846

Hon. Willie P. Mangum

Dear Sir

It is some time since, I did myself the pleasure, to write to you, and I beg now, that you will hear me with patience, for I am one of the people, and I talk to you Sir, directly from amongst them.

I have received glad tidings from afar, "I hear from the Mississippi river, Ill^s. and so on, through the "Western States" that the people there, are determined, to take their own business, into their own hands, and to manage it for themselves. That the people's man, John M^c.Lean, of Ohio, is the very one, to break down, this uproarous democracy. That they are resolved, that no man, shall be forced upon them, not even, in the person of Mr. Clay. And they desire not, a "general officer," to take command, of their civil concerns. The Whigs of the West, will not support this Mexican war, of conquest; and so says, very many of the democracy. They sigh for the day, to arrive, when they can go to the ballot boxes, and speak through them, to Jim Polk & Co. in this wise. Go ye into everlasting retirement, thou unworthy servants, for we have had enough, of thy misrule.

I shall be most happy, to hear from you. I desire to hear from one, who is in a position, to know, (if any one can) the designs, of this administration, in prosecuting this mexican war, of conquest. Is it to be a long, or a short one. Will England and France, look on quietly, and see America, take possession, of this rich and fertile country, and what shall we do with it, after we have obtained it. Or, will the war be prosecuted, with vigour, to the end, that will cause the Mexicans, to sue for peace, if so, I say Amen. But Mr. Senator, we say here, no war, for conquest of territory.

I remain my dear Sir,
very sincerely your friend
J. B. MOWER

Hon Willie P. Mangum)
)
  U. S. Senate   )
)
   Washington   )
)
     D. C.   )

[Addressed:]

Hon. Willie P. Mangum
U. S. Senate
Washington
D. C.

_____

Willie P. Mangum & W. S. Archer to James Watson Webb[128]

WASHINGTON CITY 11th. June 1846

My dear Sir,

Mr. Archer & I think, we have reason to complain of your Wine Merchant, in sending us Wine which we do not drink nor can our friends be induced to drink it - I received Six boxes - M^r. Archer I think, a larger number.

---

[128]The original is in the Ford Collection, New York Public Library.

I opened one on its arrival, & have not used it all - The other five remain unopened.

It is the more unlucky for us, as our neighbour M^r. J. M. Clayton received from the same House an excellent article - He paid one dollar more p^r. doz. - As We did not mean to place any restriction upon the price, we feel that we have not been quite so well treated by him. We would like to return it, & receive in lieu of it next Winter, a better article, of course, indemnifying for any proper Cost above the price of this, which was $11 p^r. doz.

Will you have this placed before your merchant, & be so obliging as to advise us of his determination in this behalf?

> With great respect
> Yrs truly
> Willie P. Mangum

Dear Sir

Mr Mangum has shewn me the above letter, and I am under the necessity of concurring fully, in his representation as regards the entirely valueless character of the wine sent me, being Mansanilla, the wine drunk by only the lowest class of People in Andalusia, instead of Amontilliado the wine which Mr. Mangum and myself expected, and which Mr Clayton did receive.

I did not return the wine, because I had paid for it before receiving it, and because a reluctance to inpose any concern on you who I was aware had no knowledge of the Imposition we had sustained. I do not now, wish you put to inconvenience, though I do not regard the wine as worth a single dollar for the entire quantity sent instead of $11. per doz.

> Respectfully
> Yr obt St etc.
> W. S. Archer

Mr Webb.
[End:] 11 June 1846 Washington

WPM-LC

Thos. J. Green to Willie P. Mangum

PHIL. June 12th /46.

My Dear Friend:

You will find enclosed a faithful minature Likeness of my brother Colonel Chas. P. Green, which I beg you to accept;[129] for a truer or more devoted friend you never had.

Your friend truly,

THOS. J. GREEN.

To

Hon. W. P. Mangum.
Washington city.

[Addressed:]

Hon. W. P. Mangum.
U. S. Senate,
Washington city,

By Genl.)
)
J. T. Mason)

WPM-LC

Willie P. Mangum to Charity A. Mangum

WASHINGTON CITY 22nd. June 1846

My dear Love

I was much pleased to receive your letter of last week. I fear, the wheat crop is greatly injured. The City has been quite sickly this month, not with fever, but diarhrea. I have had my share of it, but am nearly well of it.

The weather is cold enough for the first of November.- I have resumed my flannel.-

We shall not get away from here before the first of August.- Others think the 20th July, but I feel sure, it will be August.

129Charles Plummer Green died December 1, 1843, of consumption. He was thirty-four years old at the time of his death. I have been unable to locate this miniature of Green.

I have given up hope of seeing you all before the end of the session- The business has been & will be so important, that I ought not to be absent.

I thank God, that War with England is averted.[130] That with Mexico can & ought to be speedily settled, yet will it? I fear not. There are too many objects of personal ambition & avarice to be gratified by its continuance. We must however, one & all fight it out, or sustain it with vigor.- I have not heard whether [my] boy William has volunteered- I think, he is too young, yet if Mr. Piper thinks otherwise he is a volunteer, let him go to the War[131]

I cannot say my Love, how much I [desire] to see you & be at home.- This session [has] in the main, been the most unpleasant I have ever passed here- My health for more than [torn] of it, has been decidedly bad- & yet I have been so careful of it.-

I fear my lungs are incurably affected [torn] trip to Virginia two years ago, I fear, [torn] shorten my life, if other causes shall not [torn] the thread more speedily.-

> Give my Love to all the children, &
> believe me my dear Love,
> as ever,
> Your affectionate husband
> WILLIE P. MANGUM

To
    Mrs. Charity A. Mangum

WPM-LC

Josiah Randall to Willie P. Mangum.

[22 June, 1846]

Dear Sir

When I saw you, you promised to be here on the 4th July, the day is favorable & you need not be absent one hour from the Senate. I reported you would come. The Comt. & our

---

[130]On June 15, 1846, Buchanan signed a treaty with Pakenham settling the Oregon dispute. McCormac, *James K. Polk*, 609.
[131]William Preston Mangum was born July 13, 1837.

friends expect you; I exact of course the promise that you will stay with me- Write an answer immy.

Yours &c.

J. RANDALL

Phl.

June 22/46

Hbl Mr Mangum

Willie P. Mangum to Messrs. Gales & Seaton[132]

Monday 29th. June '46

4½ O. C.

Gentlemen

Mr E. Johnson called to enquire this morning, whether I knew anything of the movement intended by Mr. Mc. Duffie, & referred to in the public prints on the subject of the Mexican War.[133]

I have talked with Mr. M^c. D. - There is no foundation for the rumor. -

I suggested, that an idea thrown out by Crittenden & others I thought of value. -

He seemed to *seize upon it,* & said he w^d. urge it upon the Pres^t. -

To take some occasion, (if he had to go out of his way to do it in a Message) to say, that whenever he might receive satisfactory evidence, that the Mex. Govt. desired to negotiate, that he w^d. be ready to send a mission of three or more gentlemen, without regard to party, to negotiate a treaty of peace upon foundations solid & enduring, Clay, Calhoun & Benton for ex:

It's moral effect upon the world w^d. be good & show, though at home divided upon internal policy as regard to foreign

---

[132]The original letter is in the Ford Collection, New York Public Library.
[133]At this time George McDuffie was chairman of the Senate Foreign Relations Committee.

powers we were as one man, & upon grounds, liberal, generous & magnanimous. This is all.

Yrs truly
W. P. MANGUM

Messrs. Gales & Seaton

[Addressed:] To Messrs. Gales & Seaton
Intell: Office

WPM-LC

Dudley Selden[134] to Willie P. Mangum

NEW YORK July 8th 1846.

Dear Sir

When at Washington I did not express any opinion as to the general merits of the Tariff Bill, My interest being confined to the article of sugar alone, I only endeavored to give information upon that subject, and to shew, that the enormous duty levied upon sugar under the Act of 1842 ought to be reduced, whether any thing was done with regard to other articles or not. On my return here it being known that I had visited Washington a great many conversed with me with regard to the probability of the passage of McKays bill,[135] and I have been surprised to find how many of those who belong to the Whig party, have expressed a willingness to see the new plan adopted, some assigning as a reason that the measure coming from the South will likely prove permanent, that nothing was more mischievous than constant agitation of the question, and the derangements of private interests, based upon protection, that until the south had their own way, they would not leave the country at rest, Others have said that if any great mischief was to arise from the House Bill it would fall upon those who brought around this state of things, whereby the act of 1842, was to be changed,

[134]See above, III, 213n.

[135]In 1844 James J. McKay, Chairman of the Committee on Ways and Means, tried to revise the Whig tariff of 1842. In 1846 he presented to the House what was later known as the Walker Tariff. Under this bill all duties were ad valorem. Commodities were put in several groups and the rates varied with the groups. On July 3 the House passed the bill with few changes. The Senate began debating it on July 6. Because of the radical changes proposed, Senator Will H. Haywood, of North Carolina, broke with the administration and resigned. His resignation made possible the passage of the bill by the vote of 28 to 27, McCormac, *James K. Polk,* 672-678; Norton, *Democratic Party in N. C.,* 119-120.

I mean those, who were engaged in various handicraft work, most of whom by their vote manifested a preference, to a policy, which would reduce the price of articles of consumption other than that which will keep up a high rate of wages.

I am very desirous of knowing, whether the House bill, will pass the Senate, for should I have reason to believe it would pass I would order at once, a change in my present apparatus for manufacturing sugar, with the view of bringing to the market an improved article, and I think many other sugar planters in Cuba from the United States will do the same thing, If I make the change I ought to give my orders for machinery at the earliest possible day, which by the way will prove a job for the mechanics here of some $15,000 I suppose the result of the bill, is doubtful arising out of the uncertainty of Mr. Jarnegan and Mr. Athertons vote, and herein I assume that you will vote against the bill.

Yours very truly and with great respect
DUDLEY SELDEN

Hon. W. P. Mangum

[Addressed:]

> Hon^l.
> W. P. Mangum
> Washington
> D. C.

WPM-LC

George Constantine Collins[136] to Willie P. Mangum.

PHILADA. July 14th. 1846

Hon: Sir.

I hope it will not be considered a presumption on my part, to drop you an occasional line, inasmuch as, your exalted station should, and doubtless does afford you correspondents better suited to your official dignity and literary lore. Yet from the opinion which I formed of your attachment to those noble principles of equality, which characterize our blessed Institu-

---

[136]See above, 25n.

tions, and which you have so eminently sustained in your public life, I am emboldened to address you.

Some time since, I wrote you a Letter respecting the difficult[y] which I had to encounter since the defea[t] of our illus [trious] Candidate in endeavouring to obtain a profession [I] still have 5 months to put in before I shall be [a me]mber of this Bar. Mr. Randall my Precep[tor] ha[s] been kind [toward]s me, Alfred du Pont of Delaware has been [torn]er,- a benefactor. Both of those Gentlemen [are] warmly devoted to your interests an[d] honor. Mr. [Ran]dall told me a few days ago, that your name [was] associated as V. P. with that of Jud[ge] McLean of Ohio, who it is thought will be our Candidate for the Presidency. To this I am opposed, from this I dissent. I told Mr. Randall, that you should not be placed in that position, as your standing required perhaps the first position. Frelinghuysen more than anything else, defeated Mr. Clay. He was a bitter Sectarian, McLane is a little more moderate, but the same objection lies. He is already called the psalm-singing Candidate! I informed you in my last letter, that your name was freely used, in connection with the Presidency. Josiah Randall, thinks your nomination would be hailed with popular acclamation. I am still a Clay man, though I am instructed by many to say nothing on that score. Next to [him] your flag shall float above my 'sanctum.' N[otwith]standing you did not deem my last letter worth[y of n]otice, I yet shall remember your former kindness [with] undying gratitude. Your opposition in private convers[ation] to that greatest of all political heresies, 'Nativism' endeared you to my heart, and your letter of [instru]ction to the Whigs of the Union still remains in [my no]tion as a monument of the liberality of the Senator from [Nor]th Carolina.

But, I regret that the nomination of McLane cannot receive my approbation, as I recognize in him a bitter enemy to my Faith, and the same objection, which applied to Frelingn. will also be against him: Let me have a line, if your leisure will permit to the care of J. Randall Esq. In all events, come what may, sink or swim, I shall never forget you, though I should seem to you but a small speck on the great ocean of humanity. I have a soul which shall always be grateful to him

James Turner Morehead, 1797-1854. From an oil portrait, painter unknown, in the possession of the Kentucky Historical Society, Frankfort.

who once treated me with respect, though when the storm of politics should blow over, would be forgotten by him.

With Sentiments of profound regard
Hon: Sir, your
Friend, and humble Servt

GEO: CONSTANTINE COLLINS
(Author of "50 Reasons," & once respected
by Whigs but now forgotten though as
good a Whig now as ever).

Hon W [P. Man]gum
Senator f[rom N.]C.

WPM-LC

William H. Thomas to Willie P. Mangum and Enclosure[187]

WASHINGTON CITY
July 17, 1846

Hon. W. P. Mangum
of the Senate,

Dear Sir,

I have obtained another statement from General Scott relative my claims provided for in the Resolution before the Senate which I herewith enclose. May I ask of you the favour at the earliest opportunity to show it to Mr. Jarnagan and as soon as you can have the opportunity to have the Resolution called up and acted on.

I have been waiting and must continue to wait until sometime next week to ascertain whether the investigation now going on before a board of Commissioners will result in a treaty being made with the Cherokees by which their difficulties will be settled and the [payment] of their claims provided for,[138] The President, [torn] has authorised the Commissioners to em-

---

[187]See above, 421.
[138]On August 6, 1846, a treaty was signed at Washington with the Cherokees of the West allowing the eastern band of Cherokees, who remained in North Carolina, to participate in the benefits of New Echota Treaty of 1835. Mooney, "Myths of the Cherokees," in Smithsonian Institution, *Nineteenth Annual Report of the Bureau of American Ethnology to the Secretary of the Smithsonian Institution,* I, 165.

brace [torn] [ex]amination and report- on which a treaty will probably[torn] claims of the North Carolina Cherokees,

> With the highest respect
> your obt. servt.
>
> WM. H. THOMAS

Enclosure

Winfield Scott to W. H. Thomas

> Head Q uarters of the Army.
> WASHINGTON, July 17, 1846.

Sir:

In answer to your inquiries, I refer you to my reports to the War Department, from Athens Tennessee, dated Nov 6, 1838, relative to the means to be used for the capture of certain Cherokee murderers, &c. In that report I say: "Col Foster (Com^{dr}. 4 Inf) will also have the aid, as runners, guides & interpreters of some of Mr. Thomas's Oconolufty Indians, as well as the personal services of Mr. Thomas himself, who takes a lively interest in the success of the expedition."[139]

The reports of Col Foster speak of the valuable services rendered by yourself & Indians up to the successful accomplishment of the objects of the expedition; & I cannot doubt, that this result would have been longer delayed had other instruments, less acquainted with the localities, been used. Such delay, besides the expense attending it, would have retarded the march of the 7th. Inf, then awaiting the arrival of the 4th. at Fort Gibson, before proceeding to Florida.

> I remain, Sir, respectfully,
> Yrs.
>
> WINFIELD SCOTT.

To
    Mr. W. H. Thomas
    Washington City.

---

[139]See above, 421n.

WPM-LC

Jon. H. Jacobs[140] to Willie P. Mangum

DURANT'S NECK Nº. CA.
July 20ᵗʰ. 1846—

My dear Sir,

My health for the last two years has been very bad and for the last twelve months it has been a struggle for me to live -(the Chronic Diarrhia) A trip to the Mineral Springs of Va. last Summer, I am well satisfied has protracted my life-. and I contemplate travelling in the Western part of this State this Summer and Fall, as soon as I am able to locate my family at my Cabbin at Nag's Head-

Not being *politically* represented in Congress I have recᵈ. few documents this Session, indeed I may say none, if I except "B [illegible]", & Mr. Bigg's speech on the Tariff, sent me by Mr. Bigg's, & the report of the Coast Survey, "House Document No. 38" which I think was sent me by my Friend Mr. Barringer- I have somehow, been generally much neglected in that respect, I think, and could not be reconsiled were I not a subscriber to the Nat. Intelligencer & "Niles' Register"-

This is principally addressed you, my old Friend, (if I can be permitted to use the expression & I think I should) to ask a favor of you & through you my other Friends in Congress, to send me some few of the Valuable Documents which have be[en] printed, this Session, by order of Congress- Confined as I am a great deal within doors, reading and writing are my principal occupations, and have a tendency to wile away the tedium of a sick room-

Well I suppose we shall have a "Democratic Tariff," and once more be guilty of the folly of trying to increase the revenue by reducing the duties!- I should really think that the "Compromise" Tariff, had already convinced all sane persons, that no such result can be expected- But I suppose Demagogues must rule us so long as they rule the "majority"-

But of all the wild measures and positions of the present dominant party in Congress, none gave me so much uneasiness as the "Oregon" Controversy- The "54.40" and "all or none"

---

[140]See above, III, 296n.

men- Thank God, the good sense of Benton and Calhoun & some few others, induced them to unite with the Whigs & we may *hope* that affair is settled- But the "Mexican War," I much fear, will yet involve us with Europe, for it seems, we *must* go to the Rio Grand and of course follow up to its head, and we *must* have California, and New Mexico- Then after this is all accomplished, I think Mexico it self will be another "Texas," and "annexed" by "Joint resolution"!

I fear you will have to make yr. "Bow" on the 4ᵗ. of March next, and to use a common expression of an old friend, be "turned to grass"- The retirement of Rayner, the death of Cherry, and defeat of Outlaw have ruined we poor Whigs in this Dist. We are very unfortunate too in the candidates in this 1st. Senatorial Dist. both as to Senate & Commons- I fear we shall be beaten - tho' I have been almost bed-ridden, know nothing of myself & only from others-

Present my respects to Messrs. Haywood, McKay, Biggs, Barringer, Dockery, and all other Friends and believe me Dʳ. Sir,

Yr. Friend & ob Sert

JON. H. JACOBS

Honˡ. W. P. Mangum

[Addressed:]

Honˡ. W. P. Mangum
Washington City
D. C-

Mail.)

———

WPM-LC

Charles Miner¹⁴¹ to William A. Graham.

WILKES-BARRE, LUZERNE Co. P. July 20/46

To his Excellency William A. Graham
    Governor of North-Carolina.
Sir,

I take leave, most respectfully to invite your attention to a matter, which appears to me not only interesting to North-Car-

---

¹⁴¹Charles Miner, 1780-1865, was a journalist in Wilkes-Barre before he moved to Philadelphia. He endeavored to popularize the silk industry in various parts of the country, experimenting on a farm of his own. He also tried to increase the use of anthracite coal. *D. A. B.*, XIII, 22-23.

olina, but to the whole Union. I refer to the culture of Silk. The severity of our northern winters, retarding the growth, and injuring the tender branches, of the Mulberry, renders our position less eligible for the business, than a more southern climate. South of you the heat would become too intense; South virginia and your state I apprehend, possess that favourable temperature, best adapted to the growth of the mulberry, and the perfection of the silk-worm. I am therefore extremely anxious that with you, and under the auspices of the State Government, the experiment should be fairly and faithfully tried, not on an expensive, but yet on a liberal scale: neither doubting, nor entertaining a shadow of a doubt, but the result would prove a perenial source of incalculable wealth and abiding prosperity to your noble Commonwealth - and reflecting to after ages the highest honour on the public authorities whose spirit and forecast should introduce and effectually establish the inestimable benefits of rearing the silk-worm and the productions of silk-

Reading a few days ago, the eloquent description, in the 7th volume of Gibbon, of the rise and extension of the Silk-culture, in eastern Europe and Asia, it gave new impulse to a Resolution, long since formed to bring the matter, expecially to the consideration of your Government; and various treasury statistics upon my table enable me to present to your Excellency, some highly curious comparative views, shewing the importance of the subject

Cotton, Tobacco, Rice and Flour are regarded, and truly, as our leading staples of exportation:

In the ten years from 1836, inclusive, to 1845 the exportation of cotton, was in value $578,037,882

In the same period the importation of Silks amounted to the enormous sum of $124,870,326

From a fifth to a quarter the value of our great staple!

During the 10 preceding years the imports amounted to $ 93,392,934!

Shewing an aggragate increase of 31 millions; or more than 3 millions a year.

The exports of Tobacco from 1836 to 1845 amounted, in value to $ 85,598,727

Exhibiting a Silk import of   39,271,599
greater than the whole export of Tobacco

During the same period there were exported
of Rice $ 20,868,266

The two, Tobacco and Rice, falling short of the value of Silks imported nearly 20 millions.

The export of Flour during the same period amounted in value to $ 58,288,108.
Less than half the value of importations of Silks.

It must be obvious to your Excellency that these figures are exhibited to show, impressively, the great and steadily growing value of Silks consumed in the United States:

When the increase of opulence, and consequent advance of luxury, combined with the rapid augmentation of Population, are considered, must it not be among the things of moral certainty, that the consumption of silk will proceed with an equal if not accelerated pace? Is it not equally clear, that the overproduction of Cotton, must certainly transfer its culture, exclusively to the more southern and better adapted locations, leaving it desirable that some new and more profitable staple should be introduced into North-Carolina?

I write under the fullest persuasion that your State may be made, four-fold, the richest in the Union: that her least fruitful hills - her fertile valleys, and even her sterile plains, may "by the education" of the Silk-worm, and the production of the white mulberry, be made as valuable as the low southern lands yielding the Sea-Island Cotton. It is understood that on light and sandy soils, the Mulberry leaf, though less luxuriant, produces a counterbalancing fineness of Silk.

My Plans would be simple, involving little comparative outlay; avoiding the common fault of Governmental schemes; that is of beginning on too large a scale, and expending unnecessary sums in the experiment

A Farm of 100 acres, in the immediate vicinity of the seat of Government, it is presumed may be bought for $60 an acre - $6,000.

Obtain from the Town of Mansfield, Connecticut, two families, which should embrace at least 4 males, accustomed to the Silk-culture, (their habits are simple - their expectations moderate, while industry and economy are familiar from childhood).

Such could probably be obtained, they having the use of the Farm to subsist upon, by paying the two men 20 dolls a month - the two young men 15 - making 840 dolls a year

Five acres of the Farm to be sown in beds carefully with white mulberry seed, for nurseries - each year - for 3 or 4 years, until sufficient young trees should be raised to supply, gratuitously (or at a very small price) every family in the State, that would accept of them, with a Mulberry orchard or field, of from 100- to 3 or 400 Trees.

Domestic, or Household culture, diffused throughout every County, giving easy employment to old men - to women and children, whose labour would otherwise be of little value, may well be regarded an object of great importance. Some families might be careless; not a few indifferent, for fixed habits are slow to change; but many of the rising generation, giving the experiment a fair trial and proving successful, would ensure an ultimately favourable issue

In three years from the first planting, Silks, in moderate quantities might be made. Ten years prudent management would give a product, surprising to the incredulous - and cheering to the sanguine.

The Nursery farm would, of course, be under the immediate eye and supervision of the Legislature, and here, at the earliest suitable period, young persons might be brought from different parts of the State, to learn the simple process of gathering the leaves and feeding the Silks-spinning-gold-coining, insect.

So far from recommending, I would dissuade from costly experiments - large buildings - heated rooms; or any early attempts at fine manufactures. The Coccoons being produced for market the more expensive processes by machinery, and manipulation, might be left, solely to individual capital and enterprise. But it would be well to consider whether a Legislative bounty on the production of Coccoons and Sewing silk might not be advantageous to the business while in its infancy

The Farm, remaining the property of the State would, probably, appreciate in value.

The action of the Government in the matter, could scarcely fail to give a favourable impulse to the business of the Capital.

And would not the promising commencement of the Silk-Culture, in the state, offering such rich returns, have the effect to turn the tide of emigration, from the teeming hives of New England, into North-Carolina? It is known many of the New England race are now settling in Virginia, desirous of enjoying a middle climate and more congenial sky.

It has been estimated that the product of an acre in the white mulberry, would be $200 a year. Looking for no excessive returns, it is yet firmly believed, that, with the same outlay of Capital and Labour, it may be made to equal, if not exceed, the product of Sugar, or the general returns of the finer sorts of Cotton.

I need not say to your Excellency, that the Statesmen, who, with liberal forecast and firm resolve, make those embrio arrangements, demanding time and expenditure - patience and perserverence, the results of which are new and valuable harvests to the husbandman - increased profits to labour, and the consequent diffusion of plenty and happiness among the People, are indeed Patriots, and deserve the Public gratitude.

I pray your Excellency to allow the purity of my motives, to plead my apology for this intrusion; as I have no personal interest to advance, and to permit me to subscribe myself

Your obedient Servant
CHARLES MINER.

[Addressed:]

His. Excellency
William A—Graham
Governor of
North-Carolina.

WPM-LC

J. W. Carr[142] to Willie P. Mangum and Enclosure

CHAPEL HILL 24th July 1846

Hon W. P. Mangum—

Dear Sir

You will see from Mr Utley's letter that he wishes you to look into a patent which he obtained in Septr last from the

---

[142]See above, 299n.

patent office of the U. S. It seems that there is some misunderstanding about the knife &C- & unless it can be explained satisfactorily it may cause a suit— Dr Jones of this place Jones Watson Aliegh[?] Hutch & myself are all concerned & wish to establish the Letters patent & to show that no infringement has been made on Gaylords patent of 1843 or any improvement that he may have made up to the 27th. Septr. 1845—

You will please see Edmond Burke and Dr. Page who we think will do a way all doubts about the matter—we have written to Edmond Burke Comm^r. of patents this day about it. please attend to it & write us as soon as you possibly can together with your own opinion about the matter—

I am Sir with great respect
Your obt servt
J. W. CARR

If you can send us any documents that will be of any service in our approaching Election we should like to have them—It will be a hard contest in Orange but we hope the Whig Ticket will succeed -

J. W. C.

[Addressed:]

Hon
W. P. Mangum
(Senate of the U States)
Washington City

Enclosure

Grey Utley to W. P. Mangum[143]

CHAPEL HILL July 24th. 1846

Dear Sir-

I obtained a patent on the 27th day of Septr last from the patent office of the United States for an improvement in a straw-cutter- Since which time there has some difficulty arisen

---

[143]This letter is in the handwriting of J. W. Carr.

in this section of the country about it. It is contended by two persons here through malace that my patent is an infringement upon a patent obtained by Gaylord in the year 1843— they also say that the teeth of my knife should each be one inch apart, & I contend that I have a right to make four teeth within an inch so they are made in the same manner and the principle not altered—

Will you do me the favour to look into the matter- & please examine Gaylords patent & see if it has been extended so as to cover the different shapes of his knife—

Now your attention to the above will greatly oblige me & save me from going to Washington City my self—

Please let me hear from you soon

Respectfully
GREY UTLEY

Hon W. P. Mangum
     Senate U S—

[Addressed:]

        Hon
          W. P. Mangum
            (Senate of the U States)
              Washington City

WPM-LC

Benjamin Coleman[144] to Willie P. Mangum.

KINSTON LENOIR COUNTY N C.
July 28, 1846.

Dr Sir

Any speach or document which would throw any light upon the issues now before the people would be greatfully received. The Whigs are useing their utmost endeavours in their section of the county, to dethrone the reign of Loco-Focoism. I feel confident that Gov. Graham will be elected by an increased majority; we shall also elect a whig Legislature, and thereby

----

[144]See above, II, 355-356.

secure a United States Senator! furnish me with all the Documents you have have [*sic*] to spare and believe me your friend and Obedient Servant

BENJ COLEMAN

[Addressed:]

To the Hon W P Mangum
Washington
City
D. C.

WPM-LC

P. U. Murphey[145] to Willie P. Mangum

NORFOLK
July 31st 1846

My dear Sir

I called to see you the evening before I left & much regret that you were out. as I wished to thank you for your kindness to me, & to have explained to you what I wished you to do for me, in the case of the date of my Commission. When I spoke to you about it you thought, there would be no difficulty in the case- When the vacancies which existed were filled, Now Sir since the Secretary has concluded to fill those vacancies I am most anxious to call your attention to it. I should have had my Commission dated back to the 1st of December last, at which time, Comodore Elliott died: but instead of which it was dated the last of May. The difference of pay to me is nearly four hundred dollars, which to a poor officer with a family is a great deal. I ask for nothing more, than the old established customs of the Navy Department- I know Sir, you will see that justice is done me, & know what course to pursue better than I can tell you,

I am sorry to write you, my wife's health was such on my arrival I could not leave to send you the figs I told you, I would,

---

[145]See above, 123.

but will certainly send them by the next boat, & I will procure you some of the cuttings, if you wish them

In great haste
Yours truly
P. U. MURPHEY
U. S. N.

Honble Judge Mangum

N. B. I have writen to Captain Ramsey to call on you, & explain to you the former custom of the Dept. in my case, as its a matter which interests me very much.

The report in this place is, that the old North state will do her duty

[Addressed:]

Hon^{bl} Judge Mangum
United States Senate
Washington City

WPM-LC

J. B. Mower to Willie P. Mangum

NEW YORK 2^d. Augt. 1846.

Hon. Willie P. Mangum)
)
    U. S. Senate   )
)
    Washington   )

Dear Sir

Well Sir, in a few days, Congress will have adjourned, & you Honorable Senators gone to your respective homes. But, before you go, I beseech you, my good Sir, to give me your views, of the Great political chess board, of the Nation, and please say, how you think, it can be played, how you think, it ought to be played, & how will it be. For Sir, I hear such contradictory reports, about you Gentlemen of Congress & parties, that I am sometimes, at a loss to know, what to think of you, in Washington. But you will inform me. This much, I can assure you Sir, that in this quarter, the ticket, of the Ohio & North Carolina candidates. Let me speak out plainly. The names, of John Mᶜ.Lean, of Ohio, & Willie P. Mangum, of North Carolina, are, the most popular, *the very strongest,* and will, as you will shortly see, the most available candidates, that the people, can rally on, for the Campaign of 48, having a view, to the welfare of this great, growing, and beloved country of ours. I have the very best reports, of the disposition and intentions, of the good people of the West, towards the Peoples candidates. I am informed, that Mr. Clayton, adhears very strongly, to General Scott. How is this? He is a frail candidate. Whoever embarks, on board of that Ship, will most assuredly founder. And if any portion of the Whig party, attempt, or do in fact, bring forward Mr. Clay, as a candidate, it is as surely defeated, as that it is manifested. What man, is there, in this nation, that loves his country, that can say Henry Clay, ought not to have been elected in 1840. In 1844. I actually thought, he was elected. The identical clique, (Scott & Co) that prevented his nomination in 1840, went against him, with the addition of the vile Abolitionists in -44. And this wicked combination, is ready, at a moments warning, to do effective battle, against him again in 48. And I can further say, of all men in these U. S. Henry Clay, of right, and with a single eye, to the best interest of North America, ought at this moment, to be sitting in his arm chair, in the White House, as President. And so you, and thousands of others, all honorable men, say. But Sir, what avails all this lamentation. All great, towering geniuses, like Mr. Clay, have ever had, and always will have, strong, vindictive, powerful, tremendous opposition, and which, regarding Mr. Clay, seems, that no time can chill, no circumstances, can allay. We must take men and circumstances, just as we find them. There is no altering them. It is very true of Mr. Clay, as you remarked, on a certain occasion, "His, history constitutes, a large portion, of our national renown."

Pray take good care of your health, for I desire much to see you, again and again. I hope my eyes will open in 48.

> I am D^r. Sir,
> with the Highest regard,
> Your friend
> J. B. MOWER

[Addressed:]

> Hon. Willie P. Mangum
> U. S. Senate
> Washington
> D. C.

WPM-LC

Abram R. Laurence[146] to Willie P. Mangum.

NEW YORK Augt. 4th, 1846

To
> Honble. Willie Mangum
> In Senate - Washington City

Sir

Several Members of the Whig General Committee have been urged to press upon that Body a call for a Whig Meeting in this city to express their opposition to the new Tariff and make arrangements for effecting its repeal- The subject was considered in our Executive Committee last evening - and as acting Chairman of the General Committee I was directed to address you and some other eminent members of the Senate in regard to its policy at this time - and to ask the favor of your opinion whether at this or at any other time such a precedure would be approved of by our friends in the South—

It is proper in explanation to add that however unanimous we may be in this quarter of the Union upon the blighting influence of the new tariff we cannot forget the obligation due to you and other distinguished Southern Senators for their honorable and disinterested course in regard to the Tariff of 1842

146See above, 383n.

Suggestions have been made that a more effective and less embarrassing hostility, to the law may be produced by associations of manufacturers formed without party distinctions and embracing operatives as well as their employees

Oblige us by imparting your advice as soon as your leisure will permit-

                    Most respectfully and truly
                        Your friend & Servant
                    ABRM R. LAURENCE.

P. S. Not having time before the departure of the mail to address Messrs Crittenden and Berrien - to whom I had directions to write *and sollicit* a like favor, allow me to impose upon your kindness the task of submitting this letter to their perusal

                                        A R L.

_____

                                            WPM-LC

A. G. Hodges[147] to Willie P. Mangum.

                        FRANKFORT, KY. Aug. 4th 1846.

Hon. W. P. Mangum

        Dear Sir:

        I received your letter announcing the receipt of the Biography of Capt. John W. Russell. I was greatly gratified with your warm expressions of approbation of the Captain. For he is a noble and generous fellow. I showed your letter to Capt. Russell, and the kind expressions of him by you almost melted him to tears. He said he had the warmest friends of any man upon earth. I am gratified today to inform you that Russell will be elected in the Senatorial District by a majority of between 800 and 1000 votes.

_____

[147]From his youth, Albert Gallatin Hodges worked in newspaper offices. Beginning as a reporter on the *Kentucky Reporter*, he later established the *Kentuckian* at Lancaster but was unable to finance it for long. In 1824 he published the *Louisville Morning Post*. Two years later he and James G. Dana established the *Frankfort Commonwealth* which he continued until 1872. A fiery editor, he exerted considerable influence in Kentucky politics. Thomas D. Clark, *A History of Kentucky*, New York, 1937, 347-349.

At the close of the vote today for dinner, Russell had in

Franklin County	622 votes
Drake had	149
	———
Russell's majority	473
Russell's majority in	
Shelby County last night	
at close of Polls	179
	———
	652

Franklin & Shelby compose the District. Our election continues 3 days, and the voting will go on until to-morrow night. I believe we shall give Russell about 650 or 700 majority here, and I think he will get about 300 majority in Shelby county.

I see the Locos have passed the Tariff for the *Relief of the British Laborers!* Well, I hope they will now consummate all their schemes of destruction to the best interests of this country, and let them come before the country upon those measures. If ever there were a set of corrupt scoundrels upon the face of the earth, the Leaders of the Locos are such.

Please show this letter to Crittenden & Morehead, and much oblige

Truly, your friend
A. G. Hodges

[Addressed:]   [Postmarked:] Frankfort Ky. Aug 4

Hon. W. P. Mangum
U. S. Senator
Washington City
D. C.

WPM-LC

Benjamin H. Brewster[148] to Willie P. Mangum.

1 Sansom Street
Philada. [Aug. 8, 1846]

My Dear Sir:

Today I directed a copy of the North American to be sent you containing the notice of you. While I was pleas'd with its

---

[148]After graduating from Princeton in 1834, Benjamin H. Brewster, 1816-1886, became a successful lawyer in Philadelphia. In 1846 he held a minor Federal post in settling the Cherokee Indian Claims. He was later attorney general of Pennsylvania and attorney general of the United States. His most famous accomplishment was his successful prosecution of the Star Route fraud in 1881-1884. *D. A. B.,* III, 26-27.

phraseology and the handsome way in which it did but justice to your high claims and lofty position yet I would rather that it had been more *pointed* in the conclusion. As it is a Whig press you must acquit me of all power to guide the pen editorial though I may give tone to their purpose and good will for you. Had it been *our* rabid Loco Foco organ, and had you been sanctified in the grace of Democracy the broad folds of our banner should gleam'd with your name. As it is remember I've only given earnest of my love by pitching the key note even of my "enemies in war, in peace friends."

They dare not boldly leap and do but timidly step, and did they know you as you are known they would proudly herald your name for that post which from your party you so much merit and which you would fill with so much honor.

"Glamis, and thane of Cawdor;

"The *greatest is behind.*—

Remember "the Earldom of Herefordshire" and when you are King do not make a Buckingham of me or even treat me as Edward treated the Great Neville - Earl of Warwick to whom in your pleasantry the other day you likend your young and frolicksom friend. Remember I am to be Great Emperor of Morocco and that is my Earldom of Herefo[r]dshire.

Ever with respect and
sincerity
BJN. H. BREWSTER
8 Aug 46.

To Honble. Willie P. Mangum
Washington City

[Addressed:]

To
Honb. Willie P. Mangum
Washington City
Senate. D C

WPM-LC

Asa Whitney[149] to Willie P. Mangum

WASHINGTON D. C Aug 12/46

Sir

I am desirous of seeing Mr Packenham to explain my project for a Railroad to the Pacific, and show him how much and when I think England interested-

If you will be so kind as to give me a note of introduction, (addressed to me through the Post office) I shall feel myself extremely obliged and as I have no claim for such a request, the obligation will be considered the greater

Most Respectfully
Your obt Servt
A. WHITNEY

Honl. W. P. Mangum

[Addressed:]

Honl. W. P. Mangum
Washington
D. C

_____

WPM-LC

James Auchincloss[150] to Willie P. Mangum

NEW YORK, August 19th. 1846.

Dear Sir,

I trust that it will not be deemed by you too great a liberty if I urge upon you the absolute necessity of doing something to appease the clamors of the people here for *a* bank of some description or other that will furnish a good currency for the whole Union, and at same time equalize the Exchanges. Mr. Clay's bill would have done this if it had been sanctioned by Mr. Tyler, but seeing we are not to have it, let us have that if

---

149After traveling extensively for a New York dry-goods firm, Asa Whitney entered business for himself. In the Panic of 1837 he failed. Soon thereafter he went to China for a New York firm and became aware of the value of a transcontinental railroad. In September, 1844, he presented his plan to get Congressional aid. When Congress gave him little encouragement, he began an extensive campaign to convince the people. In 1849 he published *A Project for a Railroad to the Pacific*. Two years later he turned to the English for help. *D. A. B.*, XX, 156-157.
150See above, III, 216n.

possible which will subserve every useful purpose. I have given my idea in brief and very hurriedly to Mr. Tallmadge, and although it may not furnish you with anything novel on the subject, permit me to ask you to read my letter to him. I have spoken to Mr. T. as a practical merchant, and let me say to you, my dear Sir, that my experience in Exchanges, first and last, has not been limited. My views, such as they are, are corroborated by such men as Saml. Jaudon Esq. and Morris Robbinson Esq.,[151] both long connected with the late U. S. B. in its palmiest days and before the "old Roman" resolved on its destruction. A bank of *Exchanges* and issues is what we want in this quarter: Give us this and rely upon it we shall soon have "peace and plenty"! If I were allowed by that noble specimen of true and devoted patriotism, I would say to Mr. Clay- "give the whole energies of your mind to the accomplishment of this plan, and the gratitude of all parties awaits you." But I forbear.

I trust and hope that you will not separate without carrying *every* measure you started for at the commencement of the session; if you do separate without effecting this, and the cry of defeat ringing in your ears from your noisy and factious opponents, be assured that the consequence *here* and elsewhere will be most disastrous to us. I look forward to the *Ides of November* in such an event with unfeigned alarm.

Do me the favor to write to me and I pledge myself in advance that your communication shall not be improperly used.

My best regards to Gov. Morehead and other grave Senators at No. 2.

With great respect
Your friend & servant,
JAMES AUCHINCLOSS.

Hon. W. P. Mangum.

[Addressed:]

Hon. W. P. Mangum,
U. S. Senate,
Washington-
D. C.

---

[151]Samuel Jaudon was cashier of the United States Bank at Philadelphia. On the New York board was Morris Robinson. Reginald C. (ed.), *The Correspondence of Nicholas Biddle dealing with National Affairs, 1807-1844*, Boston, 1919, 81; Tuckman (ed.), *Diary of Philip Hone*, II, 231, 347.

WPM-LC

John B. Fry[152] to Willie P. Mangum

WASHINGTON, August 24th. 1846.

My dear Sir:

I did not have an opportunity, on yesterday, of saying as much to you as I desire in relation to a thorough organization of the Whig party, and of commencing at the opening of the next session of Congress, to distribute the most suitable speeches or documents over the entire Country- to both Whigs & locofocos.

If I could be assured that yourself- Messrs Crittenden, Clayton, Corwin and other influential gentlemen of our party would co-operate heartily in giving the plan efficiency, I would, at once, take steps to procure the fullest possible list of *names,* in every section of the Country, and be ready next December to begin a regular & systematic circulation of approved speeches, to be kept up till the Presidential Election in 1848.

I submit to you whether a circular letter emanating from a committee of Whig members of both branches of Congress, addressed to Whig capitalists in different parts of the Country, would not be responded to with sums of money sufficient to put the plan into immediate operation? If it would, and it shall be the desire of your committee, I will undertake the matter with the utmost zeal.

I am Sir, very respectfully,
Your friend & obt Serv[t].

JOHN B. FRY.

Hon: Willie P. Mangum,
U. S. Senate.

———

WPM-LC

T. L. Clingman to Willie P. Mangum

ASHEVILLE Aug 25th 1846

My dear Sir

I was in hopes that I should have had a letter from you ere this, but I know too well how you have been occupied at Wash-

---

[152]See below, 499-500.

ington to complain of your silence, Gen Waddy Thompson now here informs me that he left you looking uncommonly well at Washington and doing in all things as becomes a senator from the old North State. Our elections have gone off right and I have the satisfaction of thinking that your efforts both in this district and elsewhere contributed something to the result.

I take it for granted that you will give to the whigs the use of your name for reelection to the senate, though in your letter to me of last fall you you [sic] expressed yourself differently, yet I did not suppose that you would be permitted by the Whig party of the State and nation to decline, connected as your name has been so frequently with the first and second offices in the nation, Accordingly to my own suggestions therefore the Whig candidates in this region came out for you against all the world as their first choice, and afterwards having understood that some persons a little this side of you and a few Whigs in this district who have lately been indirectly connected by a democratic link with a certain prominent whig in Guilford of whom you told me that you had a little right to complain, understanding I say that they were for substituting that person in your stead, I made it a point myself in my replies to Mr. J. B. Sheppard[153] at various points especially at Burke & Rutherford to tell the people that it was the duty of the Whigs to make every effort to secure the legislature and that it would be discreditable to the state to allow you to be driven from the position you occupied with such distinction to yourself and the State You will therefore I have no doubt be supported for a reelection by all the whigs from this quarter as against any one. Mr. Haywoods resignation came on us very unexpectedly a few days before the election and though I am informed that Col. G. and one or two others profess to wish to elect Badger & Morehead yet you will lose no member of the legislature, These matters of course I write in confidence as I do not care to be unnecessarily embroiled with any body, but you know I am not a man to shun responsibility whenever a proper occasion is presented. As to the second vacancy (Mr Haywoods) there will be diversity of opinion.[154] Some of my friends are desirous of presenting my name for that appointment and I feel at liberty to mention the

---

[153]James Biddle Sheppard was the Democratic candidate for governor running against W. A. Graham, the Whig candidate.
[154]George E. Badger was selected.

matter to you because you alluded to it heretofore &c- Before
however any decided step is taken in the matter I must know two
or three things, And first as to whom I might be brought in collision with, If Badger is anxious to go to the Senate (though
I presume from former things and from a letter lately received
from him by me that he would not desire such a thing) then I
should not like for any of my friends to bring my name in opposition to him eminent as he stands both in and out of the State,
But I should not only wish to be informed as to whom are to be
my competitors, but also to know what probability there is of my
getting a respectable support in the middle or Eastern part of
the state. Though I might be sustained by all the members from
this part of the state, yet the number is comparitively small and
I do not besides wish to be presented merely as a sectional
candidate, I write to you as a friend in confidence to know what
you think of the matter as I am satisfied that you can from your
position give me more information than any one else and what
you may write will be not of course made public. What would
be my chance (if I should be pressed on the legislature by the
western whigs) with the deligations from yours & the adjoining counties? What are Gov. Grahams feelings towards me? I
believe from my position, I was able both in his first and second
canvass to render him more service than any one Whig in the
state, and my influence was in both instances exerted to the
uttermost both by political & personal appeals though I well
knew at the time that I was thereby greatly weakening myself
personally in the district and then believed and still am of opinion that my efforts against Mr. Hoke in '44 lost me more votes
than I was beaten by in '45.[155] If you and others whom I know
to be personally my friends are of opinion that my efforts against
the South Carolina politicians, against the democratic leaders
in North Carolina & against the Locofocoism of the Union generally afford evidence of sufficient capacity and zeal in the service of the Whig party, then I have no objection to my friends
making an effort, but of course unless I am taken up by the
whigs of the middle and Eastern part of the State, my friends
are too feeble in point of number to justify them in pressing my
name. I should like to hear from you at your earlest leisure

---

[155]See above, 316.

and I believe you know me too well to doubt but that I will take
kindly any suggestions that you might make of whatever nature.

In conclusion I will only say that if there should be any occasion for it (though I do not apprehend such necessity) I shall
use any influence I possess in your behalf as decidedly as any
friend you have in the state will do.

I am very truly yours &c

T. L. CLINGMAN

Hon Wilie P. Mangum

WPM-LC

James E. Harvey to Willie P. Mangum.

SARATOGA SPRINGS.
Aug. 25. 1846.

My dear Sir.

After parting with you, I held over a day in Philadelphia &
a week in New York, very much against my will. During my
stay, I saw many of the master spirits of the *Wards,* by far the
most important personages in regulating the sentiments of the
masses, whom to a great extent, they control - at least, direct.
The fact is not to be disguised, that the preference of the City
is for Clay & that of the Country for anybody, but him. Still
however the politicians of the former, have another idol dearer
even than him of Ashland - which is *Number one* - a deity they
never abandon, a worship they incessantly practice. Convince
these gentry, that Clay cannot be elected & that somebody else
can, who will reward as fully & punish as severely & the charm
is at once dissolved. To a certain extent, that has been already
done & some of them are now openly enlisting under McLean's
banner. The only difficulty I have encountered, is in reference
to the distribution of the patronage. Could they be assured
on that head, we should get a momentum, that no other aspirant
could resist. As it is, we have the track of Taylor, & the course
so far as Scott is concerned. He (S) has no party & the clique
which is *par excellence* & *deservedly* so, his friends, affect what
they do not feel - Even they however—Webb, *et id genus omne*

have knocked under for the Presidency & are now on the look-
out for other game. It is difficult to tell where they will go -
or rather where they will *not* go. They have very little hold
on any subdivision of the party & no affiliation with the great
mass. All things considered, the posture of affairs in New
York, is vastly better than I expected to find it & I believe I
impregnated the waters more strongly with my McLean &
Mangum Catholicon. I mean no humbug, when I tell you, the
name of the latter is a tower of strength among these same
ultras. You blazed away so "dangerously" in 1842, that they
think they smell the sulphur even now & that odor puts them
on a Crusade against all moderation & conservatism.

I halted a day in Albany to dine with Spencer (J. C.) who
invited me to do so in answer to a copy of the "Sketch" which
I sent him. We went over the whole ground from alpha to
omega & he is as true to the Whig cause as you are. This *I* knew
when you were all warring upon him in the Senate,[156] as I happened to share his confidence, during all the Tylerian time & no
greater mistake was committed, than his rejection for the Bench,
especially to us at the *South.* You have now a rank abolitionist
in disguise, in the place he should have occupied. But, there is
no use in looking back, in this age of Progress. Spencer *never*
was a Clay man, nor were any of the anti-Masons in New York
of which he was the head exponent - hence the falling off in the
vote of that section in 1844. He is thoroughly for McLean &
has forgiven you. He proposes to come out in the fall or winter
with an exposition of his remaining in the Cabinet & to place
himself on the old platform, being willing to take his place in
the ranks. There are about 5,000 men of his way of thinking
in this State, who either stayed away from the polls or cut the
electoral ticket at the great struggle. These men never were
& never can be Locofocos. They want a man, who won't ostra-
cize them because they were not born "White Charlies" & they
will concentrate on any Candidate, who will not pledge himself to elevate a few at the expense of the many. Spencer's pen
is among the most ready, powerful & almost magical in politics
of any here or elsewhere that I know of & he is willing & anxious to use it. Our manifest policy is to encourage him & his
class & not to haggle as some are inclined to do, about a seat at
the table of which we are all to be communicants in Common.

---

[156]See above, 11.

He authorized me to make known these views to Judge Mc Lean & yourself.

I reached here on Saturday night & found but few that I knew. Crittenden & Barrow had gone & accomplished nothing while here. Indeed, they did not attempt any movement. Archer, after the manner of the nobility of Virginia locked himself up in a Castle (Cottage) & appeared only at stated periods, when of course, there was a general anxiety among the fashionable & *foreign* world. The last accounts of him were that he was putting up at a *temperance* House, whose landlord had been nominated as the Native American Candidate for Governor. Hearing this, I thought it about time to drop my inquiries.

The season is over - the grand Ball has been given & our Hotel the largest & the most tonnish, is reduced to 200 very sensible & good natured people. This is by far the best part of the year & I shall hold out a week or ten days longer.

The water & exercise & relaxation of mind have improved my condition considerably even in the few days I have been here & there is every promise of further amendment. I am prudent & regular & hope to regain my health so as to render service at the next session.

I sent an Editorial to the N. A. to-day, hastily put together, in which I have said, you have consented to be a Candidate for re-election. I suppose you will see it. If it was bad I'm sure you would.

I do not ask you to write for two reasons - first because you are intolerably lazy, which your constituents ought to know, if they do not & next because I am a bird of passage & have no head quarters.

As ever your friend,
JAMES E. HARVEY.

If you have any suggestion to make or wish anything done, address me at New York & a friend will forward my letters to wherever I may be.

[Addressed:] [Postmarked:] Saratoga Springs N. Y.
Aug 26

Hon Willie P. Mangum
Red Mountain
No. Ca.

WPM-LC

John Wilson to Willie P. Mangum.

WASHINGTON 9th Sept. 1846.

Hon. W. P. Mangum

Dear Sir

Our slight personal acquaintance, was formed, so short a time; before your departure from this city; I had not the opportunity, of seeking your views; and giving my own; which I desired, in relation to the contest which is to come off, in '48, in regard to the Presidency; the success of which, I am sure both of us feel to be of great importance. That you may have a chance, to satisfy yourself, if you desire, as to "who is" John Wilson; not "Jas. K. Polk," I place before you; the following out line of my history. I was born near "Knoxville Ten^ee," raised from early childhood to mans estate; in "Augusta County Va" & afterwards, in 1811; took up my residence in "Kentucky" & for the last 25 years, have been a practising Lawyer and a resident in the "Town of Fayette, Howard County Missouri". For the last seven years, I have spent, most of my time, traveling over the U. S.; in "Louisiana" & the South generally; but also have been much, in New York, Boston, Phila. & this city.

In the course of all this period, of 35 years; I have mixed in a business capacity; extensively with the *common* people; if you will allow me the use of that expression as opposed to *Politicians*. I am without education, except, what has been *rubbed into me*, by the constant active, (I may say) energetic; mixing for more than a third of a century, with the raw, but active, and busstling materials, of a new, but at the same time, mighty country; the great valley of the Mississippi; the progress of which; for the time, has been I believe, unparalleled in the history of mankind.

My professional pursuits, necessarily led me into a close, and constant association, with the unpolished engredients of society; but yet, it is there, after all, that the germe - the diamond - of republican liberty is to be found. They, indeed need the hand of science and Literature, to polish their rough exterior; and a system of regulated liberty; to guide & restrain, the impulses of nature, but there - amongst them - is to be found the great *safety valve,* of free institutions. I intend you to infer from all this; that whatever I may have learned; I have lapped from the gushing and *uncurbed,* fountains of nature; which have spouted up around me, with such amazing and acumulating force; in that great valley, where indeed I was born; and *which;* when I first *bivouac* under a tree and the heavens; as my only shelter, on the banks of the great father of waters; was *then* but one interminable wilderness - is *now,* teeming with inteligent and energetic millions of people! while its surface- from the Lakes to the Balize; is dotted over with innumerable villages, Hamlets, Log-Cabins, & camps, of the Newcomer & the "Prairie naturelles" are swarming with beasts of the *field,* & the air is rendered, "retentissement" with the lowing of the cow; the sure and unerring sign, to the way-worn traveler; that he is nearing the abode of civilized man. A truce, however to this gushing enthusiasm; which can only be felt, and appreciated; by breathing the air, and traveling over this unparelleled valley; stretching from the alleghaney to the Rocky mountains - from the Lakes to the Gulf - to feel as the writer does, that in less than a hundred years - yes! - within the life time of his youngest son; should God spare him to the age of four-score years.- this *district* will contain a hundred Millions of people; within which the writer was born; one, of as many thousands, which was perhaps near the extent of it civilized population in 1790!! So much of myself - so much for the valley. I have digressed, but now return to say, what I set out to indite. And first I write only my own opinions, and as such, desire them only to be weighed. The Whigs of congress, ought not to have let the late adjournment pass; without having concluded; a full and energetic organization, to manage our party matters; til '48 shall have *passé.* That not having been done fully; all our leading friends, should set to work, *now;* vogorously and rest not, till such an organization is complete.

When we commenced the contest of '44, I confess I had fears of our success; because I saw amongst our friends, a determination to nominate, Mr. Clay, for whose elevation to the Precedency, I had; *against my will,* lost all hope since 1836. After his nomination, I gathered courage, and supposed we should succeed, and so inevitably we should; if it had not been; for the very thing, which has been the *bane,* if Mr. Clays whole political life: a determination to *lead*, rather than to be advised by his friends.- a disposition to *first* express, and advocate; *all* the measures of his party. This has caused most of his own mortifications; as well, as kept the whigs out of power. I do not mean this, as a sensure on his measures; but *I do mean* to say, he was always too ambitious; to *originate* and *stamp*, upon his friends, all the measures of his party, to be advocated. It is truly a laudable ambition, but to say the least, it sets at defiance the old maxim which teaches, that "in the multitude of counsellors; there is safety": and hence his *Two* Texas letters, and consequently *our* defeat: had but *one*, been written; no matter which; we should have been safe. I consider our chance for success; worse *now* than in '44, except, so far as I see a tendency, to nominate some one else than Mr. Clay, in *that* event, there is a chance, (if vigorously laid hold of) to do what could not *then*, be done under Mr. C's auspices; which is to bring about a combination, amongst all the *anti*-Regular-Loco, interests, which I have no sort of doubt; form a large majority of the voters of the Union. It is true; I believe this compromise, could have been more easily accomplished *then;* than *now* - Mr. Clay aside - But still I believe it can be done now. Then the government patronage (always the lever of Loco success) was divided, between *traitors* & Locos - it neutralized itself: then too, this patronage was weilded, by several men, who in reality had different interests to subserve - not so *now* the whole is moved, & dispensed, by one hand directed *by*, one will, & *for* one purpose, by a bold and reckless politicians. - By men who are not ashamed, in open day; to go into the house of Representatives, as they did on the Tariff bill, and drag by the very, *collar* the dissatisfied, or Tired & doubted adherents, into a vote for a bill which, these feared recusants; had in their places declared was distruction to the country!!! Hence *now,* this patronage will be used with double effect; that it was *then.* The change of the Tariff, and the establishment of the sub-treasury; widen the means of payment, to dissatisfied friends; while the army; furnishes vast facilities for bribery, and corruption, and who dare tell me; that knows the present dispensers, of the blessings of a war for the "extension of the area of freedom"; that these weapons of power, will not be vigorously used. Who can tell the power of this patronage, in *such* hands? In the days of Washington, men knew not the power of this arm, of the government; if they did; the Humblest citizen, would have scorned, to have been influenced, in his political opinions, by the bestowment on him, of the highest office: not so *now;* since Jackson taught the *dispenser;* that it was the *lever* of *power;* the *receiver;* that it was the *price,* of *obedience.* Between this, and the fall of '48; in all probability, there will be more than one hundred & fifty millions of Dollars, expended by our government, it will all, be *channelled* for the same purpose - the gathering together, under the wings of Locoism, every interest. Are you prepaired to answer, how much reason, & sound sense, this will over-rule; how much dissatisfaction, it will silence, & how much support; it will buy?

Depend upon it, I am not. Then we have a *mighty* work to achieve; and enormous evil to overcome - mark the difference in the roads, we travel - while *we* appeal to the reason, and invoke the patriotism, of the people; they openly go forth, into the streets, offering honor & Gold; saying as the woman did to her victim, who Soloman saw & observed, from his window; "I came forth to meet thee, dilligently to seek thy face; & have found thee". who shall answer for the result? Nothing but the most active, most determined & energetic measures will succeed against such a combination. *It is full time to begin.* Remember, the vast territory, over which our operations, are to spread themselves. *Our* lines of communications, are not yet established.- Those of our opponents, are complete. and in operation, to the centre of every neighborhood - in each; paid agents are already on the ground, actively engaged in the distructive work: But how is it with us? Which of us knows what another is doing? What is our plan of operations? Who are our helmsmen? Where are we to look for our flag? To whom report the countersign of our friends? We are good Whigs, give us an *open organization,* & an efficient set of leaders, who shall devise *the way,* that is the best & we shall travel it. Let this be done, before *individual* ambition, or local interests, shall seize hold of parts of our forces; so that when we shall come to ask their support, they have, by their own supposed interests; or by the wiles of our adversaries; determined, only to give it, if we yield some of our dearest principles;- This we cannot do.- Yet, if they were applied to at an early day, would be fully satisfied, with what we, can readily yield. Something ought to be done, *and at once,* to soothe the nativists, to moderate the aboli-

tionists, - To run *"a muck"* with the anti-Calhoun-Loco-interest
in the south, - to win a coalition with the anti-veto-Loco, & 54.40 -
interests, of the west & south. These are all small, but in some
instances determined parties; who, no doubt, if set about wisely
& in time, much that is salutary may be done; without yielding
any of our main principles; and especially the natives, who are
a growing party, mostly, taken from the Whigs; who in fact
ask nothing, but what I believe, the Whigs feel absolutely to be
necessary (if I abate the name they assume), for the preservation of republican Liberty - If that be so, and we both are sincere, & I feel the Whigs are; where is the great matter to be arranged? The Whigs, I trust will ever be on the side, of those
born at home if indeed, there shall come a necessity, *to resist
too much foreign influence;* and who that has carefully noticed,
all the phases of Locofocoism, for several years, & especially for
the last congress, shall be able to declare, that that party do
not especially, and particularly, look to, & *demand* and expect,
support from all foreigners *as such.* I confess with shame, that
this appeal is to be found, in nearly every speach of the full
blooded order of Locofoco-ism, & that I fear, such a contest has,
or will soon; become inevitable - If so, *I am for the home party
against the world.* If it is asked, *how* all these arrangements,
are to be concluded, & by whom? I answer by a committee for this
city - of our noblest spirits, in whom our friends delight to
trust - Subordinate Committees, of the same class of men, all
over the country, by whose influence money can be raised by
private donation; with which to buy, & send documents, statistics, & debaters (where needed) for all public assemblies & to
the people in general; to give them the light of truth the
faithfullness of true patriotism - seeking & dispensing nothing,
but the truth - That when we do succeed, it may be a victory, of
truth & true patriotism - over the spoilers of the country - Such
a victory will last. But who, without these exertions, can expect, that we shall succeed. I confess I am not among the number. The next thing of importance - yes - demanded - I had
almost said - we could not succeed without it - Is a *press* in
Washington with editors of the new school of events - In fact
at least of the present age, - possessing, talents energy, policy
& efficiency, who can write pointed paragraphs, of from two
to four inches long, instead of whole columns of long & tedious
articles, whose length insures that none but the man of leisure

or the "gentleman & schollar" will read them - exclude them
from the colums of all country papers, unless they leave out all
their advertisements, & Local news. - Editors who will not stop
in the heat of an excited campaign, on the termination of which,
is staked the liberties of a nation, to write a long criticism,
showing their knowledge of gramar - or fill a whole colum,
with an apostrophy to the beauty of some classic quotation,
from Homer or Tacitus, to show the depth of their learning.
But men who can condecend, to write articles, that even the
busy labourer, may read, & country news papers copy, & who
are natives of the greatest of all countries - men too who would
likely, be able to to save enough out of millions of patronage,
to keep up the fire upon the enemy. - And who were not too
dignified, to watch, as well behind, as before. - to fight enemies
in the front, & also "in the rear," & to be willing & capable to
drag to the light, without so much pretended delecacy; the
midnight schemes of our opponents; & thereby crush, in the
bud many of their distructive & selfish purposes; or if not able
to do that; at once to excoriate, the political backs of these dark
workers of distruction; that the anti-dote may go forth with the
poison, that the people may know, before they imbibe, the loath-
some nature of their doings: & who, too can do these things
without either Tongs or Gloves. I bear testimony with the
greatest pleasure, to the high moral stand of the Intelligencer;
to the gentlemanly & courteous articles, that therein appear,
and to the *general* correct mode of thinking displayed in its
colums, but "Jo. Gales," is farther behind the present light-
[n]ing speed of the times, in all that regards political usefully in
such a contest; as a leading editor; than Fultons Old first North
River Boat, was behind the Princeton, the Cambria, or the
Knickerbocker, of the present day. It is one of the things certain, not to be disputed; that, if any man or set of men, were
so simple, as to attempt to run Fulton's Old North River Boat
(were she here in the same plight she first left the Wharf at
N.Y. for Albany) in competition with such boats, & ships above
named; every New Jersey Bumpkin, or Lazeroni of the Wharfs,
of N. York, would laugh them to scorn; and yet the whigs are
resting, to that extent at least, the whole destinies of the nation,
upon the services of an editor, still farther in the rear of those
he is expected to out-run.

It is no answer to say, that our opponents have for the present, selected a simple old Jesuit as a counterpoise, to our "gentleman & schollar" for they will soon change him for 'a Blair'; but if they do not, the refined & classical gentleman, has ever been an easy prey, to that jesuistical system, which is all things to all men, where the spoils are concerned. In fact, the Intelligencer should be bought out, by our friends, at once; and the same policy persued with Mr. Gales, that was played off successfully with Blair & Reeves. If you leave him there; & a Wreck as it were of centries gone bye, and establish a new paper, his necessities & the sympathies of good men; will cause a division when patronage is to be given out; & your new editors, will not only not [be] rewarded, but Gales & Seaton, will be none the richer & this will endanger a victory. Remember I do not propose an immediate nomination of our candidates; but the establishment of committees, the collection of money, the buying and distributing such documents and other political information; as will be useful in inlightening "the Boys" the spirit of which last expression the Whigs, have always; (*except in 1840*) neglected: then we went to them, for the first time on their own terms, then they rallied to us, by thousands, & so they will again, if we seek them on their own ground. We have courted & won, the city "Belles & Beaux" & have won & still retain their ardent desire, for our success; Let us have these publick documents & debaters, armed with truth & patriotism, to send to every nook & corner of our beloved country; to show the honest labourer & husbandman, the true distructive schemes, of our oponents in their true light, and in this manner "the hearts of the people will be prepaired for war," not indeed for an onslaugh, upon either England, or Mexico, but against a power, far more destructive & dangerous, to the stability of our institutions; *than both these nations together*.- a power, whose chief aim, is to embroil the poor, against the rich - a party who openly proclaim that "to the victors belong the spoils." These two things both strike, directly at the very root of all free government- This spirit must be rebuked by the Whigs, or else your children, will not all have departed this life, in all probability - till a mighty Empire is established on the ruins of this our republic— When the great struggle, will be for the purple, instead of the Presidency. If any one should take exception to my proposition, to prepair the people beforehand, not only for the election, but to dissignate the candidates also; my answer is easily given - It is of necessity, the only mode of success. I was raised & still am a politician of the old school, & have always, do now, & I have no doubt forever shall; consider the course as pointed out by the Vanburen School under the denomination of caucus, & now *almost* universally adopted by the Loco foco party, *in place* of the *ballot box;* as intirely anti-Republican & distructive in its character of all free government & if it is continued and once is fully adopted by the people in general we shall soon be a nation of slaves, enstead of free men. In our State, it is a finable offence, to set fire to the prairie; and yet without the exception appearing on the face of the statute, it is usual for all our people, when at a distance they see the devouring flames, raging towards them, with an inevitable tendency, to consume their fences, their Hay stacks, & their houses; they at once go to "firing against fire" & so, save their own premises, from distruction, & are justified in the eye of the law; by inevitable necessity, for self preservation. Indeed in the art of healing, we have in modern days something of the same kind; tried it is said by late experimenters, with great success; as when a person is prostrated, with the most raging fever; the successors to the old quacks familiarly as "number sixes" who now adopt the cognomen of "Hot drops venders" They give in these extreme cases of the most violent fevers, these drops; said of all other substances, to be the most inflamatory in the chemical Laboratory; & thereby, beat the fever *at its own game.* It is consumed by a substance, still more raging. I therefore see, no anti-dote to this abominable caucus system; but to *burn it up,* by administering in constant doses that which is more powerful - the light of truth & correct information— These, & these only, vigorously administered, & in the proper manner, will drive this shameless system of caucussing - This ruling this Thinking - of the few - for the many - give truth & light to the latter, & they will hurl from their illgotten places the former. This if done, must be done by others, than the party in power, at present- The Whigs alone must to do this; if they do it not they are equally to blame for having let the heritage of their fathers - a free & happy government - dwindle in the worst of humbugery. The duty of the Whigs now can only be done, by the dissemination of truth, to all corners of the country, by *compromising* FORMS, & in forcing & adhering to the *great land* marks, of republican freedom, as handed down to us, by the fathers of the revolution at least- *"Them's my sentiments."*

You are aware, there are many isms struck off into little squads, all over the Union, many of which I feel sure if treated in a proper manner - if something is yielded to them - and if assurances are given to them, by our accredited agents-our properly organized committees, headed by our most trusted & leading men, can easily be brought into unison, with the Whigs & yet the whigs hold on to the main, principles of their creed. This is a work of time, & can only be done by committees, or some such organization, which are authorised, or at least accredited, to speak for the whigs in general. And this is why I address you. Your position has not only the highest in office amongst us, but whose public course, I believe has given general satisfaction, to every body but especially to all Whigs; it is therefore they look with confidence to you to give direction, & energy to whatsoever movement is necessary to insure our success.

I as one of the Whig party, have given you my views, not however with any expectation, that they will be litterally carried into effect. I know too well the very great difference of opinion, that is sure to seize upon different minds, even when all are bent upon the same end; to look for this. I have already received answers, to similar suggestions, from some of our truest friends, says one "its too soon to begin yet" another if we establish such committees "our opponents, will make a great handle of it" and yet another - a kind of political predestinatian - "Let the people alone, they'l do right." My answer is, that whatever is worth doing at all, is worth being done *now* & in the manner, that will do it best, and to the predestinan portion of our friends, their views are very much like, one of Mr. Clay's foolish maxims; foolish as far as applied to the *general affairs of this life-* "Truth is mighty & will prevail" - so it will in heaven - on earth it never did - as to man doing right that is let alone - he *may* hereafter- There are, if any, but few proofs it - so far as the same is applied to general politics. Were the people let alone, previous to & during the Revolution? did not the old patriots of '76 attempt in this same way, to prepair the hearts of the people for, war, & when it was commenced did they not in the same way, encourage them to nerve their arms, in so unequal a contest- If they did not, do this why was old John Hancock, Samuel Adams, & others so ardently sought for over their fellows by the British, if they had not urged, by speeches, by writing; nay by every means in their power; attempt to rouse their fellow citizens to the defence of their rights. - are not we now trying, to defend these same rights, not indeed at "le pas d'arms", but at the ballot box, where indeed our institutions are according to the Creed of the Whigs equally as infamously attackted, as were our rights by England before the revolution - England then declared, what our opponents do now to "the victors belong the spoils" Then the British taxed, us without allowing us any representation, in parliment - is not that the open effort of our opponents- It is true, in spite of all their efforts, we have some nominal representatives, in Congress But do they meet us there, in open debate to reason upon the matter, - *no sir,* they gather beforehand *in midnight caucus to themselves,* & decide what is to be done, & go into the Hall to register what *King caucus has determined* - and if any one of the party - as for instance a member from Ohio, or New York, should show a spirit of recusancy, by saying *I'll defeat your bill;* do not their chiefs, who hold the loaves & fishes in their hand, come down intirely out of their sphere & shake them openly by the collar, till they are brought back to caucus standard- Is not this done, in open day? can it be said it, is too soon, to begin to eradicate this damning iniquity. are we not taxed without representation recollect we went to the people in 1840 for the first time, on their own terms; they came to our suppt with a *vengence* on evil doers Let us try it again, & we shall not be deceived. I leave for home in a day or two, *where* I shall be happy to hear from you.

Your friend

JOHN WILSON

[Addressed:]

Hon.
Willie P. Mangum
Red-Mountain
North Carolina.

WPM-LC

John Hogan[157] *to Willie P. Mangum.*

UTICA NEW YORK, Sept 17th. 1846.

Private

My dear sir

I hear with regret that you became indisposed before you left Washington. I hope that your health is again restored & that you enjoy your usual good health for no one knows better than myself the want of that blessing- but since my return home my health has much improved still I am a little under the weather & fear I shall be for some time- Your friends in this State (and let me here say you have many) are highly gratified & rejoice that you will come back to the Senate (it is needless for me to say that no man in this State is more highly pleased & rejoices over your success than your humble *Servant,* for my dear Judge let me here say that the interest of our Country demands at this period her most true and experienced Statesmen to keep within bounds of prudence legislation in our National Councils- it is true by the united efforts of you Gent in the Senate at the last session of Congress our Ship of State was kept from the quick sands believe me when I say to you that in my opinion another storm is gathering. The imprudence of Some Gent will still spur them on and their disappointment last winter will only spur them to greater efforts whether for weal or for woe- but I must throw aside those misgivings and hope for the best- I will take a glance at the political prospects of this State, N. Y) We are all divided into Sixes and Sevens Wright & ante Wright helter skelter every one for himself, unfortunately the Gen Administration does not exercise one whit of influence neither can it from its its [sic] present untoward position in this State

Your People are settling down on Fillmore & they are uniting all through the State from present appearances they all have a maj of members of Congress. Should they continue their efforts as they have commenced they will Elect Fillmore by a large maj We Calhoun men are looking quietly taking but little *part* in fact *none*

---

[157]See above, 419.

The Abolitionests in my opinion will not get more than 6000 votes in the State probably less the Natives will do but little. *We* will try & defeat your friends if *we* can but the effort will *I fear* prove an abortive one. Although not having the pleasure of having acquaintance of Mrs Mangum & family I hope they enjoy good health- Drop me a line & let me know the State of your health

The weather here through August & up to this time has been oppressively warm-

Accept Sir for your self & family my best wishes for your health ad happiness & prosperity

I have the honour to be your
Obt servt
JOHN HOGAN

Hon W. P. Mangum
Private

[Addressed:]

Hon. Willie P. Mangum
Red Mountain
North Carolina

WPM-LC

James E. Harvey to Willie P. Mangum.

CHEMUNG, N. Y.
Sept. 22d. 1846.

My dear Judge.

Since my letter to you from Saratoga Springs, I have traversed something like 2000 miles, between the East & this region. In Massachusetts, there is no sort of sympathy for any demonstration in favor of Webster. Indeed, the repugnance is stronger than I was led to suppose. Many, very many old-school Whigs have not even yet forgiven his Fanueil Hall Movement & toleration,[158] rather than admiration is the true light in which he is regarded in important quarters. A very excellent feeling prevails towards McLean, but as yet there can be said to be no classification or siding of interests. From what I could gather

---

[158]See above, III, 302n.

among the Whig Editors & others in Boston, it is clear to my mind, he will eventually constitute the choice & concentrate the force of that region.

During the past week, I attended the great Agricultural State Fair at Auburn for four days, where there was a Collection of some 20 or 30,000 people, mostly substantial & intelligent Farmers. I made it a special point to mingle among the masses & after ascertaining political preferences, to draw out an expression of opinion in reference to the Presidency. Many were already impressed with the policy of running McLean, because he lives in a free State & therefore is presumed to be sound on questions, in which they feel concern - others on account of his great purity of Character & still some because he was a self made man, & raised himself from his own exertions. Generally speaking, there was a want of information as to his history. & when I entered upon the incidents of his life, as I did every night after the parade, to groupes of 10 & 20 in a Conversational tone, I found not only ready listeners, but new & decided friends. I distributed all the numbers of the "Sketch" I had in my portmanteau & afterwards the farmers came to me with thanks & expressed a degree of enthusiasm, that I have rarely witnessed on such occasions. I am now confident, it is of the *utmost importance*. We should spread some 100,000 copies of it at the opening of the next session, to be read & reflected upon in the long winter nights—this will enable the people for once to indicate their own candidate & to get the start of the Leaders. If you concur in this View do send me a letter to that effect & upon the general policy to Cincinnati by the post after this reaches you, so that I may be backed by the weight of your name and judgment, in laying the matter before the Judge's friends, as I intend to do, upon my arrival there, which will be about the time I may expect your answer. If this document is properly disseminated in New York & Pennsylvania, trust me there will be no difficulty about the Convention & still less about the election, if we unite as we undoubtedly will in such an event.

In this State & particularly in this County, Cayuaga & others, the Locofocos are split into the most irreconcileable divisions & I find all my opinions about a concentration on the day of election erroneous. In this County, Saml. Young the atlas of Wright

Democracy, was thrown overboard for the Convention, though regularly nominated & in the face & eyes of 700 majority. That feud has widened every day Since & the Old Hunkers,[159] who produced that result by the help of the Whigs, proclaim publicly they will either desert the polls or vote for the Whig Nominee if Silas Wright is again presented. My hope of the result is strengthened by the fact, that that interest will control. Every cause of strife, difficulty & complaint is embodied in Wright on account of the partial distribution of the spoils & all the vengeance of the opposing faction will be vented on his head.

Our Whig friends, I am gratified to say are united & harmonious over the Country parts & there is not a ruffle upon the surface, except among the unadulterated herd of assinine editors in the City. The people exhibit very little interest, as to the nomination of State officers & are prepared to support zealously whomsoever the Convention will recommend. The appearances are that John Young[160] will be nominated for Governor & he or whoever else is chosen will call out a great vote - such as not been given at a State election in years. The prospects are really flattering & I can conceive of no serious mishap that can blight them, notwithstanding my experience in disappointments, between this & november. There will be a large *slipping off* among the locofocos & the example of Maine (for which 9 cheers) will stir up the blood of those who have either principle or integrity left. Things look quite as well as you would disire [*sic*].

I have been staying here for nearly a week under the hospitable roof of my friend John C. Clark[161] whom you remember in Congress & who is firm in our faith. He is making mischief among the enemy & has a candidate "ready salted" to be started against the regular nomination, which is the true way of breaking up their discipline & efficiency.

---

[159]When Polk became President, the two New York factions of his party became bitter rivals for patronage. Marcy, who led the Hunkers, was appointed to the Cabinet. Van Buren, the leader of the Barnburners, was disappointed. Wright, as governor, worked for harmony. When the legislature met in 1846 the Hunkers proposed resolutions endorsing Polk's administration. On this resolution the Barnburners made a fight. In the convention which followed, Wright was renominated, but the disaffection in the Democratic ranks led to the election of the Whig candidate, John Young. Herbert D. A. Donovan, *The Barnburners: A Study of the Internal Movements in the Political History of New York State, 1830-1852*, New York. 1925, 67-73.
[160]See below, 513n.
[161]See above, 366.

My health is considerably improved & I am gaining ground beyond my expectations, which necessarily lightens my spirits.

Pray do not neglect the letter, referred to

> As ever
> Your friend
> JAMES E. HARVEY

Judge Mangum

[Addressed:]

> Hon. Willie P. Mangum
>
> Red Mountain
>
> No. Ca.

WPM-LC

Weston R. Gales to Willie P. Mangum.

RALEIGH, Sept. 22, 1846.

My dear Sir:

I think it i due to our long friendship, to say to you, that in all Communications I have received, and in all the conversations, I have heard, not one individual has expressed himself in terms towards you, other than those of decided favor, in connection with the Senatorial appointments. Perhaps, this information is unnecessary, but I know, if you do not, that some person or persons for reasons of their own, have very studiously kept before the public, the idea, that you contemplated declining a re-election. Fearing, that if nominations were allowed to be made in the Newspapers, predicated upon such intention on your part, pledges might be given, and difficulties thus thrown in the way of the party, of carrying out its true feelings and wishes, I have steadily resisted, as I shall do, all nominations through the Press. Of course, when two individuals are nominated, (as Badger & Osborne[162] were in the "Star") it presents the idea either of pretermitting your claims, or that you have declined a re-election.

---

[162]He refers to George E. Badger and James W. Osborne. The Whigs put up Badger and Mangum. The Democrats supported Asa Biggs and James J. McKay. The two Whig candidates were elected. Norton, *Democratic Party in N. C.,* 147-148.

I trust that either Mr. Badger or Gov. Morehead may be associated with you, and I think it will be the latter, if he will permit his name to be used. *Entre nous*, I have no idea that Badger would accept. But, if neither of these gentlemen are taken up, and we go upon the small-fry, as *Gaither* calls them in a letter to me, when shall we touch bottom? By the way, alluding to Gaither's letter I will copy a passage: "If Mangum does not positively decline, he should be re-elected by all means, by an unanimous vote, and the Haywood vacancy filled by Mr. Badger or Gov. Morehead. Badger is my first choice, Morehead next. I wish it could be known that Badger would accept, as it would put a stop to the electioneering for the *small-fry* of the party."

I have written this hasty letter, my dear Sir, not to elicit a reply, but simply to explain my course of action, and to express to you the very high regard which I entertain for you personally.

Truly your's
WESTON R. GALES

P. S.   Rayner has just stepped in, and says that the Communication in the *Star*, nominating Badger & Osborne was written by Henry W. Miller- so he is informed.

[Addressed:]

Hon. Willie P. Mangum,
   Red Mountain,
     Orange,
      N. C.

Via. Franklinton)

[Postmarked:]
Raleigh N. C. Sep 22

WPM-LC

Charles Nichols to Willie P. Mangum.

NEW YORK Oct. 1st 1846

To The
   Hon: Wm. P. Mangum

     Dear Sir,
       Availing myself of the pleasure of my slight acquaintance with you, through our mutual friend the hon: N. P. Tall-

madge and being about to leave for Amsterdam I take take [*sic*]
the liberty of troubling you with a few remarks relative to my
Post: as I understand Mr. Buchanan is preparing a report on
the Consular establishment. It is not generally known there
are two appendages connected with my station; one at the Texel,
the other at Hartigen. At both of these Ports I am obliged to
have established agents under compensation which imposes upon me a heavy tax. I have spent of my private means rising six
thousand dollars in sustaining this Consulship - living in the
anticipation of a fair salary. You may therefore imagine, dear
sir, my disappointment when I heard Mr Campbell's report assigned only $1500 to my Post. With the exception of London,
Amsterdam is the most expensive living in Europe and as it is
a diplomatic station all acknowledge it should have a salary
at least equal to that of Paris. I trust the hon: Wm. P. Mangum
will allow these facts their due weight and be kind enough to
aid me in obtaining a fair and adequate salary for the Amsterdam Consulate which will will [*sic*] ever be gratefully remembered.

I have the honor to remain
Your Obedt. Servt.
Charles Nichols.

P.S.   This communication I have requested to be forwarded
after the convening of Congress.

[Addressed:] To The
>   Hon: Wm. P. Mangum
>   U. S. S
>   Washington
>   D. C.

WPM-LC

N. Sargent[163] to Willie P. Mangum.

Phila. Oct. 16. 1846.

Hon W. P. Mangum

    My dear Sir,

        Our election is over, & we are triumphant.[164] The proba-
bility is that we have gained six members of Congress - five

---

[163]See above, III, 410; Michael Kraus, *The Writing of American History*, 1953, p. 315.

[164]In Pennsylvania the Whig vote in 1846 was 7500 larger, the Native American was 7000 less, and the Democrats 20,000 less than in 1845. The Whigs gained Congressional seats, and in the legislature they controlled 18 of the 33 seats in the senate and 66 of the 100 in the house. Henry R. Mueller, *The Whig Party in Pennsylvania*, in *Studies in History, Economics, and Public Law of Columbia University*, New York, 1922, Vol. CI, No. 2, 132-133.

certain - & that we shall have a decided majority in the House
of Rep. We have also gained several Senators. The Whig
Candidate for Canal Commissioner, the only officer for whom
the whole state voted, is probably elected by from 5000 to 8000
votes! Counties which never before failed to give large Loco
majorities have given Whig majorities of from 200 to 300
votes.- This is the reply of Pa. to Mr. Sevier, who, you remember, said she voted with her eyes open in '44, & would give the
same vote again. I only fear our victory is too soon, & will induce the Locos to modify the tariff, & make extraordinary exertions to elect their governor next year. The result in this State
decides N. Y. I look upon Young's election in that state as now
safe, & *not the less so* for Webb's impolitic opposition to him.

> Very sincerely
> Your friend
> & Obdt Servt
> N. SARGENT

WPM-LC

John B. Fry[165] to Willie P. Mangum.

WASHINGTON, D. C. Oct 23d. 1846.

My dear Sir:

The election returns continue to be of the most cheering
character to the Whigs. I have received letters from some of
our best informed Whigs in New York; all of which encourage
the expectation of a Whig triumph in that State on the 3rd
proximo. It looks, now, as if we were to have a majority in the
House of Representatives, in the 30th Congress. Is it not your
opinion that we shall? The President & his Cabinet are in sad
spirits. Unless something shall turn up to check their reverses,
I do not think they can survive much longer. They are politically
dead already.

You will recollect, that before you left Washn. we conversed together upon the necessity of obtaining a list of the
entire voters in New York - of all political parties - to enable
us to send speeches & documents to them from the opening of
the next Session of Congress until the termination of the next

---

[165]See above, J. B. Fry to W. P. Mangum, August 24, 1846.

Presidential election. I believe this to be a very important step, and one which would be more effective than any other we could adopt. If we take it, I verily believe that all the powers of loco-focoism in that State, could not take it from us in 1848. As soon as the election in New York on the 3rd Novr. is over will be a good time to take the matter in hand. If you still think well of it, will you write a letter to me, urging the plan? It would inspirit our New York friends.

I hope your health has been good, and that our bright political prospects are as gratifying to you as they are to your many friends here and elsewhere.

I am with great respect
Your friend & Obt. Servt
JOHN B. FRY.

Hon: W. P. Mangum.
I write in great haste.

WPM-LC

James E. Harvey to Willie P. Mangum.

PHILADELPHIA
Oct 24. 1846.

My dear Judge,

I returned here yesterday after a tour of more than 3000 miles, embracing Ashland and many other points of interest. In this jaunt, I have endeavored to acquaint myself with the sentiment of the masses of the people in various quarters as to the Presidency and upon other topics. I think I have gleaned something in this respect.

In Ohio, McLean is stronger than the Whig strength by from 10 to 20,000 votes-[166] There is no enthusiasm for him, but a deep-rooted respect for his intergrity, character & ability. I have heard influential Locofocos in different regions of the State, say they would support him in preference to any other candidate & I know the fact personally, he could secure another

---

[166]In 1845, under the leadership of Mangum, Crittenden, and Clayton, the Whigs had turned away from Clay as their prospective party candidate in 1848. Feeling then turned to Scott and Corwin as the candidates, but Scott got into a controversy wih Marcy that hurt him. By the latter part of 1846 there was considerable feeling among the leaders for John McLean and Mangum for candidates. Before the campaign got well under way, however, McLean had lost popularity. Poage, *Henry Clay and the Whig Party*, 153.

influence which no other candidate can touch- this too in the face of his well-known decisions supporting the constitutional principle to the fullest extent. I have now in my possession a letter from Charles Sumner Esq. of Boston, the great leader of that interest in New England, stating his unqualified friendship &c &c- pressing the opinions on this matter, which the lamented Story used to him in relation to it, in his last illness- Every important print in Ohio is in favor of McL. & so are all the old & safe leaders of the Whig party. Corwin's friends under the direction of Schenck are endeavoring, to produce a temporary diversion in his favor by appealing to the young men of the State, but it will amount to nothing unless resisted & that our friends are determined not to do. It is a sort of the dog-in-the-manger game with Corwin, in whom *we were not deceived.*

Mr. Clay is not without hope for the future & the recent result will encourage him exceedingly- I was at Ashland when Maryland sent forth the first note- I can therefore estimate what the others produced- particularly that in this State & to what account it is credited. More occurred on this subject than I can trust to the honesty of Cave Johnson's mail bags, but all of which, you will be informed when we meet.

Here there is a growing inclination & strength for our ticket, which is improving hourly also in the Western parts of the State.

I conceive it of the highest consequence that your legislature should make a demonstration in favor of the Ticket as now understood by the Country- McLean & Mangum. Let Resolutions be passed expressive of confidence in his character & his ability to secure success. These with a proper letter will bring him fairly out & he will reply in a manner that will give the fullest satisfaction. If this is not done, I fear our victories will be bootless- they will be appropriated as evidences of personal justice in a region that you know of & will make serious difficulties to our future progress. Whereas, if this movement is made in North Carolina, Tennesseee & other legislatures will follow it up & the country will gladly rally on a conservative candidate- There are tens of thousands who only want a pretext to join our ranks, which they will never find while Mr. Clay is in the field.

I tell you after a calm & patient investigation of the matter-
after much personal observation & inquiring & some acquaintance with men, I believe McLean can produce just such a revolution as occurred in '40. It only needs to be properly started &
you have now got the game in your own hands.

If you think I can be serviceable at Raleigh in any way to
bring this about, do notify me by the next post- I consider it of
the very last importance. This move made & the game is ours-
Whig success in 48 is no longer doubtful.

As Ever

Your friend

J. E. H.

I have been urged to press this upon you from very high sources-
We shall carry New York!

WPM-LC

Henry A. S. Dearborn[167] to Willie P. Mangum and Enclosures.

Hawthorn Cottage,

ROXBURY MASST. Octo, 26, 1846

My Dear Sir,

As abolitionism has, unfortunately, been blended with political organizations, in the *North,* I have considered it a duty,
as a citizen, of the whole Republic, who is a zealous & determined
advocate, for the maintainance of the *Union* of the *States,* &
the *intergrity* & *entirety* of the *National Constitution,* as the
Palladium of our *safety* & *Prosperity,* to endeavor to refute the
erronious statements, which are made, as to the conduct of the
Southern portion of the American people, & to forewarn *those*
of the *Northern States* of the disasterous consequences, which
are to be apprehended, from the exasperating speeches, resolutions & other reprehensible proceedings of the leaders of the
abolitionists; & enclose two articles which I wrote & were published in the Boston Daily Eagle,[168] on the 8th & 24th. inst-
signed, - "The Union of the States" & "American Citizen."

----

[167]Henry Alexander S. Dearborn, 1783-1851, was a lawyer, collector of customs of Boston, and brigadier general in the period before 1829. He was a member of the state legislature in 1830, Congress in 1831-1833, and mayor of Roxbury in 1847-1851. *Biog. Dir. of Cong.,* 892.
[168]The [Boston] *American Eagle* was established in December, 1844.

John Jordan Crittenden, 1787-1863. From a photographic negative by Brady in the
collection of Frederick H. Meserve of New York City.

If you will think them worthy of republication in your state, as the *views* of a *New Englander*, I should be gratified to have it done; & should it be, you will do me a great kindness, by transmittin[g] the papers, in which they may appear.

Very respectfully,
Your most obt. St.
HENRY A. S. DEARBORN

[Addressed:]

Hon. William P. Mangum,
U. S. Senate

WPM-NC

Enclosure I

Daily American Eagle

Thursday Morning, Oct. 8

ABOLITIONISM, THE SYNONYME OF REBELLION.— The spectacle, which was presented in Faneuil Hall, a short time ago, by the Whig Convention and the abolition meeting, must be regarded by every true friend of the Union, as of a most lamentable and dangerous import.

Has it come to this, that a few fanatical, ignorant, deluded and unprincipled demagogues, can expect that the people of Massachusetts, are so lost to every principle of duty—so regardless of the solemn admonitions of the most illustrious patriots of the Revolution, as that they will have the effrontery to proclaim their determination, not to be longer governed by the constitution and the law of Congress; but will set up *conscience* as an infallible code for their guidance. A code, which the remorseless bigots, and hypocritical ambition, in all ages, have adopted, and under its pretended holy sanction, deluged the earth in innocent blood.

As to the abstract question of slavery, there is but one opinion throughout the civilized world; but as to its political application in regard to the States where slavery exists, under the protection of law, the citizens of other portions of the Union have neither the *right* or the *power* to interfere; or is it possible that they can, but by revolution and a civil and servile war; for it is impracticable to so alter the Constitution of the United States, as to change any of those provisions which formed the elements of compromise between the North and the South. and resulted in the establishment of the Great Charter of the Republic.

There are but two modes in which the constitution can be amended. viz:—'The Congress, whenever TWO-THIRDS of both houses shall deem it necessary, shall propose amendments, or on the application of TWO-THIRDS of the several States shall call a convention, for proposing amendments, which in either case shall be valid, to all intents and purposes, as a part of the constitution when ratified by the legislatures of THREE-FOURTHS of the several States, or by convention in THREE-FOURTHS thereof.'*

Is it to be expected, that *two-thirds* of the States will propose, or *three-quarters* of them ratify amendments if recommended by Congress, which shall impair the rights they now enjoy, when *half* of the States tolerate slavery,—as do fourteen of the twenty-eight which now form the Union.

For the purposes of gaining partizans, the abolitionists have resorted to unjust, unfeeling, unchristian and erroneous accusations and statements, to exasperate the north against the south, and have charged upon its citizens that anti-protection policy which has characterized the administrations of Jackson, Van Buren, and Polk, when the great States of New York, Pennsylvania and Ohio, with Indiana, Illinois, Michigan, Maine and New Hampshire, have given such decided votes against discriminating duties. Was not Polk, whose partizans in Congress, have repealed the Tariff of 1842 and passed the ruinous act of the last session of Congress, elected by the votes of the *Free* States, when it was well known that he uniformly had been, and was, a decided and ultra opponent of all measures which had for their object, the developement and advancement of all branches of National Industry.

The result of that election was as follows:—Of the 164 votes of the *free* states, Polk received 103, and only 67 of the 111 *slave* states votes; while Clay, the distinguished father of the American system of protection, obtained 44 slave states votes, and but 61 of the free states. If the 164 free states votes had been given for the latter he would have been chosen by 53 majority, if all the *slave* states had voted against him.

Thus, while nearly *two-thirds* of the *free states* were given to the antiprotection candidate, nearly half of the *slave states* votes were in favor of the *tariff* candidate, who had labored, daring his whole political life, for promoting the interests of AMERICAN CITIZENS, on the ocean and on the land,—in the work-shops and manufactories,—for the extension of lines of inter-communication, by roads, canals and railways, and for the prosperity of the whole country.

The reiterated declaration of the leading abolitionists and of the anti-slavery tariff politicians, that the South is hostile to the North, is as fallacious as it is illiberal and reprehensible. Every Southern President, from Washington down to Jackson, earnestly recommended the encouragement of AMERICAN MECHANICS and MANUFACTURERS, as well as LETTERS, SCIENCE and the ARTS. In fact the *Protective Policy* originated in the South, and the tariff of 1816 was established by Southern advocates and Southern votes, while it was strenuously opposed by Massachusetts.

From the dawn of the Revolution to its triumphant conclusion, did not the South as zealously and fearlessly contend for NATIONAL INDEPENDENCE, as the *North?* and during the last war with Great Britain, for *Sailors' Rights* and the *Freedom* of the *Seas*, did not the South evince a like devotion to the honor and glory of the Republic?

What portion of the Union has produced more sincere, able and eloquent advocates for protective duties than numerous Senators and Representatives from all the slave states? Who in the North has done more for the advancement of AMERICAN LABOR, in all its forms, than Brown and Johnson, of Louisiana, Lowndes, of South Carolina, Leigh, of Virginia, Pinkney and Johnson, of Maryland, Clay and Crittenden, of Kentucky, and a host of other zealous and eminent Statesmen beyond Mason and Dixon's lines.

After such demonstrations of the most exalted patriotism, is it decorous, manly and honorable in the North, to indulge in vituperation against the South, and clamor for a *dissolution* of the *Union*, because a temporary cloud has passed over the South, and a portion of its citizens have been deluded by the modern deceptive cry of 'free trade,' when it is notorious, that it is the *free* states which have established the infamous Anglo-concocted tariff bill of 1846. With 136 votes in the House, to 92 from the *Southern* states, is it not the *free* states which have brought down themselves the evils that portend, to every portion of the country, while many of the *slave* states were generous, faithful and able allies of the *Protectionists* of the North.

The effort, therefore, which is now being made, to excite an enmity in the north against the south, is not only unwarrented by facts, but treasonable in its import and consequences; for if the views of the ultra abolitionists are carried out, in their fullest extent, there must be open rebellion, and a vindictive and remorseless civil war. How important is it then, that we should revert to the teachings of the wise, honest, and venerated founders of the Constitution; and well may we ponder on the grave and parental advice of the immortal Washington, which is contained in the following extracts, from his ever memorable Farewell Address:—

'The *unity* of Government, which constitutes you one people, is the *main piller* [sic] in the edifice of your real *Independence;* the support of your tranquility at home, of your peace abroad, of your prosperity, of that liberty which you so highly prize. It is, therefore, of infinite moment, that you should properly *estimate* the *immense value* of your *national Union;* that you should accustom yourselves to *think* and *speak* of it as of the *palladium* of your political safety and prosperity; watching for its preservation with jealous anxiety; discountenancing whatever may suggest evan a suspicion that it can, in *any event* be abandoned; and indignantly frowning upon the first dawning of every attempt to *alienate any portion* of our country from the rest, or to enfeeble the *sacred ties* which now link together the various parts.

'The name of *American,* which belongs to you, in your national capacity, must always exalt the just pride of patriotism. You have, in a common cause, *fought* and *triumpted* [sic] together; the *Independence* and *Liberty* you possess are the work of joint counsels and joint efforts, of common dangers, sufferings and success.

'These considerations speak a persuasive language to every reflecting and virtuous mind, and exhibit the continuance of

the *Union* as a primary object of patriotic desire. To listen to
mere speculation, in such a case were *criminal,* with such
powerful and obvious motives to *Union;*— and there will always
be reason to *distrust* the *patriotism of those,* who in any *quarter,* may endeavor to weaken its bands.'

Citizens of Massachusetts!—reflect seriously upon this solemn
advice, of the greatest and best man that ever 'lived in the
tide of time,' and like him, support to your last hour of existence,—

THE UNION OF THE STATES

WPM-NC.

Enclosure II

Daily American Eagle

Saturday Morning, Oct. 24

For the Eagle.

MR. PALFREY AND THE NATIVE AMERICANS.—It is as
extraordinary, as lamentable, that a gentleman of the intellectual attainments of Mr. Palfrey, should be so far deluded by
abolitionism, as to pervert facts and deduce conclusions, in
such an unwarrantable manner, as has been illustrated in his
letter to the Committee of the Native American party.

He stated that 'there is going on, under the pretended admission of the national government, a sudden importation of
dangerous foreigners, to an extent vastly greater, than what
enters through the Atlantic. Sixty thousand such, with their
slaves to swell their votes have just been entered by act of
Congress, at the south west.'

With what propriety can the citizens of Texas be called
'dangerous foreigners,' when nearly the whole of them were
Native citizens of the United States, who had emigrated to that
country and formed an independent Republic, on the principles
adopted by our State and national gove[r]nments? Are they to
be branded as 'dangerous foreigners,' when they had been
born and reared in the United States, and were Mr. Palfrey's

fellow countrymen, during most of their lives, and contained among them as able and as good men as himself?

Are Native born Americans to be classed with the mass of more than 200,000 aliens, who are annually landed upon our shores from Europe, and most of whom cannot *speak* our language, or *read* or *write* that of any other country? Is it patriotic or just, to hold up to public scorn and denunciation the citizens of a new State, which has been constitutionally admitted into the Union, not by *'slave power,'* but by the votes of the *free States;* for while they have 136 votes in the House the *slave States* could not have done it with their 86 votes. Besides, were not those citizens descendants of the soldiers and patriotic freemen of the 'Old Thirteen States,' who achieved our Independence and established the charter of our rights, and therefore entitled to our respect and affection? They well knew the value of civil and religious liberty, and wished the broad aegis of their native country to be extended over them.

Are the owners of slaves, in the southern States to be called 'vagabonds,' because they do not concur in opinion with a northern man, who sits [sic] himself up as an umpire, to decide how the people of the south are to manage their own affairs, and provide for the security of their property and lives, in conformity to the rights secured to them by the Constitution of the United States? Were the Washingtons, Jeffersons, Madisons, Patrick Henrys, Pinkneys, Lees, Rando[l]phs, and Carrolls, of Revolutionary renown, designated as 'vagabonds,' by their northern compatriots, because their lands were cultivated by negroes? Let northern men attend to their own concerns, and have the magnanimity and justice to allow to those in the south the same freedom of conduct.

The people of the South believe that they are competent to decide what it is proper for them to do, as any of the fanatical teachers of morals in the North. Men who are so clamorous for reformations in distant parts of the country, should recollect that it is not certain they are free from sectional prejudices, and erroneous conceptions of duty, and may be guilty of wrongs which strike at the very foundations of the Union. We are bound, as citizens of a vast and common country, to cherish a respect for the interest of each State, and endeavor to render the name of American dear to every individual, who has the right to call himself a citizen of any of these United States.

Mr. Palfrey further states that 'the passage of a bill which takes the bread from the mouths of the free and intelligent workingmen of Massachusetts, was carried through the Senate by the votes of two persons from Texas.' Now what are the facts in relation to the passage of the tariff bill of last July? Was it the result of that 'slave power,' which seems to have been created by the imaginative terrors of the man who deals in such round yet baseless assertions? So far from it, the *free States* established that act; and in the Senate, instead of the votes of the 'two persons from Texas,' as the Senators of that State have been insultingly designated, there were *ten* votes given for it by *seven* of the *free States,* while there were *nine* votes against it from *six* of the *slave states.* If, therefore, all the votes of the *free States* had been against the bill, it would have been defeated, in the Senate, by a vote of 37 to 18, notwithstanding the votes of 'the two persons from Texas,' in favor of it.—Was it then candid and correct? was it honest and proper to state that the bill was carried through the Senate by the votes of 'two persons from Texas?' Are such declarations decorous, or even excusable in any man capable of reading the daily published proceedings of Congress; and more especially in a gentleman, who, from his high public station, should have known better, and who assumes to speak with such a confident and authoritative tone of intelligence.

In the House there were *fifty-one* votes in favor of the Tariff, on its final passage, from *eight* of the fourteen *Free States,* and *twenty-one* agains[t] it, from *seven* of the fourteen *Slave States.* If, therefore, all the *Free States* had voted against the bill, it would have been rejected by a vote of 146 to 63.

Thus, it is apparent, that nearly *half* of all the votes in the House, in favor of the Tariff bill, were from the *Free States,* while a *third* of those opposed to it in the Senate, were from the *Slave States,* when more than a *third* of the votes of the *Free States* in that body were given in favor of the bill.

It was not to have been expected, that an aged and educated man could have been so infatuated by an abstraction,—a visionary and impracticable conception, as to so pervert his powers of ratiocination, and so completely paralyze the judgment, as to render him incapable of comprehending facts and giving them that influence, which they must ever command;— that he should not only err in results, but be induced, from false conclusions, to utter unjust and aggravating epithets against a large portion of his countrymen, when the exalted conceptions of duty as a citizen, the dictates of honor, and the precepte of morality required, such liberality of sentiment, integrity of principle, charitable magnanimity and enlarged views of patriotism, as would have effectually restrained reproach and silenced animosity.

We became an independent nation by the united valor of the south and the north, and have gloriously advanced in prosperity by the harmonious co-operation of all the states in the establishment of laws for the development of the natural and industrial resources of all parts of the country.—For more than sixty years has this Republic gloriously advanced in the career of individual happiness and national grandeur; and it was not until a few fantatical demagogues raised a rebellious clamor of hostility against the South on the subject of slavery, that there was any animosity in thought or action in one section of the Union against another. The sable flag of abolitionism was unfurled more from the hope of gaining political power, by the leaders, than a philanthropic regard for the condition of the blacks. There were as honest, and honorable, and christian men in this country during the revolutionary war and from its close to the baneful advent of that treasonable spirit, which puts the Constitution and laws at defiance and acts from a presumptuous reliance on its own infallibility, as are now to be found among the arrogant declaimers for universal emancipation; and those venerated patriots here in the north, rightfully considered that the subject of slavery was confined to those states where it existed; for they formed and acted on the opinion which that distinguished champion of the constitution, the Hon. Daniel Webster, honestly and independently declared in the presence of the assembled delegates of Virginia 'under an October sun,' viz: *'that Congress has no power, directly or indirectly, to interfere with the slave interests of the South.'*

The wild leaders of a corps of desperate men, may hurl the torch of destruction into our magnificent temple of liberty, because the African does not participate in all its rites; but where are the enlightened and able architects among their maddened and furious partizans, who can re-edify that venerated structure, when rashly reduced to a mass of broken and blackened fragments.

To destroy is the passion and vocation of the visionary and unprincipled,—of folly and of ignorance; but to create,—to conceive and establish, requires that rare combination of genius, intelligence, firmness, and indomitable perserverance, which characterised the illustrious men, who laid the deep and broad foundations of this vast Republic; while the chimerical reformations of the modern transcendental hierophants of morals, are to be accomplished, like the conquests of the Sythians by the indiscriminate destruction of every institution of government, and of every individual who does not adopt their creed and follow in their ranks. With the words of peace on their lips, they wage a war of extermination against their fellow-countrymen in the South. Alas! for the infirmities of the mind and heart of man. He sees not the terrible consequences of his desperate acts, nor does he hear the mild voice of reason when extravagant assumptions have usurped the throne of intelligence, and he becomes a lamentable object of pity and fear, instead of a revered apostle of wisdom to direct the triumphant march of the human race in the grand route of civilization and moral excellence.

We must be wary how we listen to the ravings of a maniac, lest we also become demented and degraded from that lofty position, which it is desirable should be attained by every

AMERICAN CITIZEN

WPM-LC

Thos. J. Green to Willie P. Mangum.

WASHINGTON CITY
October 31st. 46

My Dear Sir:

As you may have seen by the New York papers I was married to Mrs. J. S. Ellery of Boston on the 24th. instant.- My

brother Majr. N. T Green,[169] was with me on the occasion &
left this city this morning for home.— Before leaving I promised
to write to you for him-, to say that, on Tuesday the 10th. Novr.
he will have many of your and my friends to meet myself and
Lady at his house and beg that you and family may be present.-
His present residence *"Forest Cottage,"* is in two miles of *An-
drews Tavern* where you will get an easy direction.-

Let me my Dear Sir, add my wish also that, you will come
down even if it be that your Lady and daughters cannot accompany you.- We will have quite a blow out if old wine,
pretty women, good music & eating and a boundless welcome
can make one.- Many of *your friends* will be there so come to
spend some days and the Majr. and myself will go to Raleigh
to help you if necessary in your election.-

With sentiments of warm and devoted friendship I subscribe
myself,

Yours truly -
THOS. J. GREEN.

[Addressed:] Hon. W. P. Mangum.
Red Mountain P. O., Orange Co.
No. Carolina.

WPM-LC

J. H. Clay Mudd[170] to Willie P. Mangum.

Planter's House,
ST. LOUIS, Nov 2, 46.

My dear Sir,

I left Burlington three days ago. Enclosed are all the returns from the election, known up to that time. They were
furnished the "Republican" here, from which I cut this slip.
Iowa is, however, certainly Whig, and nothing under Heavens
can prevent the election of two Whigs, good and true, to the
Senate. You must go back to welcome, and urge them on.

---

[169]Major Nathaniel T. Green was a member of the North Carolina Council of State in 1848-
1850. *N. C. Manual*, 437.
[170]He wrote a campaign biography of Taylor in 1848. Hamilton, *Zachary Taylor*, II, 119.

All told, the Legislature will most probably stand;-

	Senate.	House.
Whigs	11	23 .
Locofocos	5	13 .
Independents	3	3 .

Most truly

J. H. CLAY MUDD.

Hon. Willie P. Mangum.

WPM-LC

P. C. Cameron to Willie P. Mangum.

ORANGE Co. Sunday noon. Nov. 46

My dear Sir

"Show yourselves joyful - all ye lands," sing, rejoice and give thanks - sing to the harp with trumpets also and shawms-." I have just this instant received a letter from my father in the city of Philadelphia and the Polictical news it gives is so *good* that I cant keep it from you. The old Gentleman says "This city is *alive* to the results of the elections which took place in N. York and N Jersey on tuesday the 3rd inst: in the former the *Whigs* have elected their Gov. - Young vice Wright - a majority of the members of the State Legislature - and of Congress! in the latter the Whigs have elected four out of five members of Congress - and a decided majority of the Legislature![171] So much for Polk - Dallas and the Tariff of 1846. After reading this you will hardly fail to sleep soundly-: Did any poor devils ever have such a time as he of the White House and his friends.

I was promised by our friend Mr Cain a visit from you; but now hardly hope to see you- I leave Home next Sunday morning for Raleigh on my way South - as you no doubt contemplate being at Raleigh (as you should) let me propose that you come this far next friday evening and we will travel down together.

---

[171]In the fall elections in 1846 the Whigs carried many former Democratic states. In New York John Young, the Whig candidate, defeated Silas Wright, the popular Democratic leader, by 11,572 votes. See the next letter also.

I desire to be named in proper terms of respectful regard to Mrs. Mangum and Daughters.

faithfully your friend.

P. C. CAMERON

Hon W. P. Mangum
    Orange Co-

Mr Bennehan has a letter from Col Ed: Yarborough (of the Hotel Raleigh) who says that Youngs majority in New York is from 8, to 10,000—

[Addressed:] Hon W. P. Mangum
        Home.
Jim/   Orange Co.

Willie P. Mangum to Paul C. Cameron[172]

At home.
Sunday night 8th. Nov. 1846

My dear Sir.

I cannot sufficiently express my thanks for your favor, by my old friend Jim Cameron.-

The news is glorious; & to me, not unexpected.- We must avoid a *collapse,* and the victory is certainly ours, at the next Pres: election.-

My family has been sick, & my youngest daughter is now confined to her chamber.

I regret not to have been able to see you & your family; & especially, my old & constant friend, your excellent uncle.-

I am extremely gratified to learn from various sources, that he looks better than he has for two years.- I go to Franklinton on Friday, & to Raleigh on Saturday.- I am not done sowing wheat, otherwise, I should take your route.- I hope to See you in Raleigh and also, Mr. Bennehan before I leave. I have southern notions also- We can't live here with slaves, unless we have accumulated Capital to support them & us.-

------

172The original is in the Cameron Papers, University of North Carolina.

In a word, accept my best thanks & present me to your excellent wife in the best manner.- & to your brother Tom, & your uncle as they know me to feel towards them, & all of you.

Most truly
your friend
WILLIE P. MANGUM

To Paul C. Cameron esq.

[Addressed:]

Paul C. Cameron esq.
Farintosh, N. C.
Jim Cameron

WPM-LC

J. B. Mower to Willie P. Mangum.

NEW YORK 17th. November 1846.

My dear Sir

There was a good reason, why you did not give me a few lines, on your departure from Washington last summer, after the adjournment of Congress, because you was sick. But I now hope Sir, that you will do me the favor, to let me hear from you in regard to your health. I congratulate you, and all good Whigs, throughout the U. S. on the prospect before us, of better political days, and as a consequence, better every thing. Has not Penna. and New York, done well? And Sir, I assure you in this quarter, there is a very decided change, in public opinion in regard, to bringing Mr. Clay forward again in 48. I percieve a decided change, since August last. The people, whom I see every day in our streets, and from all parts of the Country, appear to consider it dangerous, to bring Mr. Clay forward again,[173] notwithstanding all this Whig gain, in Penna. New York & other States. They reason in this wise, that the same accusations against him, by the democrats, will be brought

---

[173]Clay refused to announce his candidacy in 1846 and 1847 although he still hoped to obtain the nomination. When he found that his life-long friend Crittenden was one of those grooming Taylor, he was very much disappointed. He continued to hope for the nomination up to the time of Taylor's selection. On the first ballot at the convention he received 97 to Taylor's 111. The results were a great disappointment to Clay and his followers. Van Deusen, *Life of Clay,* 384-393.

forward with increased virulence, with the Texas affair, and its consequences, newvamped. And some of his warmest, old friends, begin to think, it will be dangerous to rely on him, as a candidate in 48. For say they, should he be elected, the chances are against him, that he never will see the end of his administration. They all speak of him, just as we all feel towards him, in the most kind and affectionate manner.

In selecting a Whig candidate, for Governor of New York, the Whigs have acted with great wisdom; because Mr. Young united all the little "isms" in the state. And I daily tell these same people, that if they will act as prudently, in selecting judge McLean of Ohio, for the Presi'y. and Senator Mangum of N. Carolina, for vice Presdt. they will elect them, with the same overwhelming majority. This has long been my opinion. It has been slowly increasing ever since, I had the pleasure of seeing you. It has become in a great degree, public opinion. For instance, such men as Frank Granger,[174] (although he is not fully orthodox for me) yet he sees and knows "everybody"- He says, it will be very hazardous, to think of bringing Mr. Clay, out again in 48, for the Presidency. That judge McLean of Ohio, is the most safe, strong and reliable man. One of our most active and influential speakers and writers, (a merchant) a devoted friend of Mr. Clay's, told me last week, that he began to doubt, the propriety of placing Mr. Clay again, before the People, for the Presidency in 48. and gave the same reasons, pretty much that Granger did. He said, it could not be disguised, that judge McLean of Ohio, was a very popular candidate, and observed, that independent, of his great and good political character his good moral, and methodist religious name, would secure him, a most triumphant majority. And today, I've just seen a leading Whig from Buffalo, the brother in law of our Governor elect, John Young, who says, that he has no idea, that Mr. Clay will be a candidate again for the Presidency, that in his opinion, it would endanger the great Whig party to think of him again. He says, there is a strong impression, on the minds of the people, in his part of the State, that Mr. Clay does not desire, to be a candidate.

One of our most able Whig writers, an editor of a popular magazine, said in Wall St. last Saturday, (and who had just

---

[174]Postmaster General under Harrison. *D. A. B.,* VII, 482.

returned from Washington) that if the Whigs, would be wise enough, to select John McLean of Ohio, for the Presidency, and Willie P. Mangum of North Carolina, for vice President, they would elect them, "with a rush."

Some of our *good democrats* are desirous, that the Whigs should bring forward Mr. Clay, for the Presidency again, so that, they may have another opportunity, of beating him, in 48. it is said by some of the "would be family," that the elevation of Mr. Young, in our State, has killed two candidates for the Presidency. *Henry Clay & Silas Wright.*

From every section of the U. S. I have good tidings, of the popularity of judge McLean and Senator Mangum.

I avail myself of this opportunity, to renew to you, Sir, my very great respect & kind feelings.

Your friend & Servant
J. B. MOWER

Hon. Willie P. Mangum
  Red Mountain
    N. C.

[Addressed:]

> Hon. Willie P. Mangum
>   U. S. Senator
>   Red Mountain
>   N. C.

WPM-LC

John W. Norwood to Willie P. Mangum.

HILLSBOROUGH Nov 20th 1846

My dear Sir

When I offered my boy Jacob[175] to you I thought you seemed disposed to purchase him, but it was not then convenient for you to advance the money.

----

[175]See below J. W. Norwood to W. P. Mangum, December 8, 1846.

I have it now in my power to make the time of payment such as you may desire.

I am daily expecting a meeting of the family to dispose of the remaining negroes belonging to my father's estate, my mother having declined to keep house longer. And as I am to take the land it will be necessary for me to have hands, and disposing of Jacob will enable [me] to retain one of the family negroes in his place.

I bought him for a carpenter, to which trade he had been regularly brought up. Not having as yet had any building to do I have kept him in the field and cannot say what sort of a workman he may be. He is a good field hand & good domestic servant. I gave for him $600 & will sell him for the same.

If you will take him you can send me your note for that sum with Mr. Cain or any other good man security, and the money will not be needed during the life of my mother, but the interest must be paid annually as she will need that as part of her income.

Be so good as to allow me to hear from you without delay. To be certain of reaching you I have written to Red Mountain also.

Yrs very truly

J. W. Norwood.

[Addressed:]

Hon W. P. Mangum

Raleigh

N. C.

The post master will)
please deliver this   )
immediately.   )

WPM-LC

Winfield Scott to Willie P. Mangum

WASHINGTON, Nov. 20, 1846.

My Dear Sir:

The President & the Sec. of War, have acted nobly towards me.[176] Please make no audible speculations at present on the subject; but wait for a while.

Yr friend,
WINFIELD SCOTT.

Hon. W. P. Mangum
&c &c &c

[Addressed:]

Hon. W. P. Mangum,
U. States' Senator,
Red Mountain,
No. Carolina.

―――――

Willie P. Mangum to Charity A. Mangum.[177]

Senate Chamber.
Monday 7th Dec. 1846

My dear love,

I have arrived here safe and well. The Senate has just met.- I feel uneasy about Mary- I hope you will have advice for her without delay.- I write simply to let you hear from me.

My love to all the children.

Your affectionate husband
WILLE P. MANGUM

To Mrs. Cha. A. Mangum

―――――

[176]Polk did not like Scott. In September Scott had requested that he be sent to Mexico, but Polk refused. On November 17, in a Cabinet meeting, the majority concluded that in spite of his faults Scott ought to be sent. Polk was reluctant to make the appointment, but, after consulting Benton, he gave in. Scott was delighted at the appointment. Justin H. Smith, *The War with Mexico*, I, 354; McCormac, *James K. Polk*, 455; Quaife (ed.), *Polk's Diary*, II, 239-246.
[177]The original is in the possession of Mangum Turner, Winston-Salem, North Carolina.

John W. Norwood to Willie P. Mangum.[178]

WILMINGTON N. C. Decr: 8th 1846

My dear Sir

I left home with a part of my family for this place on the 10th instant. To day I learn from home that you have agreed to take Jacob & the terms stated by you are entirely satisfactory to me. Agreeably to instructions which I left, the boy was sent down to you. The note was not attended to; I presume it was forgotten in the hurry of your starting for Washington.

My purpose in now writing is simply to say, that I am satisfied with the arrangement, and will execute, & send down to Mrs. Mangum, a proper bill of sale as soon as I return home, which will be about the last of this month.

I wish you a pleasant Session of Congress & that you may preside over Clingman or some other Western man "from and after" 4th of March 1849.

Yrs very truly
J. W. NORWOOD.

[Addressed:]

Hon: Willie P. Mangum
U. S. Senate
Washington City.

[Postmarked:]

Wilmington N. C.
Dec 9

_____

N. P. Tallmadge to Willie P. Mangum.

FOND DU LAC, W. T. [Wisconsin Territory] Decr. 8th. 1846

Private

My dear Sir.

I have a sort of presentiment that the President will feel a necessity to get *Marcy* out of the Cabinet,[179] and that he will

---

[178]See above J. W. Norwood to W. P. Mangum, November 20, 1846.
[179]Marcy served for Polk's term.

attempt to do it by sending him on a Foreign mission- If his name is sent to the Senate, I trust that body will not advise or consent to any such nomination. He is a *dishonest* as well as a *dishonorable* man, and the sooner he is permitted to retire to private life, from which he ought never to have emerged, the better for the interests and honor of the Country.

Previous to the extra session of 1837, *Marcy,* then Governor of New York, called on me at my house, to advise in relation to the contemplated *Sub-Treasury Scheme,* which it was supposed Van Buren was about to recommend. Suffice it to say, he advised me to go against the scheme,[180] and assured me I should be sustained by him, as the Executive, and by the whole party in the State, of which he was the reputed head. This advice being in accordance with my own views, I took my ground accordingly, when the scheme was brought forward- The bill was defeated- On my return to New York, I happened to meet Marcy on board the boat, and conversed with him most of the way from New York City to Poughkeepsie, where I landed— In this conversation, which was in the public cabin, he approved of all I had done at the extra session - said Van Buren was ruining himself, ruining his administration, ruining his party, and if he persists in his schemes, said he, he will ruin the country - and, by the bye, he added, when I come to make out my message to the Legislature he will want me to endorse the scheme, but with an oath, said he, would do no such thing. Notwithstanding all this, he did endorse it in his message! and then united in denunciations of me for doing what he recommended me to do, and what he approved after it was done. These conversations with me were public, and on a great public question- After these denunciations, I stated in a speech at a public meeting, what his course had been- He denied it in an editorial article in the Argus- I then wrote him to know if he sanctioned that article, or if he would pretend to deny the truth of my statements? To this letter he dared not give a reply- After waiting a reasonable time, I came out with the proofs of his having acknowledged to others what he had said to me, and of his having denounced the *Sub-treasury scheme* to others in the same manner as he had done to me - and

---

[180]For a good discussion of the Democratic factions in New York and the split between Tallmadge and Marcy see William Trimble, "Diverging Tendencies in New York Democracy in the Period of the Loco Focos," *Amer. Hist. Rev.,* XXIV, 396-421.

convicted him before the public, by the most respectable witnesses, of being a LIAR. The proofs &c were published in the New York papers of that day, and a part of it will be found in *McKensie's* publication.— A course so *dishonorable* should prevent any such man from receiving the sanction of the Senate of the United States— Had I been in that body, when he was nominated as Secretary of War, I should have opposed his confirmation as being unworthy to preside over a Department, where the highest sentiments of *honor* should characterise its Head. I say nothing of his unfitness for such a place in other respects - but, as a *dishonorable* man, he should receive no countenance from the *Honorable* men which compose your body.

I have nothing here that will specially interest you. We look to Washington for news. I should be glad to hear from you.

                              Very truly yours,
                              N. P. TALLMADGE.

Hon. W. P. Mangum.

———————

                                        WPM-LC

Josiah Randall to Willie P. Mangum.

                                  PHILA. Decr. 13/46

Dear Sir.

I feel a deep solicitude about our position as a party. If Mr. Garret Davis' views[181] are carried out, we shall lose Penna. at least I think so. It is evident Mr. Davis is doing what the friends of Polk desire, they wanted to induce him (as Josiah Quincy was) to move to impeach the Prest. We are in the war and all these movements are more or less paralyzing the Administration and likening us to the Hartford Convention.[182] You will ask me

———————

[181]When Polk delivered his war message in May, 1846, Garrett Davis, of Kentucky, asserted that " 'It is our own President who began this war." Again as a result of Polk's message in early December, 1846, Davis introduced a resolution requesting the President to submit to Congress "all orders to military and naval officers relating to the establishment of civil governments in the conquered provinces." His purpose was to show that Polk had acted illegally in establishing governments in California and New Mexico. McCormac, *James K. Polk*, 415, 459.

[182]From the first, many Whigs had opposed our entrance into the war, but they could not afford to oppose its prosecution. At the same time that they voted for appropriations to prosecute the war, they criticised Polk for getting the country into war. They blamed Polk for the mistakes of the war, and yet they gloried in the victories won by Whig generals. They were constantly in a dilemma. They could not afford to seem unpatriotic, and at the same time they blamed Polk for bringing on an unnecessary war. Smith, *The War with Mexico*, II, 272-280.

what I desire. It is, to vote all supplies and postpone the settlement of the conduct of the Admn. till the war is over, there is time enough to settle the acct. after the war and before the Presidt. Election. Penna. is in for the War and desires it concluded to the honor of the Country, and I firmly believe if you go on attacking the Admt. at every assailable point, we shall be identified with the enemy. Do these attacks change *one* vote? I do not believe they do. If I remember right, Mr. Crittendin took this ground, when the war commenced. If we had not come out for the War; even the ground of the Tariff would not have saved us. I am so accustomed to differ from you at W. that I write rather to gratify myself than in the expectation of doing anything which will dissuade our Hotspurs from destroying our prospects.

Yours truly

J. RANDALL.

W P. Mangum Esqr

WPM-LC

J. B. Mower to Willie P. Mangum.

NEW YORK 13th. Decr. 1846.

My much esteemed friend

Dear Sir

I thank you most respectfully & kindly, for your very friendly letter, of the 1st & post marked "Rl. Rd. Way," the 10th. decr. yesterday. And I hasten to reply to it, promptly because, I think from the advices, I have received from Washington, & other places, that there is some mischief brewing. And if it is possible, it must be amicably prevented. I concur most cheerfully, to all your "inquiries & observations," to "the opinions I held when, we last had an interview," and my faith, has grown stronger, every month, since I left Washington, that there is no name, among the Whigs, that can secure so large a vote, and with so much confidence, and good feeling, and not one word of abuse, as John McLean of Ohio. I also, most cordially agree with you, that I had "rather see him

(Clay) *now* Prest. than any man in the Union." In short Sir, we perfectly agree, in every particular. I am sorry, to see such a disposition, to bring him forward again. Just so sure, as he is made a candidate again, just so certain, the democracy, from Maine to Texas, is firmly united, against him. And defeat, is the consequence.

"The candidate must be selected, at the proper time, who is likely to be the best, under all circumstances" there is no verse in holy writ more true, than the above, from your letter. And how is this, most desireable end, to be brought about? Suffer, me Sir, to recommend one mode. J. M. Clayton, J. J. Crittenden of Ky. and yourself are old and steadfast friends, of H. Clay, when you three Gentlemen become satisfied, that the bringing out of Mr. Clay, will endanger the great Whig party (and you will most certainly be brought to that conclusion, before the last of February next), who will you most confidently, and with a sure prospect of success, rally on. *Judge McLean of Ohio.* And to the end, that all things, shall be harmoniously and honorably done, Judge McLean, in his own proper person, must converse freely and frankly, on this topic, with you three Gentlemen, and no others, at present, that when you four Gentlemen, are united, then bring in a few confidential friends, to advise with. And as you are, (as all the people say) to run on the same ticket, with the judge - and which, two good names, and first rate locality, makes so very acceptable to all, concerned, there is no difficulty there. Mr. Clayton & Mr. Crittenden, must be satisfied by the judge, that in the event, of his being elected, they will be placed in as good ground, as if their friend Clay was.

Is not this an important preliminary? And how is it to be consummated. The Judge must not be timid. He must not have any scruples in satisfying the friends of Mr. Clay. An honest man, with a well balanced mind, never need fear, to say to another honorable man, what he will do, in case of a certain contingency. I suppose Tom Corwin of Ohio, is at work for himself. And our little Ex Governor Seward, is also trying to do something here, but I consider all these attempts, as mere feelers. One reason, is said for bringing forward Mr. Clay is, that the *Empire Club* is unanimously for him. It was said here, some time ago, that a part of this club, had become friendly to

Mr. Clay. That club, of this city, is made up of the veriest hard characters, of the Tammany Hall people. They are mostly, without brains, money, or manners. God help the man, that puts trust, in the New York Tammany Hall politicians. That pretence is ridiculous, on the face of it.

There was a Clay supper, in this City, last week, got up by that crazy, "old man in Spectacles," M L Davis,[183] and a number of very respectable Citizens attended, and some warm toats [sic] drunk, speaking in most unmeasured praise, of Mr. Clay, as they ought to have done.

The Whigs as a party, acted with great wisdom, the last session in aiding the administration, to fight the Mexicans, in order the sooner, to bring about a peace. This war with the Mexicans is, with the masses, rather popular than otherwise, and Polks message to Congress, is cunningly put together, to please this same mass, or superficial readers & hearers. Therefore, I hope that the friends of the judge & yourself, will not rush into too deep opposition, in appropriating funds necessary to carry on the war, our gallant and thus far, successful army, has begun. The great majority of the people, don't care a straw, who the Presdt is, or who governs, all they appear to care for is, conquest and subdue the enemy. The word is now, kill the Mexicans. I am not now prepared, to oppose this mighty torrent of a war feeling. Is it not better, to jump into the stream, and help direct it?

I beseech you my dear Sir, that you take good care of your health, and I am

> with the Highest esteem
> & good will
> Your friend
> J. B. MOWER

Hon. Willie P. Mangum

    U S. Senator.

    Washington

---

[183]See above, III, 290n.

WPM-LC

Job Worth to Willie P. Mangum.

MT A[I]RY, SURRY Co. N. C. Decr. 17th 1846

Hon. W. P. Mangum.

Dr Sir.

Altho a stranger to you personally you will pardon me for addressing to you a few lines.

I feel in common with the whigs of this County much anxiety to see the glorious principle of that Patriotic party rise and remain in the ascendancy and there is probably no County in the State in which the Battle is more Bitterly fought than in "Old Surry" But the whigs have had a small majority for the two last elections, and in order to retain it they are anxious to have disemanated among the people such documents and information as will necessarly lead their minds to a proper conclusion. Any such information intrusted to my care shall be disposed of in such a way as will Best promote that object.

The whigs of Old Surry Rejoice much to perceive that the Legislature will probably remove that Infamous Gerrymander[184] By which they are now misrepresented in Congres 3 to 6.

You will permit me to congratulate you upon your recent reelection to the Senate of the United States and assure you that the Whigs will have a fearless and able champion and defender of their Political faith in the Senate for the next six years.

> I am Sir very Respectfully
> Your Obedient Servant
> JOB WORTH

Hon. W. P. Mangum.
W. D. C.

[Addressed:]

> Hon. Willie P. Mangum
> Senate of U. S.
> Washington City
> D. C.

---

[184]After the Whigs gained control of both houses of the legislature in August, 1846, a bill drawn by Kenneth Rayner was passed to regroup the counties in the Congressional districts so as to increase the number of Whig Congressmen. After the census of 1840 the Democrats had passed a bill which gave them an advantage. In the next Congressional election after Rayner's bill passed, the Whigs elected six of the nine members to Congress. Pegg, "Whig Party in N. C.," 250-251.

WPM-NC

Willie P. Mangum to the Editor of the Union

Senate Chamber
21st. dec^r. 1846

To The Editor of the Union.-

Gentlemen,

A Neighbour of mine "a democrat," requests me to have sent to him, the best democratic paper, here or at Baltimore.-

Will you be so obliging as to send to *"Williamson Parrish*[185] *esq^r.- Red Mountain North Carolina,"* the Country Paper? - Send the bill to me any day, at the Senate & I will pay it.

Your ob^t.Ser^t.

WILLIE P. MANGUM

WPM-LC

William H. Thomas to Willie P. Mangum

Senate Chamber
Dec. 24. 1846,

Hon, W P. Mangum,
of the Senate,

Dear Sir,

I herewith enclose the copy of a Resolution introduced by you last session,[186] which for want of time failed to pass. Allow me to ask of you the favor to ask Cain[?] to introduce it again and have it referred to the Committee of Indian Affairs.

Also the memorial of the Cherokee Indians of No Carolina bearing date June 25, 1846, submitted by Mr. Haywood last session but the committee was discharged without making a Re-

---

[185]In 1844 he was the Democratic candidate for the House of Representatives of North Carolina. He was defeated. *Hillsborough Recorder,* August 8, 1844.
[186]See above, 421n.

port. I have some additional evidence in both cases, to submit after they are referred

Your Obt Sevt
Wm. H. Thomas.

Ps. I am preparing to leave for Raleigh early in next week and would like to see the committee on the subject before I go.

W H T

WPM-LC

John Cameron to Willie P. Mangum.

Hillsboro 25th. Decr. 1846.

Hon: Willie P. Mangum

A merry Christmas to you my dear Judge & a happy New Year! I have not had much of a Christmas myself, as I have had my hands full of business of a half a dozen different sorts; among other things striving to draw up a company in the Old County, to join Gen. Scott at Tampico. Our success has been but partial so far, tho I am in hopes that I will be able to render a better account in the course of another week.

I wish you would be kind enough to drop me a line of introduction to the Gen. as in case we do not succeed in raising a company *here,* I am determined to go out on my own hook—

I had the honor of an introduction to him in Columbus Georgia during the Creek War, where in consideration of his acquaintance with my father he was pleased to offer me a situation in his military family: It was out of my power to accept it then, though if I cant go with a lot of *Orange boys,* I should like exceedingly to do so now.

He doubtless will have forgotten me ere this & I would gladly be called to his recollection by so intimate a friend: Your kind attention to this, will assure you be gratefully chronicled by

Yrs.
Ever truly & Sincerely
Jno. Cameron

N. B.   If you could procure me a few other letters to that quarter of the world, I would be obliged.- Our mutual friends
are all well.—

WPM-LC

John McLean to Willie P. Mangum

[26 December, 1846.]

My dear Sir,

My friend Mr Sheets[187] who will hand you this resides in
Indianapolis, Indiana, and is a gentleman of high character
and is universally respected. He has filled important offices in
Indiana. I have requested him to become acquainted with
you and he has promised me to call on you. He is worthy of
your entire confidence.

Very truly yours
JOHN M^CLEAN

Hon. W. Mangum
26 Decr 1846.

[Addressed:]

Hon. Mr-Mangum
Mr Sheets)

WPM-LC

Calvin Colton to Willie P. Mangum

NEW YORK, Dec. 28. 1846

Dear Sir,

We feel a concern here, lest some of the Whigs of the House,
should put the party in a false position before the country, as to
the *War*, & hope that you, of the Senate, will keep things
straight.

187William Sheets was Secretary of State for Indiana and a good friend of Harrison before 1840.
Virginia Magazine of History and Biography, XVIII, 109.

We shall also be concerned about taxing tea & coffee[188] until we know more. As to the *specie clause*,[189] we shall think you are all poor Doctors, if you do not keep it in their stomachs till they vomit up the whole bill.—

It seems evident you must have a floating dry dock at Pensacola. I pray you to leave the kind of dock to a commission. Knowing you to be personally in favor of that course, I only mean to express the hope that you will make it convenient to advocate it in Committee & in Senate.—

Very respectfully Yours

C. COLTON

Hon. W. P. Mangum

Willie P. Mangum to the President of the United States[190]

The Committee of arrangement have the honor to inform the President of the United States, that the funeral of the Honorable Alexander Barrow,[191] a Senator from the State of Louisiana, will take place from the Senate Chamber, on Thursday the 31st. instant, at 12 o'clock. M

WILLIE P. MANGUM

In behalf of the Committee

Senate Chamber, Dec. 30th 1846

Willie P. Mangum to J. J. Crittenden[192]

WASHINGTON CITY. 31st. decr. 1846.

10 O'Clock A: M: -

My dear Crittenden,

The scene of yesterday in the Senate, & the part you bore in it, have dwelt upon my mind, my heart, & my memory, the whole time; as if it were burned in *all*, with a brand at white

---

[188]To obtain more revenue for prosecuting the war, a bill was proposed to levy a special tax on imported tea and coffee. This was entirely separate from the Walker Tariff. The Whigs opposed the tea and coffee tax possibly for political reasons. The bill was defeated in the House, January 2, 1847. Smith, *The War with Mexico*, 285, 482.

[189]This clause in the Independent Treasury Bill of 1846 requiring specie payments for government debts was not to go into effect for six months after passage. McCormac, *James K. Polk*, 668-672.

[190]The original is in the James K. Polk Papers, Library of Congress. The signature is Mangum's, but the letter was written by someone else. Mangum had charge of the funeral service.

[191]Alexander Barrow was the Whig Senator from Louisiana from 1841 until his death December 29, 1846. *Biog. Dir. of Cong.*, 674.

[192]The original is in the J. J. Crittenden Papers, Library of Congress. This letter has been previously published in Mary Ann Coleman, *Life of John J. Crittenden*, Philadelphia. 1871, I, 265.

heat.- You know me well enough to know; that I never flatter my Friends. I have never flattered you.- I will therefore say; that the more I know of you, the more I respect & love you.-

I would not exchange such a heart as yours;- were it *mine* or my friend's; for one that the world, would ordinarily, call *good,* & for all your high & brilliant eloquence & undoubted abilities.-

Could our lamented & excellent friend Barrow have witnessed the scene, His high & noble soul, would for such a Tribute have been almost willing to meet his fate- premature- as we short-sighted mortals regard it- for himself- for his family & for his Country.-

Your friend,
Willie P. M[angum]
[torn]

To

The Hon: Mr Crittenden
K-^y

[Indorsed:] Mangum 1846
Crittenden on
Barrows death

WPM-LC

John Beard to Willie P. Mangum.

St. Augustine, Decr. 31st. 1846

My Dear Sir,

I take the liberty to trouble you with a little business, by attending to which you will not only oblige me, but also some of your neighbors & friends in N. C.

By reading Mr. Mickle's letter,[193] and my explanation on its back, you will understand the whole matter.

I have committed it to your charge because you know all the parties concerned. Be so good as to see that the business be speedily arranged.

---

[193]This letter is not in the Mangum Papers.

Although we are not now of the same party I know you will do me the justice to believe me when I say that I was gratified by your recent re-election.

There are *very few democrats,* & there is *no Whig* in N. C., whose election would have pleased me so much.

Very sincerely

Yours

John Beard.

Hon. W. P. Mangum

[Addressed:]

Hon: W. P. Mangum

Senator, U. S.

Washington City

D. C.   [Postmarked:]

Augustine Fla.

Jan 2

INDEX

(Except for the chronological section under Mangum, Willie Person, this index is in alphabetical order.)

praised 124; speech of requested, 126; views of praised, 125.
Examiner, mentioned, 34.
Excelsior Society, elects Mangum a member, xvi.
Ezell, Robert A., mentioned, 43.

F

Faneuil Hall convention, abolitionist sentiment expressed in, 503-504; proceedings of reviewed, 66; referred to, 493; speech of Webster in, 82.
"Farmer of Ashland," *see* Clay, Henry.
Farmer's Library, mentioned, 373.
Faucett, C. F., candidate for state senate, 433.
Fayette Hill, removal of post office from, 97.
Fayetteville, young men of build library, 246.
Fayetteville Library Institute, date of establishment, 246n; documents sought for, 246-247.
Federal appointments sought, 70. *See also* under the names of offices and individuals.
Federal appointments, by Polk, commented on, 265; by Tyler, approved, 260-261.
Federal marshal for Alabama, appointment of, 266.
Federal expenditures, as a campaign issue, 112, 329.
Felisola, mentioned, 322.
Fenner, James, mentioned, 415.
Fenton, Quartermaster, mentioned, 357.
Ferguson, Captain Isaac, mentioned, 361.
Ferris, Mr., mentioned, 199.
"Fifty-four forty," as war cry opposed, 116.
Fifty Reasons, mentioned, 457.
Fillmore, Millard, campaign of, 200; considered for Vice President, 66, 81, 104-105; mentioned, 418; respected in New York, 105; strength in Baltimore Convention, 123; weaknesses of reviewed, 81.
Finley, J. J., invites Mangum to Memphis Convention, 311; letter from, 310.
Fish, Hamilton, mentioned, 182, 258.
Fisher, General C. F., mentioned, 357.

Fisher, Charles, letter to, 384; mentioned, 295, 303n.
Fisher, Redwood, advises confirmation of Atwood, 258; expresses his devotion to Whigs, 258; removal of predicted, 258; letter from, 258; mentioned, 21; party maneuvers of, 23; sketch of, 258n.
Flat River Baptist Association, mentioned, 196.
Flat River Clay Club, elects Mangum a member, 158.
Floating batteries, method of making, 249; recommended for forts, 248.
Florida, admission of sought, 238; appointments in discussed, 238-239; congressional contest in, 411-412.
Foreign diplomatic corps, oppose Texan annexation, 268.
"Forest Cottage," mentioned, 512.
Forsyth, Samuel, mentioned, 150.
Forsyth Clay Club, meeting of, 149.
Forsythe, S. P., mentioned, 325.
Forsythe, William, mentioned, 325.
Forrester, John, mentioned, 360, 361.
Fort Pickering, favored for navy post, 109, 110.
Foster, Colonel, reports on Cherokees, 458.
Foster, Ephraim, accused of favoring Texan annexation, 269; opposes annexation of Texas, 269n; mentioned, 49, 202.
Fourth Installment of distribution fund, 229. *See also* Distribution of funds.
Fowle, James, reports on Boston Whigs activities, 335, 336.
Frankfort Commonwealth, mentioned, 471n.
Franklin County (Ky.), election results in, 471-472.
Franklin County (N.C.), Democratic Party in, 163; election results in 1844, 166-167; speakers at political rally in, 166; vacancy of clerk's office in, 296; Whig barbecue planned in, xiii.
Franklinton, public discussion planned in, xii.
Fraud in 1844 election, claimed, 238; investigation of, 244-245. *See also* election fraud.

paigns for Congress, 319; circular to his constituents, 319-324; controversy with Houston, 324n, 352-362; describes Texas lands, 331-332; explains his absence from Texas, 319; explains his views on Texan issues, 321-322; hositlity of Santa Anna to, 356; invites Mangum to his wedding reception, 512; letters from, 331, 352, 451, 511; mentioned, 348n; political background of, 323; prisoner in Mexico, 319; relates story of his escape from prison, 360-361; reviews basis of Texan boundary claims, 322-323; sends brother's picture to Mangum, 451; tries to vindicate his Mier conduct, 320.

Green, Wharton, J., sketch of, 319n.

Green, Willis, directs mailing of Whig documents, 160, 164; money raising efforts of, 291.

Green-Houston feud, 321-324.

Greene, Albert Collins, mentioned, 416.

Greensborough Patriot, mentioned, 273n.

Greenville (N. C.) rally, mentioned, 151.

Griffis, Elizabeth, seeks a pension for her husband, xi.

Griffis, Joshua, pension sought for, xi.

Grinnell, Moses H., endorses Webb's views on tariff, 64-65; letter from, 64; mentioned, 63; opposes a change in the tariff, 64-65.

Guilford County, barbecue planned in, xiii.

Guion, Benjamin S., seeks appointment to West Point, 261; sketch of, 261n.

Guion, Haywood W., letter from omitted, xiii; mentioned, 387, 426; sketch of, 184n.

H

Hacker, W. P., invites Mangum to speak, 338-339; letter from, 336.

Hackney, Daniel, identified, 410n; seeks documents, 410.

Hale, Justice, publication of views of recommended, 430.

Hale, E. F., mentioned, 151.

Hall, E. W., asks Mangum's aid for repairs of University, 307-308; letter from, 307.

Hall, Willis, explains the activities of Clay Clubs, 132; letter from, 132.

Hallett, William Paxton, appointed as consul, 270; mentioned, 20.

Hamer, Thomas L., criticises Congress for timidity on Oregon, 88-89; identified, 88n; letter from, 88.

Hamersly, George W., advises Whigs to support Porter, 33; letter from, 33; strength in Pennsylvania, 32.

Hamilton, John, mentioned, 172.

Hamilton, P., letter from omitted, xiii.

Hammond, John H., mentioned, 143n.

Hammond, Nathaniel, member of Whig Committee, 335; reports on Boston Whigs activities, 335-336.

Hancock, John, mentioned, 296.

Hannegan, Edward A., mentioned, 116.

Harbaugh, Leonard, mentioned, 45.

Harbor Improvements, recommended, 247-250.

Hardee, W. H., concerned over "Corrupt Bargain" as an issue, 192; letter from, 192; urges Clay to publish correspondence with Blair, 192.

Hardwick, Kezziah, mentioned, 266n.

Hardy, J. F. E., letter from omitted, xi.

Hargous, Mr., mentioned, 360, 361, 362; offers compensation for sufferers in Mier incident, 358-359.

Harkness, George W., mentioned, 45.

Harper, James, mentioned, 86.

Harris, Captain Robert, mentioned, 356.

Harris, Major, suicide of, xiv.

Harris, Robert, offers invention for steam machine, 168.

Harris, S. H., favors Mangum for Vice President, 71; letters from, 70, 168; seeks Mangum's assistance for nephew's appointment, 70-71; sends Mangum's letter on brother's invention, 168; urges Mangum to attend rally, 168.

Harrisburg Convention, 75n.

Harrison, William Henry, mentioned, 30, 160, 219, 236, 242.

to dedicate a book to Clay, 187; letter from, 186; prepares a book of maxims, 187-189; seeks chaplaincy of Senate, 186-188.

McKay, James J., mentioned, 303n, 387, 496n; provision of tariff bill of, 454n.

McKennon, Thomas M. T., proposed for Vice President, 123.

McKerall, William, informs Mangum of his election to literary society, 324; letter from, 324.

McKibbin, John S., accused of dishonesty, 35; appointed New York appraiser, 18; mentioned, 20, 21.

McLean, John, of New York, concerned over Whig course, 10; letter from, 10; seeks Mangum's opinion on politics, 10; sketch of, 10n.

McLean, Judge John, candidacy of opposed, 282; considered for Whig candidate in 1848, 393, 403, 431, 432, 435, 438, 448, 456, 479, 500, 516, 523-525; letter from, 529; presidential ambition of, 287; recommends Williams Sheet, 529; resolutions endorsing his candidacy, 501; strength in Ohio estimated, 500-501; strength in Massachusetts, 493.

McLemore, J. C., mentioned, 110.

McLeod, General Hugh, mentioned, 361.

McMackin, William, invites Mangum to speak, 336-337; letter from, 336.

McMahon, J. H., invites Mangum to Memphis Convention, 311; letter from, 310.

McMichael, Norton, letter to, 33; sketch of 32n.

McMillan A. B., mentioned, 303n.

McMannin, John A., book by, 308n.

McNeill, William Gibbs, letter from, 388; opposes Moore's promotion, 388-389; sketch of, 388n.

McRae, Duncan, mentioned, 150.

McRae, John, mentioned, 289.

Macon, Nathaniel, mentioned, 172, 173.

Madeira, mentioned, 86.

Madison, James, mentioned, 327.

Madison (Ga.), Whig rally in, 133.

Magnetic Telegraph, Mangum's reaction to, 127; mentioned, 250. See also telegraph.

Mahan, Captain, Patrick, mentioned, 356.

Mail, federal subsidies for advocated, 259.

Mail routes in North Carolina, changes in proposed, 386-387.

Maine, abolitionist strength in, 83; campaign of 1844 in, 119, 193n; political maneuvers in, 119; temperance movement in, 40; Whig strength in, 183.

Maine Democrats, campaign tactics of reviewed, 195.

Maine Whig Central Committee, Circular of, 193; list of members of, 196.

Maine Whigs, attribute defeat to ineffective organization, 194; explain their defeat in 1844, 193-196; neglected to vote, 194; satisfied with their 1844 campaign, 194.

Mallory, Daniel, bemoans threat of war with England, 341-342; identified, 340n; letter from, 340; praises Mangum's speech, 341; urges settlement of French spoliation claims, 340-341.

Man, Samuel F., letters from, 402, 405, 409; reviews Rhode Island campaign, 409-410; seeks information on Simmon's standing, 402, 406; sketch of, 402n.

Maney, Thomas, identified, 27n.

Mangham, James C., criticizes Mangum for supporting Clay, 210-211; intimacy with Mangum's family, 212; letter from, 210.

Mangum, Augustus, mentioned, 232.

Mangum, Charity A., health of, 232; discusses family news, 231-233; has piano tuned, 232; letter from, 231; letters to, 1, 7, 8, 25, 34, 251, 277, 280, 403, 434, 445, 451, 519; mentioned, 257, 289, 295, 305, 344, 345, 347, 348, 350, 493, 514, 520.

Mangum, Ellison G., letter to, 299; mentioned, 325, 402.

Mangum, Joseph, mentioned, 120.

Mangum, Martha Person (Pattie), invited to a party, xvi; let-